Marx Went Away—But Karl Stayed Behind

Marx Went Away— But Karl Stayed Behind

Updated Edition of *Karl Marx Collective: Economy, Society and Religion in a Siberian Collective Farm*

CAROLINE HUMPHREY

Ann Arbor
THE UNIVERSITY OF MICHIGAN PRESS

For Edmund Leach

Revised edition copyright © by the University of Michigan 1998
Originally published as *Karl Marx Collective: Economy,*
Society and Religion in a Siberian Collective Farm,
by Maison des Sciences de l'Homme and Cambridge University Press 1983
All rights reserved
Published in the United States of America by
The University of Michigan Press
Manufactured in the United States of America
♾ Printed on acid-free paper

2001   2000   1999   1998   4   3   2   1

A CIP catalog record for this book is available from the British Library.

Library of Congress Cataloging-in-Publication Data

Humphrey, Caroline.
  Marx went away—but Karl stayed behind / Caroline Humphrey.
    p. cm.
  Rev. ed of : Karl Marx collective. Cambridge, New York : Cambridge
University Press; Paris, Editions de la Maison des Sciences de
l'Homme, 1983.
  Includes bibliographical references (p.   ) and index.
  Romanized record.
  ISBN 0-472-09676-1 (alk. paper). — ISBN 0-472-06676-5 (pbk. :
alk. paper)
  1. State farms—Russia (Federation)—Barguzinskiĭ raĭon—Case
studies. 2. Barguzinskiĭ raĭon (Russia)—Rural conditions.
3. Russia (Federation)—Economic conditions—1991– I. Humphrey,
Caroline. Karl Marx collective. II. Title.
HD1493.R92B274 1998
338.7'63'09575—dc21   98-8341
                                                                CIP

Contents

Preface to new edition

When I returned to Bayangol in summer 1996 the monument to Marx was standing at the entrance as before.[1] The great thinker's massive concrete head was flanked by the name of the farm – but someone had hacked off the word "MARX." The farm's name had become "COLLECTIVE FARM OF KARL." The villagers' cows grazed peaceably around. Seeing my curious glance, a local driver joked, "So Marx has gone away, but Karl has stayed behind." His quip provides me with an entrance to the subject of this new edition. In the agricultural hinterlands of Russia the Marxist ideology has indeed disappeared. But its shadow remains, indeed perhaps something personal and nondogmatic like a first name, something people have not been able to give up.

The new chapters will paint a portrait of rural life in one of those seemingly conservative parts of Russia[2] where the most violent consequences of the end of Communism are absent. It is not just that in Buryatiya[3] there has been no war, no rabid nationalism, and relatively little aggressive commercialisation or mafiaisation, but even the tenor of everyday life seems continuous with that of the past. Elsewhere the very mechanisms for determining society's winners and losers have undergone rapid change (Ruble 1995, 2), but in Buryatiya despite the demise of the Party, political leadership remains largely in the hands of the old *nomenklatura*. To some extent this can be explained by the continued reproduction of the economic dependency of Buryatiya on Moscow and of the rural areas on the capital and by the fact that the few successful commercial firms work in tandem with the government rather than challenging it. Buryatiya's "quietness," however, belies a cultural ferment which is not at all separate from economic turmoil. The flow of credits from Moscow is in fact erratic and has to be constantly renegotiated. Increasingly, "wild" commercial sponsors are feverishly sought to save collapsed state services. The maintenance of the tenor of daily life, most crucially electricity supplies, winter heating, and fuel for the most basic travel, is at the edge of disaster. Within this fragile balance indigenous notions of polity are stirring and surfacing. These are post-Soviet ideas (or they could be termed "ex-Soviet" to indicate a certain quality of continuity with the past), and yet in some ways they are also deeply historical, a refiguring of culture in the *longue durée* of Asia. In the chapters that follow I show how rural people, and not just the urban intellectuals, are generating indigenous proj-

vii

ects for the future of their communities. It is a neglected aspect of the Soviet heritage that even villagers, perhaps particularly in Buryatiya, are well educated and until recently had a small proportion of people actually engaged in directly agricultural work. Similarly, little attention has been paid to people who see themselves as loyal to the Federal state, not as oppositional or marginal, and yet who maintain profound ties to specific district homelands and use kinship as the crux of their identity. The extraordinarily globalised and yet locality-producing worlds that Buryat *kolkhozniki* are attempting to create around them as the Soviet structures slowly disintegrate are the subject of the new chapters.

What has happened in the Buryat countryside with the demise of Communism? The collectives remain in one form or another. Basically, they created a way of life that was not sustainable, and yet for most rural Buryats this is felt to have been a legitimate order with mistakes in policy, not a system "contrary to human nature" as was the case among Hungarian peasants (Lampland 1995, 339). True, Buryats say they resented the restrictions on individual smallholdings, and they remember the arbitrary campaigns and the fear. I met no one who really wanted to return to those conditions. But still a constant refrain in 1996 was, "We Buryats have no grudge against Soviet power." Unlike Russians, whose sense of their own responsibility for the Revolution gives rise to immense and contradictory outpourings of pride, despair, and anger, the Buryats talk of the Soviet regime as something that happened to them. Its massive impact, its totalising interpretation of society and history, seems disjunct from their own inner, domestic, knowledge of what really happened, and they do not care to (maybe do not dare to) confront the two. With some exceptions mostly among intellectuals, rural Buryats tend to speak like people who were absorbed into, and absorbed, the Soviet ideology, and their stance is to be grateful. Indeed, by 1996 there was a wall of silence about who could have sawn off the word "MARX." It was children playing, people said, averting their eyes.

Yet the two collective farms named after Karl Marx have had rather different fates. Today the farm in Selenga retains its Soviet-type organisation and still calls itself the Kolkhoz imeni Karla Marksa. Its monument to the great bearded German is intact, and a separate monument for the farm itself has become a ritual site for marking its troubled existence with a libation of vodka when people make a journey in or out. As during Soviet times, the other collective at Bayangol in Barguzin district was more "progressive" in following government policy. Its members decided to take the path toward individual farming which was promoted in the early 1990s. In 1992 it became a Union of Peasant Holdings (OKKh),[4] and it is now known as the OKKh Bayangol. Constant reorganisations have destabilised this farm, whose rump nevertheless continues to function like a collective of old. This is the farm with the broken monument, and it is here that the farm's history museum, so devotedly set up in 1987 with an invitation to Marx's great-granddaughter to travel from Paris to attend the opening, is closed and boarded up.[5]

Thus, the historical resonance of being "named after Karl Marx" has been construed differently in the two farms. In the auditorium of the Selenga farm's club at Tashir, a line of portraits of the chairmen hang in chronological order on the wall, and no one mentions any breaks or scandals of the past (p. 349). I was told with some pride that farms named after lesser dignitaries like Stalin had been amalgamated with the Karl Marx in the 1940s, rather than the other way around, "because Karl Marx was the senior" in the revolutionary genealogy. Now the people of this farm are engaged in continuous, active generation of local sociality, going their own sweet way under the unquestioned sign of Marx. In Barguzin, on the other hand, the farm's 50th anniversary in 1987 was the occasion for taking Marx seriously. The new museum featured an interpretation of his life and works, thus inadvertently disclosing the historicity of Marxism-Sovietism as a tradition and the tangentiality of the farm's link with the great man. If such *lieux de mémoire* (sites of memory) are established when "natural memory" is lost (Nora 1989, 7), we can see the museum as an attempt to shore up and perpetuate a tradition that was already questioned. Now even that late 1980s interpretation of history is out-of-date, and the museum may never reopen, since not only has no agreed on interpretation of the past emerged, but the collective farm itself as a unity for local identities is under threat and may soon split up into constituent villages.

I have decided to reissue *Karl Marx Collective: Economy, Society and Religion in a Siberian Collective Farm* (1983) because it is still one of the few detailed studies of the great Soviet experiment of collectivised farming. Of course, the book is now historic, both in the sense that had I been writing it now I would have done it differently and in the sense that the phenomena it described have irrevocably changed. Many would argue, both inside and outside Russia, that the collective farm as a type of economic organisation is doomed. This may well be right, yet it will be argued here that collective enterprises of one kind or another are still highly relevant to our times. Why so? First, and very simply, large numbers of collectives still exist in Russia, and in many regions they and other forms of joint agricultural enterprise are indispensible to the way farming is now organised and the way people imagine their lives. In Buryatiya even those committed to reform acknowledge that the attempt to replace collectives with private commercial farms has failed. In Russia as a whole only 3% of agricultural workers are "private farmers," and their number is falling,[6] though much larger numbers live off tiny subsidiary plots in an economy which is neither collective nor fully privatised. Second, there is the far broader globalised context in which we may consider collective action in economic practice. It is not just in Russia that people see that the problems facing them cannot be resolved simply by a choice between the State and the Market (Gregory 1997). In the hinterlands of Buryatiya both are regarded with despair. Indeed the two are seen as inextricably intertwined in political corruption and mysterious monopolistic deals. Yet battling it out as a lone household

– though many people actually have to do this – is not regarded as a solution either. Not only is the household farm weak and incapable of feeding the populace at large; it is morally suspect, seen as a potential incubus of selfishness and exploitation of others. The only solution, people say, is local, community-based collectives.[7] They are not referring here to a theoretical concept like civil society, with collectives appearing as intermediate institutions (Anderson 1996, 112–14), but to a real intervention in postsocialist life.

I should go no further before saying that agriculture in Buryatiya is now in a state of economic collapse. The Republic as a whole is one of the poorest in Russia, with 52% of the population having incomes below the minimum living standard (in Russia as a whole in 1995 the proportion was 24.7%).[8] Birthrates have gone down, death rates risen,[9] health problems increased, and there are reported cases of near starvation. The crisis of the Buryat economy caused the President, L. V. Potapov, to announce an "extraordinary regime" in 1996, and this enabled him to negotiate a large one-off credit from Moscow to pay state wages and pensions.[10] In agriculture, with the exception of grain, the prices received do not cover the costs of production. Agricultural subsidies create large regular debts with Moscow.[11] Collective herds have been decimated, ploughed areas reduced, and production and productivity are down to around a half of late Soviet figures. Of the six "collectives" in the Barguzin district in 1995, only one made a small profit, while the Bayangol farm made a massive loss of 1,667,000,000 rubles.[12] Webs of indebtedness trap farms and reduce their options. Wages in rural areas have not been paid for years, so money is virtually absent. As a result, private village shops set up hopefully in the early 1990s have mostly closed.

Just as the Buryat state budget depends on annual transfers of money from Moscow, most of the districts of Buryatiya are also in debt. Their leaders go to the capital, Ulan-Ude, personally to negotiate annual transfers to cover their budgets, and this procedure is one reason for the perpetuation of "people with good contacts" in leadership roles. These transfers much exceed the amounts raised locally by taxes. Of course, in Soviet times Buryatiya also depended on the state, but then this was generally regarded as normal, as it was part of the intricately complex planned economy of the USSR in which goods and credits flowed across the whole country (pp. 95–102). Now, however, the credits go only to government organisations, and even then they are usually paid months late and often in smaller amounts than promised. Farmers are suddenly aware of being economically on their own. Collectives, which are supposed to be independent, find it almost impossible to negotiate money loans.[13] The idea of becoming a self-supporting unit has become a desperate goal for each administrative level and each enterprise. The impossibility of attaining this goal results in a schizophrenic anxiety. Reform-minded officials denounce the "dependency culture," and yet, when the President of Buryatiya made a state visit to the Barguzin region in 1996, the local newspaper ran a great pleading headline:

"Please help the district, Leonid Vasil'yevich! We need a new flour mill. We produce enough grain to feed ourselves, but we have to import flour for bread because we have only one mill."[14]

Villagers feel they are living in an extraordinary, incomprehensible epoch. The accustomed parameters of "progress" have melted away. Many collectives have abandoned their most technologically advanced methods, while villagers have to hone the arts of domestic production to survive. Newspapers are full of advice about when to plant onions or how to store carrots. Yet there is no post-industrial concept of "small is beautiful." Rather, villagers feel they are in the grip of de-modernisation (Platz 1996), a shameful turn "backwards into the past," as herders lamented to me, showing me their car lying unused (no petrol, no spare parts) and the horse they now rely on. At the same time, the other worlds of TV soaps – "Santa Barbara" especially – fascinate almost everyone; work stops, people watch together, blotting out the hardship outside, even when the cows are bellowing to be milked in the frosty evening. Turning back to everyday life is to confront endless difficulties: how to eke out hay for the sheep, how to get shoes for the children, how to cure the sick cow that has stopped giving milk, where to exchange a piglet for a video. These are the practical circumstances in which people will not let go of the collectives, and which I attempt to explain in Chapters 9 and 10.

In the present edition *Karl Marx Collective* has been left intact without changes, as a record of its times.[15] So as not to produce too gigantic a book, I have decided not to comment extensively on points in it about which new information is available.[16] The new chapters focus on the two farms in their district contexts rather than on issues concerning Buryatiya as a whole. Contemporary rural attitudes can only be explained, however, if we understand Buryat people in relation to their imagined vistas as well as their lived practice, and here there have been immense changes since the 1960s–70s. Global dimensions and historical perspectives have shifted and in some ways opened out, as I briefly discuss in the remainder of this preface.

Recent anthropology has destabilised the notion of culture as a taken-for-granted local entity, but, as Hastrup and Olwig suggest (1996, 3), rather than discarding the idea of culture, "it should be reinvented, as it were, through an exploration of the 'place' of culture in both the experiential and discursive spaces that people inhabit or invent." I understand this statement to suggest an exploration of the spaces and places made by culture, with the implication not only that histories may intertwine and overlap and thus engender conflicts but also that such narratives may be disjunct from practices which crosscut discursively created borders. In the case of the Buryats it was argued at the beginning of this book (p. 2) that even a remote Siberian collective farm could not be understood except in the wider context of the Soviet state, but I did not pay sufficient attention to the imaginative dimensions of this observation (using the word *imaginative* not in the sense of "untrue" but as pertaining to the conceptual). Today there are important differences from Soviet times: not only has the imagined domain of the USSR been replaced by the ethnicised and hence more ambiguous one of Russia, but the encompassing capitalist world has changed from being a straightforwardly enemy terrain to a space which the Buryats themselves must now engage with and enter. Accompanying this bouleversement is the reevaluation of Buryat history in its Asian context. At the same time, the 1990s have seen a remarkable intensification of the production of locality, i.e., a distinctive, self-differentiating, and yet self-regenerating life-world constituted by shared histories and understandings. As Appadurai (1995, 215) points out, the production of neighbourhoods in this sense is often at odds with the projects of the nation-state, because the latter designate localities as mere instances of a generalised mode of belonging to the wider imaginary of the polity. And alongside these irreconcilable discourses there is yet another layer, that of everyday practice, which may be hardly narrativised at all and yet which may in different ways counteract rationalising accounts.

Today, as *de-collectivisation* is being promoted by the reformists in Buryatiya, it might seem that the history of collectivisation (1929–33) would be the subject of intense local scrutiny, especially since the opening of archives has revealed new facts about those times. This is an extremely complex subject, however, which foregrounds both conflicting views and silences among Buryat people. Not only does collectivisation tragically highlight the conflict over modernisation or the struggle between European ("Russian") as opposed to Asian ("Mongolian") ways of life which had engaged Buryats since the beginning of the century (pp. 48–50, 418–20), but it lays open the ghastly and irreconcilable two-sidedness of Stalinism itself. On the one hand, Stalin's policies caused the unjust deaths of thousands of people, destroyed Buryat Buddhist culture, and split the Buryat nation into separate administrative units (p. 24) amid hysterical accusations of "Pan-Mongolism." On the other hand, people lived their lives through Stalinism. That is, their everyday practices and rewards, the rules they observed, the careers they planned for themselves and their children, or the "symbolic capital" they struggled for, were all found in the structures set up first by the Stalinist state. Even now there is a kind of gut loyalty to this former everyday life, which older people especially cannot abandon. For some people there is simple continuity, while for others there is a sudden new consciousness that the old ways are indeed "historic" (cf. the situation in the former East Germany, where objects from the old *alltag* (everyday life) have suddenly become museum material [Ten Dyke forthcoming]). All this means that it is impossible to delineate "a Buryat view" on collectivisation, as irreconcilable and bitterly opposed views surface in various contexts. A historical topic can be like an anti-focus, from which centrifugal rationalisations fly in different directions, and collectivisation is one of these.

There is now evidence of widespread armed risings against collectivisation in 1929–32 in the south, east, and west of Buryat lands. In the 1960s and

1970s, when I made my first studies, such topics were unmentionable and systematically excluded not only from books but also from conversations. One of the uprisings was based at Noyokhon, a settlement neighbouring the Selenga Karl Marx Collective, in 1930. At its height this rebellion encompassed several settlements of Russian and Buryat Cossacks, Old Believers, other Buryat and Russian villages, and virtually all of the nearby Zakamensk district; it had organised links with resistance elsewhere in the region and had raised around 300 men to leave their lands and take up arms.[17] The slogans were: "For a Democratic Republic!" "Down with the Dictatorship of the Proletariat!" and "For the inviolability of property and free trade!"; and, in the village of Khonkholoi: "Collectivisation is a straight path to slavery!" "Hail the liberation of all those arrested!" and "Hail the freedom of worship!" (Dorzhiyev 1993, 65, 72). This was not an anti-Russian nor a class-based uprising. It seems to have been initiated mostly by Old Believers, and it included not only *kulaks,* so-called rich peasants, but also people of middling and poor economic status. The large number of such uprisings, although they were small, separate, and quickly put down by troops of the OGPU (NKVD), indicate that there was in most areas a widespread resistance to collectivisation in Buryatiya. The slogans show that this was not just a matter of "peasant" resentment of the expropriations and forced egalitarianism of the collectives. People were taking up arms for principled ideological and political concerns in opposition to Communism. The defeat of the peasant uprisings left only the Buddhist monasteries as centres of resistance during the 1930s. Their legitimacy was weakened by the accusations of obscurantism and corruption made earlier by the Buddhist reformists (p. 419) and by the socialist education campaigns, which had grabbed the high ground of modernisation for the Bolsheviks, taking it from the hands of Buryat educationalists, and which succeeded in turning many young people against the lamas.

By 1938 virtually all the early Buryat leaders, of whatever political hue, had been killed or purged (Naidakov 1993, 63–8) and the monasteries annihilated. A whole generation of eminent Buddhist lamas as well as writers, historians, artists, and social activists perished. Only recently has it been revealed that the entire Party and governmental leadership of Buryatiya was purged in 1938, including, on one terrible night of June, the shooting of nine ministers and senior managers of the economy (64). The accusations, of "Pan-Mongolism" or collaboration with the Japanese, were designed to cut the Buryats from Asiatic ties, separate them from one another, and enforce loyalty to Russia.

While this history is not hidden, being available in newspaper articles and books, it is significantly not a public preoccupation of ordinary rural people today.[18] There are other parts of Buryat history which are also curiously obscured and very difficult to talk about in public, notably any events which cast Buryats and Russians against one another, particularly when Buryats suffered disproportionately. These include: the "voluntary entry" of Buryats into the

Russian state in the seventeenth century, in fact a time of fierce fighting in some areas (Forsyth 1992); the mass mobilization of Buryats for war work during World War I, in which many lives were lost;[19] the takeover by Russians of Buryat lands at many points in history but especially the land revisions of 1917;[20] and the very high loss of Buryat lives in World War II.[21] In a republic numerically dominated by Russians and with a Russian President, these topics, which were opened in the early 1990s, are now rarely broached in public.

Dorzhiyev comments (1993, 82) that the peasant rebellions over collectivisation constitute the largest of the "blank spots" in the history of Buryatiya. He notes that, while the subject is relatively well covered in Russia in general,

In Buryatiya there is so far not a single historical work specially devoted to the given theme. Furthermore, in the opinion of the author, the social consciousness of the republic is still in fact under the influence of a simplistic and negative attitude to the peasant risings of the 1920s and 30s. . . . According to such stereotypes, the peasants who took part in the risings are still seen as ordinary bandits "brutalized by the kulaks."

It is true that there may be some (nonaccidental) misinformation about history among young people,[22] but Dorzhiyev's remarks point more to a characteristic layering and hierarchisation, as well as diversification, of views, a point I explain with the example which follows.

In summer 1997 the leaders of Ust'-Orda Okrug, the Buryat region cast off into the Russian Irkutsk Province in 1937, celebrated the 60th anniversary of the founding of the Okrug by holding a magnificent *suur-kharbaan* festival. The Soviet official co-option of this Buryat festival was a regular matter (as described on pp. 380–2), but the irony of the event in 1997 aroused furious comment in the newspapers. How could Buryats participate in the celebration of the splitting up of their nation? A farmer explained, "We all know very well about 1937, when our unified people (*narod*) was divided up by Stalin. It's the leadership of the Okrug who are busy with the 60th anniversary, but the people know their tragedy. We are just celebrating *suur-kharbaan*."[23] Even though the Buryat leaders of the Okrug had just been removed in favour of Russians, it would be naive to see the farmer's statement just in terms of dominant (official, pro-Russian) as opposed to oppositional (people's, Buryat) discourse. There is plenty of economic realism among "the people" too, which acknowledges advantages in being a separate financial unit from Buryatiya in the long-standing structural competition between administrative units vying for resources (Verdery 1995). This strategic layering of responses is not unlike the reactions to the issue of collectivisation, in which evolutionist teachings – that the collectives were the instruments of the modernisation process in the twentieth century and Buryats are modern people – overlie painful historical knowledge.

Understandings of history and identity inevitably involve self-definition in relation to the discourse of the Soviet, now the Russian, state. It is important to understand that this discursive space does not "just exist" but is drawn forth by specific interlocutionary situations, such as political arguments, public statements, and indeed discussions with foreigners such as myself. There is a public genre in which many rural people are prepared bitterly to criticise current government policies and personalities, but they draw back from anything that might cause them to reconsider *gosudarstvennost'*, the abstract notion of the powerful State itself. The very existence of rebellions against collectivisation or the labour camps in Buryatiya[24] would impugn the moral legitimacy of such a state, and therefore knowledge of such matters is thrust inward and hidden. The Soviet state is said to have performed its duty, i.e., positive advances for Buryats in education, medicine, technology, hygiene, and housing. Crucial to Buryat self-definition in this particular imagery is the rejection of ethnic identification with the Mongols, who are often said to be "backward," "Asiatic," and a different nation. People may even identify themselves not as Buryats but as *Rossiyan'ye,* citizens of Russia. They celebrate the idea of the strong state and their place as patriotic citizens in it. Now, discordantly with this line, there are voices which call on the Buryat government officially to register the Buryats as a "repressed people" of the Russian Federation. This would entitle the Buryats to apply for compensation for the sufferings of the 1930s and support for their culture, but, at the same time, it would place them in a "complainant" position vis-à-vis the state and undoubtedly rile the Russian majority in Buryatiya. We are dealing here not just with discourse but with effective decisions with long-term implications. The Buryat government has steadfastly refused all such calls to register the Buryats as "repressed"; instead, the stance is to be "loyal."[25]

The ethnicisation of the notion of Russia, however, imposes a hierarchisation of different views. Looking not across the frontier to Mongolia but toward the wars and uncertainties in the west and south of Russia itself, Buryats' identification with Russia is more equivocal. In this perspective it is they who are Asiatic, and the buried memories of 1937 colour a justified fear of a Russian nationalist backlash against even small public encouragement of Buryat distinctiveness.[26] Buryat enthusiasm for actually joining up with Mongolia in the early 1990s was limited and short-lived.[27] Nevertheless, alternative theories inspired by diverse Mongolian and Asian themes have recently surged to the surface in intellectual circles. Energised by constant new interpretations of history, religion, and literature and sustained by a thoughtful press, some of these ideas not only create extended perspectives for discussion but are also put into action. For example, the Buryat National Congress is a forum for all ethnic Buryats, cross-cutting the divisions of the Russian nation-state,[28] the Festival of Geser is a celebration of mythic Asian heroism,[29] and in places environmental projects have been started to reintroduce "traditional pastoralism" with native breeds from Mongolia and China. The revival of Buddhism has created another significant space, linking Buryatiya with Mongolia, Inner Mongolia, Tyva, Kalmykiya, Tibet, and India. This is again a highly differentiated realm, impossible to discuss adequately here. In Buryatiya alone there are government-sponsored rituals,[30] fierce conflicts over precedence among lay Buddhists and lamas, new initiatives such as a monastery for women in the capital city,[31] and widespread renovation of old temples. Shamanic practice is just as active. An Association of Shamans has been established in Ulan-Ude. Famous Buryat shamans not only travel to the villages to conduct rituals, but many of them also recognise the power and seniority of shamans living in Mongolia, while others have links with new religions and are invited all over the world. All of this cultural ferment is not just a one-way movement from the centre to the periphery. The cult of Soodei Lama of Barguzin (p. 505), for example, was a matter of local oral transmission until spreading rivulets of interest brought grand lamas to the remote valley to take part in the revival of his memory in 1996. Just because people live in distant areas does not mean they cannot imagine vast space or are debarred from pontificating discourse. There is nothing new about this for Buryats: Soodei Lama in the late nineteenth century corresponded with Turgeniyev and with people in France, Germany, Tibet, and India. Thus, there are rural as well as city projections about the grand subject of "What is to be done?"

Oral genealogies are like bridges between private remembrance and more shared forms of discourse. *Karl Marx Collective* discussed genealogies as shaping the historical imagination (pp. 52–63) and kinship strategies such as exogamy and adoption (pp. 343–9) as part of the accumulation of political capital. The new chapters outline different ways in which the genealogical imagination has changed in post-Soviet times. But I must emphasize here that genealogies are also practices of remembrance. Thus, the *individual people* who died in the fight against collectivisation (and in the numerous wars fought by Soviet troops) are not at all forgotten. They are remembered in their families, as personalities, and they are never categorised in terms such as "resistance fighters" or "bandits." This is why, when I discussed *Karl Marx Collective* with the villagers, they pored over the kinship diagrams and were taken aback and disappointed that I had changed most of the names of people in recent generations. They wanted all of the real names to be there.

To illustrate some of these points and show how the shifts of the last few years have affected individual lives, I end with the stories of two people whose photographs appeared in the first edition. Oyuna Lubsanova Ukhanayeva is the real name of the little girl who appears sitting on her shepherd father's knee on p. 413.[32] I have a vivid memory of taking this photograph in 1967 in the dusty sunshine at the remote pastures of Selenga, of the shepherd tired and motionless leaning on the veranda of his hut. I remember being so impressed that Lubsan and his wife, Medegma, with just one other helper, were herding nearly 700 sheep with over 600 lambs. I recall how Lubsan explained that when they were successful as shepherds, which meant raising 100 lambs from 100 ewes, they were rewarded with all-expenses paid holidays at the Black Sea. In 1996 I heard the rest of the story of this family. When they reached school age Oyuna and her siblings were sent from the pastures to the family's village house, where they were brought up by Lubsan's mother. After Lubsan died, Medegma continued for a time as a shepherd. Now Medegma says, "I could hardly read or write, but my daughter is a scientist." Oyuna grew up to take a *kandidat* degree in anatomical morphology. She lives in the city of Ulan-Ude, and shortly is to do a doctorate if she gets a grant. In August 1996 Oyuna had come back home on a visit to take part in the hay cutting. Charming and well dressed, she brought the aura of the town to the village, speaking about the competition for places at the Institute, the new reading she had to do on zoology to prepare for a temporary teaching job, the comparison of Moscow and provincial academies. But recent circumstances have given her admirable career a new twist and seem to have altered the mother-daughter relationship.

After she retired as a shepherd, Medegma had returned to the village, bringing her few privately owned cattle, sheep, and pigs and no doubt expecting a quiet old age. As times grew hard in the 1990s and wages from her children stopped coming in, however, Medegma taught herself vegetable and fruit production. Her plot is a model of proficiency: there are glasshouses and raised beds, which are fertilised and ingeniously irrigated. Rows of salads and vegetables are sown to ripen at regular intervals. In her light, clean, spacious house Medegma's eyes gleamed as she joked with her daughter and piled on the jams, conserves, creams and yoghurts, meat patties, and baked goods for me to consume. All of these were the produce of her own hands. Overwhelmed by her hospitality, I remarked what hard work must be involved these days. "No," replied Medegma, "It was hard work *then,* in the collective." I could see that she found great fulfillment in her present life, and I sensed the unique value of the things entirely made and given by the person sitting before me.

Here then are the altered vistas in the life of one ordinary family. Soviet organisation outlined a space constituting the pastures and the weekly visit by horse cart to the village, in which the holidays at the Black Sea were like the wonderful promises of socialism come true. The drudgery of the Soviet era always held a channel of hope for young people who could move upward by study.[33] Today education and TV have given the family a more globalised space in imagination, but everyday practice has contracted their options. They are limited to the run between the village and the capital city (where Oyuna's brother also works, on a building site), education now costs money, which they do not have, and Black Sea holidays are altogether impossible. Oyuna achieved the Soviet dream, but now she does not know if she will get her grant; she has put off marrying, and I had the impression that her mother's marvellous self-sufficiency was a great comfort to her. Thus, the town turns to the village, the younger to the older generation.

Viktor Dabayevich Chimidtsyrenov, whose picture appears on p. 137, was at that time (1975) Chief Engineer of the Karl Marx Collective in the Barguzin Valley. Now in 1996 he is retired, but he has become the head of a "private

xvii

farm" (see p. 449) within the OKKh Bayangol. Viktor decided to call his new farm Arbijil, on the precedent of the famous commune of that name of the 1920s (pp. 142–7). It might seem curious to use a name so redolent of communist traditions for a new commercial enterprise, but, as I attempt to show in Chapter 10, this is not strange when we see how Buryats are frequently turning to history as inspiration for the future. Viktor is someone who was always attracted to history and literature. His house in the collective has shelves of well-thumbed Pushkin, Gogol, Lermontov, Stendahl, and so forth, and he told me how in Soviet times, when there was no TV, he used to read aloud to his family in the evenings. Being one of a tiny group of local administrators who moved from post to post between the collective, the Soviet and the Party, Viktor can only be seen as a stalwart of the Soviet system. Yet it is he who was one of the first to set up a commercial farm, in fact a fairly common situation, and, more unusually, it is he who is the main genealogist of Bayangol.

Viktor studied the genealogies I published in *Karl Marx Collective* and said he could do "better than that." Just before I left he provided me with several handwritten scrolls containing hundreds of names and mapping all the major clan groupings. What was most interesting to me was that neatly written around the names were extensive notes on certain ancestors. Viktor had interviewed old people to verify oral narratives so the information would be "correct," but at the same time the tone of the stories was not quite matter-of-fact. In fact, the same means of mythicisation were used to elevate these narratives as in classical legends of inner Asia, namely the *fixing* of story themes to particular places in such a way as to render them both experiential-believable and at the same time make them archetypal and supra-mundane. Lack of space precludes me from proving this point, which would require analysing many examples, but at least I can cite one of Viktor's stories to show how the era of *Karl Marx Collective* is a source of heroic images for today. The Karalik irrigation system was mentioned earlier (p. 206) as a perennial technical and financial problem for the collective farm, but in what Viktor wrote it appears as an authored creation, inseparable from the people who built it, and thus given the hue of the genealogical imagination. Attached to the Butama Shono genealogy is the following:

When collectives were first organised, on the initiative of Sangadin, the first chairman of the Arbizhil commune, the Karalik system was begun. First, using the plans of an Austrian prisoner-engineer, they laid foundations for the magistral canal at the place called Khügshööl, but because it required a huge amount of digging and concrete they could not finish the head work, and to this day this canal has no water in it and stands as a monument to the people's effort and engineers' mistakes. But a simple blacksmith, the illiterate Lobkhaarov Nanzan, crafted a home-made level from a gun-barrel and used it to construct another Karalik system, and to this day the main canal runs along the stream which was defined by this local hero-smith of the Butama Shono clan. Later, the system was supplied with engineering equipment and recently it has been in the hands of Garmayev Dashi Zabitorovich of the Butama Shono clan. It gives enough water to irrigate 5,000 hectares of land.

In 1996 there was a lightening of the atmosphere as compared to Soviet times, a new openness and realism, and my presence itself was as good a sounding-board for this as any. In the 1960s I was evidently suspected of being a spy, it being only puzzling who could have sent such a young and inexperienced person.[34] But in 1996 I was able to travel to the Bayangol farm with Buryat friends to stay with their relatives, and to visit the Selenga farm quite unannounced. An elderly woman said, "We are not afraid of you now." Afraid or not, I shall never forget the extraordinary generosity of Buryat people on all of my visits. Whatever 'reasons' anthropologists might provide to explain generosity, or dissolve it in 'discourse', it is in the end simply very moving to be surrounded with the warmth of people to whom one can give so little in return.

This is a time of uncertainty in Russian history in which it would be inappropriate to attempt the delineation of a clear temporal succession of epochs and transitions. In this book I do not aim to sum up 'the lesson' of collectivisation, because the process is not finished. My more modest goal is to describe the fate of the farms and their people with the demise of Communism and the ways they are engaging with the present critical situation. Some general arguments will be made, but I do not claim for what I depict that it is the embodiment of any abstract principle. More valuable at this point is an attempt to unite the material and the interpretation of the material in such a way as to achieve an understandable representation, embracing the plasticity of the here and now.

Acknowledgements

I would particularly like to thank Bair Gomboyev and Balzhan Zhimbiyev for travelling with me in Buryatiya and for their immense generosity and that of their families and relatives. I owe a great debt to all the people in Buryatiya who helped me. My particular thanks go to Eza Grigorievna and Pavel Ivanovich Tenetov, Tserenzhap Arsalanovich Zhimbiyev, Oleg Khobituevich Batuyev, Lev Budayevich Radnayev, Chinggis Muizitovich Bazarov, Viktor Dabaevich Chimidtserenov, Leonid Bazarovich Linkhoyev, Aleksei Dashinimayevich Gomboyev, Butidma Damdinovna Badmayeva, Daba Laidapovich Galsanov, Nina Tserenovna Danzheyeva, Tsetsegma Baldarzhayevna Tapkharova, Sergei Aleksandrovich Galsanov, Dulma Tsydenovna Galsanova, Medegma Ochirovna Dashiyeva, and Ayuna Lubsanovna Ukhanayeva.

I would like to acknowledge the friendly discussions of the following scholars whose comments helped me clarify my ideas: Galina Manzanova, Lyuba Abayeva, Tanya Skrynnikova, Tsymzhit Vanchikova, Sergei Panarin, Hibi Watanabe, and Natasha Zhukovskaya. I am also very grateful to Balzhan Zhimbiyev, James Laidlaw, David Sneath, and especially Frances Pine, for enormously helpful comments made on early drafts of the new chapters.

Preface to new edition

For tape recordings and photographs made in 1993 I would like to thank the volunteers of Raleigh International. I gratefully acknowledge the financial support of King's College Cambridge for fieldwork done in 1996.

Notes

1 The new chapters are based on a short visit to the Bayangol Karl Marx Collective in 1990 and a longer visit in summer 1996 to this farm and to neighbouring farms in the Barguzin region and the Selenga Karl Marx farm.

2 In the 1995 Presidential elections Buryatiya as a whole gave Zyuganov, the ex-Communist, a narrow win over Yeltsin. This was also the case in both Barguzin and Selenga districts.

3 Buryatiya's name was changed from Buryat ASSR to Buryat Republic (*Buryaad Respublika*) in March 1992. There are around 421,600 Buryats in the CIS, most of whom live in the Buryat Republic of Russia. A further 28,000 Buryats live in Mongolia, and some 20,000 live in China, a portion of these being old inhabitants from the eighteenth century onward but many having escaped from war and collectivisation in Russia in the 1920s–early 1930s. In the Buryat Republic the proportion of Buryats rose slightly by 1995 to 24% of the population, the rest being mostly Russians. Today, around 60% of the Buryats live in rural areas, and they still tend to specialise in livestock herding. However, under a third of the employed rural population had jobs directly in agriculture, as opposed to administration, services, teaching, etc.

4 *Obyedinenye krestyanskikh khozyaistv* (OKKh).

5 In 1990 the museum was a source of pride. Dominated by Marx in the first room, with a quotation from Lenin, "Marx's ideas are great because they are true!" other rooms displayed early Buryat utensils, farming implements, etc. Photographs and documents illustrated regional history, from the nineteenth-century princes through the communes of the 1920s and the amalgamations to the productive achievements of recent years. There was a photo of the previously unmentionable revolutionary Rinchino (pp. 31, 60) but no account of his arrest or his rehabilitation. "Everyone will know about that," I was told by the museum director.

6 "Russia survey," *Economist,* 12 July 1997, 17. In Buryatiya there were officially registered 3,352 private farmers in 1996, but they produced little (a total 870 tons of meat, e.g.), and the great majority do not function as farmers (Manzanova 1997).

7 Opinions have swung firmly in this direction since the early 1990s. In 1992, according to studies in many districts of Buryatiya, 15–20% of villagers supported individualised farming, but by 1995 the proportion had dropped to 3% (Manzanova 1997).

8 In 1996 real incomes in Buryatiya were 69.4% of those in 1991, and the value of pensions was 28.3% of those in 1991. The minimum subsistence level was defined as around $70 a month. In 1995, 65% of the households with incomes below the poverty line were classified as "extremely poor" (in Russia as a whole the proportion was 37.6%), and 52.1% were in a state of continual poverty (in Russia, 19.3%) (Naidanova and Dumnova 1997, 134–5).

9 In 1994, in comparison with 1988, the number of births had gone down 1.7 times, and the number of deaths had risen 1.5 times, according to a study of Buryat demography. The average family size declined from 4.2 to 4 members. Life expectancy of men reduced from 62.4 to 57.2 years and of women from 72.8 to 70.5 years (Naidanova and Dumnova 1997, 133).

10 Chernomyrdin sanctioned a credit of 128 milliard rubles in December 1996 (*Selenga,* 31 January 1997, 1).
11 In 1996 the "commodity credit" system for agriculture (see p. 467) required loans worth over 92 milliard rubles from Moscow. The Republic could only repay around two-thirds of this sum by the end of the year (*Buryatiya,* 25 July 1997, 2).
12 *Barguzinskaya Pravda,* 13 March 1996, 1.
13 As land is still, in practise, state owned in Buryatiya, it is deemed to have no value. Therefore, banks will not treat it as collateral, so credit is virtually unobtainable on this account. This is true in most of rural Russia ("Russia survey," 17).
14 *Barguzinskaya Pravda,* 22 May 1996, 1.
15 As in the first edition, the names of people still alive have been changed unless they specifically agreed to be named.
16 On the early history of the Buryats, readers can consult Forsyth 1992; on the Buryat revolutionary Elbekdorzhi Rinchino (pp. 31, 60), see Nimayev et al. 1994; on ethnopolitical relations of the late 1980s, see Buyakhayev 1993; on Buryat Buddhism, see Snelling 1993; and on its recent revival, see Zhukovskaya 1992, 1995, 1997b; on local cults and shamanism, see Hamayon 1990a; Abayeva 1992; Galdanova 1992; and Zhukovskaya 1997a; and, on contemporary Buryat national identity, see Hamayon 1996; and Zhukovskaya 1995.
17 In other regions the resistance was greater. In 1931–2 12 antirevolutionary organisations were liquidated, including 824 people in Mukhorshibiri, 250 in Ekhirit-Bulagat, and 575 in Kabansk district (Dorzhiyev 1993, 56).
18 For example, a small book published locally in 1993 on the history and culture of Noyokhon does not mention the uprising, even though this was one of its main centres. The section on history consists almost entirely of genealogical materials.
19 There were 20,878 Buryats mobilised during World War I (Naidakov 1993, 20).
20 In Irkutsk Guberniya, to the west of Lake Baikal, Buryats lost 53.3% of their land, and the Khori Buryats to the east lost 49% of their land in this revision. This caused a reduction in livestock numbers and significant impoverishment of Buryats, between 11 and 25% of whom had no stock at all in 1917 (Naidakov 1993, 21). It is not clear to what extent, if at all, land was restored to Buryats during the 1920s.
21 A beautiful war memorial stands on the hill above the Selenga Karl Marx farm from which I took the photograph on p. 142. It is engraved with the names of around 350 soldiers killed in World War II. This must have been a high proportion of the male population of the Iro Valley.
22 Absence of new school textbooks has created a gap in knowledge. For example, young people in Bayangol in 1993 were convinced that it was Lenin, not Stalin, who was responsible for collectivisation.
23 *Buryatiya,* 23 July 1997, 3.
24 As far as I know, there are no publications giving information on the camps in Buryatiya, though the existence of a "huge army of camp labour" is acknowledged in Naidakov 1993, 68. Young people in Barguzin in 1993 said there had been a camp in the neighbourhood but then hurriedly said they did not know where it was.
25 Accusing the Buryat government of cowardice, Buryat intellectuals have written, "The non-recognition of repression is an agreement to its repetition. The Ingush, Kalmyks, Tatars, Bashkirs, Sakha, and Chuvash have created through their leaderships, through their passion and energy, the face and form of their nations in Russia and in the world. But what about us, the proud descendants of the World Shaker? (Chingghis Khan)" (*Buryatiya,* 23 July 1997, 3).
26 As Khazanov (1997, 136) notes: "Stateism was always an important ideological factor in Russia; its current merger with nationalism seems almost natural. Under

the circumstances, the claim that the Russian Federation is above all the Russian national state has a certain appeal for Russian audiences." In Buryatiya in the early 1990s a tiny "Teach Yourself Buryat" column in the main regional newspaper aroused fierce objections from Russians; "Why should this native language be forced on us?" etc. Another example is an organisation calling itself the Committee for the Protection of the Rights of Peoples, which objected to a decision taken by the Supreme Soviet of Buryatiya to allow the territorial status of the Republic to be changed if over half the Buryat population vote for it. This would mean that 13% of the population (Buryats) could decide the fate of the Russian majority (76% of the population). The Committee's document continues: "Why should the Buryats have power over us? Did they conquer us? We live on our own Russian land, Siberia is Russian land. Our ancestors acquired this land, brought European culture and civilised the local peoples. The Buryats received statehood (*gosudartvennost'*) from our hands, and if they cannot use it, we should take it back."

27   Rather, this imagined terrain seems to suggest the advisability of keeping heads down in the face of the long-standing Russian state paranoia about political disintegration and borders (Humphrey 1997). Indeed "an extraordinary situation of frontier security," requiring even local people to have permits to travel in the Selenga area, which borders on Mongolia, was the explanation farmers gave in 1996 for why I had not been allowed to revisit the collective in the 1970s.

28   The Congress is one of a number of Buryat nongovernmental movements. It has an organising committee and members from all over Russia. The Congress discusses issues of Buryat concern, especially the preservation of language and culture and the possibility of reuniting the three separate regions of Ust-Ordynsk, the Buryat Republic, and Aga. The latter question is raised frequently, but union is recognised to be unrealistic in the near future.

29   Geser, the mythic hero of the epic story, was promoted as a national symbol by the Buryat government in 1990 and was subsequently made the subject of a series of local festivals in the villages of famous bards. Significantly, these festivals involved the passing of a flag (*tug*) from place to place, linking the three administratively separate regions of Ust-Ordynsk, the Buryat Republic, and Aga (Hamayon 1996).

30   For example, the 1991 celebration of the 250th anniversary of the official recognition of Buddhism in Russia was a massive event, held in the national stadium and attended by the Dalai Lama. Zhukovskaya (1992) describes the officious, quasi-Soviet style of this occasion.

31   Traditionally, only men became monastic lamas. The women's monastery was opened in July 1997 with a prayer to the goddess Tara (Dara Eke) in the presence of the Vice Premier of the government and religious leaders, including the head of the Russian Orthodox Church in Buryatiya (*Buryatiya,* 25 July 1997, 1).

32   Lubsan Ukhanayev's genealogy is on p. 343. I discovered in 1996 that Oyuna is Lubsan's daughter, not his granddaughter.

33   Young Nikolai, the Russian helper-shepherd, in 1967 used to take books to the pastures and attended evening classes from six till ten o'clock.

34   Even on my unexpected visit to Bayangol in 1990, I later learned that it was a KGB official who had taken the responsibility of conducting me back to the farm.

Maps

Figures

Tables

Tables

xxvi

Tables

Acknowledgements

I am grateful to the following institutions for their generous support of my research in the USSR, of which this book is one result. The British Council awarded me an exchange studentship in 1966–7, 1968, and again in 1974–5. This studentship enabled me to become a research student at Moscow State University in 1966–7, and I am grateful to the staff and students of the Kafedra Etnografii in Moscow for their advice, help, and administrative support. While in the Buryat ASSR I was given every facility by the Buryat Filial of the Academy of Sciences, including accommodation in Ulan-Ude, transport by light aircraft and by jeep to the collective farms, and, most important of all, academic supervision and advice while in the field. I am deeply grateful to the director and staff of the Filial for their support, and I would like to add that I am solely responsible for the conclusions and perspectives of this book, which do not necessarily reflect either the opinions or the policies of the Filial.

In the long period of writing up the Buryat materials I was generously supported by grants from the Wenner Gren Foundation for Anthropological Research, by Girton College, Cambridge, which gave me a research fellowship, and by the Fortes Fund of Cambridge University Department of Social Anthropology which awarded me a grant for typing expenses. I would like to thank the Scott Polar Research Institute, Cambridge, for the help given me in the period of writing, and in particular Mr Harry King, Librarian of the Institute, and Dr Terence Armstrong for their understanding long-term loans of Siberian materials.

I am deeply indebted to Edmund Leach, to whom this book is dedicated, my teacher and friend, without whose inspiration I would never have become an anthropologist. He supervised my research in the USSR and provided that enthusiasm for the interesting questions of anthropology without which I would not have persevered with this book. He followed my work and read and criticised my early writings with the thoughtfulness of a great teacher.

In Moscow I was given kindly support, far beyond what was my due as any research student, by my supervisor Professor Sergei Aleksandrovich Tokarev. I was also much helped by Natasha L. Zhukovskaya, S.A. Arutyunov, and V.N. Basilov, and other staff of the Institute of Ethnography. In Ulan-Ude K.M.

Acknowledgements

Gerasimova, who accompanied me to the collective farms in 1967 and who made my visit in 1975 possible, gave me cheerful and practical companionship, useful advice, and many insights into Buryat culture. Despite the trouble which I may have caused her, she gave unfailing support, as well as criticism, and hospitality, which I cannot forget. I am also grateful to A.A. Plishkina, K.D. Basayeva, I.A. Asalkhanov, and T.M. Mikhailov for their practical help and academic advice while I was in Buryatiya. May I add again that, although I benefited from the suggestions of my Soviet colleagues, I alone am responsible for the contents of this book.

Many other people have given me help and read and commented on portions of this work. I would like to thank first of all Professor Meyer Fortes, my initial supervisor, who backed this research and subsequently on many occasions discussed questions arising from it with his own blend of wisdom and sympathy. I would like to thank the following for their comments and suggestions: Terence Armstrong, Paul Sant Cassia, John Dunn, Ernest Gellner, Maurice Godelier, Jack Goody, Roberte Hamayon, Robert Hecht, Istvan Hont, Christine and Steven Hugh-Jones, Nicholas Humphrey, Michael Ignatieff, Raoul Itturra, Everett Jacobs, Owen Lattimore, Urgunge Onon, Quentin Outram, Teodor Shanin, Peter Skalnik, Michael Small, Keith Tribe, Terence Turner, Piers Vitebsky and Peter Wiles.

For typing and other editorial assistance I am indebted to Mrs Pat Little, Sally Roberts, and Lucia Szeto. Mary Bouquet helped me by preparing the maps and genealogues, and I am grateful to Mrs Patricia Williams of the Cambridge University Press for her encouragement and assistance with the production of this book.

Finally, I owe an essential debt of gratitude to the officials and kolkhozniks of the Karl Marx collective farm in Selenga and the Karl Marx collective farm in Barguzin, Buryat ASSR. This book is about them and is intended to convey the respect which I feel for their way of life and their endeavours. Most personal and some place names used in this book are pseudonyms, although Selenga and Barguzin are real districts. The photographs, all taken by the author, depict life in the collective farms but are not of identifiable persons in the book. The map of the Barguzin Karl Marx collective (Map 3) was prepared by the Secretariat of that kolkhoz.

I have used a standard system of transliteration of Russian words and extended this to Buryat words when written as they were spoken by the collective farmers. Barguzin and Selenga districts each have their own dialects, neither of which correspond with the official Buryat written language, which is based on the Khori dialect. In the glossary I have added to my version of the dialect word the official spelling taken from Cheremisov 1973. Many Buryat words (e.g. *ulus*, *aimak*, etc.) have Russianised versions which are used in the ethnographic literature, and where I have quoted from the literature I have used these. For Mongolian words I have used the spellings given in Lessing *et al.* 1960.

Acknowledgements

The tables given in this book are taken directly from Soviet sources and I am aware that in some cases the figures are added up incorrectly, but rather than tinker with the data I have left the tables as they stand.

C.H.
Summer 1981

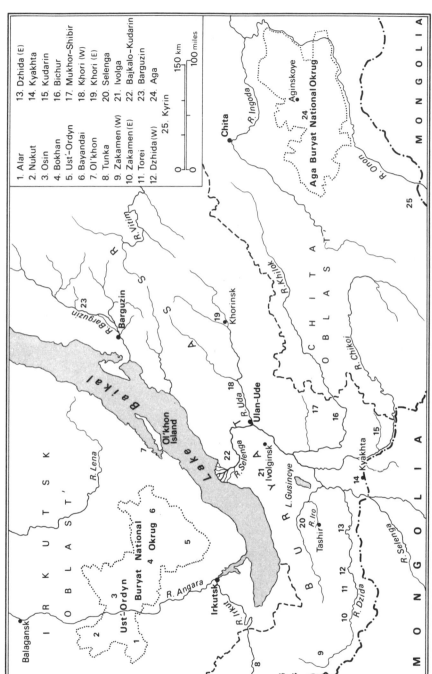

Map 1. Places of Buryat settlement around Lake Baikal.

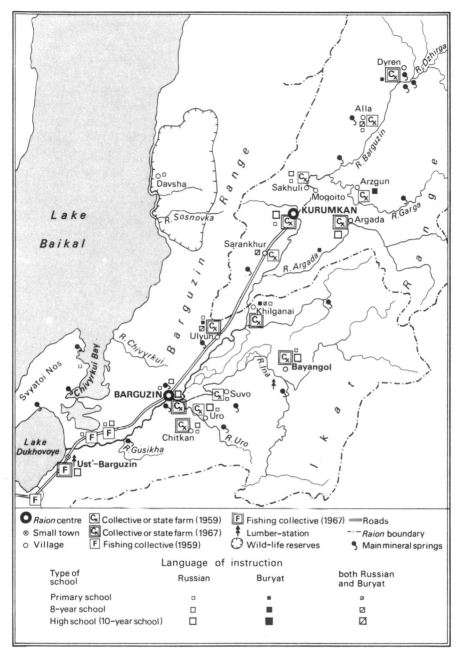

Map 2. Map of the Barguzin valley. From Buyantuyev 1959 and *Atlas Zabaikal'ya*, Glavnoye Upravleniye Geodezii i Kartografii pri Sovete Ministrov, Moscow–Irkutsk, 1967

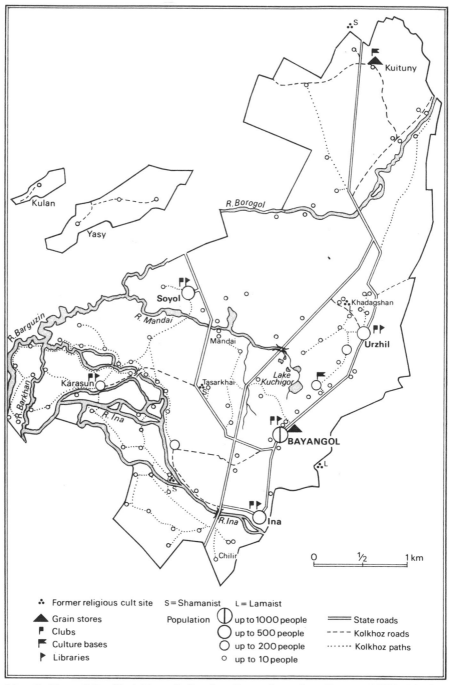

Map 3. Map of the Karl Marx Collective, Barguzin region, Buryat ASSR, 1975. Prepared by the Secretariat of the farm.

Introduction

The collective farm was a massive economic and social experiment. The unique-
ness in its time of the Soviet solution has often blinded observers to the generality
of the problem, one facing all new states which are ethnically diverse and which
have not industrialised in a comprehensive way: the need to integrate local cultures and rural economies at different stages of development into one national
political economy. It is against the background of this task, the immense difficulty of which the experiences of the 'Third World' is now revealing, that we
should assess the Siberian case. In what follows I describe the Buryats, a nationality with a mainly pastoral economy and traditions of nomadism. My research
was carried out in two collective farms, both incidentally called after Karl Marx,
in the Selenga and Barguzin districts, just north of the Mongolian border, in the
Buryat ASSR (Buryatiya). The Buryats, of Mongolian origin, were at the time of
the Revolution experiencing a burgeoning of Lamaist Buddhism and the first
stirrings of nationalism. The book discusses in this context the relation between
the collective farm as an economic institution and its role as an instrument of
political and cultural integration.

The period studied is the 1960s and 1970s, and this should be emphasised,
since there have been continuous changes in aspects of agricultural policy, and
developments in education, industry and external trade have affected and will
affect all citizens of the USSR. Nevertheless, the collective farm as a *structure*
has remained remarkably constant since its inception in the late 1920s, a point
which is discussed in relation to the two Buryat farms in Chapter 4.

The main policy change in the early 1980s was the greater encouragement
given to private domestic production and subsidiary farming in enterprises such
as factories or construction camps. The low productivity of collective as opposed
to private farming has been seen as *the* crisis of Soviet agriculture. But it would
be mistaken, in my view, to make an analysis in terms of a simple opposition
between these two, since the 'rights' over the means of production and the
produce are in fact distributed in a complex way over the entire range of 'private'
and public spheres. In other words, the 'private' is not as private as it may seem,
nor is the 'public' as public. This matter is discussed in greater detail below, and
also in Chapter 3, but for the moment we can note that the products of the

1

domestic economy are in the early 1980s included in the *state* plan for the district. It is probable that this change in emphasis will have less effect, for the present, than might be imagined, mainly because few funds appear to be allocated specifically to help private production. But the reader should be aware that the Soviet government is by no means complacent about the performance of collective and state farms, and that the problems mentioned in this book for the 1960s and 1970s are the kind of difficulties which the government is trying to deal with today. The government will probably make further changes in organisation, but only those consistent with its vision of socialism. The nature of this vision, and the role in it of collective farms, is discussed in Chapter 2.

The collective farm cannot be understood in isolation from the Soviet state.[1] This book does not attempt to deal with the nature of the state as a totality, but it does present a study of local communities embedded within the specifically Soviet state structure. The Buryats were at a pre-industrial, pre-capitalist stage before the 1917 revolution. Although the economic and political functions of their communal institutions (clans, land-holding communities) were destroyed by collectivisation, the Buryats were provided with Soviet institutions of an equally non-individualist, non-capitalist kind. This history makes their present situation unlike that of minorities embedded within 'capitalist' states. Its vastness and great geographical diversity, combined with an unprecedentedly centralised administrative system, ensures that the USSR is quantitatively as well as qualitatively different from other state systems. The USSR creates an impression of unfathomable complexity — complexity certainly quite out of the range of the social anthropologist, who is traditionally at home with 'simple societies'. It has been impossible not to feel daunted by this problem. But nevertheless, it being clear that small-scale societies can be extremely complicated, and that, conversely, gigantic states can be described at least in certain respects in terms of quite simple arguments, I have in fact found useful certain ideas deriving from the roots of the anthropological tradition.

Certain Soviet theorists have seen the Soviet state in terms of a simple cybernetic model of hierarchy (of government).[2] The hierarchy, consisting of vertically related sub-systems in which the higher directs the lower, is seen in the Soviet case to comprise the following four territorial-administrative levels: (1) the Soviet republic, (2) the autonomous republics, the *krai*, the *oblast'*, and the autonomous *oblast'*, (3) urban and rural districts, and (4) towns, villages, and settlements. 'Each higher level receives from the succeeding lower levels information about their conditions, works on this information, and then transmits orders from above to below, altering the activity in the lower systems in the necessary direction.'[3] In the USSR three institutions form the structures which transmit information and instructions through these levels: the departmental Ministries, the Soviets, and the Communist Party. The use by Soviet theorists of a cybernetic model to discuss their political system is in itself highly significant, but whatever we may think of such an approach as an analysis, the collective farm was in fact set up in such a way as to conform with this view of society: in a formal sense, it is a microcosm of the state. The collective farm has an administrative hierarchy (the enterprise management, the brigade or sector, the production team, and the household), and the structures transmitting information and commands between these levels again are three: the functional organisation of the kolkhoz, the Soviets, and the Party. In a state farm (*sovkhoz*) all three of these are direct continuations of the national institutions, while in a collective farm the lowest level of ministerial organisation is replaced by the semiindependent structure of the kolkhoz administration.

But the cybernetic or command model is manifestly inadequate, in that it takes no account of conflict, nor of what might loosely be called 'informal social relations'. Both of these must be present at all levels of the Soviet state, but it is in analysis of the microcosm (a collective farm has some 3,000—5,000 members) that a specifically anthropological approach may be most valuable.[4] Detailed and intensive study of a small community may enable us more easily to discover not only unplanned for, or hidden, or heterodox, but even non-cognised, economic and social phenomena. Soviet theorists tend to see what they call random or arbitrary phenomena as characteristic of capitalism, where the top of the hierarchy is constituted by the incalculable interplay of market forces, while in the Soviet Union centralised planning ensures an infinitely greater *regulation* of economic life.[5] But of course this distinction is false, in that structured, even systematic, and yet unexpected developments occur in both kinds of economy. What is probably true is that centralised control of information, education, and communications makes such phenomena appear — perhaps even to be — fragmentary, and makes them difficult to assess, not only by outside observers but by Soviet people too. This is one of the themes pursued in this book.

I have tried in this book to describe not only the Soviet ideologue's view of the economy of the collective farm, but also the judgements of the professional sociologists and ethnographers of Buryatiya. The latter are by no means identical with the former, and they have produced fundamental work of great perception, to which this author owes very much. But they rarely attempt to come seriously to terms with that most difficult and fascinating, ultimately unknowable, subject: the way in which Buryat farm people themselves think about Soviet reality. In trying to come to some understanding of this I have, besides talking to the people themselves, read novels, letters to newspapers, reminiscences, archives of correspondences, transcriptions of autobiographical stories, myths, ritual texts, sayings and proverbs. As far as possible I have used materials in vernacular Buryat, as opposed to literary Buryat or Russian. Buryat farmers use all three of these on different occasions, but the vernacular can perhaps be expected to be more revealing of attitudes. In fact, I originally included a chapter in this book on changes in the language of Buryat kolkhozniks, but for reasons of space this will be published separately. The present book does, however, discuss, with the necessary caution as to differences between generations and between various socio-economic groups, attitudes to labour, to wealth, to kinship and individual identity, and to the future.

Functional anthropology's characteristic approach has been to insist upon the interconnectedness, though not necessarily the mutual harmony, of social phenomena which are conventionally thought of as distinct. The correctness of such an approach is particularly at issue in a study of this kind, where a community has been relatively abruptly subject to institutional change and ideological influence of clearly 'outside' origin. I believe that certain such interrelations do exist and are very important in a socially bounded community such as a collective farm (the nature of this 'boundedness' is discussed below). We may cite, for example, the relation between Buryat affinal kinship patterns and local 'political' strategies discussed in Chapter 7. But it is important not merely to point to such relations, where they exist, but also to assess their generalisability. Chapters 4 and 7 attempt to suggest points of disjuncture between the level of the farm and that of the district. It seems to be the case, for example, that at 'higher' levels such as that of the Buryat ASSR as a whole genealogical kinship gives way to associations based on territory ('east Buryats' and 'west Buryats') in respect of political alignments. This matter is beyond the scope of this book. But it is apparent that the connections revealed here within the farms I studied exist in variants in other local communities, and it is possible that, taken together, their refractions condition certain interactions at higher levels of the hierarchy.

Although collective farms all over the Soviet Union are organised according to the same principles, varying material conditions of course make them very different from one another and there are factors internal to the organisation of the distribution of surplus which ensure that each farm will act in its own interests. Therefore even if the collective farm, no less than the state farm, can be seen as an extension of the state, in practical terms it is also true that all farms, in fact all constituent units at whatever level, jostle for position, for inputs, for personnel, and autonomy in distribution. The simple 'command model'[6] of Soviet society, whether applied for the republic, the region, the district or within the farm itself, is misleading and should be replaced by theory which takes account of the interrelations between parts of society with bases in different kinds of power, and with diverging interests.

Max Gluckman's discussion of property relations, in particular land tenure, forms the implicit background to Chapter 3 of this book. It is true that his discussion was of an African kingdom, whose concepts of property were compared with those of Western industrial societies.[7] But Gluckman's ideas can profitably be applied to the Soviet case, where the gap between legal property and actual rights is one of the themes which interest us, since it is in working out methods of analysis for *unwritten* property relations that his contribution lies.

Gluckman argues that in pre-capitalist societies the individual's rights depend on his social and political status, or to put this another way, that there is a series of overlapping rights over the same bit of property and that this hierarchy of rights is defined by the hierarchy of social relations (in the case of the African kingdom he was discussing: members of households, household heads, village headmen, chiefs of tribes, king). It is by virtue of membership of social groups, whose relation to the land differs at the different levels, that each subject is entitled to claim rights over property, not as in capitalist society, where accumulated individual property and possession of money gives people social and political privileges. As already mentioned, the Buryats never passed through a capitalist phase,[8] and before the coming of Soviet power their rights to property were based on social status deriving from membership in kinship groups or territorial communities (*buluk*).[9] I would argue that after collectivisation their rights were still based on status, but status of a new and different kind. This was the status of 'kolkhoznik', i.e. member of a collective farm, originally derived from becoming a shareholder in the collective, but subsequently passed on to succeeding generations by virtue of birth in the family of a kolkhoznik. A member of a collective farm has certain rights as a Soviet citizen, but he or she also has specific rights (and lack of rights vis-à-vis other Soviet citizens) by virtue of the status of 'kolkhoznik'. The difference between this status and others in the Soviet Union was, for decades, very marked, and Soviet writers describe 'kolkhozniks' as a separate 'class'. This definition was based theoretically on economic criteria, i.e. the relation of the kolkhoz to the means of production, but in fact the most important differences between collective farmers and others have been political (for example, the kolkhoznik did not until recently have the possibility of acquiring an internal Soviet passport). These matters will be discussed in greater detail in Chapter 3, but for the moment the main point to establish is that a kolkhoznik until recent times held rights over property, and rights of other kinds, by virtue of a politically defined status, and one, furthermore, which was virtually non-negotiable.

Rights are further defined by reference to another type of political status, that is, membership of the Communist Party, and to a lesser extent its youth branch (Komsomol). In practice the absolute distinction between members and non-members of the Party is less important than the whole spectrum of 'political reliability', in which Party office-holders lie at one end and those judged 'unreliable' for various reasons (class antecedents, religious affiliation, etc.) lie at the other. The rights deriving from this kind of status are for the most part less formally defined than the rights exercised at the different levels of the kolkhoz hierarchy, but they are interwoven with the latter.

Gluckman insisted that individual rights, for example in land, do not encroach on the community's rights in systems based on status, because these rights can exist at the same time over the same piece of land, their adjustment being determined mainly by how the holders fulfil their obligations to one another in other (i.e. social and political) respects. He distinguished, for the African case, 'rights of administration', accruing to the hierarchy of political units, from 'rights of production', which in the African case belonged to peasant households. He uses the word 'estate' to refer to the rights in the means of production conferred by status in the socio-political system. 'Estates of production lie at the base of the hierarchy, but their position there may be temporary. For an estate of production can become an estate of administration if the holder grants portions of it to others . . . who then become his subordinates.'[10] In a Soviet collective farm there are several levels of estates of production (households, work-teams, and brigades or sectors). Over the period of Soviet history since collectivisation there has been a tendency for estates of production to expand to ever higher, and hence 'wider', levels. Tasks which once were carried out by small teams are now carried out on the basis of a sector, and as small collective farms have been amalgamated units which were once whole farms have become mere brigades (i.e. a process opposite to the one mentioned by Gluckman).

Any given individual thus holds many types of rights. For example, the head of a sheep-production brigade might hold rights as a Soviet citizen, as a household head, as a kolkhoznik, as a brigadier, and as a member of the Communist Party.

After 1969 the status of kolkhoznik was no longer inherited and became a matter of choice at the age of sixteen. From around this time we notice the effects in Buryatiya of a process which had begun earlier throughout Soviet society. This was the growing importance of educational qualifications as a basis for recruitment to leading positions in virtually all institutions, including collective farms. Since educational qualifications can be accumulated and negotiated in a way which status by birth cannot, there has been an increase in personal mobility. The kolkhoz is ceasing to be the tied local community it once was.

I shall not be concerned in this book with the question of whether Soviet reality corresponds to any given concept of 'socialism'. Nevertheless, it would perhaps be begging too many fundamental questions were we not to ask ourselves whether for the Buryats 'socialism' means just what exists, and not something more. I would suggest that this question must be considered in relation not only to Soviet ideology (by which I mean the set of ideas publicly expounded by those in official positions of power), but also in relation to Buryat conceptualisations of this ideology, which are conditioned by the specifically Buryat intellectual history, for example by attitudes derived from the Buddhist view of time, or by the vicissitudes of Buryat relations with Russian political ideas from the early-twentieth-century period of nationalism onwards.

Western observers often see Soviet ideology simply as an official cover-up for 'what is really going on'. In a sense this is true, in that the reality of social life is clearly different from place to place in various regions of the USSR. And such an argument is dangerous in that it tends to dismiss the role of ideology as 'not real', as simply legitimising after the fact a domination, or grasping for domination, which already exists. In fact, Soviet ideology is one of the internal components necessary for dominance by the state. It constitutes a form of social control, as I show in detail in the latter part of Chapter 2.

6

Introduction

I would disagree with the Polish political scientist Kolakowski in two points which he had made about the nature of Soviet ideology. He insisted that because the Marxist precepts which are used to justify and legitimate current ideology are decided 'institutionally', 'Marxism' thereby becomes a doctrine without a content, its substance being supplied in every case by decree.[11] However, it is important not to confuse current Soviet ideology with precepts taken from Marx, even though this confusion is constantly promoted by Soviet writers. Whatever one's view of the 'contentfulness' of the quotations selected from Marx, this by no means exhausts existing ideology. In fact, references are more frequently made to Lenin than to Marx, and more frequently to Brezhnev than to Lenin. Soviet ideology is institutionalised but it is also specific, voluminous, and in recent years increasingly matter-of-fact in tone.

Kolakowski's second point was that because the ideology is often phrased 'dialectically' (e.g., on the one hand one should combat cosmopolitanism, and on the other one should overcome nationalism), the two sides cancel one another out and create a theory which is eternally indefinite and whose strength lies in its blurredness.[12] Opaqueness might indeed lend strength to the ideology, as Maurice Bloch has suggested,[13] but in fact it is not characteristic of the Soviet case. 'Dialectical' phrasing of ideological statements is comparatively rare, and where it does occur the opposed concepts stand in practice for quite specific policies or institutions. These are indeed in opposition in political life. Soviet ideology is intended to deal with virtually every aspect of life, and enormous effort is devoted to seeing that there is an ideological instruction for every social phenomenon.

This condition means that Soviet ideology does have to keep shifting ground, but where outsiders have been mistaken is in presuming that these displacements are viewed by internal theoreticians as damaging or invalidating. On the contrary, as I have come to realise, they are entirely consistent with the Soviet view of social evolution, and in particular with the idea that ideology is 'scientific'. As with scientific theories, ideological theories can become outdated, since they emerge from constantly developing economic and political practice, and this means that, while remaining within a very broad Marxist framework, they *should* be superseded.

Thus it is a mistake to see the official ideology simply as counterposed to a distinct sphere called 'real life' or 'everyday life'. For the very reason that ideology is institutionalised it has to be seen as integral with the power structure which is itself part of 'everyday life'. This does not mean, of course, that the ideology encompasses all of people's consciousness, only that it forms part of everyone's consciousness.

Let me explain what I mean by 'part of everyone's consciousness'. In the Soviet Union great pressures are put on people to work, and in fact it is illegal not to have some officially designated occupation. Labouring in the kolkhoz, i.e. carrying out the tasks assigned, implies necessarily giving practical support to the

7

ideology in the sense that economic positions in the farm are inseparable from 'political' ones (see p. 456 n. 61), and the political raison d'être of every post, however lowly, is defined by the ideology. Even if the dominant part of one's consciousness is alienated from the task at hand, even if one thinks in a general sense that what one has been asked to do is pointless, nevertheless in order to go through the motions of carrying out the job one has to take account of its form and aims. *Pokazhukha* (Soviet slang for doing something for show) is in a sense even more tightly defined by ideology than genuine work.

The relation of activity to ideology results in a characteristic and all-pervasive *liability* which is peculiar to Soviet society. In the case of a collective farm for example, the economic structure is supposed to coincide with the managerial (or 'political'), but orders from above do not always specify an accompanying rationale, nor, of course, do all activities take place according to order. A worker or an official is often in a position where he must decide on a course of action which might be referred to two different ideological principles; or, he might be in a situation where a course of action is illegitimate at one level but justified by overall ideological principles at another. Furthermore, it is not possible, often, to know which principle will be applied by superiors in any given case. The very fact that the Soviet ideology is so multifarious and variable means that no action can be interpreted by it in only one way, and yet there has to be an officially valid rationale for every act. People often resort to having official, but bogus, papers made up in advance, to carry round 'just in case'. In other words, however great one's powers, one is always responsible to a greater extent. 'Responsibility' in the Soviet context is an enormously elastic concept. It stretches to all those ideological specifications of what someone in power might think one ought to do. As is shown in Chapter 5, the competence ascribed to any given position is always less than the responsibility attached to it. The difference between these two is the liability which hangs like an uncertain penumbra round so many activities.

Participating in the collective farm in any way constitutes a practical support for the ideology. At the same time, kolkhoz activities do not make sense except in terms of the ideology. There is no other general, easily understandable rationale, such as 'making the best use of resources' or the 'profitability of the enterprise', to which the individual can refer when carrying out his duties. Both of these ideas are in fact *subordinate* categories within the ideology. I show in Chapter 4 that all farms have centrally decided production specialisations, and that some farms are planned to make a loss, or to make a loss in certain of their sectors. The results of inappropriately planned specialisation can be disastrous, as was in fact the case in the Karl Marx kolkhoz in Barguzin. No one is better aware of this than the Buryat economists and planners themselves. Nevertheless, no radical solution has yet been proposed. While it is true that tasks are closely connected to plans, the plans themselves are formulated according to ultimately ideological criteria, in particular the idea that the product of the kolkhoz,

8

whether profitably produced or not, contains a 'surplus', which may be removed for the benefit of society as a whole. This idea dominates in general, and therefore problems tend to be solved by recourse to it alone, i.e. by short and long-term devices for producing more 'for society'. Examples of these, discussed in Chapter 4, are *subbotniki* (days of voluntary, usually unpaid, labour) and 'socialist competitions' between farms or work-groups in some particular field. These are employed at precisely those points in the production process which are not 'profitable' (*vygodno*) for any unit except 'society as a whole'.

But if consciousness is conditioned to a partial extent by the ideology which gives form and aim to kolkhoz work, there are clearly many conditions which give rise to other ways of thinking. One of these is the existence of privately owned livestock and the plot of land given by the kolkhoz for domestic production by each household (*dvor*). Each member of a collective farm is included in an officially registered household, with a head, who may be a man or a woman, and each household is entitled to own a limited number of livestock and to make use of a limited amount of land for its own production. Although I have argued that these rights do not differ essentially from rights held in 'collective' property, the household economy is seen by many people as 'what is left' of the pre-collectivised system and it is therefore still *managed* in culturally specific ways. In the Buryat case the 'private plot' is very rarely used for growing crops such as vegetables or fruits (which are seen as a Russian tradition) but is devoted to the production of fodder for the domestic livestock, and the latter are managed in most processes of production (pasturing, shearing, breeding, etc.) by non-kolkhoz social groups, usually groups of kin. The main form of distribution and realisation of the products of 'private' production is by means of ritualised exchanges, a tradition which goes far back into Buryat history. The chief social occasions for these exchanges are: the autumn culling of livestock for meat (*üüse*), betrothals and marriages, the Buddhist new year (*Tsagaansar*), birth celebrations, ritualised visiting, and funerals. Although patrilineal kin groups remain one framework for such exchanges, Chapter 5 shows that new social groups, which have emerged on the basis of communal work, neighbourhood, and the increased mobility of women, are also involved. In other words, while the structure of ritualised exchange continues, the social constituent units are changing.

The kolkhoz itself, and units such as brigades within it, also sometimes create products surplus to the obligatory delivery plan and which are not used in reproduction. I have called these products 'manipulable resources'. The existence of such resources is important because, so long as their presence is not officially taken into account, there is no ideologically specified way of dealing with them. Indeed, their presence in most circumstances is seen as illegitimate (see Chapter 4 section 4). They can rarely be used to make good a deficit in production by some other unit without an intervening exchange transaction. Characteristically, 'manipulable resources' of the work-teams and brigades enter the sphere of exchange in the same manner as the surplus of 'private' production. Sometimes they are divided up and distributed through the very same structures as domestically produced goods, and sometimes they are realised in gross, by sale or barter.

In the present-day Buryat kolkhoz such exchanges are no less important than they were in the pre-collectivisation period. They are a means towards the creation of, or maintenance of, socio-political status. They are used to obtain desirable positions in the division of labour, and, increasingly, in the prerequisite for such positions, educational opportunities.

It is significant that the nature of the goods exchanged has continued to change according to a tendency apparent even before the Revolution. Whereas in the nineteenth century the goods exchanged tended to be items of value in production, notably livestock and utensils, they are now almost always converted into items of consumption via the medium of money. Often they are things mostly for show: expensive clothing, crockery, samovars and electrical equipment, radios, gramophones, refrigerators, etc.

Sociologically, this development can be related to the classical anthropological discussion of the different function of rights to chattels as opposed to immoveable property. The anthropologist Jack Goody showed that land may be inherited in a patrilineal descent group while moveable property in the same society is distributed after death according to quite different, sometimes matrilineal principles.[14] Meyer Fortes pointed out that rights to chattels, for example those belonging to the mother's brother in patrilineal societies, enable individuals to build up stores of property independent of rights of ownership in their own lineages. This serves to break up the exclusiveness of 'corporations aggregate' by drawing their members into other relationships.[15] In the Soviet Union the collectivisation of agriculture and the law restricting the rights of individuals in the means of production to a small plot has served to emphasise the distinction between immoveable or productive property and chattels. In fact, individuals hold much stronger rights to the latter than to anything else: these are the only property rights which can be disposed of and transmitted to heirs. Socially, these rights are important, since they serve to differentiate individuals who otherwise have only common, theoretically equal, rights in collectively held estates.

In fact, as I show in Chapters 3 and 4, the rights *actually* held by people in the various positions of the kolkhoz are anything but equal: pay, conditions of work, and esteem are very different in different jobs. It appears that the exchanges I have mentioned are therefore used in two different modes: firstly, the equalising, according to the ideology of kinship or neighbourliness, of differences inherent in the division of labour, and secondly, the negotiation of access to the most desirable positions themselves.

Perhaps this requires further explanation. Private rights to chattels are not subject to the same hierarchy of rights as collective property, and although they are not held simply by individuals they can be converted into a certain kind of personal social influence by means of gift-debt relations (i.e. chattels are disposable by donors at public social gatherings). Such social advantages can be used in the sphere of the kolkhoz as well as outside it, for example in manoeuvring for advantageous working conditions. This does not contradict the basic point that economic power depends on socio-political status in the Buryat collective farm, and not the other way around. The prohibition, which is by and large enforced, on the private employment of labour, on private transactions involving interest, on investment in production, etc., means that individual accumulation of money or goods cannot on any general scale turn into exploitation of them as capital in the Western economic sense. Consequently, individually owned goods tend to be used as leverage for attaining status in the public sphere, or at least for negating the differences inherent in that sphere. Once obtained, an advantageous position in the public sphere can be used to create a variety of personal rights, for example, the freedom to travel, to use restricted shops, or to obtain locally unavailable goods.

But, in remote Siberian farms in the period we are considering, office-holders were more concerned with simply maintaining their position. All officials are nominated from above and appointed in the vast majority of cases by means of unopposed elections. They can be dismissed with equal facility. Because of the constant shifts in agricultural policy, the frequent impossibility of fulfilling delivery plans, and the real difficulty of organising a capital-intensive agriculture on the basis of a semi-nomadic pastoralism, officials have stood a very high chance of failure and of being sacked within a few years of taking office. In Chapter 7 I discuss the biographies of some officials, relations between the farm management and the local Soviet and the Party, and criteria of success.

Often the success of an official is largely outside his control, but a condition of any success is that he should have the support of his workforce. Thus there is a double system of dependence in the farm: the ordinary working people are always finding themselves in circumstances where they need an official to make an exception in their favour, while the officials need to win support, i.e. honest labour, from the workers in order to maintain their positions. The Soviet ideology and institutions provide few mechanisms by which these adjustments can be made. One solution, in the case of the Buryats, is to make use of the system of ritualised exchange (if this latter is understood in the widest sense). It would perhaps be misleading to see these exchanges as 'strategies'; they are carried on because one is always in a relation of obligation as a result of previous gift-giving, exchanges which were perhaps not undertaken by oneself but by parents or kinsmen. One word for 'gift' in Buryat is *khariu* ('reply' or 'return'). The decision which has to be taken is not to initiate a 'strategy' of gift-giving but to stop the endless process.

The ritual exchanges are the continued manifestation of a structure which was born in an earlier society. The traditional basis for this was in the herding economy which required collaboration between households, and in a more

11

general way, in mutual collective security in the face of droughts, floods, epidemics among the herds, the need to migrate, and other chance calamities of pastoralism in Siberia. Buryat kolkhozniks today are protected by the state, via the collective farm, from personal ruin as a result of natural disasters. In this sense the state itself is coming to take the place of nature as the potential source of prosperity and ruin, and it is in relation to this that mutual security must be organised. Mutual security is the overall effect, even if myriad small transactions are what is seen. There is no reason why we should expect Buryat rural people to have adopted an individualistic stance vis-à-vis the state, i.e. personal economic accumulation and the end of exchange. Up to the 1960s or so, their kinship structure, the consciousness of having a place as one among the elders or the juniors of one clan among other clans, the lingering notion of reincarnation of the soul of an ancestor, has served them adequately. If this kinship system becomes *merely* a mental form, that is if it ceases to influence the way in which people organise social relations — and there are signs that this is coming to be the case — then this must be due to changes in the modes of recruitment and operation of the Soviet state itself, in relation to which the Buryat kinship system is itself reproduced. The functions of kinship have already changed and been differentiated. The ways in which all of this is understood and represented symbolically is the subject of the final chapter — an impossibly complex subject and one for which, more than any other, I owe a debt to the Buryat ethnographers who have studied their own society.

The question which obviously arises, with a very localised study of the kind I have undertaken, is the extent to which the material can be generalised to other areas and other types of farm. I have tried to indicate throughout the book the degree to which the collective farms I visited are typical of Buryat kolkhozy. Both the Selenga and the Barguzin Karl Marx farms are well known, but for different reasons. The Barguzin Karl Marx kolkhoz was one of the earliest to be founded in the district and was associated with a very active section of the Communist Party in the late 1920s and early 1930s. It was a farm 'in the vanguard', was given special facilities, was a training ground for managers sent to other farms, and was the subject of several books and articles. But by the mid-1970s it was no longer in the forefront, either politically or economically, and by 1980, as described in some detail later in the book, it had fallen behind most local farms in many respects and was subject to much criticism in the local press. The Selenga Karl Marx collective, on the other hand, was a farm without a particularly distinguished early history, but under the management of an energetic Chairman it had become brilliantly successful from the economic point of view by the mid-1960s. However, a scandal involving the Chairman in mismanagement rocked the farm soon afterwards, and I was not able to make a return visit in the 1970s as I did to the Barguzin farm. Local newspapers giving production figures for the Selenga farm in the 1980s indicate that it was average for the district.

12

Two questions which remain are: in what ways are Buryat collective farms different from other types of rural enterprise in the region, such as state farms, and what is the range of variation in different parts of the Soviet Union within the category of collective farm itself?

In 1976 there were 28,000 collective farms (excluding fishing collectives) in the USSR, and 18,000 state farms.[16] Although a number of collective farms are being transferred to the status of state farm, the Soviet government does not intend to abolish the distinction altogether and we may assume that the collective farm will go on being the major form of rural enterprise.[17]

The historical origins of state and collective farms are different. State farms emerged on the basis of the estates of large landowners, where labour was employed for wages. The state, in a sense, simply took over the role of the landowner. Collective farms, on the other hand, were formed on the basis of the cooperation of many small peasant farms employing family labour.[18] However, this historical distinction has long ceased to have any significance, since the majority of state farms today are those which were previously collective farms. The two types of farm are now so similar that, in any one region and given a similar farming task, they are essentially alike from the socio-economic point of view. Differences in farming task (agriculture as opposed to fishing or cotton-growing, for example) make for a greater variation in the lives of rural workers than the distinction between sovkhoz and kolkhoz.

The ideological distinction between the two types of farm is mentioned in Chapter 2. We shall note here only the main practical differences. State farms operate, like state factories, on the basis of a guaranteed basic wage tariff, and also pensions and insurance, which permit of only minor adjustments in individual farms. State subsidies cover these and other costs if the farm makes a loss. Collective farms, on the other hand, have to make ends meet, and they pay whatever wages they can manage from their own income at the end of the year. Until the mid-1960s they did not have to pay pensions or insurance, but on the other hand they were able to award wages well above the norm if they were successful. In effect there has always been a far greater range of variation in socio-economic conditions within the collective farm sector than within the state farm sector.

In the 1960s the great majority of state farms ran at a loss, i.e. the income from their total product, which had to be sold to the state, did not cover costs. In western Siberia, only 82 out of the 630 state farms made a profit in 1964.[19] Since that time, state farms have been put on *khozraschet* (made self-accounting) and various policies have been implemented to make them more profitable.[20] At the same time, collective farms have become more dependent on state, as opposed to outside market, sales. They have had cheap long-term loans made available from the State Bank, and a minimum guaranteed basic wage linked to, but less than, sovkhoz rates was introduced in the mid-1960s. Ceilings were placed on high wages. Many of the specialists employed in collective farms were sent directly from the Ministry of Agriculture and paid by the state, just as in state farms. Since kolkhozy have always been 'on *khozraschet*' in effect, the two kinds of farm are now on a very similar footing, even if the kolkhoz does still have more room for manoeuvre. A kolkhoz can decide between priorities for internal allocation of funds, and the management can — with difficulty — resist the sending in of Ministry specialists. State farms may still have some advantages vis-à-vis the government as a result of their superior ideological standing, e.g. in the prices they pay for inputs and in the state delivery prices; but if this is the case the differences between them and collective farms cannot be very great since the general policy is to make conditions similar for the two types of farm.[21] Other factors of rural life (obligatory production and sales plans, the sizes of private plots, medical and educational facilities, passport regulations, and the relation with the Party and the Soviets) are not substantially different in the two cases. It is true that collective farms negotiate their delivery plans with the Ministry of Agriculture, whereas state farms are direct subsidiaries of the Ministry, but it may be doubted how much practical difference this makes.

Life for a worker in a sovkhoz may be grimmer and more rule-bound than in a collective farm. This is because it lacks even those formal democratic institutions which exist in a kolkhoz. In a sovkhoz there are no committees or meetings of workers which have even formal precedence over decisions of the officials.

In the past, the great majority of sovkhoz workers were either seasonal or temporary, and even today there is a larger proportion of temporary labour.[22] By contrast as we have seen, in collective farms, until the change of statutes in 1969, all children born in the farm were bound to work there after the age of sixteen unless they were specifically given permission to leave. For this very reason pre-revolutionary social organisation tended to be preserved in the kolkhoz to a greater extent than in the sovkhoz. It is perhaps consistent with this that in the sovkhoz, at any rate in the 1960s, the workforce consisted overwhelmingly of manual labour and a tiny proportion of specialists and managers, whereas the collective farm had a more diverse membership, with more people in intermediate specialised positions.[23] By now, however, most of these differences have been removed as a result of policies aimed at equalising conditions for all rural workers.[24]

As the Buryat material indicates, there are wide differences in the economic conditions with which kolkhozy operate even within a single region. A recent book on rural development in Soviet Central Asia, which compares five collective farms in Tadjikstan and Uzbekistan for the mid-1970s quantifies some of the most important economic differences, and also enables us to compare these with Buryat kolkhozy.[25]

If we take the five Central Asian collective farms, we find important variations between them in the following: (a) the number of households in each farm (from 854 to 2,338 households per farm, whereas the USSR average is 486 and the Buryat ASSR average is 336);[26] (b) the average number of man-days worked by a kolkhoznik (from 142 days in one farm to 193 days in another, where the USSR average is 247.9 days; see Chapter 4 for the Buryat case); (c) the hectares of total sown land per kolkhoz and the hectares under different crops; (d) the state delivery prices paid to the farms for cotton (from 660 rubles per ton of raw cotton paid to one farm to 430.6 rubles per ton to another); (e) the average payment per man-day (from 4.02 rubles in one farm to 7 rubles in another, where the USSR average is 4.77 rubles and the Buryat average is 5.36); (f) the average annual family income from work in the kolkhoz, a function of the variations in (b) and (e) — the range in the Central Asian farms was from 531 rubles in one farm to 2,277 rubles in another (see Chapter 6 for a comparison with the Buryat case); (g) the average family income from employment outside the farm (from 479 rubles per annum in one farm to 1,299 rubles in another, this being negatively correlated with the average pay from the kolkhoz per family in these farms); (h) the gross income of the farms, and factors related to this such as current inputs, value added in collective production, and investment as a percentage of value added; (i) the output per hectare of the domestic plots as a ratio to that for collective land (from 6.5 to 2.3); and (j) the monthly average earnings of the kolkhoz Chairman and brigadier (from 300 to 500 rubles per month for Chairmen and from 170 to 300 rubles per month for brigadiers; these salaries depend on the economic performance of the farm, and so such a variation is to be expected; see Chapter 5 section 1).

There were smaller variations between these five kolkhoz in the following: (a) average size of household (from 5.9 to 7.7 members, much larger than in Buryatiya, where, in the farms I visited, there were between 4.2 and 4.6 in a household); (b) the female workers as a percentage of all workers (from 43% to 56%); (c) the size of domestic plot per household (from 0.12 hectares to 0.17 hectares; however, the USSR average is 0.33 hectares and the Buryat average is 0.4 hectares); (d) the yields of cotton and grain per hectare; (e) the total household income from the combination of domestic plot, outside employment, and kolkhoz (from 2,513 rubles per annum to 3,669 rubles per annum); and (f) the minimum guaranteed income for twenty-five days work per month (range between 60 and 70 rubles a month).

The five Central Asian collective farms were more or less similar to one another in the mid-1970s in the above respects, but they were very *unlike* other kolkhozy in the USSR in several important ways, some of which are mentioned above: the large number of households in each farm and correspondingly low area of land per worker, the large size of households, the availability of outside employment and the correspondingly small number of days worked in the farm on average by each member (166 days, where the USSR average is 250 days a year). In all these respects Buryat farms are closer than the Central Asian ones to the USSR norm.

It is clear that hunting and fishing collective farms are in a somewhat different category from other kolkhozy in the USSR and this is recognised in Soviet statistics which usually list them separately. This is because not only are they subject to the variations in size, quality of land, prices and delivery plans of any collective farm but they are also organised differently in the specialised hunting and/or fishing sector.

Philip Lineton visited a fishing collective in the Khanti-Mansi National Okrug in western Siberia in the 1970s. According to his report,[27] the farm was small (118 households) and apart from some milk and vegetable production was entirely devoted to fishing and hunting. The farm had a total annual delivery plan for fish, but fishermen were not organised in brigades with their own plans, nor, apparently, were they given individual plans. Each man, working with his own private equipment (motor-boats and nets), simply went out into the marshes and rivers around the Ob and fished for what he could get. Fishermen were paid for the amount they chose to give to the kolkhoz, as opposed to selling privately. There was a guaranteed minimum pay of 70 rubles a month, but the average income from the kolkhoz was 250 rubles a month in 1976 (heavily concentrated in some months as fishing was not possible all year round). Although a small brigade for looking after the livestock (68 cattle, 110 horses, 5 sheep and 2 pigs) did exist, and a temporary brigade was put together each year for hay-cutting, the usual Soviet kolkhoz hierarchy of sector—brigade—work-team—individual was absent.

This farm was also untypical in its apparently haphazard organisation. People did what jobs they felt like. It seems that there was bargaining over how much the kolkhoz paid the men for their catches. Essentially, their 'wages' were the proceeds from individual sales to the kolkhoz. The Chairman of the farm lacked authority, and even routine kolkhoz administration was carried out by the Chairman of the *sel'sovet*. The vital accounts of the farm were kept by the young Secretary of the *sel'sovet*, one of the few Khanti in the place who was not almost permanently drunk. Party membership in the farm was not large enough for there to be an independent primary Party organisation. In effect, the farm was run by the Chairman of the *sel'sovet*, somewhat hampered by the activities of a succession of drunken Chairmen of the trading organisation (the 'consumers' union'). It was the *sel'sovet* Chairman who decided everything: when to cut the hay, what the consumers' union should sell in the shop, and when the 'dry law' (*sukhoi zakon*) should be imposed in order that some job be carried out. The place was wild and violent. Dispirited boys hung around in the village 'refusing to work' (many of them were 'hooligans' sentenced to exile in Siberia from other parts of the USSR). Unlike the Buryat farms I visited, this farm had no policeman, and it was said that it would take a brave man to accept a posting in such a place.

The Buryat farms were busy and cheerful, if dull, by comparison. Work was carried out, new houses and schools were being built, the Chairmen seemed to know what was going on and to be respected by their officers. The kolkhozniks bowled up and down the dusty paths and roads on their motorcycles or little carts, stopping to chat to one another or to say hello to my companions.

What can the rich but dejected band of fishermen in the arctic taiga forest have in common with the successful, populous organisations of Central Asia or the quiet and industrious villages of Buryatiya?[28] It is beyond the scope of this book to explore this question in detail. Nevertheless, it is of fundamental importance to my theme that the ideology of the collective farm is the same all over the USSR and that constant efforts are made to try to bring about a state in which real conditions are equal. One result of these efforts is an astonishing and perhaps admirable uniformity in material life. In the most distant corners of the Soviet Union rural workers live in the same standard house, wear the same padded jacket (*vatnik*), eat the same brand of tinned sprats. The similarity is not only material, since kolkhozniks everywhere are subject to the same code of ideological *intent*, embodied in the stream of instructions and teachings from centralised ministries, Party Secretariats, and the Academy of Sciences. One of the purposes of this book is to discover the extent to which such instructions influence people's behaviour and ideas.

The materials for this book have been drawn partly from my own field-work in two Buryat collective farms and partly from published sources. I visited the USSR first in 1966–7 as a research student at Moscow University, the topic of my work being Buryat kinship. I worked on the unusually rich published ethnography of the Buryat for eight months, and then was able to go to the Buryat ASSR Filial of the Academy of Sciences, in Ulan-Ude, for research in the field. I was in Buryatiya in May and June 1967, the journey being financed by Moscow University. Before I set out, a plan was drawn up (by myself and my supervisor in Moscow) for the research I was supposed to do, and this plan was agreed by the Buryat Filial. Having this plan, which concerned the survival of traditional Buryat kinship relations, was very useful to me, since it enabled me to insist on covering topics that might otherwise have been considered best left alone. I did not envisage writing a book of this kind and gathered material on economics more or less as a matter of duty. On arrival at Ulan-Ude an itinerary was handed to me immediately. It was, given the limitations of time, well thought out and representative of many sides of Buryat life. My supervisor at the Buryat Academy of Sciences was anxious to help me, and was distressed that I arrived a day late and thus missed a Buryat wedding which she had planned that I would visit.

I spent the first few days in Ulan-Ude, where ethnographers at the Academy explained something of present-day Buryat rural life, the terminology used in collective farming, and the organisation of sheep production groups. Unfortunately, thinking only the 'traditional' was interesting — I intended to write a dissertation on Buryat shamanism and later did so — I did not make the best use of this opportunity, nor of that which followed, some days spent visiting Buryat factory-workers in their homes.

For the field-work in the collective farms themselves I was allotted a woman supervisor from the Academy, who travelled with me. We went first to the *kolkhoz imeni Karla Marksa* in the Selenga *aimak* (district) to the south of Ulan-Ude towards the Mongolian border. On the way we visited the Ivolga *datsan*, the only remaining Buddhist monastery in the Buryat ASSR.[29] We arrived at the kolkhoz in the evening and were settled in a room of a house belonging to a Buryat woman. She did not work much in the farm because she had four young children and she cooked the meals I had at home: ground buckwheat with butter in the morning, and mutton broth with noodles at other times.

However, I was rarely at home because from the moment of arriving in the farm I threw myself into frenzied visiting, interviewing, and note-taking, which the members of the farm were kind enough to indulge with great patience. The officials of the farm were particularly helpful. I can remember no occasion on which they refused to answer a question, or to show me their books of accounts and minutes of meetings. Often they thrust information at me which I was not able to note adequately (I did not use a tape-recorder, partly because of discretion where individuals were concerned and partly because I did not have many batteries left). As soon as I decently could, I left the officials and went to visit the kolkhozniks, thinking that perhaps I might find new material on shamanism — a more or less forlorn hope in this farm where the people had long since been almost entirely Buddhist. However, they seemed genuinely happy to talk about kinship, their genealogies, the clans, their families and children, their work and life histories. I was very lucky that the kolkhozniks liked talking about what I wanted to hear about, otherwise as a young Russian-looking girl I would probably have got nowhere. They were immensely hospitable, and in every house we were offered tea, vodka, meat and even Buryat delicacies normally reserved for high occasions (for example, *zööhei*, flour cooked in cream). Since we went to around four houses a day, and vodka or *arkhi* (distilled fermented milk) was obligatory in every one, and also at dinner in the evening with officials, the round of visits soon became exhausting to my supervisor and she stayed at home much of the time. As far as I could tell, I was not taken to specially chosen houses, and I was later able to drop in on people uninvited. The interviews were in Russian, and on the few occasions on which I met someone who did not speak Russian some member of the family translated for me. On several occasions the kolkhoz put a jeep at my disposal so that I could talk to shepherds in distant settlements.

During my time in this farm, tormented by bed-bug bites which swelled to great size, I was treated in the kolkhoz hospital, which was a clean and informal place where the patients wandered in and out in pyjamas. The doctor who treated me was born in the kolkhoz and had returned to it after training. I also visited the high school, the kindergarten (which was light, airy, and well-provided with comfortable dormitories for boarders), and the kolkhoz library. This latter contained political texts, collected editions of Russian literature, some agricultural journals, and the central newspapers, all of these being locked in glass-fronted bookcases. The place appeared to be seldom frequented.

I was invited to an amateur performance by a kolkhoz theatrical troupe at the farm cultural club. The club, run by the local Soviet, was a large wooden building with seating for around 200 people. On this occasion it was crowded with the members of the farm and their families, dignitaries and officials being seated in the front row. Under a leaning portrait of Lenin hung over the stage, the group performed sketches, songs, and small dramas. The language was Buryat. The subject matter was historical (a shepherd outwits the cruel and wily lamas and aristocrats), or political (songs about the war in Vietnam), or local (jokes about district personages). The audience was happy and enthusiastic.

I also visited the kolkhoz shop (*selmag*), but it was largely empty of goods, except for boots and tinned fish. There was a canteen, run by a rough-looking but cheerful Russian woman, which served inexpensive meals of broth and meat stew. It was used mainly by temporary labourers, and I gathered that the kolkhozniks preferred to eat at home. The house used by the farm as a hotel was occupied during my visit by a party of geologists. Also living in the farm was a team of Armenian building workers (*shabashniki*), who were carrying out construction work on a private basis for the kolkhoz.

Apart from a few old women who wore the Buryat Mongolian gown (*degel*)

Farm shop, Bayangol, Barguzin, 1967.

19

everyone in the farm wore European dress, and a young girl instructed to put on her Buryat clothes for my benefit was clearly unwilling. Her mother kept the Buryat clothes and other traditional valuables (snuff-bottles, knives with silver decoration, etc.) in old painted chests (*avtar*). The national dresses are worn mainly at festivals, and even then, not by everyone. The kolkhoz club keeps a store of such clothes, but much of this stock was 'theatricalised' and not authentic. Apart from national winter working clothes, still used on distant settlements by some people, the Buryats have not followed the Mongolian pattern of continued use, in a simplified form, of traditional dress. The Buryat clothes worn at festivals are a mere approximation to the former garb, often just a sign of nationality. It is common to wear only one item of Buryat clothing, such as a hat. In everyday life on the kolkhoz non-working clothes are neat and smart, and Buryat girls eagerly follow town fashions as far as they are able.

The interiors of the houses were similarly 'un-Buryat' to my eyes. They were furnished with plain wooden tables and chairs, and the most noticeable features were Russian: large samovars, and lace-covered cushions heaped up on the bedsteads. All of the houses in the main village, Tashir, had electricity, but they did not have running water, which was fetched from a well. Cooking was done on wood-fired stoves constructed of brick. The kolkhoz had a bath-house in Tashir, a log cabin sauna, with shelves on which the bathers could sit in the steam.

After two or three weeks on this farm, I returned to Ulan-Ude, where I did some work in the archives of the Buryat Filial of the Academy of Sciences. Shortly afterwards I set out northwards to visit the *kolkhoz imeni Karla Marksa* in Barguzin *aimak*. The journey from Ulan-Ude took two full days (three to four days on my return when the rivers were swollen), with an overnight stop at the town of Barguzin. This is an old trading town, and on its main street stood several former merchants' villas, wooden houses of two or three stories, with pillars, verandas, and pediments. We crossed two large rivers by pontoon-raft to reach the kolkhoz centre at the village of Bayangol. Working conditions and daily life were very similar to those in the Selenga farm. The officials and kolkhozniks were equally friendly and helpful. The Barguzin farm had a large well-built central office (*kontora*), with a carpeted corridor where workers waited their turn to see the Chairman, a young agricultural college graduate in his early thirties. In the Selenga farm the Chairman had almost never been in his office; he rushed around the farm in his jeep, surrounded by groups of men, energetically discussing what was to be done.

I returned to the Barguzin farm seven years later, in the winter of 1974–5, on a visit again kindly arranged by the Buryat Filial of the Academy of Sciences. I was travelling from Mongolia, and on this occasion was accompanied by a Buryat girl student whom I had known in the University of Ulan Bator. Interviews on this occasion were often conducted in Mongolian on my side, and Buryat on the kolkhozniks' side — perhaps a mistake, since I understood less of their replies than when I had been working in Russian of which I have a fluent knowledge.

Introduction

What had changed in the interval between my two visits? The most noticeable changes were a frequent air-service, operational even in mid-winter, between Ulan-Ude and Barguzin; a new bridge over one of the two rivers; improvement of the roads, which though not hard-surfaced were now relatively solid; the building of a new high school, and improvement of the supplies to the village shop (the empty shelves of 1967 were now full, with a range of warm clothing, boots and shoes, books, stationery, crockery, and a wide variety of foods such as rice, macaroni, buckwheat, salt, conserves, tinned milk, sweets and wines). Near the *kontora* a large hoarding with a painting of the head of Karl Marx had been erected. Some nearly finished heated cow-sheds and milking-parlours, together with new wooden houses for the workers, stood in the snow not far from the village. Fencing had been built and the land improved, so that the cows to form the new milk-production unit could pasture in fields, rather than out on the open steppe. In the village everything was as it had been before, though perhaps rather more dilapidated. In mid-winter the snow lay crisply everywhere; the kolkhozniks travelled by horse-drawn sleigh, appearing almost silently across the steppes. People stayed indoors to avoid the intense cold, night fell early, and it was very, very quiet.

Apart from the material obtained on these visits, this book is based on published data: the very rich and valuable work of Buryat ethnographers and economists, the statistics of the Buryat ASSR, and local newspapers. The material on

Barguzin Karl Marx kolkhoz central office. To the left a portrait of Marx, centre a bust of the farm's founder, Sangadiin, to the right the honour board of hard-working kolkhozniks.

21

the history of the Karl Marx kolkhoz in Barguzin was obtained from a book on the farm written by a local Buryat school-teacher, whom I met. Comparative data from a nearby sovkhoz came from a book written by the head of its trade union, a man who took a deep interest in Buryat traditions and had set up a small local museum. For a remote valley in Siberia, Barguzin is extremely well documented. Although this is a long book, I have had to exclude not only great amounts of economic and historical data, but also whole categories of material which I have left largely untouched: material on Barguzin food,[30] housing,[31] material culture,[32] language, dialect[33] and songs,[34] historical chronicles and genealogical mythology.[35]

1

The Buryats and their surroundings

1. The Buryats and other ethnic groups in Buryatiya

The Buryats (Bur. *buryaad*) are a people of Mongolian language, physical type, and cultural traditions, living in the region of Lake Baikal in south-east Siberia and northern Mongolia. This book is about the Buryats who live in the Soviet Union. They consisted originally of several different tribes or clans, with no common political leadership, and they can be said to have been formed as a 'people' by the establishment of a border between Siberia and Mongolia in the early eighteenth century. But even after that date tribes of Mongolians, Altaians, and others crossed the border and 'became Buryats'. In 1979 there were 353,000 Buryats in the USSR, of whom 90.2% counted Buryat as their native language.

Buryats have a Mongol appearance, but the 'western Buryats' (i.e. those living west and north of Lake Baikal) have a distinctly more European physical make-up, probably because they are to some extent descended from Turkic-speaking tribes living in that area around the ninth and tenth centuries AD.[1] The spoken language of Buryats consists of many dialects, some of which are barely mutually comprehensible. Nor have the Buryats ever had a common religion: 'shamanism', a series of cults as various in content as the linguistic dialects, was overlaid by the Tibetan form of Lamaist Buddhism among the 'eastern' and 'southern' Buryats during the eighteenth century, and by Russian Orthodoxy among the 'western' Buryats during the nineteenth century.

For centuries Buryats have lived interspersed with tribes of Tungus (also called Khamnigan and recently called Evenki), which are as fragmented as the Buryats themselves, if not more so. Since the seventeenth century, Buryat lands have been increasingly settled by Russian peasants, both Orthodox and Old Believers, and the border with Mongolia has been guarded by regiments of Cossacks, jointly made up of Russians and Buryats. By the 1970s, the Buryats were greatly outnumbered by the Russians, even in their own republic, the Buryat Autonomous Soviet Socialist Republic (ASSR).[2] People of other nationalities also live among the Buryats: Ukrainians, Jews, Chinese,[3] Tatars,[4] and others.

The Buryats and their surroundings

After the Revolution, the Buryat-Mongolian ASSR, which was established in 1923, included most of the area within the Soviet Union settled by Buryats. However, the boundaries of the Buryat-Mongolian ASSR were substantially cut back in 1937,[5] and two 'national *okrugs*' were set up within the Irkutsk *oblast'* and the Chita *oblast'* to provide administrative units of a lower level for two important centres of Buryat population now outside the ASSR. These are the Ust'-Ordynsk Buryat National Okrug to the west of Lake Baikal in the Irkutsk *oblast'*, and the Aga Buryat National Okrug far to the east of Lake Baikal in Chita *oblast'*. At the same time, the name 'Mongol' was cut out of the Buryat ASSR. Even in Ust'-Ordynsk National Okrug Buryats are outnumbered by Russians and others.[6]

Large numbers of Buryats (about 28,000) also live in the People's Republic of Mongolia, mostly in the districts which border on the USSR. Almost twenty thousand Buryats have spread even further afield and live in the People's Republic of China, in the region of Barga in Manchuria. Some of these are from tribes which settled, or were sent, there in the eighteenth century or earlier, and others are Buryats who emigrated from the Soviet Union after the Revolution and Civil War.[7]

This brief outline gives rise to two questions: what is 'Buryat' about the Buryats, and what are the relations between them and other people with whom they live interspersed?

Buryats

People calling themselves 'Buryat' belong to several tribes about whose origins there is no agreement even in Buryat mythology, let alone in scholarly history. The most important of the tribes are: the Ekhirit, Bulagat, and Khongodor, whose ancestral homelands lie to the west of Lake Baikal; the Khori, who are thought to have migrated between eastern Mongolia and western Baikaliya, but since the sixteenth or seventeenth century have lived in the region east of the lake; and some tribes of 'Mongolian' origin, such as the Khatigan and Tabangut, who arrived from Mongolia in the seventeenth century to live in the Selenga River area south of Lake Baikal. The picture is complicated by the fact that numerous small groups of other ethnic origin, Tungus, Altaian, Uighur, Dzhungarian (west Mongol), etc., attached themselves to the main tribes and called themselves 'Buryat'; and by the fact that all of the important tribes have numerous sub-divisions, many of which have migrated here and there during the last few centuries.

As a very general observation we can say that most of these migrations took place in a sweeping movement 'clockwise' around the Sayan Mountains (Altaians and western Mongols up into Cis-Baikaliya, western Buryats eastwards and southwards to Barguzin, Kudarinsk, and Selenga), and in a more recent general movement eastwards (Khori Buryats from Trans-Baikaliya to the Aga steppes and even into Barga in Manchuria). Although I have identified a pattern to these migrations, they in fact occurred as separate ventures, often involving tiny groups of people, and for many different historical reasons. The Buryats I shall be describing in detail in this book are no exception: the Barguzin Buryats are mainly descended from western Buryat tribes who crossed over the lake in the eighteenth and nineteenth centuries, and the Selenga Buryats are a mixture of western Buryat, Khori, and Mongolian clans.

Buryats have in common their sense of a common historical fate, their oral traditions of myth and legend, their genealogical conception of society, their deep concern for kinship relations, their ideas about time and the seasons, their concepts of right and proper behaviour, their respect for animals and often tender care for them, and their love of nature – even that seemingly barren landscape of dry, grey steppes, marshes rimmed with salt, and dark, decaying, mosquito-ridden forest which surrounds them. It is impossible to do justice to these ideas and feelings in a book devoted primarily to economic and political life, but I hope that some of these things will emerge in the later chapters by implication.

Evenki

According to the 1897 Census there were about 24,000 Tungus (Evenki) in Trans-Baikaliya.[8] Many of these were Tungus groups now forming administrative units outside Buryatiya. Very many Tungus, and their herds of reindeer, perished in epidemics of smallpox, tuberculosis, and other diseases in 1895, 1907–8, 1923, and 1925.[9] There is every reason to suppose that in south-east Siberia as a whole, as well as in Barguzin in particular (see p. 64), the number of Evenki has been drastically reduced since the end of the nineteenth century.

The Evenki were traditionally nomadic reindeer herders and hunters. Under Buryat and Mongolian influence many of them took up horse and cattle herding, and even by 1897 more than 15% of all the Tungus in the Trans-Baikal region spoke Buryat as their native tongue and knew no other language.[10] In general, they have had a history of conflict with Buryats. When the Russians arrived in the seventeenth century, they found the Tungus already *kyshtym* (tribute-paying subjects) of some of the Buryat groups, and even as late as the twentieth century rich Buryats engaged Tungus to hunt furs for them.[11] In many of these operations, and similar ones with Russian merchants, the Tungus were cheated and forced into debt. Poppe says: 'the Buryat–Tungus enmity was great. It is understandable that at the first appearance of the Russians the Tungus deserted to the latter and joined them, served them as guides, and were faithful allies of the Russians in their struggle against the Buryats.'[12]

Collectivisation took place more slowly among the Evenki than among the Buryats.[13] The Evenki living in the Bauntov *aimak* (district) of the Buryat ASSR were given privileges as representatives of one of the 'small peoples of the North', while those living in other *aimaks* had no special treatment.[14] To speed collectivisation, some of the Evenki population was moved out of Bauntov *aimak* to the Dyren *sel'sovet* in Barguzin in 1930.

By the 1960s all Evenki lived in collective or state farms together with Buryats and Russians. They now take some agricultural jobs and some work in livestock, but their main occupation has reverted to the hunting and breeding of fur-bearing animals. Both men and women hunt. However, the goal of the hunt today is almost exclusively valuable furs for export, whereas in the past Evenki had hunted a wide range of animals for meat, bone and skin utensils, and leather and fur clothing.

Siberian Russians

The appearance of Russians in Trans-Baikaliya was part of the general process of the conquest of eastern Siberia. The first Russians to arrive, in the 1630s, were Cossacks who had mercantile interests: they demanded a tribute in furs (*yassak*) from the native inhabitants, Tungus, Buryats and Mongolians. Having superior weapons — guns — to any of the Siberian peoples, they were able to move very rapidly through the country, establishing fortresses along the main rivers. By 1689 they had reached the River Argun, beyond which to the south was Mongolian steppeland, less rich in furs than the Siberian forest.

Most of the Cossack soldiers stayed to live in Siberia, establishing hereditary regiments paid by the Russian government. Merchants, administrators and missionaries soon followed them and the fortresses gradually became towns. Since the native hunting, gathering and nomadic pastoral economies did not provide the grain necessary to support a Russian way of life, the Tsarist administration sent out peasant serfs to farm in the Russian way. Peasant life in Siberia was thus market-oriented from the start. By the end of the seventeenth century, voluntary settlers began to arrive, but for a long time the great majority of Russians in the region were fettered in some way: they were landowners' serfs sent for the provision of corn (*na pashnyu*), state serfs allotted land in various places by an edict of 1799, or runaway serfs, criminals, or political exiles.[15]

The Siberian Russians were divided by religion. The Cossacks, landowners' serfs, and merchants (Sibiryaki) belonged to the Orthodox church, but the state serfs, exiled for their religious beliefs (called Semeiskiye because they arrived in family groups) were Old Believers. Often the two groups lived in the same villages, but they did not inter-mix or inter-marry. The Semeiskiye were, and still to some extent are, intensely conservative and inward-looking. The Orthodox Sibiryaki, on the other hand, were outward-looking, interested in trade with native peoples and not averse to inter-marriage with them.

In the early nineteenth century another wave of settlers arrived, the 'Khokhli' — Ukrainians and Belorussians attracted by privileges granted by the government.[16] These people were followed by further waves of Russian peasants from various parts of the country, especially after the freeing of the serfs in the 1860s and after the completion of each separate stage of the Trans-Siberian railway. Small towns arose along the railway, and small manufacturing, mining, transport and trade activities gave rise to a Siberian working class. Political exiles of various kinds were sent to villages and remote settlements — Barguzin, where I worked,' was a favourite place for this — and although they did not usually remain for long they had a strong political and cultural influence, especially in the early twentieth century. After the Revolution more Russians were sent as administrators, teachers, doctors and specialists, most of them living in the towns.

Russians built large villages of up to 1,200 houses in the river valleys, closely surrounded by their fields. Buryats, on the other hand, lived scattered in the hills and steppes with their herds. This meant that there was relatively little contact between the two groups at first. Children of inter-marriages and Buryats who took up a settled Russian way of life (*karymy*) tended to be ostracised by other Buryats. By the late eighteenth century there were conflicts between Buryats and Russians over access to land, particularly in the narrow valleys of Cis-Baikaliya, but these were generally solved by the Buryats moving away, sometimes with and sometimes without permission from the Tsarist authorities. The conflict became acute, however, at the beginning of the twentieth century when a land reform was proposed by which all groups of the population, whether engaged in small mixed farming or extensive pastoralism, should be granted an equal amount of land per household (an amount just adequate for a peasant family farm). In many areas Buryat communities stood to lose over half of their land. At the same time it was proposed to administer the entire population on a territorial basis, thus bringing an end to indirect government of Buryats via their clans and clan-leaders.

All of this suggests an essentially antagonistic relation between the two communities, but there are several reasons why it would in fact be incorrect to summarise relations between Russians and Buryats in this way. The question is important because long-standing attitudes influenced the Buryat view of the Revolution and present-day relations with Russians.

Russian–Buryat relations

The historical origins of this relation show that the simple formula 'conquerors–conquered' is misleading. Western Buryats put up comparatively little opposition to the Russian advance, and most of the eastern and southern Buryats voluntarily took up citizenship in the Tsarist Empire during the eighteenth century. The relatively low tax burden of the *yassak* and the freedom of movement allowed under the Tsarist system of indirect rule were seen by them as much preferable to the heavy state duties, including military service, and the internecine warfare which were prevalent in Khalkha Mongolia at that time. Indeed, 'the Buryats' can be defined virtually as those northern Mongol tribes which decided they wished to remain in the Tsarist Russian Empire.

On the other side, the Russian peasants who arrived in Siberia were mixed farmers who were adaptable to local conditions, and indeed they were in some ways more influenced by the Siberian natives than the other way around. By the late nineteenth century most Russian settlers in districts such as Tunka and Barguzin spoke Buryat, and it was common for Russians to be employed by rich Buryats, sometimes as seasonal labourers and sometimes as permanent employees.

It is important that even by the time of the 1917 Revolution class differences appear to have been more significant than ethnic divisions. Lattimore has pointed out how in its historical beginnings the relation between the Russians and the Buryats or Mongols differed from that between the Chinese and the Mongols. The Russians had a rainfall agriculture, capable of being combined with livestock herding and the exploitation of the forest, which could be carried out by small numbers of individual peasants interspersed with native populations.

. . . when the Slavs were defeated, Turco-Tatar-Mongol khans had the upper hand; but they admitted Slav chieftans and nobles to the lower ranks of their own nobility. When the final conquests went in favour of the Russians, they in turn took into their own service chieftans of the Asian steppes. Whichever way the tide turned, there was no racial prejudice; there was intermarriage both among commoners and nobles.[17]

By the eighteenth century Buryat society was highly stratified in a semi-feudal manner, and the princes (the heads of the clans) were taken into the Tsarist administration as rulers of the Buryat population. By the nineteenth century they were assuming items of Russian dress and delighting in honours and insignia of the Empire. The Chinese pattern of intensive irrigated agriculture, densely clustered villages, and mercantile restrictions formed a radical disjuncture from Mongol pastoralism. The Chinese displaced a part of steppe society in Inner Mongolia, but they were unwilling to enter into relations implying interdependency with the steppe society not yet penetrated. Trade with the Mongols always took place against Imperial edict, but for Siberian Russians trade with native peoples was a fundamental part of the regional economy. Differences in attitude were reflected in marriage: Chinese traders took Mongolian concubines for the periods they were in the steppes, but Cossack families had some intermarriage with Buryats, not only the taking of Buryat women as wives but also allowing their daughters to marry Buryat and Mongolian men.[18]

The question of the mutual influence upon one another of Buryat (or more generally north Central Asiatic) and Russian forms of agriculture is an interesting and complex one. It cannot be discussed in full here, but in summary we can say that Russians took up important Buryat agricultural techniques (the *ütüg*[19] form of hay cultivation and the Central Asian type of irrigation[20]), while the Buryats, especially the western Buryats, began under Russian influence to cultivate grain crops which were expressly aimed at market sales.[21]

The designation of grain for the market and the growing value of arable land led to parallel changes in the land-tenure systems of both Russians and Buryats. It is not generally recognised that in both communities there was an evolution of land tenure from simple possession by use (*zakhvatnaya sistema*), to the establishment of land 'norms' per male soul and periodic re-allocation of plots within the village community (*peredel'naya sistema*), and then the inheritance of land by individual families which were able to 'take out' certain plots from the village community (*nasledstvennaya sistema*). It is true that this evolution happened at different rates, and to a varying extent, among Russians and Buryats. Most Russian peasants, both Sibiryaki and Semeiskiye, had carried out land measurements and gone over to the re-allocation system by the 1840s or 1850s, and furthermore this encompassed the basic farming land of the community.[22] Western Buryats followed them in the succeeding decades, but eastern and southern Buryats, most of whom placed little emphasis on arable farming if they did it at all, still used the *zakhvatnaya sistema* until the end of the nineteenth century. Since they were primarily livestock herders the land most prone to division, re-allocation, and inheritance was hay-meadow.[23] Similarly, we find that Russian peasants began to fence in common pasture-land earlier than the Buryats.[24] Nevertheless, we observe a similar development towards individual ownership systems in the two communities, this being most clearly visible among the Buryats in densely populated areas near towns (e.g. in Cis-Baikaliya and the region around Verkhneudinsk (Ulan-Ude) where Buryats cultivated grain for sale). Capitalist farming also developed on a small scale in both communities near towns.

Despite an initial marked divergence in social structure — the Russians never had the large patrilineal clans and exogamous lineages of the Buryats — the development of similar forms of land tenure had the effect of producing emergent class relations which were common to the two communities. In both cases rich farmers directed their operations towards the market, engaged in small-scale manufacturing (milling, leather goods), employed wage-labour, and undertook transactions of an 'interest-bearing' kind (money-lending, advantageous contracts with Tungus for furs, etc.). Both communities also had a small number of land-less and livestock-less households which, even if they only stayed in this condition for a short period of the developmental cycle, provided labour for market-oriented production. Siberian Russian peasants, with their serf or Cossack origins, did not have a culturally superior attitude to the Buryats. Buryats were early on recruited to form Cossack regiments of equal status to the Russian ones. Buryat families made long-standing trading-partner relations with Russian families, and it is significant that the Buryat word for this was *tala* — friend.

Although there was a certain amount of economic exchange between Buryat and Russian households, and both communities used common markets or bazaars (*yarmark*), the cultural interaction between them was not very great.

The Russians, on the whole, continued to use Russian styles of architecture, clothing, food, utensils, songs and stories. Almost no Russians became Buddhists, although a few sometimes consulted shamans. The Semeiskiye in particular cut themselves off from any outside community, including the Russian Sibiryaki.

In the village of Verkhne Zhirma in the late nineteenth century, an Old Believer, Ivan Kitayev, fell in love with a 'Sibiryak' girl and married her. The Old Believer elders accused him of treachery for this heinous act. He, in reply, took up the Orthodox religion and began to smoke a Buryat pipe (*ganzy*). This was completely unheard of in Old Believer communities. To this day [1969] in Verkhne Zhirma the descendants of Ivan Kitayev are nicknamed 'gonzy'.[25]

The Buryats, however, were more visibly affected by Russian culture, particularly in the area west of Lake Baikal. Prosperous men among the western Buryats wore Russian clothes by the late nineteenth century, though women did not, and they built themselves Russian-style wooden houses for winter. Large numbers of primary schools were opened by Orthodox missionaries among the western Buryat villages, and by the beginning of the twentieth century 85,000 Buryats had been baptised.[26] However, the acceptance of Orthodoxy was in the great majority of cases a mere formality, and it never had the authority among the western Buryats which Buddhism held among the eastern and southern Buryats.

In 1897 the census recorded 161,658 people in Trans-Baikaliya who claimed to be Buddhists, over 80% of the Buryat population of the area.[27] Among both eastern and western Buryats shamanism continued to provide the fundamental religious way of thinking among ordinary people, even though the deities were sometimes given Russian or Lamaist, rather than shamanist, names. Many individuals carried on all three religious practices with no feeling of contradiction, even though the clergy tended to be at loggerheads. It was more common, however, for individuals to profess one religion, and not necessarily the same as that of their relatives.

By the late nineteenth century a remarkable intelligentsia had emerged among the Buryat, with members from the Russian-educated elite and from well-to-do families oriented towards Mongolia and Tibet. Many of these people were scholars, who studied Buryat mythology, shamanism, and Lamaism, but by the beginning of the twentieth century they became increasingly involved also in politics: above all in the land question, which threatened the Buryat transhumant way of life, and in the problem of a new script for Buryat which would more accurately reflect the spoken language than the Mongolian script. Essentially these Buryat leaders opposed the new Tsarist policy of Russification, which was being carried out by means of increased settlement in Buryat lands, by a single system of government for the two peoples (to be based entirely on territory, doing away with the separate Buryat administration by clans — *rod*), and by intensified Orthodox missionary work and education in Russian. It is unfortunately impossible to discuss this fascinating period in adequate depth here. We should, however, note that the Buryat intelligentsia, though tiny in numbers, was internally divided into several factions ranging from those who advocated a separate 'pan-Mongolian' state to those who identified with socialist revolutionary ideals and saw Russification as a progressive phenomenon. By 1917, however, most of the Buryat leaders joined together in a Buryat nationalist movement, which was socialist but not Bolshevik, and aimed for autonomy within the Russian state rather than complete separation from it.

A bizarre episode of the revolutionary period illustrates the complex relations between Russians and Buryats at that time. In 1918 the population of Trans-Baikal was divided into Russian and Buryat administrative districts. The Buryat nationalist leaders of the time did not wish to be part of any joint administration, and the Buryats were given their own areas, called *aimak*, scattered among the Russian villages. In Barguzin and other districts, Land Commissions proposed giving some of the Buryat land to Russians. The amount proposed for Barguzin was 115,200 of the 235,439 *desyatinas* belonging to the Buryats. The *aimak* leaders walked out of the meeting in protest and shortly afterwards took steps for military defence of the Buryat territories. However, certain other groups of Buryats, motivated by the desire to avoid war with Russian neighbours, the dislike of the new taxes, and the overweening style of the new leaders, rose against the *aimak* group. This occurred in several regions of Buryatiya. In Barguzin, the *aimak* leaders, amongst whom was Rinchino (mentioned below, p. 60), were opposed by people from Khilganai and the region which now forms the Karl Marx collective. The 'Khilganaitsy' quickly over-ran most of Barguzin and set up their own, conservative, administration. This, however, was soon re-taken by the *aimak* leaders, though sporadic fighting continued until 1922. Both sides accused the other of being Bolsheviks, but in reality neither were.[28]

It is impossible in a book of this scope to do more than sketch the political history of the Buryats since the Revolution. In the Civil War, some Buryats fought on the side of the Whites, some joined the Red partisans, and some conducted their own diversionary skirmishes with vaguely pan-Mongolian aims, but most of them stayed out of the conflict altogether. 'War communism', 'de-kulakisation', and 'all-out collectivisation' had disastrous effects on Buryat society and economy, but it is arguable that the worst excesses of all of these policies took place in Russian rather than Buryat communities. From the point of view of the central government it was Russian peasants, not Asiatic natives, who were counted on to produce and deliver the agricultural products to feed the armies and the urban working class. By far the great majority of Communist Party members in east Siberia in the 1920s were Russians, not natives, and the crucial battleground of agricultural policy was the Russian, not the Buryat, village. Early Buryat nationalist revolutionaries of note virtually all perished by the late 1930s, but the same is true of many Russian figures of equivalent standing.

The exception to the parallel fate of the two communities is the brutal destruction of the Buryat Lamaist church in the 1930s. This was qualitatively different from persecution of the Orthodox church because Buddhism and the organisation of Lamaist monasteries represented for the Buryats not only a religion but also the institutional form of all that was most developed in their culture; literature, medicine, the arts, and education were all based in the monasteries, which were also the main repositories of wealth.[29] The action itself was carried out by radical Buryats, mainly young Komsomols and members of the Union of Militant Atheists in the countryside; and there is evidence that the central organs of the Party, where Russian influence was concentrated, opposed the most repressive measures against the monasteries up to 1936, when the great majority of the lamas had already left.[30] By this time the monasteries had long become centres of armed resistance to Soviet policies, and the final closure of all but two of them was carried out as part of a general policy of securing the border zone (twenty-two out of twenty-nine Buryat monasteries were in the frontier zone with Mongolia). It would thus be a mistake, in my view, to see the destruction of the Buryat Buddhist church primarily in ethnic terms, even though the effect was the annihilation of the most distinctive, sophisticated and serious part of Buryat culture.

This then is the background to the present relations between Buryats and Russians in the Soviet Union. It is, in fact, very difficult to discover any material of a general kind relating to ethnic relations in Buryatiya today. This is partly because many aspects of the subject, with its political implications of 'nationalism', are left almost untouched in the scientific literature. The Buryat press, collections of statistics, articles on economic life, etc., designed for the local public, almost never mention ethnic affiliation. In newspaper reports, for example, there is no hesitation in mentioning intimate details about named individuals (age, job, family circumstances, illnesses, criminal record, morals and sexual exploits, and so on), but it is officially considered irrelevant whether the person is Russian, Buryat, Tatar, or Ukrainian. This in itself contributes to the carrying out of the policy of 'the growing together of the peoples' (*sblizheniye narodov*).

2. Ethnic relations and inter-marriage in Buryatiya

Soviet sociologists commonly divide the population into the following 'classes': workers (*rabochiye*), employees (*sluzhashchiye*), and peasants or kolkhozniks. These categories are not quite what they seem, since the 'class' of 'workers' includes people on state farms, whose economic conditions may be more similar to those of workers in collective farms than to those of factory-workers. The procedure for assigning people to these groups is also questionable: the statisticians identify a head of each household, assign him or her to one of the three groups primarily on the basis of employment, and then assign all members of the family to the same group.[31] Thus the adult children of a collective farmer will be

Ethnic relations and inter-marriage in Buryatiya

Table 1.1. *The 'class' structure of Buryat ASSR and of the Buryat population in the republic in the Soviet period (%)*

	1926	1939	1959		1970[a]	
	Buryat	Buryat	Buryat	Total	Buryat	Total
Workers	1.2	23.0	24.5	51.4	48.5	62.8
Employees	0.5	16.1	18.7	20.1	31.0	27.4
Kolkhozniks (peasants)	98.2	60.9	56.8	28.4	20.5	9.8
Other	0.1	–	–	–	–	–

Source: Belikov 1974a, pp. 141–3.
a. The figures for 1970 refer only to the employed (*zanyatoye*) population, which is a few per cent different from the population as a whole (workers 63%, employees 22.8%, kolkhozniks 14.2%).

designated as kolkhozniks if they live at home, even if they are employees of the state. The seriousness of the distortion this creates depends on the degree of social mobility, which is now considerable in Buryatiya. Nevertheless, even on the basis of these data (Table 1.1), we can perceive important changes in the pattern of employment in Buryats during the Soviet period.

Whereas Buryats were overwhelmingly classified as 'peasants' in 1926, almost half of them were 'workers' by 1970 (although, unfortunately, we do not know what percentage worked in state farms as opposed to industry). Buryats are not in the majority in the Buryat ASSR (22% of the total population) and they formed in 1970 an even smaller proportion (14%) of the total of the 'workers' of the republic.[32] If Buryats have not entered the urban working class to an extent equal to other nationalities, they have been relatively successful in acquiring positions as 'employees', i.e. 'white collar' work (see Table 1.1). On average both industrial workers and state employees in the USSR earn more than collective farm workers (in 1970 they earned 135.3% and 124.3% of the kolkhoznik's income per family respectively),[33] but the category of 'employee' includes also the great majority of jobs which are attractive because they imply a certain amount of power. Therefore, in the most general terms, we can see Buryats as occupying a relatively influential place, given the population distribution, in the structure of employment in the Buryat ASSR.

In Ulan-Ude I was told that Buryats and Russians tend to live in different areas of the town. There are considerable problems of alcoholism in both communities. In the long Siberian winter nights, with inadequate transport between the factories and housing estates, queues for food, and a rationing system (since 1975) on the sale of alcohol, the town can be a grim place to live. It is apparently unsafe for Russians to venture at night into Buryat quarters, and vice versa.

33

In collective farms with mixed populations, it is usually the case that Russians live in separate villages, or separate parts of villages, from Buryats.[34] Most collective and state farms, while having a mixed population, are dominated by one nationality or the other. The 'Buryat' kolkhozy I visited were typical of the Buryat ASSR in having around 90% Buryats, 5% Russians, 3% Tatars, and 2% other nationalities.[35] However, in the Ust'-Ordynsk National Okrug Buryats live closely interspersed with Russians, who numerically dominate most collective farms, e.g. the *kolkhoz imeni Kalinina* in Bokhan *raion* (district), which around 1970 had 363 households, of which 50.1% were Russian, 25.6% Buryat, 11.9% Ukrainian, 1% Tatar, and 5.3% of other nationalities. In the Aga National Okrug, on the other hand, Buryats and Russians live separately, and collective farms contain only small numbers of people who do not belong to the main group.[36]

There is no evidence that 'Russian' collective and state farms are in any way officially favoured over Buryat farms. Indeed, the reverse may be true, as we can perhaps surmise from the scanty information available, for example the fact that the 'advanced' (*peredovyye*) farms of the republic mentioned in the literature are mainly Buryat, or that wages quoted from Russian farms were lower than those in the Buryat farms I visited.[37]

There is not very much inter-marriage between Buryats and other nationalities, though the incidence is growing. This is the case despite the fact that inter-marriage is officially encouraged, as evidence of the 'growing closer' of the nationalities. Most of the inter-marriage which does occur happens in the town of Ulan-Ude. In the farms I visited the register of marriages from 1964 to 1967 revealed no cases of inter-marriage with Buryats (see Table 1.4), and I met only one mixed family, a Buryat Hero of Labour and former kolkhoz Chairman who had married a Russian woman. In this family the wife did not speak Buryat, and the children spoke in Buryat with their father and in Russian with their mother.

A study of inter-marriages in Ulan-Ude provides some interesting data, which give some indication of future tendencies (presuming that the incidence of inter-marriage will increase) even though the numbers in the studied example are obviously very small.[38] The exact numbers are not revealed. The first interesting point shown in this study is that there are significant differences in the incidence of inter-marriage according to sex. Buryat men marry Russian women far more often than the other way around (30.2% of all inter-marriages in the ASSR are between Buryats and Russians, and of these 27.2% are between Buryat men and Russian women, and only 3% are between Buryat women and Russian men). Buryat women hardly marry men of other nationalities at all. The same pattern is true for other nationalities in relation to the Russians: Ukrainian men marry Russian women more than Ukrainian women do Russian men, and the same is true of Jewish men, Tatar men, and Belorussian men.[39] The only national inter-marriage in which this is not the case is Russians—Mordvinians, but here the sample is probably too small to be significant (there cannot be many such marriages in the town of Ulan-Ude). Zhalsarayev, the author of the study, explains these imbalances by the greater mobility of Buryat men as opposed to women, and by the greater 'susceptibility to national stereotypes' of the latter. Both of these observations seem to be justified, even if they do not fully explain the phenomenon: Buryat women are less mobile *before marriage* than men, mainly because they do not have to do military service. Military service of two years is obligatory for all young men from the age of eighteen except those who are students in certain privileged institutions of higher education. Even these have to spend two months in military camp and do regular military training courses at their institute. But most colleges do not 'save' their students (*ne spasayut*), and sooner or later they have to go. However, since the military commission takes a specified number of young men every year, and the population of eighteen-year-old men may exceed this number, there is some leeway for negotiation: a kolkhoz may ask the commission not to take its young men one year, pleading lack of labour for essential tasks of production. Generally, though, the great majority of young men do military service, and training courses available in the army enable some of them to take up urban jobs afterwards. Only those who return to their native villages marry local girls. As people said to me, 'You can't expect a girl from the village to wait two years, not knowing if you will really come back.'

In Buryatiya it appears that most young men do come back to their native districts, and this explains why it is in fact women who appear in the statistics as more mobile: women almost invariably go to live with their husbands at marriage, and they also move, just as men do, in connection with changes of job before marriage.[40]

Buryat women have always preserved more of 'national culture' (religious practices, Buryat clothing, etc.) than Buryat men. It might well be the case, since marriage choices even today are much influenced by the male elders of the kin-group (see Chapters 6 and 8), that Buryat women are *kept* in this mode by men. Buryat women are supposed to preserve the purity of blood of the Buryat people.

The general pattern in which men of national minorities marry Russian women cannot be explained by particular features of Buryat culture. There are several other possible explanations: men of national minorities marry Russian women in Ulan-Ude in order to get permission to live in, and hence get a job in, the town; or Russian women tend to have 'comfortable' jobs which would support a husband in a less good job; or Russian women have 'good connections' which would be useful to an ambitious young man from a minority group. However, as we saw earlier, Buryats in the Buryat ASSR do comparatively better in relation to their total population than Russians in the acquiring of desirable jobs (as 'employees'), and so it is unlikely that these economic-strategic explanations for the imbalance are adequate.

Other interesting facts from the Zhalsarayev study suggest that the explanation may lie in a status hierarchy of nationalities in the USSR — a status hierarchy whose basis probably lies in the ability of given nationalities to dominate positions of political power (it is difficult to say whether this is the case, in the absence of comparative data from other republics of the USSR). The evidence for a status hierarchy can be seen from Table 1.2. This shows that Russian nationality is slightly preferred to Buryat, and that Buryat nationality is decisively preferred to most others (the exception of Belorussian is probably due to the small size of the sample — only 0.8% of all mixed marriages are between Buryats and Belorussians). Zhalsarayev explored the possibility that the choice of nationality might be influenced by some tradition, such as a preference for the father's nationality. He found that where the father comes from the higher-status nationality, the tendency for children to choose this nationality is greater than if the mother comes from the 'higher' group. In the case of Jews, Tatars, Belorussians, and Mordvinians, children only choose these nationalities if their father came from them, but if the father is Russian, then 100% of the children

Old women sometimes wear Buryat clothing. Selenga 1967.

Table 1.2. *The choice of nationality at age sixteen by the children of mixed marriages*

Parents		Choice of nationality by children (%)	
(a)	(b)	Choose (a)	Choose (b)
Buryat	Russian	49.0	51.0
Buryat	Ukrainian	80.0	20.0
Buryat	Belorussian	50.0	50.0
Buryat	Other	69.2	30.8
Russian	Ukrainian	88.5	11.5
Russian	Jewish	98.2	1.8
Russian	Tatar	91.0	9.0
Russian	Belorussian	75.0	25.0
Russian	Mordvinian	94.1	5.9
Russian	Other	86.1	13.9

Source: Zhalsarayev 1974, p. 133.

chose Russian nationality. However, in an equivalent situation in Russian –Buryat mother families, 33.4% of the children chose Buryat nationality.[41]

Although the first generation of children of mixed marriages between Russians and Buryats do not become assimilated either one way or the other, there is evidence that by the second generation there is a noticeable tendency towards Russian-ness: 83.3% of the children of Russian–Buryat families marry Russians.[42]

As inter-marriage in rural districts is so infrequent, we have little data on it of any statistical significance. However, there is some information on inter-marriage in the Bauntov *aimak* which adjoins Barguzin. This is a remote mountainous and forested area, populated originally almost entirely by Evenki (Tungus) and a few Buryats, but now dominated by Russians and others who work in the mines and on the Baikal-Amur railway construction. The total population of the Bauntov *aimak* in 1977 was 11,000.[43] Over the twenty years preceding 1974 there had been about forty or fifty mixed marriages.[44] It is interesting that the pattern of these marriages conforms to that identified for the capital, Ulan-Ude.

Although the numbers in Table 1.3 are so tiny, the pattern is nevertheless evident by which men of the minority nation marry women of the majority nation more frequently than the other way around. The corollary of this is that *women marry down*. In the case of Buryats this is what we should expect from the pre-revolutionary marriage traditions. Buryat women in Ulan-Ude told me that they would like to marry Mongols, even though in another context they remarked that Mongols are 'uncultured' and 'backward'. However, it is interesting that the hierarchical marriage pattern seems to be much more general, and it suggests that this is a phenomenon of Soviet kinship as a whole. In countries

Table 1.3. *Number of mixed marriages in Bauntov aimak*

Number of marriages	Nationality	
	Man	Woman
17	Evenk	Buryat
8	Buryat	Evenk
11	Evenk	Russian
1	Russian	Evenk

Source: Tivanenko and Mitypov 1974, p. 132.

with a similar ethnic situation (e.g. Canada, Alaska) but a different political structure, the pattern is reversed: Eskimo women, for example, marry Anglo-Saxon Canadians far more frequently than do Eskimo men.[45]

Although neither Buryats nor Russians engage in much inter-marriage, Buryats do so more per 1,000 of the population than Russians.[46] Mixed marriages in which Buryats are one of the partners tend to be stable relative to divorce rates in the USSR,[47] but it is unfortunately not possible to compare them with Buryat—Buryat marriages, for which divorce rates are not known (although they may be presumed to be very low, see p. 45). Most of the Buryat men who marry women of other nationalities are either 'workers' or 'office employees', and Buryat women marrying out are mostly 'office employees' or 'teachers';[48] these occupations are, not surprisingly, ones in which there is more than average mobility.

To summarise: Buryats, Russians, and other nationalities work together, but they tend to live separately, and to preserve cultural differences. Data on inter-marriage and choice of nationality indicate that there is a status hierarchy among the ethnic groups of the Buryat ASSR, and that men tend to marry up and women down. The tendency towards inter-marriage is rising, particularly in the capital of Ulan-Ude where, between 1959 and 1970, mixed marriages were 19% of all marriages involving Buryats.[49]

3. Population and migration in Buryat collective farms

No studies of specifically Buryat rural populations are available, apart from the data I gathered myself in 1967 and 1974—5. Although the scale of my data is very small, there is no reason to suppose that it is not typical of rural Buryat life.

In 1966, the Karl Marx kolkhoz in Selenga *aimak* had a total population of 1,724.[50] Of these, 740 were children aged up to twelve, and 198 were children aged from twelve to sixteen. Thus 54.4% of the population were aged up to sixteen, and 42.9% were aged up to twelve, figures which reflect the large families of Buryat kolkhozniks. There were 369 households in the farm, giving an average household size of 4.6 people. Unfortunately, I do not have figures for the numbers of males and females, but the numbers of registered workers on the farm, 270 women and 254 men, suggest that the absolute number of females was considerably higher than the number of males, since many women do not register for work if they have to look after children.

In 1975, there was a total population of 2,126 in the Karl Marx kolkhoz in Barguzin *aimak*.[51] Of these, 1,099 were children under sixteen, i.e. 51.6% of the total population. This was a slight decline from 1966, when the percentage of children under *twelve* in the total population was 52.1%. The average household size in this farm was 4.22 in 1975. Of the 503 households, about fifteen were Tatars, ten Russian, and the rest Buryat. Of the 685 people registered for work,[52] 382 were men and 303 were women. The Chairman of the farm confirmed that large numbers of women did not register for work, and we may suppose that as in Selenga and other parts of Buryatiya[53] there were more adult females than males in the farm.

It is worth noting that the number of 'households' given above for both Selenga and Barguzin was the number registered in the farm for official purposes, *not* the number of households actually conducting a life as separate socio-economic units. For reasons explained in Chapter 6, the number of the latter is probably rather smaller than the number of official 'households', and consequently the real size of the average rural Buryat household is probably larger than the figures I have given above.

The Karl Marx kolkhoz in Selenga is located in the Iroi *sel'sovet* (or *somon sovet*, as it is called in Buryat), the lowest administrative level of the Soviet government. Besides Tashir, the centre of the kolkhoz, the villages of Udunga and Ust'-Urma, which are brigade centres, are also part of the *sel'sovet*. The population of the *sel'sovet* is larger than that of the farm, because it includes school-teachers, specialists, doctors and nurses, librarians, and people working for local industries and organisations as well as the kolkhoz members. The total population of the Iroi *sel'sovet* on 1 January 1967 was 2,483. In 1966 there were ninety-five births in the *somon*, of which seventy-one were Buryat and the others Russian, Ukrainian, or Tatar. From January 1967 to the end of May 1967, there were thirty-five births, of which twenty-five were Buryat. In 1966 there were twenty-one deaths in the *somon*, and eleven of these were Buryat. All were the deaths of old people, rather than children. There were twenty-six marriages in 1966 — sixteen between Buryat and Buryat, eight between Russian and Russian, one between a Ukrainian man and a Russian woman, and one between a Tatar man and a Russian woman. There were no divorces between 1964 and May 1967. The secretary of the *sel'sovet* estimated that about 90% of the *somon* population was Buryat.[54]

It is interesting to look at the marriage data from the Iroi and Bayangol *sel'sovets* in more detail (see Table 1.4). The Barguzin Karl Marx collective farm was located in the Bayangol *sel'sovet*. In Selenga (Iroi) the average age of marriage

39

Table 1.4. Marriages in Bayangol sel'sovet, Barguzin raion 1964–7, and in Iroi sel'sovet, Selenga raion 1966

Date of birth		Nationality		Birth-place		Present residence		Children		Occupation		Previous marriages	
H	W	H	W	H	W	H	W	H	W	H	W	H	W
Bayangol 1967													
1938	1936	Rus	Rus	Bayangol	Karaftit	Bayangol	Bayangol	—	—	tractor-driver	housewife	1st	1st
1942	1940	Bur	Bur	Bayangol	Bayangol	Bayangol	Bayangol	—	1	driver	housewife	1st	1st
1940	1945	Arm	Tat	Armenia	Tatar SSR	Ina	Ina	—	—	brigadier constr. brig.	sales-woman	1st	1st
1937	1941	Bur	Bur	Talla	Talla	Talla	Talla	—	—	tractor-driver	housewife	1st	1st
?	?	Bur	Bur	Bayangol	Bayangol	Bayangol	Bayangol	?	?	driver	teacher	2nd (div.)	1st
1937	1939	Bur	Bur	Irkutsk oblast'	Alar (Irk. oblast')	Bayangol	Bayangol	—	1	worker	prim. school	1st	1st
1940	1939	Bur	Bur	Bayangol	Bayangol	Bayangol	Bayangol	—	1	elec.-gas mechanic	sanitary worker	1st	1st
1941	1929	Rus	Rus	Ina	Ina?	Ina	Ina	—	2	fitter	housewife	1st	1st
Bayangol 1966													
1943	1941	Bur	Bur	Bayangol	Chita oblast'	Bayangol	Bayangol	—	—	fitter	pharmacist	1st	1st
1940	1940	Bur	Bur	Bayangol	Bayangol	Bayangol	Bayangol	—	1	electrician	nurse	1st	1st
1925	1927	Rus	Rus	Barguzin	Moscow oblast'	Bayangol	Bayangol	—	2	retired	lav. attendant	1st	1st
1939	1946	Bur	Bur	Bayangol	Bayangol	Bayangol	Bayangol	—	—	driver	shepherdess	1st	1st
1937	1940	Bur	Bur	Bur ASSR	?	Bayangol	Bayangol	—	2	machine-op.	milkmaid	1st	1st
1938	1938	Bur	Bur	Bayangol	Bayangol	Bayangol	Bayangol	—	1	kolkhoznik	kolkhoznitsa	1st	1st
1940	1938	Rus	Rus	Barguzin	Barguzin	Bayangol	Bayangol	—	2	kolkhoznik	kolkhoznitsa	1st	1st
1918	1935	Bur	Bur	?	?	Bayangol	Bayangol	3	3	vet. assistant	kolkhoznitsa	1st	1st
1940	1942	Rus	Rus	Bayangol	Barguzin	Chilir	Chilir	2	2	carpenter	cook	1st	1st
1938	1940	Rus	Rus	Bayangol	Dugsl. raion	Ina	Ina	—	1	mechanic	housewife	1st	1st
1939	1941	Bur	Bur	Bayangol	Bayangol	Bayangol	Bayangol	—	1	driver	kolkhoznitsa	1st	1st
1937	1943	Bur	Bur	Bayangol	Bayangol	Bayangol	Bayangol	—	—	driver	cook	1st	1st

40

1939	Bur		Bayangol	Bayangol	Bayangol	Bayangol	–	–	driver	milkmaid	1st	1st
1938	Bur		Bur ASSR	Bayangol	Bayangol	Bayangol	–	–	–	–	1st	1st
1939	Bur		Bayangol	Bayangol	Bayangol	Bayangol	–	3	kolkhoznik	kolkhoznitsa	1st	1st
1947	Rus		–	–	Ina	Ina	–	–	joiner	head of canteen	1st	1st
1941	Ukr		–	–	–	–	–	some	metal-work	plasterer	1st	1st
1940	Bur		Bauntov raion	Soyol	Soyol	Soyol	–	–	driver	milkmaid	1st	1st
1938	Bur		Bayangol	Bayangol	Soyol	Soyol	–	–	kolkhoznik	kolkhoznitsa	1st	1st
1940	Bur		Bayangol	Bayangol	Ulan-Ude	Karasun	–	–	student	schoolteacher	1st	1st
1913	Bur		Bayangol	Bayangol	Bayangol	Bayangol	2	2	kolkhoznik	shepherdess	1st	1st
?	Bur		Bayangol	Bayangol	Bayangol	Bayangol	–	–	kolkhoznik	kolkhoznitsa	1st	1st
1939	Rus		R. Kuda BASSR	R. Kuda BASSR	Ina	Ina	2	2	driver	worker	1st	1st
1917	Rus		Suvo	Karabash	Bayangol	Bayangol	6	6	kolkhozrik	kolkhoznitsa	1st	1st
1942	Bur		Barguzin	Bayangol	Bayangol	Bayangol	1	1	kolkhozrik	kolkhoznitsa	1st	1st
Bayangol 1965												
?	Tat	Tat	Tat ASSR	Tat ASSR	Ina	Ina	–	–	kolkhoznik	housewife	1st	1st
1933	Bur	Bur	Bayangol	Yarigta	Bayangol	Bayangol	–	3	kolkhoznik	kolkhoznitsa	1st	1st
1947	Rus	Rus	Suvo	Uro	Ina	Ina	–	–	student	kolkhoznitsa	1st	1st
1935	Rus	Rus	Barguzin	Belgor. oblast'	Barguzin	Barguzin	–	–	mechanic	hydrologist	1st	1st
1940	Bur	Bur	Ulyun	Bayangol	Bayangol	Bayangol	–	–	teacher	teacher	1st	1st
1905	Bur	Bur	Borogol	Karasun	Ina	Ina	4	4	administrator	housewife	1st	1st
1904	Bur		Bayangol	Bayangol	Bayangol	Bayangol	3	3	pensioner	pensioner	2nd (widower)	2nd (widow)
1921	Bur	Bur	Bayangol	Bayangol	Bayangol	Bayangol	1	1	stockman	milkmaid	1st	1st
1938	Bur	Bur	Bayangol	Sev. Baik. raion	Bayangol	Bayangol	–	–	veterinary assistant	shop (selpo)	1st	1st
1940	Bur	Bur	Bayangol	Bayangol	Ina	Ina	–	–	tractor-driver	worker	1st	1st
1938	Tat	Rus	Tat ASSR	Sakhalin oblast'	Bayangol	Bayangol	–	–	driver	housewife	1st	1st
?	Gyp	Gyp	Irkutsk oblast'	Uro	Ina	Ina	1	1	worker	various	1st	1st

Table 1.4. (*cont.*)

Date of birth		Nation-ality		Birth-place		Present residence		Children		Occupation		Previous marriages	
H	W	H	W	H	W	H	W	H	W	H	W	H	W
1942	1942	Bur	Bur	Bayangol	Bayangol	Bayangol	Bayangol	1	1	electric repairs	–	1st	1st
1907	1907	Bur	Bur	Khabartai	Ulyun	Bayangol	Bayangol	5	5	pensioner	housewife	1st	1st
1941	1941	Bur	Bur	Bayangol	Bayangol	Bayangol	Bayangol	–	–	driver	kolkhoznitsa	1st	1st
1936	1941	Bur	Bur	Bayangol	Bayangol	Bayangol	Bayangol	–	2	driver	shepherdess	1st	1st
Bayangol 1964													
?	?	Bur	Bur	Bayangol	Darkhan	Bayangol	Bayangol	2	5	kolkhoznik	kolkhoznitsa	2nd (div.)	2nd (div.)
1936	1937	Bur	Bur	Bayangol	Bayangol	Bayangol	Bayangol	–	1	agric. mach. repairs	kolkhoznitsa	1st	1st
?	?	Bur	Bur	Ulyun	Ulyun	Bayangol	Ina	–	1	metal-work	housewife	1st	1st
1932	1941	Bur	Rus	Barguzin	Bauntov. raion	Ina	Bayangol	–	–	head of IRM	accountant	1st	1st
1939	1942	Bur	Bur	Chilir	Yarigto	Karasun	Karasun	–	–	kolkhoznik	kolkhoznitsa	1st	1st
1932	1933	Bur	Bur	Bayangol	Bayangol	Bayangol	Bayangol	–	–	administrator	school-teacher	1st	1st
1935	1935	Bur	Bur	Karalik	Bayangol	Bayangol	Bayangol	–	1	*feldsher* (medical asst.)	milkmaid	1st	1st
1940	1940	Bur	Bur	Bayangol	Shergino BASSR	Bayangol	Bayangol	–	–	kolkhoznik	kolkhoznitsa	1st	1st
?	?	Bur	Bur	Bayangol	Kurumkan	Bayangol	Bayangol	–	–	kolkhoznik	kolkhoznitsa	1st	1st
1937	1943	Bur	Bur	Bayangol	–	Bayangol	Bayangol	–	–	teacher	housewife	1st	1st
1940	1938	Bur	Bur	Tolgoito BASSR	Bayangol	Bayangol	Bayangol	–	–	metal-work	teacher	1st	1st
1939	1946	Rus	Rus	Barguzin	Ulan-Ude	Ina	Ina	–	–	various	turner (lathe operator)	1st	1st
?	?	Bur	Bur	Chilir	Suvo	Chilir	Bayangol	–	–	kolkhoznik	kolkhoznitsa	1st	1st
1941	1944	Bur	Bur	Bayangol	Bayangol	Bayangol	Bayangol	–	–	driver	kolkhoznitsa	1st	1st

Iroi 1966

1941	1941	Bur	Tashir	Bur	Arbuzovo (Seleng. raion)	Tashir	Tokhoi (Seleng. raion)	–	–	secretary of committee	–	1st	1st
1942	1945	Bur	Udunga (Seleng. raion)	Bur	Ust'-Urma	Arkhangelsk	Ust'-Urma	–	–	army	school-teacher	1st	1st
1929	1920	Bur	Udunga	Bur	Udunga	Tashir	Tashir	–	–	tractor-criver	housewife	1st	2nd (widow)
1943	1943	Bur	Tashir	Bur	Novo-Selenginsk	Tashir	Ust'-Urma	–	–	army	teacher	1st	1st
1939	1941	Bur	Udunga	Bur	Udunga	Udunga	Udunga	–	1	tractor-driver	milkmaid sales-woman	1st	1st
1935	1942	Bur	Udunga	Bur	Ust'-Urma	Tashir	Tashir	3	3	driver	asst hydrometry	1st	1st
1940	1938	Rus	Cheremkhovo (Chita oblast')	Rus	Tulev. oblast'	Ust'-Urma	Ust'-Urma	1	1	forestry	packer at selpo	1st	1st
1945	1939	Rus	Ulan-Ude	Rus	Novo-Selenginsk	Tashir	Tashir	–	–	loader at selpo	teacher	1st	1st
1938	1942	Bur	Iro	Bur	Ust'-Kham shigadai (Kudar. raion)	Tashir	Tashir	–	–	teacher	teacher	1st	1st
1938	1940	Bur	Seleng. raion	Bur	Udunga	Tashir	Tashir	–	–	teacher	teacher	1st	1st
1938	1945	Bur	Ust'-Urma	Bur	Ust'-Urma	Ust'-Urma	Ust'-Urma	1	1	worker	housewife	1st	1st
1943	1945	Bur	Udunga	Bur	Nur-Tukhum (Kyakht. raion)	Ust'-Urma	Ust'-Urma	–	–	teacher	teacher	1st	1st
1936	1937	Rus	Verkh. Kaz. (Bashkir ASSR)	Rus	Kamirovo (Bashkir ASSR)	Tashir	Tashir	4	4	shepherd	shepherdess	1st	1st
1920	1917	Rus	Dzhida (Bur ASSR)	Rus	Dzhida (Bur ASSR)	Tashir	Tashir	5	5	tractor-driver	housewife	1st	1st
1939	1946	Rus	Poloskovo (Bur ASSR)	Rus	Tsushan. oblast' (RSFSR)	Irkutsk	Irkutsk	–	–	geologist	student	1st	1st

Table 1.4. (cont.)

Date of birth		Nationality		Birth-place		Present residence		Children		Occupation		Previous marriages	
H	W	H	W	H	W	H	W	H	W	H	W	H	W
1947	1946	Bur	Bur	Ust'-Urma	Ust'-Urma	Tashir	Tashir	–	–	teacher	dispatcher	1st	1st
1947	1946	Ukr	Rus	Kiev oblast'	Irkutsk oblast'	Tashir	Usol'ye-Sibirskoye	–	–	geophysicist technician	student	1st	1st
1938	1940	Bur	Bur	Tashir	Ongoi (E. B.r. Irkutsk oblast')	Tashir	Tashir	–	–	electrician	fel'dsher	1st	1st
1948	1947	Rus	Rus	Pribaikal	Bur. ASSR	Tashir	Tashir	–	–	accountant	cashier	1st	1st
1943	1947	Rus	Rus	Ust'-Urma	Khabarov. krai	Ust'-Urma	Ust'-Urma	–	–	tractor-driver	teacher	1st	1st
1941	1943	Tat	Rus	Tat. ASSR	Akmalin. oblast'	Tashir	Tashir	1 (1966)	–	carpenter	housewife	1st	1st
1927	1921	Bur	Bur	Kheltegei (Bur ASSR)	Auula (Seleng. raion)	Ust'-Urma	Ust'-Urma	2	–	teacher	in school	1st	1st
1942	1948	Bur	Bur	Udunga	Udunga	Udunga	Udunga	–	–	kolkhoznik	student	1st	1st
1942	1943	Bur	Bur	Tashir	Tashir	Tashir	Tashir	–	–	teacher	teacher	1st	1st
1947	1947	Rus	Rus	Ust'-Urma	Ivolga (Bur ASSR)	Ust'-Urma	Ust'-Urma	–	–	electrician	at boarding school	1st	1st
1940	1946	Bur	Bur'	Tashir	Zakamensk (Bur ASSR)	Ust'-Urma	Ust'-Urma	–	–	driver	teacher	1st	1st

44

among Buryats was 26.1 years (26.8 for men, and 25.3 for women). The average age for Russians, Ukrainians, etc. was slightly lower (25.4 for men and 25.6 for women). In Barguzin (Bayangol) the average age of marriage was even higher among Buryats (31.86 years for men and 29.51 years for women) and Russians (29.5 years for men and 27.8 years for women). One explanation for this high age of marriage may be that registration of marriage at the *sel'sovet* was distinct from sociologically significant marriage (the wedding), which occurred earlier. Several couples registered marriages at an advanced age when they already had children.

In Selenga, four of the sixteen Buryat couples had children before registration of marriage, and four of the ten other couples also had children before registration − in one case, five children. In Barguzin, twenty-two of the forty-five Buryat marriages, and nine of the eighteen Russian and other marriages, had offspring before registration of the marriage. It is interesting that the register, which gives both the paternity and the maternity of the children, attributes the children in the majority of cases to the wife only. This suggests that in many cases registration of marriage is not with the acknowledged father of the children. In fact, Buryats in the farms told me that illegitimacy was no longer considered a disgrace. Contraceptives were easily available,[55] and it was not difficult to obtain an abortion, but Buryat women did not like to use either. A woman with a child could marry easily, as it was evident that she was fertile.

In both Selenga and Barguzin, most marriages take place between partners born in the same kolkhoz or nearby. In Selenga eight out of sixteen Buryat marriages were between partners born in the Karl Marx kolkhoz and intending to live there after marriage, and in another seven cases one of the partners (the husband in six out of the seven) was born in the kolkhoz, while the other partner came from outside, mostly from neighbouring areas of Selenga *aimak*. In only one marriage were both partners from outside the kolkhoz, but even so they were both from within the Selenga *raion*.

In the Barguzin Bayangol *somon* the number of marriages taking place between members born in the same farm/*sel'sovet* in the mid-1960s was even greater than in Selenga: out of forty-five Buryat marriages, twenty-eight were between spouses born in the territory of the *sel'sovet* (Table 1.5). In a further seven marriages one partner was born in the farm. The picture in both Bayangol and Iroi is thus of a very localised range of unions, with a strong tendency to virilocal residence.

The Buryat rural community, as opposed to the Russian, seems to be fairly static in general − that is, not only are marriages made within a narrow geographical range, but few people once working in the kolkhoz leave it for another job. It is true that about 50% of school-leavers enter the army or go for further education and do not return. It is also true that the Soviet government has kept kolkhozniks tied to the land until very recently (see p. 133). However, there is no legal hindrance to a kolkhoznik leaving one farm for another farm. But even

Table 1.5. *Birth-places of people marrying between January 1964 and May 1967, Bayangol*

	Bayangol *somon*	Barguzin *raion*	Buryat ASSR	Elsewhere	Not recorded
Buryats					
Men	35	3	4	1	2
Women	28	9	3	2	3
Russians					
Men	4	7	1	–	1
Women	1	4	4	3	1

this does not occur very often according to my data (though it should be remembered that the farms I visited were among the most successful in the republic). From interviews in the Selenga Karl Marx farm I was able to make notes on the movements following change of residence of 106 women and 95 men, all of Buryat nationality, the sample being probably weighted towards the better paid and more qualified kolkhoz members. Table 1.6. as given certainly underestimates the number of people in such a sample who would have undertaken further education, e.g. many of the women whose reason for leaving was 'marriage' might have spent some time as students and met their future husbands when away from the farm.

Nevertheless, the evidence of stability of population in the Selenga farm is remarkable. There is material suggesting that kolkhozniks from other areas, especially those distant from any large town, are more mobile, but since this data is based on a sample of mixed nationality, predominantly Russian, it is not possible to tell how mobile the Buryats are in particular.[56] Most movement, according to this study of the Ust'-Ordynsk and Aga National Okrugs, is fairly localised and takes place within the *raion*, but nevertheless there is a general tendency for rural areas to become depopulated.[57]

It is interesting to note from the same study – since it did not occur to me to ask this question – that a slight majority of the migration takes place voluntarily as opposed to migration by order (*po napravleniyu*). Of the people arriving in the Aga National Okrug,[58] 47% came for the purpose of work, and of these a majority came of their own wish. Another batch of people returned to their native *okrug* after finishing educational courses; of these, 58% came voluntarily and 41% were sent by order.[59] Most of the people sent by order come into one of the following categories: members of the Party,[60] specialists working for government organisations such as the Ministry of Agriculture, and young people who have finished training (all Soviet graduates have to do two years of work in a place designated by their educational institution). Despite this, we find that in the age structure of the rural population of Buryatiya there is a lack of young

Table 1.6. *Reasons for arriving in or leaving the Selenga farm and immediate environs (radius of about 30 km)*

	Men	Women
Arriving in/leaving the farm		
Arriving for work	9	3
Leaving for work	12	–
Leaving for army	1	–
Leaving for education	2	2
Leaving for marriage	–	18
Arriving to stay with children	–	2
Arriving for marriage	–	17
Total	24	42
Staying in the farm from birth	71	64

people in their twenties, which indicates that somehow these people are escaping to the cities.[61]

Thus, we may summarise by saying that Buryat population shows the following features: a high rate of birth, a high age of marriage, the condoning of illegitimate children, but at the same time a low rate of divorce, very localised marriage among those who remain on the farm, a tendency towards virilocality, and a very low rate of mixed marriage. All of this is consistent with a population markedly immobile after the age of thirty or so.

4. Concepts of Buryat society and kinship

The pre-Revolution period

Many people in Buryat collective farms today remember genealogies going back twelve or more generations, and literally everyone knows an extensive network of kin, amounting to well over a hundred names in the present generation. In making marriages the principles of lineal exogamy are still observed. It is clear that kinship as a social phenomenon beyond the immediate family has not lost its significance. But the Soviet political economy has had the effect of changing the forms of kinship and its place in society. In order to assess this change and its meaning for the Buryats, we need to know about the operation of the kinship system – on both the ideological and the practical level – before the Revolution.

In this section I shall consider the kinship system of the Barguzin Buryats, mainly because it is directly historically linked with my own field material from that district. The Barguzin Buryats are emigrants from the clans living to the west of Lake Baikal. They began to arrive in Barguzin in the late seventeenth or early eighteenth century. But they were influenced over the years by the Khori Buryats (known as the 'eastern Buryats', see Map 1) living directly to the south of them, and their kinship system may therefore be said to show an interesting conjunction of the 'western' and 'eastern' features which I have described elsewhere.[62]

Until the time of the twentieth-century revolutions, the Barguzin kinship system also constituted the indigenous political system. In other words, under the conditions of Tsarist indirect rule, the political leaders of the Buryat were defined by their position in the system of patrilineal clans. It is possible to trace the historical evolution of these clans in some detail because the Barguzin Buryats were deeply interested in their past and wrote a series of chronicles describing their history as they saw it.[63] The chronicles were mostly written by the clan princes themselves, or by scribes or Buddhist lamas closely connected with them, and so it is not surprising to find that the 'history' of the valley differs according to the clan origin of the author. What these sources represent, in fact, is a strange amalgamation of a Buryat view of the past, based on cyclical and genealogical views of time, and a linear concept in which events are dated by the Gregorian calendar of Russian origin. This latter was used primarily to date events in which the Buryats were involved with the Tsarist governmental process. The fact that the Buryat authors were operating simultaneously with two historical genres, or 'languages', is extremely useful from our point of view, since it allows us to distinguish between the genealogical development of the clans through time, a matter of continual but variable fissioning, and their petrification as units of the governmental structure.

The chronicles say that the Barguzin valley was first settled by a cultured agriculturalist people known as the *aba khorchin* Mongols. These people subsequently moved away, and the only remains of their culture are their irrigation canals (some of which are still used) and occasional bronze arrowheads and implements. When these are found by the Buryats they are worshipped as sacred. At least one of the chronicles then proceeds to identify the Barguzin valley with the place of origin of the 'Mongols', i.e. the Imperial Mongols of the Yuan Dynasty. The son of Heaven, Bürte-Shono (Bürte-Wolf) married the earthly beauty, Goa Maral (Goa-Deer), and gave birth to the Mongol people. This legend is common to all Mongol peoples, and most variants agree that Bürte-Shono lived on a mountain called Burkhan-Khaldan. The Barguzin chronicle[64] identifies Burkhan-Khaldan with a mountain called Barkhan-agula, the most sacred peak in Barguzin. Bürte-Shono's descendant in the thirteenth generation was Bodonchar, ancestor of the Bordzhigit clan, the famous 'golden family' (*altan urag*) which constituted the aristocracy of the Mongols. In the ninth generation from Bodonchar, Yesügei-Bagatur was born, and in the sixteenth water-horse year of the third *rabdzhun* there took place the birth of Temuchin (Genghis Khan). In order to reassure readers of the truth of this statement, the author of the chronicle slips into his other genre, and points out that a famous Buryat historian, Dorzhi Banzarov, personally said to the Barguzin prince Sakhar Khamnaev when they met in the 'Christian' year of 1854, that 'The ancestors of the great *khagan* lived in Barguzin'.

Here perhaps it is in order to say something about the status of these chronicles. Since they emerged from the literate aristocracy of the late nineteenth and early twentieth centuries it might justifiably be questioned whether they represent the ideas of the ordinary people. Two points can be made: first, the legends cited are of a type which is common to Buryat culture as a whole; that is, although the emphasis given to particular ancestors may vary from one group of Buryats to another, the idea of historical origins based not on whole peoples, or classes of people, but on single heroes and their kin, is genuinely common to all Buryats. Secondly, the chronicles indicate in themselves a consciousness of alternative views, such that it is impossible to regard them simply as the ideological productions of an aristocracy concerned to legitimate its position. They did fulfil this latter function without doubt – many paragraphs are devoted to the awarding of medals to the ruling prince and such details – but the important fact is that they show clearly that Buryat culture by the nineteenth century was located at the intersection of at least three civilisations, the Mongol-Tibetan, the Russian, and the Chinese, and that the Buryats were by no means unaware of the contradictory ideologies which these represented.

The common Soviet view that the ordinary Buryats before the Revolution were illiterate, 'backward', and ignorant is unjustified. Even by 1800 Mongolian Buddhist lamas were teaching in Barguzin – and Barguzin, it must be remembered, was perhaps the most remote of all areas populated by Buryats east of Lake Baikal. A *datsan* (teaching monastery) was established shortly afterwards, and by the 1840s the Tsarist government was already concerned about the number of lamas. In the mid-1850s the number of official lamas attached to the Barguzin *datsan* was cut down from about seventy to six.[65] But this did not stop the spread of Buddhist teaching nor the wide cultural links it brought the people of Barguzin. By the 1860s people were regularly travelling to Mongolia on trade journeys, and visits from Tibetan and Mongolian lamas were common. Sometimes religious and financial aims were combined: thus in 1869 a high Lamaist dignitary came to Barguzin from the U-tai region of China bearing a large quantity of goods for trade. The reigning prince in 1879, Tserenzhap Sakharov, obtained 'according to the desire of the whole people' a copy of the *Danzhur*, a commentary on the Tibetan religious text *Ganzhur*, in 225 volumes, from Peking via a Buryat agent in that city. Meanwhile, Russian missionaries also were active, and a much more powerful Western influence was the flow of political exiles condemned by the Tsarist government to live in Siberia. In Barguzin, two Decembrists, the brothers Kyukhel'beker, opened a school in which Buryats as well as Russians studied. The princely lineage of the Sakharovs was itself actively and seriously interested in education. Sakhar Khamnaev founded the first Buryat secular school in 1844. Who would imagine that a Soviet Buryat, a native of the Barguzin sovkhoz at Deren (Dyren), would write about this prince, a class enemy, in the following terms?

By the way, it should be mentioned that the passionate initiator of enlightenment among the Buryat, the teacher and poet, D.P. Davydov, wrote about Sakhar Khamnaev: 'Among all the respected clan elders and the officials of the Barguzin region, only one man takes trouble over the school . . . and it is because of his efforts that the school exists at all, the classroom having been built by his means . . . and this is a Buryat, an official of the fourteenth class, Sakhar Khamnaev. He is known for his loyalty and is exceptionally respected by everyone in general, and by the Buryats in particular . . . he knows excellent Russian and Mongolian, and has visited almost every academic institution in St Petersburg.

'With fatherly care, Khamnaev watches over the school, grows potatoes for the children, helps the poor by gifts from his own property, rewards the diligent and directs the lazy, and the school keeps going by his efforts.' Despite the fact that teaching at that time brought no material rewards, Sakhar Khamnaev educated both of his sons, and they both became teachers after graduating from the Verkhneudinsk school.[66]

During the latter part of the Sakharovs' period in office, the following secular schools were opened in Barguzin: in 1908 in Khargana, in 1910 in Nur and Ina, in 1916 in Dyren, in 1917 in Murgun, Kharamodun, Argada, and Garga. One particularly influential teacher at the end of the nineteenth century was Aimpil Galsanovich Gal'cheev, known as Aimpil-*baksha*. Although he was a Buryat, he taught, as an old kolkhoznik remembers from his youth in 1906—8,

the Buryat language, Russian, and arithmetic . . . To this day I shall never forget the enthralled interest with which we listened when he read us *Dyeti Kapitana Granta* ('The Children of Captain Grant') by Jules Verne. He had a great influence on the people of Ulyun. For that time, he had a very large library in the Ulyun school. Aimpil-*baksha* always dressed very neatly, in a Russian suit.

Aimpil taught his pupils at home, and there was also a variety of other teachers, outside the school system, who gave instruction in the Mongolian-Tibetan tradition: lamas, scribes, and assistants to the princes.[67]

It is thus clear that the Buryats who wrote the genealogical chronicles, and the Buryats who still think in genealogical terms about their history (see Chapter 8), were not doing so in any unconscious way. They were making a statement about their kind of history and their view of the nature of their society. The contemporary implications of this will be discussed in detail later, but meanwhile it is worth bearing in mind that if a Buryat social system could be conceived in terms quite distinct from the Tsarist political structure — despite the fact that the latter apparently made use of the former — the same can be true in relation to the Soviet political economy, which in principle envelops the whole of society.

Let us look at this initial disjunction. The Cossack armies established a fortress in Barguzin in 1648. All over Siberia the natives were subdued, often with no fighting involved, and then left more or less to their own devices so long as they paid taxes. The tax-collectors were the native 'princes', who were to transfer the tax to the Russians according to the number of 'male souls' (counted from the time of birth until, occasionally, long after death) in their fealty. Many of the Siberian peoples did not have 'princes' in this sense, and were forced to invent them more or less from scratch, but the Buryats had a category of people who had an analogous social role, the heads of the patrilineal clans (*taisha*). The Russians began to set up collection points (*mirskiye sborniye izby*) throughout Siberia from the middle of the seventeenth century, but the Buryats east of Lake Baikal seem to have been left alone until the mid eighteenth century. From this time until 1811,[68] the Barguzin people were governed at a distance, a local tax-collection office (*kontora*) only being set up in that year. The *kontora* was at Ulyun (see Map 2). It was re-named a 'steppe *duma*' after the Speranskiy reforms of 1822, but its function remained essentially unchanged. In 1904 the steppe dumas were replaced, and a district (*volost*) government of 'aliens' (*inorodtsy*) based on territorial as opposed to 'kin' divisions was set up at Khargana. This had authority over eight territorial divisions (*buluk*), but it was still the clan headmen who were politically dominant despite the clans themselves (or rather their administrative equivalents) having ceased to be tax-paying units. In the 1918–23 period, after the overthrow of Tsarist power, but before the Bolsheviks had established a government in this region, Barguzin was administered by Buryat nationalist revolutionaries. As in the preceding 1903–17 period, the Buryat population of the valley (classed together with neighbouring Tungus as 'aliens') was administered separately from the Russian settlers. The Buryat part, called the Barguzin *aimak*, was divided into four *khoshun* or districts (Bayangol, Baragkhan, Argadin, and Dede-Gol), each of which consisted of several *somon*.

Until 1903, the Buryats were governed on the basis of clans alone. However, these administrative clans, called *rod* in Russian and *otok* in Buryat,[69] soon ceased to correspond with the genealogically based clans (*yahan*, or *esige*) recognised by the Buryat.

For the Buryats a clan is in principle a strictly patrilineal unit descended from a male ancestor. The clan – or its divisions, which are structurally the same thing – is called *esige* (father). Clan divisions, or lineages, are formed from the descendants of brothers, who are always ranked by age. There is general agreement, both in the chronicles and among the Buryat kolkhozniks of today, that there are eight clans (*esige*) in Barguzin. They are called the 'eight foreign' (*nayman khari*) because they are not counted kin of one another, and can therefore take wives from each other. The eight exogamous clans are:
(*cinggüldür*) Hengeldur in present pronunciation
(*cino*) Shono in present pronunciation
Bayandai
Abazai
Galzud
Emkhenud

Tsegenud

(*bulgad*) Bulagat in present pronunciation

The Hengeldur, Shono, Bayandai and Abazai clans are all in fact descended from a common ancestor, Ekhirit. In order to achieve their present 'foreign' status vis-à-vis one another, the ancestors in legend performed a rite, breaking their common cooking-pot and bows, which established the legality of marriage between them. The genealogy at this point is shown in Figure 1.1.[70]

The Emkhenud clan is not considered to be part of the Ekhirit, because it is descended from the illegitimate son of one of Shono's daughters. The Tsegenud and Galzud clans are also distinct from the Ekhirit, and from one another. Their ancestors fled to the west of Lake Baikal during the war between the Dzungar Khan Galdan and the Khalkha Mongols in the seventeenth century, and they subsequently came to Barguzin.[71] The Bulagat tribe is represented in Barguzin by the *esige* called Khuranski.

The eight *esige* of Barguzin are of very different size. There were always more of the Hengeldur and Shono people than of any of the others. The Bayandai and Abazai numbered only a few hundred households at the end of the nineteenth century, and the Emkhenud, Tsegenud, Galzud and Bulagat were even smaller.

Since the Tsarist government's relations with the 'aliens' of its empire were concerned primarily with tax payment, and tax was collected on the basis of the number of 'male souls', the *esige* themselves rapidly became unmanageable as fiscal units. As early as 1786 the Hengeldur were divided into three 'administrative' lineages (*otok* or *rod*): the Buura, and the first and second Hengeldur. Of these the Buura was genealogically senior, and the line of princes of Barguzin came from this group. The title of the main chief was *zaisan* or head *taisha*. By the early nineteenth century there were six *otok*: Buura, first Hengeldur, second Hengeldur, Shono, Bayandai, and *Izbooron* (a Buryatisation of the Russian word *sborniy*, 'collected', i.e. all the other small *esige* collected together). Later there were eight, and then twelve *otok*, arising from the fissioning of the Shono and Hengeldur clans. In 1846, although the number of clan sub-divisions went on multiplying, the administrative *otok* were reduced to six, on the grounds,

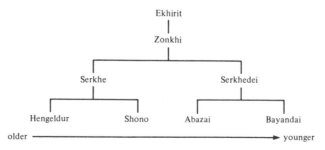

1.1. Idealised representation of relations between the Barguzin clans (*esige*).

52

according to one of the chronicles, that the existence of twelve separate units was socially divisive. It is thus apparent that by this time the administrative units consisted not of the *esige* themselves, but of political unions of the clans or their sub-divisions. In other words, the early attempt to keep pace with the growth of population (which multiplied both naturally and by further immigration into the valley) by creating more and more administrative units was abandoned in 1846. This also coincided with the point at which the line of Buura chiefs established definitive control.

During the second half of the eighteenth century, the line of Buura chiefs descended from Ondaroi (Russianised as 'Andreyev') Shibshe competed for the head *taisha*-ship with various other groups. The Buura aristocratic line was still closely linked with its homeland west of Lake Baikal, even though the founder of the Barguzin dynasty, Bosgol Andreyev, had gone to Barguzin as early as 1762. Thus a descendant of Bosgol, perhaps a grandson, Khamnai Sankirov (Sakharov), made an attempt to acquire the Verkholensk *taisha*-ship from his Buura kinsmen in the west some time at the beginning of the nineteenth century.[72] When this failed, Sankirov returned to Barguzin, was elected *taisha* and established his family definitively in power. It is through this account that we learn how succession in office worked: the principle was one of primogeniture in the male line, but each *taisha* had to be elected into office by the clan elders and so the way was open for other candidates to insert themselves. The elders formed political parties, usually two in each administrative unit, and these parties manipulated the vote by naked use of bribery and coercion.[73] A standard method of legitimation of claims by the candidates from either side was the reconstruction of the genealogies. The writing down of the Barguzin chronicles by the Sakharov *taishas* was perhaps at least in part aimed at preventing such re-interpretations of seniority being put forward by their opponents.

In theory all of the eight *esige* are exogamous groups. Furthermore, they are also recognised to be in some sense qualitatively unlike one another, in that each possesses a different supernatural ability (*udkha*: root, essence). The different nature of each clan is associated with distinct natural abilities, as well as shamanistic ones. Thus, of the four main clans in Barguzin, the Abazai are notionally ironsmiths, the Bayandai are huntsmen, the Shono are silversmiths (and are also supposed to be crafty and deceitful), and the Hengeldur are herdsmen. When women marry into another clan they bring the spirits of their natal group with them, and this, it was thought, could be dangerous because shamans of the husband's clan could not necessarily control the foreign *udkha*'s kind of power.

Like many Asian peoples the Buryats make a distinction between paternal links, conceptualised as 'bone' formed by the father's semen, and maternal links, seen as 'blood' or 'flesh' contributed by the mother. A common word for the patrilineal lineage is, in fact, *yahan* (bone).

The Buryat kinship system contains an underlying possibility of 'generalised exchange' between clans or lineages. This can be seen from the fact that marriage with women of the F's Sis D category was absolutely forbidden over nine generations, while marriage with the M's Br D, even a first cousin, was possible. Marriage was accompanied by the payment of a large brideprice (*aduu*: horse herd) consisting of livestock, money, and other gifts. Since the brideprice was considerably larger than the amount of property owned by given individuals, the system as a whole depended on balancing the flow of wealth into the group from daughters and sisters given away in marriage with the flow out of the group of wealth allotted to sons as brideprice. There is an implicit status difference between a wife-giving and a wife-receiving lineage. This can be seen from the kinship terminology diagram (Figure 8.2), where the line of the mother's father/brother (*nagatsa*) is conceptualised as a category of seniors in relation to Ego, while the line of people accepting women of Ego's group (F's Sis Son, Sis Son, etc.) (*zee*) is seen as junior to Ego. Even today Ego should not call any of the *nagatsa* males by their names, nor use the familiar *shi* (you) rather than the formal *ta* (you) with them. He can, on the other hand, call any *zee* by his name and use the *shi* form.

Certain local lineages in each district were renowned for producing good wives. And if a marriage had been successful (i.e. fruitful in terms of children) people were anxious to repeat it. As one western Buryat put it:

Every kinsman was anxious to take a wife from a good lineage. A good lineage was considered one which was first friendly and honest, second healthy and multiplying in numbers, and third work-loving and industrious.

If we follow up the kinship relations of the various *ulus* [villages] of the Yangut lineage we see an interesting picture. The inhabitants of Ongosor *ulus* of this lineage took their wives, for the most part, from the Tarasa and Buret' *ulus* of the second Gotol lineage, and the inhabitants of the Yenisei *ulus*, particularly the Matuushkha and Mat'bi kin-groups (*urag*) of the Yangut, took their wives from the Zaglik *ulus* of the third Gotol lineage, etc. This phenomenon can be explained not only by the desire of bridegrooms to get wives from good lineages, but also by the fact that it was easier for him to find a wife in a foreign lineage where the people were already known to his own kinsmen.[74]

The Buryats had no explicit rules for marriage with any particular group, nor does the kinship terminology imply that the father-in-law is one of the same kin category as the mother's brother (see Figure 8.2). However, the tendency for marriage with groups from which wives have already been taken, together with folk sayings, which one occasionally comes across in the literature, implying that marriage with a woman of the mother's group is to be preferred,[75] indicates a certain tendency in pre-revolutionary Buryat society for generalised exchange.

The terminology for the marriage exchanges is instructive. The Yangut and Bokhan western Buryats used the expression *aduu-baril* for the brideprice. *Aduu* as we have noted means 'horse herd', but *baril* has the meaning of gift (from one below to one above), tribute, or even bribe.[76] Baldayev, himself a Buryat, explains further that the word *baril* or *barilga* means a payment to a clan chief for some misdemeanour.[77] Another term for the brideprice is *basaganai khudaldaan* – literally price for the daughter. The phrase *khudaldaan khudal* has the meaning of 'lie' or 'cheat'. But the bride's dowry brought with her at marriage, that is her jewellery, furniture, and household equipment, were described in terms which have quite different implications. The most common term was *zahal*, meaning 'correction', 'improvement', or 'proper outfit'. This category clearly must be distinguished from the endowment (*enzhe*) paid after marriage by the bride's father in order to set up the young household. The *enzhe* was paralleled by a similar contribution made by the bridegroom's father to the young couple (*anza*). Neither of these terms have any moral implications. But the categories *aduu-baril* and *zahal* are clear statements as to the different intentions of the payments at marriage itself by the two sides.

It seems probable, in fact, that 'generalised exchange' was a practice of the upper status clans only. Here we need to examine the other kinds of marriage which were possible. There is a good deal of evidence to suggest that families of middling wealth and status used to practise exchange-marriage (*andlya*). The advantage of this form was that it avoided the brideprice payment on both sides. The sources are clear that the only 'correct' form of *andlya* marriage was between two previously unrelated (*khari*) lineages, but economic necessity may well have over-ruled considerations of propriety and Baldayev suggests that some pairs of lineages practised repeated exchange-marriage.[78] The high brideprice prevented some men from marrying at all. Manzhigeyev gives several cases of families at the beginning of the twentieth century in which there were three or four sons where only one managed to marry, and that only after a long period of gathering together the brideprice.[79] A third kind of marriage, and the least 'respectable' from a man's point of view, was one where he worked for some years in the bride's father's household instead of paying brideprice.

Thus the Buryat kinship 'system' in the early decades of the twentieth century was consistent with three rather different kinds of marriage: the 'respectable' alliance type, in which repeated marriage with women from the mother's lineage (or another 'good' lineage) was preferred; the exchange-marriage, in which both sides were equal, and expensive weddings were avoided by both groups; and the least 'honourable' kind, where the primary factor was the working capacity of the incoming spouse in the restricted family.

This is consistent with the practice of 'generalised exchange' at the higher status level, and 'restricted exchange' among the ordinary people. Let us see what happened to this pattern in Barguzin after the Revolution.

The post-Revolution period

The *esige* present in the Bayangol area of Barguzin are shown in Table 1.7. Before collectivisation many of the *esige*, if not all, were divided into local kingroups named by their place of residence or by a description such as 'northern', 'southern', 'middle', etc. Thus, for example, the Barbinsho-Hengeldur were

Table 1.7. *The esige of the Bayangol area of Barguzin*

Hengeldur clan	Shono clan	Bayandai clan	Abazai, Tsegenud, Emkhenud clans
Buura	Buga	Khonkhoi	
Iyekhüi	Sheptekhüi	Tokhoi	
Khodoi	Butuma		
Khonkho	Tümentei		
Ordo	Borsoi		
Nomol	Basai		
Barbinsho	Otorsho		
Büübei			

divided into the Baruun-Barbinsho (the 'west' Barbinsho, living west of the Ina River), the Dunda-Barbinsho ('middle' Barbinsho, living the other side of the Ina), and the Urdo-Barbinsho ('south' Barbinsho, the junior line, living near Karalik).

The great majority of marriages of Bayangol men took place with women of the same district of Barguzin. A typical marriage pattern can be seen in the genealogy of Donsan Zhigzhitova of the Ordo-Hengeldur *esige* (see Figure 1.2). This is a characteristic example of 'restricted exchange', in this case between the Ordo-Hengeldur and the Buga- and Butuma-Shono. It should be noted that these genealogies were volunteered by the informants, whom I did not press for further information. Thus, since it is extremely unlikely that Donsan Zhigzhitova would have 'forgotten' the lineage of her own sister's husband, it is possible that this marriage was an 'incorrect' one.

However, most people did not appear to be trying to hide 'incorrect' marriages — indeed, many insisted that the concern with exogamy was a matter of the past and that young people no longer take it into account. We shall look at this question later, in Chapter 8. Meanwhile, it is apparent that, if we take the 149 marriages in which the *esige* of both spouses was mentioned for a period from approximately 1920 to the 1960s, there is in fact a definite tendency towards exogamy of the *esige* and a preference for marriage with what one might call the opposite moiety; i.e. Hengeldur men marry Shono women, and vice versa (Table 1.8). The other six marriages, making up a total of 149, were between members of the small groups (Galzud, Emkhenud, etc.).

It is not possible to see any repeated alliances of the 'generalised exchange' type between the various *esige* among the ordinary people. Rather, as the Ordo-Hengeldur genealogy shows, small groups of *esige* belonging to the opposite 'moiety' tended to conduct exchange-marriage amongst themselves. The sample was not large enough to tell whether these affinal groups related by exchange were themselves in some sense discrete units, i.e. whether a caste-like series of essentially endogamous groups has emerged, each containing *esige* from both

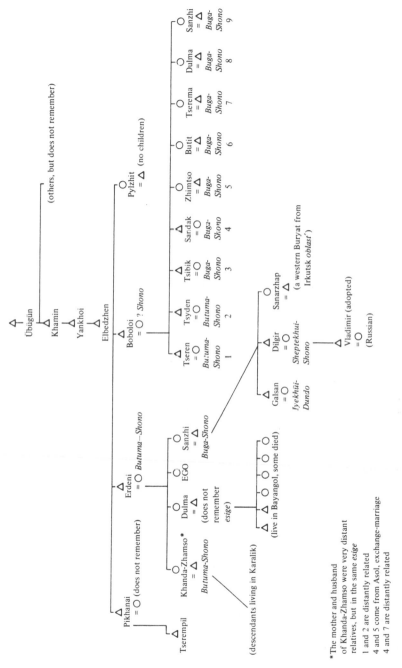

1.2. Genealogy of the Ordo-Hengeldur *esige* given by Donsan Erdinieva Zhigzhitova, 14 June 1967, in Bayangol, Barguzin. The Übügün-*tang*.

Table 1.8. *Marriages amongst the esige of Bayangol, c. 1920–66*

Marriage partner	Shono *esige*		Hengeldur *esige*	
	Men	Women	Men	Women
Shono, same *esige*	2	2	⎫ 47	⎫ 43
Shono, other *esige*	7	7	⎭	⎭
Hengeldur, same *esige*	⎫ 43	⎫ 47	4	4
Hengeldur, other *esige*	⎭	⎭	21	21
Emkhenud	1	1	–	–
Bayandai	3	2	4	2
Tsegenud	–	2	–	2
Galzud	–	1	–	–
Russian	1	–	–	–
Total	57	62	76	72

Hengeldur and Shono. The evidence I have suggests that this was probably not the case, and that all Hengeldur *esige* could take wives from all Shono, and vice versa. We are reminded of what Lévi-Strauss wrote about 'restricted exchange': that it is not a system, but a procedure. What emerges from the Barguzin material seems to be that of a series of affinal alliances between *esige* of Hengeldur and Shono, alliances which may not last over the generations, but which at any one point involve a relation of reciprocity between essentially equal partners.

The exceptions to this pattern occur at either end of the status range. At the lower end are the Emkhenud, a small group which had no political power in the Tsarist system, and related illegitimately to the Shono (themselves junior to the Hengeldur by ranking of brothers) through a woman. The Tsegenud are also few and their lack of political status was summed up in the saying: *Otogtoo noyobei segeenut, oroidei uhebei segeenut*; 'The Tsegenud have no chief in the *otok*, the Tsegenud have no hair on their heads.'[80] It is noticeable that Hengeldur men did not take wives from either of these groups, although it was possible for Hengeldur women to marry into them. This is consistent with the suggestion made above that the marriages of Buryat women reflect status hierarchies.

At the other end of the scale is the Buura *esige* of the Hengeldur clan. The Hengeldur are 'senior' to the Shono not only because they are descended from the older brother of the two, but because, according to Barguzin myth, when they decided that their families must inter-marry in order to reproduce, it was Hengeldur who gave a daughter to Shono's son. The Buura have always been perceived as in some way separate from the other Hengeldur lineages. The separation, which also had a political dimension (it will be remembered that the Buura had a separate *taisha* by the middle of the eighteenth century), although it stems initially from a genealogical seniority within the Hengeldur clan, became so marked that, paradoxically, it allowed some of the Shono people to claim that Buura was a Shono lineage.[81] This is what we should expect, if the Buura were ever to conceive of themselves as outside the balanced 'moiety'-type exchanges between Hengeldur and Shono.

The Buura lineage was differentiated from the other *esige* of Hengeldur by a criterion which in one form or another was often used to separate off aristocratic lines in Mongolian kinship: the differentiation of wives of the founding ancestor.[82] According to one Barguzin informant, Hengeldur had three wives. The Buura are descended from the first and most senior, all of the other Barguzin *esige* are descended from the second wife, and the descendants from the third wife still live west of Lake Baikal (see genealogy of Zhambal Upanov, Figure 1.3).

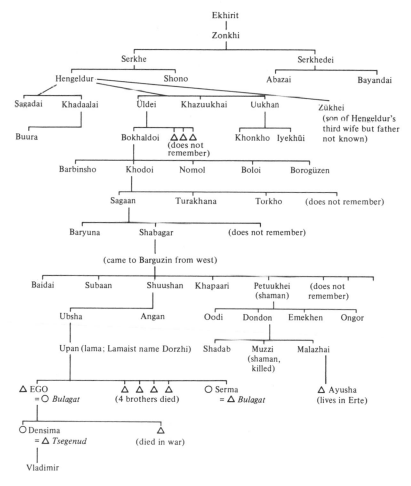

1.3. Genealogy of the Hengeldur-Khodoi *esige* given by Zhambal Dorzhiyevich Upanov, aged 70, 16 June 1967, in Bayangol, Barguzin. He was Chairman of Bayangol *sel'sovet* in his youth.

It can be seen, by comparing Upanov's genealogy with that of Buura Butoyev (Figure 1.4), himself a member of the Buura lineage, that genealogies by no means coincide, even those provided by men from the same village.

The early modern Buryat nationalist leaders derived their position initially from the clan system, if only in the minimal sense that they came from families which were rich and influential enough to provide them with education. The domination of education in Barguzin at the beginning of the century by the Sakharov line has already been mentioned. But this line of the *taisha* himself, however liberal the individual holding the *taisha*-ship might have been, was defined by the politics of the revolutionary period as belonging to the 'class enemy', and the early nationalist and socialist leaders tended to come from other privileged, but not aristocratic, lineages.

The most famous and influential of these leaders, born in Bayangol in Barguzin, was Elbekdorzhi Rinchino, of the Barbinsho-Hengeldur lineage. Rinchino, born around 1885, graduated from the Faculty of Law in St Petersburg, at one time worked on Buryat language reform, made studies of the east Siberian Tungus, and later became Chairman of the Military Council and Comintern Representative in the government of Tseren Dorzhi in Mongolia in the early 1920s. Rinchino, originally a Social Revolutionary, not a Bolshevik, later became a Communist, and was an important figure in the complicated politics of Mongolia and Buryatiya – he has been called the '*de facto* dictator of Outer Mongolia'.[83] Like many other revolutionary Buryats of the time, he was an ardent pan-Mongolist. In 1924, at the Third Congress of the Mongolian People's Revolutionary Party, he said, 'We must be the cultural centre for our races, we must attract to ourselves the Inner Mongols, the Barga Mongols, etc.'[84] In 1928, with the 'left turn' in both the USSR and Mongolia, he was recalled to Moscow, and he died in the 1937 purges.

The genealogy of Rinchino's family was given by one of his relatives, a kolkhoznik in the Karl Marx farm (Figure 1.5). This family history is interesting because it illustrates the process of class division of the local patrilineal group, which began to occur in the economic and political cataclysms of the early twentieth century. The local kin-group descended from Morkhosei (Morkhosei-*tang*) was strongly Lamaist, very prosperous, and closely cooperative. Erinchin, son of Balzhar, became a leader in the *volost* – in local terms he was a *noyon*, a lord. He was able to give education to all of his children, and they left Barguzin, only Tseren, the youngest, remaining to inherit the property. Badma's property, however, was divided between Zhigmit and Pydan-tseren, each of whom had numerous descendants, and this side of the family became poorer. Erdene was ill, lost all his wealth, and died young, and so his children, including my inform-ant, were brought up by their uncle Bobei in a state of dependence. The two halves of the family were divided between on the one hand violent state politics, and on the other the humble collective farm.

The principles of Buryat kinship outlined here still remain in people's minds.

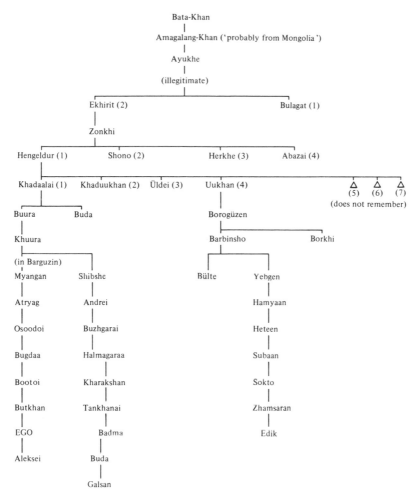

1.4. Genealogy of the Buura-Hengeldur *esige* given by Buura (Viktor) Butoyev, aged 70, June 1967. He arrived in Barguzin as a youth.

The informant has included the *taisha*'s line, descended from Shibshe, although he did not mention that this was an aristocratic lineage. In general, all the kolkhozniks avoided talking about the previous political system, and I did not press them on this point. It was only possible to establish who the *taishas* were from other published sources. Buura Butoyev also gave a detailed genealogy of the men and women and their descendants within the *Bootoi-tan* (i.e. group descended from Bootoi), but I have not included it here for reasons of space. He would also have given all the descendants of Bülte (a section of the Barbinsho-Hengeldur), but I wanted to ask him about other matters and stopped taking notes on the genealogy at this point. There were many stories about Myangan, who was a rich man, and about Osoodoi, who was a famous singer. Zhamsaran was a well-known performer of epics and legends.

Seniority of brothers is given in parentheses.

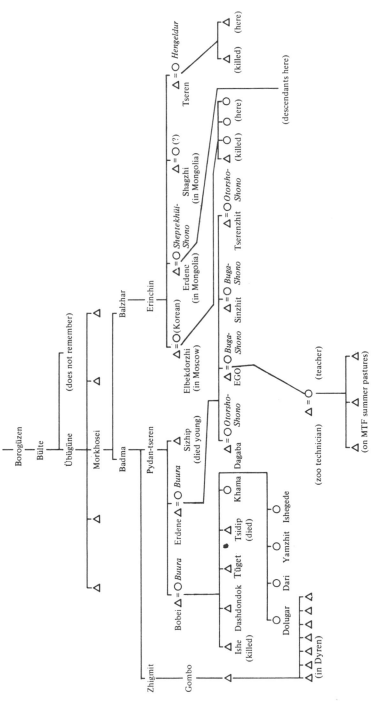

1.5. Genealogy of the Hengeldur-Dunda-Barbinsho *esige* given by Tseren Pydanovich Erdeneyev, aged 68, on 17 June 1967, in Bayangol, Barguzin. The marriages of Dagaba and Tserenzhit were exchange-marriages. Khama, whose husband was from the Buga-Shono lineage, was the mother of the farm Chairman.

The breaking up of many local kinship groups in the pre-collectivisation period for economic and political reasons (e.g. land re-allocations in the 1920s,[85] the taking of different sides in the *'aimak'* and 'anti-*aimak*' movements,[86] the civil war of 'de-kulakisation', the different reactions which individuals had to collectivisation[87]) did not destroy the cultural *concept* of the group. Such patrilineal groups still exist in the kolkhoz, but their function has totally changed, to the point where one might say that they have become almost purely cultural self-reflections, existing by virtue of their dissimilarity to Soviet institutions. This, together with the present forms of practical kinship (i.e. kinship ties used in practice but not necessarily culturally formalised) will be discussed in Chapters 7 and 8.

5. The Barguzin valley

Karl Marx Collective has its centre in Bayangol in the remote region of Barguzin. Extending north-eastwards from the shore of Lake Baikal, and enclosed on all sides by mountains, the valley of the River Barguzin is one of the most inaccessible of the inhabited areas of south-eastern Siberia. The densely forested Ikat range forms its southern and eastern boundary, and the craggy Barguzin range, covered in snow and ice even in summer, cuts it off from the lake to the north and west. These two mountain ranges meet near the mouth of the Barguzin, allowing the river to force its way out past a rock, the 'Shaman's Threshold', which juts out from the northern ridge. Behind this narrow entrance the valley opens out into an area of salty bogs and swamps, and then rises to some of the most northern steppelands in Asia, the Kuitun.

It was on account of these steppes, good sheep-herding land, that the valley has long been known to the Mongols. 'Barguzin-tukum' was mentioned in the thirteenth-century chronicle 'The secret history of the Mongols' as the birthplace of an ancestress of Genghis Khan. In more recent centuries the valley, which was relatively little populated, was renowned among Buryats as a place to flee to:

Khotiggoe mikha olkho
Hükhegee tülyee olkho
Khuligae khee khadan buyykha,
Khudlaar khelee khadan
Khorgolkho gazar.

You can get meat without a knife
You can find wood without an axe
If you've stolen you can hide
If you've cheated there's somewhere to stay concealed,
It's that kind of place.[88]

When the Russians arrived in the area in the 1640s the Barguzin valley was inhabited by both Buryats and Evenki.[89] In the decades after this many of the Buryats migrated southwards to Mongolia to avoid the taxes and other demands made by the Russians. The remaining Buryats apparently assimilated with the more numerous Evenki. By 1680 some Buryats returned from Mongolia, where they had found conditions worse under the warring Khans than in Siberia. They were told by the Irkutsk governor to move out of Barguzin, however, and they went to the western side of Lake Baikal with the intention of migrating back to Mongolia. It is not until 1783, when a census was carried out, that we know for certain that there were again Buryats in Barguzin — 597 males, to be precise.[90] These were people of western Buryat origin and the direct ancestors of the present Barguzin Buryats.

The Buryats soon came into conflict with the Evenki, who tried to forbid them hunting rights and the use of pastures. In the end the two communities built a fence, called by the Buryats *uta khürei*, which became their boundary. Subsequently, the Buryats themselves forced the Evenki further and further north up the valley, and during the nineteenth century the Evenki were much reduced in number from epidemics.

Russian settlers began to arrive in Barguzin in the seventeenth century around the same time as the western Buryats. The town of Barguzin was first primarily a fortress, but soon developed into a trading centre. Manufactured goods from Russia, and cloth, tea, and other products from China were exchanged here for agricultural and livestock products and furs. Barguzin was famous for its fur-bearing animals, particularly the sable, which was sold for very high prices. By the 1930s sables had become so rare that hunting of them was stopped, but it has recently been restarted under licence.

A street scene in Bayangol with the Ikat hills behind.

The Barguzin valley

In 1812 the Barguzin Buryats of the Hengeldur clan first invited Buddhist lamas from the Khori region to initiate Lamaist teaching. In the same year a man from Barguzin went to the Egutuyev *datsan* in Khori, was consecrated as a lama, and learnt Tibetan. Under the patronage of the Barguzin *taisha* (prince) the first lamas of the valley learned about Tibetan medicine, taught children Mongolian and Tibetan, constructed the first temple, and went to Kyakhta to obtain religious books. The first wooden monastery was built in 1828 and Lamaism continued to grow, but in 1854, with the publication of the Tsarist government 'Directive on the Lamaist clergy in eastern Siberia', which aimed to reduce Buddhist influence in the border regions, the number of lamas was cut down from about seventy to eight.[91] Despite this, the monastery was re-built in 1861 and Lamaism continued to grow in influence, as there was a host of unofficial lamas besides the eight official ones. The Barguzin monastery was re-built again after the 1917 Revolution by the nationalist head lama, Agvan Dorzhiyev, close to the famous mountain worshipped by shamanists, Barkhan Öndör. This *datsan* was closed sometime in the early 1930s.

Today, the Barguzin *krai* is part of the Buryat ASSR, itself part of the RSFSR. From the time of the Revolution until 1944 the region was known as the Barguzin *aimak*. It was divided in 1944 into two *aimaks*, the Barguzin and the Kurumkan. The region as a whole has an area of 47,400 km², and the total population in 1977 was 26,000 people in Barguzin *aimak* and 18,300 people in Kurumkan *aimak*. The upper end of the valley is a narrow, rocky gorge which cuts through the taiga for about 100 km until it meets the River Dzhirga (see Map 2). The central part of the valley, in which most of the Buryat population lives, opens out below the Dzhirga to form a basin 200 km long and between 35 and 40 km wide. This extends as far as the town of Barguzin. The floor of the valley is between 500 and 700 metres above sea level, while the surrounding mountains reach 2,700 metres. Most of the cultivable land, and Kuytun steppes, are on the left bank of the Barguzin. The valley narrows again below the town of Barguzin and forms a ravine in which the river flows under cliffs hung with fir and pine trees for about 40 km. Finally, at the mouth of the river the valley opens out into a swampy area, about 15 km square, which debouches onto Lake Baikal.

The valley is rich in useful and precious minerals, including gold, copper, and manganese. Large amounts of copper have been discovered in the forested area north-east of the valley, and the Baikal-Amur magistral railway now being built north of Lake Baikal will bring these into full exploitation. For the moment the most important mineral source is manganese, found near the River Garga.[92]

In the forested mountains and hills surrounding the valley are brown bears, lynx, wolves, elk, wild reindeer, wild goats, boars, and several different kinds of deer. Otters, which were introduced into the valley in 1936, have spread in the numerous marshes and rivers, and are hunted for their thick, gold-tinted pelts. Squirrels, ermine, martens, and polecats also have valuable furs. Maral deer are hunted for their horns, from which a costly medicine called 'Pantakrin' is made.

65

Barguzin has long been famous among Buryats for its unique number of mineral springs. Such springs were considered to have healing properties by the Mongols, and 'spirit-owners' (*ezhid*) of the water were supposed to live in them. Most of the springs even now have not been scientifically studied. They are known in general to include natrium—sulphur, natrium—carbonic acid, and natrium—carbonic acid—calcium components. Many of them are hot, the two most famous springs, at Garga and Alla, reach temperatures of 70 °C to 75 °C. The local people have their own, unsupervised, 'health resorts' (*dikiye kuroty*) at the springs, primarily to cure rheumatism and nervous diseases. At Garga the neighbouring collective farms have built an official rest-home for their members, with houses, regulated bathing, a cultural centre and a canteen.[93]

The natural features of the region are crucially important for the operation of local collective farms. The land available for exploitation varies from the bogs and salty meadows along the River Barguzin, to the Kuitun steppes, the wooded hillsides along the Ikat range, and the high mountain pasture used in summer. Each of these has its problems as well as its advantages. The most serious drawback of the region is the flooding of the River Barguzin, which completely destroyed the low-lying hay-meadows in 1929, 1934, 1942 and 1949.[94] In Karl Marx Collective the 1971—5 five-year plan was ruined by devastating floods in 1971—3; there were floods again in 1980 (see Chapter 4), when no hay was obtained at all. The river floods to some extent every year after the summer rains. Half of Barguzin's rainfall occurs in the two months of July and August, and this not only threatens the hay but also causes harm to the grain crops standing in the fields.

The problem of flooding has apparently become much worse in the last thirty years. Buryats of the older generation remember homesteads, meadows and roads in places where there is now only marsh. Geologically, in the long term, the valley floor has been sinking, while the mountain ranges, including the Shaman's Threshold, have been rising. The Shaman's Threshold, of hard crystalline rock, slows down the flow of the Barguzin River and consequently of its tributaries also. But the reason for the intensification of flooding in the last thirty years is not fully understood. We know only that in many of the formerly prosperous Buryat settlements, Ugnasai, Khatai, Uksakhai, Murgun, Elysun, Yarikta, Ulyuchikan, and Topka, the hay-meadows on which the people depended in order to feed their herds through the winter have now turned into bogs and lakes.

At the same time, Barguzin suffers from drought. The annual rainfall is only 219 mm in Kurumkan, and less than 200 mm on the Kuitun steppes. Of this 80% falls in the summer and autumn, while the months of May and June are regularly almost completely dry. This makes it difficult to grow any crops in the region without irrigation.

The climate is sharply continental. In January the average temperature in Kurumkan is −30.3 °C, and the winter is generally very cold, dry, and windless.

The spring is also cold, with wide variations in temperature. During the period of vegetation (April, May) the temperature can vary by as much as 30–35 °C within a single day. This is also the period of the least rainfall in the year, and high winds raise storms of sand and even gravel. On the Kuitun steppes the spring wind-storms carry off the useful top-soil. A Buryat chronicle written in 1917 notes that 18,670 *desyatinas* (20,540 hectares approximately) of good land had turned into useless sandy waste since the mid nineteenth century, and every year land continued to be destroyed.[95] The use of the Kuitun steppes for pasture has increased the problem, especially since collectivisation and settlement into villages. The herds are pastured in too large numbers in the relatively well-watered areas near the farms. This causes destruction of the grass cover and unnecessary erosion even in comparatively good land.[96] Irrigation of the Kuitun steppes for agriculture is difficult because of the hilly relief and lack of even underground water in many areas.

Late frosts, into May and June, sometimes kill off young crops. But these are not as dangerous in Barguzin as the early autumn frosts, which start in the second half of August and frequently harm the harvest, particularly maize and vegetables. The growing season is thus extremely short. The rivers freeze at the end of October, which makes transport considerably easier, and thaw at the end of April. In July the average temperature in Kurumkan is +20.1 °C, and there are periods of much warmer weather in summer, interspersed with heavy downpours of rain.

Only a tiny proportion of the valley's land is used. Recent figures are not available, but in 1959 only 1.5% of the total was cultivated, 0.08% was fallow, 1.3% was hay-meadow, and 2.3% was pasture. Collective farms had 11.8% of the land area (including a certain amount of unusable wasteland), state farms 0.6%, the state forestry commission 87.2%, and other users 0.4%.[97]

Since 1917 the pattern of land-use has altered significantly. The figures from various sources may not be strictly comparable, in that it is not certain that they apply to exactly the same area, but the fact that the Barguzin valley is so enclosed means that the difference cannot be very great. The total amount of land used has increased by nearly one half. In 1959 there was already nearly twice as much hay-meadow as in 1917 and about twenty times as much land under agriculture. But the area used for pasture has gone down by one-fifth, from about 136,500 hectares in 1917 to 109,000 hectares in 1959. During the same period, however, there has been a large increase in the sheep herds. In 1917 there were 28,800 head of sheep and goats in the Barguzin valley. By 1976 there were 76,600 head. This causes pressure on the reduced pastures, particularly on the steppes, the best sheep-grazing land.

Climatic conditions have always made herding difficult in Barguzin. A heavy snowfall, which then freezes (Bur. *zud*), makes it impossible for the animals to get through to the underlying grass. Sudden late frosts in spring, when the grass has grown a little, can also ruin the pastures and cause widespread loss of livestock. The spring is the time when the animals are weakest, exhausted by the long dark winter and the dry spring, with its quick changes of temperature and air pressure.

The difficulty of the comparability of the areas covered by various surveys applies to population figures also. However, if we suppose that the 'Barguzin *okrug*' of 1897 covered approximately the same area as the 'Barguzin *aimak*' of 1917, and that the boundaries of the *aimak* did not significantly change between then and 1959, the figures in Table 1.9 give some idea of the Buryat population. We can probably conclude that the number of Buryats living in Barguzin region has not greatly multiplied since 1897.

In the Soviet Union quite small settlements count as 'towns', and there are three of these in the valley of Barguzin: Ust'-Barguzin, a predominantly Russian fishing settlement on Lake Baikal; Barguzin, the *aimak* or *raion* centre of the lower part of the valley, and Kurumkan, the *aimak* centre of the upper district. Barguzin has a food factory for processing the various products of the region, an electricity station, an airport, and also schools, a cinema, a hospital and a hall for cultural events. Kurumkan also has a food factory, a high school, a hospital, cultural institutions, and an inter-kolkhoz hydro-electric station. Russians are the main inhabitants of the fishing villages, the lumber-stations, and the gold mines in the north.

In 1959 there were sixteen collective farms in the valley, of which twelve were mixed herding and agricultural and four were devoted to fishing. But shortly after this the government initiated its policy of transforming collective farms into state farms and continued amalgamating smaller enterprises into large ones. By 1975 there were three collective farms in the Barguzin *aimak* (figures are not available for Kurumkan *aimak*): 'Karl Marx', 'Ulyun', and 'Khilganai'; and three state farms: 'Bodon', 'Barguzin', and 'Chitkan'. Two fishing collectives, 'Put' Lenina' and 'Baikalets', remained on the coast, and two wood factories worked on the slopes of the Ikat ridge, 'Barguzin' and 'Ina'.

The Barguzin valley is connected with other parts of Buryatiya by a non-metalled road running from Kurumkan to Barguzin to Ust'-Barguzin and south-wards along the shore of Baikal. In the rainy season the road is frequently impassable. In 1967 I had to cross two rivers by raft in order to reach Karl Marx Collective, but by 1974 a wooden bridge had been built across the River Ina. A regular air service connects Kurumkan, Barguzin, and Ust'-Barguzin with the ASSR capital of Ulan-Ude. When the lake is not frozen a steamer service runs between Ust'-Barguzin and ports at the south end of the lake.

6. Health, sexual life and child care

In the late 1920s, on the eve of collectivisation, the Buryats suffered extensively from venereal diseases, tuberculosis, gastro-intestinal diseases, smallpox and typhus. Leprosy, which had been widespread in the nineteenth century, had

Table 1.9. *Population of Barguzin 1897–1958*

Date	Region	Total population	Buryat	% Buryat
1897	Barguzin *okrug*	25,467	11,510	45.2%[a]
1917	Barguzin *aimak* (before division)		11,562 (males 7,224)	–[b]
1923–4	Barguzin *aimak* (before division)		13,550 (males 6,598)	–[b]
1958	Barguzin *krai* (i.e. both Barguzin and Kurumkan *aimaks*)	approx. 30,000	–	over 40%[c]
1971	Barguzin *aimak* Kurumkan *aimak*	26,100 18,300	– –	–[d] –

Sources:
a. Rumyantsev 1956, pp. 48–9.   b. *Obyaznitel'naya zapiska* 1929.
c. Buyantuyev 1959, p. 4.   d. *Narodnoye khozyaistvo buryatskoi ASSR* 1976
pp. 26 and 45.

almost died out by this time,[98] but it still inspired terror in people's minds. Victims of leprosy were shunned and no one could be found even to bring them to clinics. Meanwhile, the really serious medical problem of the age, venereal disease, was taken by the Buryats relatively lightly. The transmission of venereal diseases was not generally understood. Yet this seems to have been the main cause of the low fertility and high infant mortality of the period. We should consider this matter here, since although venereal disease has now been eradicated it has left a shadow of fear, just as leprosy did for an earlier generation, and this goes some way towards explaining present Buryat attitudes towards fertility and the reproduction of the family. To have many children is also to make a statement in respect of the future, beliefs about which will be discussed later in this book.

A Buryat ethnographer has written, 'For the Buryat the notion of "being happy" is connected first and foremost with children, with heirs.'[99] The most widespread and most appreciated expression of good wishes is, 'Have sons so as to live amongst your own "warm" kinsmen, have daughters so as to find affinal kin.'[100] In many of these formal blessings, which are widely used among the Buryats, a direct link is made between having sons and wealth in livestock, for example, 'May your house be full of sons, may your pens be full of livestock!'[101] A man without sons was considered to have extinguished the sacred fire (*gal gulamta*) of his patrilineage, and a woman who had borne no children was disliked and feared. It was thought that she would become an evil spirit (*ada*) after death, and that even during her life she could harm babies by her glance. She was *seertei* (sinful) and a bad omen. If she had a child, people said, 'She has become

69

a human being, she has come out from sin.'[102] These are 'traditional' beliefs, but they were collected by the ethnographer in the 1960s.

The high infant mortality and low fertility of the Buryats in the first part of this century was a tragedy for the people. Reports from Bichur, Kudarinsk, and western Buryatiya indicate that the situation was general.[103] In 1921 a study showed that 69% of children born in that year did not survive in Kudarinsk district. The 1890 census of Irkutsk and Balagansk districts indicated that the Buryat population had significantly fewer children aged up to fourteen (as a percentage of the total of males and females) than did the neighbouring Russian peasant population.[104]

Doctors working among the Buryats attribute much of this to venereal disease. Romashev, working in three *sel'sovets* of western Buryatiya in the late 1920s, found 42% of the population investigated to have syphilis, most of it tertiary and inherited. Archives showed that syphilis had been common in the area at least since the 1870s. Romashev further found that not a single male was free of gonorrhoea, and that the majority of the women attending his clinic came with gynecological problems associated with gonorrhoea.[105]

A Barguzin Buryat woman, born around 1900, described the circumstances of birth as it took place in her youth. The house was prepared by spreading dung on the floor, tying a rope across the room for the woman in labour to hold, and putting a fir tree at the door as a sign (*seer*) to outsiders not to enter. Since birth was considered polluting, it could take place only in the women's side of the house. The father was present to hold his wife on his knees as she gave birth, and an old woman was invited to receive the child. After the birth the child was never washed, but smeared with cream or fat, wrapped in a sheepskin, and placed on cushions. Three days after the birth a lama came to read prayers and make a libation, after which the house was no longer considered polluted. But the fir tree stayed at the door for a year to keep outsiders away, a baby being especially vulnerable to spirits brought by strangers or by people entering the house at night. One month after the birth the baby was ceremoniously put in its cradle. Relatives on both sides of the family gathered. The midwife took the hind thigh-bone of an ox, a bone even larger than the baby, and asked, 'Which is dearer, good meat or the baby? Who shall we put in the cradle, the bone or the baby?' and everyone cried, 'The baby! The baby!'[106] The afterbirth was buried with further rituals under the floor of the house, this spot being known as *huuri* (origin). Old women and successful mothers present at this ritual smeared childless young men with the fat used in the ceremony, and in some parts of Buryatiya they took off their underpants and beat the young men with these saying, 'Why have you had no children? Next year may you have a son/daughter.'[107]

Hung with amulets, with the ritual ox bone, with the umbilical cord wrapped in a little bag, the cradle was the precious baby's throne. The baby was hardly ever taken out. Buryat mothers often did not feed their children at the breast, this sometimes being forbidden by the lamas for a religious reason. Babies were fed by means of a hollow horn, with a teat at one end made from a cow's udder. Frequently the milk or other food placed in it was first taken into the mouth of the person caring for the baby, who warmed it or chewed it before spitting it into the horn.

Romashev accounts for the high mortality of babies by this very custom among others, but he describes the Buryats as quite unaware of medical theory. They attributed illness and death to the activity of spirits.[108] In the late 1920s some people from the area where Romashev was working emigrated eastwards to Barguzin, and they explained this by the death of their children from spirits which had arrived in the area. Previously these spirits had lived east of Lake Baikal, but as a result of the activity of lamas there they had been driven to the west. There were few lamas in the west and hence the spirits were able to flourish.[109]

Doctors working among the Buryats also attributed the widespread venereal disease to sexual custom. In a study of 5,167 male and 2,719 female Buryats, Pesterev found that most began sexual activity in their early teens, more or less with the onset of puberty, that the majority had several partners, and that the great majority of married people of both sexes had liaisons on the side.[110] Romashev confirms these findings and explains them by the great desire to have children. The age of marriage was largely determined by economic factors,[111] and the birth of children thus seems to have been regarded as a somewhat separate matter. It was an advantage to marry a woman with children if a man was too poor to marry in his youth, and a childless husband allowed his wife freedom in the hope that she might give birth. Childless husbands took two or three wives in order to beget heirs, and those who could not afford to marry again entered side liaisons for the same reason.[112] That illegitimacy was at the same time considered shameful only contributed to the despair of those who were forced to resort to it.

Adoption was the honourable way to acquire children, and this was common and widespread among Buryats. Families with many children agreed to give one or two to kinsmen without heirs. Sometimes children were adopted from Russian families, as they were considered to be stronger. As a sign of thanks, the adopting family gave *ümedkhel* (clothing) — fur coats and shirts — and a horse and a cow to the parents.

By the 1960s and 1970s medical conditions had been transformed. Venereal disease was eradicated[113] and every large collective farm had its own hospital, maternity home,[114] and several subsidiary clinics. The Barguzin Karl Marx farm in the mid-1970s had two kindergarten schools, including sections for toddlers aged from one to three, each of which had medical staff attached.[115] But the attitudes associated with child deprivation still persist. To have a large family is sufficient to give a man and wife status.[116] Adoption is very common (see Chapter 6). An indication of these attitudes is the custom of retaining a tuft of hair (Barg. Bur. *yalo*) on the otherwise shaven heads of little boys. In Mongolian culture the hair, especially of males, contains power and is a symbol of fertility and longevity. The manes and tails of stallions are never cut. Mongols and Buryat men used to wear their hair in a pigtail. The first hair-cutting of a child, the removal of the first fluffy hair of babyhood (*daakh'*), is a ritual occasion of great joy. Loving parents, in a characteristic gesture, always stroke the remaining tuft, a kind of blessing for long years of life.

A kindergarten class in Barguzin, 1974.

2

Ideology and instructions for collective farms

1. 'Objective laws' and the establishing of a model for society

The justification of the moral and prescriptive nature of economic institutions in the Soviet Union is that their statutes, or charters, have been established by the Party and government according to immutable laws derived from the political economy of Marx and Lenin. Such laws by definition are 'objective', that is not subject to purposive human intervention. In fact, of course, the specific relation between these laws and the written charters of particular institutions such as collective farms has changed since the Revolution according to central government policy. But such changes are thought of as the rectification of earlier 'mistakes' in interpretation. The present position is always assumed to be correct. This is what gives such charters their ideological character. It also provides a certain inertia and resistance to change on the part of the government. Nevertheless, it is the government, or rather its policy centre, the Communist Party, which is the source of such changes. Indeed, it is really the source of the laws themselves.

Many of the 'laws' which are in fact adduced to provide the theoretical basis for Soviet institutions today are not clearly attributable to Marx, and indeed their origin is uncertain. We may cite as instances of these 'laws', quoting from a Soviet textbook: 'the law of the objective necessity of the planned development of the socialist economy', 'the law of the objective relations of economic calculation', and 'the law of distribution according to labour'.[1] These 'laws' apply to all economies in all modes of production, and it is their discovery by Marx which has revealed them as truths. We, on the other hand, might see these 'laws' as neither primary nor immutable. The second of those quoted above, for instance, has only fairly recently become prominent in Soviet writings. The attribution of the status of 'law' to such formulae might seem best interpreted as the practice of a culture accustomed to operating on the basis of sacred texts. But to the Soviet writers such 'laws' have an objective existence, and it is only deficiencies of understanding which explain why some of them have not emerged into prominence until recently, why others have been over-emphasised, and so on.

73

From the point of view of the workers, the statutes created by the government assume the form of a set of obligatory rules. The rules have pre-determined meanings, given by the official explanations in terms of the 'Marxist laws'. Such official explanations, which we might see as the theoretical practice which in fact gives rise to the 'laws', are subject to debate within the academic echelons of the Party, but as they appear in many of the publications designed for the workers they take the form of precepts. For the recipients the discussion is over, almost as though it had never been, and what the workers are presented with is a bundle ('laws', statutory rules, and explanations for the rules) of which the internal links have to be taken on trust.

It goes without saying that the statutes are to some extent removed from actual practice, and that the official explanations are separate from people's own ideas about the institutions they are working in. The gap may be substantial. Widely differing conditions in the various regions of the Soviet Union make it impossible for the statutes to be realised in an identical way. One must also assume imperfect understanding of the 'laws' and their explanations (certainly in a Buryat community which has only recently become generally literate), and a time-lag in the local appreciation of the reasons for new rules. This gap is well understood by the theoreticians of the Soviet state — for whom it is yet another 'law' of the political economy of socialism that it should not exist.

Thus for the Soviet Union we must separate out a level which hardly exists in many societies, distinct from either local practice or local aims and understanding. This is the level of the *theoretical model* of collective production in agriculture. It comprises not only the statutes and instructions, or what people ought to do, but also the explanations of them in the countless publications of the Ministry of Agriculture; these, in effect, are what people ought to think.

It is the purpose of this chapter to elucidate the relations between Marx's political economy, the 'laws' set up by the Party theoreticians, and the statutes and rules of the collective farm. This is a necessary stage towards understanding what happens in reality in the Soviet rural economy. People do try, amongst other things, to follow the rules. But, to put it very crudely, because the relations between 'laws', explanations and statutes are confused, and because collective farms themselves in practice extend beyond the rules and in ways unforeseen by them, the kolkhoz in reality only partly makes sense in the terms given for understanding it. This should become clear even in the present chapter, and will be demonstrated on the basis of specific field material in Chapter 4. The question then becomes: how do Buryat farmers make sense of their world? The rest of this book puts forward material which provides an answer.

As we have seen, there are two main kinds of productive enterprise in agriculture, the state farm (sovkhoz) and the collective farm (kolkhoz). Inter-farm units (*mezhkhozyaistvenyye ob'yedineniye*) constitute a third type of enterprise; they have until recently been fairly small, employing some members of neighbouring kolkhozy and some outsiders, and they process agricultural materials, make

bricks, run small electricity generating stations, etc. The state also runs 'subordinate enterprises' (*podsobnyye khozyaystva*) which are small-scale agricultural
and vegetable-growing units to supply factory canteens and shops. Kolkhozy also
sometimes include such enterprises. Finally, there is the private sector, which
accompanies all of the other enterprises. Each kolkhoz member, or state farm
worker, or other agricultural employee, is entitled to a private plot of land and
some animals.

The state farm is considered to be a 'higher' form than the collective farm.
The grounds for this are that a state farm is state property and therefore it is a
stage closer to communism than the kolkhoz which is owned collectively by its
members (see section 3 below). State farms have been given huge subsidies and
have had other advantages over collective farms. For example, they used to be
entitled to buy producers' goods at wholesale prices, which were lower than the
retail prices paid by collective farms. Most regions have enterprises of both
kinds, and this, as Nove has pointed out, has led to lack of coordination in planning: the kolkhozy are controlled by the regional (*raion*) Party organisation
(formerly until 1958 also by the MTS — machine and tractor stations), while the
sovkhozy have a separate line of authority from the Ministry of Agriculture.
Since 1960 this situation has been improved by the introduction of a regional
agricultural union in which both categories of farms are represented by their
Chairmen or Directors.[2] State farms lie outside the scope of this book and I shall
say no more about them in this chapter, except insofar as economic theories
affect both types of enterprise.

The collective farm is in theory a kind of cooperative. This is expressed as
follows in the master statutes or charter (*ustav*) used by Buryat kolkhozy. 'A
collective farm is a cooperative organisation of peasants voluntarily associated
for the purpose of the common conducting of large-scale socialist agricultural
production on the basis of socialised means of production and collective labour.'[3]
This definition has a legal status, and certain important organisational and
financial characteristics of collective farms stem from their cooperative nature.
These mainly concern the election of collective farm officials from within the
kolkhoz and the decision within the farm as to the allocation of income against
various financial priorities. However, as will become clear later, the connotations
of the word 'voluntary' and 'cooperative' in Soviet conditions are not what
might be supposed, and the actions of kolkhoz committees and officials are
strictly limited by externally imposed obligations and restrictions. The kolkhoz
has a set of internal rules (*vnutrennyi rasporyadok*) which, like the statutes, are
based on an all-Union master-plan. Besides this there are a host of other regulations. These are set out most fully in the massive *Directory for the Chairman
of a Collective Farm.*[4]

The theoretical, as opposed to the legal, basis of collective farming is set out
in a constant stream of publications designed to reach present and future
kolkhoz leaders. Some of the books are written in a pedagogic manner, with

questions to answer at the end of each chapter; others are for theoretical discussion. Agricultural colleges use such books and they are to be found in kolkhoz libraries. I also saw a row of them on the bookshelf in the home of the young Chairman of the Barguzin kolkhoz in 1966. No kolkhoz official could entirely escape their influence.

In these books it is immediately noticeable that while the standard notation for certain Marxist economic concepts is adopted, for example the formula $c + v + m$, the ideas themselves are clothed in a new terminology designed for a socialist economy. To the extent that the Soviet economy is in fact different from a capitalist economy the creation of a new terminology is obviously justified. But the striking thing is that the concepts employed are often taken *directly* from Marx's analysis of capitalism. A collective farm does not work like a capitalist firm, but the ideas used to explain it are nevertheless disguised elements from Marx's analysis of capitalism. The Soviet justification of this would be that the 'laws' deduced from Marx are abstract truths which apply to any economic system in any society. The authors of these textbooks have not been in a position to abandon the idea of 'laws', and use Marx critically to establish a new economics for socialism. The effect has been to deny, except by a trivial alteration of terminology, the historic difference between capitalist and socialist economies. It is as if the ideas employed by economists at this popular level have not caught up with the economic reality of the Soviet Union. The reality of collective farms is determined by many factors outside their organisational structure: the price systems, hierarchical planning, scarcity of resources, and various kinds of official and unofficial markets. None of these enters into the ideal world of the economic 'laws' used to explain collective farming in the textbooks, or to be more precise, these factors tend to be discussed separately in a less exalted, more practical, context. This does not mean that there are not economists in the Soviet Union who grapple with these real problems on a theoretical level.[5] But their work, which is still the subject of deep political disagreement, is hardly perceptible at the textbook level. Thus what the collective farmers have to deal with is a simplified and popularised set of ideas, still more or less unchanged from Marx's analysis of nineteenth-century capitalism, but a little disguised by a new terminology.

The view expounded in these textbooks is that extraction of 'surplus value' by the state is legitimate in much the same way that 'extraction' of profit is regarded as legitimate in capitalism. For ordinary workers local publications and regional newspapers endlessly make the same point in a more concrete way: specific examples from the experience of local workers, citing the names and kolkhoz affiliations of those involved, are described in detail to show how herdsmen, tractor-drivers or milkmaids should understand the tasks allotted to them. The obligatory deliveries to the state are to be understood not as a direct loss to oneself or to one's team, but as production for society which any honest person will undertake. This moral obligation is seen not simply in terms of the benefits which workers receive from society in return, but as an absolute commitment to improve and enrich society by producing ever more in the way of 'surplus'.

The basic outlines of kolkhoz structure are defined legally by a document called the 'provisional statutes' (*primernyy ustav*) of the kolkhoz, which was affirmed by a Resolution of the Central Committee of the Communist Party of the USSR and the Soviet of Ministers of the USSR on 28 November 1969. This document differs in some ways from the earlier version issued in 1935.[6] In theory, each collective farm should work out its own statutes (*ustav*) on the basis of the 'provisional' or master example, taking into account its own conditions of production and the way of life of its members. Each kolkhoz should have its own statutes confirmed by a general meeting of all of its members.

However, in practice a printed booklet of statutes, identical to the master statute of the USSR,[7] is issued from the Soviet of Ministers of each republic. The one used by the Karl Marx kolkhoz in Barguzin in 1973—4 was published in Ulan-Ude in 1970. It was entitled 'Statutes (*ustav*) of [name of kolkhoz] of [name of *aimak*/region] of the Buryat ASSR, accepted at a general meeting of the kolkhozniks on [date] 1970.' The users of the booklet had not bothered to fill in the blank spaces.

2. Theoretical basis for the internal economy of the collective farm

One general instruction book, printed in Moscow in 1977 in a large edition of 30,000 and at the low price of 22 kopeks, is clearly aimed at a wide readership, and I shall take this as the basis for a description of the theoretical structure of a collective farm.[8] It sets out the basic economic structure of a kolkhoz, starting from the first principles of the original Marxist concepts. The authors, Kosinskii and Mikhailik, explain that the value of annual aggregate production (*valovaya produktsia*) is equal to $c + v + m$, the formula Marx used to explain his concept of 'value'. It is understood that Soviet readers will already know that c stands for 'constant capital', v stands for 'variable capital', and m is *mehwert* ('surplus value'). In the collective farm c forms the 'compensation fund', while $v + m$ constitute the 'aggregate income' (*valovoi dokhod*). This latter is divided into the 'consumption fund' (*fond potrebleniya*) and the 'savings or accumulation fund' (*fond nakopleniya*). The category of c is also divided, into the means of production ('basic production fund') and the objects of production, i.e. produce ready for realisation on the market within that year ('circulation fund' and 'realisation fund', *oborotnye fondy*, *fondy obrashcheniya*). This gives an accounting structure as shown in Figure 2.1.

What is not clear is how the farm management is to use these concepts in practice. The very word 'fund', as I have translated the Russian *fond*, indicates the problem. The textbook says that the word *fond* should be reserved for the expression in terms of value, i.e. the theoretical economic expression, of the 'means'. A *fond* is thus a theoretical division of the farm assets, which will be expressed in practice as the actual means (*sredstva*) of the farm: cows, machinery, buildings, etc. But which 'means' are to be entered in which *fond*, and when during the agricultural cycle are these operations to take place?

The ideas involved in the structure above may be unfamiliar, and so I shall explain them briefly here. There have been many critiques of sophisticated formulations of these ideas by Western economists, since this is also the structure by which the Soviet economy as a whole is understood, but they are to a great extent irrelevant to the concern of this chapter, which is to examine the use of rudimentary Marxist concepts in the theory of collective farming. I shall hardly refer to them here. But insofar as run of the mill Soviet economists have become conscious of failings in the Marxist body of ideas, or rather, since this is inadmissable, of 'mistakes' in the application of these ideas in a socialist context, I shall try to indicate this.

The labour theory of value is the foundation of the argument. According to Marx an article has value only because human labour in the abstract is embodied in it. 'Value' is analytically separate from either 'use-value', the utility of an object to people, or 'exchange-value', i.e. what is equal between two commodities which may be exchanged for one another. Exchange-value, or market price, is easily perceived by people, but Marx saw as his task the uncovering of the 'value' which lies behind it, which is given by 'socially necessary labour-time' (the time required for production under normal conditions, with average degree of skill and modern machinery).

Here we are concerned with the implications of the labour theory of value for the organisational structure of collective farms. Soviet attitudes have changed radically since the Revolution. There was a period, from the end of the New Economic Policy to 1941, when the theory of value was not thought to apply to the Soviet Union at all, since in a planned economy the principles lying behind the random, unorganised workings of capitalism were not applicable. Even the word *ekonomika* which had historically been associated with these principles was avoided, and replaced with *khozyaistvo*, a more general word for the management of material resources. But in 1941, an article, thought to have been

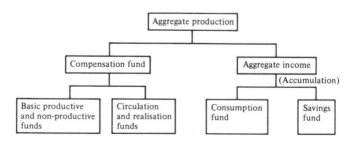

2.1. Accounting structure of a collective farm.

written by Stalin, was in preparation, and this was directly concerned with the 'law' of value in the Soviet system. The article appeared in the middle of the war in an influential party journal; it stated, 'To deny the existence of economic laws under socialism means sliding down to vulgar voluntarism, which consists in the substitution of arbitrariness, accident, chaos, for the orderly process of development of production.'[9] The author deduced the survival of the 'law of value' from the fact that labour is not paid an equal sum for each hour of work, that it is paid in money, that purchase and sale occur, that money is used. But the role of the 'law of value' is limited, because it cannot affect the distribution of resources within the state sector, or the production programme of state enterprises. It applies, 'in a transformed form', to all operations where purchase and sale take place, i.e. to the sales by collective farms and individual peasants to the state, and also to the sales by state retailing enterprises to the citizen, and on the foreign market. The goods exchanged in these transactions become 'commodities' in the Marxist sense, while the goods distributed within the state sector are not commodities.

Soviet attitudes to the 'law of value' have undergone many vicissitudes since the 1940s, some of which will be discussed later, but the main change is the general acceptance in the mid-1950s that *all* goods in circulation are commodities. This has had the effect of re-establishing collective farms, at least in theory, on the same ideological level as the rest of the economy. However, it is politically important that for many years the collective farm sector was one of the main areas of the economy where the 'law of value' was thought to 'survive', since this has been the justification for many discriminatory policies against this form of enterprise.

Marx's labour theory of value when seen in the context of a capitalist economy necessarily implies the existence of 'surplus value'. The connotations of exploitation which this concept brings to mind are clearly unacceptable in the socialist context, and so the term 'surplus value' was replaced by 'surplus product'. Some Soviet economists also took to referring to v and m respectively as 'product for self' and 'product for society'.[10] This is interesting and significant, since it is a clear indication of how Soviet workers are expected to think about the production process in which they are engaged.

The two Marxist concepts which are most relevant to the theory of the productive cycle in collective farms are the ideas of constant and variable capital. 'Constant capital' refers to that portion of the value of machinery and materials which is used up in production and added to the value of the product. 'The means of production can never add more value to the product than they themselves possess independently of the process in which they assist, i.e. the amount of labour time necessary for their production.'[11] But labour-power in the process of production undergoes an alteration of value; it both 'preserves and transfers to the product the value of the means of production, and at the same time, by the mere act of working, creates each instant an additional or new

79

value'.[12] The labourer's time can thus be divided into two parts: (1) the period during which the amount of the value he creates is equal to the value of the wages he receives from the capitalist ('necessary labour time'); (2) the period during which he creates value over and above that received in wages, i.e. 'surplus labour time'. It follows that the value of a commodity in capitalism is made up of three components. The first represents the value of the raw materials and machinery used up in production (constant capital). The second is that which replaces the value of the workers' labour power (variable capital), and the third is made up of the surplus created by 'living labour'.

The theory of constant and variable capital is difficult for the authors of the collective farm textbooks to deal with. They cannot ignore it altogether because without it the explanation of 'surplus value' (or 'surplus product' in Soviet terms) does not make sense. The major stumbling-block is that labour under socialism does not form part of capital. One way of avoiding the issue is to use different terms, while making essentially the same distinction. The acceptable terms are 'objective and subjective factors', identified by Marx with 'constant and variable capital'. A textbook author, from Central Asia, gives the following formula for socialist economies:

In the conditions of socialist production the objective and subjective factors of production certainly exist, but they cannot now take the form of constant and variable capital since they do not function as capital; they must function in a different form within a socialist content. The objective factor of production appears as the productive fund, and the subjective as labour-power, but the latter under socialism is neither a commodity nor capital and therefore cannot be included in the productive fund.[13]

But the author still cannot ignore the presence of constant and variable factors:

It is without doubt that the means of production and labour-power cannot be identified under socialism with constant and variable funds (*fondy*), since labour-power is not a fund. But they do function in a concrete historical form with a socialist content, and therefore their forms of functioning should be in some way defined. We suggest that they should be called *constant and variable factors of socialist production* . . .
   First of all, is there any need to recognise and acknowledge constant and variable factors of socialist production? Undoubtedly there is, for two reasons: the first is the known and accepted fact that the material and personal factors of production take different forms in different socio-economic formations, and thus they function in a concrete form in each case, for example in the form of 'capital value' under capitalism. Therefore, such concrete forms of functioning exist objectively also under socialism, independently of whether we recognise or reject them. Secondly, the different form and meaning of the factors of production exist also under socialism . . . [14]

One wonders what collective farmers can make of such a complicated explanation. And it is far from clear how they are to identify constant and variable factors of production in their own farms. The author himself has the greatest difficulty in explaining what he means. We are led to explanations such as the following, which I quote because it is a good example of the kind of contorted reasoning which agricultural trainees are expected to follow:

The means of production and labour-power, which function under capitalism in the process of increasing value and in the labour-process as constant and variable capital, from the point of view of the process of transformation are divided into basic and circulating capital.

'From the point of view of the process of transformation', wrote K. Marx, 'we find on the one hand the means of labour, i.e. basic capital, and on the other the materials of labour and wages, i.e. circulating capital.'

Under socialism the category of capital is liquidated and labour-power is not a commodity, and therefore only the means of production are included in the funds (*fondy*). And with regard to the means which go towards the reproduction of labour-power, they are not included in the funds in themselves as the form of the existence of the objective conditions of production.

However, K. Marx underlined that personal consumption is a constituent of productive consumption, and that it is a condition of any production.

Therefore, the functioning of productive funds (*fondy*) on the level of society demands the presence of a special fund of life means (objects of use or consumption), this being necessary for the reproduction of labour-power.[15]

In practice, the Soviet economists appear to operate with a combination of the classical dichotomy between fixed and circulating capital and the Marxian distinction between constant and variable capital. The 'basic productive fund' is equivalent to fixed capital, and the combination of this fund with the circulation fund is equivalent to constant capital. Because labour-power is not supposed to constitute any kind of capital it is removed from the 'circulation fund' category (in which it occurs under capitalism) and is given a separate existence in the collective farm theoretical structure. In fact it is placed, according to Kosinkskii and Mikhailik, in the category 'aggregate income' (see Figure 2.1). This is an interesting sleight of hand, since from the point of view of the farm as a whole, wages are expenditure, not income, a point implicitly recognised by Kosinskii and Mikahilik in their discussion of bonus pay (see below). Furthermore, this procedure creates confusion among farm managers, who are uncertain of the distinction between the aggregate income (*valovoi dokhod*), the money income, and the money profit.[16] In fact the money income (*denezhnyi dokhod*) should not include wages, but the money profit (*denezhnaya pribyl'*) should, since it consists of all moneys coming in to the farm. It is thus a larger category than the money income, which is the income from sales of the product and services by the kolkhoz, and includes income from the sale of the basic means of production, insurance payments for losses, and loans from the state as well. The most important category, but one which again has a theoretical rather than practical nature, is the pure income (*chistii dokhod*). This is defined as the 'surplus product' after wages have been deducted. However, kolkhozy have difficulty in calculating it, and it appears that there is no agreed method in the USSR as a whole. The *chistii dokhod* includes a part which the kolkhoz never sees, that is the difference between the delivery prices paid by the state and the 'social prices' (retail prices) of its product. In the collective farm the *chistii dokhod* is the difference between the delivery prices it receives and the cost of production. But it is difficult to know how to assess the cost of items like fodder, for which there are two prices. And in calculating the cost of production the problematic position of wages is raised again: in theory this should be assessed at the 'socially necessary' rate, but in practice farms vary widely in the amounts they actually pay. Although it would appear to be theoretically essential to establish a level at which 'variable factors of production' can be assessed at 'socially necessary' rates, this has not been possible, and there is no defined rate either for state farms or collective farms.[17]

The 'compensation' of the basic production funds takes place by means of a specially created amortisation fund. This consists in theory of the value transferred from the means of production to the newly created product. In practice the annual amount to be counted into the fund is to be reckoned according to the following formula:

$$\frac{\text{original cost of object} + \text{cost of capital repairs} - \text{remaining value}}{\text{length of service}}$$

Here the 'remaining value' means the amount of the total value of the object (original cost + maintenance) which has not yet been amortised in any given year. The textbooks advise farm economists to make calculations of some complexity,[18] by means of all-Union standard amortisation norms for all categories of production goods. The amortisation fund should be used for two purposes: firstly for capital repairs of existing means of production, secondly for the renewal of these by providing new machines and materials for those which have been used up. It is interesting that the authors point out that the amortisation fund, in a situation of developing technology, may be used not only for the 'restitution' of the basic production fund, but also for 'the reproduction of this fund in a larger form'.[19] By this they presumably mean that more efficient tractors, for example, may be acquired to replace old models, and that a form of capital investment is possible via amortisation.

Another recommendation of the textbook authors Kosinskii and Mikhailik (in fact it is a legal requirement) is that collective farms should keep the money set aside for amortisation in the State Bank, 'thus allowing the state temporarily to use free kolkhoz money for the development of socialist production, including the development of technology, and the advancing of credits to collective farms'.[20] This raises, but neatly avoids answering, the awkward ideological question of interest on money in a socialist economy. The equivalent of interest paid by the State Bank to farms which do bank their money is presumably thought of as a payment for allowing the state to use the money, rather than as 'interest' on 'capital' as such.

The idea of 'constant factors of production' does run into certain trouble in practice, as Kosinskii and Mikhailik admit. They raise the problem of tractors, whose period of life is reckoned to be twelve years, after which according to Marx they must have transferred all of their value to the product; but what if some of these tractors are still in good working order? Insofar as they go on being used after the period has elapsed in which they have transferred their value (reckoned in theory as the socially necessary labour time required to manufacture them) they are in a sense creating *more value*. Collective farms have been in the habit, Kosinskii and Mikhailik say, of destroying such machinery because of the unreckoned-for amortisation payments required for their maintenance. However (regardless of Marx), they themselves recommend that such tractors should go on being used, without setting aside amortisation money, on the very pragmatic grounds that 'the demand for new machines by collective farms is not fully being met' by industry.[21]

From the diagram given by Kosinskii and Mikhailik (Figure 2.1), it is apparent that the 'basic production funds' are divided into 'productive' and 'unproductive' sections. This distinction has nothing to do with Marx's differentiation between 'productive' and 'unproductive' labour, where what is at issue is the production of surplus value. Here, it is a matter simply of the directness of the involvement in production. 'Productive' funds are such things as tractors, ploughs, or working horses; 'unproductive' funds are nevertheless still involved in production, but not directly — for example, the houses workers live in, administrative offices, etc.

The 'circulation fund' and the 'realisation fund' are further stages in the process by which materials are transformed by living labour into products with exchange-value. The concept of the 'circulation fund' includes that of the 'realisation fund'. The 'circulation fund' differs from the 'basic production funds' by the fact that it consists of means of production which are fully used up in one cycle. Thus it includes such things as fertiliser or colouring matter, as opposed to tractors and milk cows.[22] This distinction was also made by Marx, although not in such a concrete way as the setting up of separate funds. However, Kosinskii and Mikhailik give a quotation from the collected works of Marx and Engels when explaining the idea: 'Coal, which is burnt in the furnace of a machine, disappears without trace, just as the grease which is used to smear on the axle of a wheel also disappears. Dyes and other such materials disappear, but re-appear in the characteristics of the product. Raw materials create the substance of the product, but in doing so change their form.'[23] The 'circulation fund', which it will be remembered is part of the total 'compensation fund', is renewed in agricultural enterprises not so much by a money fund but by the return of natural products, such as grain, seed vegetables, milk for feeding calves, etc. A great part of the total production of a farm is thus returned for the 'restitution' of the used-up materials. In the Soviet Union as a whole 35.2% of the total production of grain was set aside to 'compensate' the 'circulation funds', 16.9% of this being seed grain, and 18.3% going as fodder seed.

When a large part of the 'compensation' for a certain fund is in natural products from the same enterprise, as is the case with the 'circulation fund', the question arises of how these products are to be valued for accounting purposes. In most collective farms at present such products are valued by their actual prime cost, or cost of production, *sebestoimost'*. Thus in each farm the same product, for example a given weight of seed grain, will be given a different value in rubles. Kosinskii and Mikhailik see this as creating unnecessary confusion in the inter-kolkhoz enterprises to which several farms contribute. They recommend the use of retail prices instead. But it is easy to see why the collective farmers do not use this method: retail prices would in almost all cases be higher than the *sebestoimost'* and to use them for the 'compensation fund' would put up the total cost of production. This would not affect the amount available for wages unless the natural products were actually bought by the kolkhoz in order to put them into the compensation fund, but it would make a difference *on paper* to the total cost of production. Since lowering the cost of production is one of the main indicators of success, collective farm leaders might have to forgo some of their own prizes and bonuses if they changed to the new system.

Kosinskii and Mikhailik also give theoretical legitimation to the course they advocate. The retail price of natural products, they say, is much closer to their 'value' than is the cost of production (*sebestoimost'*). 'It is obvious', they write,

that seed, fodder and other products of one's own enterprise have exactly the same use-value as the same things bought outside, and therefore their valuation in no way differs from bought ones. In all cases the basis of the value of a given product is the material expenses, the payment for labour, and the surplus product (clear income). It is wrong to suppose that surplus value is contained only in the commodity or trade part of production, and that it is lacking in that part set aside for seed, fodder, etc. within the enterprise. There can be no question but that clear income is created in the process of production, and its presence does not depend on the channel by which the product is moved.[24]

The 'realisation fund' is a subdivision of the 'circulation fund' consisting of products ready for realisation, such as cattle fully fattened for slaughter (as opposed to cattle in the process of, or designated for, fattening for slaughter). The 'realisation fund' also includes money which has not yet been allocated to some other purpose.

The actual behaviour of collective farms is influenced strongly by the 'indicators' (*pokazateli*) of success, since the level at which wages and bonuses are paid is closely tied to them. A collective farm has greater freedom in this respect than a state farm or factory. In the latter wages are set by the planning and financial departments of the Ministries at a level corresponding to the aggregate production (*valovaya produktsiya*) achieved in each enterprise. In collective farms the workers' wages are decided internally, though guidelines are issued by the Ministry of Agriculture, but the salaries of the Chairman and the administrators tend to be linked to aggregate production. This, strange as it may seem, has an effect not only on the total direction in which the farm chooses to produce, but also on the internal distribution of resources between the various *fondy*.

Aggregate production, colloquially known as *val*, is the success indicator par excellence. *Val* is usually calculated by the ruble price of the product, and therefore all factories and farms have an interest in producing *expensive* products (or *heavy* products when *val* is calculated by weight). In factories, which sell their products to other factories, the effect can even go as far as choosing to use not local but imported raw materials, since the transport costs make these inputs two or three times more expensive. The 1965 economic reforms attempted to change this situation by substituting, as the main success indicator instead of aggregate product, 'realised' (i.e. sold) product. But in fact *val* continues to determine the level of 'realised' product. As a Soviet newspaper remarked: 'The chief planning indicator and the measure of success of enterprises, groups of enterprises and ministries is the growth of global product, expressed in money. There both individual enterprises and whole sectors are interested not in economising but in increasing the amount of their expenditure.'[25] This leads farms to produce types of grains, meat and vegetables with high prices at the expense of those with low prices, even if the latter are in great demand in the shops. Farms now sell some of their product directly to retail outlets, where they negotiate prices, rather than to the state, where prices are fixed from above, but they have an interest for these items too in using costly raw materials which will push up the price and hence the level of 'realised' *val*. This occurs because *val* is a more powerful success indicator than lowering the cost of production.

Another important success indicator is labour productivity, i.e. *val* divided by the number of workers. One way to improve this indicator is to increase work-norms temporarily; this is called a *shturm*. Of course the annual increase by the planners of the level of *val* for a given enterprise without a corresponding increase in the number of workers automatically raises this success indicator. In practice though, labour productivity is subordinate to *val* itself. Thus managers will encourage workers who invent more efficient methods but only if the introduction of a new technique does not halt the flow of production. If the *val* goes down even for one year the management risk losing their prizes, bonuses, and congratulatory bouquets of flowers at the New Year celebrations.

A third main success indicator is *fondootdacha*, i.e. *val* divided by the value of the basic productive funds. This figure also should rise from year to year, and this means that any attempt to modernise equipment is likely to run into trouble: it will raise the value of basic productive funds and ruin the indicator *this year*, even if it is due to pay its way by two or three years' time. If a farm goes on using its old machinery, with the amortisation payments mostly made, its value becomes smaller and smaller, and the *fondootdacha* indicator goes up. Were it not for the fact that *val* has precedence over this too in most circumstances enterprises would have an interest in letting equipment run on until it fell into pieces in the hands of the workers.

These three indicators, *val*, labour productivity, and *fondootdacha*, are what give an enterprise its prestige and reputation. It can be seen that allocations within the farm between the various *fondy* will depend on the importance given to specific indicators in different regions at different times. There are other success indicators — lowering the cost of production, improving the quality of product, economising in materials and energy, rationalising methods, etc. — but they all count for less than the main three.

After realisation of the products of the farm by sale to the state (both in fulfilment of the plan and in over-plan sales) and by sales to other collectives, to members of the public, and to the members of the farm themselves, and after allocation of a specified proportion to the compensation fund, the resulting income should be divided, according to Kosinskii and Mikhailik, into two funds: the consumption fund (*fond potrebleniya*) and the savings fund (*fond nakopleniya*).

Since the amount of money or natural products available to pay the workers on the farm depends on the amount not allotted for other purposes, it becomes very important *in what order* the annual income is designated to the various funds. Until the mid-1950s the wages fund had very low priority, there being no guaranteed levels of pay for kolkhoz workers, and in effect the wages fund simply consisted of whatever was left over after everything else had been accounted for. The resulting sum was divided up and paid to the workers in proportion to the work they had contributed. These proportions were reckoned by conventional work units (*trudodni*, 'workdays') which were graded according to the kind of work performed. This intricate system will not be discussed in detail because it is well described in the literature. The main point is that because the wages fund (known as 'the fund for the payment of labour') was in effect residual, i.e. determined last, the workers could not know until the final reckoning at the end of the year how much their 'workday' was worth. Payments fluctuated greatly from year to year, and varied widely between different farms.

This system was changed in the early 1960s to one of guaranteed minimum monthly wages for each type of work. The 'amount and quality of work' were to determine how much a worker actually received. The 'amount' was in fact limited at the lower end by a minimum number of days to be worked in order to become eligible for basic pay. If a kolkhoz was not in a position to pay the minimum wage it could borrow money from the state for this purpose.

Writing in 1977 Kosinskii and Mikhailik say that the setting up of the wages fund is now the *first* obligation of the kolkhoz. Their explanation of this is interesting. Although for obvious reasons they do not quote Marx at this point, their account of the necessity for according primacy to payments to the workers is distinctly reminiscent of Marx's description of the role of wages in capitalism.

The primacy of the formation of the fund for the payment of labour is determined by the fact that the socially necessary requirements of the workers are formed objectively and do not depend directly on the levels of pay occurring in different enterprises. The satisfaction of the necessary requirements of the workers, i.e. the reproduction of their labour-power, is an absolutely necessary condition for the process of reproduction in general.[26]

We are reminded of Marx's own words about capitalism:

Labour-power exists only as a capacity, or power of the living individual. Its production consequently assumes his existence. Given the individual, the production of labour-power consists in his reproduction of himself or his maintenance. For his maintenance he requires a given quantity of the means of subsistence. Therefore the labour-time requisite for the production of labour-power reduces itself to that necessary for the production of those means of subsistence; in other words, the value of the labour-power is the value of the means of subsistence necessary for the maintenance of the labourer. Labour-power, however, becomes a reality only by its exercise; it sets itself in action only by working. But thereby a definite quantity of human muscle, nerve, brain, etc. is used up, and these require to be restored. This increased expenditure demands a larger income. If the owner of labour-power works today, tomorrow he must be able to repeat the same process in the same conditions as regards health and strength. His means of subsistence must therefore be sufficient to maintain him in his normal state as a labouring individual.[27]

But after all the authors are discussing only the *minimum* wage and one might expect more benign criteria to be introduced in relation to the amounts above this actually paid by collective farms. The guaranteed minimum is fixed at a level more or less equal to that paid in state farms in the same geographical zone of the USSR. The question then becomes: how far should successful collective farms be able to raise the basic pay of their own members? At the moment the amount permitted to be allocated to the wages fund is proportional to the 'aggregate production' (*val*). The recommendation of Kosinskii and Mikhailik is that farms should *not* be allowed to pay higher wages simply because they are successful in terms of profit. Thus there should not be a fixed percentage of the annual income set aside for wages. This would create too much disparity between the pay of workers doing the same type of work in different farms. Kosinskii and Mikhailik suggest egalitarian criteria for higher wage payments. They say that the minimum pay should be determined by the amount necessary to maintain 'average' living conditions, and that any raising of basic pay should only take place on the basis of a *general* raising of the productivity of labour in that enterprise. Until 1966 at least there was a maximum level of basic pay for kolkhozy.

In fact, with the exception of administrators and specialists, the 'quality' aspect of productive labour in collective farms is already determined approximately by labour productivity. Thus, for example, tractor-drivers and other machinists are paid a much larger basic wage than ordinary kolkhozniks who might do the same type of work using more primitive tools (horse-drawn ploughs, scythes, etc.). In Marxist theory this should be accounted for by the idea that a greater amount of labour time goes into the production of a tractor and a trained tractor-driver than into the creation of a working horse, plough, and ploughman, and therefore the 'value' of the former is greater than that of the latter. But obviously such calculations are almost impossible in practice. It seems more likely that wage distinctions of this kind are inspired at least in part by a different section of the work of Marx, that dealing with the advance of technology in capitalism:

The introduction of power looms into England probably reduced by one half the labour required to weave a given quantity of yarn into cloth. The hand-loom weavers, as a matter of fact, continued to require the same time as before; but for all that, the product of one hour of their labour represented after the change only half an hour's social labour, and consequently fell to one half its former value.[28]

Another practical reason for such wage discriminations (which did not exist in the early communes) is now recognised to be the need to provide incentives for people to train as tractor-drivers, etc.

The kolkhoz textbook observes that basic pay rewards the productivity of labour as regards organisation and mechanisation, but it cannot stimulate individual productivity since it does not reflect experience, enthusiasm, or initiative. A system of bonus payments is recommended to reward these qualities.

In fact, a large part of bonus payments is for higher productivity *tout simple*. This can be seen from the all-Union payments quoted by Kosinskii and Mikhailik as examples for collective farms to follow. Over-plan production by individuals was the citation for 50.8% of bonus payments in 1971 and 40.7% in 1975. Other citations were for quality of work (14.7% in 1975), length of service and training qualifications (34.5%), economy of production (3.7%) and other reasons (6.4% in 1975).[29]

A question arises which is of both theoretical and practical significance: what is to be the financial source of the bonus payments? The present practice is the financing of bonuses from the 'pure income', in which case the amount cannot be counted in the prime cost or cost of production (*sebestoimost'*). Kosinskii and Mikhailik, however, maintain that since bonus payments aid production they should be counted among necessary outlays and be drawn from the running costs of the farm, i.e. from the wages fund. The issue here is the cost of production, which farmers are always being urged to lower. Indeed, farm Chairmen and specialists sometimes get bonuses themselves for lowering the cost of production. Kosinskii and Mikhailik observe severely:

The distribution of means from the 'fund of material encouragement' [which is drawn from the 'pure income', i.e. the income left after wage and basic investment have been accounted for] allows certain collective farms not only to conceal frequently unjustifiably high payments to their workers by comparison with other farms but also to show a high profitability and low cost of production which is a distortion of the real productive-financial activity of these farms. And here the 'fund of material encouragement' is often enlarged at the expense of the basic productive fund and other funds, and this contradicts the economic principles of the correct conduct of the enterprise.[30]

They urge that the payment of bonuses from the 'pure income' should be strictly limited, and that it should not be thought of as an automatic addition to basic pay. The *possibility* of bonus payments should be guaranteed by the farm, but they should be neither continuously nor necessarily guaranteed for particular levels of work.

Given that in practice the bonus payments are taken from the 'pure income', Kosinskii and Mikhailik can only sit by and regret the large increase in this type of payment (doubled from 1970 to 1975).

The fact that 'surplus product' is also called 'clear income' (*chistii dokhod*) does not mean that it constitutes something in the nature of profit as we know it. Several obligatory payments must come out of it each year. Apart from bonus wages two other outgoings from it occur under the heading of the 'consumption fund'. These are the obligatory payment of social security (*sotsial'noye obespechiniye*) and social insurance (*sotsial'noye strakhovaniye*). Until recently kolkhozy were expected to provide for and administer the distribution of these funds themselves internally. But since 1965 social security has been administered centrally by the government. This means that now people know how much pension they will get, whereas previously the amount might fluctuate as widely as workers' wages. The collective farms are now obliged to allow 5% of their aggregate income each year, which they despatch to the social security department. The state covers the difference between what the farm provides and the amount its members need in the event. Social insurance works in much the same way. The collective farm sends off 2.4% of the money or products allotted for wages (including bonuses), and receives insurance payments when needed. In this case, however, more is paid by the kolkhozy than they reclaim, and the remaining money is used by certain trade unions and a body called the All-Union Soviet of Collective Farms.[31] In fact, social insurance and security payments are often made not from the 'clear income' but from the productive funds of the farm.[32] This reflects the fact that, contrary to theory, collective farmers see such payments as expenditure, not income, and in any case they wish to preserve the maximum amount in the most freely disposable part of their budget (the *chistii dokhod*, source of bonus payments).

The 'clear income' also has two further demands made on it by the state, but in this case the payments are separate and do not form part of the 'consumption fund'. The first of these is an annual tax (*podkhodnoi nalog*) and the second is the obligatory insurance of the farm's buildings, animals, fields of crops, etc. The tax is described by Kosinskii and Mikhailik as 'that part of the kolkhoz income designated for the whole society'.[33] It is imposed only if the profitability of the farm is over 15% (meaning 'pure income' is higher than 'cost of production' by 15%) and the average monthly wages of the kolkhozniks is not below 60 rubles. The tax is 3% of each percentage of the 'clear profit' over the 15%, but in all no more than 25% of the taxable 'clear profit', and it is also 8% of the sum set aside for wages over the level of 60 rubles per worker per month.[34] Since farms which have an average wage below this level do not have to pay the tax at all, and since the tax comes from the fund from which the management's salaries are drawn, there is some incentive to avoid the tax by maintaining a workforce which is low-paid on average. This may be one reason why farms do not object to having large numbers of workers on their books who only put in a few days' labour per month.

Another major annual expenditure of the collective farm is made to the accumulation fund (*fond nakopleniya*) designed for investment. This fund is formed entirely from the 'clear income' or 'surplus product'. It consists both of money (from products which have been sold) and natural goods, such as cattle to add to the size of the adult herd. This fund can be used to increase the stock of any of the other funds of the farm, including cultural and educational facilities. There is a sub-division of the accumulation fund which is the last of all to be allotted; this is the reserve fund (*rezervnyi fond*). It is intended to provide a reserve in case of natural disasters, accidents, bad weather, or mistakes and mis-judgement in previous years. Thus it seems to take over many of the functions of insurance, which may indicate that the state-operated insurance is not as access-ible as it might be.

Finally, there is a separate fund for capital investment, belonging to neither the accumulation fund nor the consumption fund, which is set aside in good years from the 'clear income'. Most general investment seems to be financed from either the compensation fund or the accumulation fund, and this separate fund appears to be devoted primarily to new building (houses, stables, baths, clubs, canteens, etc.). Kosinskii and Mikhailik advise their readers to make sure that such constructions quickly become economically effective. They note that the proportion of the capital investment fund taken up by *uncompleted* building rose to 35% during the last five-year plan. They urge economy in building costs and immediate productive exploitation of the new premises.[35] The reason for the huge amount spent on unfinished building is that capital construction counts in the aggregate productive output of the farm for which 'indicator' bonuses are paid to managers, and at the same time is financed largely from state grants and loans. Consequently there is an incentive to use expensive materials, and to start buildings which can never be completed.

Though the distribution of the aggregate product has now been described, an understanding of the working of collective farms requires an indication of the size of the various funds in relation to one another. Each kolkhoz is allowed to decide this according to its own circumstances, but nevertheless there are guide-lines which farms are supposed to follow. It is interesting that these guidelines are constituted by what the kolkhozy of the USSR as a whole practise: in other words, individual farms are supposed to follow the norm.

In the compensation fund of Soviet collective farms taken as a whole, the great majority of resources went (1971–5) into the circulation fund (88.9% in 1971 and 88.5% in 1975). The remainder (11.5% in 1975) went into the basic

Table 2.1. *Allocation of resources between compensation fund and aggregate income in two collective farms*

	Kolkhoz 'Rossiya'	Kolkhoz 'Gruziya'
Aggregate production, thousands rubles	20,430	7,100
Compensation fund, thousands rubles	6,787	3,172
% of value of aggregate production	33.2%	44.7%
Aggregate income, thousands rubles	13,643	3,928
% of value of aggregate production	66.8%	55.3%

Source: Kosinskii and Mikhailik 1977.

productive fund. Of the aggregate income the amount going into the accumulation fund has risen from 23.8% to 28% from 1971 to 1975, while the consumption fund takes about 70%. Because of large increases in wages the proportion of aggregate income to the whole has risen greatly since 1965. These figures are given by Kosinskii and Mikhailik in their textbook as indications which the farms should follow.

However, in the most important allocation of all, that between the compensation fund and the aggregate income, it is clear that farms differ greatly in the amount they can allot to aggregate income. In the example given by Kosinskii and Mikhailik of two farms in South Russia, the kolkhoz 'Rossiya' was relatively more economical in its productive costs, i.e. its allocation to the compensation fund, and therefore its aggregate income was proportionately larger. For every ruble of aggregate product the 'Rossiya' spent only 33.2 kopeks on 'compensation', 11.5 kopeks less than in the kolkhoz 'Gruziya'.[36]

This example reveals one of the central paradoxes of collective farms. They are intended to constitute a particular type of organisation of production, and much of Soviet agricultural planning (including the textbooks themselves) is devoted to seeing that they do conform in detail to this type. The specific attributes of the type have changed during Soviet history, but whatever they are at any given period the planning organs and district/regional authorities have an interest in being able to demonstrate that the farms under their authority conform to it. The forcing of kolkhozy into a particular mould which occurred in the Stalinist period, for example by ordering farms to allocate their resources in specific ways, has now ceased, but there is still a tendency to expect and hope that they will independently come to resemble one another. The example of the 'Rossiya' and the 'Gruziya' shows, be it in a very schematic way, that they are actually very different from one another in quantitative terms, if not in structure. In the last two decades the policy has been to attempt to regulate kolkhoz activity by means of external regulations limiting choices and by setting up examples to follow. Direct interference in productive decisions by district and regional authorities also sometimes occurs (see below) but now the phrase *dopustit' shablon* (to perpetrate over-patterning) has come into increasingly common use in newspapers, which indicates that the authorities should not take this too far. In the next section we shall look at the relation between the kolkhoz and the state and at some of the theories by which the intervention of the state is justified.

3. The collective farm and the state in Soviet theory

The state

The policy of the state towards collective farms is carried out by the law, plans, prices, taxes, and loans. However, we need to begin this section by examining briefly the theoretical concept of the state itself in Soviet socialism. If we are to understand the rationality of collective farmers we must address the question of whether the state is actually seen as in principle distinct from its economic institutional creations, or whether it acts within and by means of them. Are Soviet collective farmers taught to see themselves as the object of state planning, or as the instrument by which state planning is executed?

Marxist theory assigns the state under capitalism to the superstructure, but the question arises for socialism whether it remains in this status, or whether, in view of its creative and participant role in the socialist economy, it should be seen as a direct actor (as 'subject' in Soviet terminology) in the infrastructure. What is perhaps remarkable is that it appears that this central problem has not been resolved.

In the Stalinist period the state was thought of as part of the infrastructure. The state plan *was* the 'main economic law' of socialism, the 'living practice of the dictatorship of the proletariat'.[37] This view was criticised in the 1950s as allowing 'voluntarism' in economic policy and the prevailing view came to be that the state in socialism has a dual nature: superstructural, in that it fulfils political, military, and ideological functions, and infrastructural, in that it carries out the organisation of economic development. However, a recent textbook on collective farms rejects this formulation. In a characteristically convoluted argument it points out that such a position would involve a contradiction: since relations in the infrastructure are 'objective' and develop independently of human volition, the dying away of the state envisaged in the transition from socialism to communism would imply that conscious human policy-making would also disappear.[38] Therefore the author, Peshekhonov, suggests that the state must be seen as part of the superstructure, perhaps all of it, in socialism too. The state consists of those people who perform state functions, but they do not form a separate class because, in their economic position, i.e. their infrastructural relations, they are no different from any other members of Soviet society.

92

The state, in this view, *acts on* the economic base. However, and this is important, it would be incorrect to infer that the economic base simply goes its own way, developing erratically and in ways unforeseen as a result of the interaction of numberless related factors. 'We must not forget', writes Peshekhonov, 'the classical proposition of Engels that in socialism the laws of social activity will be applied by people who have a full knowledge of the state of affairs, and it is because of this that the population will submit to their rule.'[39] The state thus has the right and the duty to know what is going on; we can see this as one important legitimation of the vast documentation of everyday life in the Soviet Union and the general absence of a notion of privacy of information.

We are still left, however, with the problem of how the present activity of the state is to be understood: the state has an 'objective' existence, whereby it will wither away with the advent of communism, but at the same time it continues to have a 'subjective' role in directing the economy. The problem is solved, at least for the benefit of collective farmers, as follows: besides the economic 'laws', which have an objective existence, there are also the actions of people, which are a sub-system within the sphere governed by the 'laws'. These actions are 'subjective', in that they are consciously worked out as forms of economic-social organisation. They are divided into two types: 'economic organisation' and 'technical organisation'. It is in the first of these that the state has its role: it is the 'subject' of economic organisation. On the basis of its understanding of the economic 'laws', the state puts forward methods and principles for the organisation of the economy, and it also has the responsibility of regulating other human activity, for example in the sphere of technical progress, which is to some extent independent in its nature from the society it happens to occur within.

The main economic 'law' to be understood and acted upon by the state in the economy is that in socialism the form taken by the organisation of production should correspond with the level of development of the productive forces. It is in putting this 'law' into practice that the Soviet state created collective and state farms and other economic institutions.

As we have already mentioned, it is considered that the state farm is the 'higher' of the two types. This is because the relations of production are expressed above all in property relations, and the state farm assigns the ownership of the means of production to the state, whereas in collective farms they are owned in common by the members of the farm. Accordingly, the 'higher' form was appropriate to the more developed areas of the country.

Collective farms were initially seen as transitional, to disappear with the development of the productive forces. Recently, however, it has been acknowledged that the kolkhoz is more economically flexible than the sovkhoz farm, and that this organisational form should remain as an integral part of socialist society.[40]

It is important to remember here that Soviet historians divide the post-revolutionary period into two stages: the first, which lasted until approximately the 1960s, they designate as the stage of 'socialist construction'; the second is the stage now reached, 'developed socialism'. In accordance with this the collective farm itself is held to have undergone a qualitative change.

This internal transformation has, in Soviet theory, two aspects, both of which relate to ownership of the means of production. In the early collective farms the members contributed their private property to the kolkhoz and received a certain number of shares (*pai*). These shares were subject to repayment by the kolkhoz if a member wished to withdraw. However, a certain proportion of the farm's assets were the 'indivisible funds', i.e. funds not subject to repayment. These consisted of property confiscated by the state from 'kulaks' and also some of the peasants' contributions which were simply put into the 'indivisible funds' in order to 'strengthen the farms and create economic equality amongst the members'.[41] In 1932 about half of the total property of collective farms was in the form of shares and about half was the 'indivisible funds', but by the period of 'developed socialism' the *pai* (share) form had virtually disappeared. Today only 0.5% of kolkhoz property consists of shares.[42] The second aspect concerns the scale of ownership. Whereas the small early collective farms are said to be examples of 'group ownership', the present large farms represent 'collective ownership', in which the direct participants in production and appropriation are big collectivities of people.[43]

It will be shown in Chapter 4 that these arguments are misleading. The Buryat material shows convincingly that the structure of the collective farm has not changed essentially in the Soviet period. We need say here only that the 'share' was really a legal fiction, since it was not practically possible for kolkhozniks to withdraw and claim their recompense. Furthermore, the disappearance of the *pai* as an important part of the kolkhoz assets does not coincide historically with the supposed advent of 'developed socialism'. By 1940 the 'indivisible funds' already comprised 92.3% of all assets.[44]

State delivery plans

The state farm engages in what is known as a 'direct exchange' of products with the state. In other words all of its product is appropriated by the state in return for inputs of various kinds (machinery, raw materials, money, etc.) which form the productive resources of the enterprise. The collective farm, on the other hand, disposes of its product and acquires its inputs by sale. It engages in transactions not only with the state, but also with other organisations and individuals. The concept of the 'state' here means the buying/storage departments (*zagotoviteli*) subordinate to the Ministries, while other organisations such as factories or retail shops, even though they are state-owned, are not in this respect considered to be part of the 'state'.

The state appropriates the products of the kolkhoz by means of obligatory delivery plans. These form the basis for other plans for the general production and development of the kolkhoz over the five-year period of the delivery plan. The general plan (*orgkhozplan*) is worked out according to guidelines established by the Ministry of Agriculture and is confirmed by the Ministry, but it is no longer (post-1965) handed down to the farm, as used to be the case.[45] Within the framework of the *orgkhozplan* the kolkhoz draws up several further plans: plans of 'social development', plans of current production, plans of use of labour, investment plans, etc.[46]

It is the delivery/sale plan (*plan zakupok*) which is now the key to the relations between the kolkhoz and the state. It is seen theoretically as the means by which the socialist state organises the exchange of products between the town and the countryside, the distribution of the products of agriculture, and it is intended to express the leading influence of the working class of socialist industry on the development of agriculture.[47] The *plan zakupok* is obligatory and, furthermore, the kolkhoz is obliged, according to a directive of the 24th Congress of the CPSU for the 1971—5 period, to sell to the state a minimum of 35% of its grain produced surplus to the plan, and a minimum of 8—10% of its livestock products over the plan.[48] The plan is formally constituted by contracts made between the kolkhoz and the *zagotoviteli* for each type of product. The contract specifies the amount, quality, and assortment of the product, the timing and place of the sale, the responsibility of the kolkhoz for transportation[49] and packing, and the obligation of the *zagotoviteli* to receive, store, and sometimes process the deliveries. The methods and timing of payment by the *zagotoviteli* are also specified, as are the fines to be incurred by the kolkhoz if it does not fulfil its obligations. The theory of state planning in agriculture is already well known in the literature on the Soviet Union, and it will not be further discussed here, except to say that its general outlines have changed remarkably little, despite several changes in policy towards collective farms. The latter have been directed towards improving the efficiency of the appropriation of the surplus by the state, rather than to changes in the principle of centralised distribution.

Prices

The system of obligatory deliveries to the state at fixed prices is expressly seen as a way of counteracting the non-socialised nature of kolkhoz property. As Kosinskii and Mikhailik explain:

On the whole, retail prices for agricultural produce are higher than the delivery prices for which these products are obtained from collective farms. The difference between these two prices, i.e. the deduction of expenditure on preparation, storage, and realisation (turnover tax), is an important part of the income of the state budget. Thus, the 'clear income' created in the kolkhoz can be divided into two parts: the income of the kolkhoz itself, and the centralised state clear income, i.e. the income created in the kolkhoz and realised by means of the

95

system of state deliveries. The transfer of part of the aggregate income to the state takes place in view of the fact, primarily, that the plan-orders of the state as to the sale of products have a directive character.[50]

The Soviet pricing system is so very different from our own, and so fundamental to the functioning of collective farms, that it deserves some discussion, even though it will be impossible here to indicate more than a small part of the complexities involved. The most important point is that, since prices in the Soviet system are not determined by market forces, a *decision* has to be taken as to their level, and this opens the way to pricing in such a way as to create a tax.

From 1929 to 1953 the prices paid by the state virtually did not change at all. As Isayev has pointed out, agricultural prices in many cases did not pay half, and sometimes not even one-third, of the cost of production of the goods by the kolkhozy.[51] Furthermore, from 1939 onwards most Soviet wholesale prices, including those for agricultural produce, have been fixed 'delivered to station of destination'. They therefore include an allowance for average cost of transport.[52] The supplying organisation thus bears the brunt of transportation costs. For many remote collective farms this cost itself was frequently higher than the price paid by the state.

The difference between the price at which the state disposed of products and the delivery price received by collective farms was often huge, and the delivery prices were not responsive to inflation. For example, in 1948 the price at which the state sold rye to wholesalers was 335 rubles per 100 kilos, but kolkhozy were receiving only 7–8 rubles, a few kopecks more than in 1928. The price of rye bread meanwhile rose from 8 kopecks in 1928 to 2.70 rubles in 1948.[53] There have been massive rises in delivery prices since the 1950s, but in livestock production particularly they sometimes still do not cover costs (see Chapter 4).

Over-quota deliveries to the state are paid at a much higher price than those delivered up to the level of the planned quota. This system of multiple pricing has three main faults: it is difficult to calculate rationally what to produce if there is no way of telling which price basis will be applicable; the prices are not rationally related to one another, or to costs of production – for example, at one time fodder was expensive relative to bread at retail prices, and so it paid peasants to buy bread in the shops to feed their domestic animals; thirdly, the principle of two or more prices with a large gap between them does not make rational economic sense – it means that a farm with a high delivery plan will receive less for its total product than a successful farm (receiving to a much greater extent the over-quota prices) would obtain for the same amount. This whole system has the result that for the Soviet Union as a whole average prices would be higher in a good harvest year than in a bad one, i.e. prices would be lower in the event of scarcity.

The theoretical basis of pricing is supposed to be the average cost of production of all enterprises producing the commodity in question, plus some addition for profit. 'Prime costs' (*sebestoimost'*) are reckoned by most Soviet

96

economists to include: materials used up, depreciation of basic capital, and the rewards of labour. But in the absence of a market how are 'prime costs' actually to be determined, let alone 'values'? For the Soviet Union as a whole m or 'surplus product' equals that portion of the total value of the product which is not paid out in the rewards of labour or capital compensation. But for each product separately m is not known because its total value is not identifiable.

The problem is to find an 'objective' basis for prices. From the literature one can only conclude that no such 'objective' basis has been found, certainly not one which is acknowledged by Soviet economists as a whole. Ultimately, the government has had to set prices more or less arbitrarily. Controversies continue as to how the inconsistencies arising from such arbitrariness can be avoided by reform of prices. And of all kinds of prices, agricultural producers' prices have perhaps been most affected by political as opposed to economic factors — by the particular attitude of the state to peasants (see Chapter 3). Until recently there has not been any serious attempt to base prices on 'cost plus' — and indeed this would be difficult in principle, as we have seen. In general, unless it is assumed that a centralised system, with a limited role for prices, is superior to a decentralised planning system, the greatest problem of the various rival 'cost plus' theories is that whatever is added to cost the resulting formulae must be static and based on what is already the case; in a planned economy prices should be capable of influencing decision-making, whether by planners or enterprises. Arbitrarily determined prices can give no positive indication of scarcity or utility, and may frequently distort any attempt to discover these factors in the economy.

A second theory was developed in the 1960s to deal with the question of values and hence prices. Instead of basing value on 'cost plus', this theory, which has not yet reached the kolkhoz textbooks *as a theory*, suggests that values are derived from the tasks to be performed and from the plan. It is wrong to regard the costs of producing one item in isolation as a basis for its value, since the production processes of all goods, and the needs they fulfil, are inextricably intermingled.

One of the main exponents of the new theory, Novozhilov, says:

Marx noted that with a proportional division of social labour: 'products of different groups are sold according to value (in their further development in their prices of production) or even according to prices which are modified values, corresponding to prices of production, defined by general laws'. Marx and Engels, *Collected Works*, p. 185.

This remark of Marx has not attracted sufficient attention. Nonetheless it has great significance. It means that *modified value* 'defined by general laws' *also expresses socially necessary labour cost just as value does* . . .

What then are those general laws which determine the formation of modified value?

The mathematical model of the national economy helps to answer this question. It shows that prices based on the law of value are partial derivatives of the value of the final social product, dependent on the quantity of the given product.

In the absence of any resource restraints these partial derivatives are in direct proportion to value. When there are constraints on material resources then prices are proportional to a value modified to take account of these constraints . . .

The scarcity of the best resources (machines, installations, natural resources) leads to the necessity for social norms for the permitted margin of effectiveness of their use. This is vividly demonstrated in the mathematical models of the optimal plan: with constraints on resources for the construction of the plan auxiliary multipliers are essential.[54]

The quotation from Marx himself is obscure (a feature of his economic writings which one feels must be both an insurmountable obstacle and a saving grace for Soviet economists), but Novozhilov himself is clear enough.

The real measure of the costs of producing one item is not only prime cost (*sebestoimost'*) but also opportunity cost, a variable charge reflecting the use of scarce capital, natural and other resources. Prices of factors of production, according to their theory, are to be derived from linear programming on a computer in relation to the general requirements of the plan. According to some of these economists the computer can replace the market.

The theoretical propositions suggested by this school of economists (which are a good deal more sophisticated than I have been able to indicate here) do not penetrate the kolkhoz textbook level of publication. Nevertheless, the fundamental point does appear in a simple form: 'value' is not of course tied specifically to scarcity, but it should take account of the conditions of production in relation to means and needs, which can lead to similar practical conclusions.

However, the authors of the kolkhoz textbooks complain that practice falls far behind this ideal. Prices are still tied to centrally defined (prime cost) *sebestoimost'*, and they are always underestimated, since kolkhozy have to pay out social security, insurance, and costs of transport and realisation, none of which are commonly counted in *sebestoimost'*. This is one reason why prices are still too low. Another is failure to compute the increase in costs in particular branches of production. The idea of prices based on *average* costs means that in any case some enterprises will be operating at a loss. In particular cases whole sectors of production operating at a loss are covered by profit from another sector at the republic level, or else have to be heavily subsidised by the state. This is the case with livestock farming, which from 1971–5 has operated at a loss in Azerbaijan and probably also in other areas of the USSR.[55]

The result of the pricing system is that individual collective farms still operate at widely different rates of profit or loss irrespective of their efficiency. The plan given to a collective farm may instruct it to produce something which is frankly unprofitable in those conditions, with those resources, and those prices. Of course, for many years profit-making was not an important criteria for judging an enterprise. But recently the view has prevailed that economic enterprises *should* be profitable as well as socially useful. The 'law of value' is cited to justify this conclusion too:

Another rule of the law of value states that all socially necessary methods of production of the given commodity must be profitable. If, therefore, costs of production differ in various factories and all these factories are essential to satsify demand, the price must cover the highest level of necessary costs. Pricing practice does not satisfy this requirement of the law of value either. Prices are based on average branch costs. This method does not only give rise to enterprises making planned losses but, what is more important, deprives economic practice of criteria on the basis of which it would have been possible to separate justified from unjustified costs.[56]

The idea that each enterprise as a unit should be profitable, or at least not loss-making, is known as *khozraschet* ('enterprise account-settlement'). Profits are expressed as a percentage of costs, not of capital. Costs, it will be remembered, exclude land rent. To calculate profits, costs are compared to sales (*tovarnaya produktsiya*), not to gross output. Thus the fulfilment of the plan, which includes unfinished gross output, is not directly related to profits. Prices, which are related only to average costs, and which leave out adequate compensation for variation in scarcity and natural conditions, are likely to perpetuate the disparity between the goals of plan fulfilment and *khozraschet* for any individual enterprise.

Another policy, as yet as far from present reality as the theory that all sectors of the kolkhoz economy should be profitable, is the notion that all kolkhozy should be left with the same disposable income at the end of the year. 'Levelling-out' (*vyravnivaniye*) is to be carried out partly by differential state buying prices and partly by differential taxing (*podkhodnoi nalog*). In theory this would mean that the more successful farms would be paid lower prices by the state for producing the same items as less profitable farms.[57] This acknowledges the fact that some farms do make a loss even if they are operating as effectively as possible in given conditions, but it does not offer much incentive to productivity on a general scale and could even result in negating the first-mentioned policy that all enterprises should be profitable. The aim here is directly opposed to significant profit-making of individual enterprises, since it is concerned with the 'perfection of the economic inter-relations of the kolkhoz with the state, and the attraction of surplus "clear income", created in the more favourable natural conditions, into the disposition of the state'.[58] At the same time, the policy of levelling-out is a measure for *social justice*: it is clearly wrong in a socialist society for some kolkhozy to have a much greater disposable income than others, since it is difficult to prevent the rich farms from simply awarding themselves more wages. However, since these differentiated prices which would result in levelling-out only in fact exist at zonal levels, rather than at local levels as envisaged, we need not dwell on the matter further here. It should be noted only that levelling-out by differential prices is the policy, even if it is not effectively carried out in practice.

Taxes and loans

The policy of levelling-out is in fact more effectively realised by taxation. As we mentioned earlier, the state takes an annual tax from collective farms proportional to 'clear profit' and the total amount paid in wages, including bonuses. Previously, kolkhozy had been taxed according to income, not profit, and the tax had come directly from wages. No allowance was made for regional climatic differences, and the result was that the tax was crippling for certain disadvantageously situated kolkhozy. The present system is fairer, but some of the textbooks comment on its disincentive qualities; they advocate instead a tax based on the quality of land:

Among the numerous factors influencing the clear income received by collective farms the most important is the quality of their land. The land-improvement and irrigation works carried out by kolkhozy and the state cannot in a short period lessen the differences in the quality of land of different zones, and in fact the full liquidation of these variations is impossible. Therefore, collective farms with better land, disposing of the same quantity of labour and material resources as farms with less good land, receive a much greater product. In order to attract the surplus clear income produced in this way into the disposition of the government it is very important to establish a land register. A land register for each enterprise would make it possible to value land of different kinds in a more economically rational way, and thus to establish a tax by zones, and within zones by individual enterprises according to their quality of land. The rate of tax would thus be determined without reference to profitability, which would allow the main part of the gain from the intensification of production to remain in the hands of the kolkhozy themselves.[59]

Although this tax is not called a land rent paid to the state, it is difficult to see the practical difference between the two. Indeed, some economists such as Novozhilov do argue the necessity of such a rent. Nove mentions that this suggestion was put forward as early as 1960, but rejected on the grounds that it would presuppose that prices would cover costs even on the worst land for kolkhozy, while prices in the state sector, including state farms, would continue to be based on average cost.[60] It appears that this objection has won the day, since a land tax has not yet been put into practice. One cannot help supposing that the ideological objection to rent in a socialist society is one of the crucial stumbling-blocks.

Collective farms which fail to deliver the amount specified in their plans have to pay fines (*neustoiki*). This yet further intensifies the financial problems of farms which are unable to negotiate appropriate plans. It is only since 1965 that collective farms have been able to borrow directly from the State Bank. Before this credits were granted only through the *zagotovitel'* organisations in the form of advances for sales. We can see from this that, while the state took tax from collective farms, the general idea was that it had no financial obligations towards them. This has now changed, together with the acceptance in principle of the idea that collective farms are an integral part of 'developed socialism'. But even so, it is not easy for farms to obtain loans. Short-term loans are granted to cover money running costs, and are only given by the bank if the farm presents its accounts (its financial plan and budgets for its sectors for the year and the quarters) which have been previously inspected by the *raion* Soviet executive committee. Loans are not granted for more than a sum payable within the year according to the farm's financial plan. Interest is payable at 1% for short-term loans and 3% for loans whose period of repayment has expired. Long-term loans are available for construction projects, putting virgin land into use, buying farm machinery, land improvement, buying breeding livestock, and setting up inter-kolkhoz organisations. These are repayable at very small interest, 0.75%. Such loans can be seen as 'socially necessary redistribution', but in practice it is the successful farms, which can demonstrate that they can repay, which receive them most easily.

In conclusion, we can say that the pricing system combined with planned deliveries is above all what ensures economic 'rationality' of the individual kolkhoz. In practice Soviet agricultural prices do not adequately take into account scarcity of producers' goods or quality of natural conditions. Prices may be inconsistent with plans, and the plans themselves may not be related to demand. The highly important policy of levelling-out the residual income of kolkhozy by prices and taxes must have (if it is properly carried out) the effect of depressing the productivity of those farms which manage to operate success-fully in the agricultural jungle. All of this creates a genuine difference between the socialist and capitalist economies which is masked by the misleading expression 'state capitalism' for the USSR.

We can say that this situation must inevitably cause alienation, in the sense that collective farmers do not have real control over, or fully understand, the economic system in which they live their lives. The structure of the farm set out in section 1 above looks like a functioning whole in which resources can be allocated in the way best suited to the farmers themselves. But however admir-able the structure, the economic organisation will in practice run the risk of going seriously out of control if prices cannot be used as indicators of real costs. At the moment neither the prices at which kolkhozy buy production goods (e.g. fertiliser, fodder, seed) nor the prices at which they sell their own products really reflect costs, and therefore they cannot be used to plan profitable pro-duction. And even if profitability for any one enterprise is not a very important criterion of success from the point of view of the state, it is still the only cri-terion which is in the interests of the farmers themselves — since their wages come out of the income after the plan has been fulfilled and capital 'compen-

101

sation' paid. Collective farmers would only *not* feel alienated in this situation if they genuinely identified themselves as members of a *service* profession, providing as much wool, meat, milk, etc. as possible to the rest of society in return for the basic wage.

The legal obligation to fulfil specific plans is what keeps the system operating. Here it is necessary to have some idea of the structure of command within farms, in other words the political organisation which ensures that production is directed towards the plan at all.

4. Principles of government and social control in collective farms

The theoretical model of the collective farm is put into practice by means of defined structures of authority. These structures are themselves conceptualised theoretically and described in numerous publications. They differ from the economic principles mentioned earlier in their relative clarity and in the general unanimity towards the ideas lying behind them. It is not difficult for farms to act in accordance with these principles, indeed they are legally bound to. Nevertheless, in practice, as I shall show in subsequent chapters, many farm managements do not act on, but *act out*, the principles, and what we have to consider is the gap between the formal performance (which itself has a certain weight of a ritual kind) and the real patterns of authority which lie behind it.

Two aspects of administration are mandatory for all collective farms. The first is that the production units form a hierarchy which itself should constitute the chain of authority relations. The second is that political activity[61] should be carried out by means of defined orders of varying degrees of compulsion, depending on the hierarchical status of the actor. Authority relations as a whole are defined according to certain general principles of government, in other words according to a specific political theory.

The structure of government

The term 'structure of government' refers to what is in fact a hierarchy of productive units. Collective farms are divided into a variety of such units: production sectors (*tsekh*), sections (*otdeleniye, uchastok*), brigades (*brigada*) and other smaller units (*ferma, zven'ya*, etc.). A textbook published in Moscow in 1977 gives three ways in which these units can be combined.[62] The most 'progressive' is held to be the *tsekh* type, in which farms are divided into sectors (agricultural, livestock, etc.) specialising in a certain kind of production and under the authority of a trained specialist. The other types are division into sections or complex brigades (i.e. a three-tier structure, as it is known), or into simple brigades (a two-tier structure).[63] In the two-tier system the brigadiers organise the work of their own brigade, allocating the task to the teams and individuals within it, and checking the results. The three-tier system is similar, except that several

102

varied brigades, as well as a team of secondary specialists, unite to form a section (sometimes known as a complex brigade) which mediates between the Chairman and the brigadiers. Farms do not have to follow these models consistently. In some cases the whole farm is divided into sections, in others the section system is combined with the simple brigade structure.

What is significant is that this model is described in the textbook as a 'structure of government'. There is in fact a separate hierarchy, which subordinates individual office-holders to the decisions of meetings and committees (see Figure 2.2) and which is supposed to formulate policy. However, its organisational features in real life have left this latter structure with a largely formal character and its function is mainly to act out the principle of collective decision-making without which no actual decision on policy would be valid. Thus the term 'government' (*upravleniye*) referring to the hierarchy of economic managers is in fact correct, since it is they who both make decisions and carry them out. Figure 2.3 shows how a farm Chairman visualised the configuration of governing officials in his farm.

According to the statutes of the collective farm the highest authority in policy formation is not the Chairman, but the general meeting of the members of the farm (*obshchee sobraniye kolkhoznikov*). This meeting, which should take place at least four times a year, elects a governing committee (*pravleniye*). The committee, of nine to fifteen members, which has authority when the general meeting is not in session, elects a Chairman, who is at the same time Chairman of the committee and of the farm as a whole. He is formally the third authority after the general meeting and the governing committee. This whole

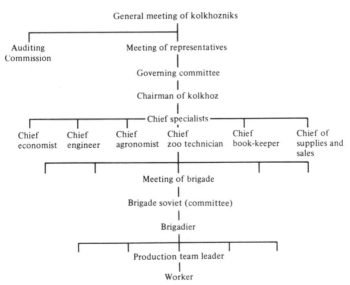

2.2. Formal decision-making structure of the kolkhoz.

103

structure, i.e. (1) meeting, (2) committee, and (3) leader, is repeated at the section or brigade level.

Another textbook, designed for the use of kolkhoz Chairmen, makes clear that these collective organs are responsible for 'general leadership', while the hierarchy of officials are charged with 'operative leadership' (*operativnoye rukovodstvo*).[64] The latter comprises: directing the work of the productive units, planning their future work and their interrelations, and distribution of resources. This 'operative leadership' is to be carried out on the basis of *yedinonachal'ye* (single authority), with distinct subordination of the levels in the hierarchy. The democratic aspects of kolkhoz management are diminished in the following ways. If it is difficult to call the general meeting of the kolkhozniks the committee of the farm is told that it may replace this meeting by a meeting of representatives (*upolnomochenniye*), usually one representative for four to five members. The method of selection and length of service is to be decided by the committee. Clearly this gives the officials the possibility of excluding argumentative kolkhozniks from the meeting.

Questions to be placed before the meeting of representatives, and the decisions taken by them, are discussed by ordinary kolkhozniks at the open brigade meetings. But although the brigade meetings can table their opinions ('for' or 'against') on the matters decided, the textbooks give no guidelines for procedure in the case of disagreement. It states simply: 'If, at the meetings of the sections (or brigades), all the questions lying in the competence of the general meeting of kolkhozniks are recognised to be more expediently decided at the meeting of representatives, then in this case the meeting of representatives becomes the highest organ of government in the kolkhoz.'[65]

Officials appointed by the governing committee, the 'chief specialists', have full responsibility for the matters under their competence (planning, agriculture, book-keeping, etc.), and thus take precedence over the brigadiers. This introduces another level in the hierarchy, between the governing committee and the brigade soviets. The only other element in the formal governing structure is the Auditing Commission (*revizionnaya komissiya*), which has wide powers to check the financial and economic affairs of the governing committee and Chairman. The Auditing Commission is elected by the general meeting (or its substitute, the meeting of representatives) and presents its report to that meeting. The difference between this formal structure and a Buryat kolkhoz Chairman's own picture of the farm organisation can be seen by comparing Figure 2.2 with Figure 2.3.

In my view, this structure, in which individual leaders are subordinated to committees, can in fact be reduced to the 'structure of government' referred to at the beginning of this section. Because of the procedural forms of political action, the role of general and representative meetings becomes one mainly of assent, and the power of the governing committee and the brigade soviets is also limited. Factual administrative authority lies with the hierarchy of individual officials, and this as we have seen is recognised by the textbooks.

This situation is the result of the practical implementation of Leninist political ideology, specifically, the precedence given to the principle of the 'single leader' (*yedinonachaliye*) over the principle of 'kolkhoz democracy' (*kolkhoznaya demokratiya*).

The kolkhoz textbook gives six 'principles of government' for socialist organisations. It is significant that the authors no longer refer to Marx on this matter.

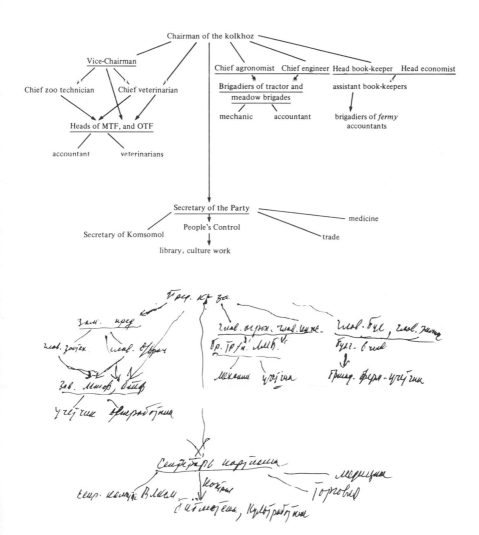

2.3. Translation of the diagram of the administration of a collective farm, drawn by the Chairman of the Karl Marx kolkhoz, Barguzin.

105

All references and quotations are from Lenin. The first general point is that political principles are considered to 'flow from the character of productive relations'; they are not, like laws, given an existence independent of the will and wishes of people, but are themselves created by people engaged in socialist production relations. However, they are formed by and develop under the specific influence of economic laws. The textbooks give several examples of the emergence of principles of government from economic laws. These principles are somewhat general ('the continuous and regular tendency towards the achievement of the maximum result in given conditions of production').[66] Officials of the farm are instructed to guide their activities in these matters according to more specific rules, sometimes known as 'laws of government'. These appear in all of the textbooks and they are worth mentioning in some detail.

(i) *The principle of the unity of political and economic (khozyaistvennogo) leadership*, also known as the principle of 'party discipline' (*partiinost'*). This 'is expressed by the fact that the Communist Party, as the guiding and leading power of our society, defines at each period the main economic task, and the tempo of development of socialised production, on the basis of objective-economic and other conditions'.[67] One of the tasks of the Party is the selection, distribution, and education of leadership cadres, and it is by the direction of cadres in particular sectors of the economic organisation that the Party has its effect on the process of production. This principle presupposes that the economic leadership of any part of the organisation should operate from the point of view of state interests.

(ii) *The principle of democratic centralism*. This means 'the union of the centralised state-planned socialist economy with the development of the creative initiative of local organs and the masses in the direction of production'.[68] The socialist economy is a single, unified system, the textbook says, and cannot function without centralised leadership which directs the activity of all enterprises according to a single plan.

(iii) *The principle of the 'single leader' (yedinonachaliye) and collegiality (kollegial'nost')*. The concept of 'single leadership' means the submission of the members of the collective to the will of one leader (*yedinonachal'nik*). As a consequence of this power he has personal responsibility for the matter in hand. This is the most frequently cited principle in the textbook, and it is worth dwelling on it further. Lenin explained it as follows:

Every large machine industry, i.e. the very material and productive source of socialism, demands the absolute and very strictest *unity of will (yedinstvo voli)*, directing the work of hundreds, thousands, and tens of thousands of people … But how can the strictest unity of will be achieved? By the submission of the wills of the thousand to the will of one man.[69]

He adds that this power must not be abused:

The more decidedly we now stand up for hard, ruthless power, for the dictator-

106

ship of individual people in *definite* processes of work, in definite moments of *purely executive* functions, the more varied should be the forms and means of control from below, in order to paralyse the slightest shadow of a possibility of the perversion of Soviet power, in order to tear out the incessant weed-grass of bureaucratism. [70]

Collegiality consists of the collective discussion of matters of common concern, and it is opposed to the principle of the 'single source', just as democratic centralism is opposed to the encouragement of the 'creative initiatives of the masses'. Lenin explained how the former principles are reconcilable: 'Just as collegiality is necessary for the discussion of basic questions, so "single source" responsibility and "single source" administration is necessary in order that there should be no red tape, in order that it is impossible to escape from responsibility.'[71]

How is this to be achieved in collective farms? The textbook answer is revealing. The group is to decide upon important matters and the leader is to carry out the decisions:

The reconciling of kolkhoz democracy with the principle of 'single source' consists in the operative direction of production being preceded by common discussion of the basic questions of the life of the kolkhoz and its sections and by the taking of the corresponding decisions . . . For example, in the case of a brigade, these are decisions as to the ways and means of fulfilling productive tasks, as to measures for strengthening labour discipline, suggestions as to awards and fines, and the distribution of income among the members.

After the collective has taken a decision on a certain question, the leader carries out the will of the collective by means of individual orders and administrative acts . . . [72]

In fact, as will be clear later, the 'decisions' taken by a brigade collective are relevant only to low-level brigade concerns. The important concerns of the farm, such as the annual production plan, the level of wages, and matters of discipline, have already been decided at a much higher level of the hierarchy. The same is true of the all-kolkhoz meetings, where what can be 'decided' is limited by what has been decided at higher levels. Only certain kinds of decision are appropriate at each level. Also, the principles of *partiinost'* and 'democratic centralism' state that important decisions *should have already in effect been taken* by the corresponding section of the Party or state in almost all cases. I shall describe later how this happens. The collective merely confirms the 'decisions' (*resheniye*). The effect of this is for operative power to revert to the *yedinonachal'nik*, who takes the decisions which are left to be taken at this level, thus limiting the sphere of action at the level below.

The remaining three principles of government are less complicated and can be summarised quickly.

(iv) *The principle of scientific management.* This means that the enterprise must be run on 'scientific' lines, according to 'economic laws', and making use of advanced methods.

(v) *The principle of material and moral interest in the results of labour*. This consists of seeing that the workers are encouraged to maintain their interest in socialised production. The leaders of the kolkhoz are to achieve this by both material interest (wages, prizes, bonuses) and moral means (the good opinion of fellow-workers).

(vi) *The principle of socialist observance of laws*. This means observance not only of state laws, but also of the internal regulations of the enterprise (*vnutrennyy rasporyadok*). The governing officials of the kolkhoz have the responsibility of seeing that people obey both of these types of laws, as well as the orders given within the enterprise.

This last principle gives individual officials and the governing committee the right to act as in a limited sense *judiciary* bodies:

The governing committee investigates the cases of violation of the statutes of the kolkhoz as well as the internal regulations, and decides on measures of punishment for those guilty.[73]

The leader of a division [i.e. a 'specialist' official] has the right to reject work of low quality and demand that it be done again, to dismiss from work those people who violate the technology of production [i.e. who break machines and tools] and the rule of exploitation of technology [i.e. those who use machines wrongly].[74]

Of course, kolkhoz officials do not constitute the only legal authority within the farm, but they are the first level of such an authority. They have serious punishments (fines, dismissal from work, etc.) at their disposal, and can, and indeed should, report on misdemeanours outside their competence to the police and other bodies.

These six principles of government indicate that collective farm administration does not discriminate between economic, political, and legal powers. Any official holds all these powers in some degree. But what is the system of precedence?

Here, two different lines of seniority are laid down by the textbook. The first hierarchy is known as *lineal* government, and consists of the submission of each worker to one official only, the one senior to him or her (i.e. workers → team-leader, team-leader → brigadier, brigadier → official, official → Chairman). The second kind of hierarchy is the *functional* or *specialist* system, which operates within each productive speciality. Here the top of the hierarchy is the chief specialist, who is able to give orders even to the Chairman or to brigadiers on questions of his own speciality. The 'functional' line of command runs: chief specialist ← senior specialist ← specialist ← other worker. The textbook comments that the drawback of the 'functional' system is that the chief specialists of different professions (e.g. agronomist, zoo technician, book-keeper) may come into conflict with one another. In view of this, most farms combine the two systems.[75]

The textbook comments: 'As a result of the fact that the chief specialists are subordinate to the farm leadership by the lineal system, and that the other specialists are subordinate to the chief by the functional system, as a whole in all sections of the administrative system leadership operates on the basis of the "single leader" (*yedinonachaliye*).'[76] Because the principle of the 'single leader' is so important, the textbook instructs leaders on the economic, administrative, and socio-psychological methods of getting their orders obeyed. A lesson is also given on how to take decisions ('consider all the alternative possibilities', etc.). It becomes clear that for those in the *lineal* system of government the political aspects of the office are far more important than economic ability. A quotation is given from Kalinin:

Leadership of a collective farm is a very difficult matter, and demands many qualities from the Chairman. Firstly, the Chairman should have sufficient authority that his orders will be carried out not only as the orders of the Chairman, but on the basis of his *personal* political and economic authority. Secondly, he should have some agricultural experience, or at least some organisational ability. thirdly, he should have enormous patience, and not lose his self-control because of thousands of little annoyances. And the main thing is that he should be a good practical politician. If the kolkhoz has found such a person, it goes without saying that he should be protected by the higher authorities; they should follow Lenin (*postupat' po-leninski*), i.e. aid the growth of such a leader.[77]

Whatever the official's means of getting people to obey his orders, the 'principle of the single leader' means that he himself cannot be criticised, punished, or dismissed, without referring first to the general meeting of kolkhozniks. In theory, it is *because* of the official's personal responsibility for what occurs under his command that he is given this comparatively inviolate position. But as we shall see later, the form of internal kolkhoz meetings ensures that officials are rarely required to take personal blame from within the farm for the lack of success of their section in the normal run of things. If an official is criticised it is very rarely at the general meeting, and virtually never at the instigation of the general meeting, but much more likely to be by means of some outside organ such as a newspaper. Deliberate malpractices, uncovered by the Auditing Commission or the People's Control (see below), render officials liable to criticism or punishment by the invoking of outside senior authority, but almost more likely is an unexpected accusation as a result of changes in policy from above (see Chapter 7.)

Rarely in the history of the world can there have been a society which has codified ways of ordering people about in civil life to the extent that the Soviet Union has. Let us look at the battery of commands available to officials of the kolkhoz and sovkhoz.

The first of these is the command itself (*prikaz*). A *prikaz* is a written or oral command which can be given only by the Director of a state enterprise. Very often the *prikaz* is the form in which the Director carries out orders he himself has received from above, i.e. administrative Acts (*rasporyaditel'nyye vozdeystvyye*) from the central government, or directives (*direktivy*) from high

Party or government organs. The *prikaz* is used for commands to do with the economy of the farm, for accepting new members, for dismissing or transferring workers, for awarding prizes and extracting fines, for ordering working trips outside the farm (*komandirovki*), for regulating the working day, and so on.

In collective farms the *prikaz* is replaced by the decision (*resheniye*), in other words the decision taken at a general meeting of the members or their representatives. But, as I have indicated, the term 'decision' is misleading, for two reasons: firstly, the matter may be one where no decision is actually required (for example, the presenting of periodic reports on progress by various production teams); secondly, the agenda together with proposals for decisions is drawn up beforehand and then voted on or confirmed at the meeting. The *resheniye* has the same power as the *prikaz*: it must be obeyed. It is interesting that the kolkhoz textbook gives no instructions as to what to do if the meeting votes against the proposed 'decision'. Probably, a wise Chairman would never introduce such a controversial matter to a general meeting. He would use instead some means of command which his subordinates can do nothing about.

One of these is the order (*rasporyazheniye* or *direktiva*), which in theory comes second to the *prikaz* or *resheniye*. The order may be given by 'lineal' officials and specialists, and must be obeyed. It is used most often for expressing work tasks to the members of the farm. The last form of obligatory command is the 'instruction' (*ukazaniye*), which may be given by lower officials such as brigade and team-leaders.

For all of these obligatory commands, the textbook warns that the official must make sure that his subordinate has understood what to do, where, when, and to whom, and how. Furthermore, the authors touchingly advise that 'The form the command is couched in should not lower the human dignity of the subordinate.'[78] Any absolute command, when seen from a negative point of view, is known euphemistically as an 'administrative method' in the Soviet Union. The textbook warns, 'If administrative methods are used without reference to objective conditions, without consideration of the economic facts, and have signs of despotism or subjectivism, they transform themselves into naked administrativeness (*goloye administrirovaniye*).'

After the obligatory commands, there are a series of lesser methods. In order of forcefulness they are: the 'advice of a leader' (*soviet nachal'nika*), the 'advice of a senior' (*soviet starshego*), and finally the 'comradely request' (*tovarishcheskaya pros'ba*). The last of these is suitable if the person issuing the request is well-qualified in relation to his subordinate and trusts his honesty and competence. In other cases, the more categorical forms of 'advice' should be used.

Written work-orders to teams are called *naryady*. They are given out by brigadiers or team-leaders at weekly or daily conferences (*soveshaniye*). They are not strictly obligatory, but workers can be punished for disobeying them. Pay is assessed by the fulfilment of *naryady*.

Punishments, like commands, are in a series graded according to severity. The least serious is the rebuke (*zamechaniye*), followed by the reprimand (*vygovor*), the severe reprimand (*strogiy vygovor*), transfer for a period to lower-paid work and dismissal from the present job.[79] Lastly there is exclusion from the farm. Punishments are proposed by officials of the farm in documentary form and then ratified by the Chairman, or the governing committee. Sometimes a fine is imposed, but more serious is the fact of documentary evidence of misdemeanours in a person's work record (*trudovaya knizhka*) — somewhat like endorsement of a driving licence in Britain — since this will affect promotion, success in the Party, and possibilities of transferring to other jobs. Fines and *vygovory* are also noted in the worker's pay-book (*uchetnaya kartochka*) which can be used in assessing his 'character' when references (*kharakteriskiki*) are written.

The rewards for approved behaviour are also graded in carefully defined categories. Predictably, the *ustav* cites as the main criteria for rewards, 'the achievement of high results in production and the introduction of rationalising suggestions'.[80] The list of possible honours and rewards is: (i) a declaration of thanks, (ii) giving out of prizes, awarding of valuable presents, (iii) awarding of a Diploma of Honour (*pochetnaya gramota*), (iv) mention on the honour board or in the honour book, (v) conferring of the title 'Merited Kolkhoznik' (*zasluzhennyy kolkhoznik*) and 'Honoured Kolkhoznik' (*pochetnyy kolkhoznik*).

Apart from orders, punishments, and rewards, there is widespread use of the idea of competition to encourage increased production. This kind of competition (*sorevnovaniye*) is claimed to be, and is, different from capitalist competition in market economies. The prize is not direct material gain (more sales), but increase in prestige and indirect material benefits (cash awards, presents, diplomas, etc.). Local newspapers publish the production indices for the kolkhozy and sovkhozy at intervals through the year. Within the region *sorevnovaniye* is somewhat like a school examination system where, however badly you do, you have to go on competing. I shall discuss later the particular 'socialist competitions' which are set up at all levels, from the regional (i.e. whole groups of kolkhozy and sovkhozy) down to the individual tractor-driver or milkmaid.

Competition in general has implications for social control because it is seen also as a means to internalised self-discipline on the part of workers. A booklet issued to workers, in which details of production are to be listed for each month, shows this clearly. Besides pure production, the worker is given spaces in which to record economies in materials, his part in rationalisation of production, study, the work of the comrade he is competing with, new events in his family, participation in voluntary work, cultural activities, social work and help given to colleagues. The booklet is prefaced by thirteen 'Commandments' (*zapovedi*, the same word used for religious commandments) which are worth quoting for the light they throw on an ideology which instructs the individual to identify with the group by making himself worthy. Incidentally, it should be noted that the intimate (*ty*) form of the second person is used throughout.

111

Commandments of the Collective of Communist Labour

Give the very highest productivity of labour — that is our slogan!

Show courage in everything. Think how to do better.

One for all, all for one!

Think this way: one idler is a disgrace for the brigade, one truancy is a black mark for everyone, one spoilage is a disaster for the whole collective.

When you have finished work, don't waste time for nothing. School, technical college, and institute are waiting for you.

If you have a free minute — pick up a book.

Learn to bring even more help to your people.

Be concerned with your culture [i.e. with civilised behaviour].

Have done with swearing, rudeness, drunken bouts.

Never allow incidents of hooliganism, drunkenness and uncivilised behaviour to pass.

If someone offends under your eyes, you also are guilty!

Respect old people — on the streets, at home, and in the family.

Be polite, welcoming, and tactful.[81]

The booklet begins with a page in which the worker fills in his name, date of birth, education, party affiliation, job and work-group. Then a promise is given:

Entering competition for communist labour I take upon myself the following obligations:

1. Obligations and their fulfilment in 196___

	Norms of work		Quality	
Months	promised	fulfilled	promised	fulfilled
January				
February				
etc.				

The same format continues throughout the booklet. Several pages are set aside for 'Checking of obligations', presumably to be filled in by someone in a supervisory capacity. Each section is headed by a small device or slogan. The 'Checking of obligations' heading reads, 'You gave your word — keep it!' The section on voluntary labour is headed by a quotation from Lenin: 'We call communism an order of society in which people are attracted to carry out social obligations without any special apparatus of enforcement, when unpaid work in the common interest becomes a general phenomenon.' At the head of the section devoted to help to colleagues is the slogan: 'The brigade is your hearth and home (*rodnoi dom*). Your success is the success of your comrade!' The section of new events in the family is headed: 'Everyday life and the family are not private matters. A person should strive in all his doings and thoughts to be pure, pure as truth. In everything, including the family.'

Any worker issued with such a booklet is clearly under strong pressure to involve himself in the work ethic, to measure his successes not only against others, but against himself. The sanction is guilt, guilt at not carrying out one's word, at letting other people down. Although I do not know how widely such booklets are used and did not see one myself when in the field, the attitude they embody seems very general. This is the constant, all-pervasive, moral pressure which is deployed to shame people into putting the collective above their individual interests.

Each collective farm has its own flag (*znamya*) which symbolises

the union of peasants for socialist agricultural production, their labour honour, glory and valour, and it also serves to remind each kolkhoznik of his duty in the government and development of the communal economy, the growth of production and sale to the state of the agricultural product, the raising of the material and cultural standard of living of the peasants, and the building of communist relations in the village.[82]

The size of the flag is specified. On one side there should be a silhouette of Lenin, 36—40 cm high, with the inscription 'The collective farm is the school of communism for the peasants.' On the other side is the republic emblem, with the name of the kolkhoz and its address. The orders and medals won by the kolkhoz should be attached to the flag. The occasions on which the flag should be paraded are specified in the Directory for kolkhoz Chairmen.

The life of a collective farm official is beset with documents. All *prikazy*, *resheniye*, *narady* and *rasporyazheniye* should be in writing, in several copies, as should minutes of meetings (*protokoly*), petitions and applications (*zayavleniya*). The central government has set out standard forms for such documents, which officials are obliged to follow. These define the size of paper to be used, the information to be included, the place on the page for various bits of information, even the size of the margins.[83] Letters written between officials, either within the farm, or from the farm to outside organisations, also have standard forms. They consist of: accompanying letters covering the expedition of other documents, letters of information, requests for materials, inquiries, and replies. These letter forms also have to be complied with by ordinary workers if, for example, they wish to apply for leave, to go on a visit, to change their kind of work, to join a library, and so on. All of this formal documentation has the goal of controlling people's movements at the same time as ensuring that people are *officially* treated in the same way, above board, and according to law. That this penetrates to the minutiae of people's working lives can be seen from the following document, given as an example to follow in the textbook. This is a report or memorandum (*dokladnaya zapiska*), one of the commonest forms of documentation in use; it is employed by officials, brigadiers and team-leaders to report on work done, to comment on conditions of work, to propose improvements, to make complaints. It is the main official form of communication between lower officials and the Chairman or governing committee.[84]

Sovkhoz 'Banner'	To the Director of the Sovkhoz
Complex brigade no. 2	comrade Gran'ko V.Ya.

Memorandum
24. 04. 77
On violation of labour discipline

On 23 April workman P.D. Ershov was given the assignment (*naryad*) of unloading a lorry of feed concentrate which was to arrive in the brigade in the second half of the day. But comrade P.D. Ershov did not come to work after lunch. The lorry waited idle for two hours.

The reason for staying at home was not sufficient.

I suggest that comrade P.D. Ershov should be punished.

Enclosed: an explanatory note from P.D. Ershov dated 24.04.77 consisting of one sheet of writing.

Brigadier   [signature]   *V.G. Petrov*

It is the task of the Auditing Commission to check on malpractices among the officials. The Auditing Commission is elected by the general meeting of kolkhozniks and may not include members of the farm committee or their near relatives. However, its membership is limited to people from the farm, and from what we know of the way in which elections are managed we may deduce that it is not as independent a body as the statutes envisage.

Evidence for this is the existence of another body to perform the same job, the People's Control (*Narodnyy Kontrol'*). This was reorganised by the Soviet government in 1963 within every productive institution in the USSR. It was formerly known as the 'Party-State Control', which gives some idea of the idea behind it. The People's Control exists to combat dishonesty, inefficiency, and laziness among all levels of workers, including officials. The difference between it and the Auditing Commission is that it has a base outside the kolkhoz and can always appeal to higher authorities if local officials do not cooperate. Buryat ASSR has fourteen Committees at district level of the People's Control, each consisting of one paid full-time worker and nine or ten volunteers. Within the kolkhoz or sovkhoz the local organisation of People's Control again takes the form of a hierarchy: i.e. 'head', 'section', and 'brigade' groups, as well as numerous 'posts' in rural settlements. The members of these groups are elected among the populace at open meetings of the *sel'sovet*.[85]

A small booklet published in Ulan-Ude entitled *People's Control in Action* describes the state of the organisation in the late 1960s:

Now [1967], in rural areas of Buryat ASSR there are about 8,000 'controllers'. In the process of representation [of the populace] the quality of the members has been improved and has been renewed to the extent of 50% new membership. This is a pretty fresh power! More than two-thirds of the controllers are members of the Party of Komsomol, and around 20% are women.[86]

The work of the people's Control is never-ending, and ubiquitous. Here is one story given in the booklet:

114

Principles of government and social control in collective farms

One day in the spring of 1965 the 'people's controllers' of one of the enterprises in Barguzin *aimak* arrived at a shepherds' camp (*otar*). They dropped in on the yards and pens to look at the sheep and lambs. The winter had been a hard one, the sheep had lost weight, and many of them were beginning to drop their wool. But nobody picked it up. The head of the unit, although he blamed the shepherds for not collecting the wisps, clearly thought the matter was unimportant.

What to do? How to influence the shepherds? After discussing it amongst themselves, the controllers decided to spring a trap. One of them strolled into the sheep-pen and scattered some coins on the ground so that they would later be noticed. Then he asked the shepherds to come in and explain some working matter. They walked about the pen talking. Suddenly, one of the shepherds picked up a coin, adding 'These kids of mine throw money all over the place, the *sholomsy* [devils]!' Another shepherd saw a second coin, picked it up, rubbed it clean, and put it in his pocket, saying, 'I'll show my son Bator how to fool about with my hard-earned wages!' Got them! The controller asked the shepherds, 'And why don't you pick up this too?' The shepherds looked carefully round but could not see more money. They asked, 'Where is it? There isn't any more money.' And only then, when the controllers showed them a pile of fallen wool and explained that it also was worth money, did the shepherds understand what was going on, and that they had been made fools of. They were ashamed and said, 'Thanks for the lesson, we'll correct our mistake and pick up the fallen wool.'[87]

But the work may be on a larger scale:

A few years ago the sovkhoz 'Yeravninskiy' was one of the most backward in the Buryat republic and made an annual loss of 300,000 to 400,000 rubles. But in recent years the sovkhoz has made many advances with the help of the Party organisation of the district and region, and here a certain amount is due to the People's Control. In 1963 the question of the unsatisfactory situation of the sovkhoz was discussed at the regional (*oblast'*) level of the People's Control, and it emerged that the sovkhoz was making wrong use of its land. The Committee requested the Director of the sovkhoz to alter the structure of the land use. With the help of regional and district officers of the People's Control practical steps were worked out and initiated on the spot: the administrative-governmental apparatus was cut, the accounting mechanism was improved, mistakes were corrected in norms of pay. In every brigade and section meetings were held, at which concrete cases of inefficiency were discussed, and measures proposed to improve work in hand. The use of land was changed fundamentally, with a far greater amount of fodder grown. In the next few years the sovkhoz showed a great improvement and the loss was reduced by two to three times. In 1965 the sovkhoz was the initiator in the republic of industrialised feeding of cattle.[88]

If the kolkhoz or sovkhoz officials do not obey the recommendations of the People's Control, or even accuse them of petty-minded interfering, the latter can address the Party organisation and expect to find immediate support. At the local level, many of the people involved in the two organisations must be the same. The People's Control is really a specialised extension of Party initiatives into the everyday working lives of the farmers, and it often involves criticism within the Party from higher to lower levels. We can see this from a case discussed

115

in the booklet *People's Control in Action*, where the local Party organisation of the kolkhoz 11th Party Congress was accused of 'serious faults in directing the posts and groups of the People's Control in the kolkhoz'. The accusation was made at the district (*raion*) meeting of the Party by the district level of the People's Control. The fault was apparently at the section (*otdeleniye*) level of the kolkhoz:

The party organisation of the sections completely failed to direct the groups, not a single Party organisation during three years listened once, with the exception of the election meetings, to the reports of the work of the People's Control. The Party meetings, committees, and secretaries of the sections did not give orders to the controllers, and therefore they basically did not work at all.[89]

The account suggests that little initiative from the people is to be expected from the People's Control.

The 'People's Control' is one of the main channels for criticisms, and it should represent not only Party views. In the Selenga Karl Marx farm twenty-five deputies were elected for a period of two to three years from the entire population of the *sel'sovet*, and there were also separate People's Control posts in each of the brigades. The deputies saw their job as 'helping the militia' and as a 'prophylactic' against corruption, the favouring of kinsmen, etc. But the organisation is itself controlled by the Party, and it seems clear that criticisms will be of a certain kind only. They will reveal inefficiency, laziness, dishonesty, etc., insofar as these hinder the carrying out of Party policies, and they may criticise lower level branches of the Party itself, but they cannot attack the policies themselves because the People's Control is in a sense a functional extension of the Party. This matter will be discussed further in Chapter 7, but meanwhile we can see that the intention of the People's Control is to be another organisation entitled to check the others in the mutually vigilant circle of the farm management, the auditing commission, the local branch of the Party, and the rural Soviet.

Trade unions played very little role in the life of collective farmers in the period studied. There is a Union of the Workers and Employees in Agriculture and State Deliveries, which has branches at the republic, *oblast'* (region) and *raion* (district) levels, but none of the documents I have had access to mention branches in the kolkhoz, although state farms do have trade unions. No one mentioned the trade union in either of the farms I visited. From the literature it appears that trade unions are relatively powerless because many of the matters with which they are concerned (pay, unfair dismissal, work conditions, etc.) are decided upon by the various other bodies, and it is understood that the trade union's task is to carry these decisions out. Only in the sphere of social security and safety at work does the All-Union Central Committee of the Professional Unions appear to have the main role in decision-making.[90]

Thus the collective farm is established by law as a hierarchical, highly formalised framework, in which rights, duties and procedures are in theory clearly defined. For officials with rights of *yedinonachaliye* political power is not differentiated from economic management or legal authority within the farm. The system distinguishes policy-making from executive powers, defining the latter as the 'structure of government'. The somewhat strange formulation is understandable when it is realised that policy-making actually takes place outside the formal organisation of 'meetings' theoretically responsible for kolkhoz policy decisions. Similarly, the structure for social control is overseen by another organisation (People's Control), itself directed by a third body (the Party). This chapter has described the authority structures as they *should* work given ideal conditions. As we shall see in subsequent chapters all things are not equal, and the complex relations of the collective farm structure with material circumstances, with outside organisations (the Party and the Soviets and other enterprises, etc.), and unauthorised interests, creates a situation which is far from that laid out in the textbooks; indeed, it is this intractable complexity which is the reason for their existence and constant up-dating.

3

The hierarchy of rights held in practice

This chapter will describe briefly the *de facto* rights held by individuals and groups in Buryat collective farms. The approach is different from the classical Soviet analysis, which discusses society by means of the concept of 'relations of production', based on different types of ownership of the means of production.[1] It also differs from Western Marxist analyses of Soviet history, such as those of Charles Bettelheim, which use the idea of 'possession' or 'proprietorship' of the means of production in order to separate classes of state functionaries and managers of enterprises from the workers.[2] It differs again from the approach of present Soviet sociologists, for example Arutyunyan, who use statistical techniques to establish 'strata' in Soviet society based on a variety of criteria, such as type of work (physical or mental), pay, and level of education.[3] I shall be using the anthropological approach to property rights initiated by Malinowski and developed by Firth and Gluckman. There is nothing new about this. It simply provides a useful tool by which we can look at the collective farm community in terms of rights, which are defined by specific usages.

Malinowski wrote: 'Ownership can be defined neither by such words as "communism" nor "individualism", nor by reference to "joint-stock company system" nor "personal enterprise", but by the concrete facts and conditions of use. It is the sum of duties, privileges and mutualities which bind the joint owners to the object and to one another.'[4] Gluckman made the point that in certain African societies, as opposed to Western capitalist society, the individual's rights to property depend on his social and political status.[5] I suggest that in the Soviet Union too rights over the means of production, including labour, accrue to groups and individuals by virtue of their social-political status. They cannot be summed up by reference to the legal statutes outlined in the previous chapter, nor can they be defined by reference to purely economic criteria, since, as we saw, even the legal statutes do not differentiate the economic from the political. Essentially, the *de facto* rights held by people in Soviet society, and even more so, the system of socio-political statuses from which they derive, remain to be discovered. This book can only put forward some material towards the accomplishment of that task.

118

The lineal structure of production and administration

It has been traditional in the anthropological literature to use the word 'right' for the *de facto* power exercised by individuals and groups. This usage perhaps came about because of the absence of a separate legal code in the societies anthropologists were discussing. In those societies powers deriving from social status have a moral legitimacy and can well be termed 'rights'. But in the Soviet Union the *de facto* powers exercised by people can be both more and less than their publicly acknowledged rights. Because people have possibilities of action which are not necessarily part of public legitimate knowledge, and may even be opposed to it, I shall here use the terms 'powers' or 'capacities', as well as 'rights'.

I give below a preliminary outline of the *de facto* powers held by individuals and groups which are derived from the interrelation of three socio-political structures: the kolkhoz, the Party, and the Soviets. Each of these organisations has not only its own overlapping hierarchy of rights (in the statutory sense) but also specific *de facto* capacities accruing to the members of the organisation at different levels. An individual may have rights and powers in all three organisations at once, and furthermore, he or she may have capacities of action stemming from other systems, such as kinship or education. In this sense a collective farm is very much a community of multiplex relations. The complexity of the relations involved will only become apparent as the text of this book unfolds. In this chapter I describe only those powers deriving from the first three systems mentioned. In the period studied, they dominated over the others such as kinship or education. A discussion of the factors behind this domination is continued in later chapters, but here we should mention only the main reason: the structures of the kolkhoz, the Party and the Soviets are congruent and therefore can be said to form one interlocking system.

At the level of the local community it is the primary structure of the collective farm to which the other two organisations are linked, although in different ways (see below).

1. The lineal structure of production and administration

The Karl Marx kolkhoz in Selenga district in 1967 was an 'estate of production' organised on the 'lineal' model described in the previous chapter. The distinguishing feature of the 'lineal' system is a line of authority from the Chairman of the farm through brigadiers to the leaders of production teams within the brigades and down to the individual workers. Parallel to this, on the same territory, were the hierarchies of the Party and the Soviets, which we may term 'estates of administration' in Gluckman's phrase.

The Party organisation is directly attached to the farm rather than to the Rural Soviet, the latter being the lowest organ of the Soviet government, of the same territorial area as the farm but including non-kolkhoz personnel, that is workers for other organisations, such as teachers, nurses, geologists, etc. The Party in 1967 had one hundred members, and the Komsomol (youth branch)

119

had fifty-eight, these together being around one-fifth of the members of the farm aged over sixteen. The Party had a committee (*partkom*) of nine members at the all-kolkhoz level, led by its Secretary, called the *partorg*. It was sub-divided into branches at the brigade level, each with their own small committee, and further divided into cells within the production teams. The Party also had its own informal organisation within the local Soviet, the 'Party group' (*partiinaya gruppa*), responsible for overseeing policies.

All adults over eighteen living in the territory of the Rural Soviet are its constituents.[6] It is because, for historical reasons, the Rural Soviets coincide in territory with the present large farms, are administrated from the farm centres, and are financially dependent on them, that we can say that they are linked to the farms. In formal terms, however, the kolkhoz or sovkhoz is a constituent of the Soviet, not the other way around. Sometimes a Rural Soviet has more than one farm on its territory. In the case of the Selenga farm, the Rural Soviet (*sel'sovet* or *somonsovet*) had a constituency of 2,438 people, including children, of which 1,724 were members of the kolkhoz. The Rural Soviet had a council (*sessiya*) of twenty-five deputies. This body elected an executive committee of five, headed by a Chairman. The Rural Soviet had no sub-divisions at brigade level. However, it administered the People's Control organisation (twenty-five deputies and a Chairman) which was in operation both in the kolkhoz as a whole and in the brigades, where there were posts of a few members each.

In the Party and the Rural Soviet only two people, the Party Secretary and the Chairman of the *sel'sovet*, worked full-time in these organisations. All other members and activists were simultaneously occupied in the kolkhoz or in other jobs.

If the three organisations, kolkhoz, Party and Soviet, are mapped on to one another at the local level, we see that the Soviet has the widest constituency, the collective farm a smaller one within the Soviet, and the Party the smallest of all. With regard to 'vertical' links, the Party coincides with the kolkhoz at each of its levels, and all three organisations have executive committees with leaders at the top. The membership of these committees overlaps to a considerable extent (see Chapter 7). It is the very small number of people who hold office at this level who have the greatest concentration of *de facto* powers derived from their 'socio-political status' (if we restrict the reference of this term for the moment to the three organisations discussed here).

The Chairman of the kolkhoz

The dominant person in the Selenga kolkhoz in 1967 was quite clearly its Chairman, Dorzhiyev. The Chairmen of collective farms are elected by the general meeting for a period of three years, extendable for another three. However, Dorzhiyev had been in office since 1946 and continued in the post well into the 1970s. He was a member of the Party committee of the farm, and he was also a

Table 3.1. *The organisation of production and administration in Karl Marx kolkhoz, Selenga 1967*

Farm	Brigades	Production units	Workers
	Brigade 1	MTF 1	about 8 in team
		MTF 2	about 8 in team
		MTF 3	about 8 in team
		Field station	1 watchman, 1 mechanic
		Hay team	15–20
		Calf-raising units (about 4 *gurtas*)	2–3 per unit
	OTF 1	Lambing units (about 5 *otaras*)	3 per unit
		Other sheep units (about 6 *otaras*)	2 per unit
Kolkhoz	Brigade 2	MTF 4	about 8
		MTF 5	about 8
		Field station	1 watchman, 1 mechanic
		Hay team	15–20
		Calf-raising units (about 4 *gurtas*)	2–3 per unit
electric	OTF 2	Lambing units (about 5 *otaras*)	3 per unit
shearing		Other sheep units (about 6 *otaras*)	2 per unit
planning)	Brigade 3	Field station	1 watchman, 1 mechanic
		Hay team	15–20
		Calf-raising units (about 4 *gurtas*)	2–3 per unit
	OTF 3	Lambing units (about 5 *otaras*)	3 per unit
		Other sheep units (about 6 *otaras*)	2 per unit
	Brigade 4	MTF 6	about 8
		MTF 7	about 8
		MTF 8	about 8
		Field station	1 watchman, 1 mechanic
		Hay team	15–20
		Calf-raising units (about 4 *gurtas*)	2–3 per unit
	OTF 4	Lambing units (about 5 *otaras*)	3 per unit
		Other sheep units (about 6 *otaras*)	2 per unit
		KTF (horses)	2

(building
garage
workshop
mill

deputy to the Supreme Soviet of the Buryat ASSR and the Supreme Soviet of the USSR in the Soviet system. In the period 1959–65, when most kolkhoz Chairmen in Buryatiya were dismissed in order to make way for better educated cadres, Dorzhiyev remained at the job.[7]

Dorzhiyev was a man both energetic and physically dominant. He supervised the operations of the farm closely, travelling out to distant production units, surrounded by a little group of other officials. His house and its interior furnishings were no different from that of the other kolkhozniks. Dorzhiyev could always be distinguished from other kolkhozniks by his white trilby hat, his 'sign', his air of authority, and by the fact that he had a car at his disposal.

In a farm with a 'lineal' structure the Chairman's job is concerned with both production and administration. He is responsible for work discipline, issuing permits for travel, sick-leave, insurance and pensions, taking on and dismissing workers, and the honesty and quality of their work, as well as the directly productive activities of allotting products and money to different funds, obtaining inputs, fulfilling the plan of deliveries to the state, allocating machinery and workers to the brigades, and so on. These functions are shared with the kolkhoz committee, but the Chairman is not only formal head of this committee, with rights of *yedinonachaliye*, he is the only member of it without sectional interests. His *de facto* powers can therefore be far greater than those envisaged in the statutes. In fact, the possible sphere of power of the Chairman is so large and subject to so few *specific* institutional counterbalances that his personality accounts for most of what actual powers he wields. In the Aga National Okrug, for example, the Chairmen of farms were responsible for setting up the rural cultural club, although this was officially under the *sel'sovet*. As we shall see, the possible spheres of power of the *partorg* and the Chairman of the *sel'sovet* are also large and ill-defined, and the only way in which we can analyse the actual relations between these three is to look at the economic and political resources they have under their control. The specifically economic resources at the disposal of the Chairman of the farm are described in Chapter 4 section 4.

The Chairman of a kolkhoz is nominated for election by the district Party committee or by a higher-level branch of the Party (see Chapter 7). As we saw in Chapter 2 section 4, according to Leninist principles the head of an organisation is supposed to bear personal responsibility for its success or failure, and in theory he is answerable for mistakes to a greater extent than officials placed lower than him in the hierarchy. However, numerous cases described in a book about the activities of the People's Control in Buryatiya show that for run-of-the-mill negligence, disorganisation, and cheating offences it is much more common for lower officials and workers to be punished than the Chairman himself. This is the case even when the management has been asked to improve matters and has not done so, in other words when the fault can be directly attributed to the management of the farm.[8] But, although protected by the fact that the

Party and the People's Control have to work with and through the farm management, the Chairman is vulnerable to unpredictable check-ups and investigative
commissions. A Chairman can be fined, demoted or dismissed without any
public legal proceedings being instituted.

If the Chairman is relatively invulnerable to sanctions such as fines, in comparison to the people working under him in the farm, this is because of his
pivotal position between the kolkhoz and the district authorities. The Chairman
is often called upon to act *for* the district in relation to the farm-workers. However, the head of any enterprise, precisely because he represents both the farm to
the authorities and vice versa, is very vulnerable to moral sanctions. The publicity of his position makes this so. Moral sanctions, such as the various 'reprimands' mentioned in Chapter 2 section 4, operate through public admission of
fault. Usually this takes place at Party meetings (farm enterprise heads are
virtually always members of the Party) where the Chairman may be required to
admit before a room crowded with his subordinates to having been somehow in
the wrong. Occasionally the district or regional authorities may carry out the
same procedure in the even more public circumstances of a general meeting of
the kolkhoz. People told me that such sessions are dreaded more than fines, or
even prosecution in court (what is of major significance within the enterprise
may be a minor offence outside). At a public meeting, even if, as is sometimes
the case, everyone knows that the offending Chairman was acting in good faith,
or is otherwise being unfairly blamed, nevertheless some aura of guilt remains,
with a corresponding *involuntary* sense of shame.

In all collective farms, in deference to the 'democratic' charter, the Chairman
is legally not permitted to carry out administrative acts except by authority of
the managing committee (*pravleniye*) of the farm. This committee, elected,
according to the statutes, by the members of the farm, is in fact nominated for
election by the local Party organisation, one of whose members is the Chairman.
Thus, for example, the Chairman is not supposed to fine workers without first
having consulted the committee. But this rule is so often broken that most
people do not know of its existence. It conflicts, in any case, with the principle
of *yedinonachaliye* (single source of leadership), and it is not clear which of the
two rules would prevail in any given case in a court of law. A kolkhoz Chairman
has very extensive powers in respect of the ordinary members of his kolkhoz. In
the Stalinist period they were virtually unlimited: a Chairman could beat someone almost to death and people were too frightened to do anything about it.
This could no longer happen; the balance of power between administrators and
workers has shifted (see p. 304) and there is greater general confidence in
external Soviet law. However, it should not be forgotten that such events did
take place. The position of the Chairman 'above' that of the rest of the farm
members is demonstrated by the fact that during the 1950s, 1960s, and 1970s
the Chairman alone was issued with an internal passport allowing travel within
the Soviet Union. During the early part of this period, many Chairmen sent to

work on farms by higher organs as 'plenipotentiaries' (*upolnomochenniye*) did not even bother to join their farms as members.

It is the Chairman, above all, who is responsible for getting people to work. With luck, as in Selenga in the 1960s, he may manage the following: obtain enough money to pay wages, adjust work-norms so that people come out to work, use the income from products to raise wages, and so on. But the whole cycle may go the other way: if there is no money to pay wages kolkhozniks are unwilling to work, and if few people work there is less money for wages, and so on. With all the Chairman's powers, he cannot drive the whole workforce out to the fields with a gun. The sad Chairman in Abramov's story of rural life, trudging from house to house at silage-making time, listening to plausible excuse after excuse, is a case in point.[9] The situation virtually requires there to be 'non-official' ways of getting people to work (see Chapter 7). Even if it is this very 'un-official' network which is the cause of disapprobation of the Chairman on the part of higher authorities, its strength may be such that no one else sent to replace him can operate in his place. This appears to have been the case in Selenga in the early 1970s, where the authorities were forced reluctantly to reinstate Dorzhiyev as Chairman of the Selenga farm after he had been dismissed for alleged malpractices because no one else could do the job in his stead.

The committee (pravleniye) of the kolkhoz

In the Selenga farm this committee consisted of the Chairman, the Vice-Chairman, the Party Secretary, the brigadiers and the heads of some of the production teams. In the Barguzin farm in 1975 the *pravleniye* was made up of the Chairman and Vice-Chairman, the Party Secretary, and the chief specialists responsible for production sectors. Thus in both cases the majority of members of the committee represent sectional interests. Minutes of meetings in the Selenga farm suggest that most meetings take the form of reviews of activity by the various sectors, or proposals for their development, these reports being made by the section heads represented on the committee. Decisions are taken by an open majority vote. The Chairman does not have an extra vote, but since he is not only head of the committee but also represents the general meeting of kolkhozniks, which by statute has precedence over the *pravleniye*, his say has far more weight than that of anyone else. Since most decisions concern the allocation of central kolkhoz resources to the various sectional groups, and all sections are represented, as it were in competition with one another, only the Chairman, Vice-Chairman, and Party Secretary can be said to gain powers extra to those belonging to their offices from sitting on this committee.[10] None of the members of the committee has any direct say in the nomination of a Chairman for election, and the statutory period of his office can be easily overridden by superior authorities of the district or regional Party.

The lineal structure of production and administration

The Party Secretary

The *partorg* of the local Party organisation is elected for a period of three years, renewable indefinitely. He has the responsibility of overseeing the general policy decisions of the farm and checking that they are in accord with directives received from above. As with the Chairman, his possible sphere of activities is so wide that much depends on his personality as to what he actually does.

In the Selenga farm, the Party Secretary was in charge of all documentation, procedures and minutes of meetings. He said that the main part of his job consisted of personnel work: selecting people for jobs, encouraging and publicising good work, and issuing warnings to slackers. He maintained that the Party was the highest authority on every question, and indeed he thought that Party members could not be arrested by civil authorities unless they had first been asked to leave the Party. Nevertheless, he was not regarded with as much respect as the Chairman.

The Party Secretary is nominated by, and responsible to, his seniors in the Party at district level, but his success is judged largely on the ability of the farm to fulfil its production plan. The Party members within the farm are bound, according to notions of Party discipline, to obey his orders. But, in view of the fact that most of his activities will be concerned with raising productivity in the farm as a whole (organizing 'socialist competition', ordering an unpaid voluntary workday, and so on), he has relatively few resources at his command. Those he has are of two kinds, ideological and political, but the latter restricted to the sphere of career aspirations: it is the Party which controls placement in all official posts, and insofar as people wish to take up these posts the Party Secretary can use his power of recommendation as a resource. The Party has its subdivisions in the brigades, production teams, *sel'sovet* and organisations subject to the latter, but none of them have specific funds of their own. Members of the Party pay dues, a small percentage of their salaries, to the local branch, but it is not certain whether this money remains in the control of the *partorg*. Any other finances coming to the local branch are allocated from above, usually for specific purposes.

The Party sub-divisions are directly under the command of the Party Secretary, as is the *agitbrigad*, a band of about fifteen volunteers who engage in general propaganda, giving lectures, putting on films, and so on, in the distant parts of the kolkhoz. The Komsomol or youth branch, however, is somewhat separate, with its own hierarchy at district and regional levels. In some farms it is more or less dormant and of no direct help to the Party Secretary, while in others such as the Barguzin Karl Marx kolkhoz in 1975 it acts closely with the Party and its Secretary attends Party committee meetings. The *partorg*'s ability to influence decisions and activities of his own subordinates, let alone other people, is thus limited (a) by the fact that higher authorities may act directly without consulting him, and (b) by the lack of material resources under his single control.

The Chairman of the Rural Soviet

The *sel'sovet*, being the organ of the Soviet government, has responsibility for all civil administration. According to the 1968 'master constitution' (*primernoye polozheniye*) the *sel'sovet* should 'control' the enterprises on its territory in matters of planning, budgeting, payment of insurance, social security, fulfilment of delivery plans, use of land, allocation of private plots to citizens, building, transport and communications, construction of housing, education, culture, historical monuments, provision of employment, pensions, registration of births, marriages and deaths, passport control, identity and other documents, policing, law courts, and the organisation of vigilante groups. It is also charged with supervising trade, retail shops, restaurants, baths and wash-houses, the upkeep of villages, and religious activity. In effect, the *sel'sovet* can be asked to do almost anything which another organisation finds difficult. In the Selenga farm the Chairman of the *sel'sovet* said he was given various tasks which one might imagine were purely the concern of the kolkhoz, such as recruiting labour for harvesting, or unsnarling blockages in supplies. The 1968 law states that the organisations 'under' the *sel'sovet* must obey it.[11] This law was passed precisely because the Soviets lacked authority. However, it is doubtful if the 1968 law has changed very much. The reasons are not difficult to find. The *sel'sovet* is not even planned to have financial resources sufficient to carry out all of the tasks it is charged with; several of the organisations on its territory and 'under its control', such as the schools, hospitals, or trade organisations, are actually subordinate to their own higher authorities; around half of the budget of the *sel'sovet* comes directly from the collective farm or other enterprises on its territory, and it is by no means always the case that they pay in time or in the correct amount.

The *sel'sovet* operates through its deputies and a number of voluntary organisations (see Chapter 7). But people who take part in these are not freed from their productive work, except for committee meetings, nor, as far as I could gather, are they paid. The policies enacted are decided for the most part by the Party, which puts them forward through its 'groups' inside the Rural Soviet. The *sel'sovet* has few, or no, resources to offer its active members and it relies almost entirely on the goodwill of people who wish to take part in local government. It is interesting to note that deputies to Soviets (as in the case, according to my informants, of Party members) cannot be arrested without the written permission of the executive committee at the level they are accredited to.[12]

Brigades

In the Selenga farm in 1967 there were four complex production brigades, i.e.

126

four 'sub-farms', each with their own territories. Each brigade was supposed to make the best possible use of its land, and since the terrain was varied this meant that one brigade placed more emphasis on cattle-breeding (4th brigade), while another concentrated more on grain production (3rd brigade). Nevertheless, with the exception of the absence in the 3rd brigade of a milk-production unit (*molochno-tovarnaya ferma*, or MTF), all of the brigades engaged in every type of production (see Table 3.1).

Besides the production brigades, there was a 5th brigade, consisting of some ten men, set up for the purposes of building and repairs. This brigade was based at the farm centre, Tashir, as was the mechanical repairs workshop, the mill, the garages, and the fleets of cars, tractors, lorries and other agricultural machines.

Each brigade is led by a brigadier. In theory the brigadier is elected by the 'brigade soviet' (a committee elected from among the members of the brigade), but the distance between theory and practice can be seen from the fact that in many farms there are no brigade soviets. The brigadier is appointed from above. If there is a soviet, its members are appointed by the brigadier! In a 'lineal' system a brigadier has rights of *yedinonachaliye* and his orders can be reversed only by the Chairman or the *pravleniye*. In theory the Party or the *sel'sovet* can intervene, and can even suggest the dismissal of a brigadier, but in practice — at least in the Barguzin farm — these organisations operate through the Chairman of the farm committee, who may protect 'his' brigadier (e.g. see p. 361).

The brigadiers spend more time actually involved in the organisation of production than does the Chairman.[13] A brigadier in the Barguzin farm, Anatolii Khaptayevich Tadnayev, head of a sheep-products brigade, described his work as follows. He was responsible for distributing the members of his brigade among the tasks to be done (it was significant that he saw the *workers* as the fluid quantity, rather than adjusting the tasks to the workers available). He observed their work and reported on it, and he worked out the pay for each man in consultation with the book-keeper. An endless series of documents had to be filled in (orders, receipts, instructions, complaints, etc.). He saw to the receiving and distribution of production goods among the teams (*otary*): hay and other fodders, firewood, and maintenance and building materials. He organised political meetings at the 'red corner' (*krasnyy ugolok*) in the brigade centre at Karasun. Much of his time was spent in conveying information, in travelling from the kolkhoz centre to the brigade centre, and from there to the various herding camps (the *otary* are not, of course, on the telephone). The present brigades in the 'lineal' structure are as it were the geographical remnants of the previous farms, and the settled milk-production units within the brigades are 'survivals' of even earlier and smaller farms.

To a great extent this geographical structure is the result of a succession of political planning decisions rather than a 'natural' emergence of villages in environmentally suitable sites. In the *kolkhoz imeni Stalina* (now probably called by another name) in the Selenga district the earliest village communes of the 1920s were built on patrilineal kinship territories, but they were superseded by an amalgamated kolkhoz situated on a barren no-man's land, with the aim of eradicating lineage loyalties. This place had a completely insufficient water supply and later had to be moved.[14]

Brigades have a permanent membership — that is, workers who are attached as members of the various production units cannot leave the brigade of their own accord. They can only be moved by the central management. Apart from these 'attached' (*prikreplennyye*) workers, there is a pool of unskilled labour at the kolkhoz centre which can be sent out to the brigades by the management for specific jobs.

The great majority of all production is carried out by the brigades within their own territories, just as though they were separate farms. The only exceptions to this in the Selenga farm in 1967 were the grazing of the cattle of the 4th brigade on the land of the 3rd brigade (which had far fewer cattle), and the fact that the hay-fields were all in one place which did not belong to any of the brigades. Each brigade sent its hay-cutting team (*zveno*) to the common hay-meadows. The total hay was then assigned (*zakreplen*) to the four brigadiers in accordance with their needs, and then sub-divided and assigned within the brigades to the production units. Concentrated feed, bought from outside the farm, was distributed in the same way. A brigade is expected to produce enough of other fodders to feed its own herds, but if this does not happen the central farm management can request other brigades to contribute, or it can buy from outside the farm altogether.

A brigade should use its own labour to carry out the tasks which arise through the year on its land, but even here the brigadier can ask the management to obtain workers from other brigades. Thus, in the 3rd brigade, which has the largest grain fields, the brigadier regularly obtains outside labour for the harvest from brigades 1, 2 and 4. But at most other times of year, the pool of labour kept at the centre is sufficient to cope with variations in the amount of labour needed throughout the farm.

Probably the area in which brigades can most clearly be seen to have a separate existence is in planning. The farm as a whole has a five-year plan which is divided into yearly plans of increasing magnitude (see Chapter 4 section 4). Each brigade has an annual plan, divided into two parts, summer and winter. The brigade plans are drawn up by the economist and 'specialists' of the farm (agronomist, zoo technician, etc.) together with the brigadiers, and they are ratified at a meeting of the management (*pravleniye*) and Party committee. In effect, since all of the brigadiers sit on the management committee (*pravleniye*), this amounts to a matter of bargaining between the brigades, under the eye of the Chairman and Party officials, for the dividing up of the total to be produced by the farm. Once the brigade plan has been drawn up, the brigadier is responsible for allocating it among his various production teams.

The brigades in the Selenga Karl Marx therefore have only qualified independence as productive estates. Each brigade has its own territory, but is liable to have to allow other brigades to use it; a brigade has its own productive stock and fodder, but may have to give some to another unit if the central management requests; a brigade has its own labour, but again may have to relinquish some workers at busy periods. Mechanised equipment and transport — and it goes without saying electricity — are centrally allocated. The only machinery kept in the brigades is, where it exists, equipment for milking; ordinary tools are also kept there. A brigade does have its own plan and yearly accounts — but it does not have to make the accounts balance (*khozraschet*) (costs may be planned to exceed the money value of products in the brigade, and there is no charge made for production goods transferred from other brigades). All of these factors almost certainly erode the 'historical' consciousness of identity based on the prior existence of the brigade as a kolkhoz in its own right.

Production units within brigades

With the exception of the hay-cutting team (*zveno*) which consists of people sent out each year to harvest the common hay-meadows and at other times engaged on odd jobs, all of the production teams have their own territories, permanently attached labour, twice-yearly plans, their own accounts, and some instruments of production of their own. Nevertheless, their capacities for independent decision-making are severely limited.

Milk-production units (MTF — molochno-tovarnaya ferma)

MTF appears to be the general name given to cattle-herding units, even if subdivisions of the units are not directly engaged in milk production.

The Selenga farm in 1967 had eight MTFs, all of which were seasonally transhumant. In winter they were located in three villages, Shuluta (fourteen houses), Verkhne-Iro (thirteen houses), and Murtoy (thirteen houses), in the territories of the 4th, 1st and 2nd brigades respectively. In summer, the herds divided into eight and moved to the open pasture. Each of the eight units had around one hundred head of cows.

Besides the units directly engaged in milking, there were also in the farm as a whole eighteen calf-raising teams (*gurty* in Russian). These were scattered among the various MTFs and brigades. Twelve of them were engaged in raising young calves up to eighteen months or two years. The remaining six teams raised slightly older calves in separate herds of about forty to fifty head. The *gurty* consist of one or two families.

The tasks of individual workers, together with their annual production plans, are given out by the brigadier, not the head of the unit. Thus the brigadier would decide which workers would join the unit, who would replace them if they fell ill, would allocate the number of cows per milkmaid, and so on. In the nomadic *gurty* the brigadier, rather than the team-leader, decides where the cattle are to

129

graze, checks the pasture and watering facilities in advance, provides concentrates for weak animals, sets targets for weight-gain over the pasturing season, arranges to weigh the cattle regularly, and so on. The problems of an MTF team-leader are discussed in the local Selenga newspaper for 25 May 1967. The head of the Ekhe-Tsagan MTF of the sovkhoz 'Selenginskii', Lubsanov, complained to the newspaper that by this time of year (end of May) his milk team should have moved to summer quarters. But they could not move to the place allotted, Eladut, because ten herds of sheep were already there, and the grass was not yet thick. The kolkhoz should have sown more fodder crops to cope with such a situation. Now the milk cattle would probably suffer and the team would obtain lower yields.[15] It is clear from this that the work-team is at the mercy of the organisational powers of the brigadier, who is responsible for directing the movements of all herds, both cattle and sheep, on his territory. He in his turn may have little choice in the matter, since the kolkhoz management may have decided to over-stock with sheep. As we shall see later, the kolkhoz may not have much choice in this 'decision' either.

Sheep-production units (OTF – ovtso-tovarnaya ferma)

The Selenga Karl Marx farm has its total sheep production divided into forty-eight teams (*otara*). Each team, consisting of two or three families, looks after 700–800 head of sheep. The teams are divided among all four brigades and those *otaras* assigned to a single brigade constitute an OTF. The head of the OTF is the brigadier himself in many cases. Each *otara* has its own leader, subordinate to the head of the OTF (for a detailed description see Chapter 5 section 1).

Horse-production unit (KTF – konno-tovarnaya ferma)

The Selenga Karl Marx farm in 1967 also kept a large herd of horses, 458 head. These were tended by two or three herders, one of whom was the leader (*zaveduyushchyi*). In the 1950s the horse herds had been even larger and were highly nomadic: in summer they moved across the mountain pastures, the herdsmen rapidly travelling between camp-sites where there were temporary huts. The pastures were so high that even the sheep herds could not reach them. The whole unit had considerable freedom from the brigadier in the summer (May to September), but for the winter the horse herds returned to a place near the kolkhoz centre, and here the herdsmen had to keep a strict regime, since the herds had to be pastured in shifts, night and day.

Around 180 of the horses were kept for working purposes in the farm. The remaining 270 or so had no very clear productive function, especially since the farm had no horse products, neither milk nor meat nor horsehair, in its state delivery plan. I was told that the horses were kept for racing, and one can perhaps assume that they were milked in summer to make *kumiss* in the Mongolian tradition – though I saw no sign of this in May when milk would be plentiful. Kolkhozniks were not allowed to keep horses privately, and yet they are an essential means of transport. It is likely that the kolkhoz allotted some of its horses to individuals for their domestic use.

Hay-making team (senokosnoe sveno)
Each brigade of the Selenga farm in 1967 had a hay-making team consisting of some fifteen to twenty-five people with a leader (*zaveduyushchyi*). The members were permanently attached (*zakreplen*) to the team through the year. In the non-hay-making periods of the year they were assigned by the brigadiers to work as carriers, to load silage, to help the shepherds, and so on. They were responsible for the irrigation and manuring of the hay-fields. During the hay-cutting itself they were joined by as many other people as the brigadiers could muster. They lived for a month in a temporary shelter near the hay-meadows. For the rest of the year they lived in the kolkhoz centre or the brigade settlements.

Agricultural field stations (polevoy stan)
Each brigade had its own agricultural fields with a nearby threshing-floor and storage barns. The only people who lived permanently at the field stations were the watchmen of the storage barns. A mechanic was assigned in each brigade to maintain the threshing and grain-sorting machinery, but he did not live at the field station.

There were no permanent production teams within the brigades for agriculture: tractor-drivers and harvester-operators were assigned to each brigade by the central management as the times for the various agricultural operations came up. Much of the work seems to have been done by hand, by unskilled labour. During the sowing period, the field station at Talim-bulak in the 3rd brigade housed about sixty people in dormitories. At harvest-time the number at the station rose to about 160, plus some cooks. About fifty people remained behind for sorting the grain, and finally they too were assigned to other jobs, only the watchman being left behind. Milling of the grain was carried out centrally.

Thus in this kolkhoz the level of the 'production unit' in the agricultural and hay-making processes hardly existed. The hay-making teams had no permanently assigned meadows of their 'own', and the amount of the final production of hay each year was crucially dependent on outside labour drafted into the team.

To summarise this material on production units in the 'lineal' structure: they have a certain social, even historical, identity – articles appear in the press blaming or praising their work, and certain teams are famous in the district. Nevertheless, their autonomy is crucially limited by the following circumstances: production plans are determined from outside, usually at brigade level; team-leaders are by-passed by orders from brigadiers; production units are not mechanised, and they only engage in parts of any given cycle of production, and lastly, the units officially have no control over the disposal of their products. Even if certain of the products of a team remain with, or return to, that team (for example, lambs from one year entering the basic herd in the following year), the decision as to whether this would be the case is always taken outside the production unit itself.

Households

The household (*dvor*) has an anomalous position in the collective farm. The lowest level of the hierarchy of production is officially the individual worker, not the household. It is an ideological tenet that the household should no longer be a unit of production under socialism though it may remain as a unit of consumption.[16] However, the household is the unit which is allotted a limited smallholding for private production.

The household must consist of the kin (family) of a kolkhoznik, and it must have a recognised head. Non-kin may only become members of the household if all the adults in it request the *sel'sovet* that they be admitted. It is not permitted to belong to two households, nor is it allowed for the household to hire outside labour. A member may leave the household, taking his share of common property or money compensation for it, at the age of sixteen or over.

The household has possession, but not ownership, of its private land. It does, however, own in common its house or houses, barns, furniture, livestock and poultry, implements and constructions such as wells or irrigation channels on its plot. The household head is responsible for the distribution of assets among the members.[17] In the 1970s, a tax was paid on household property.

Individual members of the household are legally permitted to own clothes, footwear, and consumer items, their wages from the kolkhoz, and items they inherit or are given. These cannot pass into the property of the household unless the individual so desires.

In practice the distinction between household and individual property is a hazy one. The history of the private small-holding, the changes in rules regarding its size, the amount of tax, and ideological attitudes towards it, is a complex one, the more so when we consider how social status is reflected in differential use of the private plot and the nature of the social channels by which the product is distributed in the community. These matters have been made the subject of a separate chapter (Chapter 6).

Individual workers

Until 1969 and the publication of the new Provisional Statutes the status of 'kolkhoznik' was an inherited one. Children of farm members automatically became members themselves at the age of sixteen. Even up to 1979—80 it was difficult for Buryat kolkhozniks to leave the farm, because it was not until this date that they were issued with internal passports. It is this general situation which enables us to talk about the kolkhoz as a community through time. However, the status of 'kolkhoznik' is a complex matter, the practical implications of

132

which will only become clear gradually throughout this book. Here some brief preliminary details are provided.

Before issue of the internal passport, civil identity was defined in relation to membership of a household (*dvor*) belonging to the collective farm. One member, at least, of the household had to be a registered worker in the kolkhoz, issued with a 'work book' (*trudovaya knizhka*) as a form of identity. Even though civil identity is no longer defined in this way, pressure is put on people living in the kolkhoz to become registered workers. Under the laws against 'parasitism' an able-bodied person over the age of sixteen can be ordered to find a job within fifteen days, and an RSFSR law of 25 February 1970 provides for imprisonment or corrective labour of up to one year for people who refuse. It is easier for women not to take jobs, since housework and looking after children are recognised, or half-recognised, as alternatives to kolkhoz jobs. Once a member of the farm, invalids, people who leave for military service, education, service in Soviets and cooperatives, work in inter-kolkhoz organisations, and people who reach the retirement age retain their membership.[18] Permission is given by the kolkhoz managing committee (*pravleniye*) to leave for education, military service, and so on for specific periods of time.

A kolkhoznik can only leave the farm permanently and legally if the *pravleniye* (in fact, often the Chairman) gives permission. Marriage to someone living outside the farm or going to live with parents or children, is virtually the only count on which permission is easily given. By a 28 November 1951 decree of the USSR Council of Ministers, enterprises were forbidden to give work to kolkhozniks who did not have permission from their farms to take up other jobs. In fact this rule was often broken, especially in Siberia where there has long been a chronic shortage of labour. Before 1969 the farm members who could take up such opportunities were limited to those who were able to leave, for example, for military service, and make their own arrangements. Now, young people who do not become members are able to leave freely. Members who leave of their own accord are not given back their work books, and it is legally forbidden to employ someone who does not have this or another proof of identity. Furthermore, without his work book a person cannot claim the years worked in the kolkhoz towards his pension, and this is a disincentive to older people who might wish to leave without permission.

For the worker who wishes to leave to take up a job in a city, there is also the factor of the 'residence permit' (*propusk*). Cities have limits on the number of permits they can issue, and it is necessary for a citizen to show that he or she has work before a permit will be issued. One well-tried method of obtaining such a permit is marriage to someone who already has one. It is not difficult, on the other hand, to obtain a permit to live in another rural district. The result is that once registered in a kolkhoz many workers never leave, except perhaps to try their luck in another farm.

It is illegal to take another job at the same time as a kolkhoz one, unless permission is given by the *pravleniye*. This law is often disobeyed, particularly when collective farms are near towns where part-time work can be obtained. But Buryat collective farms are mostly situated miles from the nearest town, and 'moonlighting' is not a practical possibility.

However, since collective farms generally pay less than comparable enterprises, there has been a steady outflow of labour, especially among young people, who try to get themselves other work by hook or by crook. This process accelerated after 1969, with the result that farm managements attempt to hold on to those people who do register with them, especially those who have specialist qualifications. Thus cases are known of farms refusing young specialists permission to leave, even though there is no appropriate work for them in the farm and they have other jobs waiting for them elsewhere.[19]

It is difficult for the farm to dismiss a worker who wishes to stay. Persistent infringement of the rules of the kolkhoz, or failure to work over a long period, must be proved by the farm before it can dismiss someone. In the Soviet Union the attempt to ensure that the whole population has work is taken very seriously, and cases of appeal against wrongful dismissal are often decided in the worker's favour.[20] Thus, from the farm's point of view, the ranks of workers are swelled by numbers of people who do little work and who leave only if they decide that things are better in another farm. From the worker's point of view, the more conscientious he is and the more he improves his qualifications, the greater the pressure on him to stay.

An individual kolkhoznik cannot do much about punishments less than dismissal, since he has only the right to appeal to the *pravleniye* which itself is the body administering them in the first place.[21] Reprimands and fines are noted in the work book or in the individual account (*uchetnaya kartochka*). The great majority of such cases are decided inside the kolkhoz itself, without involving outside legal authorities. In 1967 the case came up in the Selenga Karl Marx kolkhoz of a herdsman who had lost several head of calves. In the somewhat stilted language of the minutes of a governing committee (*pravleniye*) meeting on 12 February 1967, the matter was described as follows:

Comrade Chagdurov, brigadier: Through the fault of Comrade Shkol the brigade lost nine head of calves. He was in charge of them and left them out in a storm.

Comrade Shkol, herder: I recognise my mistake, but claim that it was not entirely my fault, as there were other calves that did not die in the storm. These calves must have been weakened by illness, or they would not have died. However, I do recognise that calves should not be left out in a storm in any case.

Zoological technician Batorov: I was called in to examine the bodies of the calves. There were no signs of illness.

Comrade Shkol: I will pay for them.

Comrade Chagdurov: Comrade Shkol must pay for them. He must give as many of his own calves as he has, and must make the rest up in money. How much were the calves worth?

Zoological technician Batorov: 50 rubles each.

Comrade Shkol: I will give three calves now, and pay the rest when I can.

In relation to wages, fines such as these can be ruinous. The average monthly wage for a calf herdsman in Karl Marx kolkhoz, Selenga, in 1967 was 72 rubles.[22]

While an ordinary kolkhoznik can be fined or otherwise punished by the *pravleniye*, the Chairman of the farm, the members of the *pravleniye* and the Auditing Commission may only be brought to justice by the general meeting of kolkhozniks. Since this body has no other leadership and is hardly in a position to have information about misdemeanours by its officials unless these are very obvious, such action takes place very infrequently, and almost always at the instigation of some outside organisation such as the district auditors.

When a worker is accepted by the kolkhoz, he can claim certain benefits, but these are not rights because each farm negotiates them according to its own circumstances. In the Selenga farm he could claim a cow from the kolkhoz as his private property, and the use of a plot of land for growing hay or vegetables of 0.4 hectares. On this farm, workers were allowed, according to my informant, as much hay as they needed from the communal meadows for their private livestock, and private animals were pastured on communal land. In Barguzin the members were given large stacks of firewood free of charge. (I am not sure whether this applied to all members, or only to some, e.g. widows, disabled people, etc.) A member of the farm is entitled to housing, some of which is of high standard. Thus the house given to the chief veterinarian in the Barguzin kolkhoz, which also served as his surgery, was allotted free of charge and was a spacious dwelling by the standards of the farm. Other workers, such as shepherds who live on a succession of distant and less well-appointed *otaras*, can build, or have built, their own private houses. Often the farm will help them with loans, reasonably priced building materials, and labour. Probably most farms give kolkhozniks the use of one or two horses. Workers in Barguzin used some of the grain given in lieu of wages to make fodder for their private animals, and they were able to use the kolkhoz mill for this purpose (as far as I remember they did not pay for this service).

However, members of the kolkhoz cannot automatically make use of the natural resources of the farm territory. Mushroom-gathering and berry-picking are free, but a licence from the regional centre had to be obtained for hunting in the Barguzin farm.[23] Holders of licences are allotted special areas for hunting, and they are fined in the same way as non-licence-holders if they hunt outside them. I am not sure if a licence is required for fishing, but the practice is certainly regulated. The Barguzin rivers are rich in fish, many of which are species that come up the river as far as the kolkhoz to spawn and then go back to Lake Baikal. There are restricted fishing periods for this reason.

Workers with defined and permanent jobs, as opposed to those on general

135

duties, usually have their 'own' tools and other means of production. The quality of these makes a considerable difference to working conditions: a milk-maid with good cows can earn far more than her neighbour in the brigade with poor cows, and a tractor-driver with a new machine does far better, at least for a time, than his mate with a broken-down old tractor. Here, workers are very much at the mercy of the team-leader or the head of the garage. A worker's 'rights' to his tools are always conditional on the goodwill of the team-leader, just as the 'rights' of the production team itself are dependent on the brigadier.

Individual workers in production units are also in the hands of the team-leader as regards documentation of the work done. Out of laziness, semi-literacy, or spite, a team-leader may note down incorrectly the work done. Workers may also be prevented by the brigadier from excelling at work. A reporter asked the workers of a brigade what 'socialist obligations' they had taken on. The brigadier answered that no one had taken any, because how would he otherwise move them from project to project?[24]

A kolkhoznik who is a member of the Party may be asked to take on some particularly arduous job. However, since the point of this is quite largely ideo-logical, he or she is also more likely to be given help of various kinds (good machinery, supplies which arrive on time), to have the work correctly assessed, and to have successes publicised.

Thus, an ordinary kolkhoznik has rights of *use* in the productive estates of the farm; he is not concerned with administrative estates. Wages are related to productivity (see Chapter 5), but their level is decided upon centrally by the farm management or, as in the case of the Selenga farm, a special wages com-mission.[25] A kolkhoznik has the right to use productive assets only according to the orders (*naryad*) he is given by the brigadier. A milkmaid can be punished, for example, for consuming the milk of 'her' cows. In practice it is nearly impossible for the kolkhoz to guard against use of kolkhoz property without orders, and prosecutions are very rarely brought for such offences, either within the kolkhoz or outside it. In 1967, the Selenga farm had a series of incidents in which people were removing the skins and hooves of livestock killed by wolves for their own use. This was not defined as 'theft' but as a 'violation of work discipline', and it was decided to deal with the matter by making the brigadier personally respon-sible for any future occurrences. In practice, when people talk about 'theft' they mean stealing from one another. The practical capacity to make use of kolkhoz property can thus be seen as a matter of negotiation, depending on the position of the individual in the social hierarchy. The farm Chairman always has a kolkhoz car at his disposal. A blind eye may be turned to the violation of the hunting regulations. In these circumstances, it is worth noting a complete absence of private theft. The secretary of the *sel'sovet* in the Selenga farm smiled at my question and said that there had been no single case in the last ten years.

136

2. The 'specialist' structure of production and administration

The 'specialist' type of structure is an ideal type which did not exist in the farms I visited in 1967–75. However, the Karl Marx Collective in Barguzin came close to it. The effect was to eliminate the 'complex' (i.e. mixed) brigades based on the previous small kolkhoz territories. In the Barguzin farm there was a livestock sector, sub-divided into sheep, cattle and horse production teams (called brigades), an agricultural sector, divided into grain/root crop production and hay production teams, an accounting and book-keeping sector, and a building and transport sector (see Table 3.2). Machinery was placed in the hands of the production teams themselves, not held at the kolkhoz centre. The livestock sector was headed by a chief zoo technician and a chief veterinarian, the arable sector by a chief agronomist and a head engineer, and the planning and accounting sector by a chief economist and a chief book-keeper. All of these people had specialist higher education, and they were 'sent' to their present jobs by the Ministry of Agriculture. Brigadiers were subordinate to the chief specialists. It was the chief specialists who dominated the *pravleniye*.

Specialists do not necessarily become members of the farm, but may be employed by it for given periods on lease from the Ministries. In such cases the relation between the outside specialists and the Chairman becomes problematic, since the specialists are in the position of serving two masters. Since appointments and transfers are controlled by the Ministry via the district branches, it is

Chairman and chief economist of a kolkhoz at work in the farm office.

Table 3.2. *The organisation of production and administration in Karl Marx kolkhoz, Barguzin, 1974*

Farm	Specialised sectors (*otrasli*)	Specialised brigades	Production teams	Workers
Kolkhoz (economics book-keeping)	livestock			
	milk/ beef/ (pork)	MTF 1 (Bayangol)	2 milk units 1 beef unit? and other *gurty*	approx. 8 in each approx. 2 stockmen
		MTF 2 (Urzhil)	5 milk units 2 beef units and other *gurty* 1 pig unit	approx. 8 in each approx. 4 stockmen 2–3 workers
		MTF 3 (Soyol)	4 milk units 2 beef units and other *gurty* 2 sheep *otaras*	approx. 8 in each approx. 4 stockmen approx. 3 shepherds in each
	wool/ mutton/ (horsemeat)	OTF 1	5 lambing *otaras* 6 young sheep/ ram *otaras*	2–3 shepherds in each 2–3 shepherds in each
		OTF 2	13 *otaras*	2–3 shepherds in each
		OTF 3	1 horse unit 5 lambing *otaras* 9 young sheep/ ram *otaras* 1 horse unit	? 2–3 shepherds in each 2–3 shepherds in each ?
	hay (mutton)	Meadow amelioration brigade	1 hay meadow/ irrigation team 5 ram *otaras*	15 machine-operators 20 hay workers 2–3 shepherds in each
	agriculture			
	grains/ fodder	Tractor field brigade 1	1 team of machine-operators and field-workers	50–55 people altogether
		Tractor field brigade 2	1 team of machine-operators and field-workers	50–55 people altogether
	technical			
	building/ (eggs)	Building brigade	1 team 1 poultry unit	10 men 2 workers
	transport	Transport/repair brigade	1 team	34 drivers/mechanics

often the case that specialists have this line, rather than the interests of the farm, as their priority.

In a farm, such as the Barguzin Karl Marx, which retained vestiges of 'lineal' organisation, i.e. the presence of non-specialised administrators such as brigadiers and team-leaders, the possibilities of contradictory orders also multiply greatly. In a fully specialised farm, with only one kind of production on an 'industrial basis', this would not occur, because all officials would be specialists within the same sector (*otrasl'*).

Although we should perhaps not place too much weight on what was a quickly drawn sketch, the diagram drawn by a Chairman of the Barguzin farm (Figure 2.3) does show how internal relations are perceived. Placing himself at the top, though in rather under-emphasised writing, the Chairman divides the farm into three sectors: livestock, headed by the Vice-Chairman, arable farming directed by specialists, and accounting, also headed by its specialists. The Party Secretary is removed from farm matters altogether, placed at the bottom of the diagram where he has his own domain of Komsomol, Control, culture, etc. The farm Chairman's *de facto* powers seem to include direct authority over the brigadiers and team-leaders in livestock production, the most important sector of the farm, bypassing the Vice-Chairman and livestock specialists, and a single clear line of authority over the Party Secretary. In theory, of course, the Party Secretary should have an outside controlling function over the whole farm. We see from this diagram that even officially perceived relations between holders of important positions in the farm diverge from the textbook structure (see p. 103), and we shall see in later chapters how unofficial activities serve to transform what should be simple relations of domination into something quite different.

The practical powers of production brigades in the Barguzin farm with regard to 'property', i.e. *de facto* rights to land, materials and equipment, were not very different from those in Selenga. All powers were conditional on the place occupied in the hierarchy, but in this case the situation was more confused. Although the brigades (MTF, OTF, tractor-field teams, etc.) in Barguzin did not have their 'own' territories with boundaries, they did have areas where they habitually worked at different times of year. However, these were changed in the interval between my two visits with the reorganisation of the farm on a more specialised productive basis. It is not simply the farm management which carries out reorganisation of land-use; the district (*raion*) authorities may intervene directly to put specialisation plans into effect.[26] Although the kolkhoz has a legal right to claim compensation for land lost to other enterprises in this process, it cannot claim for production losses as a result of re-arrangement of its use of land. If the kolkhoz cannot make such claims, still less can the brigades and production teams. Nevertheless, the teams are organised on a self-accounting (*khozraschet*) basis, and they do have a greater control than in the Selenga farm over the means necessary for production. The significance of this will be discussed in the next chapter.

139

4

The collective farm economy

1. History and structure

At any one time the kolkhoz has a bounded territory which defines 'its' resources, and from which it must produce what is laid down in the plan-order. In order to understand the structural position of the kolkhoz with regard to the state (the higher Party, ministerial, and Soviet organs), it is necessary to investigate the nature of these boundaries and the degree of control, if any, which the farm has over them. Collective farms have increased hugely in size in the period of their existence, and it might be supposed that this has altered their position with regard to the state. We need to find out whether this is so or not. Does management of an enormously larger unit of resources put the farm officials in a more powerful position?

Table 4.1 shows that the number of collective farms in Buryatiya has been reduced from 1,068 in the days immediately after collectivisation to fewer than sixty at the present time. Since the area of land used by farms has gone up slightly from 3,229,000 hectares in 1940 to 3,806,000 hectares in 1975, it is clear that the size of the farms must have increased dramatically. The number of households per kolkhoz has gone up from an average of 110 in 1940 to an average of 377 in 1975.[1]

It would also be interesting to establish whether the increasing size of farms has affected the structure of their internal economic organisation. It will be suggested later in this chapter that, even if the administrative structure has changed very little, the quantitative changes in kolkhoz farming have had certain qualitative effects. The larger the size of a farm within limits, the greater the opportunities for economies of scale and the use of more complex and expensive plant. A much larger farm also has the possibility of establishing a more extended division of labour than a small farm: in theory, a large farm should provide enough work for each specialised worker to be engaged full time on his specific task. If this has occurred, it would be a possible hypothesis that social relations within the farm would have undergone some corresponding change, especially in the sphere of the 'political economy' of the farm. The present section describes

140

Table 4.1. *Number of state farms, collective farms, and machine—tractor stations in Buryat ASSR, 1923—62, and 1975*

	1923	1928	1932	1940	1950	1953	1958	1962	1975
State farms	—	1	3	3	4	4	8	42	94
Collective farms	5	46	1,068	525	396	303	229	81	59
Machine—tractor stations	—	—	7	30	36	38	28	—	—

Sources: Narodnoye khozyaistvo buryatskoi ASSR 1953, p. 19; 1976, p. 53.

aspects of the history of the Barguzin and Selenga farms as a means of elucidating the structural position of the farm vis-à-vis the state. The next section shows how this structure, combined with ideological pressures from the government, has created a new pattern of the social organisation of groups inside the farm.

The history of the Barguzin and Selenga farms shows that neither farm has had a decisive role in determining its own size. On the other hand, we can observe a quite systematic growth in their land area, such that at any given time they approximated to the average kolkhoz size for the republic. In this, though not in the absolute size of the farms, they were undoubtedly characteristic of Soviet collective farms in general. By 1967, both Selenga and Barguzin Karl Marx Collectives were the results of a series of amalgamations of smaller farms in their districts. The concrete administration of the mergers was carried out by the district (*raion*) Party committee, but the decisions to amalgamate were made at the Buryat ASSR level (which is hierarchically equivalent to the *oblast'*),[2] and, significantly, the timing of these decisions correlates with Soviet central government instructions ordering the amalgamation of collective farms.

However, since the farm has always been seen ideologically as a unit with its own identity — which the workers are encouraged to 'identify with' — the fact of amalgamations and other changes is disguised by claiming a line of earlier farms as the 'history' of the present farm. Thus, despite changes of name in the historical series of farms, it can be claimed by Soviet writers that progress has taken place within the given unit — while blurring over the fact that the 'unit' was something quite different at earlier periods. In fact it is the Party organisation which has provided continuity in the Bayangol community.[3] Originally, the farm in Barguzin designated as the ancestor of the present Karl Marx had only about 100 hectares of land. It now has 37,000 hectares. The other small farms, which were one by one absorbed, are now being forgotten, and the younger generation which never knew them in life does not even know their names — a process not unlike the 'structural amnesia' observed in certain patrilineal lineage systems.

One could suggest, in fact, that the kolkhoz 'system' is like the obverse of the classic patrilineal clan system (as observed, for example, among the pre-

141

revolutionary Khori Buryats).[4] In the clan system there is a process of fission into structurally similar units, and 'structural amnesia' applies to the higher level links which formerly joined the new separate clans. In the 'kolkhoz system' there is a process of fusion into structurally similar units, and 'amnesia' occurs in relation to the previously distinct components of the present whole.

The present *kolkhoz imeni Karla Marksa* in Barguzin district traces its history back to the founding of a commune called 'Arbijil' in 1927. ('Arbijil' is a Russification of a Buryat word, *ar'bajal*, meaning 'increase'.) This was not the first, nor the only, socialist-inspired organisation in the district. But its organiser, Buda Sangadievich Sangadiin, was later chosen as the leader of several amalgamated communes, and this is probably the reason why the 'Arbijil' is now reckoned to have been the foundation of communal agriculture in the area.

None of these early farms had unified territories of their own. They used the scattered fields and hay-meadows of their owners and this naturally made 'collective production' something of a euphemism. The 'collective' sheep were divided among the herdsmen. In the first year of the existence of 'Arbijil', Sangadiin asked the regional Party committee for a grant of land, and when they did not grant it simply took the land he had selected, a good patch of about 2,750 hectares at Khadyn-Bori near the Karalik irrigation system, with the permission only of the local land society.[5] At this period a certain independence from the Party was possible: a directive in 1929 for the *artel'* 'Soyuz' to join up

General view of Tashir, main settlement of the Karl Marx kolkhoz, Selenga, 1967. Dark areas are *ütüg*, hay-fields.

Table 4.2. *Collective organisations in Bayangol somon, Barguzin district, in 1929*

Name	No. of households	No. of people
Commune 'Arbijil'	35	136
Commune im. Lenina	47	184
Commune 'Soyol'	42	163
Commune 'Zorik'	23	91
Commune 'Pakhar'	18	50
Artel' im. Sakhyanovoi	12	51
Artel' 'Urzhil'	17	68
Artel' 'Chebukchen'	9	52
Artel' 'Ulan Ochin'	11	47
Artel' 'Toyaga' Karasun	11	37
Artel' 'Toyaga' Borogol	12	42
Artel' 'Soyuz' Baragkhan	12	60
Total in communes	165	624
Total in *artels*	84	357

Source: Ycgunov 1952, p. 91.

with the commune 'Soyul' was highly unpopular and resulted in a flow of members out of the commune.

In 1929 there were 799 households altogether in the Bayangol *somon* (which corresponds more or less with the present territory of the Karl Marx kolkhoz). Of these, 249 households, or 991 people, were members of communes or *artels*. The size of these organisations was very small, and it is probably not by accident that their range in size corresponds closely with the range in size of the pre-revolutionary settlements in Barguzin.[6] In some areas of Buryatiya the early communes were indeed simply transformations of the earlier settlements (*khoton*),[7] being defined primarily by kinship ties (see Chapter 5). But in Barguzin, where settlement was not so closely tied to kinship, the early communes appear to have been created voluntarily by people who believed in them. Thus, while they were of a size consistent with certain communal operations in the Buryat economy of that time, they did not include all of the households of any one given winter village. For example, the settlement of Karasun in the early 1900s had fifty-eight households, acording to Patkanov,[8] but the *artel'* 'Toyaga' at Karasun in the 1920s included only eleven households (see Table 4.2).

'Arbijil' was regarded as the most progressive of the communes and it provided leaders for the four others. Its internal organisation was truly communal: there was a total absence of individual property rights within the commune. Even domestic utensils and food were shared. Poor members who had contributed little property on entering nevertheless received just as much from the commune as the formerly rich members. Only the charismatic leadership of Sangadiin and a school-teacher called Tubchinov kept the tensions resulting

143

from this situation at bay. Clearly chosen as a 'model farm', the commune could hardly but prosper economically. It received credits of 13,000 rubles to build a cheese factory, a loan of 12,250 rubles, and a herd of Merino sheep.[9]

It is from the end of 1929 that we begin to see the emergence of the 'kolkhoz system', the combination of a specific external articulation with the state and an internal politico-economic organisation which lasted, essentially unchanged, from that date until the present.

Let us start with the external political relations. I shall approach this problem by looking at the historical sequence of events in the Barguzin Karl Marx farm. Very early on, from the first beginnings of collectivisation, we see the emergence of patterns which were to hold good at least until the end of the Stalinist period, if not beyond.

The first event was the purge of the leadership of the 'Arbijil' which took place in late 1929, only two years after the farm was founded. Certain prominent men, but not Sangadiin himself, were dismissed on the grounds that they were of 'kulak' origin and antagonistic to the needs of the poorer members. Shortly afterwards, Sangadiin himself was transferred to a bureaucratic post elsewhere in Buryatiya.

The removal of the local leadership of the farm was related politically to the arrival of the 'twenty-five thousanders' (*dvadtsatipyatitysyachniki*), volunteers from the urban working class sent to correct 'distortions in the Party line' in the farm. This movement, which was paralleled by a similar injection of outside leaders into collective farms in the 1950s (the *tridtsatitysyachniki*, the 'thirty-thousanders'), was of decisive importance for the political status of the farm as a unit in the Soviet economy, and it is worth considering it in some detail here.

The 'twenty-five thousanders' sent to the 'Arbijil' were two Russian factory-workers from Leningrad. The Leningrad shoe factory 'Skorokhod' (the 'Walk-Fast Shoe Factory') took over the patronage or leadership (*sheftstvo*) of the Buryat ASSR in 1930. This was part of the state policy of subordinating the peasantry as an economic category to the working class, of placing the peasantry directly under the leadership of the working class by means of Party activity. Tyushev, describing the movement in Buryatiya, writes:

The patronage of industrial enterprises and cities over individual rural districts, collective farms, national *oblast's* and republics, which became widespread during the first five-year plan, was one of the ways of bringing into actuality the Leninist teaching of the union of the working class and the peasantry, the leading role being taken by the working class and its vanguard – the Communist Party.[10]

What did this mean in practice? The factory's Party organisation proposed to send 100 workers to different rural enterprises in Buryatiya. When the campaign was announced 400 people volunteered. Letters they sent later from Buryatiya to the factory newspaper show that many of them were young people, including women, and they appear to have taken to their work in the Siberian countryside with ardent determination. Indeed, they operated in danger of their lives, and a few of them were killed by opponents of collectivisation.

One aim of the movement was to stiffen local resistance to openly anti-Soviet attacks directed by the lamas and the remnants of the aristocracy. But even more important was the 'correction of the ideological line' in the collectives themselves. This took on both a political and an economic aspect. Politically, it had to be ensured that the local leaders of the farms would subordinate themselves to the wishes of the higher Party and state organs, even if these were expressed indirectly as 'advice', 'confirmation' of elections, and so on. Economically, it had to be established that farms would fulfil the plan-orders for products and would deliver the planned amounts to the state buying agencies. The communes in the days of the New Economic Policy had operated in an economic context in which they had a great deal of choice as to how to dispose of their product. After collectivisation this was no longer the case: quite apart from the obligatory nature of the plan-orders themselves, the entire rural population was rapidly absorbed into the collectives during 1929–33, peasant markets were closed in many areas, trade in grain became illegal, and the economic space in which the communes had previously operated was fairly quickly closed off. It was still possible during these years for individual peasants to remain outside the collectives, existing in the penumbra of clandestine black markets, but this market-related activity was impossible on a general scale for the collectives themselves.[11] The 'twenty-five thousanders' were to see that the local leaders on the farms understood this point. By 1933 or so virtually all of the remaining individual farmers were collectivised.

During 1930 and the first part of 1931, the collectives in principle had to sell all their product to the state at prices much lower than those of the black market. This, together with the anger and despair of the large numbers of peasants collectivised against their will, resulted in huge losses of livestock and very low grain production. During 1930 the various kinds of collective in existence (communes, *artel's*, TOZy,[12] etc.) were reorganised internally on the uniform basis of the kolkhoz. All new collectives were set up on this same basis. The task of the 'twenty-five thousanders' was to preside over this reorganisation in the face of general confusion and antagonism between the various groups now forced to become members of the same kolkhoz. In October 1931 the Soviet government decided on the compromise of allowing the collectives access to rural markets, the 'kolkhoz markets', in order to dispose of their over-plan surplus. But almost immediately this was limited by a decree stating that collectives could sell their surplus only if all the collectives of the region had fulfilled their plan.[13] The fundamental message was clear: the collectives were to produce for destinations designated by the state.

In an ideological sense this was represented by the link between particular rural regions, known to produce certain raw materials, and the urban enterprises manufacturing products from these materials. This was the link between the

'Skorokhod' shoe factory and the Buryat ASSR. Thus, the factory newspaper, addressing the volunteers, wrote: 'Considering that Buryat-Mongolia is one of the bases for raw materials in the leather industry, we ask you always to remember the necessity of carrying out the tasks set by the Party in strengthening the livestock economy. In this way you will support our leather factory by providing for its essential material base.'[14] This link did not of course actually represent the economic function of Buryat products, since the great majority of these were things other than leather, but it provided an ideological rationalisation of the role of the 'twenty-five thousanders' in the countryside.

In Buryatiya, the young volunteers from the factory were immediately 'voted' into leading positions in rural institutions. It seems not to have mattered very much whether these positions were officially political (i.e. positions in the Party, the Komsomol, or the Soviets) or officially economic (i.e. positions in the collective farms themselves). In the 'Arbijil' one of the volunteers, a man called Zhigarev, was made Vice-Chairman, and then, when Sangadiin was transferred, Chairman of the collective. The other, a girl called Gavrilova, was elected Secretary of the Komsomol. What can these people have known about the organisation of what was still semi-nomadic sheep-farming in Mongol-speaking Siberia? It is clear that their real role was to replace local Communist leadership. In these circumstances the factory-worker volunteers came into direct opposition with the existing officials of the locality. The way in which they established predominance — despite the total absence of a support base among the Buryat herdsmen themselves — is very instructive. It is in fact a paradigm of the structural relation between the kolkhoz and the organs of the state.

An example is the case of the volunteer Tsarev, who was sent to the Kaban region of Buryatiya. He wrote to the factory newspaper:

For the past two months we have been experiencing great difficulty in correcting the mistakes made during collectivisation. The deviationists have been terrifying the poor and the working people in our region. Using administrative methods they have 'de-kulakised' [i.e. expropriated the property of] even middling herdsmen . . . There was a case of such illegitimate 'de-kulakisation' in Khandalay village, and when I protested the deviationist tried to threaten the herdsmen, even going so far as to wave a revolver at him. The deviationist, the head of the collective, Burilov, threatened me too, and it was not until I put the matter to the bureau of the *raikom* [District Party Committee] that the matter was regularised and Burilov dismissed from work.[15]

As the author of an article on the 'twenty-five thousanders' observes, both Tsarev's predicament and his solution of the problem were entirely typical. 'They [the volunteers] were successful when they carried out their work under the leadership (*rukovodstvo*) and with the help of the Party organisation. In a difficult moment Tsarev appealed to the *raikom* for help.'[16] It is significant that Tsarev did not appeal for help to the local Party branch — these people might well have been in opposition to him themselves — but to the next higher organ, the *raikom*.

146

Jerry Hough has shown in his classic study[17] how disputes between different institutions at the same level are resolved. In a disagreement between the *raikom* and a Soviet or ministerial institution at the same district level, appeal is made to the level above, the *obkom* (*oblast'* Party committee). This is how the 'leadership' of the Party is made manifest: at any one level the Party Secretary cannot force the enterprise head to do his bidding, but he can appeal to higher Party organs which can then order the active members at his level (which would normally include the head of the enterprise) to carry out the required order. Because the Party has control over appointments and dismissals for all important posts, such an appeal to the higher organs frequently has the effect of ensuring the removal of the existing enterprise head. A new man is installed who is identified precisely with the carrying out of the policy supported at the higher level. This matter will be discussed in more detail later, but for the moment the outlines are clear: if he is a Communist, the local leader is forced to obey the commands of his Party superiors even if they are directly against his interests, as he understands them, as enterprise head. If he is not a Communist he may simply be removed (*snyali ego*) in virtue of the Party's control over personnel.

Many decisions do not involve local opinion at all and are simply transmitted from above (the *oblast'*) to below (the enterprise), bypassing the *raion* as a decision-making point. This is what occurred in Barguzin, shortly after the arrival of Zhigarev and Gavrilova, when it was decided to amalgamate the 'Arbijil' with the 'Soyol', the 'Zorik', and the 'imeni Lenina' communes. The united farm, called 'Arbijil', was organised on the kolkhoz or *artel'* principle on the same lines as all others in the USSR. After a certain time, Sangadiin was brought back to be Chairman. Perhaps the Leningrad workers were better politicians than they were farmers. At any rate, they were recalled to the city in 1932. The 'Arbijil' now had 155 households (268 people), a sown area of 466 hectares, 1,359 head of cattle, 1,571 head of sheep, 40 pigs, and 208 horses.[18] At the end of the same year Sangadiin was again sent off to other work, this time in the Kyakhta region. In none of this can the ordinary members have had any say at all.

The disappearance of Sangadiin was disastrous. The next leaders, deliberately, according to the local historian Dymbrenov, caused the destruction of the 1932–3 fodder crop, and most of the collective herd perished as a result.[19] After another purge, the kolkhoz gathered itself together and proceeded fairly successfully through the 1930s. This may have been due at least partly to the fact that no further organisational changes were implemented until 1940. However, there were two changes of name: the 'Arbijil' became the *kolkhoz imeni B. Sangadiin* in 1934 after the death of Sangadiin, and was changed to *kolkhoz imeni Karla Marksa* in 1937.

It was during the 1930s that Party 'traditions' of selecting leading cadres for the collective farms became established. Each Party organ has a list of important posts, its *nomenklatura*, for which it has the responsibility of 'confirming' appointments and dismissals. Any given post may be on the *nomenklatura* of more than one Party organ, and indeed some Ministries also have lists as well. It appears from the Buryat data that the *obkom*, i.e. the level of the Buryat ASSR, concerned itself directly with the appointment of kolkhoz Chairmen, and indirectly with the appointment of other cadres (accountants, brigadiers, etc.). Cadres were 'mobilised', 'moved forward' (*vydvinut'*), 'sent' (*napravlyat'*), 'selected' (*vydelit'*), and 'expelled' (*iskluchit'*), and it is clear from the following descriptions that in practice the role of the Party went far beyond the mere 'confirmation' of cadres in office.

In April 1931 the Bureau of the *obkom* listened to a paper 'On the progress of collectivisation and preparations for the spring sowing'. In the decision which was taken it was proposed to all the *aimak* [*raion*] Party committees that they should send to the collective farms, within three days, a total of one hundred book-keepers for permanent employment.[20]

The local Party organisations played an important part in supplying the collective farms with leading cadres. Thus, in August 1933, the political section of the Selenga machine—tractor Station sent (*napravlyal*) five people to be Chairmen of collective farms.[21]

The political departments of the Bokhan, Tunka, Bayandai and other machine—tractor Stations succeeded in moving forward (*vydvigat'*) women into positions of leadership. Thus, the Women's Organiser (*zhenorg*) of the Bokhan MTS, V.I. Khogoeva, carried out a great deal of work among women. On her initiative ten women were sent on courses for book-keepers. In the Shunta kolkhoz, she sought out Elena Ikhenova, a milkmaid, in whom organisational potentialities were discovered. On Khogoeva's suggestion, Ikhenova was moved forward to be head of the Milk-Production Team. She took to the work with enthusiasm, and her team became one of the best in the district.

Khogoeva then turned her attention to Tat'yana Prokop'yeva. Khogoeva succeeded in having her moved forward (*vidvinuli*) as Chairman of the farm. Prokop'yeva was summoned to the political department. At first she refused, but the political department convinced her, and promised that they would help her to work. She agreed.[22]

The *oblast'* committee of the Party paid much attention to the quality of the leaders in collective farms. They organised in 1932–3 a check on the leaders in a series of districts. The check (*proverka*) showed that in some kolkhozy there were alien class elements, who were trying to undo the work of the farm from inside. Thus in the Bokhan *aimak*, as a result of the purge from 1 December 1932 to 15 February 1933, 385 kulaks were expelled from the collective farms, and of them 124 had been in responsible positions, such as Chairman, brigadier, accountant, or head of a production team.[23]

The *obkom* gave a strict order to . . . all *aimak* Party committees and *aimak* Soviet organs [i.e. *raion* level organs] to make an inspection immediately of the total leadership of the collective farms, to carry out a 'self-cleansing' (*samochistka*) operation of the kolkhoz activists revealing the disguised alien elements, and to move forward in their place trusted activist-*udarniks* [shock-workers] from the poor and middle classes, and to put an end to the harmful practice of moving around and dismissing Chairmen of farms without the authority of the NKZ [People's Commissariat of Agriculture] of the Buryat ASSR.[24]

In 1940 the Karl Marx kolkhoz was amalgamated with the neighbouring 'Urzhil', a medium-sized farm of seventy-nine households. These two farms were approximately equal in livestock per kolkhoznik, but the 'Urzhil' was significantly better off in land (79.74 hectares per household, as opposed to 63.0 hectares in Karl Marx). The amalgamation therefore was to the benefit of Karl Marx. In 1941, after the joining up, there were 11.8 head of cattle per household in the collective — a figure not remarkably better than the 9.8 per household in the founding year of 1927 — but the amount of sown land had greatly increased, from 2.8 hectares per household in 1930 to 10.4 hectares in 1941.[25]

The next amalgamation, in 1954, under the direct influence of Khrushchev's instructions on the unification of agricultural enterprises, does not seem to have gone so smoothly. Again, the Karl Marx swallowed one of its neighbours, the *kolkhoz imeni Kalinina*. We know that the amalgamation took place on the initiative of district Party officials who were themselves obeying the instructions of the September Plenary Session of the Central Committee of the CP USSR 'On measures for the further development of agriculture in the USSR'.[26] The matter was fiercely debated at kolkhoz meetings in the two farms. Each farm had established its own work-norms per 'labour-day' (now a cash wage with a minimum level, see Chapter 5 section 2), but low work-norms were preferable only if the farm could pay well for labour-days. The amalgamation in 1954 was evidently to the long-term benefit of Karl Marx, since that kolkhoz had too many animals for the pasture and hay-meadow available, and it also had too few workers for the size of herds present. Kalinin, on the other hand, had much unused pasture and a lower work-load for its members. For the individual members the advantages and disadvantages of the amalgamation were much less clear: in terms of dividends the Kalinin workers probably gained at the expense of their neighbours, since the Karl Marx, as the most successful farm in the district, almost certainly paid its workers at better rates per labour-day than the Kalinin, but on the other hand the absolute amount of work to be performed after joining up with the Karl Marx was greater. At any rate it is clear that the amalgamation cannot have benefited both sets of workers, since a new level of work-norms was established in the unified farm. The main effect must have been to create uncertainty among the kolkhozniks — particularly since the rate at which the labour-day was paid in the new farm could not be known until the end of the year.

It is not difficult to understand the reasons which might impel regional authorities to make this kind of amalgamation in a planned economy. In a capitalist economy, if farm X has good summer pasture and farm Y has good arable land the two farms can exchange the use of land or the products themselves via the market. In a planned economy this cannot generally be done, and a merger, which combines a balancing of factors of production with the possible benefits of economies of scale, seems the obvious answer.

However, not all amalgamations of kolkhozy in Buryatiya resulted immediately in a reorganisation of production. The Selenga Karl Marx farm, when I visited it in 1967, consisted of four production brigades, each of which still carried out its own mixed economy. There is evidence that economies of scale occurred primarily in the arable, rather than the livestock, sectors of the farm (see section 2 below). But even in the arable sector production was carried out in the four brigades separately in 1967.

In the Barguzin Karl Marx farm, however, the merger with Kalinin was followed by an immediate reorganisation of production. The two farms were no longer recognisable as separate units. The total of six agricultural brigades and thirteen livestock brigades of the two farms was reduced to four and eight respectively. However, it should be noted that this amounts to a reorganisation of the productive process, not an alteration in the structure of production: the farm was still structured into brigades, sub-sections or brigades (*fermy, stany*), and sub-divisions of these sections, the same relationship was maintained between these units and the Party hierarchy, and orders were transmitted in the same way as before.

The merger with Kalinin is also interesting with regard to the position of the farm officials. Clearly, one of the two Chairmen had to give way. The head of Kalinin was demoted to brigadier of the building brigade in the new joint farm. Ten full-time officials were reduced to working jobs, and a total of 6,000 labour-days of administration per year were saved.[27] This is interesting because, according to certain economic theory relating to capitalist firms, mergers whose rationale is the introduction of economies of scale are normally accompanied by an increased division of labour and this in itself requires greater administrative supervision than before. In the new, larger collective farm, however, administration was drastically cut back. We can only suppose that the reasons were unrelated to the economy of the farm − or that the administrators had previously been under-employed.

The now much reduced leadership made a dismal failure in organisation of the new farm; the people would not come out to work. The leading officials were removed at the next general meeting, and a new chairman. G.B. Tsydenov, a nominee of the district Party committee, was duly elected as head of the farm. This was part of a general move to strengthen kolkhoz discipline after the mergers which swept the country in the mid-1950s. The 'thirty-thousander' (*tridtsatitysyachniki*) movement, in which reliable cadres (often not farmers at all) were sent as Chairmen to virtually all Buryat collective farms, recalls the earlier 'twenty-five thousander' movement, although there was no attempt this time to make direct links between urban and rural enterprises. Tsydenov personally went round to the houses of all those who were refusing to work. 'He helped many to realise their mistakes, to overcome the limi-

150

tations which had got in the way of their active participation in communal work.'[28]

I have come across only one case in Buryatiya of refusal to comply with the administrative mergers. This occurred in the utterly remote forested North Buryat district, where, again in 1954, it was decided to merge the *kolkhoz im. Budennogo* at Taksimo with the even more desolate kolkhoz *Put' k kommunizmu* situated some 400 kilometres up the River Amalat. The Taksimo people refused to go to live in the infertile and bleak Amalat region. But this cannot be seen as a victory for self-management, since the *kolkhoz im. Budennogo* was disbanded all the same. The result was simply a collapse of collective enterprise, and in 1966 the question of 'socialised' work for the inhabitants of Taksimo had still not been decided. The entire female population of the village supported the community by individual small-holdings.[29]

It is interesting to discuss this kind of data in relation to Charles Bettelheim's theory, in his early book *The Transition to Socialist Economy*. Here he suggests that in a socialist economy the form and level of 'ownership' of the means of production, i.e. the level at which the collective farm is located, should correspond with the degree of 'socialisation of the productive forces', i.e. the extent to which the inputs and products of the farm emerge from and reach a wide social community.[30] In other words, Bettelheim is suggesting that the 'development of the forces of production' can be identified with increasingly 'social' inputs, for example utilisation of chemical fertilisers from industry rather than the dung of one's own cows, and with an ever more 'social' sphere of disposal of outputs. He recognises that, according to these criteria, the 'level of ownership' in Soviet collective farms (in effect, the size of the farm) has advanced 'beyond' its proper level of correspondence with the degree of development of the forces of production (the latter in any case has been artificially held back by the existence of individual peasant plots). But he suggests that this was a necessary step in order to be able to introduce new technology inappropriate in small farms, and in order to create opportunities for full employment for the farm-workers. In essence, he is making the classic proposition that in a socialist economy it is possible to reach a state in which forces and relations of production are not in contradiction with one another. Several comments could be made about this theory in the light of the actually existing socialism of the USSR. But firstly, any anthropologist would ask the question: how is it possible to identify the development of the 'forces of production' with the extent of their 'social' range? The meat from Buryat livestock production, even in the days of the semi-nomadic household economy, probably reached Western Europe;[31] and even in a 'stone age' economy items essential in production are traded from far away.[32]

The Buryat material, with its differential level of mechanisation between the arable and livestock sectors, suggests that it would have been difficult, if not impossible, for planners to establish any *generally* valid criteria for the level at which farms should be established — especially if they were to base their judgement on assessment of the 'development of the forces of production'. This is because, quite apart from the theoretical difficulties involved, in practice the level of development of the 'forces of production' in any conventional definition was controlled centrally by the regulation of the network of machine–tractor stations (MTS).

Machine–tractor stations were set up in Buryatiya, as elsewhere in the Soviet Union, at the beginning of the 1930s. They contained all of the advanced technology allocated to the region, and farms could use the machinery only if they paid fairly heavily in grain. Even Dymbrenov, whose view of the history of the Karl Marx farm in Barguzin is normally rosy, points out that the local Kuitun MTS was both unable and unwilling to clear the farm's hay-meadows or shrubs, nor would it help in drainage, with the result that through the 1950s the fodder situation of the livestock worsened steadily.[33] The machinery of the MTS, particularly tractors, was such a vital element in any farm's ability to fulfil its plan that the stations themselves could naturally become instruments of control by the state. But the control was not a matter simply of allocation of vital technological resources. The MTS were the bases for Party Secretaries or commissars who were able to intervene directly in the decision-making and even the day-to-day running of the kolkhozy in their area. This system lasted until 1958, when the stations were abolished and MTS machinery was sold to the kolkhozy. From this time onwards the collective farms were able to manage their own machinery, as the state farms had done all along, and the Party organ to which the farm was directly responsible became the *raikom* (district committee), which had previously supervised several MTS. Poor farms could not afford the cost of buying and maintaining the machinery and many fell into debt. The abolishing of the MTS was therefore not a positive move in all cases, nor did it affect the structural position of the farm vis-à-vis the state: the farm still was obliged to fulfil plans set by the Ministry of Agriculture and its performance continued to be directed and regulated by the Party.

The pattern which emerges is thus one of an enduring organisational structure operating with a changing set of material resources. The changes were essentially outside the control of the people 'in charge' of the structure. This can be illustrated by a further example from the history of the Barguzin farm. Up to the 1970s all changes in the land resources of the farm had been in the direction of their increase. In 1967, the area of the farm, which had been 19,282 hectares in 1935, had grown to 37,000 hectares. But shortly afterwards the farm was required to give up some land. A forestry station was set up on the River Ina at Chilir. The workers in the camp were almost entirely people sent from other parts of the Soviet Union, and the timber they felled came from the eastern hills outside the farm boundary. Nevertheless, the forestry station itself, together with its workshops and plots of private land, grew rapidly to take up a good section of the farm hay-meadows. In theory, state-run organisations such as forestry stations are not allowed to take over useful agricultural land from farms, and furthermore, they are supposed to pay compensation for any land they do take. It is not clear if compensation was paid in this case. The matter can be presumed to have been an issue of debate, since the book of kolkhoz statutes given to me by the farm Chairman had been underlined heavily in ink at the paragraphs referring to compensation. Re-named 'Yubileiny' after the jubilee on the fiftieth anniversary of the Revolution, by 1974 the forestry station was already bigger than the central village. Its population of 2,000 people was double that of Bayangol. In 1973 the handover of land was administratively ratified by the formation of a separate *sel'sovet* for the lumber station. The Bayangol *sel'sovet*, which had included both kolkhoz and forestry station, was divided into the Bayangol *sel'sovet* on the one hand, and the Yubileiny *sel'sovet* on the other.[34]

The advent of the forestry camp raises the more general issue of the control by the kolkhoz of its own workforce.[35] During the Stalinist period it was a widespread practice to use kolkhozniks for labour in the forestry camps of Siberia. In 1974 I was told specifically that the Yubileiny lumber camp did not 'like' to use kolkhoz labour and that the workers in the two organisations were separate. However, the existence of the camp was not even mentioned to me in 1967 and it is possible that the Karl Marx farm had supplied labour before that time.

In the Stalinist period collective farms had both more and less control of their labour supply than they do today. On the one hand, until the change in the kolkhoz statutes of 1969, all children born in the farm automatically became members at the age of sixteen unless they managed somehow to get away. On the other hand, farms, like other institutions, could be obliged to provide labour for purposes quite outside their control (forestry, road-building, and so on). They were also obliged to accept labour sent to them from outside, and this applied not only to small numbers of convicted exiles, or people from ethnic groups punished by Stalin, such as the Tatars in the Buryat farms, but also to substantial movements designed to re-populate the countryside. In Buryatiya, for example, the 1953 Plenum of the Central Committee called for an improvement of agricultural production, and accordingly some 7,500 people followed the 'call' (*prizyv*) of the Party and went to work in the countryside.[36] In 1960 a further 500 specialists, 100 technicians and engineers, and 2,000 young people from Komsomol were sent to Buryat farms.[37] We may easily imagine that this situation, however much desired by the collective farms, was not much under their control.

In the 1980s, a collective farm would probably not have labour either added or deducted without consultation. But, on the other hand, young people born in the kolkhoz are now free not to join it if they can find alternative work. Although applications to work outside are to some extent controlled, there are large areas of the Soviet Union (including some areas of Buryatiya) where collective farms are being seriously depopulated.

There thus seems no reason, arising from control of resources, to regard the kolkhoz (the 'enterprise') as a privileged level in the hierarchy of institutions.

153

Brigades, work-teams, households and even individuals also have areas of limited autonomy and can dispose of 'their' means of production in a limited variety of ways. The decisions taken at district, regional, or republic levels would have to be scrutinised very carefully before it could be shown that the enterprise level actually holds rights which are significantly greater, or more enforceable, as Bettelheim claims, than those of higher levels. Available policy documents suggest that, even if collective farms are seen to have reached an 'optimum' size and are no longer subject to mergers (though this is not sure), they are likely to become increasingly involved in two kinds of even larger production unit: the inter-enterprise union (*mezhkhozyaistevnnoye predpriyatiye*) and the agrarian-industrial enterprise (*agrarno-promyshlennyye predpriyatiya*).[38]

The number of inter-enterprise unions in Buryatiya has increased dramatically in the last ten years and virtually all collective farms are now shareholders in at least one of them (Table 4.3). In the inter-enterprise union, the kolkhozy and sovkhozy of a district contribute raw materials, finance, and often labour to a permanent organisation which has the purpose of fulfilling some special function on a scale larger than that which any of the individual farms can manage. The greatest number of unions are concerned with building, but others fatten livestock, operate as lumber camps, make fodder concentrates, manufacture products such as cheese or leather, conduct artificial insemination, and so on. The products are distributed among the farms, or sold on their behalf, according to the number of shares each farm has in the union. Farms 'volunteer' to join such unions, but the fact that *all* farms are members of at least one suggests that pressure is put on them — for example, to have building work carried out by the union rather than do it themselves.

The inter-enterprise unions are described in the Soviet literature as examples of 'horizontal cooperation'. However, they are run on principles of *yedinona-chaliye* (one-man management), and this implies that the resources which farms commit to the unions are thereby removed from their control. Furthermore, there also exists a yet higher level of 'cooperation'. There is a category of boards or trusts whose job it is to direct the activity of the inter-enterprise unions.[39] In Buryatiya I have been able to discover the existence of only one such board, the Buryat Republic Organisation for the Administration of the Inter-Kolkhoz Buildings Organisations (*Burmezhkolkhozstroy*), but others may well be present. *Burmezhkolkhozstroy* is not simply concerned with administration. It carries out work itself at the 'meta-level' of coordination between the unions: it has therefore a road-building department, an experimental projects department, a factory for building materials, its own fully mechanised work-team and so on.[40]

An important political issue has been the method of Party supervision of the workers assigned to teams and units set up by the inter-enterprise unions. According to Miller, a general solution was found in the model of the Party structure based on the Gor'ky Automobile Plant, the subject of a special Central Committee decree in 1976. In this arrangement the Secretaries of the primary

Table 4.3. *Inter-enterprise organisation in the agriculture of the Buryat ASSR, 1965–75*

	1965	1970	1971	1972	1973	1974	1975
Number of inter-enterprise organisations	4	12	15	18	19	23	24
Shareholders*							
State farms	—	—	16	25	37	54	65
Collective farms	16	63	64	76	68	90	89

*Some farms are shareholders in more than one organisation.
Source: Narodnoye khozyaistvo Buryatskoi ASSR 1976, p. 120.

Party organisations of the participating farms and organisations form a council of Secretaries, which meets periodically to coordinate Party work. These councils have only advisory status, but since they are directly subordinate to the Party *raikom* they can be seen as an intermediary between the farms and the *raikom*. By the late 1970s there had been some retreat from Brezhnev's earlier policy of encouraging inter-enterprise associations without reservation, and there is debate on the form which such unions should ultimately take,[41] but the general line is still that integration is the 'high road' of agricultural development. It should, however, be strictly regulated from above:

Even if a group of kolkhozy and sovkhozy have their own (in the case of sovkhozy only relatively their own, of course) accumulation of money funds for the creation of some joint complex, nevertheless the realisation of these financial means in a functioning enterprise depends on whether the state makes possible the materialisation of these funds in building materials, machinery, implements, etc. . . . In other words, the state should not allow the position to arise in which this or that kolkhoz or sovkhoz, under the pretext of moving to the new form of organisation, curtails the production of sectors of agriculture which are necessary to society . . . [42]

The kolkhoz is not, therefore, at the apex of a hierarchy of production. Increasingly it functions as a constituent in larger-scale enterprises conducting essential work in the maintenance of a material base for the collective farm's own production. In 1974 the Karl Marx farm in Barguzin had twenty-three building and reconstruction projects on its books (Table 4.4). Of these, twelve were due to be carried out by various inter-enterprise unions, and eleven by the kolkhoz itself. Fifteen of the projects were to be funded by outside organisations, and eight by the kolkhoz. Only five projects were completely under the control of the farm, i.e. to be funded and built by it.

The second type of large-scale production enterprise, the agrarian-industrial union, is described in Soviet writing as an example of 'vertical cooperation'. The idea is that a series of farms join up with workshops and factories to make a

Table 4.4. *Construction projects on the books of Karl Marx kolkhoz, Barguzin, in 1974*

Construction project	Timing		Finance	Body carrying out work
	Begin	End		
1 'Dom Kul'tury'	1975	1976	kolkhoz	Mezhkolkhozstroy
2 Extension of school to 350 places	1975	1976	Minpros (Ministry of Education)	(Inter-kolkhoz Building Org.) Irkutsk lesstroy (Irkutsk Timber-Construction Org.)
3 House for teacher	1975	1976	Minpros	kolkhoz
4 Reconstruction of sports hall	1975	1976	Minpros	kolkhoz SSZ
5 Children's hygiene centre	1975	1976	Minpros	kolkhoz
6 Trading centre	1975	1976	Burkoopsoyuz (Buryat Co-operative union)	MSO
7 Kombinat Bytovogo Obsluzhivaniya (KBO: workshop for domestic repairs, decoration, etc.)	1975	1976	Ministerstvo bytovogo sluzh. (Ministry of Services)	kolkhoz, Barguzin KBO
8 Communications centre	1975	1976	*Raion*	kolkhoz
9 Polyclinic for 100 patients	1975	1976	Minzdrav (Ministry of Health)	kolkhoz
10 Asphalting of the central road in Bayangol village	1976	1976	str-vo avtodorog (Road Construction)	DU – 599
11 Electrification of the cattle *fermy* at Bayangol, Zorik and Urzhil	1975	1976	Bur-energ.	Mekhkolonka no. 56 (Mechanical Con-struction Team)
12 Irrigation and fertilisation of 208 hectares of pasture	1975	1976	Min. mel. vod. kh-va (Ministry of Water Improvement)	Burvodstroy (Buryat Water Construction Org.)

Table 4.4. (*cont.*)

Construction project	Timing		Finance	Body carrying out work
	Begin	End		
13 Reconstruction of the Karasun irrigation system	1975	1975	Min. mel. vod. kh-va	Burvodstroy
14 Completion of Karalik irrigation system	1975	1976	Min. mel. vod. kh-va	Burvodstroy
15 Drainage of the Manday swamps	1975	1976	Min. mel. vod. kh-va	Burvodstroy
16 Irrigation and fertilisation of 1,500 hectares of arable land	1975	1976	Ministerstvo Sel'skogo kh-va (Ministry of Agriculture)	SKhT
17 Improvement of meadows, 1,000 hectares	1975	1976	kolkhoz	kolkhoz
18 Completion of cattle-shed for 400 head	1975	1976	kolkhoz by *gossud* (state loan)	MSO
19 Construction of ten sheds for sheep	1975	1976	kolkhoz (*gossud*)	kolkhoz
20 Reconstruction of shed for calves being fattened	1975	1976	kolkhoz	kolkhoz
21 Conversion of cow-shed to shed for sheep, 2,500 head	1975	1976	kolkhoz	kolkhoz
22 Building of forty houses	1975	1976	kolkhoz (*gossud*)	kolkhoz
23 Mechanisation of livestock *fermy*	1975	1976	kolkhoz	sudostroit. zavod

giant production-manufacturing complex. The one enterprise would see through the process of production from raw materials to finished products. These giant agrarian-industrial unions, associated more with sovkhozy than kolkhozy, exist only in certain areas of the Soviet Union. There were none as yet in 1975 in Buryatiya. They are a further development of the idea of zonal specialisation, which does already exist everywhere in the USSR to a certain extent. Every single Buryat farm, whether kolkhoz or sovkhoz, is designated as a specialist producer of certain products according to the geographical zone of the republic in which it is situated. As yet, farms do not confine themselves in practice to their 'specialities' (see p. 222). But the theory is that such specialisation, when refined to a greater degree than it is at present, will naturally provide the ground for an agrarian-industrial complex. The policy is particularly identified with Brezhnev, who first put it forward in his report to the 24th Congress of the Communist Party. Speaking in 1974 in Alma-Ata, Brezhnev said:

The development of specialisation leads to the emergence of ever higher forms of cooperation, when together with collective and state farms, government-run industrial enterprises will join up to form agrarian-industrial unions. In some parts of the country, for example in Moldavia, Rostov *oblast'*, and Krasnodar Kray, they already exist. We should study their experience carefully. The more so, in that we are concerned not simply with actual organisational, economic problems, but also with a problem of principle — the future coming-together of state and cooperative forms of property.[43]

But by the 25th Congress the policy had apparently been reversed. Yanov, a political scientist now in the USA, suggests that this is because the creation of these giant complexes *could* give the managers power; in other words it would destroy the structure of relations between farms and the state which has existed up to the present, and in doing so it would strike at the interests of certain people who now hold powerful positions in the hierarchy. Yanov argues that these people, the regional (*oblast'*) Party Secretaries, have succeeded in keeping the Brezhnev proposals at bay by making alliances with centrally placed conservative groups in the government.[44] Yanov suggested that the reason for the lagging development of the agrarian-industrial combines is opposition from the First Party Secretaries, whose main task is to act as intermediary between existing low-level managers of enterprises. It is very difficult to tell, with the kind of information at our disposal, whether this is the case. There are likely to be in any case many other reasons of finance and technology why the giant combines have not been built on a large scale. However, what Yanov says about the role of the *obkom* secretaries does seem to be confirmed by other studies of a more detailed kind.[45] The Party's own definition of its task is that it should be involved in policy-making (*politicheskiye*) decisions. The Party is not supposed to intervene in the day-to-day running of factories or farms. But, as Hough points out, it is because of the complications, the multiplications of directives and plans, that, paradoxically, the *oblast'* and *raion* Party organs thrive: it is precisely when competition arises between different hierarchies and enterprises that a *politicheskiy* question arises. It is here that the Party has authority to countermand orders and insist that an enterprise takes a certain action.[46]

This matter will be discussed further in Chapter 7. But meanwhile we may summarise the argument of this section as follows: it has been suggested that the size of the farm enterprise as such does not affect its structural position vis-à-vis the state and Party organs. Nor has it substantially altered the organisation of production within the farm up to now, i.e. the hierarchical division into brigades, work-teams, and smaller production units. It is the policy of specialisation which is as yet very incomplete, rather than the policy of 'horizontal integration', which is beginning to have organisational effects on production. But by the 1970s the managers of specialist farms were still not necessarily in an advantageous position vis-à-vis the district authorities. As we shall see later, the larger but more 'old-fashioned' Selenga farm with its mixed brigades was in a better position and economically more successful than the specialised Barguzin farm. This suggests that, even as it is, specialisation may have proceeded too fast and at too high a level for the fragile Buryat productive base (see pp. 230–2). The next section will investigate briefly to what extent one farm, the Karl Marx kolkhoz in Barguzin, did follow state policies, including those for specialisation, and will attempt to assess the effect of this endeavour on the farm's social organisation.

2. State campaigns, ideology and social groups

In this section I discuss the pressure on farms to comply with state production campaigns, the related, and to an extent contrasted, growth of an ideologically voluntarist organisation of production, 'socialist competition', and the consequent partial emergence of units engaged in economic competition as social groups.

Our evidence on state campaigns comes from Dymbrenov's history of the Karl Marx farm in Barguzin. From this account it appears that the farm no sooner heard of state agricultural campaigns than it put them into action. But to what extent can we trust Dymbrenov's history? His book was written for a local readership, and it is probable that he was fairly accurate about facts which were verifiable by anyone, such as changes in leadership or the building of a new school. But, on the other hand, his detailed figures about the acreage under wheat, or the number of ewes, might be quite misleading.

We know that there were three sets of figures, purporting to represent the same facts in the same year, current in the Selenga Karl Marx farm in 1967 (see section 4 below). All three sets of figures were 'official', in that they came from different official sources. This suggests that even if Dymbrenov were using 'official' figures in good faith, there would still be doubt as to the relation between them and the facts on the ground. The Selenga figures were different from one another in interesting ways, but they were not grossly divergent. However, a reliable informant suggested, in relation to the Dyren sovkhoz in Barguzin, that the gap between these 'official' figures and *unofficial* ones can be very great indeed.[47] We might therefore be justified in thinking that sources such as Dymbrenov's history are very unreliable guides to the actual state of affairs.

However, though it is conceded that any Soviet published figures should be viewed with caution, there are some reasons for thinking that those facts which Dymbrenov does actually provide cannot be radically misleading. The first reason has to do with the internal coherence of the materials: the book is so detailed, and is concerned with such a small community, that a year-by-year account of this kind cannot make very extraordinary claims without it being apparent. Secondly, Dymbrenov goes to some lengths to hide certain data – for example, the acreage from which particular harvests were gathered – and we may suppose that he would not take these precautions were it possible simply to alter the grain harvest figures. The third reason is that there are, surprising as it may seem, fairly extensive corroborative sources: the local newspaper *Barguzinskaya Pravda*, the article by Yegunov on the history of the Karl Marx farm,[48] my own materials collected in 1967 and 1974–5, and various other publications in which the farm is mentioned. Finally, while one cannot rule out the possibility of collusion, it is also true that farms, brigades, and work-teams do get criticised individually and publicly in the *raion* First Secretary's speech at the end of each year. The speech is published in the local newspaper, and it would be difficult for an author writing for a local audience, like Dymbrenov, to contradict this public information.

What is absolutely clear from Dymbrenov is that, if the farm leaders did not actually follow the central government policies, they certainly had to make it appear that they had.[49] For the period covered in detail by his book, the end of the Second World War until 1958, his materials suggest, furthermore, that the farm moved forward economically in a rhythm directly related to central government campaigns.[50] It is the mechanisms by which this occurred that I now seek to elucidate. A full-length description of Dymbrenov's materials would be tedious, so I give here simply an abbreviated list of the main central government decisions and their 'results' in the farm (Table 4.5).

The September 1946 Plenum of the Central Committee of the Communist Party and the Soviet of Ministers is important because it established the basis on which post-war government decisions could be put into effect. It is clear that during the war all pretence, or indeed reality, of democratic forms of organising the kolkhoz economy had disappeared.

The general meetings of the kolkhozniks were held irregularly, the farm officials and Chairman rarely answered to the members for their actions, and for long periods of time there were no elections. Leaders were appointed and dismissed without consulting the kolkhozniks. This led to certain Chairmen ceasing to feel any responsibility before the members. There was a desire to govern in an individualistic way, to make use of kolkhoz property, avoiding decisions of the general meeting. There were frequent cases of the *raion* organisations making use of kolkhoz property and finances by direct orders, without the authority of the kolkhozniks.[51]

There is evidence also that in some areas of the Soviet Union there emerged a kind of collusion between farm chiefs and workers during the war: the chiefs had more or less complete control over the communal economy, while the workers largely ignored them and expanded their private plots as far as they could.[52]

The 1946 decision ('On methods of liquidation of violations of the kolkhoz charter') was designed to put an end to this state of affairs, and more specifically, it seems, to teach a lesson to the local and district Party organs which had been dictating the affairs of the collective farms. This is apparent from the fact that the commissions set up to investigate the said 'violations' were composed of officials of the *Soviet* apparatus and kolkhozniks, not Party officials.

However, Zaitsev, writing about this period, notes that while there was a widespread move to change the leadership in collective farms as a result of the government decision, old habits of pushing forward unsuitable *raikom* nominees, against the wishes of the kolkhozniks, continued to have force even after the war. Thus, 'In Novosibirsk *oblast'* alone, the [1946] elections in 107 collective farms were designated *by higher organs* to be invalid, on the grounds of violations of the procedures of kolkhoz elections and selection of candidates, and these elections were held a second time.'[53] Thus the higher, presumably the *oblast'*, organs were concerned to ensure that the post-war leadership in collective farms would take the members' views into account, at least to a certain extent.[54] But, paradoxically, the very idea of removing the existing farm leadership was a central government one. There were cases where kolkhozniks were satisfied with their Chairman, and in some places the *raikom* was forced to hold the elections three times in order to force a new man in.

The 1946 campaign thus illustrates the central paradox of the kolkhoz situation, a paradox which obtains to a lesser degree today. During the war democratic institutions were more or less in abeyance. But after 1946, while it was still imperative that central government decisions should be implemented, it had to appear, even if only as a matter of political rhetoric, that the implementation was the result of grass-roots activity. This follows from the slogan, 'The Party and the People are One!' In effect the policies were decided in Moscow and transmitted via the *obkom* and the *raikom* to the kolkhoz, where they were explained by Party workers to the farmers. Here a switch in direction took place. The kolkhozniks 'took a decision' at a general meeting to plant maize, or whatever the policy was, and their decision was then administered by the management committee and the Party cell, which then transmitted the results of the campaign back upwards to the *raion* and the *oblast'*. It should be noted, however, that initiatives of the Soviets, as opposed to the Party and Ministries, were often left unheeded in this period!

Table 4.5. *Central agricultural policy and the Karl Marx kolkhoz, Barguzin*

Date	Decision-making body	Decision	Action taken in Karl Marx kolkhoz, Barguzin
1943	Central Committee of the Communist Party of the USSR (CC CP USSR and SNK USSR)	Raising of minimum number of *trudodni* (labour-days) to be worked by kolkhozniks	In 1941 there were still 47 able-bodied kolkhozniks who worked less than 100 'labour-days'; after 1943 no one worked less than 100, and the number working from 201 to 400 increased[a]
March 1946	Supreme Soviet of the USSR	Post-war five-year plan	The kolkhoz 'accepted' the plan, and opened a 'socialist competition' to fulfil it (see below)[a]
September 1946	Soviet of Ministers of USSR and CC CP USSR	Liquidation of violations of the kolkhoz charter	A 'decisive blow' dealt to anti-kolkhoz elements in the farm[a]
February 1947	CC CP USSR	Raising of the agricultural economy	124% rise in milk production in 1949 as against 1945; 300% rise in grain production in 1949 as against 1945[a]
April 1949	Soviet of Ministers of USSR and CC CP USSR	Three-year plan to raise the productivity of the livestock economy	By May 1950 kolkhoz had already fulfilled the year's plan for horses (101%), cattle (104%), sheep (114%). The three-year plan for the development of livestock economy over-fulfilled, and the kolkhoz awarded the Red Banner of the Soviet of Ministers[a]
April 1948	Soviet of Ministers of USSR	New work-norms and reorganisation of labour	Average number of 'labour-days' worked by one kolkhoznik rose from 274 in 1946 to 325 in 1950 and to 366 in 1954. The Barguzin average in that year was 304 'labour-days'[a]
September 1953	CC CP USSR	Methods of raising productivity in agriculture	Amalgamation in January 1954 with *kolkhoz im. Kalinina*[a]
end 1953–1954	CC CP USSR	Maize campaign	In 1953 the kolkhoz sowed no corn (maize); in 1954 it sowed a little, in 1956 it sowed 35 hectares, and in 1957 60% of its fodder sown was maize[a]

163

Date	Organisation	Subject	Description
February–March 1954	CC CP USSR	Specialisation of production in farming	The kolkhoz specialised in sheep-farming. Number of sheep raised to 15,513 head in 1956 and to 22,413 head in 1958[a]
February–March 1954	CC CP USSR and Soviet of Ministers of USSR	'Virgin Lands' campaign ('sharply increase production of grain by significant increase in acreage of grain, grain-fodders, etc., by means of use of virgin and long-fallow soil . . .'[b])	The Karl Marx kolkhoz increased its acreage of fodder grains sown from 561 hectares in 1954 to 1,081 hectares in 1958, and 1,340 hectares in 1959[a]
October 1955	Soviet of Ministers of the Buryat ASSR	Increase in production of fine and semi-fine wool in kolkhozy and sovkhozy	Change to production of fine wool; by 1958 95% of the flock were fine-wool-bearing sheep[a]
September 1957	Bureau of the *obkom* of CP of Buryatiya and Soviet of Ministers of Buryat ASSR	Methods of improving sheep-breeding	Introduction of artificial insemination for sheep. The best shepherdess of the kolkhoz, Sh. Tsyrempilova, won many prizes for her work in artificial insemination[c]
February 1958	CC CP USSR	Reorganisation of machine-tractor stations	The kolkhoz members agreed to put over 30% of their money profits into the 'indivisible fund' as opposed to the usual 12–15%, in order to pay for MTS machinery[a]
1968	Soviet of Ministers of the RSFSR	Help to the collective farms of the Buryat ASSR in developing sheep-herding	Kolkhoz accepts specialisation plan as a farm specialising in sheep

Sources:
a. Dymbrenov 1961, pp. 34–56.
b. Bazheyev 1968, p. 162.
c. Drykheyev 1958, p. 190; Kotlykova and Erenprais 1963, pp. 10–15.

Meanwhile, the kolkhozniks' own concerns were neglected. This can be seen from three facts dating from the post-war period in Buryatiya. First, when a 'Soviet for Kolkhoz Affairs' (*sovet po delam kolkhozov*) was set up, it received between 1946 and 1950 a total of about 120,000 letters and 10,000 visits from kolkhozniks with suggestions, complaints, and declarations. A large number of the letters proposed that an All-Union Convention of Kolkhozniks be called, so that the statutes of the kolkhoz charter could be changed. This, however, did not occur until 1969, twenty years later.[55] Secondly, the greatest number of letters called for a secret ballot, instead of open voting, at kolkhoz meetings, particularly for the election of officials.[56] This has still not been implemented in all farms. Thirdly, a large number of letters requested that the plan of obligatory deliveries should be given to the kolkhoz at the beginning of the year, and that local organs should not be allowed to give the farms additional orders for the delivery of products during the year.[57] This was implemented in the early 1970s.

It is in these circumstances that 'socialist competition' has its place. The problem is that, while it is relatively easy to ensure that a correct 'decision' is taken at a kolkhoz or brigade meeting, how is it possible to make sure that the 'decision' is put into practice? This is the crucial test of the officials' powers. With the end of the politics of terror, it was necessary to have some means (a) of picking up any slack, as it were, in people's work efforts, and (b) of giving a certain democratic expression to the will of the people at the bottom, the masses who have taken supposedly 'democratic' decisions. All the kolkhoznik has with which to express his will in this political situation is his time – he can work less, or he can work more. The rhetoric of the 'socialist competition' reflects this. It is founded in the idea of choice and voluntarism, and it takes on this form in relation to the concurrent political mechanism of central directives. In fact, however, such is the propensity of Soviet organisation to centralism that the democratic element in 'socialist competition' is often lost.

'Socialist competition' is one of a number of methods employed, ranging from those in which purely ideological incentives are offered (*subbotniki*, *voskresniki*, 'Saturdays' and 'Sundays' of unpaid voluntary labour) to those in which the incentives are directly materialist (bonus schemes, prizes for productivity, etc.). It is probably true that there has been a move from predominantly ideological incentives to material incentives in the period we are considering. Both extremes have their drawbacks: *subbotniki* are only appropriate to urgent occasional tasks, and the more frequently they are called by the Party or Soviets the less willing is the participation in them. Often they tend to acquire a purely formalistic character, in which the main point for the organising official is to show that the *subbotnik* happened, and the only concern of the participants is to be able to say that they participated. Little work tends to get done on these occasions. Material incentives, on the other hand, do encourage people to work, but the kolkhoz may find it difficult to pay for them (see section 3 below).

'Socialist competition' has none of these drawbacks. It works in theory as

164

follows: a worker, or a group of workers, 'discovers' some particularly efficient method of attaining a certain production target, or a target is simply declared ('one kilo of added weight per day in the next 100 days' for calves). This 'initiative' is then supported by the local Party branch, or the *raikom*, which then promises to publicise the competition and open it widely to other workers. At the *raion* level, the Party will see that teams from the various farms of the district enter the competition. At the *oblast'* level, workers from one district will be encouraged to 'take up the challenge' of the kolkhozniks of another district. Some 'socialist competitions' spread right through the USSR. There are always many of them in existence at the same time, and it is virtually impossible for a worker in either industry or agriculture not to become involved. Hough quotes Soviet sources indicating that in both 1945 and 1965 some 90% of workers, engineering personnel, and white-collar workers in the Soviet Union were said to be involved in socialist competition.[58]

In the Karl Marx farm, socialist competition began in 1934, when the kolkhoz was still called the *artel' im. Sangadiina*. Dymbrenov describes this as follows:

On the initiative of the Party organisation and the directorship of the kolkhoz, a socialist competition was organised with other collective farms, and this played an important role in developing the economy of the *artel' im. Sangadiina* as it did in advancing its competitors. In 1934 the kolkhoz made a formal agreement with the Zagustai *kolkhoz im. Stalina* of Selenga *aimak*, according to which the two kolkhozy would engage in competition. The kolkhozniks of the two competing farms visited one another and exchanged work experience. The results of the competition were calculated quarterly.[59]

Today, the pages of *Barguzinskaya Pravda* are frequently taken up with the mechanics of socialist competition. In one case, the matter began with a declaration by the initiating workers,[60] accompanied by a newspaper leader in heavy type on the front page explaining the importance of the target and the difficulty of attaining it.[61] Side by side with the leader was an unsigned article entitled 'In the *raikom* CP USSR', containing three resolutions: to support the initiative, to 'oblige' or 'commit' (*obyazat'*) the kolkhoz managements in the district to make a decision on the competition, and to oblige the editor of the district newspaper to publish the results.[62] Subsequent issues contained articles by the heads of production brigades and Party organisers in various farms explaining why they were entering the competition.

It would be a mistake to dismiss such newspaper articles as empty ideological formalism, and to assume that the real life of the Soviet Buryats is completely hidden and is something quite different. The fact is that the newspaper articles do describe reality — not all of it — but an ever-present part of Soviet life. The Party Secretaries do select targets and persuade workers to sign an announcement, countless meetings are held to discuss how the target can be achieved, articles are written, workers fill in their 'socialist competition' booklets, overseers

165

check the results, notices and graphs are displayed to show the progress of the competition, meetings are held to discuss the quarterly results, to chide those lagging behind, and to award those who do well. It happens, and it takes a great deal of time.

Socialist competitions are always declared 'in honour of' a forthcoming Congress of the Communist Party, or in order 'to be worthy to meet' the fiftieth anniversary of the October Revolution, or some other imminent ceremonial event. At the same time they are 'inspired' by the 'thoughtful' and 'far-reaching' decisions of a previous Plenum or Congress. A substantial part of the economic life of the country thus takes on the rhythm of the great socialist rituals, and is in its turn directed by them. It is noticeable that, however lowly the competition is, it is always the great all-Union occasions which are invoked. This means that all over the USSR, whatever the local conditions, and whatever the subject of the competition (fattening for beef in Buryatiya, growing sugar-beet in central Russia, mending tractors in Kazakhstan), a quite extraneous, 'non-economic' rhythm is imposed. This is superimposed, as it were, on the ordinary process of production. But it is clear that, even here, the 'ordinary' does not mean the 'natural'. For long periods under Stalin and Khrushchev, and even in some things today, events such as sowing, harvesting, or artificial insemination have to take place by a certain date *by order*, and the date specified is related more to the necessity for the *raion* to get the figures in on time than to local natural conditions of weather, etc.

It is not difficult to see that the appearance of voluntariness in socialist competition is largely an illusion created by the newspapers and radio. In fact, *oblast'* Party organisations are instructed to pick out specific innovations in individual enterprises and see that these 'initiatives' are taken up throughout the area. It is clear that the crucial moves are strategic; not all innovations are 'picked out' by the Party, and not every branch of every enterprise engages in socialist competition all the time. There are political interests behind the timing and the extent of each competition.

One interest is certainly the demonstrative carrying out of central government special campaigns. An example is Khrushchev's meat delivery campaign of 1958–60. In the Barguzin Karl Marx farm the amount of meat produced had already risen from 6.5 centners a hectare in 1954 to 27.5 centners a hectare in 1959, and in 1958 and 1959, the first years of the campaign, they were awarded the Red Banner of the District, and three stockmen received the titles 'Best Herdsman of the *Aimak*'. In 1958 the kolkhoz seven-year plan was based on the December Plenum of the Central Committee and the 21st Congress of the Party. In 1959 they produced 4,704 centners, which was 582 over the plan, and in 1960 they were 'inspired' by the July Plenum of the CC CP USSR to increase the plan they had been given (5,127 centners of meat) to the huge figure of 9,400 centners.[63] This of course was the year of the explosion of the 'meat competition' at *oblast'* level – the year when rivalry among *oblast'* First Secretaries to win Khrushchev's favour by fulfilling his inflated all-Union plans led to widespread and disastrous over-slaughtering, and even the suicide of one over-zealous First Secretary. The sources do not say whether the huge 1960 meat plan for Karl Marx was fulfilled or not. But it seems unlikely, given that the 1971 plan was only 4,650 centners and the 1975 plan 5,720 centners, when the beef herds of the farm were about the same size as in 1960. In 1974 the Chair-man of the farm said to me that they would find it difficult to fulfil the 1975 plan for meat.

The other purpose of 'socialist competition' seems to be the nudging forward of *unsuccessful* enterprises. A minor demonstration of this comes from the Selenga district. The milkers of the Tel'man kolkhoz declared a socialist com-petition, which was taken up by the milkmaids of the Selenginskii sovkhoz. The target of the competition, however, was to achieve 2,100 kg per fodder-fed cow in 1967, and 1,750 kg by the anniversary of the Revolution in November of that year, a very low target which was already being achieved in the normal course of things in the Karl Marx kolkhoz of the same district. The competition thus must have been a special 'low-level' event, a competition which the Karl Marx was not supposed to enter.[64] Similarly, the widely advertised competition to add 1 kilo of weight per day per animal in the beef herd looks less remarkable when it is realised that the good stockmen of Karl Marx kolkhoz were achieving 1.2 kilos in 1958.

A little study of the articles by the brigadiers and Party activists entering their groups for a competition reveals that there are troubles in their units.

A meeting has just been held of the machine-operators of the Khilganai kolkhoz. The question of the initiative of the engineer-technicians of the Selenga *raion* 'Selkhozteknika' union, supported by the neighbouring 'Ulyun' kolkhoz, was discussed.

. . . The meeting also noted serious faults in the work of the machine-operators.

. . . The main reason for the poor use of the car and tractor plant is the inadequate organisational service, which does not control the runs of the machines, particularly those without a load. Chronometric measurements are not made. The main people guilty of this incorrect use of the plant are the chief engineer of the farm, V.P. Morgonov, the head of the garage, M.B. Budaev, and the head of the machine—tractor workshop, Z.B. Bazarov.

It was made clear at the meeting that many machine-operators do not observe the order of the day, accidents and wrecking occur for various reasons, they often go out of the garage without route documents, or they fill them in after they get back. Therefore, it is difficult to establish where, and why, each car or tractor left the park.

As of today, of thirty-one lorries, special machines, and cars, only twelve are working. And even they are not in good order, and not a single car is working. So some of the special machines have to be used as cars. The cars of F. Pirtanov and Yu. Dondupov have been under repair for three, five and more months. Neither the head engineer, nor the head of the garage have taken any measures to hurry this up . . .

167

At the meeting, the machine-operators took on the obligation to get all the earth-turning machinery mended and in full readiness for work by the opening of the 25th Congress. At the same time, they promised to train twelve new tractor-drivers and carry through the attestation of twenty-five machine-operators.[65]

In other words, socialist competition is not necessarily what it appears to be, a voluntary striving (*stremleniye*) for more efficient production at the forefront of technical possibility, but is often a selective, patching-up operation, whose generality is related to the fact that most collective farms tend to do badly in some respect quite frequently. The targets are, however, always somewhat beyond those given in the normal obligatory plan.[66]

Often the workers do not know until the end of the year how their results compare with those of others. This is what a driver from the Barguzin lumber-station wrote:

Imagine this picture. The shift is over. Driver Valentin Andreevich Gagarin puts his car in the garage, goes to the office, and there are all the drivers gathered together. Valentin cannot think why they all look so cheerful, with smiling faces. And they hand him a bunch of flowers, and congratulate him on his labour success – it appears that on this day Gagarin completed his target for the five-year plan . . .

But all that is the realms of fantasy. Nothing like that ever happened with us. Usually someone finds out that he has accomplished some task, or his plan, at some meeting or other. They read out his surname on the list of front-line workers, and that's all. Well, and he gets his prize money from the cashier when he goes for his wages. It is all boring. And this is how our difficult work and successes are valued; no wonder enthusiasm is quenched. And how many ways might be found for providing moral rewards for a hard-working person! Why not, for example, put up a star on the cabin for every thousand miles, or why not have a banner which passes from driver to driver, showing which one was the winner in the previous week?[67]

If lack of knowledge of what is going on is as general among individual workers as this implies, it is relevant to kolkhozniks' explanations of success and failure (see section 3 below).

On the ideological level, socialist competition serves to link the individual or group *directly* with the state. The form and timing of the competition make it appear that the working unit is personally and voluntarily inspired by events of state importance, transcending all the federal levels of organisation which lie in between.

There are other mechanisms besides socialist competition for increasing production at the level of the brigade or work-team. One of these is the touching custom of including a dead person in the membership of the team and doing his or her work as well as one's own. I was told of a brigade of eight people which 'took on' a young boy who had died recently trying to save some people in a fire. Sometimes a team 'takes on' a well-known hero, such as Yuri Gagarin, and in this case it will be known as 'Gagarin's brigade'. The motivation is entirely ideological, and 'Gagarin' is not paid for his work.

Similar to this is the notion of the 'socialist obligation' (*sotsialisticheskoye obyazatel'stvo*), by which individuals promise to fulfil a named target of extra work unpaid. A Party worker will approach a worker at the beginning of the year and ask him what is his 'socialist obligation'. Some people refuse to cooperate, but others name some target which is then publicised. For those who prefer a quiet life the trick is to name a target or some task which they would have to perform anyway. Other people who are genuinely inspired to work name a difficult target, well over their normal production plan. Sometimes these individual 'obligations' are widely publicised in the local newspapers: 'I declare that I will milk x litres per cow by . . . ', but the publicity does not in fact relate to the difficulty of the task, rather the newspaper editor's decision to ginger up some lagging area of production. Often the 'obligation' is combined with 'competition': milkmaid X of one farm challenges milkmaid Y of another farm to beat her in obtaining a certain number of litres. Again, all of this can go on at an ordinary level, well below that of the champion milkers.

It is significant that enthusiasm is only permitted if it is controlled,[68] and if it has no basis in 'unsocialist' feelings such as personal attachment to one's 'own' land or over-riding loyalty to one's 'own' people (kin or nation). What is put forward as a focus for enthusiasm in 'socialist competition' is rivalry between economically constituted groups (brigades, kolkhozy, districts, etc.).

The official rewards in a 'socialist competition' are more honorific than material (a Red Banner which moves from winner to winner, titles such as 'Best Shepherd of the District', or inscribed diplomas). However, prizes in money and/or goods may be paid to the winners. As with ordinary bonuses for productivity the hierarchy of officials of the winning group earns proportionately more than the workers. But even 'losing' workers may benefit in the natural course of things if they are on a piece-work rate and produce more by participating in the competition; and the leaders definitely stand to gain since they earn substantial bonuses for absolute production (see Chapter 2). Prizes are normally shared between the workers, but it is not unknown for them to be given up 'voluntarily' to some institution.

'Socialist competition' is as difficult, and as easy, to evade as any other work in the kolkhoz: in other words, the people who can most easily refuse to take part, or remain indifferent to 'letting the side down', are those who have least to lose anyway, the ordinary unskilled workers. For all the people who do have something to lose, whether it be a higher rate of pay, a reputation, or a career, 'socialist competition' is something in which one must take part because it is increasingly the way in which the economy is organised. People take part in the competition and by doing so create the objective conditions for the continuation of such competitions.

As we see in section 3 below 'socialist competition' can invade even the private sector of production: people may 'voluntarily' take on the obligation to provide specific products from their own household economies towards the plan. As a point of classification or terminology, the initial provisioning of private products by households is not itself called 'socialist competition' but a 'people's movement' (*vsenarodnoye dvizheniye*). However, as soon as these products reach the hands of the Soviet institution they are re-classified, and counted towards the totals of the district 'socialist competition'.[69]

Essentially, 'socialist competition' is a political-ideological mechanism for manipulating the economy. It plays on, and accentuates, regional and sectional divisions. What matters is that the community is divided in this way, and that the divisions are used to create specific obligations for individual people. The extension of 'socialist competition' to the private sphere has raised official fears that other, non-soviet social groups will become involved. This can be seen from the criticism publicly expressed when a whole neighbourhood of people got together to enter, and win, a competition for the sale of pork to the state. The Party authorities were criticised for not specifying *who* could enter, for giving too large a prize (a token enabling the winner to buy a car), and for not taking into account that private production on this scale would take away fodder resources from the kolkhoz.[70]

In fact, the main benefit of 'socialist competition' for those administering it may be an unintended one — unintended, that is, from the ideological point of view. The surplus created 'outside the plan' can be converted, by means of semi-illicit or undercover trade-offs between enterprises, into acquisition of scarce inputs, or money, or other benefits. Even if illicit or sideways ('left') dealings are not resorted to, the gains to the kolkhoz for over-plan sales to the state can be substantial. Thus the Karl Marx farm in Barguzin made the following amount from its successful participation in the 1958 meat competition: the farm's plan was for 800 centners, the kolkhoz in fact produced 1,322 centners, and it made a total of 2,180,000 rubles on its meat production in that year, of which 500,000 was for 'over-plan' production.[71]

It is this possibility, which exists alongside and independently of the satisfaction derived from 'winning', which provides a genuine impetus for workers in the competition. The economic units involved, brigades and production teams, as well as farms, become social groups to the extent that their members are collectively involved in effort, decision and in the sharing out of the proceeds. People become the subjects in action with intention. The units in the competition are for once not simply units of production, but also units of distribution; even if they 'lose', it is likely that the product will be generated over the level to be compulsorily sold to the state. The importance of such 'manipulable resources' is discussed again in section 4 below.

The farms and brigades whose raison d'être is to be units of production are becoming social units of distribution in non-political spheres too. This can be seen from the fact that they are gradually coming to take the place of kinship groups in the exchange of goods at weddings (see Chapter 8 section 2). We can perhaps see here the generation of social categories which will supersede native Buryat ones.

3. The effects of collectivised farming

This section examines the overall effects of collectivised farming at the level of the Buryat republic. The aim is to give some idea of the generality of the problems which face Buryat farmers, and to provide a context within which the particular data which I collected in the two farms I visited can be understood.

The population of the Buryat ASSR has more than doubled in the period 1926 to 1976, but the rural population has remained more or less constant. In recent years, the countryside working population has even started to go down, despite the high birth-rate among Buryats, evidence of the flow of people to town. Meanwhile the number of livestock in the republic has dramatically increased, though with large fluctuations over the Soviet period. Here we should note two important features of the situation: firstly, there were disastrous losses of animals during collectivisation, when well over half the cattle, two-thirds of the sheep, and large proportions of the pigs and horses perished, and there were also significant losses during the Second World War. This means that after each of these occasions a more or less constant number of rural workers had to increase productivity in the livestock economy even to bring the figures up to the previous level. Secondly, there has been a change in the Soviet period in the composition of the herds. There were substantially fewer cattle in 1976 than there were in 1928, but the number of sheep has more than doubled (Table 4.6).

In the same period the area under arable farming increased by over seven times, from 204,100 hectares in 1928 to 1,532,000 hectares in 1975.[72] These figures are for land under grain and root crops as well as fodder crops such as maize or hay. However, the amount harvested from these fields, while it has increased over the years, has not risen in equivalent proportion to the acreage. Thus, if we take grain production, there was a harvest of 138,400 tons in 1928, but an average of only 418,200 tons in 1961–5, and by the period 1971–5 the annual harvest was only around 510,000 tons. While the area sown with grain has increased five times, the amount of the grain harvest has gone up by only 3.6 times.[73]

The figures for the hay harvest are much worse. We have no data for the pre-collectivisation period, but the total harvested in 1940, 735,000 tons of all types of hay, has never been equalled since. Even in 1975 only 527,900 tons were gathered.[74] The acreage under sown one-year grasses has increased, from 22,400 hectares in 1940 to 145,700 hectares in 1973, and the amount of hay gathered from this type of meadow has not gone up by the same proportion.[75] Generally, however, the huge increase in sown area for all types of crops has been at the expense of the natural hay-meadows which have declined steadily in area. It has

171

Table 4.6. *Livestock and population in the Buryat ASSR, 1928–76*

	1928	1933	1946	1963[a]	1971	1976[b]
Cattle	728,600	262,900	299,000	392,000	449,000	492,100
Sheep	898,400	214,500	465,000	1,509,000	1,755,900	1,951,800
Pigs	152,100	52,100	15,600	152,400	173,200	185,200
Horses	214,200	120,700	56,400	56,800	56,600	57,900
Population[c] (total)	388,900 (1926)	545,800 (1939)		696,100 (1960)	816,600 (1971)	864,600 (1976)
Population (rural)	338,500 (1926)	378,500 (1939)		410,900 (1960)	445,300 (1971)	383,800 (1976)
Livestock per head of rural population (approx.)	5.8	1.7		5.1	5.4	7.0

Sources:
a. *Narodnoye khozyaistvo buryatskoi ASSR* 1963, p. 89. All figures for livestock up to and including the year 1963 are taken from this source. The data for 1928 and 1933 were collected in the summer; those for 1946 and 1963 were collected on 1 January.
b. *Narodnoye khozyaistvo buryatskoi ASSR* 1976, pp. 88–90. The figures for 1971 and 1976 were collected on 1 January.
c. *Ibid.*, p. 8. No data available for 1940s.
The table includes livestock in private smallholdings.

not proved possible to increase productivity on these meadows either. Writing in 1969, Galdanov observed that Buryat farms in the 1960s rarely got as much as eight centners per hectare of natural hay, whereas in 1941 the average had been 13.2 centners per hectare.[76] The total of natural hay gathered has gone down drastically, from 686,700 tons in 1940 to 310,400 tons in 1962, and had made only slight improvement, 387,900 tons, by 1973.[77]

The problem is essentially one of intensification. Between 1950 and 1965 the total agricultural product in the Buryat republic rose three times, but the amount produced per 100 hectares of useful land rose by only 58%. For food grains the product per hectare has, if anything, gone down since the 1920s (see Table 4.7). During the period 1965–75, despite huge efforts to intensify, the aggregate product (*valovaya produktsiya*) of farming rose from a value of 214,200 million rubles to 281,400 million rubles, i.e. by 31%, but the acreage rose by 26% at the same time.[78] Thus, in the most general terms, the farms have greatly increased their product during the period of collectivisation, but they have done so only by simultaneously increasing the area of land used and the number of livestock. Meanwhile, the rural working population has remained more or less constant, and if we take into account the age structure may even have gone down.[79]

Fodder

How does the decrease in productivity per hectare of fodder crops affect the livestock economy? Galdanov, the Buryat economist, was critical of the situation as it was in the 1960s (the point of his figures being counted in 'livestock units' is that this balances out the differences in fodder requirements between large and small livestock).

In 1928, within the present-day boundaries of Buryatiya there were 992,700 head of livestock (counted in livestock units), as opposed to 703,600 head (in livestock units) on 1 January 1967, i.e. there were 289,100 head more. All of these animals were kept in winter on hay alone, and in summer on the pastures, for in those days there were only 204,100 hectares of sown land, almost none of it sown for fodder crops: only 28,500 hectares of oats, and 6,300 hectares of green hay. With the exception of pigs, livestock were not fed with grain. Only horses which were engaged in heavy work were sometimes fed with oats. Of course the animals of those days were low in productivity, and were not accustomed to fodder feeding, but facts are facts: a larger than the present number of livestock was maintained exclusively on natural fodder, while today the natural hays covers only 25–30% of the herds' needs in rough fodder, and even less of their fodder requirements as a whole.[80]

It would be difficult not to see in this situation a reflection of the disastrous neglect of natural hay as a fodder which was the concomitant of Khrushchev's emphasis on maize all through the USSR in the 1950s and 1960s. During the period of the maize campaign there was a general cut-back in the production of high quality grass seed, in hay-mowing equipment, in machinery needed for working the meadows, and in finance for drainage and irrigation. The result was a fall from 64 to 47 million tons of hay gathered in the RSFSR between 1953 and 1965.[81]

In Buryatiya the decline in productivity of hay per hectare has to some extent been compensated for by the absolute rise in grain production. Improved livestock breeds require more concentrated fodder than that derived from hay. As we shall see later, the Karl Marx kolkhoz in Barguzin used all of its proceeds from grain production, as well as a certain amount of the farm's grain itself, in order to buy fodder concentrates. Inevitably, with the extending of the cultivated area, the productivity figures for grain harvested per hectare in Buryatiya in the collectivised period have not greatly increased: in 1928 there was an average harvest of 7.2 centners per hectare, and this has only advanced to an average of 9.4 centners per hectare by the 1971–5 period.[82] This is despite the introduction of new technology, high-yielding strains, a change in the crop structure (more spring wheat, less spring rye), and the advent of chemical fertilisers. A good average yield in Buryat conditions is 15 centners per hectare, and on irrigated and manured land the yield can go up to 20 or 30 centners per hectare.[83]

It is recognised by Buryat agronomists that far more grain and grain fodders could be produced per hectare if a greater proportion of the land was irrigated and fertilised. However, in the present state of farm technology these are both very labour intensive operations. Many irrigation systems in the republic have broken down, and even where they are still working the final stage of the

173

watering has to be carried out by hand. Galdanov estimates that one worker can water 0.7 to 0.8 hectares a day, and thus collective farms with, say, 1,000 hectares of 'irrigated' land require a workforce of 170–200 people for ten or eleven days in order to get the watering done.[84] Many farms do not have this amount of labour available in the early summer. Thus, even if we discount the labour problems in renovating, or building, irrigation systems – this work is not carried out by the farms but by a separate organisation – Buryat kolkhozy and sovkhozy still have difficulty in making use of the systems which are more or less in working order. The problem of fertilisation is similar. The republic has a plentiful supply of animal dung for manure, but the farms lack machinery for transporting and distributing it on the fields. Many farms also lack essential storage facilities. Without these natural manure quickly loses its qualities, and in Buryat conditions, if it freezes in winter, the transport and spreading problem becomes virtually insuperable.[85]

It is natural to ask why the fodder problem, which is general in the Soviet Union, should have occurred in Buryatiya, where the sown area is larger in relation to population than in Russia and where the composition of the herds has moved away from cattle, which require large amounts of fodder, to sheep, which require less. A part of the answer seems to lie in the abandoning not of the traditional methods of the Buryat household economy themselves (which could not in any case be employed with the present organisation of labour), but of those common-sense practices which were applied before collectivisation and which ensured (a) that the crops and hay-meadows were encouraged to grow, and (b) that they were protected from destruction by the herds. Galdanov, writing in 1966, was brought to the point of reminding Buryat farmers of practices which were quite standard before collectivisation: for example, the building of a fence separating summer pastures from the fields and hay-meadows, the setting aside of winter pasture on which herds have spread their droppings for hay, the mowing of hay only after the flowering of the grasses, allowing them to seed for the next year, and so on.[86] All of these measures are so obviously common sense that we can suppose only a mood of despair, or very severe disorganisation, in farms which do not practise them.

Buryatiya, it seems from the latest data available to us,[87] is experiencing a growing disproportion between the number of livestock and their fodder base. It is not just that the hay harvest is going down in absolute terms but also that fodder grain production is not rising as fast as food grain production. Unfortunately, data are not available for the 1970s at the republic level, but in the 1960s, when the number of sheep was rising rapidly, fodder production could not keep pace, and Galdanov estimated that by 1966 they were receiving only half of the ration per head required to keep an animal in good condition. Of the fodder which the sheep did receive, only 40% of all types, including pasture, was produced in the farms themselves. The rest had to be bought from outside.[88] It is possible that much of the bought fodder was provided by imports of hay from

Mongolia, and certainly by the mid-1970s imported hay was reaching as far as Barguzin.[89] It is unlikely that production of fodders has improved during the 1970s. In Barguzin *raion*, at least, there were disasters with the hay harvest in 1972, 1974, and 1980 (see section 4 below).

Food grains, fallow, and irrigation

In 1970 the Buryat republic managed to produce enough grain to feed its population without imports.[90] This was a big improvement on the situation in the 1950s and 1960s, when not enough was produced of any of the main food items (grain, meat, milk, potatoes and vegetables) to feed the population at the level of the 'physiological norm' established by Soviet nutritionists.[91] But this achievement in grain production was not made without serious costs. Already in 1970 Buryat economists were warning of the consequences if, with the present level of productivity, the attempt were to be made to keep pace with the growth of population. By 1975, it was estimated, a further 348,000 hectares would have to be ploughed up — as much as the total area sown with grain in 1960.[92] In fact, we know with hindsight that only 65,000 additional hectares were ploughed up between 1970 and 1975,[93] and it is possible that this reflects an appreciation of the seriousness of the problems of the republic, though it might have been due to changes in central agricultural policy.

One of the main problems in Buryatiya stems from the rapid expansion of the sown area when combined with sheep-farming: erosion. This problem only began to be appreciated, or publicly commented upon, after the 'Virgin Lands' campaign, which was energetically and disastrously carried out here as in other parts of the Soviet Union. Between 1954 and 1958, 287,600 hectares of virgin land were ploughed up.[94] It is interesting that this amount appears to have been limited by the labour available, since, while obeying the order to plough new land, most of the districts of the republic compensated by abandoning some of their old fields. In Barguzin 22% of the old fields were left, while in the Pribaykal and Zakamensk districts up to 95% of the previous fields were not re-used. In the Tarbagatay district, the 'Virgin Lands' campaign even led to a lessening of the total area of land under cultivation.[95]

There may have been other reasons than simply the lack of labour for this result (see below), but meanwhile we should try to estimate the effect of the campaign on erosion in the republic. It is well known that the campaign created vast desert-like areas in Kazakhstan, previously useful pasture, where outside labour and machinery were drafted in.[96] However, in Buryatiya, which had to use its own resources, the campaign can be seen as part of a more gradual process which started long before collectivisation. Many areas show an increase of erosion since 1895, and a particularly serious spread since the 1930s.[97] In the Selenga valley 17,000 hectares were already eroded by 1934, and in the republic the figure rose to 100,000 hectares, a quarter of the total sown acreage, by

175

1960.[98] Nearly all of the former pastures adjacent to the rivers Chikoi, Selenga, Ina, Zhargalanta, Tunka, and Argada are affected. The villages of Staroye Nomokhonovo, Novoye Nomokhonovo, and Mar'ino have had to be moved, and many settlements in other districts, including Barguzin, are no longer viable.[99] No information is available on the present state of erosion in Buryatiya, but since the sown area has continued to rise and the number of livestock has also gone up (over-pasturing, of course, also creates erosion), we may suppose that the problem has not been solved.

The situation is thus a frightening one. The population of the republic is rising, the demand for grain is rising, the harvest per hectare is on average rather worse than it was before collectivisation (see Table 4.7), more land is being ploughed up, and at the same time the amount of available potential arable land is decreasing still further because of erosion (deposits of wind-blown sand on pastures). This brings to the forefront the question of how a given bit of land is used, in particular the question of the shortening of fallow periods.

Before collectivisation the Buryat employed a rather different agricultural technique from the Siberian Russians, although both methods depended on substantial fallow. In fact the various groups of Buryats differed between themselves. Some living in the eastern steppes with plentiful land used the *zalezhnaya* system, while others, who inhabited the densely populated valley of western Buryatiya, employed a technique similar to the Russian *parovaya* system. Others, living around the shores of Lake Baikal, and including the Selenga and Barguzin Buryats, seem to have used a combination of the two techniques. In the *zalezhnaya* system land is sown each year until it is exhausted and then it is left for twenty or thirty years to recover. In the *parovaya* system the land is divided into two, and each year one half is sown and the other left fallow (*pod parom*). The Buryats living close to Lake Baikal used a combination such as: plough, plough, fallow, plough, fallow, plough, *zalezh* (several years).[100] However, Russians all through Buryatiya used the two-field system. This has generally been considered by Soviet writers to be the more advanced system, and it is a matter of some wonder to them why the Buryats did not adopt it wholesale. The Buryat answer was quite clear, however: 'We still had plenty of steppe, and the *parovaya* system needs more labour.'[101] This was clearly true. The Buryats, like other agriculturalists among the Mongol-speaking peoples, simply cleared the steppe of large stones, ploughed it once in summer, and then it was ready for ploughing and sowing the next spring. The *parovaya* system required more and deeper ploughing, raking, fertilising, weeding, and more care of the fields in general. The Buryats only used it when there was a shortage of land (clearing of the taiga forest which surrounds some Buryat settlements is even more laborious than the increased work required by the two-field system).

For a long period Soviet agriculturalists saw decreasing the fallow period as an 'advance', whatever the conditions. This culminated in Khrushchev's disastrous abandonment even of the short summer fallow period in 1962.[102] In Buryatiya,

Table 4.7. *Productivity of the arable sector in Buryatiya: the period of collectivisation compared with the 1970s*

| Types of grain (centners per hectare) | 1928–9 | | 1929–30 | | | 1971–5 average | 1975 | |
	Kolkhoz	Individual farms	Sovkhoz	Kolkhoz	Individual farms	Sovkhoz and kolkhoz	Farms of all types	Farms of all types
Rye	9.0	8.1	10.0	10.0	8.7	5.8	5.8	7.8
Wheat	9.0	8.2	11.0	11.0	10.3	10.5	10.5	12.3
Oats	9.0	8.2	10.5	10.5	9.5	8.3	8.3	9.7
Barley	10.0	9.0	–	10.8	10.0	6.5	6.5	7.4
Potatoes	–	104.3	140.0	135.0	115.4	62.0	97.0	113.0

Sources: Plenkin 1930, quoting the 'kontrol'nyye tsifry' for 1929–30 of the Gosplan of the RSFSR; *Narodnoye khozyaistvo buryatskoi ASSR* 1976, pp. 84–5.

long fallows and particularly the *zalezhnaya* system have been seen as backward. There has been a steady decline in fallow fields since the war: they were 37.5% of the total in 1940, but only 19.3% in 1962.[103] By 1975 they had declined still further to 16.5% of all arable land, and there were no lands at all classified as *zalezhi*.[104]

The decrease in fallow periods is a rational policy if three conditions can be filled: the introduction of new technology adequate to cope with the increased labour, fertilisation to counterbalance the more frequent use of the fields, and, in Buryat conditions, enough irrigation, wind-shield planting, and correct siting of fields to prevent erosion. It is probable that the amount of agricultural machinery in Buryat farms is now adequate,[105] but we should look in more detail at the other conditions. The high labour cost of irrigation has already been mentioned. Perhaps because of this the area of land inside irrigation networks in Buryatiya has gone up little since 1945, and between 1962 and 1975 it even marginally *went down* (from 177,100 hectares belonging to kolkhozy and sovkhozy in 1962, to 176,100 hectares in 1975).[106] Some 7% of this land is not used at all, a fairly large amount is used but not actually irrigated (25% in 1965), and only 17% is used to produce grain. The rest is used as hay-meadows.[107] By 1975 more of the irrigable land was in use, but still only 23% was under arable crops.[108] In absolute terms this was 41,300 hectares of land, or 1.9% of the total of arable land in the republic.[109] In other words, irrigation was being of virtually no help in the conditions of decreasing fallow for grain and root crops.

Buryat farmers now have access to chemical fertilisers as well as natural manure, these having become widely available since 1973 or so. In 1975 there were enough chemical fertilisers in the republic to provide 26 kilos per hectare,[110] but this must be inadequate. The planting of wind-breaks and siting of fields away from sandy slopes is insufficient, and the newspapers sometimes accuse farms of neglecting these matters entirely, allowing recently planted trees to die.[111]

The conclusion must be that while the reduction of fallow has brought an absolute increase in the amount of grain produced, it has at the same time brought problems which are still largely unsolved: an increasing pressure on labour, and decreasing fertility of fields. It was perhaps for these reasons that Buryat farms abandoned such a large proportion of their old fields during the 'Virgin Lands' campaign — in effect what they were doing was allowing the fields to return to a much-needed state of long-term fallow.

Livestock production and its place in the rural economy

The major reason why the fodder problem is such a pressing one is the change-over of Buryat farms to more productive breeds of livestock, which require increased and better quality fodder. In the last twenty years not only has the number of animals greatly risen, but there has also been a large increase in productivity per animal. It is true that there have been fluctuations in productivity. Writing in the late 1960s Galdanov noted a decrease at that time in productivity of milk, beef, and wool, but with the possible exception of beef, it appears that this trend was reversed in the 1970s. During the period 1970–5 productivity of milk, eggs, and wool remained at a more or less stable level. Figures for productivity per animal of meat are not given in the statistics of the Buryat republic, which may indicate that they are declining.[112] However, the general picture is of significant increases in productivity per animal since the mid-1960s (Table 4.8). This has been achieved (a) by the production of more fodder, (b) breeding, and (c) by increased labour. It is to this last factor which we now turn.

There is a very low level of mechanisation of livestock farming in Buryatiya. In 1966, only 6% of the cows in the republic were in *fermy* with mechanised milking facilities, only 10% of the cattle-sheds had mechanised cleaning-out services, and only 20% had mechanised feeding. In fact, of the major operations in livestock farming, sheep-shearing was the only branch which was adequately mechanised (90% of sheep were provided with electric apparatus in 1966). Moreover, the machinery in existence was not fully used: in the mid-1960s collective farms of the republic used only 12% of the milking-machines, 28% of the feeding apparatus, and 68.5% of the shearing facilities.[113] This disastrous situation has, it seems, got worse rather than better since the 1960s. Thus by 1973, kolkhozy of the zone near Ulan-Ude — presumably the most developed zone of the republic — provided mechanised milking for only 0.3% of cows, mechanised watering for 40.4%, cleaning-out for 1.0%, and mechanised fodder distribution for only 0.7% of cattle.[114] As the Buryat economist Ayushiyev says: 'In the last few years there has been a growth in productivity of the animals, but this has not given rise to a greater productivity of labour because there has been a significant decrease in the level of mechanisation of labour.

Table 4.8. *Productivity of the livestock sector in Buryat collective and state farms, 1973–76*

Indicator	1953	1959	1959 as % of 1953	1960	1966	1966 as % of 1960	1975–6	1975–6 as % of 1966
Head of cattle (thousands)	251.8	241.0	95.7	268.0	307.0	114.5	353.3	115.1
of which cows	73.5	74.5	101.4	82.0	103.0	125.6	115.7	112.3
Milk (thousand tons)	40.5	82.9	204.7	98.8	129.0	130.6	158.2	122.6
Milk per cow (kg)	550.0	1,205.0	219.1	1,467.0	1,331.0	90.7	1,767.0	132.8
Beef (thousand tons)	6.9	9.0	130.4	9.8	12.0	122.5	18.2	151.7
Beef per head cattle (kg)	109.0[a]	122.0	112.0	123.0	120.0[b]	97.6	n.a.	n.a.
Head of sheep (thousands)	827.1	1,326.6	160.4	1,480.0	1,459.0	98.6	1,824.5	125.1
Wool (tons)	1,386.0	3,056.0	220.5	4,068.0	3,792.0	93.2	5,416.0	142.8
Mutton (thousand tons)	3.1	4.7	151.6	5.7	6.6	115.8	7.7	116.7
Wool per sheep (kg)	1.7	2.3	135.3	2.9	2.7	93.1	2.9	107.4
Head of pigs (thousands)	37.2	52.2	140.3	84.0	125.0	148.8	116.4	93.1
Pork (thousand tons)	1.4	1.9	135.7	3.2	5.5	171.9	7.2	130.9

Notes:

n.a. not available

a. 1958

b. 1965

Sources: for 1953–66, Galdanov 1969, p. 24; for 1975–6, *Narodnoye khozyaistvo buryatskoi ASSR 1976*, pp. 95–7.

As a result the expenditure of labour in looking after the animals has increased.'[115]

How can we explain this absurdity? One factor is certainly the inadequate electrification of most farms. Virtually all kolkhozy have electricity of some kind, but if the farms rely on *raion*-level allocation of power and do not have generators of their own, the supply, even in the mid-1970s, tended to be weak, and subject to unpredictable cuts and fluctuations. Another explanation, admittedly an odd one, is that provided by Ayushiyev: mechanisation brings about an increase in the costs of production (*sebestoimost'*) through higher amortisation costs and the increased wages which have to be paid to mechanically qualified workers. It is necessary to employ extra trained workers to look after the machines, and the costs per unit of product rise.

The managements of kolkhozy have reacted by lowering the bonus paid for production of the amount specified in each worker's plan, and as a result the workers have 'lost interest in mechanisation, and have refused it'.[116] This, Ayushiyev says, is the main reason for rejection of mechanised milking in the kolkhozy and sovkhozy of the Ulan-Ude region. The Buryat sociologist, Ushnayev, on the other hand, suggests that the explanation is to be found in the attitude of managers, who attach little importance to mechanisation in the livestock sector.[117] This raises several interesting questions which will be discussed below.

The amount of labour required of livestock workers has also been greatly increased as a result of two mutually interacting policies of the collectivised economy: the settlement of people and, as far as possible, herds in fixed villages or brigades, and the specialisation of productive units. Whereas in the pre-collectivised homestead the hay needed for winter was in the main gathered from the *ütüg* (fertilised and irrigated field) adjacent to the byres and corrals, and the animal dung produced during winter pasturing fertilised the *ütüg* as a matter of course, now hay and other fodder and water have to be specially transported over large distances to reach the herds — which are kept static in their sheds because the new productive breeds cannot withstand open pasturing during the winter in Siberian conditions — and the manure has to be collected, loaded, and transported and then spread in places which are far from the herds. Because of specialisation and concentration of production the units responsible for irrigation and fertilisation of fields are not those engaged in looking after the livestock, and the coordination of the traditional system, now more difficult because of the large scale of production, is lost.

The breeding of new types by artificial insemination, a task which Buryat farms have had to carry out for sheep as well as cattle, is immensely time-consuming. In the last thirty years or so the great majority of Buryat sheep flocks have been transformed from rough to fine or semi-fine wool types, but this requires complicated organisation of the flocks as they are taken to centralised insemination points and great care on the part of shepherds to avoid the losses in fertility which occur when natural mating is abandoned.[118] Both sheep

Table 4.9. *Average work-load of one collective/state farm worker in the Buryat ASSR in comparison with that of the RSFSR in 1965 (RSFSR = 100 %)*

	Work-load (%)	
Indicator	per kolkhoznik	per state farm worker
Agricultural land	218.0	182.4
of which arable	120.0	112.0
Cattle (head)	171.0	130.0
of which cows	156.0	122.0
Sheep (head)	546.0	645.0
Poultry	112.0	49.0
Pigs (head)	80.0	110.0

Source: Galdanov 1970, p. 41.

and cattle have to be taken to central slaughterhouses which are sometimes several hundred kilometres from the farms; this operation, it appears, is done on foot, and requires complex arrangements for pasture and crossing rivers without bridges on the way.[119] The increase in labour extends beyond the purely livestock production units to the arable sector too, since the settlement of the herds has meant that proportionately more fodder has had to be produced and fed to the animals than would have been the case if they were moving over the pasture for a greater part of the year.

It is important that there are substantial differences in the work-load of kolkhozniks between different regions of the Soviet Union. This can be seen simply as a result of natural and historical conditions. Another view would suggest that, given the opportunity afforded by a planned economy to regulate the work-load in collective and state farms, the present situation is a result of deliberate policy. Table 4.9 shows that in 1965 Buryat kolkhozniks had a larger work-load than the average for the RSFSR in all the main sectors of farming except pig-keeping.

We should remember that what is tabled here as 'work-load' also constitutes wealth. The average Buryat kolkhoznik is better off than his Russian (RSFSR) counterpart. If we assume that the natural increase in population has been the same throughout rural areas of Buryatiya, this distribution of wealth is reflected in movements of population. Table 4.10 shows that there was a steady movement of workers away from the cattle specialisation zone and into the sheep specialisation and suburban zones during the 1960s. This movement took place despite the restrictions on the mobility of kolkhozniks in force at that time.

Profitability

I consider now the profitability (*rentabel'nost'*) of the various sectors of farming

Table 4.10. *Changes in the distribution of collective farm and state farm workers according to zone of specialisation in the Buryat ASSR, 1964–70*

	Number of workers per 100 hectares of farmed land			
Year	Buryat ASSR average	Sheep-farming zone	Cattle-farming zone	Suburban zone
1964	2.70	2.46	2.47	4.28
1966	2.78	2.51	2.26	4.46
1968	2.82	2.64	2.15	4.51
1970	2.91	2.77	2.06	4.59

Source: Buruyev 1974, p. 30.

in Buryatiya. The profitability of any given product is officially reckoned by the relation between the cost of production and the prices paid by the state (i.e. it does not take into account other prices, such as those on the 'kolkhoz market', which might be available to the farms). Since the great majority of the kolkhoz product that is sold is sold to the state we may, for the purposes of this chapter, value the whole product at this price and look at the implications of 'profitability' as officially defined.

The Buryat republic, until perhaps very recently, has been in the unfortunate situation of being climatically and ecologically most suited to livestock production, of having been designated as a zone specialised in livestock production,[120] but of having to operate in a situation where arable farming is very profitable, but livestock can only just be made to pay (Table 4.11).

Figures are not available for the Buryat republic since 1966, but in the USSR as a whole the profitability of both arable and livestock farming went down between 1966 and 1975, and in view of the Buryat specialisation in livestock it is unfortunate that not only did milk production remain unprofitable, but wool production began to make a loss, and the possibility of recouping by grain production is also reduced.

Although state buying prices went up in 1960, 1965, and 1970, and the 'varying prices' (*skol'zyashchiye tseny*), which went *down* in good years, were abolished in 1965, the precarious profitability of livestock farming was not improved: during this same period the cost of production also went up, largely because of the introduction of a fixed basic wage in collective farms and successive increases in wages for all types of farming work.

In Buryatiya, farms which have some success in grain production and which are able to specialise in sheep-farming can make a profit. However, there is the complicating factor that every farm in the Buryat ASSR is designated as specialising in a certain sector, and many of these are instructed to specialise in cattle products, meat and milk, and are given obligatory delivery plans with this in mind. It is supposed by at least some of the Buryat economists that the fact that

Table 4.11. *Profitability of production of items in arable and livestock farming in kolkhozy and sovkhozy of Buryat ASSR in 1966, in percentages*

Items	Collective farms profitability (+) or loss (−)	State farms profitability (+) or loss (−)
Arable farming as a whole	+ 188	+ 77
of which grain	+ 279	+ 120
Livestock farming as a whole	+ 6	− 2
of which beef	+ 6	− 4
of which mutton	+ 19	+ 7
of which pork	+ 7	− 1
of which milk	− 16	− 12
of which eggs	− 7	+ 3
of which wool	+ 36	+ 3

Source: Galdanov 1969, p. 88.

Table 4.12. *Dynamics of the level of profitability of certain products of kolkhozy in the USSR, 1966–75, in percentages*

Items	1966	1970	1975
Arable farming as a whole	+ 83.5	+ 56.3	+ 42.0
of which grain (excluding maize)	+ 177.0	+ 109.0	+ 65.0
Livestock farming as a whole	+ 5.3	+ 16.9	+ 3.0
of which beef (live weight)	+ 24.7	+ 27.6	+ 11.8
of which milk	− 8.2	+ 4.5	− 4.0
of which wool	+ 15.8	+ 26.8	− 1.0
of which eggs	0	+ 12.0	+ 10.0

Source: Vasyukin and Davydov 1978, p. 70.

the state buying prices do not vary with the specialisation zones of the republic causes severe problems. But rather than change the prices it would be simpler to alter the specialisations.

It is clear that farms specialising in cattle products, in those years when the average Buryat republic profitability of milk and beef production was around −10, would have to make their profits, if any, in some other sector of production. Deryugina, an economist from Ulan-Ude, states that farms specialising in cattle and pig production made over 200% of their income from grain, and this must mean that the specialised sector itself made a significant loss.[121] Further, it should be noted that Table 4.11 gives the republic average, and in some areas particular items made a loss even where the average for the republic was a profit. Thus some collective farms in the mountain taiga zones keep pigs and regularly make a loss from this sector, although it is generally a profitable one.[122]

183

Soviet economists now criticise the idea that a few profitable products within the farm should be expected to 'cover' for unprofitable ones.[123] Their reasons for disapproval of this situation – which actually exists – raise several questions of interest for the sociology of collectivised farming. Whereas in the past it was assumed that kolkhozy should be forced to produce particular products, it is now a matter of regret that 'administrative methods' are still needed to make farms go in for loss-making production. The persistence of this situation is a dominant factor in the political relations between the farm and the *raion* (district) Party organisation which will be discussed in Chapter 7.

Economists have also claimed that the present situation with regard to profitability contradicts the ideological emphasis on the labour theory of value. A worker in milk production makes eighty-three times less net income (*chistii dokhod*) for the farm in one hour than does a worker in grain production in the USSR on average, and in some regions the difference is even greater.[124] The difference between meat and milk buying prices, for example, cannot be explained by the greater training required in meat production, since both sectors employ manual workers. This is the direct result of pricing policy, which is tied to relatively fixed retail prices at the upper limit. The labour theory of value is in effect ignored.

Within individual farms wages are related to the net incomes derived from the different products sold to the state. This means that the pay of workers in loss-making sectors falls considerably below that of workers in profitable sectors, despite the introduction in the mid-1960s of basic minimum wages in collective farms. As we note in later chapters this situation gives rise to a certain enmity and jealousy between workers in different sectors. Although some farms equal out wages by transferring income from one sector to another, this does not altogether solve the problem. Wage rises are tied to productivity, and Soviet authors point out that to transfer income from grain to pay wages in the livestock sector 'gives rise to contradiction' (*vyzyvayet raznorechivost'*) between the interests of different groups in the kolkhoz.[125]

Here we can recall the question of the decrease in mechanisation of livestock production. It is in the interest of the managers of a farm to retain the goodwill of workers in the most profitable sector of the enterprise, and hence most farms do allow a large differential between these and other workers and do not transfer resources to livestock producers beyond the bare minimum. To introduce mechanisation, which would involve the transfer of some workers to other lower-paid jobs, is to run the risk of alienating workers to the extent that the machinery is 'accidentally' broken. Also, unless the *entire* process of production is mechanised, the manual parts hold back the rest and make it impossible for the management to increase the load (*nagruzka*) for each worker, for example by allotting each milkmaid twenty-two instead of twenty cows. As a result, partial mechanisation does not increase the productivity of labour from the point of view of the management, which cannot always make use of the fact that a milkmaid has a little more free time in each working day, and there is hence no basis for raising wages. Both management and workers, it appears, have thus resisted mechanisation in livestock production, but it is interesting that the real reason for this — the refusal of workers to cooperate in a process which would lower their wages — has only just been recognised in the Buryat literature. What follows from this, the fact that the kolkhoz management does have to bargain with its workers, is still too delicate a topic for discussion in Soviet publications.

Complete mechanisation should lower the cost of production of milk (although not enough Buryat farms seem to have tried this option to say whether this does occur), but it seems that it is only by considerably increasing fodder that the productivity per cow can be raised sufficiently to pay off the initial costs.[126] However, given the great differences in the buying prices of grain (high) and milk (low), it clearly makes sense for farms to grow grain directly for sale, rather than a variety of crops destined as fodder for cows. In Buryat conditions, where the area of land suitable for arable farming is limited, this must be one of the main factors which hold back milk production. But by concentrating on grain production Buryat farms are engaging in a hazardous pursuit. Siberian weather conditions seem to destroy much of the harvest in two or three years of every decade. All of this must be quite evident to the kolkhozniks, and must be particularly poignant to Buryat farmers, for whom the possession of cows used to be an index of security. It was only if the household had sufficient cows that it would invest in further sheep, horses, or agriculture in the pre-collectivised economy. By the 1970s, it had still not been possible to build up the number of cattle in Buryatiya to the 1928 level, and this must be largely the result of decades of pricing policy which has discriminated against the production of meat and milk. Possibly, Buryat cultural attitudes to cattle, and objections by traditionalist workers to de-personalising the milking process, are an important factor in the failure of collective farms to mechanise.

Collective farms all over the USSR sell products up to the level of the 'firm' plan (*tverdyi plan*) at the normal state buying price, but over-plan production is sold to the state at a higher rate. The effect of this dual price system is extremely unfair, since the profitability of a farm will to a great extent rest on the level of the 'firm' plan it has been able to negotiate with the *raion* authorities. The Soviet economists Vasyukin and Davydov mention farms which sell three times more than their plan, at over-plan prices of 30% above the normal price, while other farms only just manage to produce up to the level of their plan.[127] In 1970 it was made obligatory for farms to sell their surplus, up to 35% of the amount specified in the plan for grain and 8–10% of the plan in the case of livestock products, to the state. This was a measure to capture for the state the surplus which existed in some farms, and which might have been sold elsewhere. Table 4.13 shows that after 1970 the state did not, however, gain ground as a buyer of kolkhoz produce.

In the period since 1965 the prices paid by these different outlets (the state

Table 4.13. *Sales of products by the collective farms of the USSR expressed as a percentage of the total in rubles*

Year	Deliveries to the state	Direct sales to state retail organs	Kolkhoz market	Kolkhoz members	Other
1965	77.7	4.5	5.3	4.4	8.1
1969	83.3	6.8	5.9	2.7	1.3
1970	86.2	5.9	4.4	2.6	0.9
1975	85.7	8.5	3.2	2.3	0.3

Source: Vasyukin and Davydov 1978, p. 51.

retail organisations such as shops and canteens, the kolkhoz market, internal sales to kolkhozniks, and the state itself) have tended to come closer together.[128] By 1971—4 the state buying prices were in fact above the average offered by all these outlets for grain, meat (live weight), milk, and eggs. Although there is a tendency for kolkhozy to sell more of their extra produce direct to retail outlets, thereby bypassing the state and the turnover tax, this is still regarded with disapproval in some circles, and there can be no doubt of the domination of state delivery prices in the orientation of the kolkhoz economy.

This domination is held at its present level by means of fairly frequent juggling with the proportions of 'firm' plan prices and over-plan prices. The problem is that not only can kolkhozy obtain the highest prices of all from direct negotiations with retail outlets, particularly if they process produce themselves, e.g. making butter from milk, but also that the farms are sometimes cheated by the state buying organisations. This is made possible by the fact that the farms are obliged to sell to these organisations and are not always in a position to check that their produce is being correctly weighed and assessed for quality. In order to tie the kolkhoz product more firmly to the state it was made law in 1965 that not only should farms be subject to a plan of sales to the state, but also all *production* on improved land should be carried out according to an obligatory plan, which could then be used as the basis for 'over-plan' sales. By 1975 the extent of the 'firm' plan was already being extended into the area previously regarded as 'over-plan'. It is true that higher prices were offered, but at the same time a greater proportion of planned production came under the 'firm' plan, with appropriate sanctions on non-fulfilment.[129] In the autumn of 1980 it was announced that this process would be carried still further: from January 1981 the prices paid for over-plan sales would be included in the 'firm' plan prices, and in order to stimulate production farms would be paid a 50% bonus for all sales above the level of sales they had achieved on average in the previous five years.[130]

Given this situation, the sociologically interesting result, which has in no way been changed by the juggling with prices, is the necessity for competition between farms vis-à-vis the *raion* not to have a large component of unprofitable production included in their plans, and within the farm the competition among workers not to have to take jobs in the unprofitable sectors. In effect, at both levels, the political takes precedence over the economic.

Specialisation, productivity, and Buryat concepts of labour

The fact that state buying prices give such an advantage to grain producers as opposed, particularly, to milk producers, the fact that the climatic and soil conditions of the farms of the republic are very varied, and the fact that electrification, irrigation, and mechanisation are concentrated in some farms rather than others makes the initial conditions with which farms have to operate quite unlike one another. Specialisation has only accentuated these differences.

Increased specialisation in certain products does seem to have been accompanied in most cases by higher productivity per animal.[131] But, in the non-mechanised livestock sector, where can the basis of this productivity lie? The amount of fodder given to cattle only rose from 10.2 fodder units per animal to 10.4 fodder units between 1965 and 1970, and for sheep it actually went down from 2.8 units to 2.2 units in the same period. Horses suffered a drastic drop in fodder, and even chickens were given less feed in 1975 than in 1965.[132] Improved breeds of animals account for some of the increase in productivity per animal. But the most important factor must be increased labour, or more precisely, intensified labour. Buryat statistics show that the productivity of labour (man-hours required to produce one centner) has improved for every category of farm produce between 1965 and 1975, and that this out-distances the absolute growth in products over the same period.[133] In other words, Buryat kolkhozniks work more productively — but not for longer hours — than they did, if we are to take these statistics at their face value. As there has been so little mechanisation in livestock production, and since the indicator of labour productivity is one of the most ideologically stressed, it may be the case that the statistics have been presented in an over-optimistic way. Even so, they indicate that for meat and wool labour productivity began to decline between 1970 and 1975 and it did no better than remain constant for milk in this period (Table 4.14).

Wages have kept pace with productivity in the republic as a whole since the 1960s, and in the livestock sector they have exceeded it. But there are very large differences in wages between separate farms, some paying low in order to economise on costs, others paying more as productivity per animal rises. Wages can be as much as three times higher in farms which make exactly equivalent profits.[134]

Buryat kolkhozniks worked on average 256 days a year in the mid-1960s. These figures hide significant differences between collective farms — in some farms the average worked was 330 days[135] — and, more important, differences

Table 4.14. *Man-hours required to produce one centner in Buryat collective farms, 1965–75*

	1965	1970	1971	1972	1973	1974	1975
Grain	3.3	1.6	1.4	1.9	1.8	1.5	1.1
Cattle (beef)	68	63	66	62	67	60	63
Milk	19	15	15	14	15	14	14
Wool	305	246	266	232	269	260	244

Source: Narodnoye khozyaistvo buryatskoi ASSR 1976, p. 117.

between the various jobs in the farm. With increased mechanisation in arable farming agricultural workers have been able to put in less time, while the live-stock workers' load has continuously increased. Tractor-drivers' work is limited more or less to the months of May, August, September, and March. Milkmaids work all year round.

This means that workers in different jobs have unequal access to time for private production. There has always been a conflict between the private small-holding and the public sector in one respect, the allocation of labour time. We can see from Table 4.15 that time spent on private production has declined as a percentage of all time worked between 1966 and 1970. This table reflects the Soviet vision of a pool of time (100%) which should be fully 'used up', as little as possible being spent on private production (though the attitude towards private production has become more positive recently). In fact things are not like this, since many kolkhozniks have a great deal of free time. What is true is that some people, because of their position in the division of labour, have more time to devote to private production than others. And in some jobs there is the opportunity to develop private production parallel to their work in the collective, using the same time, e.g. shepherds who keep their own flocks alongside the public ones. Nevertheless, this idea of a pool of time which can be divided up is often used to stir up public feeling against people who are felt to be doing too well out of the private economy. But essentially the antagonism arises not so much from jealousy at 'wealth' obtained from private work as from anger at people who have escaped the drudgery of the farm itself. Everyone aims to make a good living somehow, and within the private economy people do not value their labour, just as they discount the time spent on arranging private 'deals'. As Amalrik remarks, since people pay nothing for the eggs and milk they themselves produce, they have the illusion of getting something for nothing.[136] On the kolkhoz, on the other hand, every hour is assessed carefully for the money it will bring in, and, for those in badly paid jobs, it would perhaps be fair to say that every hour is begrudged.

Table 4.15. *Time spent as a percentage of the whole in production in collective farms of the cattle specialisation zones of Buryat ASSR, 1966–70*

Time spent in producing	1966	1968	1970
Agricultural products	25.8	27.9	30.6
Grain	6.6	7.0	7.4
Potatoes	1.2	1.2	1.1
Vegetables	1.1	1.3	1.5
Other	16.9	18.4	20.7
Livestock products	56.2	62.1	65.4
Beef	17.5	20.7	23.4
Wool	4.9	5.8	7.1
Milk	23.1	23.9	23.9
Mutton	8.7	6.4	6.9
Other	6.4	5.3	4.1
Private production	18.0	10.0	4.0

Source: Buruyev 1974, p. 54.

The peasants disliked the teacher — not because he was a bad teacher or a bad man but because he was outside the system of compulsion within which they themselves were confined. They resented the fact that his work was lighter than theirs, that he was paid more for it and yet also, like them, had his private plot as well. For the same reason they disliked his wife, who managed the village shop, and Vera who ran the recreation room.[137]

As will be discussed in later chapters, there is a tendency for the 'lighter' and more mechanised jobs in the farm to be taken by Russians and people of other nationalities, while the local Buryats are concentrated in the livestock sector.[138]

If Buryat kolkhozniks today very probably work harder than their parents did before collectivisation, this is only regarded in official circles as a beneficial result of the rationalisation of labour resources. Ushnayev remarks, perhaps disapprovingly, that the pre-collectivisation Buryat household used only 45% of its working potential.[139] This observation, however it was arrived at, fits rather uneasily with the insistence elsewhere in Soviet writings that the early-twentieth-century Buryat household was burdened with endless, back-breaking toil. It is impossible to make an accurate assessment of this matter, but what does seem clear is that work was distributed among people in a completely different way (see Chapter 5). The division of labour in those times was traditional and was based on age and sex; while it would not be correct to say that this division was regarded as natural, since there is no reason to suppose that Buryats ever perceived a 'natural' or 'biological' order underlying social categories, it does appear that the traditional division of labour went largely unquestioned. To work, and to be seen to work, at the appropriate tasks was to be a good person, as we see from the novel *A Buryat Girl* by Ch. Tsydendambayev, which has been praised for its accurate depiction of Buryat psychology of those times. A woman thinks about her daughter-in-law, Zhargalma:[140]

'How good she is,' is Khanda's pleasant thought, 'she is strong and she can do everything. Her father and mother were lucky to bring up such a daughter. And I am also lucky now that she is living in our *yurt* . . . When I was young I could not milk cows as well as that. But when Zhargalma is milking the milk makes a noise in the pail as though ten shamans were beating their drums. Not a drop falls outside the pail. She's a work-loving daughter-in-law, both in the *yurt* and outside, and she doesn't leave me any work to do. But I can't sit long empty handed. Without work I'll soon get old.'

Later she says to Zhargalma:

'So you want to sit me on the right-hand side of the fire? I am to sit and sit and wait with an open mouth for a tasty bit of food from a foreign hand? No, my girl. We women were made by god to work day and night. You know how horses work, well, our fate is the same as theirs . . . my daughter, don't sit me on the other side of the fire, I am still healthy.'

One day, Zhargalma, having got up early to milk the cows, falls asleep again:

Zhargalma did not hear when Norbo, her husband, got up. That was bad, and she worried: 'What a long time I slept. The neighbours will find out, they'll say I am lazy, that I lie around in bed till mid-day. From being one of the good, it's easy to become one of the bad, that's what my mother told me.'[141]

While it is possible that this attitude still persists in the private domestic economy, there are at least two factors which act against it in the kolkhoz. One is the valuation of all work in rubles, but with an allotment of rubles to tasks in a way which is seen to be unfair:

Carting twenty barrels a day at a rate of ten kopecks per barrel, I was due to get more than sixty roubles in March, if I took no days off. 'See how much Andrei is getting,' the kolkhozniks grumbled. 'We shan't get as much as that. And there's nothing to the work: he just holds a hose in his hands and the water flows in the barrel by itself.' In fact I didn't even hold the hose, as I had made a hook out of wire to attach it to the rim of the barrel, while I just walked around. This only made the kolkhozniks madder still. Even Leva was very upset at earning only twenty roubles, and he no longer asked my forgiveness for living better than me but hinted that it was uncomradely for one 'parasite' to earn three times as much as another.[142]

The other factor is the removal of the possibility of organising one's own work in an efficient way, and the probability that saved time, as soon as it is noticed by the officials, will be put to use in some other way, again outside the wishes of the worker.

Not all tasks in the kolkhoz are seen to be dead-end jobs (see Chapter 5), and indeed some are much sought after. But whatever job one has, that is all one has, and, in the case of a job which is seen as unpleasant, its justification in terms of

190

the contribution to the farm as a whole is lost because it is valued in terms of its own internal indicator of success (barrels per day, litres milked per day, etc.). In the pre-collectivisation household, on the other hand, tasks, pleasant and unpleasant, came round with the seasons, and they had to be done simply because they were a necessary part of the total farming cycle – in which to play one due part was to be a worthy human being. It appears that this attitude has not survived the transformation of the unit of production from the household to the kolkhoz. It is true that those who do not work hard in the kolkhoz are criticised, but not for the same reasons as before. Zhargalma feared the neighbours' gossip because to get up late was to show oneself careless in looking after oneself, in preserving one's own social identity. In the kolkhoz, non-workers are criticised for somehow getting by without the drudgery of labour, and this is expressed in terms not of moral worth *for oneself*, but as a direct relationship with those who do work. The idea has taken root of a 'fair share' of work owed to one's comrades, in which credit accrues to those who contribute more, and debt to those who contribute less. Although everyone in fact works to a large extent for themselves, there are institutionalised circumstances (party, kolkhoz, and *sel'sovet* meetings) in which it is appropriate to deny that this is the case, thus providing the opportunity to vent feelings of resentment.

Characteristically, these ideas are expressed in terms of money. 'They work a kopeck's worth, but they eat a ruble's worth', is a saying among the Buryat.[143] In my view, even though what kolkhozniks say on formal occasions appears to be couched in terms of blame and guilt, this kind of grumbling does not in fact amount to a condemnation of moral worth. The speeches at meetings have an artificially prepared quality:

'I am ashamed that I did not contribute to the kolkhoz and led such a [bad] way of life,' said Prokopii Elanov. 'Property and my personal economy took a hold of me and killed all responsible feeling in me. Thank you very much, fellow-villagers, for your intervention. If you will take me back in the kolkhoz, I promise to become worthy of your trust by my honest labour and good behaviour.'[144]

But in day-to-day talk among themselves people speak in terms of money. Through the medium of wages, money comes to stand for the relation between people, yet it is not an index of moral worth in Buryat Soviet society. Money is characterless and at the same time a mediator, utilisable for the interaction of the most diversified objects. The very use of the money metaphor removes the question of labour from the sphere of truly ethical judgements. Money is the metaphor for something like a weighing balance, and those who grumble in the kolkhoz are not so much making moral judgements as lamenting the fact that the scales are weighted against them. The querulousness of such complaints becomes more marked with the perception that the amount of work to be done inexorably increases. And the distinctions between the categories of ethics, work, and money become sharper as it is more clearly understood, with every

191

'change' in prices and wage rates decided from above, that the relation of work to money remains for the kolkhozniks quite arbitrary. The fact that work is measured by internal indicators of success and is paid according to these indicators separates each job from the whole, and yet the fact that all jobs are paid in money makes comparison between them inevitable. In the official ideology personal accumulation is 'wrong', as Prokopii Elanov makes clear, but at the same time wages are becoming ever more clearly the most important motivation to work.[145] Wages do not represent moral worth, and, as will be described in Chapter 8, the Buryat, apparently in realisation of this fact, transform them into something else in the gift system.

Information and criticism

The above discussion raises the question of what the kolkhozniks know about their situation, and the closely related questions of the extent to which they are able to formulate criticism on a basis of knowledge and the nature of the criticism they can publicly express.

There is no doubt that kolkhozniks have access to a great deal of local economic information. The publicity given to 'socialist competition', which is coming to embrace almost all production at the various levels of the enterprise, work-team, and individual worker, ensures that the kolkhozniks are aware of the relative and particular measurements of their productive efforts. They know that their best efforts may indeed produce less than those of another district, and that, despite the rhetoric of success, the targets for 'socialist competition' are strictly related to circumstances. With the widening of competition to ever more groups, targets may even be going down. These targets and the attempts to surpass them are periodically read out at kolkhoz meetings and are published in the local kolkhoz or *raion*-level newspaper – in such a way that it would be hard for a collective farm worker to avoid them. But each batch of seemingly meaningful and related numerical indicators (the kilograms milked per cow in this half year as a percentage of the average for the last five years, the centners of hay harvested per hectare in 1975 in Barguzin as opposed to Tunkinsk, etc.) serves only to particularise the causes of success or failure. Furthermore, certain particularly unsuccessful items of production (classically, fodder), which certainly play their part in the totality of the farming cycle, are omitted altogether from the recitation of results. This means that, on the basis of this information alone, it would be very difficult to draw any general conclusions about the state of agriculture as a whole.

It could also be argued that the practice of farming itself as it is organised in the Soviet Union has the effect of confusing the criteria for judgement of the system. Those who *in fact* reproduce the system, the farmers, measure their efforts in politically determined time-spans (the five-year plan, the next plenum, etc.) which cut across time as reckoned by the seasonal rhythms of agricultural production. Politically oriented timing affects not only the presentation of results, but also the process of production itself, as when the farms of a district compete to accomplish some task by some ceremonial date. Of course there is no agricultural system which is not part of a political economy; but in this case the political organisation of time conflicts with other expressed aims *internal* to the system. These aims are purely 'economic' — productivity per hectare, net output, etc. — and require a different organisation of time from the political. But if farmers have to see the future refracted through the prism of political time, as embodied in multiple plans, it must be difficult for them simultaneously to envisage another 'economic' arrangement of time, and still more difficult to see beyond this opposition altogether. 'Economic efficiency' becomes the image of what has not been achieved, and its hold on the imagination does not depend on the means to attain it being clearly visible.

While detailed information of a factual, if sporadic, kind is readily available to the kolkhozniks for their own locality, it is probably true to say that such information becomes more difficult to attain the greater the level of generality. Thus Buryat republic statistics, though not hidden, are available only in specialist publications with a small circulation,[146] and certain information relating to crucial operations of the republic (e.g. gold-mining in the north of Buryatiya) is not available at all, clearly because of its all-Union and international significance.

The particularisation of information does not mean that kolkhozniks are shut off from all general comment on Soviet agriculture as a whole. Articles on general problems are published in central newspapers such as *Pravda, Komsomol' skaya Pravda*, and *Izvestiya*, which are easy to obtain anywhere in the Soviet Union. If we look at the content of newspapers at the different levels of the Soviet hierarchy, from the kolkhoz self-produced newssheet, through the *raion* (district) and *oblast'* (ASSR) papers to the central Moscow publications, it is apparent that criticism can become more general in its nature the more central the newspaper. This is true in particular of criticisms of management and planning: a district-level paper cannot criticise *oblast'* (regional) planning, nor can the regional paper find fault with Moscow planning. Conversely, it is only a Moscow paper which can condemn *oblast'* administration, and it is only a regional (or higher) paper which is able to criticise the districts. The district newspaper or radio station can do nothing but seek causes for failure in the individual enterprises 'under' it. What this means is that on the level for which the kolkhozniks have information, their own district and locality, generalised and systematic criticism cannot be expressed, while, on the other hand, the more reflective comment to which they have access usually floats divorced from factual information of a relevant kind and is certainly far removed from the local realities.

Let us contrast, for example, the content of two articles on the problems of agriculture published in 1980, one from the central Moscow *Pravda* and the other from the district-level newspaper *Barguzinskaya Pravda*.[147] While both are essentially dealing with the same problems, the central newspaper phrases the central subject matter as 'The relationship between man and his duty', but the district paper particularises: 'Failure of fodder production will make us unable to cope with livestock as a whole.' The central paper gives a small amount of not very relevant factual information – in an article on agricultural difficulties it provides a list of regions which have done well – but the local paper gives a great deal of very relevant information: the half-yearly production figures for all of the farms of the *raion*, the amount of hay which needs to be harvested in order to keep the herds alive through the winter, the exact number of animals which died during the spring and summer, etc. The central paper's article makes several comments of a general kind on the system: it says that planning from the 'achieved level' should end, that planners at regional levels should equalise conditions between farms by adjusting prices and taxes, that material rewards should be more closely tied to labour, etc. The local paper cannot make such comments, but instructs the managers of farms to do specific things: take out loans to construct fodder storage sheds, repair machinery for the hay-harvest, organise day and night pasturing of the herds for the rest of the autumn, see that hay-workers are adequately paid for their work. The two articles take rather different positions on the question of labour. Moscow *Pravda* stresses the need for initiative and responsibility among the workers, the desirability that managers should avoid authoritarian styles of command, and above all it stresses the role of material rewards: with adequate rewards 'any infringement of labour discipline will be punished by the ruble'. The local paper, on the other hand, knowing that these pious hopes cannot possibly help in the coming hay-harvest, tells the managers to get out there and organise *subbotniks* ('voluntary', unpaid labour-days), making sure that every single person attends. Both articles criticise specific categories of officials, but true to their roles they do so at different levels: Moscow *Pravda* accuses the regional authorities of protecting inefficient district officials and managers by finding good jobs for them when they have failed in one position already; the *Barguzinskaya Pravda* accuses individual specialists and officials in specific farms, sometimes citing them by name, holding them directly responsible for recent losses in fertility of the cows of the district.

Of the two articles, the one in the local paper is probably the more redundant for readers in general. This is because the newspaper does not have the authority to advise readers of general changes in policy, and because the information it contains – although the precise figures are usually subtly altered[148] – is made available to kolkhozniks on numerous other occasions. Knowing this, we need not be surprised to learn that when a survey was done of readers' interests for the newspaper *Pravda Buryatii* (a district-level paper), it was found that of all categories of articles (leaders, 'Party life', industry and transport, agriculture, science and technology, life and morals, politics and ideology, *belles lettres*, international events, local information, sport, and letters to the editor) those on agriculture were far and away the least read.[149]

194

This aversion can be explained, however, not merely by the redundancy of the information on agriculture, and not merely by the fact that news about agriculture is often bad news, but also by the nature of the social allocation of blame. No one in the Soviet Union can publicly blame the system of collectivised agriculture itself. This being the case, censure can be directed outwards and objectified; for example, by blaming the weather, which both articles do. But clearly there is a limit to the plausibility of the weather as an explanation for failure. Alternatively, censure can be directed inwards and subjectified. Centralised planning does not permit the farmers to make the system more efficient by questioning its mode of operation, but, on the contrary, what it does is to make the operators question themselves and their labour (the human element). Therefore, according to this view, the means to make the system more efficient is to transform the human element rather than the structure of the system. But, as has been mentioned, and this will be explored further in Chapter 5, the organisation of work and pay does not make it easy for kolkhozniks actually to identify the job with morality. The institution of the 'socialist obligation', abbreviated to *sotsobyazatel'stvo* in Soviet jargon, is aimed specifically at overcoming this disjunction. Almost everyone who is cooperatively inclined takes on some kind of 'socialist obligation', so who wants to read in their newspaper that this is still not enough? In the newspapers, blame is almost always shifted to the level below that from which the author writes. Frequently, it is specifically directed at some person or group. 'In inefficiency there is always a concrete guilty man' (*'U beskhozyaistvennosti vsegda est' konkretnyi vinovnik'*), says *Pravda*.[150] But for the local level, where such accusations become easily identifiable, the kolkhozniks know that they are not always justified. A scapegoat can be found, but a question remains.

4. Economic life in two collective farms

Although both the Selenga and the Barguzin kolkhozy were considered to be among the most successful in the republic, and although they both claimed to have a 'clear profit' or 'clear income' of hundreds of thousands of rubles, in fact one of the farms had a large gross output surplus to the plan, while the other was struggling to produce enough even to preserve the cycle of reproduction. This suggests that it is necessary to make a distinction between what is called in Soviet terminology 'clear income' (*chistii dokhod*) on the one hand, and what might be termed real profits on the other (that is, a disposable surplus over and above the delivery plan and reproduction obligations in the enterprise). The existence of such a surplus is not illegal, but could be described as non-legitimate. I shall discuss the difference between these two categories on the basis of my field data, and I shall suggest that it is the latter, for which I use the expression 'manipulable resources', which actually denotes the success of the enterprise from the point of view of those running it.

The collective farm economy

Two things are crucial to the nature of 'manipulable resources' in the kolkhoz economy: firstly, they are usually goods, not money, and secondly, they are obtained in circumstances of production in which the main controllable element is labour. Part of the 'manipulable resources' is thus used to establish relations of an 'exchange' or 'debt' type with the workers, over and above the regulated payment of wages. And, since 'manipulable resources' are in essence those products which are really surplus, or extra, to the state delivery plan, another part of them can be used in political manoeuvring to negotiate a low, or at least attainable, delivery plan. Such resources may be obtained in legal or illegal ways, and it is apparent that farms which are unable to meet their delivery plans are under strong pressure to resort to undercover methods. These include the obtaining of means of production and finished products from the 'manipulable resources' of the private household economies.

The use of field data makes it possible to give a more realistic description of the household economy than that obtainable from official statistics. It is suggested (see Chapter 6) that the nature of 'manipulable resources' in the domestic economy is essentially similar to that obtaining in the farms. In both types of production the scarce factor is labour, and what has to be 'realised' are goods of a parallel kind (meat, milk, wool, and fodder). The dichotomy between 'public' and 'private' production seems to me to be misleading: there is one economy. The same kind of operations occur in both sectors – indeed the operations are inextricably intertwined. Kolkhozniks obtain a large part of their surplus from the farm itself; after all, sale, or some kind of transfer, to the individual farm members is one of the most convenient ways for the kolkhoz to 'realise' its profits. Conversely, in lean times for the kolkhoz, the household economies can be tapped, either by using political pressure, or by making some 'bargain' involving long-term obligations. The nature of the 'manipulable resources', whether at the household, brigade, or farm levels, to a great extent determines the kind of operations in which they can be used, and consequently the kind of social relations such transactions establish. This matter – i.e. the channels of disposal of 'manipulable resources' in the context of the formal structures of power (the kolkhoz, soviet, and Party hierarchies) – will be discussed in Chapter 7. Meanwhile it is necessary to locate the 'manipulable resources' themselves, both in the kolkhoz (this chapter) and in the household economy (Chapter 6).

First, however, it is necessary to turn briefly to the question of the 'truthfulness' of the farm accounts. I would like to emphasise that these may show discrepancies which are of an entirely legitimate kind. When I was in the Selenga Karl Marx farm in 1967 I came across three sets of figures representing the production for the year 1966. One set was given to me by the chief economist of the farm, reading from her own handwritten book of figures. Another was obtained from the minutes of a general meeting of the kolkhoz at which the achievements of the previous year had been explained to the kolkhozniks. The

196

third set came from an interview with the chairman of the farm published in the local newspaper, *Krasnaya Selenga*. The three sets of figures are given in Table 4.16, and it will be seen that barely one figure is the same in the three cases. Instinctively I placed most trust in the figures given to me by the economist, perhaps because the information was given person to person, and the book, which I was able to examine, did seem to be a working document. In the rest of this section, these are the figures I used, unless otherwise stated. However, I realise that there is no very good reason to trust these figures in an absolute sense. An ethnographer visiting the Dyren sovkhoz in Barguzin in 1978 was given official figures of livestock belonging to the farm:[151]

   24,000 sheep
    4,700 cattle
     580 horses

whereas the 'spontaneous' figures which slipped out in a private conversation were

   13,000 sheep
    1,500 cattle
     300 horses

I find it difficult to believe that such a large difference between the official figures and 'reality' could exist in the Karl Marx farm, if only for the reason that, given the plan, the productivity claimed per animal or per hectare would otherwise be absurd. Another factor to be borne in mind is the time of year when livestock calculations are made. The flock of sheep may grow by about one-third depending on whether calculations are made in the autumn or the early summer. This may explain, at least in part, the Dyren discrepancies. However, it is clear that this cannot be the whole explanation, and we should remember that the farm leaders themselves, entirely legitimately, as in any business enterprise, operate with more than one set of figures. Even the plans for deliveries to the state exist in several versions (see Table 4.18).

Textbooks on book-keeping in the Soviet farms indicate that the operations involved in keeping accounts are extraordinarily complicated. This is partly because the farm accounts concern themselves with so many things which in Western life would be the concern of individuals (e.g. food to take on journeys to visit relatives). It is partly because certain important elements of the accounts are planned (amortisation rates, 'accounting prices', the *sebestoimost'* of products, etc.), but these do not correspond to reality, and corrections, deductions and so on have to be made. These latter corrections are allocated 'allowable' rates which may not cover actual expenses. Book-keeping is carried out by two methods, the 'analytic' and the 'synthetic',[152] which may introduce an element of confusion. The intention of book-keeping practice is to leave no possible gap for illicit operations, and thus every single production unit is accounted for in a variety of over-lapping documents. The theory is that these should provide checks for one another.

197

Table 4.16. *Output of Karl Marx farm, Selenga, according to three different sources, 1966*

	Economist of Karl Marx farm, Selenga, figures for 1966	Minutes of general meeting in Karl Marx farm, Selenga, 23 February 1967	Newspaper interview with chairman of Karl Marx farm, Selenga, 25 May 1967
Grain, total produced[a]	82,918 ct	—	—
sold to state	12,555 ct	12,160 ct	over 12,000 ct
Wool, total produced	945 ct	—	—
sold to state	945 ct	1,214 ct	995 ct and (later in same interview) 945 ct
Meat, total produced	5,059 ct	—	—
sold to state	5,059 ct	5,224 ct	—
Milk, total produced	16,462 ct	13,382 ct	13,574 ct
sold to state	13,652 ct	—	—
Fodder, total produced	36,059 ct	35,182 ct	—
Hay, total produced	—		—
General income[b]	1,222,348 r	—	1,222,348 r
income from agriculture	251,208 r	—	—
income from livestock	964,959 r	—	—
Clear income[c]	—	—	414,000 r
Pay to kolkhozniks	629,987 r	—	—
Av. monthly pay basic	—	—	90–115 r
Sown area, grains	7,505 h	—	7,897 h
Av. yield per hectare	11.04 ct	*aimed at for 1967*	15.2 ct
No. of cattle[d]	3,127 (summer)	3,656	2,900
cows	954	1,150	about 1,000
No. of sheep, total	44,522 (summer)	36,000	over 33,000
ewes	—	16,500	—
lambs	16,000	14,025	—
Milk per cow[e]	—	1,884 kg	1,827 kg
Wool per sheep	—	3.2 kg	over 3 kg

Notes:

a. *valovaya produktsiya* b. *obshchii dokod* c. *chistii dokhod* d. includes cows and calves e. average for fodder-fed cow

For one livestock production unit alone the following documents should be filled out: (1) a list of the individual workers, with the kind of herd (e.g. bulls from one to two years, heifers from two years, etc.), the number at the beginning of the month, the number sold, dying of disease, bought, 'disposed of', etc., and the number remaining at the end of the month; (2) a list of each named animal, its weight at the beginning of the month, the fodder given to it, weight at the end of the month; (3) a list of the movements of animals in and out of the production unit (bought, sold, slaughtered, etc.); (4) classification of the animals by weight, age, and breed; (5) a calculation of the value of various categories of animal on the basis of live weight; (6) an 'act' giving the details of slaughtered animals, a list of the products (meat, skin, horn, etc.), the units of weights (kilos, litres, centners, etc.) and the price for each. All of these documents (and others too numerous to mention) have to be signed by a number of responsible people. For example, the 'act' of slaughter has to be signed by the calf-herder, the head of the unit, the *zootekhnik*, the veterinary attendant, and the stockman.[153]

Most of the initial documents are filled out by the heads (*zaveduyushchiye*) of the production units, who spend a great deal of their time on this (see Chapter 3). However, some of the data has to come from the individual labourers. A large proportion of livestock workers are only semi-literate, and mistakes may appear for this reason.

It is by no means unknown for the unit heads to falsify production figures for individual workers with whom they have private feuds. The very fact that some people have to sign the papers, while others do the work, can lead to an attitude of irresponsibility. As soon as one mistake or discrepancy occurs all the figures begin to diverge, and it is more or less impossible to trace the source. Another frequent reason for discrepancies is that accounting does not take place simultaneously in all institutions.[154] It is thus probably fair to say that all units, and therefore to a greater degree all farms, operate in an atmosphere of approximation; no one quite knows which figures are exact representations, which ones a little false, and which ones positively misleading.

This very fact becomes the equivalent of a sword of Damocles hanging over the heads of the kolkhozniks. For years they may muddle along. But one day the district Party authorities can decide to make a real check. The heads of production teams are at risk, the Chairmen of the kolkhozy even more so.

I would therefore argue that the book-keeping system itself, entirely legitimately, creates the possibilities for the emergence out of nowhere of 'manipulable' products. Of course it is also true that the opposite can happen: accounting muddles could lead to the appearance of high costs or debts where they do not exist, but there must be strong pressures on book-keepers not to let this happen. The various documents of the production units are correlated and added up by a team of book-keepers whose sole job this is. They are organised hierarchically, like all other teams within the farm, with the most junior, young girls working with abacuses, doing the initial sums, and the most senior collating the final totals. The heads of the production units have nothing to do with this office-work except to hand in their own papers, and it is highly unlikely that the young cashiers and book-keepers ever have any say about the final accounts. The system lends itself to the introduction of error at every level. It is thus not surprising that the Karl Marx farm in Selenga had three sets of figures for 1966, nor is it necessary to suggest any double-dealing at work in the fact that they are different from one another. I simply point out that the social system of accounting in Soviet farms lends itself to the possibility of 'creating' manipulable resources at each level if people are so minded.

The farm accounts are checked by an Auditing Commission and may also be inspected by the representatives of the People's Control. As explained in Chapter 2, the People's Control is the more active body and the more powerful.

Kolkhoz accounts are also checked by an auditor from the *raion*. In some cases these officials are helpful to the farm, explaining to the management how to write the accounts in such a way that inevitable inconsistencies are concealed.[155] But in general in the *raion* planning departments, unless some relationship with a kolkhoz exists, every effort is made to ensure that no loophole is present by which an enterprise could deliberately engender 'unplanned' resources. Tiktina, a school-teacher from the Ukraine, recounts how the rural school where she was employed in the 1950s and 1960s used its 'special account' (*spetschet*) designed to provide food, etc., for the children to create a thriving farm run by the pupils, a much more productive and lively enterprise than the kolkhoz to which the school was attached. The profits of the school farm soon exceeded the entire school budget. But the existence of 'special accounts' at schools was made illegal, and the little farm was forced to close. The reasons given were ideological: the school farm was encouraging capitalist methods, it had an unhealthy emphasis on profitability, and it was operating for 'local' rather than 'social' goals.[156] But in fact, as Tiktina implies, the kolkhoz itself was forced in bad times to create, by manipulation of the accounts, illegal resources just in order to survive.

It got to the point where, even in our huge Michurin kolkhoz (and it was the same in others), they stopped registering part of the cattle offspring at the *fermy* in order to have reserve calves to cover the increasing mortality caused by their own negligence, lack of fodder, and overcrowding. And at the same time, the herdsmen did not forget their own interests and they stole the unregistered calves even more than before.[157]

Thus, to summarise, the category of 'manipulable' resources can be arrived at in two ways: (1) from consideration of a single set of official figures themselves, where legitimate surpluses may be manifest, and here my field data provide evidence; (2) from general sociological writing from inside the Soviet Union which suggests the ways in which book-keeping may be used to misrepresent the facts — here I do not have direct evidence myself and must refer to the literature.

What were the economic differences, judging from the figures given to me,

200

between the two farms? Table 4.17 shows that in 1966 the Selenga farm had a larger total area at its disposal, and a greater area in actual use, than the Barguzin farm in the same year. At the same time, the Barguzin farm had a larger population than the Selenga farm. It should be noted, however, that both farms were huge by Russian standards. For approximately the same size of working population, the average USSR kolkhoz had a land area of 6,500 hectares, as opposed to 59,000 hectares in Selenga and 37,000 hectares in Barguzin. Thus the two farms fully confirm the conclusion reached in section 3 above that Buryat farmworkers have a larger 'load' measured in kolkhoz-worked land than their RSFSR compatriots.

The Barguzin farm paid relatively more attention to fodder production than the Selenga kolkhoz. It had 7,000 hectares of hay-meadow, as opposed to 4,000 hectares in Selenga, and it also had more sown fodders. Selenga, on the other hand, as one would expect, had more open pasture (19,500 hectares, as opposed to 16,000 hectares in Barguzin). Selenga thus appears as a relatively more 'traditional' farm, using more open pasture and for a longer period of the year than Barguzin. This agrees with the difference already noted in the political culture of the two farms. Production based on mixed arable-livestock brigades and with a 'lineal' hierarchy of command, as in Selenga, is considered in Soviet terms to be more 'backward' than the specialised production units and 'staff' hierarchy of command of farms such as the Barguzin Karl Marx.

The amount of private land allowed each household was about 0.04 hectares in both of the kolkhozy. This was used mainly for intensive hay production, and sometimes for a small patch of potatoes. However, it is vitally important that the Selenga farm management also allowed its members to cut hay for their private animals from the communal natural hay-meadows. This hay furnished the essential element for the feeding of the private stock in winter. Without it, kolkhozniks have to sell other products in order to buy fodder for their animals and this severely limits the number they can keep.

The most complete data I have on agricultural (i.e. arable) production come from the Selenga farm in 1966. All of the Barguzin sources are fragmentary on this subject — probably with good reason, as we shall see. Even Dymbrenov's history of the Barguzin farm omits to mention progress in arable farming, and the *Barguzinskaya Pravda* district totals for 1974 and 1980 list meat, milk, wool, and eggs — but not grain production.

Let us look at the Selenga farm first. The chief economist, Mariya Dymbrilovna, gave me the following grain production figures for 1966:

total grain production	82,918 centners
sold to the state	12,555 centners (for 176,576 rubles)
sold to own kolkhozniks	2,849 centners (for 32,496 rubles)
paid to own kolkhozniks as wages	133 centners
sold to another kolkhoz	1,962 centners (for 31,966 rubles)

Table 4.17. *Population and collectively owned land and livestock in certain Buryat farms compared with pre-collectivisation holdings*

Per household useful land (hectares)	Per household hay-meadow (hectares)	Per household arable land (hectares)	Per household pasture (hectares)	Population per hectare total land	Average size of household	Per household			
						Horses	Cattle	Sheep	
90.40	9.02	1.02	56.99	0.037	4.98[a]	5.00	29.10	24.40[b]	Barguzin, 1890s
57.72	5.51	–	–	–	4.61[c]	4.80	15.00	18.00	Selenga, c. 1920
–	8.19	1.13 (incl. fallow)	–	–	–	2.60	13.10	11.10[d]	Kizhinga, c. 1922
112.80	27.75	c. 2.40	83.25	–	4.90				Eastern Buryats with 1–1½ des. arable
104.25	24.90	c. 4.70 (incl. fallow)	74.95	–	5.60[e]				with 2–2½ des. arable
32.37	12.98	10.43	13.24	0.053	3.57	2.40	11.80	12.80[f]	Barguzin, Karl Marx kolkhoz, 1941
34.35	10.28	13.48	28.97	0.048	4.25[g]				Barguzin, Karl Marx kolkhoz, 1954 (after unification)
90.50	25.70	25.70	52.80	0.029	4.61	1.26	8.47	89.35(s) 117.67(w)[h]	Selenga, Karl Marx kolkhoz, 1966
c. 58.70	13.69	c. 13.89	31.31	0.062	c. 4.55	1.10	10.17	71.72(w)[i]	Barguzin, Karl Marx kolkhoz, 1966
48.09	9.46	18.57	20.04	0.059	4.67	1.02 (1968)	5.48	47.61 (1968)[j]	Barguzin, Lenin kolkhoz, 1969
–	–	16.57 (not incl. fallow)	17.89	0.053	4.22	1.39	8.50	60.08[k]	Barguzin, Karl Karx kolkhoz, 1974

s = summer   w = winter

allocated to kolkhoz seed fund (grain)	14,262 centners
allocated to kolkhoz seed fund (maize)	300 centners
put into reserve/aid fund	30 centners
sold on kolkhoz market	—
fodder for farm animals	36,059 centners

The acreage under grain in 1966 was 6,902 hectares, so the yield that year must have been around 12.0 centners per hectare, a good result for the Buryat region where the average that year was 11.3 centners per hectare.[158]

However, other things about these figures make less good sense. Firstly, what happened to all the extra grain? All of the destinations mentioned by the economist add up to only 68,150 centners. A massive 14,768 centners of grain remained at the end of 1966, neither sold to the state, nor to another farm, not put into the seed fund, nor set aside for fodder, nor sold on the market. A certain amount, I was told, was used in an agreement (*dogovor*) with a state vegetable cooperative (ORS), by which the kolkhoz exchanged grain for a fresh supply of fruit and vegetables. However, there was no sign of fresh fruit and

Notes to Table 4.17.

a. Asalkhanov 1960b, p. 86. These data refer to the whole area of the Barguzin steppe duma occupied by Buryats and Evenks.
b. Koz'min 1924, p. 5. Koz'min compares the Barguzin Buryat with the Selenga and Chita Buryats. In the 1890s the Selenga Buryats had only half the number of cattle per household owned by the Barguzin Buryats, and only 18 sheep per household as opposed to the Barguzin 24.4. They also had fewer sheep than the Barguzin people and were generally poorer at the end of the nineteenth century.
c. Rukavishnikov 1923.
d. Koz'min 1924, p. 12.
e. *Ibid.*, p. 10.
f. Dymbrenov 1961, p. 32.
g. *Ibid.*, pp. 46–7. These figures show how the Karl Marx Collective benefited by the amalgamation with the Kalinin kolkhoz, especially in pasture. The hay-meadow area per household was already down from the 1941 figure, however, and was not markedly better than the figures for Barguzin as a whole in the 1890s. Family size had gone up by 1954 after its low point in the war.
h. These data come from my field-notes, 1967, information given by the chief economist of the kolkhoz. These figures show that the Selenga Karl Marx farm had much more land for the household members than the average individual herders of the Selenga region had at their disposal in the 1920s before collectivisation. Other kolkhozy in the Selenga region may however have had correspondingly less land per household. These 1966 figures also show the staggering change in herd composition in Selenga district since collectivisation.
i. These data come from my field-notes, 1967, information given by the Chairman of the kolkhoz. The amount of hay-meadow rose since 1954, as did the amount of pasture per household. This was despite the fact that the boundaries of the kolkhoz did not change between 1954 and 1966, and the population per hectare grew. The explanation is that an absolutely larger area of land was brought into use during this period.
j. Dambayev 1970, pp. 58–9. This example shows a kolkhoz neighbouring the Karl Marx in the Barguzin region, but somewhat less privileged in natural resources and animal stock per household.
k. These data come from my field-notes, 1974–5, information given by the Chairman of the kolkhoz.

vegetables when I was visiting (May 1967). In any case, the amount of grain used in this exchange cannot have been very large. We are left with what I have called a 'manipulable' resource, consisting of grain.

The other odd feature of these figures is that the ruble sums quoted to me as accruing to the kolkhoz for sales of grain to the state and to the kolkhozniks are larger in both cases than they should have been at the prices quoted. Thus, at the state delivery price mentioned to me, of 11 rubles 50 kopecks per centner, the kolkhoz should have received 144,382 rubles, not the 176,576 rubles the economist said they obtained. It is possible that the difference here could be explained by the higher prices paid by the state for over-plan production — according to the Chairman's interview the amount of grain sold to the state in 1966 was over three times the annual plan.[159] It is also possible that they could have received some extra money from the state if they produced the grain at a lower *sebestoimost'* than had been planned.[160]

However, the second discrepancy is more difficult to account for. The economist told me that grain was sold to the kolkhozniks at the price of 3 rubles 72 kopecks per centner. In that case the sum received by the kolkhoz would have been 10,598 rubles rather than the 32,496 rubles quoted to me. The price at which grain is sold to the kolkhozniks is decided at a general meeting, and the aim is to set it as 'low as possible' so that each member should gain. However, there is a clear disjunction here between the aim of the individual members and the interests of the farm itself. There is no way of telling for sure where this money came from. The kolkhozniks, living far from any town or market, their village shop in the mid-1960s empty of everything except tinned fish, may have in fact paid more per centner of grain than the price quoted to me. Alternatively, it is possible that the kolkhoz sold more grain to its members than the stated 2,849 centners. All we can say is that there was a sum of money unaccounted for in the kolkhoz coffers.

The kolkhozniks also ended up with a 'manipulable resource' from this deal. Even if only 2,849 centners were sold to them, each household would have received 772 kilos of grain. This is more than any household of five members could possibly consume in a year. Some must have been used as feed for private animals. But if some of the households bought more than others they could have amassed substantial amounts of grain available for use in private transactions.

As regards hay, the Selenga kolkhoz produced 35,182 centners from its 4,990 hectares of meadows in 1966. This was considered, like the grain, to be a great success. It was 11,000 centners more than the hay produced in 1965. However, the yield obtained (8.7 centners per hectare) still did not reach the average Buryat yields of 1941.[161] Possibly some of the better hay-meadows were cut by the kolkhozniks for their private animals.

Let us compare Selenga arable farming with that of the Karl Marx farm in Barguzin. The figures I have for the latter farm refer to the early 1970s. I was never told a figure for total grain production, but the amounts of deliveries to

Table 4.18. *The five-year plan given to Karl Marx kolkhoz, Barguzin district, Buryat ASSR, for the years 1971 to 1975 (centners)*[a]

		1971	1972	1973	1974	1975
Meat	plan	4,650	4,990	5,140	5,340	5,720
	over-plan (*sverkhplana*)[b]	200	490	490	490	520
Milk	plan	8,000	8,100	8,200	8,700	9,700
	over-plan	800	800	960	1,000	1,050
Wool	plan and over-plan	924	1,070	1,100	1,225	1,330
Grain	plan and over-plan	3,500	3,500	3,520	3,575	3,750
Vegetables	plan	100	100	100	100	100
Potatoes	plan	700	700	700	700	700

Notes:
a. Note the interesting differences between this version of the plan and the 'working version' given in Table 4.21. This version may well represent the original plan, given out at the start of the five years, whereas the 'working version' was probably amended by the *raion* officials during the course of the period.

Note also that the figures given in the *Barguzinskaya Pravda* (see Table 4.22) as the plan for the Karl Marx farm for 1975 do not correspond with the plan above for the same year.
b. 'Over-plan' sections of the plan are also strictly obligatory. However, distinctly higher prices are paid for the fulfilment of these sections.

the state were available. The five-year plan for 1971–5 was as follows, including the amounts of 'over-plan' production which are obligatory. (The complete five-year plan for the Barguzin farm is given in Table 4.18.)

1971	3,500 centners of grain
1972	3,500
1973	3,520
1974	3,575
1975	3,750

By the beginning of 1975, when I visited the farm, they had managed to deliver only 6,930 centners in four years, leaving over 10,900 centners to be delivered in 1975. Even with good weather, the farm Chairman knew they would not manage this. The early 1970s had in fact been disastrous. There was severe flooding in 1971 to 1973 which had affected the whole Buryat republic, and in 1974 there was a drought. In 1974 they had in fact managed to deliver 3,600 centners of grain, but if we consider that 3,700 hectares were sown that year with wheat alone, it is clear that the yields were disastrously low. Wheat yields were less than 2 centners per hectare in 1974. This should be compared with the 11.6 centners per hectare obtained in 1958, when weather conditions were good and the extent of erosion less.[162] The total grain production that year was 27,000 centners. Even if the farm produced more than it delivered in the 1970s, the difference cannot have been very great, just enough for the seed fund, since farms are obliged to fulfil the plans before using grain for any other non-productive purpose.

We therefore have to explain a drastic fall in grain production since the late 1950s — a situation which was especially serious in view of a price structure favouring grain which prevailed through the 1960s.

Studies of the Barguzin valley written as early as the 1950s make it clear that the disastrous flooding and droughts of the 1970s were nothing new. The valley was a paradigm of the difficulties mentioned in section 3 above. The Kuitun steppes, the main agricultural area of the Karl Marx farm, and indeed of the Barguzin valley as a whole, had always been dry and subject to erosion. In 1975 one half of the Kuitun steppes was badly eroded — this being half of the area which supplied two-thirds of the grain of the whole district. A local newspaper accused farms in the district of ploughing up virgin land without due attention to problems of erosion, and it complained that the Karl Marx farm in particular had neglected tree planting which might have protected the fields from wind erosion. Fourteen hectares of trees had entirely perished as a result of neglect from the kolkhoz.[163]

Furthermore, the Karalik irrigation system, originally constructed in the 1920s with much enthusiasm, had fallen into disrepair. This resulted in yields on 'irrigated' land which were no higher than those on ordinary fields. The Karalik irrigation system had been in trouble for some time, since Dymbrenov complained that it, as well as the Karasun, Borogol and Mandai systems, was in need of repair back in 1960. However, the kolkhoz was not in a position to do much about the problem, since as we have seen the reconstruction of the irrigation systems was to be both financed and carried out by other bodies. The Ulyun kolkhoz chief agronomist complained bitterly about the situation at the *raion* Party conference in 1975.[164]

The problems of water management affected hay production in this farm even more severely than grain. In 1971 to 1973 the Karl Marx lost its *entire* hay harvest. The Mandai area was permanently water-logged (see Map 3), and its drainage was another item on the list of construction projects still incomplete in 1975 (see Table 4.4). Again the financing and repair were in the hands of two separate outside organisations.

In 1975 hay was being imported from Mongolia to deal with the fodder situation (this hay itself had created another problem — a kind of mouse, which arrived with the hay and multiplied extraordinarily, requiring the kolkhozniks in Barguzin to keep cats, which they had never done before; they, like other peoples of Mongolian culture, regard cats as unclean animals). By 1980 the fodder situation was desperate in the whole of the Barguzin valley. The main hay-fields of the three collective farms were flooded, and the Soviet authorities

Table 4.19. *Hay and grain production on Selenga and Barguzin farms*

	Land area sown with grain (hectares)	Grain harvest (centners)	Land area of hay (hectares)	Hay harvest (centners)
Karl Marx, Selenga, 1966	5,005	82,912	4,009	32,182
Karl Marx, Barguzin, 1974	4,900	c. 3,600	9,000	? (they had no harvest at all in 1973)

were calling for 'every inhabitant of the *raion*, every industrial enterprise, organisation and educational establishment' to take part in cutting fodder for the following winter (1980–1). They were to cut small twigs, reeds, the grass on roadside verges, clearings in the forest, and marshes. It is apparent that although the hay harvest in 1979 had been quite good nevertheless it did not provide enough for total fodder needs. In the first half of 1980 many animals had died: 945 cows, 7,411 sheep, and over 28,000 lambs. The reasons given for this tragic loss were 'extreme lack of fodder, and organisational difficulties'.[165]

In the Karl Marx farm itself the new Chairman announced a 'complete reorganisation' of fodder production in 1980. Writing in the *Barguzinskaya Pravda*, he implied that everything would be different: the two tractor field brigades would be specialised, and the whole arable operation would be headed by B-M.Ts. Dambayev. However, the brigades were already specialised by 1975, and Dambayev had been the chief agronomist for several years. But what could the Chairman propose? As his article makes clear, the same old problems remained: the Karalik irrigation system was now apparently operating, but the Karasun system was not, and once again the *Buryatvodstroi* organisation was failing to do the necessary work. The crucial Kuitun steppes were still too dry, and summer pastures near the Ina river were also lacking irrigation.[166]

Thus we can easily see why, because of its low production of hay and other fodders, the Karl Marx farm was forced to spend its entire revenue from grain sold to the state (not a large amount, as we have seen) on the purchase of fodder concentrates.

A comparison of the arable production of the two farms in the years for which I have data is remarkable (Table 4.19). Selenga has better climatic and soil conditions for agriculture than Barguzin. The growing season is almost a month longer. The Barguzin farm Chairman complained that his soil was bad, the climate hard, and the farm situated far from any railway or large town, which made transportation expensive. In 1967, when I first visited the farm, it was necessary to cross two rivers by raft in order to reach the farm. By 1975, a wooden bridge had been built over one of these rivers, the Ina. Nevertheless it is clear that Barguzin is one of the areas least suited to agriculture in Buryatiya. The problems are exacerbated by placing vital technical remedial tasks in outside hands.

But the Barguzin Karl Marx farm had an obligatory grain delivery order which was of much the same proportions as the Selenga farm. There was no possibility for it to create the same kind of 'manipulable resources' in grain as the Selenga farm. It is very probable that the Barguzin farm made a net loss in agriculture which had to be covered from other sectors of production.

Livestock production in the two farms is shown in Table 4.20. Barguzin was relatively less successful in milk production than Selenga. It obtained a yield of 12.7 centners of milk per cow in 1959 as against Selenga's 17.25, and, although we do not know the total produced in 1974, the Barguzin farm had a larger number of cows and sold less to the state than did the Selenga farm in 1966. One reason for this must have been the fodder problem in Barguzin. A hard-working milkmaid with good cows could expect to get at least 20 centners per cow in Buryatiya.[167]

The production of milk is particularly beset with problems of quality. Obviously, if the target is simply to get a certain number of litres the milkmaids will be tempted to produce large quantities with a very low fat content. The Karl Marx farm did so badly in the quality, cleanliness, and freshness of its milk deliveries in 1975 that its best production unit, at Soyol, gave only second class

Pontoon-raft crossing the River Ina in the Karl Marx kolkhoz, Barguzin, 1967.

Table 4.20. *Livestock production on Selenga and Barguzin farms*

	Selenga Karl Marx, 1966 (data provided by chief economist)	Barguzin Karl Marx, 1959 (data provided by Dymbrenov)	Barguzin Karl Marx, 1974 (data provided by Chairman)
Milk (centners)	16,462	14,060	?
sold to state	13,652	4,032	12,000
sold to kolkhozniks	104[a]		
No. of cows	954[b]	1,100	1,129[b]
Wool (centners)	945	754	1,192
sold to state	945		
No. of sheep	44,522[b]	24,865	30,223[b]
Meat (centners)	5,059	4,122	?
sold to state	5,059		4,900 (?)
No. of cattle not including cows	2,173	3,017	3,149
No. of pigs	–	346	251

Notes:
a. Remainder to calves
b. Summer

milk, and all of the milk from its other *fermy* was returned from the factory as unusable.[168] By 1980 this problem still remained and the farm was mentioned among those of the *raion* which delivered particularly low quality milk because they had not managed to organise an adequate cooling system. It is true that the kolkhoz also had its milk returned because the district dairy worked on a single shift and was unable to process all of the milk supplied to it into long-lasting products such as butter.[169]

There does not seem to have been much room for manoeuvre in milk production in either of the farms by the mid-1960s. The delivery quotas had risen from the 1950s until virtually all the milk produced and not used to feed the calves had to go to the state. The same was true of wool production in the Barguzin farm. At an average cut of 4 kg per sheep, the delivery plan arounted to all of the wool that the kolkhoz flock could produce. This was not the case, however, in the Selenga Karl Marx farm. Even if the cut here was significantly lower, at 3 kg per sheep (which seems not too much to expect, since it was already 2.8 kg per sheep in 1959),[170] the amount produced would still have amounted to 1,335 centners in 1966, that is 390 centners over the amount sold to the state. Again, judging by our economist's figures, the Selenga Karl Marx farm seems to have ended up with a useful 'manipulable resource'.

The figures on meat production are the most difficult to interpret. Even if the Barguzin farm sold all of its meat to the state, as seems probable since it was only just keeping up with its deliveries (see Tables 4.20 and 4.22), this tells us little about efficiency as compared with the Selenga farm, because we do not know what proportion of the sheep, cattle, and horse herds were destined for slaughter.

The collective farm economy

Finally, it should be noted that the livestock itself may provide a 'manipulable resource'. If the breeding programme results in a larger number of young animals than is needed for the reproduction of the herd, then these young constitute a resource which can be turned into money (or other benefits). Livestock production units have a certain autonomy in buying and selling animals provided they can deliver the planned amount of meat in live weight. At the level of the farm itself there is even greater leeway. The Selenga farm regularly managed to sell eighty to a hundred calves to other enterprises each year in the mid-1960s. The Barguzin farm, on the other hand, had to buy young animals to keep its herds up to size. In 1973 it bought calves worth 61,912 rubles.

How successful were the farms in fulfilling their plans of deliveries to the state? I have no data on the Selenga kolkhoz plans, and full details of the Barguzin farm's plans are given in Table 4.18. Here, it is worth noting only the more general points for this farm: (1) The Barguzin farm, in keeping with its notable history and favoured treatment over the years, also had a larger plan to fulfil in all main products than the other farms of the district (they were probably also smaller enterprises). (2) The Karl Marx farm in Barguzin was unlikely to fulfil the meat, vegetable, and grain quotas of its five-year plan, although it was coping more or less successfully with milk and wool (Table 4.21). (3) In relation to other farms of the Barguzin *raion*, the Karl Marx was not particularly successful, nor was it especially unsuccessful (Tables 4.22 and 4.23).

By 1980, the delivery plans for all the farms of the *raion* had been lowered for all items except wool. Despite the fact that the delivery orders were lower in 1980 than in 1975, the Karl Marx was unable to keep up in meat and milk. However, in wool production it was successful: with a smaller number of sheep than in 1975, 25,000 as opposed to 30,200, the farm was managing to produce more wool than it had in 1975. Wool, perhaps, is the livestock product least affected by fodder shortages, since the sheep graze on natural pasture for a large part of the year. By 1980, the sovkhoz 'Bodonskii' had clearly overtaken the Karl Marx kolkhoz as the 'vanguard' farm of the district, although in 1975 it had been the least successful (Tables 4.22 and 4.23). Although it is not clear why from Table 4.23, the Bodon farm won the 'socialist competition' for the first half of 1980 in both milk and meat. Its good milk figures were the result of its selling a greater proportion of its milk (78%) to the state, rather than giving it to the calves. Other farms of the district sold only about 50–60% of their milk. If this is perhaps evidence of a short-term gains policy on the part of the Bodon management, their sheep-farming activity bears indications of the same attitude: they achieved good meat sales by selling all the farm's one-year-old lambs, a tactic which put a premium on meat as opposed to wool and which could not be carried out every year in any case. The politically favoured position of the Bodon farm by 1980 is indicated not only by its winning the competition for achievement of deliveries – this being dependent, of course, on the level at which the plan for deliveries is set – but also by the large number of

Table 4.21. *The 1971–5 five-year plan in Karl Marx farm, Barguzin (centners)*

	Milk	Meat	Wool	Grain	Potatoes	Vegetables
Five-year plan	51,200	25,905	5,609	17,800	3,500	500
Fulfilled by end 1974	46,563	19,969	4,516	6,930	2,582	376
Leaving for 1975	4,637	5,936	1,093	10,870	918	124

Source: Chairman of the Karl Marx farm, Barguzin.

articles in the *raion* newspaper outlining its methods and praising its teams.[171]

It can be seen from these tables of the results of 'socialist competition' in the Barguzin *raion* – in effect the totality of production directed towards state sales – that the Karl Marx farm was about average for the district. Grain and hay figures are not mentioned in the tables at all, presumably because the output had fallen so far behind the plan. As we have seen, these crucial elements put the whole livestock sector in jeopardy. It seems likely therefore that the Barguzin Karl Marx farm, unlike the Selenga farm of the 1960s, had few disposable resources by 1975, let alone 1980, since it was still struggling to fulfil the grain and meat obligatory delivery orders.

Here it is necessary to consider the distinction which I am making between 'manipulable resources' and the category which in Soviet terminology is called 'clear income', or 'profit'. The Soviet category of 'profit' does not correspond to a common-sense Western idea of profit, since it is almost entirely non-disposable. As we saw in Chapter 2, the Soviet 'profit' is derived from the value which the product has over the costs of production and reproduction in the accounting period. Part of this profit goes to the state in the form of taxes and another part is also never seen by the farm as it consists of the difference between the prices paid for products by the state and the rather higher prices which usually obtain on the open market (kolkhoz market) and retail outlets. Despite the loss of part of the 'profit' to the state, most farms end up after 'realising' their products with a sum of money, which they call the 'clear income' (*chistii dokhod*). Let us see how this was obtained in the Barguzin Karl Marx farm. This exercise, though somewhat tedious, shows why the 'clear income' cannot be seen as a profit (disposable surplus) in common-sense terms.

For the Karl Marx farm in Barguzin there are the data shown in Table 4.24, copied by me from the account book lent to me by the farm Chairman, for the year 1973. It is by no means obvious how to interpret these accounts. One of the difficulties in understanding them is that the total output was not revealed, either in money terms or expressed in products. Referring to Chapter 2, p. 81, it is probable that what the Chairman called 'general income' (*obshchii dokhod*) corresponds to the category 'aggregate income', i.e. the value of the total product plus wages minus the costs of production and reproduction (*sebestoimost'*).

Table 4.22. Results of 'socialist competition' of the farms of the Barguzin aimak in sale of products to the state on 1 December 1975 (centners)

	Meat			Milk			Wool			% of 1974		
	Plan	Fulfilled	%	Plan	Fulfilled	%	Plan	Fulfilled	%	Meat	Milk	Wool
Kolkhozy												
Karl Marx	5,300	5,083	96	11,795	10,577	90	1,190	1,128	95	104	96	95
Ulyun	2,900	3,073	106	7,095	6,642	94	450	470	104	113	96	104
Khilganai	2,800	2,400	87	5,320	4,228	79	520	560	108	94	82	106
Sovkhozy												
Barguzin	4,840	4,130	85	11,535	11,909	103	198	204	103	88	109	102
Chitkan	2,000	1,635	82	11,435	10,580	93	22	40	182	123	102	167
Bodon	3,000	1,639	55	4,340	3,377	78	250	227	91	85	86	98
The people	1,750	2,088	119	—	44	44	270	299	111	114	42	101

Source: *Barguzinskaya Pravda*, 2 December 1975, p. 3.

Table 4.23. *Results of 'socialist competition' of the farms of the Barguzin aimak in sale of products to the state, half-year ending 16 July 1980 (centners)*

	Meat		Milk		Wool		% of 1979		
	Annual plan	% fulfilled	Annual plan	% fulfilled	Annual plan	% fulfilled	Meat	Milk	Wool
Kolkhozy									
Karl Marx	3,650	21	9,900	43	1,280	45	170	68	170
Ulyun	1,700	20	4,450	31	465	20	50	49	—
Khilganai	1,800	13	4,250	25	560	42	39	40	107
Sovkhozy									
Barguzin	1,850	36	12,300	55	190	—	62	86	—
Chitkan	1,400	58	9,400	52	40	—	108	86	—
Bodon	1,850	54	3,700	68	255	—	105	94	—
The *raion* (including deliveries from individuals)	1,270	30	44,000	48	3,100	30	76	74	93

Source: Barguzinskaya Pravda, 19 July 1980, p. 1.

Table 4.24. *Accounts of the Karl Marx kolkhoz, Barguzin, 1973, as given by farm Chairman*

Non-productive expenditure

1	Wages for workers	753,267 rubles
2	Social security and insurance	17,299
3	Investment in 'undivided funds' of the farm	182,885
4	Cultural services	50,000
5	Capital building and maintenance	647,000
	Total	1,650,451 rubles

Productive expenditure

		Plan	Fact
1	Petrol, oil, etc.	77,589 rubles	81,828 rubles
2	Seed grain	15,038	14,293
3	Fodder	40,610	67,878
4	Fertilisers	17,064	20,258
5	Medicines, chemicals	29,390	18,200
6	Spare parts	13,115	42,718
7	Other materials	2,000	22,576
8	MGP	–	12,419
9	Running repairs		
	machinery	9,365	17,809
	buildings	20,000	14,231
10	Electricity	16,000	7,983
11	Hire of motor transport	11,000	51,897
12	Young cattle	48,834	61,912
13	Other	42,569	69,579
	Total	1,697,226 rubles	1,835,953 rubles*

Income

1	'General income' (*obshchii dokhod*)	1,641,935 rubles
2	'Clear income' (*chistii dokhod*)	232,885
3	Income from 'over-plan' sales to the state	
	wool	30,657
	milk	37,100
	meat	32,460
	Total	100,217 rubles

*By this point, no reader should expect the listed items to add up to the total! I do not know what the initials MGP stand for.

According to the rules, the first item to be deducted from the aggregate or general income is the wages bill. The farm Chairman told me that the income from 'over-plan' sales to the state, i.e. obligatory deliveries which are paid at a higher rate than the deliveries in the first-part of the plan (see Table 4.18), are used in his farm to pay the difference between the planned costs of production and the actual costs of production. In fact the difference in 1973 came to 138,727 rubles, which is more than the farm received from 'over-plan' sales (100,217 rubles). The next item to be deducted from the remaining 'general income' is a sum for capital building and maintenance, which goes into the 'compensation fund'. A loan from the State Bank covered about half of these costs. After these operations the farm is left with a sum of money corresponding to the category of 'clear income' as described in the textbooks. This must be divided up between the 'consumption fund' (*fond potrebleniya*) and the 'accumulation fund' (*fond nakopleniya*). Accordingly the Barguzin farm paid off sums for social security and insurance and cultural services into the first, and a sum for productive investment into the second. The farm thus ended up with a balance of 319,993 rubles. However, if it had not borrowed money from the state, it would have made a net loss of 47,026 rubles (see Table 4.25).

The reader will notice that no sum in the accounts as I have worked them out corresponds to the 232,885 rubles claimed by the Chairman to be his 'clear income'. It is possible to arrive at a somewhat similar figure (203,158 rubles) if the loan from the state bank is not inserted into the accounts, and if the income of the farm is assessed before it has paid out sums for social security, investment and culture. This would correspond more or less with the textbook category of 'clear income'. In view of the confusion of the conceptual categories involved, discussed in Chapter 2, it is not in practice clear what should be counted as 'clear income'. But it is evident that, wherever the line is drawn, the money income of the farm is legally due to be counted off into a variety of funds, each with a defined purpose. The Chairman of the farm did not mention a further series of payments which every farm has to make out of its 'clear income': the annual tax (*podkhodnoy nalog*), the payments of bonuses to workers and management, trade union dues, and subscriptions to the All-Union Soviet of Collective Farms.[172] These payments are obligatory, and if any money is left over, it enters the reserve fund. The 'clear income' cannot thus be seen as a profit in the usual sense of the word, because as soon as it appears in the books it is not freely disposable. It is merely an accounting statement about the temporary position of a certain, probably notional, sum of money at the end of the year.

Even bonus payments are not genuinely disposable by the management. Their size in relation to the basic wage is regulated by statute and they are tied to productivity.[173] They are a permanent part of the farm's bill for wages, and are often not even awarded by the farm itself, but by Party officials.

The 'clear income' in the Selenga farm in 1966 was about twice the size of the 'clear income' in the Barguzin farm in 1973. This allowed the Selenga farm

Table 4.25. *An analysis of the accounts of the Karl Marx farm, Barguzin, 1973*

	+ 1,641,935 rubles	income from sales to the state net of planned costs of production		+ 1,641,935 rubles	income from sales to state net of planned costs of production
	− 753,267 rubles	wages		− 753,267 rubles	wages
= +	888,668 rubles		= +	888,668 rubles	
	− 138,727 rubles	difference between planned costs of production and actual costs		− 138,727 rubles	difference between planned costs of production and actual costs
	+ 100,217 rubles	income from 'over-plan' sales to the state (in fact included in the obligatory delivery plan)		+ 100,217 rubles	income from 'over-plan' sales to the state (in fact included in the obligatory delivery plan)
= −	38,510 rubles		= −	38,510 rubles	
	+ 888,668 rubles			+ 888,668 rubles	
	− 38,510 rubles			− 38,510 rubles	
= +	850,158 rubles		= +	850,158 rubles	
	− 647,000 rubles	capital building and maintenance		− 647,000 rubles	capital building and maintenance
	+ 367,019 rubles	loan from the State Bank for capital building	= +	203,158 rubles	'clear income'
= −	279,981 rubles			− 17,299 rubles	social security and insurance
	+ 850,158 rubles			− 182,885 rubles	investment in 'undivided fund'
	− 279,981 rubles			− 50,000 rubles	cultural services
= +	570,177 rubles		= −	250,184 rubles	to be deducted from the 'clear income'
	− 17,299 rubles	social security and insurance	= −	47,026 rubles	final balance
	− 182,885 rubles	investment in 'undivided fund'			
	− 50,000 rubles	cultural services			
= −	250,184 rubles				
= +	319,993 rubles				

to pay more into the investment and reserve funds than was possible in Barguzin. But as we saw in Chapter 2, the annual tax is proportional to 'clear income' and the amount paid out in wages, including bonuses. The Selenga farm paid particularly high wages, and its bonus system was probably more generous than that in unsuccessful farms. Thus, unless we count bonus payments as profits, it is not clear that the Selenga farm gained much advantage in terms of manoeuvrability from its large *chistii dokhod* ('clear income'). Its real profits lay in its 'manipulable resources' in grain, wool, livestock, and perhaps hay.

This 'economic' fact was to a large extent politically determined: the Selenga kolkhoz management was powerful enough in local politics to negotiate a plan which fell far short of the farm's capabilities. At the same time, the management's interior network within the farm was such that the kolkhozniks had an interest in coming out to work. It is largely to gain these ends that the farm makes use of its disposable resources. If these resources were seen simply as commodities, to be exchanged for other commodities or for money, the economic pattern would be much more like a capitalist system. However, I suggest that the use made by the Selenga farm of its 'manipulable resources' in 1966 was not commodity exchange, with one small exception (the exchange of grain for fresh vegetables and fruit).

For example, the kolkhoz sold none of the surplus resources on the kolkhoz market. As Kerblay explains in his authoritative work on markets in the USSR, it is very often disadvantageous for collective farms to make use of the 'kolkhoz' markets where they are in direct competition with private sellers. The situation is explained clearly by the director of a kolkhoz market in Ashkhabad:[174]

Up to now the market has been entirely dominated by individual sellers. At the moment the kolkhozy tend to avoid it. The kolkhoz never takes any account of demand, it gets rid of what it has. There are 'gaps' in the arrival of products for sale, and the private seller, and sometimes even the speculator, takes advantage of them. Here is an example: the 'private sellers' had established a 'modest' price of 30 rubles a kilo for tomatoes a month ago, but when the kolkhoz Sovet Turkmenistana started to sell tomatoes the price went down to 7 rubles a kilo, and the private sellers had to go along with the kolkhoz price . . . There is another reason why the consumer prefers the private producer: the care and attention which are given by him to putting fresh goods on the market. The 'private' radishes will be washed and watered from time to time, while the kolkhoz just gets rid of huge quantities all at once.

Kerblay noted a general tendency for Soviet collective farms to sell less and less at the 'kolkhoz' markets during the 1950s and early 1960s. The proportion of surplus produce sold on the market depends to a great degree on the geographical location of the kolkhoz in relation to the market.[175] The farm pays the cost of transporting both what it sells and what it buys. In the case of the Buryat farms we are considering, where the kolkhoz market nearest to both farms is probably at the *raion* centres (80 km from Bayangol, 110 km from Tashir), it is understandable why the market plays such a small part in their transactions (see

Map 2). Soviet economists have estimated that transportation costs make sale of produce on the kolkhoz market for farms prohibitive if they are situated over 50 km from a railway station or market.[176]

There is another legal method by which the kolkhoz can dispose of its surplus products in a 'commodity' transaction: sale 'by commission' to a state-run cooperative. Sales 'by commission' consist of contracts made between the kolkhoz and a cooperative, which takes upon itself the re-sale of the product at a market or in retail shops. The cooperative and the kolkhoz bargain for a price, but the cooperative is bound by law to sell at a price from 10 to 15% lower than the market price, and it also takes a commission of 7%.[177] In Buryatiya, the cooperative organisation (*Burpotrebsoyuz*) buys goods from farms and individual producers at prices no higher than the state delivery prices.[178] It is thus no more advantageous for a farm to sell to a cooperative than to the state. There are other problems with cooperatives: they prefer not to buy perishables, they avoid buying expeditions to distant regions and prefer to acquire goods themselves at kolkhoz markets, and while they have to buy at more or less regulated prices, they sell in competition with private producers. This means that the cooperatives themselves may avoid doing business with distant collective farms. It is difficult to estimate how much of the collective farm surplus produce is sold via the cooperatives. Kerblay gives a table taken from a Soviet source in which it appears that Ukrainian kolkhozy sold 66.7% of their surplus on the kolkhoz market, 20.1% to cooperatives 'on commission', and 13.2% to their own kolkhoz members.[179] This table, however, presupposes that 100% of the kolkhoz surplus is disposed of in one of these three ways and it ignores the widespread payment of wages in kind. It is my view that in Buryatiya, in fact, comparatively little of the 'manipulable surplus' is disposed of through the commercial channels of the market and the 'commission' sales. The farms I visited appeared to dispose of none in this way.

A large proportion of the surplus produce is transacted *as goods*. It is moved directly between farms, or between farms and shops, or farms and factories, and here the agent is not the commercial market or the bureaucratic and largely non-commercial cooperative organisations, but a variety of adept middlemen, often including the district and regional Party apparatus. As will be seen in Chapter 7, an integral part of the 'exchange' involved in these transactions is the acquiring of political power, and, conversely, the balance of the 'exchanges' is determined by existing political power. Even if the surplus products of a farm have already been 'realised' as money via the market or 'commission' sales — both transactions being comparatively unprofitable from the point of view of the farm, as we have seen — the resulting income is freely disposable. This income, also, in the form of rubles, is likely to enter the 'politicised' economy. These 'exchanges' will be discussed in Chapters 7 and 8, but meanwhile it is necessary to mention the other use for kolkhoz 'manipulable resources', i.e. transactions involving the members of the farm itself.

Economic life in two collective farms

Collective farms sell their surplus to the kolkhozniks at prices far below the state delivery prices, let alone the market prices. In the Selenga farm, the kolkhozniks bought grain at 3 rubles 72 kopecks a centner, while the state delivery price was 11.50 rubles a centner, and the market price was around 16.30 rubles. They bought milk from the kolkhoz for 10.34 rubles a centner, while the state price was 15.57 rubles. Furthermore, the Selenga kolkhoz sold its members far more grain than they needed for purely consumption purposes. The unspoken 'payoff' for the kolkhoz is the goodwill of its labourers.

In its simplest form, this transaction is seen in the hay harvest. Kolkhozy offer the workers a percentage of the hay they cut to use for their own private livestock. Abramov gives the clearest account of this transaction in his study *Vokrug da Okolo*.[180] The kolkhoz Chairman is telephoned by the *raikom* secretary and instructed to gather in the hay harvest immediately. But it is raining, and no one will come out to work. The Chairman goes from house to house, but everyone has their own reason not to appear: some people are going mushrooming in the woods ('at least we can sell the mushrooms'), another is 'ill', a third has too much work to do in his private plot, and so on. In despair, the Chairman goes into the village bar. A kolkhoznik says to him, 'No, you can't count on me for tomorrow. If I had a cow, then maybe it would be worth it, but I haven't got a cow, so what's the point of working myself into the ground?' The Chairman thinks to himself:

'Again, the problem of cows! And this in a kolkhoz which is literally buried in grass. Every year tens, and hundreds, and if you count it all, even thousands of hectares just get left to waste under the snow, and a good half of the kolkhozniks do not have cows. Isn't it mad? And the answer's simple. Ten per cent per work-day of the total hay harvested — that's what they get. And what does that mean? It means that a kolkhoznik, to get enough hay for his cow, has to cut hay for at least ten or twelve cows, and if you reckon two tons a cow — well, it's completely impossible, even with modern equipment.'

The Chairman gets drunk in the bar in despair. Next morning he wakes up with a hangover, very late. He looks out of his window, and to his amazement, the hay-meadows are full of toiling workers. What has happened? Surely the farm Party Secretary has not created this miracle overnight? As he goes hurriedly to the fields, he hears the words, 'Thirty per cent'. It appears that the previous night, in a drunken state, he had offered someone thirty per cent and the word had instantaneously sped round the kolkhoz. Immediately he is struck with terror. The *raikom* will regard this arrangement as illegal, and they are bound to find out. Even as he is wondering what to do, the well-known *raikom* jeep drives up to the Party office. Should he disclaim all knowledge of the thirty per cent, and face the loss of the hay harvest, or should he confront the anger of the *raikom* and allow the kolkhozniks to have their hay and help the farm too?

This is only the most simple of the implicit transactions (labour exchanged for products) between the management and the kolkhozniks. These arrangements must vary widely between different areas of the Soviet Union, according to cultural tradition, and even between farms in the same region. I shall discuss specific Buryat examples in later chapters.

Kolkhoz surplus paid as 'in kind' wages and bonuses also forms an important part of the income of the individual household. In the 1950s the Karl Marx kolkhoz in Barguzin paid for one 'workday' (*trudoden'*) 1–2 kg of grain, 125 grams of meat, and 2–3.5 rubles in money. Bonuses were also paid in kind, even though this practice resulted in kolkhozniks receiving more animals than they were legally allowed to keep. A shepherdess in the Barguzin farm received eleven lambs as bonus payment alone in 1951.[181] The Selenga farm went over to money assessment of the worth of the workday in 1961, the Barguzin farm in 1960, but both farms continued to pay kolkhozniks to a great extent in produce. This practice, which exists also at higher levels (bureaucrats and officials are 'paid' in such things as the right to use restricted stores, coupons for health resorts, cars, etc.), has a significant social effect. It creates a continuing relationship. Unlike money, produce cannot easily be stored, and people are dependent on its continued supply.

This only applies, of course, if the produce is either consumable and desired for consumption, or if it is disposable. As soon as the point is reached where the goods are not wanted in themselves, and/or cannot be sold, payment in kind becomes a disincentive, or rather, it removes the burden of distribution of surplus items from the shoulders of the farm management to that of the workers. In fact, in the Buryat case, because of inherited traditions which establish social status by means of feasts and gift-giving, this point has not yet been reached. In any case, the practice removes the opportunity for people to distinguish themselves from their comrades by overt consumerism, by signs obtained with money. It is perhaps a more truly socialist way than money payment, but in Buryatiya it had the effect of preserving traditional distributions as payments in kind could be transferred into the gift sphere.

Although 'in kind' wages are becoming less important, there are structural reasons why the kolkhoz surplus will continue to be disposed of, at least in part, via the individual workers. In Buryat kolkhozy in the late 1960s a quarter of all basic wages was paid in meat, milk or grain, but for livestock workers the proportion was higher. Furthermore, all of the bonus pay of livestock workers was still in the 1960s in kind in most farms, usually in calves or lambs.[182] With the general shortage of meat in the urban centres of the USSR, kolkhozniks in most regions find no difficulty in selling or bartering any animals in their possession (see Chapter 6). There are good reasons why the surplus of kolkhoz production will still find its way 'out' to some extent via the kolkhozniks: firstly, the farm needs the workers' labour and goodwill, and secondly, it is easier to dispose of a large amount of goods via a multitude of small outlets than it is to become involved in the storage, transportation, and 'realisation' problems of disposing of a huge surplus at one go. It is, of course, in the interest of the kolkhoz management to conceal the existence of *any* surplus so as to avoid the pressure from the *raion* to raise its delivery plan. Finally, as mentioned in section 2 above, the farm can allow livestock to multiply in the household economies of the members and then stage a campaign of 'socialist obligation' by which the animals are bought back by the kolkhoz and used towards the delivery plan.

We cannot ignore the fact that, on the basis of the Buryat evidence and emigré Soviet documentation, some 'manipulable resources' may be illegal. Consider the position of a farm which, mainly through circumstances outside its control (weather, inappropriate planning decisions, lack of control of essential construction projects), ends up not fulfilling the plan, relying on a bank loan to make the books balance, and being reviled in the local newspaper. Under these circumstances, a kolkhoz Chairman has almost no alternative but to resort to some illegal methods – illegal, but so widespread as to constitute a systemic part of the Soviet economy itself. There is one major pattern to such practices, which arises from the fact that the real profits are not *chistiye dokhody* but what I have called 'manipulable resources' – and it applies whether we are talking about industry or agriculture. This consists, in essence, of producing more goods than are registered in the accounts. The extra goods are produced by using cheap materials instead of those specified, so that for the same cost two or three times the proper amount can be manufactured. The goods are disposed of through a variety of semi-legal and illegal markets.[183] In fact, such illegalities are as easy to practise in industry as in agriculture.

It can be understood that in a farm where the need to fulfil the plan was a constant nightmare for the Chairman, there would be strong pressures to resort to such methods. How could this be done? The milk could be watered down (as was the practice in a Buryat sovkhoz in Barguzin). Or the farm could neglect to sort the grain, allowing a certain amount of unusable material to be included in the end weight.[184] Or they could carry out shallow ploughing, instead of making the furrows the required depth.[185] But all of these are desperate measures which in the end will cause more trouble than they are worth. The only sure way is to acquire, as cheaply as possible, legally or illegally, the raw materials from outside, inscribe them as part of the legal *fondy* of the kolkhoz, and use the profits from expanded production to pay the creditors. It is precisely with farms in this unfortunate position that a kolkhoz like the Selenga Karl Marx could expect to make some advantageous deals. And in fact, the Selenga farm sold part of its excess grain to a neighbouring kolkhoz at a price (16 rubles 30 kopecks a centner) well above the state delivery price of 11.50 rubles. But this price was well *below* the retail price of grain, which was between 25 and 30 rubles a centner in 1966. This deal was not illegal, but one suspects that there must have been some *quid pro quo* in the arrangement.

Collective farms frequently carry out a certain amount of production which is extra to the plan in the sense that it consists of different goods, rather than a surplus of the goods which are named in the plan. The Barguzin Karl Marx plan consisted only of meat, milk, wool, grain, potatoes and vegetables. But the farm also produced eggs in large quantities, and at certain times in its past had gone in for bee-keeping. Products such as horse-hair, horn, and leather were also disposed of in some way, perhaps to the consumers' cooperative 'on commission'. The *Barguzinskaya Pravda* mentioned a fishing kolkhoz where it had been decided to breed rabbits for meat, and this kind of subsidiary activity does not always get included in the plan. Furthermore, the kolkhoz workshops can be used to manufacture useful things such as nails, glue, crude tools, etc., which are certainly disposable in the vicinity. In other words, the enterprises of a district each try to produce some goods for exchange, knowing that in all probability they themselves will lack some crucial input at some time or other.

Any farm needs a certain amount of materials such as bricks, cement, iron, glass, paint, spare parts for machinery, ordinary tools such as drills and screwdrivers, etc., but it is just these essential materials which are in very short supply. To use the Russian word, they are *defitsitnyye*. When an important product is in short supply it becomes defined by the Ministries as 'funded production' (*fondiruyemaya produktsiya*), in other words a product which can only be distributed by means of official orders (*naryad*). The shops are not allowed to sell these products freely, certainly not to individuals, and not even to enterprises unless they have the necessary *naryad*. This situation leads to endless small illegalities.

First of all, how to get the orders? In theory a farm, or any other organisation such as a school, hospital or cultural club, should be supplied with sufficient orders by the centralised planning system. But this is often inefficiently done. The management of the farm has to send someone to the planning departments to worm orders out of them (*vybit' naryady*), and even this may not be possible. So enterprises have recourse to little deceptions. Tiktina gives, for example, the case of acquiring nails and paint for the upkeep of the rural school where she was a teacher in the 1960s:

The shops did not have the right to sell building and repair materials for payment through a bank, and the school did not have the right to buy these materials with its own money taken from its budget. Payment through a bank could only be used for centralised *naryady* [orders] for building materials, but we were almost never given such orders.

But at the same time, shops were allowed to sell food to schools for payment via a bank, even though schools did not feed the children. So we took out an account in the local shop 'for sugar', and wrote in our budget that we had bought sugar, but in fact we bought . . . nails. Of course it was absolutely forbidden to re-sell the nails, so as to cover some of our costs. Luckily we had a small boarding section in the school, and 'sugar' and 'flour' could be put down to this (even though we had no right to feed the children in it and we weren't sure under what heading in the statutes we could account for the food), but the real nails bought instead of the mythical food were used by us and also distributed where they were needed without ever being registered.

All of this kind of thing gave rise to much small illegality in many schools —

and gave everyone without exception a great deal of trouble and confusion. I remember that the mythical 'sausages', bought by us to cover for the real paint we actually acquired, were on our hands for two years, and we managed to get them officially registered only with the help of the *raion* auditor Moroz.

. . . If I succeeded in getting some money at the end of the accounting year from the unspent resources of the school, . . . what I used to do was to transfer this money to the account of the kolkhoz or the *selmag* [rural shop], having made an agreement with them. This was because unspent resources of the school, *raion* and *oblast'* authorities was deducted at the end of the year, and the budget for the following year was reduced by this amount: unspent resources were counted as spare: 'They have not spent it — that must mean they do not need it.' But in fact it was often not possible to spend the money, even the miserable amount they gave us, because we did not have the *naryady* [orders]. But collective farms, shops, and other enterprises on *khozraschet* did not have their unspent resources deducted. So, at the beginning of the year, after the 1 of January, they returned our money or products to us.[186]

As Tiktina points out, this kind of juggling with resources for the sole purpose of getting the enterprise to work as it should is far more troublesome and difficult than it would be simply to pocket resources from the organisation for oneself. The one transaction is as illegal as the other. In both cases the perpetrator is under constant threat of being uncovered by one of the many checking agencies (People's Control, the kolkhoz Auditing Commission, the *raion* auditor).

One way in which a collective farm, or any other enterprise, can get round the problems which beset it is to have a representative at the places where the problems arise. Such a person is called a 'pusher' (*tolkach*). Thus, in areas where fodder is scarce, kolkhozy have their 'pushers' travelling round the district or even the region looking for farms with spare hay. Or, if the buying organisations are slow in paying up, it may be necessary to station a *tolkach* with them to ensure payment, otherwise the plan will not be fulfilled because the product has not been realised.[187] Sometimes collective farms are cheated by the state procurement agencies where officials mark down livestock delivered to the farms as of lower quality and weight than they really are. In this case, the farm may have to keep a resident representative at the delivery point to make sure that the weighing, etc., is done fairly.[188] A *tolkach* is particularly necessary for *defitsitnyye* products. A Novokuznetsk cement factory, for example, recorded some 400 visits by *tolkachi* a year, each man coming with an official visit (*komandirovka*) and staying for at least a week.[189] A *tolkach* may find it necessary to impress a supplier, for instance by putting on some kind of uniform, and efficient 'pushers' make card indexes of important people in the district, noting their birthdays and anniversaries, as well as their soft spots.[190] Sometimes 'pushers' are necessary even for the most normal operations. For example, in the third quarter of 1970 the kolkhozniks and sovkhozniks of Lithuania owned large numbers of cows and pigs which they were legally due to get rid of by the end of the year, but the slaughterhouses were unable to cope with the number. In one kolkhoz, the agronomist became a full-time *tolkach* at the slaughterhouse, trying to push through the sale of privately owned livestock.[191] Factories and state-run organisations are normally so carefully checked for financial misdemeanours that they find it difficult to resort to straight bribery. But collective farms have a relative financial freedom, and their 'pushers' do often take advantage of this.

A range of slang terms has come into being to express the multifarious tricks which make survival easier in the planned economy: *plyushkinstvo* ('adding on', e.g. to keep something aside for a rainy day), *nelikvidy* ('unsaleable products', often bartered between enterprises in a deal which includes items for which there is a demand), *levaya produktsiya* ('left production', i.e. production on the side, often using state-owned means), *dostat'* ('to obtain', often used with the implication 'by hook or crook', contrasted with *kupit'*, to buy, legally).

One trick is particularly common. This is *pripiski*, the registering of more products in the accounts than have in fact been produced. *Pripiski* are the resort of the less successful farms, but they are even more common in organisations such as construction teams, where not only the team itself but also the enterprises which employ it need to have it appear that the work has been done, e.g. to keep up their capital input figures.[192] This phenomenon is in fact the converse of the trick which we have identified as most common in collective farms, the non-registering of items which have been produced. Of the two, *pripiski*, which can be repeated and multiplied by the bureaucracy at each level, are more harmful to the Soviet economy. They result in an unreal assessment of the situation among planners at higher levels and in the continued allocation of unrealistic plans to the producers. This, of course, encourages further recourse to *pripiski* and reproduction of the gap between 'on paper' results and actual production. Essentially *pripiski* arise because 'on paper figures' are themselves a resource of the bureaucracy, used in the furtherance of careers.

It has been shown that the category of 'clear income' (*chistii dokhod*) on paper is not an indication of profit as it is generally understood, and that even a farm which is struggling to fulfil its plan can calculate 'clear income' in such a way as to appear successful. 'Clear income' is simply a temporary situation in the accounts — accounts which represent the major part of surplus value as going to the state and the rest as going towards the reproduction of the kolkhoz economy. The real profits are extra to the category of 'clear income', and in the nature of farm production they tend to consist of products rather than money. The social organisation of accounting lends itself to the concealment of such 'manipulable resources'. Also, since the accounts are expressed in money and what the farm produces is not money but goods, the very translation of one into the other, even if all the goods are registered, provides the possibility of concealment. It is by no means clear, for example, in the absence of a market economy, what money value should be assigned to products such as livestock which remain in the farm.

Real profits cannot be acquired without good labour relations in the farm, that is relations in which labour is exchanged not only for wages but also for some other benefit not defined as wages; perhaps lower work-norms, the paying of large bonuses, or the turning of a blind eye to accumulation in the household economy. Equally important is the ability of the kolkhoz Chairman to negotiate an easily attainable plan — a matter of his political power vis-à-vis the *raion* authorities. In a sense a structurally similar relation exists between each level, since the kolkhoz itself sets work-norms and plans for the production within it. At each level it is negotiations which establish the size of the plan, and here the ability of the producing unit to provide some advantage to the planning unit by means of their 'manipulable resources' may be crucial. Since such resources cannot easily be furnished for use outside the farm unless the delivery plan is attainable, their existence becomes a condition for the reproduction of the situation in which they can be produced. The relationship between planners and those planned for is a political one, and the disposal of 'manipulable resources' cannot be seen simply as an economic act. Their distribution will take the form characteristic of political relations of the society involved — a form which is different, I suggest, among Buryats from that among Russians (see Chapter 8 section 2).

Some farms, even with good relations with the *raion*, fail disastrously to produce any 'manipulable resources', through no fault of their own. Section 3 showed how precarious farming has become in Buryatiya. For unsuccessful farms there is enormous pressure to resort to illegal methods, to misrepresent by undervaluation what has actually been produced. This creates a resource, but it is less freely disposable than the real profit of a successful farm since it should be used to fulfil the plan. Struggling farms also have recourse to the means of production accumulated in the private economies of their members. But this very possibility requires the farm to have allowed such accumulation to take place — in effect an illegal policy towards the household economy. What we have said about the kolkhoz also applies to some extent to production units within it. As was mentioned in section 1, brigades, which historically were often collective farms in their own right and still retain a certain financial autonomy, no less than kolkhozy operate in unequal conditions of production. Depending on the plan they are able to negotiate with the kolkhoz, this situation may force some of them to have recourse to the private sector, some of them to resort to *pripiski*, while others can produce a surplus whose existence may, or may not, be hidden from the kolkhoz.

In a sense this entire structure results from the formal characteristics of the plan: there will be a surplus to the plan in some cases, and a deficit in others. Because they are formal characteristics, they tend to reproduce themselves. Here, however, we can see a contradiction between the political and the 'purely economic'. In the first case, 'manipulable resources' are used by the farm to gain political credit with the *raion* (e.g. by selling at a low price to other farms within the *raion*) in order to re-negotiate a low plan. In the second case, the farm may sell its surplus, probably outside the *raion*, at the highest price available. I have suggested that Buryat farms tend to follow the first alternative, partly because the strategic advantages of keeping on good terms with the *raion* may outweigh the short-term benefits of a purely economic transaction, and partly for cultural reasons. The domination of the political over the economic has the effect of reproducing vertical links between the kolkhoz and the *raion* and at the same time separating the farms of a district from one another. They are in competition for the allocation of low delivery plans which specify a minimum of unprofitable production. Even if farm X sells products to farm Y which the latter can include in its delivery to the state, this should be seen as a relation mediated by the *raion*, since it is primarily in the interests of the *raion* rather than farm X to keep 'its' products within the district. If relations between the farms of a district are characterised by competition, those between each farm and the *raion* are characterised by secrecy, or rather the concealment of the actual state of affairs and the presentation of whatever can be maintained plausibly as a good negotiating position.

We have thus identified a very complex set of relations behind which one factor is the desire, and sometimes the need, to acquire disposable resources. But in saying this I do not wish to imply that the strategies which use 'manipulable resources' as their means are somehow more important or more 'real' than the due courses of official politics. There is a tendency in certain anthropological writing on politics to see 'strategies' or 'transactions' as fundamental, perhaps because the 'strategy' is definable for the individual rather than the collectivity, and there is the possibility of attributing a motive to an individual, thus making the explanation seem more 'whole'. Such an analysis would be inappropriate to the Soviet Union for several reasons. Firstly, 'transactions' with disposable resources are not limited to individuals: individuals, it is true, manipulate the products of their private small-holdings, but brigades or work-teams also have resources they can use, and so does the kolkhoz itself. Secondly, it is impossible in a fundamentally complex society such as the USSR to attribute 'a motive' to strategies and thereby explain them. The individual, not less than the collectivity, exists in specific conditions (as regards the natural environment, the division of labour, the material difficulties of work, etc.), and furthermore, the collectivity no less than the individual has its history and its 'culture' (the kolkhoz renowned for its 'progressiveness', the work-team which has always cheated, the brigade which wishes to retain a certain autonomy). All of these factors influence what people decide to do, and in the political economy they are more important than 'strategies' as narrowly defined precisely because they are given and individuals can do little to alter them. It is the organisation of the Soviet political economy which calls forth semi-legal 'strategies', not the other way round. Therefore, while individuals may see themselves as having tactics designed to attain certain ends, viewed in general these 'strategies' appear as largely situational, inescapably tied to official political processes because the latter are the expression of the overwhelming power of the state and Party. A 'transaction' can ensure that the brigadier gives a man an easier job, but it cannot alter the fact that the brigadier has the right to allocate jobs. We cannot say that this right consists simply in the accumulation of all the jobs that the brigadier has ever distributed.

Nevertheless, 'manipulable resources' are essential in the Soviet political economy because they form the material basis with which individuals and groups can operate in terms of their own objectives at a particular time. As we have seen, these operations may be either legal or illegal, and they may be designed to legitimate ends even if the means, e.g. trickery with the accounts, are strictly speaking an infringement of the law.

5

The division of labour

1. Division of labour and the socialist transformation of work

Changes in the division of labour in collective farms during the 1960s and early 1970s are correlated with 'specialisation'. This implies the narrowing down of productive activity to officially specified tasks and goals. As will be shown later in this chapter it also implies the creation of a hierarchy among workers by virtue of the ranking of jobs, both externally defined by wage differentials and internally defined by a much more complex cultural assessment of what makes work worth doing.

In the Stalinist period a typical farm contained a few administrators, a relatively small number of people in jobs for which particular knowledge and experience were necessary, and a mass of untrained workers. By the 1970s a kolkhoz or sovkhoz had a greater proportion of administrators, specialists, and trained personnel of every kind, and the percentage of 'general workers' (*raznorabochiye*) was reduced from around 60% to 35–40%. This can be seen from a comparison of the figures in Table 5.1 (unfortunately no breakdown is available for the late 1970s). Of the 112 workers in agriculture in 1965 over half were in specialised 'mechanised' jobs in the following categories: tractor-driver, harvester-operator, machinist, driver, assistant harvester-operator, motor mechanic, electrician, fitter, turner, and welder.[1]

The Selenga Karl Marx kolkhoz was probably one of the most advanced in mechanisation in the republic in the 1960s.[2] Nevertheless it shows a pattern of the division of labour which was typical for the region as a whole. The decrease in the number of arable workers between 1958 and 1965 was the result of the acquiring by farms of their own machinery for arable farming and the switching over of untrained field-workers to livestock production. In 1952 the Karl Marx kolkhoz had only four tractors, leased from the machine–tractor station at Selenduma, and sixty-eight horse-drawn ploughs. By 1966, it had fifty-eight of its own tractors, twenty-two combine harvesters, twenty-five lorries and four cars, and it also had a variety of other specialised machinery.

By 1970 in Buryatiya there was also an advanced division of labour in live-

228

Table 5.1. *Gross division of labour, Selenga farm, 1958 and 1965*

	1958		1965	
	No.	%	No.	%
Agriculture	313	54.1	112	20.1
Livestock	200	34.5	332	59.7
Construction	16	2.8	12	2.2
Transport	13	2.2	29	5.2
Ancillary manufacture	10	1.7	10	1.8
Administration, culture, services	27	4.7	61	10.9
Total	579	100	556	100

Source: Sanzhiyev and Randalov 1968, p. 43.

stock production, where 81.5% of jobs were tied to specialised work:[3]

Milkers	24.0%
Cattle-herders	15.5%
Calf-rearers	6.2%
Pigmen	4.7%
Shepherds	30.7%

General workers
    and others, including horse herders   18.9%

There are clear correlations between the division of labour and specialisation by age and sex. Of the eighty-one people in mechanised work in the Selenga Karl Marx farm in 1965 (this figure includes a few mechanised livestock workers as well as the great majority in arable work), seventy-eight were men, while only three were women.[4] Almost all of these workers (91%) were young, aged between twenty and forty. In livestock production, on the other hand, the majority of workers were women (60–70%) and most were middle-aged. Out of 332 live-stock workers in the farm only 16 were aged below thirty.[5]

There were still a fairly large number of general workers, or workers 'by order' (*po naryadu*) as they are known, in both livestock and arable sectors. The majority of these workers were men, and they were characteristically middle-aged or elderly.[6]

The category of workers in administration, culture and services was internally highly differentiated. Of the sixty-one people in this category in the Selenga Karl Marx farm thirty-seven were in 'administration'. Sanzhiyev and Randalov in their study of the farm divide the administrators into three clear groups: (a) the leaders and chief specialists — sixteen people; (b) the heads of production brigades, workshops and field stations — fourteen people; (c) accountants and book-keepers.[7] The great majority of these were men, with the exception of the book-keepers, who were mostly young women.[8]

229

The division of labour

With the exception of families working as shepherds on distant pastures I met almost no cases where kin, even husband and wife, worked in the same production unit. Thus it appears that forms of the division of labour transitional between the old kin-based economic groups and the present 'statutory' collective farm, such as the early 'clan kolkhoz' found in some parts of Buryatiya, have completely disappeared.[9] There can be no doubt that the social relations of production have changed once and for all since collectivisation.

But things are not as simple as this statement might imply. In the intricacies of daily working life the previous ways of doing things linger on. These are the habitual ways of the old people. They even become a challenge to the proclaimed, lectured-about new farming techniques. This can happen because new methods are propounded not so much by farm leaders as by the Party and therefore the very simplest tasks of the herdsman come to have an ideological content. Quite often it is the most experienced and most 'traditional' herders who are the most successful. When yet another resolutely unmodern old man or woman trudges up to the kolkhoz stage to receive their award of honour it is the culmination and justification of a whole way of life and way of thinking. Everyone knows about this, and to some extent it places the kolkhoz officials in a quandary.

One reason for this situation lies in the fact that the material conditions of work in certain jobs have hardly changed at all since collectivisation. They have in a sense lagged behind the organisational revolution. This applies particularly in livestock production, which is the predominant sector in Buryat farms. As we saw earlier, even if the capital is available to buy new machinery for livestock farming there are many problems in actually introducing and maintaining it (see p. 180). A division of labour introduced artificially from above in these circumstances becomes a hindrance to production. In order to compensate for the vast increase in arable acreage farms have enlarged the area of land under use, and herders are sent to marginal and distant places not previously farmed. In some parts of Buryatiya these pastures are so rugged that farms have even introduced different species of livestock, yaks and reindeer, suitable to the terrain.[10] With the present organisation of production, livestock workers do not have control of essential inputs, chiefly fodder of various kinds, which used to be produced within the kin-based herding unit. In other words, it has become more difficult than it was before collectivisation to be a good herder. Knowledge of the animals, of the locality, the weather, diseases, the best grasses for pasture and fodder, the sources of salt and soda, the movements of predators, in short all the traditional knowledge of the herdsman, have come to have a golden, almost mystic value. This is not only because such knowledge is essential. In fact it is a complex phenomenon which we should look at more closely.

What used to be everyday knowledge has been transformed into 'wisdom', and one reason for this is that the normal process by which it was transmitted, from parents to children working together in the domestic unit, has been disrupted. All children in the collective farm now go to school from the age of

230

seven to sixteen at least. If their parents are on distant pastures and there are no relatives in the central village children become boarders (100 of the 764 pupils in 1974 in Barguzin). The school teaches 'subjects' (chemistry, geography, litera- ture, etc.) using Russian as a medium from the first class and with Russian text- books. There are practical classes for the older children, but these, for both boys and girls, are of two kinds only: mechanical (*mashinovedeniye*) and domestic (sewing and cooking). Farming skills as such, and particularly Buryat livestock herding expertise, are entirely neglected. Buryat rural schoolchildren are enthusi- astic about school subjects, more so than their urban counterparts. The subjects they like best, sport, literature, history and chemistry, are unrelated to the future working lives of the vast majority.[11] Very few school-leavers wish to take up jobs in livestock farming; the Party Secretary of the Barguzin Karl Marx kolkhoz even found it worthy of mention as one of the successes of the year in his speech to the 40th *raion* Party Conference that, persuaded by the Party and the Komsomol, fourteen girls had taken up livestock work.[12]

But because of the great respect in which elders are still held in Buryat society children revere the words of the old people, even though they do not wish to have to take them seriously in the sense of putting them into practice. The reasons for respect of the 'golden words' have changed. Now that livestock herding jobs are no longer desired by young people the practical use of folk knowledge is devalued, but, paradoxically, their value as culture, as emblems of ethnicity, has grown.

On the other hand, it is because of the enduring practical value of traditional skills that the Buryat Party has taken the attitude that they should be passed on to the next generation. Accordingly the prize-winning old people give interviews to the local newspapers, and books and pamphlets are written about them. But these publications fail in their purpose because of contradictions inherent in the Party position. The writers of the articles cannot actually advocate a return to traditional methods in general, nor even in particular since the overall organis- ation of production — including the advanced division of labour — should pre- clude the use of most traditional techniques. The 'golden words' of the old people as they appear in the newspaper are shorn of their specific quality and appear as advice of the most banal kind ('I make sure to give my cows a good feed in the morning'). The writers know that old people are successful because of their specific practice, but not being able to say this directly they praise them for love of work.

Most livestock workers, with the exception of those who have the advantage of belonging to well-supplied 'vanguard' brigades, have to operate within what is in effect a contradiction: on the one hand a division of labour based on the premise of specialised tasks, and on the other material conditions which are more or less unchanged since collectivisation, and in which successful production can only be achieved by devoted attention to the cycle of livestock farming as a whole. This latter, which is exemplified by Buryat traditional herding methods,

231

continues to be carried out with regard to the private herds. Livestock workers keep their own private animals alongside the kolkhoz flocks and they also frequently take care of the animals belonging privately to kinsmen who cannot herd them. Thus traditional practices live on, and to some degree extend into the sphere of public herding. The domestic production process is radically different from work for the kolkhoz, since it is not concerned only with a single task (e.g. fattening one-year-old calves) but with the whole life-cycle of several different kinds of animal for multiple purposes. The aim of domestic herding is to keep a flock on the hoof which can be used over the years in a number of ways, such as milking and shearing sheep and goats, and animals are, as far as possible, killed for meat only at the end of the life-cycle. The kolkhoz, on the other hand, divides up the flock in order to designate each herd for *one* purpose (meat *or* wool in sheep herding, for example), and certain elements of Buryat traditional herding are dropped altogether. Thus kolkhoz sheep are no longer milked, and the symbiotic relation between goats and sheep no longer obtains because the kolkhoz does not keep goats.[13] The detailed description below of herding life shows also that the division of labour in the kolkhoz sector impedes even the efficient performance of the limited public tasks. Insofar as organisational failures in collective farms lead livestock workers to 'fall back on' their private flocks, the traditional totality of practices retains a practical value. Out of sight of the kolkhoz officials, on the distant pastures, such practices to some extent spread into public work, even if the 'realisation' strategy of collective farms prevents them from doing so entirely. Of course, there are also livestock workers who are more or less alienated from public work. I suggest below that this is particularly the case with milkers, while shepherds and horse-herders are more likely to combine traditional with new methods in public work.

These contradictions do not exist in arable farming. Nothing now remains of the minor cultivation which used to exist among richer Barguzin and Selenga Buryats before collectivisation. There is no private arable farming, and the kolkhoz sector is fully mechanised, with an appropriate division of labour.

Below I describe the working life of the main categories of ordinary kolkhozniks: shepherds, milkers, stockmen, field-workers, machine-operators, drivers, and meadow-workers. It will become apparent that these jobs have very different characteristics and open up different possibilities for the people who go into them. In accordance with this, the methods of recruitment differ: for livestock work, which is unpopular with young people, ideological means are employed to 'call' (*pryzvat'*) in recruits, while for the jobs of machine-operator and driver there are examinations to control entry and promotion.

But in every case there is an ideal model of what qualities are required in a given job. I have quoted some of these, taken from local newspapers, and hope that they will speak for themselves.

Shepherds

It is in shepherding that Buryat traditions of nomadism, or more exactly transhumance, continue to operate as part of working life. In fact these traditions are strong in many parts of Buryatiya even among people who have long ceased to have any reason to migrate. Thus in the Selenga farm people who worked all year round in the kolkhoz centre built themselves small 'summer houses' alongside their main winter houses, just a few yards away, in order to have somewhere to move to at the appropriate time of year. Even more common than this is the making of a visit to relatives who are shepherds out on the pastures. The shepherd's life remains as a kind of distant cultural ideal, especially for people who do not have to live it, somewhat similar to the role of the 'farmer's life' in urbanised Western culture.

Shepherds (Bur. *honishon*) spend their working lives 'on the *otara*'. The word *otara* is Russian and means a flock, but it is also used colloquially on Buryat farms to designate the shepherding settlements. A shepherding production team with its own flock is known by a number, for example, the 20th *otara* of the 1st brigade. This team moves from settlement to settlement during the year. In some farms the area of movement is fairly discrete and coincides essentially with the pasture of an individual shepherd who may have stayed on there after collectivisation. In this case the general area may be known by the shepherd's name, for example *Prontiin tala* (Pronteyev's steppe). In other farms an *otara* team is sent to various places, and they may differ from year to year. This is generally unpopular; although Buryats like to move, they prefer moving to places they know. Individual pastures are known as *zuhalan* (Bur. summer pasture) and *übelzhen* (Bur. winter pasture), and sometimes there are also autumn and spring pastures. The general area associated with a group of people is *nyutag* (homeland). There is still a strong identification of people with such areas as can be seen from the common expression *garahan türehen nyutagmnai khübüün* ('a boy born and brought up in our homeland').

The *otara* settlement consists of a wooden house, built and owned by the kolkhoz, and some sheds and pens for the sheep. There are no gardens, trees, or field-like enclosures. A typical *otara* is in the bare steppe, near a stream, with a good wide view of the surrounding grasslands.

The number of shepherds on a lambing *otara* is usually three and on non-lambing *otaras* two. One shepherd is always designated as the 'senior' (Bur. *akhalagsha honishon*) and the others are called 'second shepherd' and 'third shepherd'. This tiny hierarchy, which is reflected in pay and responsibilities, is of course unlike anything known in the Buryat domestic economy. Furthermore, these roles sometimes conflict with traditional Buryat ideas of seniority by age and sex. Not infrequently a woman is 'senior shepherd', in command over men, sometimes including her husband. The 'senior shepherd' is nominated from

233

above, and if an *otara* is doing badly the kolkhoz will send (Russ. *napravlyat'*) a young trained person to improve its output. This frequently causes problems of managing older workers. I met one shepherding family in which a complete reversal of the normal Buryat male—female roles had occurred: the wife was 'senior shepherd' out on the pastures, and the husband, who was 'third shepherd', frequently left the *otara* to go and look after their children who were at school in the kolkhoz centre. Nevertheless, in the detail of her life this woman was very Buryat, not speaking much Russian, smoking her long-stemmed pipe, quiet and reserved.

The activities of herding are not always carried out in the same way in every kolkhoz, nor even every *otara* within one kolkhoz. In the advanced 20th *otara* of the 3rd brigade in the Selenga Karl Marx farm the year was divided as follows. Lambing began in January. In the mid-1960s it was considered best to rear the lambs in warm heated sheds, but it was later decided that this 'modern' practice weakened them and the farm went back to more traditional shelters: low walls of wooden poles, one side open to the air, and a roof covered in hay and dried dung.[14] For the first few days the lambs were kept with their mothers in separate pens. Then, according to a method which shepherds were encouraged to follow, they were separated into small groups (*sakman*) with the mothers, which were gradually added to as more lambs were born. After four or five months the lambs were separated from the mothers and formed into flocks of males and females, some designated for wool and others for meat. By summer a sheep production unit would have several kinds of flock (Bur. *hüreg*) to look after: ewes which had already lambed, divided into those which lamb in January and those which lamb in the spring, rams, male lambs, female lambs, and one-year-old females destined to lamb.[15] The animals intended for meat are fattened during the summer and taken away for slaughter in autumn.

Most collective farms divide their shepherding teams into those which keep lambing ewes and those which do not. The former have much harder work and are better paid. Ushnayev, who carried out time and motion studies in Buryat collective farms, estimated that shepherds in lambing *otaras* had an average working day of twelve hours in the first three months of the year. The setting of the lambs to suck and their removal from the ewes alone takes up to six or seven hours, besides which the shepherds have to see that they are feeding properly, give water and fodder to the ewes, clear out the pens, cart away the dung, and prepare fodder for the next day.[16] The work in summer is less arduous,[17] but even so shepherds may have to walk long distances. Buryat shepherds do not use dogs for controlling sheep, and the kolkhoz gives only one or two horses to each *otara*. This means that the less senior shepherds may have to do all their work on foot.

In the Barguzin farm (1974) a shepherd looking after a flock of one-year-old lambs described the following typical winter day. There were three people on the *otara*, a husband and wife and an unrelated old woman, and they together

234

looked after 900 sheep. They were one of the most successful teams in the kolkhoz. In this team they got up at 6 a.m. and had a breakfast of salted tea, bread, *zöökhei* (cream) and boiled mutton. From about 8 o'clock they gave hay to the sheep in the sheds, and at 9.30 they let them out. At this point the sheep were given fodder concentrates provided by the kolkhoz. In some farms very distant *otaras* are inaccessible by road in winter and the concentrates have to be flown out by helicopter.[18] We may imagine that such supplies are uncertain, since I have never heard of a farm with its own helicopter. At 12 o'clock the sheep are taken out to graze on the steppes and to water at a well which does not freeze in winter. For some *otaras* the kolkhoz transports water by lorry to the pastures (in the form of ice, which has to be unfrozen), but in this case it was not necessary. There was a new well, 52 metres deep, from which water was electrically pumped up to a central tank heated by a log stove. From this, water was let out into wooden troughs for the sheep. The work of the shepherds included operating the pump and keeping the stove going. In Barguzin in winter the snow is often too deep for the sheep to get much grass. Even in these conditions the flocks are taken out, with the herdsmen riding in a horse-drawn sleigh. The *otara* I visited in 1974 had four horses allotted to it by the kolkhoz, and its pastures were 3—4 km distant from the *otara* settlement. During the day the herdsmen check that none of the sheep have fallen, that none look ill, and that they are getting some grass. Occasionally it is necessary to clear snow from the steppe with rakes. At 4 o'clock the sheep are watered again, and if it is very cold (−30 °C or so) they are given more hay. They are taken back to the sheds in the dark, the way being lit by reflected light from the snow. The winter working day ends at about 6 o'clock in the evening.

In this *otara* the work was not the responsible and exhausting task of bringing the lambs into the world in the dead of winter, but the more gradual work of fattening the sheep and guarding from predators (wolves and bears). In summer it was necessary to prevent the sheep from wandering among thorn bushes which would harm the wool. In successful *otaras* such as this one the shepherds were able in summer to drive out to the pastures on motor-cycles as far as possible, and then walk the rest of the way. They take books to read and they often sing songs while watching the sheep. Shepherdesses knit stockings to while away the time, not a traditional Buryat pursuit, and we may suppose that the idea of 'wasting time' is something new in Buryat concepts.

After lambing the busiest time of year is shearing, which takes place at two special places in the farm. The shepherds are involved in taking the sheep to the shearing points, some electrical and some hand-shearing, and in sorting the wool. However, the shearing is directed and the machines maintained by special mechanics. The final wool sorting, before the bales are sent off to the collection point, is carried out by two trained workers at a laboratory on the farm.

The local newspaper *Barguzinskaya Pravda* published an interview with a shepherdess from the Karl Marx kolkhoz in its issue of 9 December 1975. I quote from it here, since it gives a good idea not only of the work but also of the ideological atmosphere, at least in those teams which are 'in the vanguard'. Even if most shepherds are not so dedicated, the slogans and aims ('100 lambs from 100 ewes!') are omnipresent and form a constant background to work.

Our Obligation is to get 100 Lambs from 100 Ewes

Tsybyk Obonova Dashiyeva has worked as a shepherdess in the Karl Marx kolkhoz for thirty-two years. For twenty years she has worked constantly in a lambing *otara*. Her modest labour has been repeatedly recognised by honourable diplomas of the *raion* Party committee, the executive committee of the *aimak* Soviet, and the Party committee and management committee of the kolkhoz.

She has been awarded the medal 'For Valiant Labour in the Great Patriotic War 1941–45', and recently she was given the medal '30 Years of Victory in the Great Patriotic War'.

Her *otara*, which last year took part in the 9th five-year plan All-Union Socialist Competition obtained 100 lambs from 100 ewes in 1975.

The editors of the newspaper asked Tsybyk Obonova to share with us her long experience, to tell us how the shepherds are planning to greet the 25th Congress of the Communist Party of the Soviet Union. We publish below the reply given by Ts.O. Dashiyeva.

'In my thirty-two years in shepherding I and my colleagues have had to work in various conditions. There were years when, because of bad weather, we had a lack of fodder. In my first years we had no idea of rational feeding with concentrated fodders; we had bad living conditions, and the animal sheds were dilapidated. Now, of course, by comparison with those years considerably better

A shepherd in the Barguzin Karl Marx kolkhoz at shearing time.

working conditions have been created. our housing is better, and the care of the collective herd has improved.

Timely and Good-quality Artificial Insemination is the Pledge of Success
'The basic factor in obtaining good healthy lambs is high quality insemination. We get our semen from our own elite rams, and we think it is necessary to follow a well-organised feeding programme of full-rationed fodders in order to get good quality semen from the rams.'

The Basis of High Productivity in Sheep is Good Summer Pasturing
'Pasturing must be well organised. Therefore our *otara* tries to make use of the whole period of daylight. This is particularly important in hot summer weather. The sheep are driven out to pasture before sunrise. They rest during the day, and then in the evening as the heat becomes less they start grazing again on the way back. Right through the year we constantly try to make sure that the sheep have adequate minerals and enough water.'

Preservation of Received Offspring is the Final Aim of the Work of Shepherds
'Success in receiving and preserving the lambs depends primarily on there being a sufficient number of experienced *sakman* workers attached to the team. If the team is made up well in advance then we can prepare for lambing: get temporary warm sheds built, repair the pens, whitewash and disinfect them, set aside bedding materials, and get ready micro-elements for fodder.

When lambing starts we operate a strict rota of *sakman* workers, each one taking his turn on duty according to the list. After the end of lambing, each *sakman* worker takes his own group of lambs and ewes out to graze. This helps the lambs to put on weight before they are separated from the ewes.

At the moment we have 560 ewes in our *otara*. We have undertaken the socialist obligation in honour of the 25th Congress of the CPSS of receiving 560 working lambs, i.e. 100% (*ot sta po sto*); we undertake to shear an average of 3.6 kg wool per sheep, and get our lambs to 21 kg weight before separation.'

What is clear from this article is firstly the precise but limited aims of the work, and secondly the fact that the *otara* team is crucially dependent on outside labour to achieve these aims. As we saw in Chapter 4 the narrowing of aims is due to the demands made by the state on the collective farm as a whole, and it is implemented by means of all-embracing 'socialist competition'. Herding which is 'successful' in these terms is dependent on supplies from the brigadier which are not under the control even of the first shepherd: if the lambing helpers (*sakman* workers) are not sent, if adequate fodder concentrates, minerals, fuel for the stoves, disinfectants and other veterinary supplies do not appear, if the pastures allotted are overcrowded, if the pump maintenance engineers or the shearing mechanics are inefficient (or themselves not supplied with the necessary inputs) there is nothing much that the shepherd can do except make the best of a bad job, and suffer in loss of bonus pay.

The Barguzin Karl Marx kolkhoz was unusual in 1975 in allowing their shepherds relatively wide control over their conditions of production. Each brigade was organised on *khozraschet* (self-accounting) to a certain extent, and it had its own hay-fields and its own pastures from year to year. Within the shepherding brigades, each *otara* was allotted two oxen, as well as some horses, to carry out the necessary field-work for its fodder production. But in other farms fodder was produced by different brigades and centrally allocated, with consequent problems of storage and transport; insemination was carried out centrally, so that *otaras* lost control of breeding; and pastures were switched from year to year.

Many Buryat farms were also less mechanised than the Barguzin Karl Marx: mountainous terrain made the use of motor-cycles impossible, there were no pumps for water, and an uncertain electric supply meant that shearing might also have to be done by hand.

In both the Selenga and the Barguzin Karl Marx farms in the 1960s shepherds were paid for production, though there was a basic rate below which wages did not fall if the required number of days were worked.[19] In Barguzin the shepherds got 0.80 rubles for each kilo of wool, 1.00 ruble for every kilo of weight added to the birth-weight of lambs, and 0.08 rubles for each kilo gained by one-year-old lambs. Each shepherd was given a plan of production for these indicators, and they were paid 70% of the total as an advance each month. If they fulfilled their plans the final 30% was paid as a lump sum at the end of the year, but they lost it if they could not reach the targets. Bonuses were paid for production over the plan, often 'in kind' rather than in money.[20] The senior shepherd was paid 15% more than the other shepherds for the basic indicators.

Every kolkhoz has its own differentials between the different jobs (Table 5.2). Although the level of basic wages perhaps indicates a lowering in prestige for the job of shepherding in the last few years, it is nevertheless true that a successful shepherd can earn large sums of money through bonus pay. The best-paid shepherd in the Selenga farm in 1965 earned, together with his wife, who was also a shepherd, 2,947 rubles. Part of this was paid not in money but in lambs, grain, milk, etc.[21] If approximately 2,000 rubles was earned by the couple in basic pay, this leaves about 900 rubles in bonuses. This compares well with the income of urban workers, clerks, and so on, who had more or less similar basic pay in the mid-1960s, but without comparable possibilities of bonus pay. By 1973 in the Barguzin farm a successful shepherd was earning 270–300 rubles a month basic pay, although I think this applied to a shepherding couple rather than a single person, with an annual total for that year of 4,000 rubles. Bonuses of about 700 rubles were paid in February 1974 for over-plan production in 1973. But workers in other jobs could earn even more.

The main 'success indicator' for shepherds in lambing *otaras* is undoubtedly the number of lambs per 100 ewes. Wool sheared per sheep, and live weight, were considered less important, though there were bonuses for these too. The latter indicators became more important for the *otaras* also herding young animals and rams. Other indicators are the cleanliness and the quality of the wool. But the *ot sta po sto* slogan had a magic above all others; in the Selenga farm, shepherds who achieved the 100 lambs were sent on a free holiday by the kolkhoz to far-away warm places such as the Caucasus or the Black Sea.

238

Table 5.2. *Average pay per month by occupation in Selenga (1966) and Barguzin (1973) collective farms, Buryat ASSR (not including bonuses)*

Selenga Karl Marx kolkhoz 1966		Barguzin Karl Marx kolkhoz 1973	
Occupation	Pay (rubles)		Pay (rubles)
Milkmaids	100	Builders	200—240
Shepherds	98	Tractor-drivers; machine operators	190—200
Machine operators	94	Chief specialists	192
Calf-rearers	86	Shepherds in lambing *otaras*	150—170
Stockmen	72	Brigadiers	140—160
		Milkmaids	140—150
		Calf-rearers	130—150
		Shepherds (non-lambing)	139
		Stockmen	130—140
		Assistant specialists	130
		Pigmen; drivers	120—130
		General workers	90—100

Sources: Data provided by the economist of each farm in 1967 and 1974.

What did the shepherds do with their money, and how did they choose to live? There were noticeable differences between families of 'ordinary' and 'successful' shepherds.

The Selenga farm was more traditionally 'Buryat'. The wooden house of a typical *otara* was really two one-roomed houses back-to-back, with separate entrances and verandas, one on each side. This was a standard kolkhoz building pattern, which saved heat from the log stoves in winter. The interior of the house was Buryat in many respects, with cooking arrangements on the right side from the entrance (*züün tala*) and respectable furniture and objects to the back of the room (*khoimor tala*).[22] This conceptual organisation of space persists even though the orientation by points of the compass on which it was traditionally aligned, with the door facing south, is now usually not adhered to. Each house had one square room, which was not sub-divided. There was little furniture inside. In summer cooking was done outside on a clay or metal stove.

In normal times, a team consisting of a married couple and one other shepherd would divide so that each family had one room. But the *otara* was often swollen with other people: in winter *sakman* workers came out to help with lambing, and in summer relatives who lived in the kolkhoz centre at Tashir would arrive to spend some time in the beloved fresh air of the steppes. Occasionally school-leavers were sent out to do a year or two's work. Each year almost the whole final class was distributed in twos and threes among the production teams of the farm; this was the *stazh* which school-leavers who did not pass

239

college entrance exams had to do before they could apply for further education (p. 309). Although the school-leavers sometimes lived in a separate house or dormitory, the *otara* could be quite a crowded place.

The *otara* is seen as something 'Buryat' and different from the kolkhoz centre. Firstly, for the kolkhozniks working at the centre it is the place of summer migration, in imitation, as it were, of the old nomadic life. Secondly, even for those people who live all year round on the *otara* it is a different cultural world. For example, people keep one set of clothing, Buryat winter working dress, for the *otara* and have another modish set which they wear when going to the centre.[23] This is not simply a distinction between working and evening clothes. A young shepherdess will have the full-length, thick Buryat *zubsaa* overcoat for herding on the *otara* and another overcoat in Russian style for her visits to the centre.

On the *otara* Buryats address one another by their first name and a kin-term, for example 'Lubsan *akha*', 'older brother Lubsan', as though everyone were related. Even strangers will use the familiar descriptive terms, for example *übgen*, 'old man', *töödei*, 'granny', or, if they know someone's name, they use the name and the descriptive term, for example 'Valya *basagan*', 'young girl Valya'. Often people are known by reference to their children, for example 'Serenei *töödei*', 'Seren's granny'. It appears that old people have their own way of speaking, which differs from locality to locality, but is generally contrasted with the speech of young Buryats, which is more uniform. Thus in one book about collective farms in the Oka *raion* written in Buryat for local readers the author congratulates an in-coming official on 'even being able to understand the old people on the *otaras*'.[24]

The *otara* can be very remote. The Barguzin Karl Marx farm has seventy-two such camps, some of them 40–50 km from the centre. In one farm of the Oka district it took ten days to reach some of the horse herding camps and this journey was not possible at certain times of year.[25] Shepherds even in relatively nearby camps may have to cross rivers by raft or by ford in order to get to the centre. People travel generally by horse-drawn cart or sleigh, and the fact that horses are not allowed as private property causes a certain amount of hardship, as kolkhozniks have recently complained in Soviet newspapers.[26] The successful herdsmen have motor-cycles, but very few have cars, and even if they did the state of the roads is such that for long periods of the year motorised transport is of little use.[27] On the *otara* people have difficulty in getting supplies of food, clothing, manufactures, and medical supplies. *Barguzinskaya Pravda* in 1975 complained that although two farms of the *raion*, the Karl Marx kolkhoz and the Barguzinskii sovkhoz, had organised mobile service units to tour the camps, other farms had done nothing.[28] It is interesting that the political needs of the shepherds were considered to be the most important – or perhaps they were easier to supply. At any rate the teams sent out to the Karl Marx shepherds were 'complex agitbrigades', which put on plays, lectures and political information classes, as well as providing medicines and a travelling shop. The latter two services were insufficient, according to the newspaper, since the best goods were already sold off in the kolkhoz centre, and often items of first necessity were unavailable to the shepherds. Local hospitals did not have sufficient staff to send doctors to the camps. Prophylactic, sanitary and veterinary advice was completely lacking.

All of this means that the shepherds themselves carry out many of those tasks which in the centre of the kolkhoz are removed from the workers by the general division of labour: sewing of clothes, making working tools, fetching fuel, distilling alcohol, veterinary work, and activities such as baking bread, hairdressing, games and entertainment. Thus, superimposed on a fairly rigid economic/ organisational division of labour in respect of the collective herds is an anomalous and enforced 'integration of labour' in almost every other sphere. This is anomalous in the sense that it is, from the individual contemporary Buryat's point of view, like a reconstitution of a traditional state of affairs. Thus while it is true that Buryat herding camps have never had an advanced division of labour, except for the few specially favoured 'vanguard' teams, the young people who now come out to work as shepherds have experienced a different and more 'modern' life in their schooling at the centre. For them this is an education for disenchantment. They are reminded of it constantly as their lives oscillate between the periphery and the centre. In short, they become used to amenities, and the material necessity of returning to the isolated self-sufficiency of the steppes is seen by them as a backward move.

For the *otara* itself it is necessary to make a distinction between the organisation of the economy, which is 'Soviet', and the carrying out of the heterogeneous activities of the herding life; a distinction between the rationality of the whole, and the detailed content of the parts. Insofar as the latter, which are naturally framed by Buryats in Buryat traditional categories, can be with impunity carried on within the Soviet framework, we find that the old ideas are preserved (for example the naming of places, weather, grasses, and categories of animals). In fact the shepherds operate with two sets of classifications for the livestock, their own and also the more sub-divided set of Russian terms. The sheep are actually herded in flocks divided according to Buryat categories, but for the sake of official presentation of figures they are counted in Russian categories which are linked to specific production tasks. In practice the shepherds continue to use the Buryat terms. On all those occasions on which overall economic rationality is at issue the Buryat categories are discarded. They are no longer used even by the traditional people. This applies, for example, in the case of notions of time, without which an economic organisation cannot be conceived. Thus Russian words for years, months, twenty-four hours (Russ. *sutka*, Bur. *süüdkhe*) are used in Buryat conversation and writing. The old western Buryat months, named by occurrences in nature, are half-remembered by old people in Barguzin, but they are never used in relation to production.[29] The

Central Asian twelve-animal cycle for years and months is known by everyone, but it is used in ritual and astrology, not in economic life.[30]

Corresponding to the oscillation between periphery and centre, two types of accumulation of wealth by herdsmen are spatially separated. The accumulation of livestock, which in pre-collectivisation times used to be *the* index of wealth, takes place out on the *otaras*. The accumulation of consumption goods, on the other hand, takes place in the shepherd's private house in the kolkhoz centre. The question of the private production and accumulation is discussed at length in Chapter 6, but it should be noted here that the shepherding life is one that lends itself to semi-legal opportunities; what official is there to count the lambs in the snowy mountains, and who knows what really happened to the three sheep said to have been 'killed by a wolf'? Even if the strictest legality is observed shepherds accumulate sheep inevitably, if only because their pay is to a certain extent made in lambs rather than money.[31] Sheep over the legal norm can be taken to town and bartered or sold, and the same can be done with frozen mutton and sheepskins. All shepherds also convert sheep into money and goods for local social consumption (weddings, gifts, rituals). This is inevitable since the kolkhoz has the legal right to confiscate large private herds.[32] But some younger shepherds also convert them into goods for *private* accumulation and consumption. By 1975 there were a few shepherds' houses crammed with expensive gold-painted crockery, costly nickel-plated bedsteads, wall-hangings, radios and record-players, and gleaming electrical appliances. This would never take place on the *otara*. The private houses of shepherds at the centre are mostly shut up during the working year. Some few of them when opened might be revealed as true Aladdin's caves.

Workers on MTFs (milkmaids, milkers, stockmen)

Nearly all milkers are women, and when men do the job it is almost exclusively when the operation is mechanised. Both of the farms I visited had facilities for mechanised milking in some of their *fermy*. But the problem was that the electricity supply to collective farms was so unreliable that a team of hand-milkers had to be kept in readiness in case there was a power-cut. The Chairman of the Barguzin farm was hopeful that the supply, which comes from the district centre, would soon be improved. However, the problem is a general one for the USSR as a whole. An agricultural newspaper in 1973 said that there had been 132 accidental power-cuts in Soletskiy *raion*, Novogorod *oblast'* between June and November 1972, and ten farms in Kalinin *oblast'* had had power supplies cut completely during the first six weeks of 1973.[33] In the Barguzin farm two of the three MTFs were not yet electrified in 1973. So we can take it that milking was still basically done by hand, and done by women.

A milkmaid in the Selenga farm described her work as follows. She had twelve of her 'own' cows. She got up at 5 o'clock in the morning and gave fodder to her cows at 6 o'clock. After this she milked them. While the stockman drove them out to pasture, she cleaned out the cowshed. This work was finished by 10 in the morning. The cows were milked again at between 1 and 2 o'clock. At 6 o'clock in the evening another lot of fodder was prepared and the woman milked them again. She reckoned to finish work at 8 o'clock in the evening or a bit later.

This is a very short account which does not give much idea of all the work a milkmaid actually does. Ushnayev did a detailed study of milkmaids in four Buryat farms, including the Selenga Karl Marx, in 1961–4.[34] Preparatory work (fetching the cows from byre or field, tying-up the cows' legs, massaging the udders, washing the teats) took time varying from 1 hour 55 minutes in the Karl Marx kolkhoz to 30 minutes in the Lenin kolkhoz, Dzhida district. Basic milking took from 3 hours 55 minutes maximum, in the Lenin farm, to 2 hours 10 minutes in the Karl Marx. The work of finishing-off (undoing tied legs of cows, pouring milk into churns, delivering churns and washing buckets) took around 50 minutes in all four farms. Auxiliary work (watering the cows and feeding the calves, cleaning the shed, and fetching and giving out silage) took a maximum of 3 hours 10 minutes in the Lenin kolkhoz and a minimum of 2 hours 15 minutes in the Communism kolkhoz, Mukhorshibir district. The total work of the milk-maids varied between a maximum of 10 hours 50 minutes in the Lenin kolkhoz and 8 hours 30 minutes in the Karl Marx, per day. But this did not take account of time spent waiting around before the next task could be done.

A relatively small amount of time was spent in the Selenga Karl Marx farm on cleaning the sheds, and this was explained by their new system of a mechanised conveyor belt for the removal of dung. The Lenin kolkhoz in Dzhida district, on the other hand, had a particularly time-consuming regime of feeding the cattle, involving heating water, steaming flour, and making a gruel for the cows. None of these matters is decided by the milkmaids themselves. Even the head of the unit cannot make radical changes in the work tasks. Much depends on outside decisions — not only the amounts of fodder available, but also the type of cow-shed, the number of milkings, and the availability of tools; all are allotted by the brigadier, or, in the case of a specialised farm, by the chief specialist.

In summer, because the cows mainly feed on pasture, the milkmaids have a somewhat shorter working day, varying from 5 hours 40 minutes to 7 hours 28 minutes in the four kolkhozy of the survey mentioned above. But in two of the farms the time between milkings was employed in hay-making and sheep-shearing, adding a further 4 to 6 hours to the working day. Thus Ushnayev quotes approvingly the case of the 'Friendship' kolkhoz in Yeravnin district of the Buryat ASSR.

There are kolkhozy which make a more rational use of the milkmaids' time . . . In the 'Friendship' kolkhoz during the hay-making period each group of milk-maids is allotted a horse and cart, which they use to go out to the meadows when they are not involved in their main work. As a result, the length of their working day becomes 11 hours 56 minutes. Sheep-shearing and hay-cutting are paid separately, which adds a certain material interest for the milkmaids. Furthermore, the hay they gather is given to their MTF over and above the fodder norm, again a matter of interest to all those engaged in milk production.[35]

In Buryatiya as a whole, very little of the milkmaids' work is mechanised (see Chapter 4 section 3). In a farm with hand-milking the working day, including necessary waiting time between the various tasks, averaged 13 hours 43 minutes in the early 1970s.[36]

The work of the milkmaids was thus almost literally endless. The cows had to be milked seven days a week. At the time Ushnayev was writing, the end of the 1960s, kolkhoz workers had no paid holidays. They could only take a holiday by refusing to work, with possible disciplinary consequences, or by finding some excuse. By the 1970s kolkhozniks were allowed days off in bad weather, and women in the Barguzin Karl Marx farm were given 112 days maternity leave. Nevertheless, many women worked literally all year round.

Pay for milkmaids, as for shepherds, could be quite high. There is a basic minimum pay by tariff per day, and then the workers are paid an additional sum, *raztsenka*, usually around 15% of the basic pay, for what they have actually produced towards their plan. Thus, for example, a milkmaid may be allotted twenty-two cows, and she will be given a plan by which she should produce 660 centners of milk and twenty calves by the end of the year. If she succeeds in fulfilling her plan she will be paid a *raztsenka* of 15% of her basic pay, but if she does not succeed the *raztsenka* is correspondingly lowered by an amount reckoned according to the deficit in products. In some farms the entire pay is calculated by the products, e.g. 4 rubles per calf and 1 ruble 70 kopecks per centner of milk (the *akkordno-premial'naya* system). In other farms, the time spent in clearing out, feeding, etc. is counted separately, and only the time spent actually milking is reckoned to be 'productive'; this is not so good for the milkmaids, because the *raztsenka* is calculated only against 'productive' time and amounts to 15% of a much lower figure.[37]

Some farms attempt to solve the problem of the length of working hours by having a two-shift system for each group of cows. This, however, runs into difficulties when the two women do not get on together: there are accusations of laziness, allowing the cows' condition to deteriorate, etc. As we saw in Chapter 3, the means of production allotted to each worker as 'his' or 'hers' constitute a fundamental right, and it is not surprising that the two-shift system is not popular. When wages are paid for productivity the problems of this system become even more acute.

In the Selenga farm in 1966 a milkmaid, with no husband or other earner in her family, was paid 2,088 rubles, of which about 800 rubles was bonus pay (i.e. *raztsenka* paid for fulfilling and over-fulfilling her plan). I was given this figure by the book-keeper of the farm, who was presumably quoting the best-paid milkmaid that year. Her name was Dolgorzhap Tsyrendorzhiyeva, a famous worker who had been awarded a gold medal and a car. It was difficult to believe that any other milkmaid earned more than her, and many must have been paid much less. But this does show that a milkmaid can earn more than a shepherd. However, a shepherd has many more 'on the side' opportunities than a milkmaid. As we have seen, a sheep can always be sold for meat, private animals can be mixed among the collective flock, and, in agreement with the technician who signs the certificates, a sheep can 'die', be signed off the register, and the meat shared out. But what of much value can a milkmaid do with her milk? A bottle for me, a bottle for you . . .

A milkmaid's job, on the other hand, has certain possibilities of a demonstrative kind. It can be lifted to a heroic plane by extraordinary achievements in getting more milk, perhaps simply because milk is so countable. It is thus a job which appeals to, or more usually is allotted to, dedicated enthusiasts (see Chapter 7). This was satirised by the Soviet writer Voinovich in his account of the famous milkmaid 'Lyushka'.[38]

Lyushka was one of the first to enter the kolkhoz. They gave her previously *kulak* cows. It is true that they didn't give as much milk as before, but from inertia they continued to pour out plenty. Gradually, Lyushka began to stand on her feet. She got shoes and clothes and got married to Yegor and entered the Party. Soon there began to emerge workers of the vanguard (*peredoviki, udarniki*), and Lyushka on all the evidence was fully entitled to belong to this category. The first notes on Lyushka's achievements began to appear in the local and central press. But she really took off when some correspondent or other, quoting her (or maybe he made it up himself) squeezed into the paper the sensational report that Lyushka had given up the ancient way of milking cows and was now taking to handling four teats at once, two in each hand. Then it all started. Making an appearance at the Congress of Kolkhozniks in the Kremlin Lyushka assured the delegates and comrade Stalin himself personally that the old-fashioned way was now finished with, once and for all. And on comrade Stalin's retort, 'Cadres! Cadres!', she promised to teach the new method to all the milkmaids of her kolkhoz. 'And will it work for all of them?' asked Stalin craftily. 'Yes, after all every milkmaid has two hands, comrade Stalin,' she replied smartly, and held up her two palms. 'Right you are,' said Stalin with a smile and bowed his head. From this time onwards Lyushka was never seen in her native kolkhoz: either she was sitting in conference in the Supreme Soviet, or she was taking part in meetings, or she was receiving English dockers, or she was having an interview with the writer Lion Feightvanger, or she was being awarded a medal in the Kremlin. Newspapers wrote about Lyushka. The radio talked about her. Newsreels made films about her. The journal *Ogonyek* had her portrait on its cover. Soldiers in the army wrote that they wanted to marry her.

That this is not so very far from reality we see from articles in the local Barguzin press, such as the following, which appeared on 2 December 1975.

A milkmaid – laureate of the State Prize of the USSR
The fame of our 'Kommunarka' sovkhoz has long spread through the Moscow region and far beyond. 5,000 kg of milk per cow is achieved by many of our milkmaids. The stockmen of our enterprise have often been the initiators of

excellent new methods. But the idea that everything had been done already to raise productivity never entered the head of the front-line milkmaid M.S. Gromova. It was with thoughts of productivity in her head that Mariya Sergeevna approached the director of the sovkhoz at the beginning of the five-year plan.

They sat late that evening . . . They decided to begin milking with the high-productivity apparatus 'Mayak', which is able to serve four cows at once. Gromova suggested a full division of labour: the milkmaids should only milk the cows, or more accurately, they should only see that the machines were working properly . . .

Does Gromova have a secret? The main secret is that she is a master of machine milking. To become such a master one needs not only to know the technology, but one needs also to be a patient experimenter, to understand the behaviour of one's own wards . . . Working with milking machines milkmaids lose a great deal of time in various manual operations: massaging the udders before and during milking, finishing off by hand, and so on.

The goal is to get as much milk out of the udders as possible. But the milk-maid noticed that there is a paradox: even though working with machines, the milkmaids lose much time in . . . helping the machines to work. Is this necess-ary? Apparently not . . . The matter was put right when they began to use a rational system of milking: all cows without exception were milked only by machine, with no manual work whatsoever. And this is not the only example of the creative approach of M.S. Gromova.

She now has many followers.

The outstanding achievements in labour of the front-line milkmaid, Hero of Socialist Labour, Mariya Sergeevna Gromova, have been recognised by the award of the State Prize of the USSR for 1975.[39]

This article in no way makes it clear how the master milkmaid is able to make the machinery work without manual help when other women cannot. But that is less important than the fact that a milkmaid can be awarded the State Prize for somehow or other getting enormous amounts of milk out of the cows.

The more modest achievements of local milkmaids are noted in the papers too. An article about a milkmaid from the Barguzin Karl Marx kolkhoz, Margarita Ochirovna Badmayeva from the non-mechanised 2nd MTF in Urzhil, describes her methods of getting a higher yield: she makes sure that the man who does artificial insemination of her cows actually gets them all pregnant, she finds out if any of her cows have wandered off on the pastures for too long and then gets the vet to check them, she makes sure that every bit of the daily fodder allowance actually gets to her cows, and, finally, she makes use of every single day of the 300-day lactation period. What this amounts to is that she takes the responsibility of checking that the other workers on whom her own results are dependent, the herdsman, the inseminator, and the vet, do their work properly — and then she milks the cows for all they are worth. This is how milk-maids get large bonuses and prizes.

But the trouble is that the milk itself, using such methods, may be of low quality and may even be undrinkable. In 1975 the state dairy which receives the Barguzin milk instituted a new three-tier system of classing milk. Instead of the old price of 22 rubles per centner (100 kg) for all milk, they paid 24.60 rubles for milk of the first class, 23 rubles for the second class, and 21.90 rubles for the third class. Milk below the third class is returned as unusable, and even third class milk may be sent back if it does not come up to criteria of cleanliness and purity. This is indeed what happened in the Karl Marx farm in 1975. Only the milk from the Soyol *ferma* (MTF 3) was accepted, and that was only second class. All the rest of the milk, including presumably everything milked by the industrious Margarita Badmayeva, was sent back. This may even arise directly from the exhortations to milkmaids to produce every last drop. Two of the reasons quoted by the director of the dairy for the return of milk are the non-acceptability of milk taken in the first seven days of lactation and the last seven days.[40]

The milkmaid, far more than the shepherd, is in a situation where the quality of her product is determined by the division of labour. Good quality milk has a high fat content, but the physical well-being of the cows depends on other sectors of the kolkhoz producing enough fodder, a matter of crisis by 1980 in most Buryat farms, as we have seen, and on the care given to pasturing the herd by the stockmen. The main complaint of the Barguzin dairy was that the milk reaching them had gone sour; the team of zoo technicians is responsible for matters of bacteriological testing and preservation, and the drivers are in charge of transport. How is it possible to feel enthusiastic about the production of litre after litre of milk if it may all be returned from the dairy through no fault of one's own? The result is that milkmaids care not so much about the product as about the rewards of the job: steady pay and the possibility of becoming known as a 'good worker'. Because of its high ideological visibility compared with its real life grinding work-load, this job has a particularly high turnover of team-leaders. The newspaper *Komsomol'skaya Pravda* cited the case of an MTF which had had ten team-leaders in the last ten years and now a young girl was being sent out to bring the group up to standard. She was given this position, over the heads of many more experienced milkers, because she had been educated in a technical college as a zoo technician.[41]

The constant and daily calculability of the milkmaid's product induces stress in the workers. They try to help one another. In a kolkhoz in Chita *oblast'* they have a term for this: 'to give the group [i.e. of cows] as a brideprice' – *otdat' gruppu na kalym*. This expression is used when one girl is absent without leave (Russ. *gulyayet*, goes off to have a good time) and her friend milks her cows and writes down the amount of milk in her own record book. In this same farm milkmaids were very badly paid – only 70 rubles a month in 1981, which is less than half the wages of milkmaids in the Barguzin Karl Marx farm in 1973. Many of the women appeared at work irregularly, and most of them were heavy drinkers. If a milkmaid was caught at work drunk she was 'caricatured': the brigadier wrote a laughable story about her and put it up in a public place. But this had little effect. The women were almost proud of their drunkenness, and the brigadier himself could hardly keep sober.[42]

247

Cattle-herders (stockmen) are 16.6% of all livestock workers in Buryat collective farms. Their job is to take the cattle out to pasture, both summer and winter, and their success is measured by weight gain over periods of time. The equivalent of the shepherds' slogan *ot sta po sto* is the cowboys' *za sto dnei — tsentner privesa* — 'a hundred kilograms in a hundred days'.

The cattle-herders work longer hours than anyone else. It is not possible to achieve the kilo a day weight gain without pasturing the animals for twenty or twenty-one hours a day. Many stockmen work in pairs and the load can be shared between them, but even so two men are required to work simultaneously in many of the operations, especially if the herd is a large one. In the Barguzin region it is not rare for two herdsmen to have charge of 600 young cattle. In the Selenga farm one family would look after 100–200 head. Only front-line workers, engaged in 'socialist obligations', would actually pasture the animals for twenty-one hours a day. But even so, the *average* working day in summer for a cattle-herder is fourteen hours.[43]

The main problem in grazing cattle is the lack of good pasture-land and the fact that no fenced areas are set aside. This means that the herdsmen have constantly to guard against the cattle getting into the crops. In August when the grass is no longer much good the cattle are tempted by the smell of ripening wheat and continually break away from the herd. In the forests and swamps of Buryatiya it is difficult to keep track of them. Goaded by summer flies and mosquitoes cattle easily stampede and risk breaking their legs as they charge downhill. The stockman is personally responsible for cattle which die and he has to pay not only the cost of the animal but also a fine if the brigadier decides that he is to blame.

In winter the herdsmen still take the cattle out, but the hours on the pasture are shorter. The average working day still stretches to over ten hours[44] and the work is much more exhausting. Herdsmen have to clean out the cow-sheds (not the stalls themselves which are done by the milkmaids), cart away the manure, fetch silage and heat up water.

In spite of this, the herdsmen were paid less as a basic wage than either the shepherds or the milkmaids. However, with devoted work it was possible to earn as much as the shepherds, when bonuses are added for good weight-gains. A Selenga family, with both husband and wife working in cattle herding, earned 2,997 rubles in 1966, the same as a brigadier whose wife did not work.

A typical milk-production unit (MTF) in a Buryat kolkhoz in the 1960s had nine members. The team-leader was a woman, whose special job was rearing new-born calves. She was in charge also of the book-keeping and of the artificial insemination procedures. Under her were two couples, the husbands working as calf-herders and the wives as milkmaids, three single women milkmaids, and one single man, a Russian, who was both driver and milker. Pastures were allotted not by the team-leader but by the brigadier over her. The team-leader was, however, responsible for the calf-herders' papers. As a stockman in another farm complained:

Almost a month ago I took on a group of calves. I feed them and I feed them, but the relevant documents have still not been made out. What weight were they when I took them on? I don't know. When they gave the animals to me they did not weigh them. And after all I get paid by the weight . . . [45]

The job of stockman is counted as different from that of calf-rearer and is less well-paid. Calf-rearers are always attached to production teams (MTF) on a permanent basis, but stockmen are sometimes general workers who are given this job for a season. This work is also given to casual labourers, people who are hired temporarily by the kolkhoz but who do not become members of it.

Machine-operator

The occupation of machine-operator (*mekhanizator*) has its own internal division of labour into tractor-driver, harvester-operator, assistant harvester-operator, chauffeur, machinist of various types (shearing machinery, milking machinery, etc.), electrician, fitter, turner, welder, and technical engineer. Many people do more than one of these jobs — tractor-driver and harvester-operator, for example. The two with the greatest number of workers are tractor-driver (*traktorist*) and driver (*shofyer*) and I shall accordingly describe these.

Tractor-drivers

The *traktorists* and drivers are the aristocracy of the farm-workers. Because they both undergo special training and have several grades (driver of first, second, third class, etc.), these jobs have an internal 'career' structure which does not apply to most other work. In accordance with the ideology of productivity (see Chapter 2) *traktorists* in particular are paid more than other arable workers. In the early 1960s it cost the Selenga Karl Marx farm 1 ruble 80 kopecks to cut a hectare of hay using a tractor; it cost them 4 rubles 51 kopecks to cut the same area using a horse-drawn cutter, and 35 rubles by hand.[46] The pay to *traktorists* per hour of work is almost proportional to the cut in costs. Thus in this same farm a worker using the horse-drawn cutter was paid 18 rubles per shift, while a *traktorist* was paid 60 rubles per shift.[47] The pay to ordinary field-workers was almost certainly very much lower even than the hay-cutter operator. Furthermore, *traktorists* can earn large bonuses for completing given jobs in a given period of time. Yet the job is not universally popular.

What does it involve? In the Selenga farm in the mid-1960s the following operations were mechanised: all sowing and cultivating of grain, silage and vegetable fields, all harvesting of grains and fodders, the transport and threshing of grains, and winnowing. Only hay-cutting and stacking were regularly done by hand, as well as much of the loading and unloading. *Traktorists* worked much fewer hours than livestock workers. Their average working day was seven hours in winter and eight hours in summer (in a range of Buryat collective farms).[48] But much of this time was spent hanging about, travelling to and from the fields, and in making repairs which ought to have been unnecessary. Ushnayev says that the *traktorists* he studied used only 53.5% of the working day when sowing spring wheat, 49.4% when loading peas, 73.7% when harvesting wheat, etc. Furthermore, on many days of the year *traktorists* do not work at all. In the Trans-Baikal region only 130–150 days of the year can be used for outdoor arable work in any case. In the winter *traktorists* and machine-operators have almost nothing to do. Sometimes they are set at loading fodder for the cattle. But even so, Ushnayev estimated that half of the workforce engaged in arable farming did not work at all in the kolkhoz in the winter months.[49]

Because of their training machine-operators find it comparatively easy to move from farm to farm, and even to get jobs in factories. One important movement of population in the farm is thus among this group. One of the main reasons for leaving is the irregularity of the work and hence the pay, even if it is *per diem* higher than that of everyone else. In 1965 in Buryatiya 68% of people trained as machine-operators in agriculture had left farming altogether and were engaged in other work.[50] In the Selenga Karl Marx farm in 1967 there were eighty-one machine-operators. Of these twenty-three had worked in this farm for less than a year, and eight of them were temporary hired men.

Although Soviet workers do not own the means of production, the tie between the *traktorist* and 'his' tractor is very important. A *traktorist* does not go out to

Traktorist, Karl Marx kolkhoz, Barguzin, 1967.

work when 'his' machine is under repair but waits for it to come out of the workshop. A tractor can even be 'inherited', as in the case of a father who had always 'got on badly' with his tractor and blamed it for his poor performance, but when he retired and the machine was taken over by his son it was found that the tractor was in good order and it was the father's way of using it that had been at fault.[51]

The *traktorist* is supposed to maintain his own machine, but there is also an inter-kolkhoz organisation, *Selkhoztekhnika*, which takes charge of big repairs. This causes many problems of organisation: the *Selkhoztekhnika* has spare parts for some machines but not others, the farms may not send in their machine in time, or there may be a queue at the workshop. Since the *Selkhoztekhnika* mechanics do not have to drive the tractors themselves there are frequent cases of bad workmanship. In Barguzin it appears that the district head engineer working for *Selkhoztekhnika* organises campaigns in the farms for the repair of machinery in the off-season. This means that the *traktorists* may have to serve two masters, the kolkhoz management which may require them to do some job which crops up (e.g. transporting fodder) and the district engineer.

Machine-operators have more education than other farm-workers. Of the eighty-one machine-operators in the Selenga farm in 1966, seven or eight had ten years schooling, fifty-nine had five to seven years, and only fifteen had simple primary education. The majority of livestock workers on the same farm, on the other hand, had only primary education.[52]

This can be linked with the gradual increase in specialisation and mechanisation. In the Selenga farm, with its comparatively old-fashioned values, *traktorists* in 1966 were still paid a lower basic wage than either milkmaids or shepherds. In Barguzin by 1973, on the other hand, *traktorists* were paid much more than either of these, and even more than the specialists (190–200 rubles basic pay a month). It is significant that rates of pay did not reflect success in production: the Selenga farm was extremely successful at grain production, the Barguzin kolkhoz was not.

A comparatively large number of *traktorists* and other machine-operators were Russians (see also Table 1.4). Randalov, a Buryat ethnographer writing about his own locality, quotes the growth in the number of mechanised jobs as one of the main factors bringing Russians to Buryat farms. 'In joint work activity and life in one village, there is a mutual enrichening of their cultures and family traditions.'[53]

In fact, the life of a *traktorist* is more 'urban' than that of livestock workers. He lives in one of the kolkhoz villages and does not move house with the seasons. The influx of a certain number of Russian and other machine-operators into Buryat kolkhozy has made the villages larger, more mixed in population, and more 'urban' in outlook. *Traktorists* know that the financial success of the farm depends to a large extent on their work. They will not agree to live in barracks by the fields like the ordinary manual workers. They go out to work in the mornings and return in the evenings. Randalov mentions that the idea of a definite working day, with an agreed beginning and end, is even emerging in some tractor teams, something that is unheard of in the livestock sectors.[54]

The job of *traktorist*, then, with its connotations of trained and dedicated youthful workers proceeding in their machines over the immense fields of corn — not to speak of the 'Virgin Lands' campaign instigated by Khrushchev and executed by the Komsomol — has ideological possibilities which in the all-Union culture shepherding, for example, could never attain. Because it is a job which requires training, and for fully qualified workers is very highly paid, it can be depicted as a 'rags to riches' avenue, by which ordinary field-workers can make their way up through the ranks of the brigade. The job of *traktorist* thus becomes a kind of paradigm of the ideal life:

All of Life in Labour

Dalai Rinchinovich Radnayev knows the price of labour. Yes, and how would he not know it since he started work at fifteen? He began as a trailer-man [i.e. working on trailers behind tractors]. He began here, in Khilgana. They were difficult, those years . . . The first year of war, the first year of working life . . . All the grown men had gone to defend their homeland. His father went too. So Dalai stayed behind, his own master . . . All of his care and thoughts were taken up by work. Work attracted him, it muffled the bitterness of his father's absence.

The spring was full of unrepeatable music, the earth gave out an inexplicably moving smell. He came to love it, like his own mother. With envy he looked at the *traktorists*: 'Ekh! If only I could be a *traktorist*!' The plough-shares turned over the earth. All day before his eyes in a never-ending stream there flowed earth, earth . . . From childhood he drank in her smell.

Soon the eager youth was sent on a course for *traktorists* at Bayangol [in the Karl Marx kolkhoz]. After three months he came back to his home kolkhoz, and now he saw the earth from the cabin of his own tractor . . .

Victory in the war brought a lightening in the work. The defenders came home, and the Kuitun steppe herself breathed more easily. The kolkhoz needed specialists. Dalai Rinchinovich was sent to the Selenginsk institute for machine-operators. For two years after he graduated he worked as assistant brigadier of the tractor brigade. And now he has been at its head for twenty-five years. Now it is already a tractor–field brigade [i.e. with both machinery and land of its own].

It is a long *stazh*. A whole life in one's home kolkhoz. Under his own eyes the bare feather-grass-covered Kuitun steppe has come alive and rich. The cares of the kolkhoz are his own deepest cares . . .

Dalai Rinchinovich is a communist. Labour is the meaning of his life. The success of the kolkhoz to a great extend depends on the way the tractor–field brigade works.

And the Khilgana kolkhoz has something to be proud of. Earlier than any in the district it accomplished its harvest, and it went to the help of the Karl Marx kolkhoz. They tilled 1,500 hectares of winter sowings, instead of 1,200, and they sowed 8,000 centners of first and second class wheat. The five-year plan for the sale of wheat to the state [which ended in 1975] was fulfilled by 1974.

Behind these dry figures is the life of his brigade, his own life. As the wheat turns into golden scattering of grain, his life is sweetened in its very heart. He is not only an excellent worker but also a sower.

His spacious home is full of happiness. Eleven children grow up one after another with his wife Buda Gomboyevna. And not only are the children proud of their parents, the parents too have something to be proud of: the eldest, Stepan, is a *traktorist*—combiner working in his home kolkhoz, Boris is also a *traktorist* and takes an external course at the agricultural technical school – he was sent by the kolkhoz. Sergei worked for two years in the kolkhoz and is now serving in the Red Army. Galina, the eldest daughter, is working as a tram-driver in Ulan-Ude.

'The rest are still at school, the youngest is only five. Their future is still ahead of them,' smiles Dalai Rinchinovich.

On the table are diplomas and medals. There are many of them, difficult to count. Last year Dalai Rinchinovich was awarded the medal 'Sign of Honour'. And all of this is for honest work, for work with full giving of himself.

On his temples are a few grey hairs. Wrinkles line his forehead, but in his eyes is a living sparkle.

'We have got all the machines ready for the spring sowing and we are just getting our teams organised. The main thing is to prepare the field stations now, to get things ready for the machine-operators. There is still a lot to do,' sighs Dalai Rinchinovich.

And life is before him, a life full of the cares and joys of labour.[55]

This account from the local Barguzin paper shows the ideal *traktorist*, devoted to work in his own 'speciality', with sons following in the same profession. The idea of upward mobility is clearly present (note that while the father has a Buryat name, all of the children have Russian names). The 'bare Kuitun steppe', which was always in fact perfectly good pasture-land, is transformed from its 'virgin' state to become a huge wheat field. No mention is made of the erosion, which we know this policy has caused (Chapter 4 section 3), nor of the attempts made by the collective farms to combat it – that is the concern of the engineers and nothing to do with the *traktorist*'s life.

Drivers

Of all the jobs in the farm this seemed to be the one which was most attractive. People were glad and proud to say they were drivers. As with other machine-operators, almost all drivers are men, and they tend to be young and relatively well-educated.

The job involves transporting products, machinery, fuel, fodder and even animals from one part of the farm to another, and from the farm to the district centre and state processing plants. Drivers are usually attached to brigades, but for certain tasks they may be formed into special teams. (In kolkhozy such as the Selenga Karl Marx in 1966, where the brigades were not mechanised, the drivers and other machine-operators belonged to a central pool.) In 1975 the Barguzin Karl Marx farm decided to form a special team of drivers to carry out the centralised distribution of winter fodder and fuel to its seventy-two herding camps. This involved driving right across the territory of the farm, from the

Kuitun steppes, the Yasy, and other far-flung parts where fodder is grown, to the many tiny camps dotted over the pastures. The team of drivers was given its own fleet of lorries, cars, and tractors. The timing of the journeys was worked out by one of the specialists, an economist called Omsoyev, and it was reckoned that this centralised organisation would enable each driver to make three return journeys each day. Previously, when the brigades (i.e. MTFs and OTFs) had each fetched their own fodder, the drivers had only done one or two journeys a day. What did the drivers think of this sudden 'increase in the productivity of the lorry-park'[56] which was at the same time almost a doubling of their work-load? We know only that the trade union organisation of the kolkhoz held a meeting at which the idea was approved.

In Siberian conditions the life of a driver is tough, but also full of adventures and opportunities. For much of the year everything is covered with snow and ice. Engine failure in a remote area in winter can mean frostbite or even death within hours, and there were many stories of this kind, especially concerning drivers who were drunk. In the spring, with the thawing of the rivers, driving is, if anything, even more hazardous. Even made-up roads (none that I saw were tarmacadamed) can be washed away in a few hours. Uneven thawing of perma-frost causes gaping holes to be formed, which may be invisible because of a thin layer of snow, and river crossings are always dangerous at this time of year: the driver has to get out and test the ice, but even this is never sure.

The other side of the driver's life is the ever-present possibility of private transactions. Perhaps the majority of drivers act as unofficial taxis, and all without exception take other loads as well as the ordered one. Locally unobtainable and interesting goods can be brought from the town, presents can be delivered to distant relatives, and produce from the private economy of the farm can be taken for sale. All of this brings a side income, and more important, a position of some power in the reciprocal exchange which is so important in the domestic economy.

Furthermore, drivers are generally well-paid. The family of a driver in the Selenga farm, Bato Dashiyev, whose wife was a milkmaid, earned 2,865 rubles in 1966 — about the same as the figure given for a shepherding family and a cattle-herding family (both with working wives). Basic pay may be low, but bonuses are earned for extra work taken on over the daily norm and for consistent reliability. Like *traktorists*, drivers are classed according to grades. The examin-ations for these grades include mechanical and technological tests, and a driver of the first class is qualified to have charge of a variety of different vehicles. Pay rises as higher grades are attained.

The 'ideology' of the job emphasises not so much pure love of labour, as in the case of the *traktorist*, but technical knowledge and reliability. The job, according to the local Barguzin newspaper, is a 'calling' (*prizvaniye*). In real life drivers are known for being 'sharp'. The job has great opportunities for side transactions and this is recognised in the kolkhoz by the appointment of a special official to 'control' particular transport operations.[57] Unlike shepherds, who benefit from the space between the *otara* and the kolkhoz centre, the drivers derive their opportunities from the relations between the kolkhoz and the outside world. Many of them have had experience of the army and have had other jobs, for example on geological expeditions. It was mainly among drivers and machine-operators that I met people who were impatient with talk of Buryat traditions. In accordance with their greater mobility and sophistication drivers occasionally marry the rural intelligentsia, librarians or school-teachers.

Meadow-worker

The task of a meadow-worker (Russ. and Bur. *lugovod*) is to prepare the irrigated and fertilised hay-fields (*ütüg*) and then to harvest, dry, and store the hay. It was my impression that during the 1960s, when I first visited the farms, this job was not highly esteemed. The production of hay, although absolutely vital for the livestock units, was not an area in which a kolkhoz could 'shine' in the eyes of the *raion* and it was consistently subordinated to the more glamorous and financially advantageous activity of grain production. In Buryat culture also the job was not esteemed, being only a wearisome *part* of a true man's occupation: herding. The people doing the job of meadow-worker tended to be middle-aged men, Russian rather than Buryat, aided by an army of housewives, schoolchildren, etc. when the time for the harvest arrived. Those meadow-workers whom I met were members of the Party, who had been 'sent' (*napravlyat'*) to this necessary and arduous task. As Party members they could hardly refuse. They were not helped by the perennial neglect of the irrigation systems and the reluctance of farm managements to allocate equipment (e.g. bulldozers) with which meadow-workers could repair the channels themselves.

By the mid-1970s, and particularly by 1980, this attitude had changed. The disastrous fodder situation in the Barguzin *raion* pushed the authorities into taking the job seriously, and articles began appearing in the local newspaper extolling the achievements of the *lugovod*. Whereas in the mid-1960s meadow-workers were undertaking 'socialist obligations' to harvest an average 12–15 centners per hectare,[58] by 1980 the best *lugovody* were achieving up to 66 centners.[59]

It is significant that these recent results were obtained by changing the organisation of work. Instead of having a team of meadow-workers sent to work at various places in the farm allocated by a brigadier, the best results in 1980 were achieved by giving each man his own patch, which he continued to work and improve over the years.

The work involved is clearly described by a *lugovod* from the 'Bodon' sovkhoz in Barguzin:[60]

The division of labour

'Five years ago my neighbour Nikolai Korokin obtained 54 centners per hectare from this patch (we call it Gerasimov's patch). But it wasn't a very good patch. The year before I got it it only produced 12 centners a hectare.'

Petr Alekseyevich, the *lugovod*, looked out of the window.

'If only it would rain! It would help the wheat and the grass. I was a *lugovod* up to 1961, but in those days nobody spoke about meadow-work, they just harvested whatever grew up and that was it. But now things have become difficult for the livestock, and the losses of animals are growing. They sent me to be a senior shepherd in the sovkhoz. I worked, I got prizes. But it is difficult work, or perhaps that was just me. Anyway, my health wasn't very good, and with that job I had to spend the whole day in the saddle. Last year, the director of the sovkhoz said: "Look, Alekseyevich, take the Gerasimov patch, show how the work should be done. The communists realise it is a difficult patch, but we believe in you and know you will not let us down."

'Well, as you see, I haven't let them down, though there is one year to go till I retire. But even after that I'll probably go on. I like working.'

'That's what he's like,' broke in his wife, who was fussing round the electric samovar. 'He goes out with the sunrise and comes back with the sunset.'

'What do you expect!' Petr's eyes were twinkling. 'The Bodon River flows at night too. We mustn't lose any water. The meadows need so much. By the time the water gets to my patch you could ladle out all that is left. So you have to water the fields at night, when everyone else is asleep. Last year I managed to irrigate the meadow twice completely, and that saved the grass' [1979 was a very dry year].

Petr Alekseyevich's first task, when he took on the patch, was to fertilise it with local manure . . . He spread twenty tons per hectare. He was lucky that the cattle-sheds were not far away. But you can't be lazy in a job like that. As he transported the manure in a trailer he hoped that his neighbouring meadow-workers would notice and follow his example. He even spoke about it to the agronomist. But nothing came of it — the example, it seems, did not reach to the heart.

Of course he had to clear the patch of stones, old tins, and branches . . . After clearing and fertilising, the *luvogod* gets down to harrowing. This allows the earth to breathe and at the same time conserves moisture. Then there is the pricking of the young grass, done with a special instrument which he made himself.

'It's better than the factory made equipment,' the *lugovod* explained, 'because it does not harm the upper soil so much. And the upper humus is what we must preserve, it is the most fertile. Then I start the irrigation. The first one is to give the essential moisture without which the grass will not grow. Every drop is useful . . .

The whole patch has to be fenced in. The *lugovod* has just spent several days repairing a gap in the poles [Buryat fields are fenced not with wire but with stout constructions of long poles twined together].

'It's always possible to grow a good crop of grass,' said Petr Alekseyevich, 'but that is not all. The price of our labour only appears in the autumn with the final results of the harvest.'

You can grow, but how are you to harvest? This is also an important element in the work of a *lugovod*.

'On 5 June they told me to gather some housewives and go to cut hay on the far meadows. I got together fifteen women. They found me a helper, N.F. Bel'kov, who is retired, but a good worker. And you can't really go far away with the housewives, they have to work close by. But they "threw" us on the very furthest, and in fact the most difficult, patch. We had to harvest reeds. And we scythed it. In five days we got 150 centners. It's not easy to harvest reeds. You can't get through by tractor, you'd get stuck immediately. Even horses are no use. There is water everywhere. We did the work in high marsh boots. And everything we harvested we carried out by hand or in bags to a hillock, where we laid it out to dry. And on my own Gerasimov patch we started to harvest only on the 20 August. It was a bit late. At first I thought, 'The grass is too thick, we'll never manage to cut it.' But it was all right, they helped me. The specialists of the kolkhoz, the director, and the Party Secretary organised a *subbotnik* [labour-day]', and we scythed the whole lot by hand. We got it off the fields in time, before the rains. And that's how I got 66 centners per hectare.'

Meadow-workers used to be paid at low rates, and in the 1960s they were not counted separately from the manual workers who got between 60 and 70 rubles a month in the Selenga farm. In the Barguzin farm they earned between 90 and 100 rubles a month in 1973, plus bonuses for good work. Probably, they are much better paid by now.

In conclusion we should summarise briefly the ways in which economic and political aspects of the division of labour intersect.

1. The social division of labour is preceded, as it were, by the division of the objects of labour. Sheep, for example, are divided into flocks of specific types, and these broadly correspond to different jobs. But the division of the objects of labour is not caused by the social division of labour but exists independently of it, determined by particular economic targets given in the plan negotiated by the farm with the state. Given the conditions of production in the livestock sector of most Buryat farms this segmentation of the objects of labour is not objectively necessary, and indeed it is often inefficient. Furthermore, it is to some extent subverted by the workers because it does not correspond with their Buryat traditional knowledge of herding.

2. Independently of this, and arising from the theory of the industrialisation of agriculture (see Chapter 2), there is a social division of the working population into 'professions'. Because of the different tasks, pay, ideologies, and political opportunities associated with these jobs they appeal to people of different character. There is thus a voluntary aspect to the present division of labour. At the same time the well-defined characteristics of each job serve as labels for people ('Dulma is a milkmaid'). Alongside the Buryat evaluation of different jobs there is an official evaluation, indicated clearly by pay differentials (see section 2), which influences the *younger* generation by means of the education system.

3. As a result of the process outlined above there has been a change in the status of Buryat traditional knowledge. As practical knowledge it is associated with low prestige jobs, and it is generally only held by people of the older generation. It has therefore become transformed, in the minds of young people for whom such jobs represent the Buryat 'past', into an aspect of ethnicity.

257

4. The state, in the form of the Party, *contributes* to the change in the status of traditional knowledge by its manipulation of the political and economic aspects of the division of labour: (a) Certain 'professions', for example *traktorist*, attract young educated and politically motivated people, who naturally achieve positions in the Komsomol, the Soviets, etc. (b) Other 'professions', for example shepherd, stockman, do not attract these people and are filled by recognisably 'backward', less educated workers. (c) The Party recognises all professions as making an economic contribution, and furthermore has a policy of representation of all professions in bodies such as the Soviets. Thus although such political bodies are dominated by the 'advanced professions' the Party sees that there will be representative milkmaids or shepherds in their midst. The economic achievement of such people is thus recognised *de facto*, but the Party ignores their traditional basis by transforming Buryat practical knowledge into edited 'golden words' of a rudimentary exhortative kind. 'Golden words' are published in the press in such a way as to emasculate their effectiveness as guides to economic practice (which would threaten the political/ideological esteem of more modern professions), but to justify the political recruitment of people from backward professions into the Party because they are repositories of these very 'golden words'.

2. Division of labour, pay, and the 'irresponsibility' thesis

Analysis of the whole range of working jobs in Buryat collective farms, as well as the more detailed survey of a few key jobs given above, leads us to a discussion of five main points.

1. The length of the working day and the physical exertion required in the various jobs differ greatly through the range of occupations. Soviet studies show that nearly all kolkhozniks in livestock jobs exceed the daily norm of seven hours, in one case actually doubling it, while half of all kolkhozniks in agricultural jobs *do not work at all* during the winter. There are large differences in the time worked even among livestock occupations (Table 5.3).

As we have seen from the material in the detailed studies of the main occupations on the farm, the length of the working day is very rarely in any way controlled by the workers themselves. Thus, although the pay in livestock work is fairly good, the jobs are unpopular because of the exhausting work and lack of autonomy. In the pre-collectivisation attitude to work, Mongols and Buryats valued highly their own mastery over the processes of production.[61]

The Mongol view is that other peoples are slaves to work; they lack free agency and are continually anxious about some particular undertaking or enterprise. To the Chinese, for example, the term *kuo-jih-tze*, 'passing the day', means laboring industriously every day to maintain one's security. Mongols tend to reject the approach to life in which the work governs the person rather than the reverse. A nomad prefers to see himself as controlling his own life and destiny and com-

Table 5.3. *Average working day among kolkhozniks in livestock jobs of Buryat ASSR (in minutes, and as % of seven-hour norm)*

	Time worked			% of norm worked		
Occupation	Summer	Winter	Average	Summer	Winter	Average
Milkmaid	283	516	399	67.4	122.9	95.0
Calf-rearer	330	564	447	78.6	134.3	106.4
Cattle-herder	742	620	681	176.7	147.6	162.1
Shepherd	259	677	468	61.7	161.2	111.4
Pig-herder	687	840	764	163.6	200.0	181.9

Source: Ushnayev 1969, p. 93.

monly refers to his approach to labor as *aju-törökhü*, meaning 'being involved in productive labor' [*aju* = task; *törökhü* = to give birth, to create]. In short, the Mongols see themselves as freely and deliberately involved in work and the Chinese as rather unthinkingly, automatically working from dawn till dark with no real consciousness of the process.

This sense of mastery, however, is exactly what is removed in the present system.

2. Pay and conditions of work vary enormously between different collective farms, even within the same region. The policy of 'equalising' mentioned in Chapter 2 has been unrealisable in practice. If the Selenga Karl Marx farm is compared with the neighbouring *kolkhoz im. Zhdanova*, we find that, in the early 1960s, the Karl Marx paid a horse-herder twice as much as Zhdanov, poultry-keepers five times as much, shepherds (for 1 kg wool) seven times as much, and cattle-herders (for 1 kg added weight) five times as much.[62] At the same time, the work-norms in Karl Marx were much lower than in comparable collective farms: a horse-herder in Karl Marx worked 25–30% less time per shift than he would have done in Zhdanov, and shepherds looking after rams had 25% shorter shifts than in the 'Ulan-Burgultay' kolkhoz. Meanwhile, for no special reason, shepherds in lambing *otaras* had nearly twice the work-load of those in 'Ulan-Burgultay'.[63] These dry figures say nothing of the differences which may be more important: the fact that one kolkhoz may be well run, pay its wages regularly, keep its equipment in good repair, receive subsidies for housing, etc., while another may be corrupt, poverty-stricken, and ill-equipped.

In the Stalinist period certain farms including the Selenga Karl Marx were selected to be 'model farms' in each district, and were given better facilities and more attention from the Party and state. This possibly is no longer the case, but kolkhozniks still find themselves, through no choice of their own, at the receiving end of 'decisions' to increase or decrease work-norms and/or pay. All kolkhozy are instructed not to give pay rises without corresponding increases in productivity of labour. However, successful farms are obviously better able to carry out this instruction than those existing in a permanent shadow of debt.

3. The pay received by workers in different jobs in the same farm varies widely.[64] The wage per daily work-norm in the Selenga Karl Marx in the early 1960s was three-and-a-half times higher for a tractor-driver than for a man working a horse-drawn rake. The pay of a field-worker is about half that of the man with the rake. The Chairman of the farm received ten times this amount.[65] Furthermore, these figures only apply to days worked. A field-worker can never work right through the year because of the seasonality of agriculture.

Of course, large differences in pay between various occupations are to be expected and occur in all monetary systems. The difference is that pay does not find its 'objective' level as in market economies. All pay rates are *decided upon* — in general terms by the state, which sets sovkhoz rates, which the kolkhozy are supposed to take as guidelines, and in particular by the *pravleniye* and pay commissions of the farms themselves. Because they are decided upon, pay rates come to have built into them a value judgement in terms of 'social use'. The idea of the socially valuable, but badly paid, job does not really exist in the Soviet Union. Discrepancies are explained as temporary phenomena brought about by external conditions (the low level of mechanisation at present does not allow certain farms to make enough profit to pay good wages), or by laziness and lack of motivation (kolkhozniks spend too much time on their private plots, the farms suffer and therefore cannot pay adequate wages — this argument was used by Khrushchev in the early 1960s).

However, as was noted in Chapter 4 (sections 3 and 4), this 'social value' does not necessarily coincide with the Buryat kolkhozniks' own valuation of social or moral worth. They are thus placed in the situation of seeing as perhaps 'unfair' or 'irrelevant' rates of pay which cannot be dismissed as either simply objectively there by virtue of market forces, or imposed on workers as the result of capitalist exploitation. Rates of pay in the kolkhoz are the numerical representation of a social valuation, the more irresistible because it is proclaimed to operate in the interests of Soviet society as a whole, not merely the local society of which the kolkhoznik actually has knowledge.

4. Wages do not in fact reflect the 'quantity and quality of the work performed' (see Chapter 2). This phrase gives the impression that what is aimed at is a single criterion for everyone (quantity) given the inevitable difference in human abilities (quality). But in fact wages are not determined in this way. Workers are divided into different categories, and the criteria for the wages paid to each group are different from one another. Thus, in the Selenga Karl Marx farm in the early 1960s, only the field-worker was actually paid on a 'quantity and quality' basis. The different tasks, raking hay, working on the grain elevator, sorting grain, etc., were graded according to a tariff with nine points, this presumably giving the official estimate of the 'quality' of the labour involved, and the workers were then paid by the amount of time they spent doing each task. Actually, the agricultural tasks plotted on the tariff ladder in the Selenga farm were little different from one another either in skill or laboriousness and it was

complained that the system was unfair.[66] In some farms the tariff system, later changed to a six-point scale, is used for other workers besides farm-labourers, and in this case the system is elaborated by taking into account the qualifications of people with training. Machine-operators in the Selenga farm were not paid by tariff but by the rates established in the former machine—tractor stations, i.e. much higher than kolkhoz rates, the reason being that they would otherwise never have been induced to join the farm. This was a general policy in the USSR as a whole. The Chairman was paid at a rate determined by the total product (*valovaya produktsiya*) of the farm. (In other farms an 'indicator' other than total product is used, e.g. amount sold to the state, or 'profit'.) The Vice-Chairman and chief specialists were paid a fixed percentage of the Chairman's salary, and the assistant specialists a fixed percentage of the chief specialists' pay — in all cases apparently irrespective of the 'quantity and quality' of their work. The livestock workers in the Selenga farm had their wages estimated on the dual basis of work-norms (shifts) and amount produced. Finally, the clerical administrative staff were paid regular monthly wages established by the farm's pay commission.[67]

It appears, from publications of the late 1970s, that 'quantity and quality' of *product*, rather than of work performed, is now becoming the more 'progressive' criterion of pay.[68] This is because of the problem of linking piece-rates, paid for some part of the working production process, with the final product. The problem stems directly from the fragmentation of the division of labour into many tasks performed by different production units on the lines of industrial factory production. A tractor-driver is paid by the number of hectares ploughed, and he is also encouraged to save fuel and running costs. Unless he has a strong sense of duty, the temptation to plough shallow and fast is very great. It is someone else's responsibility how much grain the field actually produces. The *akkordno-premial'naya systema* of pay is an attempt to solve this problem by linking pay directly to the final product.

The bonus system (*dopolnitel'naya oplata*), which is often combined in various ways with the *akkordno-premial'naya* system, is another way of linking pay to productivity. Bonuses are awarded for units of specified production, e.g. for 1 centner of product, or 100 rubles of *valovaya produktsiya*. But production of a large quantity is often at the expense of the quality, particularly if someone else in the system is affected: obviously the milkmaid gets more milk if the calves get less, and it is not she but the calf-rearer who suffers in pay. There are awards which try to counteract this tendency, for example a recommended reward to milkmaids who deliver cooled and fresh milk, as opposed to milk which has been allowed to sour. But clearly, if the dairy does not pay the farm for this, the farm cannot pay the milkmaids either — and this is just what appears to have happened in the Barguzin Karl Marx farm prior to the introduction of a new grading of milk at the Barguzin dairy in 1975.

Attempts have been made to overcome these problems by various reorganisations of the division of labour. In the *beznaryadnoye zveno* (a work-team which is not subject to daily orders but is simply responsible for a specified output at the end of the year) and the *kompleksnaya brigada* (a team which carries out all the work of different types associated with one main kind of production – in effect a mini-farm) kolkhozniks have far greater responsibility for the inter-related totality of farming operations. In Buryatiya these experiments have been very successful, particularly in sheep-farming. For example, in Dzhida in 1961 one 'complex brigade' was set up with eight members, 2,615 sheep, nine working horses, 100 hectares of fields and meadow for fodder production, and the necessary equipment (hay-cutters, rakes, shearing machinery, outbuildings, etc.); their plan was to produce 375 centners of meat, 60 centners of wool, and 1,000 lambs. The pay was fixed at 41 rubles per centner of wool, and 13 rubles per centner of meat. The team managed to lower the planned costs (planned *sebestoimost'*) of both meat and wool, and also over-fulfilled its plan. It received thousands of rubles over basic piece-rates for these two achievements.[69] But, although it is recognised that such teams work best, only some farms use them and only for certain kinds of production. The problems are that there is not enough equipment for all teams to work in this way, that workers in other teams become jealous, and that the brigadier in charge of the whole sector is constantly tempted to remove equipment and labour from these successful teams to make up gaps in the others. Where such teams do exist they form an elite within the farm, contributing to the general hierarchisation of the community.

In other words, instead of a unified system of reckoning pay, and hence of the social worth of different kinds of labour, there is a hodge-podge of different criteria.[70] Perhaps the overriding one in the Selenga farm, which appears to be typical, was volume of product (*val*). This determined not only the pay of the Chairman and specialists, but also the regular wages and bonuses of the majority of workers. But as we have seen, while volume of product might legitimately be seen to be the responsibility of the managers of the farm, it is almost never in the hands of the individual worker alone. Because of the rigid division of labour in collective farms each job is only a fraction of the total production process and each worker is dependent on the good performance of people working in other sectors. Volume of product thus cannot be tied directly to 'quantity and quality' of work, and in fact makes nonsense of the claim that the latter is actually the guiding criterion of remuneration.

5. Not only are some jobs markedly more pleasant and less wearisome than others, and some more or less arbitrarily paid better than others, but the possibility of making a name as a front-line worker exists to a much greater extent in some jobs than others. In many jobs a worker may be commended for good work, but he cannot really make a name for himself except by changing his job. This, as we know, is in the hands of the head of the production unit or the brigadier. And while some brigadiers certainly give people leave to go on training courses, with the eventual possibility of losing them, it is necessary to retain

some proportion of workers in unskilled jobs. This is the same situation, at a lower level in the hierarchy, which exists for the kolkhoz as a whole.

There thus comes to be a state of chronic competition among workers for allocation to preferred jobs at the outset — a situation which increases the power of the circle of managers, the headmaster of the local school, and the Komsomol and Party officials who handle such matters. At the same time there arises, in addition to the formal administrative hierarchies of both lineal and specialist types which I have already described, an informal ranking of jobs. Precisely how the jobs are ranked depends, of course, on many different factors, such as the wage-scales in particular farms, the possibility of performing the job well at all, or the preference given to free time over the opportunity to shine in official eyes.

The 'irresponsibility' thesis

Whatever the ranking that emerges among the workers, it is still possible to say that, looking at the system as a whole, as was shown in Chapter 3, each level of the official hierarchy finds itself carrying out the orders of the one above it. The lower the level, the less participation in any decision-making process. Andras Hegedüs and Rudolf Bahro have used the expression 'a system of organised irresponsibility' to describe the organisation of institutions in present-day socialist countries.[71] Hegedüs suggested that this system leads, in agriculture, to what he called a 'flight to the domestic plots'. Bahro, on the other hand, emphasised the development of 'subaltern' mentality. We should look at these ideas more closely.

Material from the Buryat collective farms, which are not unlike others in this respect, indicates that both workers and administrators are placed in positions of responsibility. They bear personal responsibility for losses of the product, breakages in equipment, and, in the case of administrators, for disorganisation of supplies and labour. The degree of responsibility becomes greater the higher the position in the hierarchy of command, and this is fully in accord with Leninist theories of leadership. The Chairman of a farm may in fact be held responsible for anything which goes wrong in it. However, as things are organised at present, the power effectively to assume this responsibility does not coincide with the liability in any given position. Thus a Chairman is held liable for more than he can actually control. The same is true of brigadiers, team-leaders, and ordinary workers. Even a milkmaid is made liable for far more than she can effectively influence, and the fact that her pay is tied to narrowly defined production goals means that she is likely to confine her activity even more tightly than the possibilities allow. In other words, what workers are given a monetary incentive to do is more confined than their possible sphere of control, but this latter is itself more limited than their imputed sphere of responsibility.

Hegedüs' suggestion was that the less responsibility a worker has in the collective economy the more likely it will be that he has recourse to the alternative of the domestic plot. However, as we have seen, the kolkhozniks with least responsibility tend also to be those who have to labour for the longest hours in the collective farm. It is not necessarily the case that people who avoid work in the kolkhoz wish to devote themselves to work on a domestic plot. In fact, since most domestic production in Buryat farms is in livestock, it is frequently carried on in parallel, not in opposition, to kolkhoz jobs. Since administrators can make unofficial use of kolkhoz labour as well as other resources, it is often those in the most responsible positions who benefit most (since they do not even have to do the work themselves) from the possibilities of 'domestic' production.

Differential opportunities for private production may be recognised explicitly by Buryats, although I do not know if this is the case. In Russian collective farms the membership is colloquially divided into those 'with horses' and the 'horseless'. This expression, which is probably an old one, refers to the fact that some workers, tractor-drivers, etc., have access to kolkhoz machinery (formerly horses) with which to work their private land, while others, such as in the Russian case livestock workers, field-workers, and ordinary labourers, do not.[72] This division does *not* coincide with the hierarchy of responsibility in the farm.

Precisely because the liability of any given position is greater than its practical possibilities of control, there emerges a second base of power by means of which individuals attempt to enlarge their effective capacities. This will be discussed further in Chapters 7 and 8, but meanwhile we can suggest briefly that it consists of two kinds of phenomena: the unofficial (perhaps semi-legal or even illegal) use of official control vis-à-vis those people and things situated lower in the hierarchy, on the one hand, and the building up of a purely social/cultural credit, akin to what Bourdieu called 'symbolic capital', on the other. The former phenomenon, of which the administrators'/machine-operators' exploitation of the possibilities of 'domestic production' is but one relatively small example, occurs to some extent in all Soviet institutions, but its scope is limited by the ever-present possibility that it will be discovered. The latter resource is equally widely cultivated, but it is more important in that it is virtually no longer a matter of choice: for any individual the sphere of blame and culpability, wider than his or her field of control, must be counteracted by 'social credit' of some kind. However, the form this 'symbolic capital' will take varies in different cultures of the Soviet Union.

The existence of other bases of power besides the official hierarchy — although these are admittedly dependent on it — points to the difficulty in Bahro's attempt to define a characteristic social personality of 'actually existing socialism' — his concept of 'subalterny'. Firstly, while it may be the case that conditions of subservience, generating an attitude of acquiescence to those above, exist all through the Soviet hierarchy, it is equally true that 'subalterns' are masters to those below them. It would be hard to say, in terms of a characteristic personality (if we can even talk of such a thing), which fact has the greater force, and it may well be that the creative possibilities of playing off different kinds of power, even for people at the very bottom of the hierarchy, make the concept of 'subalterny' inappropriate. Secondly, as Bahro recognises — and this must be particularly pertinent to the non-Russian peoples of the Soviet Union — the official Soviet system, through its management of language and doctrine, defines itself as something external and superior to everyday life (*byt*), as something yet to be attained, and therefore it cannot subsume the totality of people's consciousness. It is quite possible for anyone to live a life in a certain detachment from the official world of prohibition and exhortation, and from its anti-world of intrigue, and at the same time retain an acute sense of responsibility. Only if we assume people to be absorbed by a reality corresponding to the official representation of reality would the idea of the 'subaltern', whose responsibility ends with his narrow duty, make sense. And in fact it is within the official text, as it were, that this concept does make its appearance as a negative phenomenon to be fought against.[73]

Our main concern, however, is not the effect of the division of labour on the personality, but the nature of the social relations which it represents. In particular, what social relations are engendered by the specific division of labour found in collective farms? It has already been shown that the hierarchy of administrative-productive estates creates competition between like individuals (production units, brigades, and even farms themselves) for the material and technical resources necessary to fulfil their plan-orders. At each higher level, this competition is subsumed in the united front presented in order to compete with other units at that level. A separate division, cross-cutting with the farm hierarchy, opposes those with resources for the exploitation of private production to those without. In specialist systems, where knowledge also becomes a resource, there is an attempt to make possession of knowledge coincide with the levels of the hierarchy already present — in other words socially recognised knowledge is hoarded at each level, by means of diplomas, certificates, and degrees, and the people in a lower rank are held to be 'incompetent' to decide matters for which 'knowledge' is held at a higher level.

The material I have described on the division of labour in the farm allows us to see this system more precisely. The 'division of labour' implies both positive chains of dependence created by the generalised exchange of products, and negative relations of indifference or even competition between groups which exchange nothing (essentially because they engage in the same kind of production). Even if a given production unit contributes nothing of its *product* to the exchange within the farm, e.g. the poultry-keepers, all of whose product is, at least in theory, sold direct to the state, it nevertheless engages in the general circulation of goods and money within the farm because it must acquire or purchase chicken-feed, building materials, grit, and so on. But the positive links of exchange between groups which are dependent on one another's product are only positive if the exchange functions smoothly, and this is only likely to be the case if the interests of the groups concerned, as defined by other criteria such as wages, or rights over materials and machines, do not contradict one another. Even if we take a simplified representation of one of these chains, for example:

fodder production	→ fodder storage & transport	→ livestock	→ manure clearing	→ manure spreading for fodder production
(*lugovody*)	(general workers, drivers)	(stockmen, milkmaids)	(general workers)	(*lugovody*)

it is apparent that the general workers (*raznorabochiye*), who are paid less than meadow-workers (*lugovody*), milkmaids, or stockmen, who are often paid by time rather than piece-work, and who may have to toil with horses, carts and spades when the *lugovody* have tractors, have no particular interest in the flow of fodder and manure, and may indeed he quite happy to see the task of milkmaids, stockmen, and meadow-workers made more difficult.

We can therefore suggest at least three points at which conflict is likely to occur within a system which is ideally one of 'organic solidarity': first, when the end product is the result of several different kinds of work, any one of which may be performed badly or slowly and hold up production, e.g. when hay-teams deliver fodder in insufficient quantities to keep livestock teams stocked through the winter; secondly, when the fundamental material interests of the workers are in conflict, e.g. milkmaids and stockmen, both of whom require the cows' milk for different purposes; and thirdly, when the workers in a single job are in competition for the labour of a different type, e.g. milkmaids in a *ferma* each require the general labourer to bring water for her cows.

All of such flows are mediated by the administration, which may make an incorrect assessment of the amount of labour and materials required to service any given team. But even if this does not happen and the Chairman and brigadiers make the most efficient possible assessment of needs, the chronic insufficiency of resources (fodder, chemical fertilisers, petrol, machinery) makes it also inevitable that some teams will be favoured over others. The political pressure on farms to be able to show at least one crack team 'in the vanguard' only reinforces the perceived inequality of wages and the distribution of resources. As we noted earlier in this chapter these problems for the administration are greatest in those farms which have been given a large proportion of 'unprofitable' products in their delivery plan. An energetic and inventive Chairman can make the system work well − though it will be seen later that the use of unofficial social relations is essential − but the present material shows that precisely because the criteria of what it means to 'work well' are different for the various sectors in the division of labour his task is a very difficult one.

6

Domestic production and changes in the Soviet Buryat family

1. Limitation of private property and the 'Soviet family'

In rigidly circumscribing the amount of productive property allowed to each rural household, the Soviet Union carried out a social experiment which was unique in its time. Social anthropologists have frequently debated the role of property as an explanation for the form taken by the family and other kinship groups. If we were to take the 'economic' explanation for the forms taken by rural kinship groups to the extreme, we might expect to find, sixty years after the establishment of more or less uniform property conditions, the emergence of a single type of 'Soviet family'. However, the Buryat data and some comparative material from other parts of the USSR show that, although there have been some powerful and uniform influences on all Soviet rural kin-groups, the emergence of a standard family type has not occurred.

This can be seen from one fact alone, though it is apparent in many other ways too: even though the amount of private productive property allowed to Soviet rural workers is tiny and relatively uniform throughout the country, this minimal property is made use of in very different ways by households belonging to different ethnic groups. In part this can be explained by the variation in the conditions of rural production in different parts of the Soviet Union (e.g. the nearness of markets and industry), and in part it may be explained by the wide range of ethnic preferences for particular kinds of production, but to these explanations we must also add the inherited concepts of what kinship is and ought to be, which vary widely from ethnic group to ethnic group within the USSR.

The relations within the family have been transformed since the Revolution, and we must see this as the result primarily of economic and legal changes which have been effected more or less uniformly in Soviet rural life. But these 'transformed' relations are themselves highly specific in respect of the culturally modelled habitual actions of the past and the particular conceptions of kinship which each generation carries with it in the present.

Two 'economic' factors of a general kind have affected all rural families.

267

Domestic production and changes in the Soviet Buryat family

First, there has been a change in the relation between the 'family' as a productive group and the wider economic-political groups in society. Before the Revolution Buryat society was organised primarily in terms of kinship structures of which the family appeared as the hierarchically lowest unit. This is no longer the case. Now, the wider groups of society (work-teams, brigades, collective farms, Party organisations, etc.) are recruited by principles other than kinship, and there are no economic-political functions for kin groups wider than the family in official Soviet society. This has had important repercussions both on the internal relations within families, and on the social functions (now largely unofficial) of kinship relations beyond the immediate family.

Secondly, limitations on the private ownership of the means of production so that all households are now entitled only to the same amount in a given region, and the steady increase in kolkhoz and sovkhoz wages in the 1960s and 1970s, have had the effect that it is now labour in the public sphere which brings in most income. It follows, also, that it is individual labour in the socialised, rather than the private, sphere which is now the source of the main 'official' differentiation of wealth between families. Increasingly, the public sphere has also come to be the source of varied extra benefits, to which the individual adds the product of the 'private plot'. These together constitute his disposable goods as opposed to his non-negotiable rights and duties as a member of the collective. This process has resulted in a change in the evaluation of specific labour processes which can be carried out by different members of the family. Consequently there has developed gradually a new evaluation of socially defined kinship roles, insofar as these are identified with the work that family members do.

In this chapter I shall confine myself to discussing changes in kinship at the level of household and very local production, and hence the first of these two 'economic factors' will be dealt with only in passing here (see Chapters 7 and 8 for analysis of the role of wider kinship groups among present-day Buryats). We may begin analysis of the second problem, the effect of the Soviet property laws on the family, by observing that there have been three stages in a process which seems to have reduced the size of the 'family' to an ever-smaller unit. The first stage is the granting of land-shares, expropriated from lamaseries and kulaks in the mid-1920s, to individual households. In practice, although women were legally allowed to own land in Soviet law after the Revolution, and although the size of shares was in theory determined by the number of adult people (*yedok*) in the family, these plots were distributed among households defined by the presence of a male head with his dependants.[1] The possibility of obtaining land in this way encouraged sons to separate from their parents earlier than they would otherwise have done and establish new households. In Buryatiya the Soviets did not succeed in carrying out allocation on the same scale as in some other parts of the USSR, so this short-lived economic policy probably did not have much effect on Buryat family organisation in general.[2] The second stage, collectivisation, did however bring about a radical change, which will be discussed in detail below. Essentially what occurred was the wiping out of all distinctions between families based on ownership of the means of production. At the same time, each household was given the possibility of acquiring a limited subsistence small-holding of animals, poultry, and land (known in the literature as the 'private plot'). At this time (1930s) and perhaps even more so during the 1940s and 1950s, wages from the kolkhoz itself were tiny and sometimes even non-existent. The small-holding became the major means of subsistence. The allowance was granted to all 'households' (*dvor*) of collective and state farm members, including those headed by women. As a result families split into the smallest possible constituent units in order to obtain private small-holdings. The tendency for such units to be headed by women increased during the Second World War and after, since many men did not return, either because they had been killed or because they managed to find more attractive work elsewhere. In the final stage, with the rise in kolkhoz wages during the 1960s and 1970s, it has become possible for individuals to subsist on these alone. The small-holding, on the other hand, requires the labour of more than one person, especially if employment is also taken up in the kolkhoz. A contradiction thus arises between the possession of the private small-holding which is allotted and worked on a joint basis, and wage-labour which is individual. Most households in fact combine earnings from work in the public sector with the proceeds of the small-holding, but now there also exist a number of people who dispense with the small-holding altogether.

Thus it would appear that the general tendency is for the Soviet rural family to reach its smallest and most atomised point in the last period. However, among the Buryat and other eastern nationalities this is not actually the case. The household must in fact be distinguished from the family. The tiny households and individuals who 'live on their own' are largely fictive. They exist on paper in the *sel'sovet* in order to qualify for the small-holding, but in practice people live and share their income in larger units. Furthermore, improvements in medicine ensure that the large number of children always desired by Buryats now survive (see Chapter 1 section 6). Parents and elderly relatives are almost invariably cared for within the family; there is among Buryats an attitude of responsibility towards the old which is more or less independent of the fact that pensions only became available to kolkhozniks in the mid-1960s and are paid at a low rate. Randalov, the Buryat ethnographer, has estimated that the Buryat rural family is now *larger* than at any point since the Revolution.[3]

In other parts of the Soviet Union, especially in the west, where women work in a wider variety of jobs in the public sphere, where the birth-rate is low, and where divorce is more frequent, the small-holding is decreasing rapidly in importance. The government has now removed taxes and other impediments to private production within the legal limits, but even this has not halted the abandoning of the plots in western areas. In some national regions of the USSR, where unlike either the Buryat or the Russian cases it was men who primarily kept up household production, the persistence of a traditional division of labour has also resulted in the abandoning of private domestic production, since it has become difficult to combine this with work in the kolkhoz or sovkhoz.[4]

We can, perhaps, make the general observation that the Soviet rural family is no longer *primarily* oriented towards production. It is, on the other hand, the unit of consumption. I would argue, furthermore, that because of the legal limitations on the accumulation of property and its transmission to the next generation, the patterns of exchange and consumption have increased in social importance. This has had the effect (a) of emphasising marriage, as opposed to birth or death, as the single most significant moment in the domestic cycle, and (b) of activating kinship structures which are wider than the nuclear group, in part because there are good socio-political reasons for the maintenance of a wide network for distribution of one's resources, and in part because marriage itself creates kinship ties beyond the immediate family.

Wealth is not accumulated for the purpose of transmission between generations. The citizen can keep as much money as he pleases at home, but the risk of theft, etc., does not make this an attractive idea in the long run. As the British sociologist Matthews has pointed out,[5] the virtual devaluation of cash holdings under the 1947 currency reform has never been forgotten by the public, nor repudiated by the authorities. There is no limit on holdings in savings accounts in the State Bank, but a large balance has its drawbacks. The rate of interest is only 2–3% per annum, and furthermore, the saver has the right to bank only 'earned income', which puts a certain limit on the amount which can be credibly banked. The bank authorities can inform other organs if they suspect that money is being obtained illegally. The RSFSR Civil Code contains provision for confiscation in such circumstances. The estates of deceased persons are assessed by a notary, and although wealth is not taxed as such and maximum death duties are only 10%, the involvement of the authorities in scrutiny of bank accounts limits what is actually passed on in inheritance. Accumulation of other forms of wealth is also difficult: during the war there were campaigns for donations of gold, etc., to war funds, and precious metals and stones are now hard to find in the Soviet Union. Religious paintings and statues have been subject to confiscation. The number of houses a family can own is limited to one, plus a *dacha*. The private plot is not inherited. Such plots are allocated by the local Soviets to each eligible household.

As accumulation of wealth for inheritance by heirs has become less important, so too has the economic significance of a death; and the same can be said about birth, certainly among the Buryats, where the birth of a son used formerly to entitle a family to a further share of the community's hay-fields. Thus the economic basis, in property and to a lesser extent in joint production, for the link between generations in the family has weakened. Now, it is the occasions for the exchange, distribution and consumption of current income which are important, in particular marriage. This is because marriage, or rather the wedding, is at the same time the moment when new links are formed with affines, the moment when a household is set up which requires furnishing with consumer goods, and the moment when a new productive unit is established, entitled to register for its own small-holding and other kolkhoz and state benefits. In other words, marriage is the moment when the family enters a relationship with the state. This situation is, in a sense, recognised by the Soviet ritual system, which celebrates marriages (e.g. in the building of luxurious Palaces of Weddings), while largely ignoring birth and funerals. In many parts of the Soviet Union, marriage has become the occasion for vast, and competitive, exchanges of wealth (see Chapters 7 and 8 for the Buryat case). The significance of these marriage exchanges lies not so much in their role with regard to pre-mortem inheritance as in the 'horizontal' links which they create. It is noticeable, and not only from the Buryat ethnography but from other nationalities too, that gifts at weddings are not given only, or even mainly, to the young couple.[6]

Unfortunately, little is known in detail about the relation between private production, distribution, and the Soviet rural family. In order to discuss the Buryat case in some depth, we need first to understand the configuration of relations and the division of labour in the pre-collectivisation family. This is because the form taken by kin-based activities such as marriage exchanges in the Soviet present is not determined simply by negative legal rules. It is not enough to know that there is a tendency for distribution at marriage. We need to know for each ethnic group separately how income is generated, the amounts which come from the various sources, and to whom it is distributed. All of this depends on customary actions, ideas and values which we can discover by looking at earlier forms of kinship.

2. The Buryat family before collectivisation

In both Selenga and Barguzin before collectivisation the Buryats ordinarily lived in households based on the 'stem family', defined here as a residential unit consisting of the married heir living with his parents. At the first stage of the developmental cycle the families of non-heirs went through a phase in which the residential unit was the 'nuclear family', a couple with their children. The heir, who inherited his father's house and his father's share of the family herds and fields, was the youngest son. The ideas of the 'family' and the 'household' were not really separate in Buryat thought. The family was known as *ger büle* (literally *yurta*-family — see below) or *ail*, and the latter term was used for the dwelling or group of dwellings in which a family lived as well as for the family members.

Sons, apart from the youngest, usually established new households at marriage. A winter house was built for the young couple, who had their own livestock, fields and other property and kept a separate domestic economy. In this the Barguzin and Selenga Buryats were different from some other Buryat groups, where sons often remained with their father and only separated when he died, or where the new houses of sons were built within the same fenced yard as the father's house and the domestic economy was run in common. However, even in Barguzin and Selenga 'separated' sons continued to have economic duties towards their parents and their brothers: arable tasks such as sowing and harvesting were done together, taking turns on each field, guests were entertained together with contributions of food from each household, and the wives of sons were obliged to help their mother-in-law in her domestic tasks.

The division of labour between men, women, and children was as follows: men were responsible for the herding of the livestock, for manuring and irrigating fields, for ploughing, sowing and harvesting the fields, for hunting, for selling livestock and wool, and for cutting and hauling firewood. Women were responsible for milking cows, sheep and mares, for fetching water, for drying and collecting dung for fires, for collecting wild onions and lily bulbs, for preparing food, for curing, softening, and smoking leather, for sewing clothes and footwear, and looking after the children. The women also frequently helped the men in herding and arable work. In Selenga felt, used in large quantities for the coverings of the *yurta* (tent) and for carpets, was made by both men and women, but the women's share in the process took more time. From an early age children started to take over the task of herding, and they also took part in most of the other activities appropriate for their sex.

Most Buryat families moved at least twice a year, from the winter settlement to the summer pastures. In both Selenga and Barguzin people had more or less permanent wooden houses for their winter dwellings. Both tents and houses were known as *ger* or *ail*, referred to in the literature as Russ. *yurta*. Since the Revolution *yurtas*, used in the summer by Selenga Buryats, have been considered 'old-fashioned' and 'unhygienic' and there are very few of them left, particularly the felt tents which now exist only in tiny numbers in regions near Mongolia. Buryats instead live in wooden houses of a type which are standard all over the Soviet Union. However, the idea of a move from winter to summer quarters still has a cultural value for the Buryats. Many families therefore have two houses, even if their work on the collective farm does not make it necessary for them to move, and the two houses are adjacent in the same yard.

The Buryat house, before collectivisation, always faced south, or south-east, as Mongolian *yurtas* do to this day. Windows were built into this front wall only. Most houses had only one room, and this was conceptually divided, like the Mongolian *yurta*, into an area for men (to the west) and an area for women (to the east), a respected 'clean' area (to the north) and a 'dirty' area (to the south). The wooden summer *yurtas* in Barguzin were even more like the Mongolian round tent: they had six or eight walls, with a conical roof, and a smoke-hole in the centre over the fire.

In most areas of Buryatiya it was usual to place a tethering-post for horses (*serge*) outside the house. This *serge* also had a ritual significance. A new one was put up every time there was a marriage of a son, and so most houses had a row of them. In wedding ritual the *serge* symbolised the bridegroom or the male sexual organ.[7]

There were almost no rituals which involved only the narrow circle of the household. Even intimate festivals, such as the burial of the afterbirth (*toonto taikha*), the first hair-cutting of a child, the thanksgiving for the birth of a child (*milaagod*), the invocation of a family spirit-protector (*hakhiuuha khuruulkha*), and others, were in fact carried out by a wider circle of relatives than the immediate family.

Before collectivisation most families lived in winter settlements of three to ten houses situated at some distance from one another (*khoton*). Each house was surrounded by a fenced yard in which cattle could be kept, some outbuildings, and a manured and often irrigated hay-field (*ütüg*). The families living in such a group were often agnatic kin, but not necessarily so. The winter settlements were grouped into larger scattered villages of some thirty or more houses. These villages (*ulus*) were often associated with segments of patrilineal lineages which dominate the life of the *ulus* even if not all village residents belonged to the lineage. Even today, older members of the kolkhoz think of the territory of the farm in terms of which lineage formerly lived in which area. Several *ulus* formed a territorial administrative unit known as *buluk*.

The summer settlements were relatively less permanent than the winter ones, and in the Selenga district most people lived in tents rather than houses. The summer camp could therefore move during the pasturing season and might well be in a different place from year to year. The summer camps were usually made up of close patrilineal kin who shared a common hay-field. They traced descent from a common ancestor and called themselves by his name plus a suffix (*-tang*) indicating collectivity of people (e.g. *Dorzhi-tang* – the descendants of Dorzhi).

In most parts of Buryatiya east and south of Lake Baikal it appears that residence was more strictly linked to patrilineal kinship than was the case among the Barguzin and Selenga people according to my data. The winter settlements (*khoton*) also consisted of the kin descended patrilineally from a named ancestor.

A few *khotons* usually made up an *ulus*. Thus, for example, the seven *khotons* of the Gutai lineage made up the Gutai *ulus*, which also constituted a separate landholding community (*buluk*). The Shanagin, Shibertui, Khonkhloi and other *ulus*es were the same. The Kharlun people of the Tsongol lineage and the Khayan Ashekhabats had the same kind of settlement pattern. According to our data, residence by kinship group was characteristic for the majority of the Buryats living east of Lake Baikal and was only not observed in a few places.[8]

It seems that the *khoton* (a word which was not used by my informants in Barguzin and Selenga) was often the residential equivalent of the '*-tang*' kinship group. The *khoton*, according to Randalov, was of about seven generations depth.[9] The '*-tang*' in Barguzin and Selenga according to my informants was of around five to six generations depth, depending on the number of male descendants. The named ancestor of the '*-tang*' was a man with several sons, the descendants of whom made up the group. But as the group fluctuated in size over time through births and deaths, a new ancestor would be chosen as the named head so that the group could be redefined at a size and composition appropriate to economic conditions existing for the present generation.

Before the paying of brideprice was forbidden by law (1920s) and the brief emergence of the idea of 'free marriage' (i.e. without a wedding), it was this payment which ensured the legitimacy of sons and hence was the basis for recruitment to the '*-tang*' (see Chapter 1 section 4). Once the brideprice had been paid, sons of that marriage belonged to the husband's '*-tang*', even if there was a divorce, or if the husband was not the biological father. The brideprice often greatly exceeded the total wealth of any one household (one man told me that a brideprice worth 600 rubles was a good one for middling families at the beginning of the 1920s, see Tables 6.3 and 6.4). It was a payment from a corporation of male herdsmen which was the prerequisite for the gaining of more herdsmen (sons and grandsons). It was considered the greatest of blessings to have many sons, in part at least because there was a direct relationship between the multiplying of the herds and the amount of care herdsmen were able to give them. The payment of brideprice from the members of one '*-tang*' to the members of another in order to acquire reproductive rights in a woman thus had an essentially legal character.

The brideprice itself, called *aduun* ('horse herd') by the Barguzin Buryats, had a symbolic aspect as well as its economic one. In the Buryat nineteenth-century law codes it was specified in a formalistic way which cannot have corresponded with reality. In one case, western Buryats were instructed to provide camels in the brideprice, despite the fact that these animals did not exist in their herds.[10] There was no rule stating which patrilateral kinsmen should contribute to the brideprice. It was paid by all members of the '*-tang*', but as we have seen this was a group which could be defined at various levels.

The bride's side paid a dowry (*zahal*), composed of bedclothes, curtains, rugs, winter and summer clothing, trunks, domestic utensils, a fur hanging to go over the bed, gold and silver necklaces, bracelets, ear-rings, buttons, and decorations. Rich families sometimes gave their daughter a servant. The dowry was worth at least as much as the brideprice, and was paid for in part out of the latter.[11]

It is important to realise that marriage established a status difference between the givers of the bride (superior) and the receivers of the bride (inferior), even if this difference in most cases was of a formal nature only (see Chapter 1 section 4). By the twentieth century the fact that status was involved in the giving of the dowry, while the brideprice was seen more as a means towards acquiring a bride, began to have effect on the contents of each payment. The brideprice was paid to a great extent in money, rather than animals, and there were cases of cheating and legal squabbles over the amount that was actually paid.[12] Nothing of the kind is mentioned with regard to the dowry. It was in fact possible to marry with a minimal brideprice, or by means of bridegroom-service. These alternatives were traditionally considered demeaning for the bridegroom and all his relatives, but by the early twentieth century attitudes had to some extent changed. Certainly the ethnographic record seems to suggest that it became allowable, without losing status, to drive a hard bargain in regard to brideprice, i.e. to agree to pay a large amount but actually to pay rather less, while in the case of dowry, which was displayed at the wedding, this would have been unthinkable.

Contributions to the brideprice made by relatives, especially large in the case of those with sons, were called *xariu* ('reply'); it was expected that reciprocal help would be forthcoming when their own children married.

The point I wish to make here is that substantial brideprice and dowry were really part of the political economy of the community, rather than being simply concerned with the reproduction of kin ties (see Chapter 1). They were very important among those kin-groups which occupied strategic positions in the clan-lineage system, but were of only domestic significance among the people who never aspired to make influential matrimonial alliances. The discussion in more detail of brideprice and dowry and their present-day functional equivalents therefore belongs in the analysis of the political economy and will be dealt with later (Chapter 8).

Nevertheless, brideprice and bridegroom-service need to be mentioned in connection with family relationships because they had repercussions on the mutual status of husband and wife. If a brideprice was paid which was respectable in the eyes of the affines, marriage was virilocal and the bride occupied a servile role in her husband's family. She was required to behave with extreme respect to all her husband's senior kinsmen and women, a respect which was expressed in avoidance in the case of senior male kinsmen, and she was required to do the bidding of her husband's mother at home.[13] If brideprice was substituted by bridegroom-service, marriage was uxorilocal for the period of the service and it was the groom who had the position virtually of a servant in his wife's family. The great majority of marriages were, however, virilocal. The bride's position was improved if her family provided her with a good dowry (*zahal*).

The establishing of a new household shortly after marriage was in effect the setting up of a new economic unit and coincided with the inheritance (*enzhe*) by both husband and wife from their respective families. Each son was entitled to an equal share of the father's herd and summer hay-fields. If the father had arable land this was also divided. Usually the *ütüg* (manured hay-field at the winter settlement) was not divided and each new household prepared a new one. The husband received his inheritance when he set up a new household, usually at marriage, but the wife, whose dowry was also thought of, in a sense, as an inheritance, did not receive an *enzhe* at once. A woman's *enzhe* was paid in livestock and money only, never in land. It was paid only if her father wanted to help her household. There was no fixed share given to a daughter, but on the other hand a woman could go on receiving livestock as *enzhe* from her father over a period of years, especially after the birth of her children. Unlike the brideprice and the dowry, both of which were contributed by the entire '*-tang*' kin group, the *enzhe* was provided by the father only.

Let us look at an example of a family from Barguzin. Molon, around the time of the Revolution, was able to build up a good holding of sixty to seventy cattle, four or five horses, and forty to fifty sheep. He had 15 *desyatina* (16.5 hectares) of hay-fields. When his eldest son Lubsan married and established his household he was given a relatively small share because of the large number of other children, four brothers and three sisters. He received four cows with their calves, two mares with foals, fifteen sheep with lambs, and one working ox. His male '*-tang*' relatives provided him with a house, doing most of the work themselves but paying one cow to a carpenter. He himself made the roof of the house. He did not get a share of his father's hay-fields but was allocated land by the district office of the *sel'sovet* (this was 1927). By this time the paying of brideprice was already illegal and Lubsan did not mention whether any was paid by him or not. However, if anything was paid it would have been at about the same rate as that received for his sister Sakhandere, who married in 1926. They received one horse and two cows for her, but sheep which were promised were never paid. Lubsan's wife, from the Butumo-Shono lineage, brought a full dowry of gold ornaments, silver cups, fur coat, silk gowns, a table, crockery and storage chests. She also brought one horse and two cows with her as her *enzhe*.

In 1928 Lubsan entered the 'Soyol' commune and put all of his livestock and land into it. Everything except clothes and ornaments was communalised, and people did not even have their own food but ate in a canteen. Lubsan's wife's jewellery was sold during the Second World War. Now, everything which Lubsan owns (his house, livestock and plot of land) has been received from the kolkhoz, and nothing at all remains from his previous property.

In the pre-collectivisation economy every household desired to maximise their wealth in herds, but the problem in any individual case was how to balance labour resources with the livestock owned. Tables 6.1 and 6.2 from the 1897 census illustrate this problem.

In all Buryatiya, Barguzin was second only to the Chita region in the number of livestock per head of population, and its situation was therefore closer to Table 6.2 than to Table 6.1. According to the 1897 census, in the Khatai and Alachi *buluks* of Barguzin, there were 232 households, a population of 1,125 (average family size 4.8), and a total of 1,439 horses, 6,775 cattle, 6,264 sheep and goats, and 163 *desyatina* (179 hectares) of agricultural land. The rich class, constituting 23.7% of the households, owned 60% of the cattle and horses, and 70% of the sheep and goats. The poor class, 34.1% of the households, owned an average of eleven head of cattle, seven horses, and only four sheep per family.[14]

People whom I spoke to maintained that a household of the middle category in Barguzin could provide for itself without either hiring labour or taking on outside work. But in fact this was not strictly true. An example of a household

Table 6.1. *Family size and livestock in mixed farming areas of Buryatiya*

| Family class | Family size | Male workers | Livestock | | | | Acres arable |
			Horses	Cattle	Sheep/goats	Total	
Poor	4.4	1.3	1.0	4.8	4.0	9.8	0.8
Middle	5.2	1.5	3.4	18.3	15.3	37.0	1.6
Rich	7.1	1.6	30.5	55.3	168.4	254.2	4.1

Source: Koz'min 1924, p. 12.

Table 6.2. *Family size and livestock in livestock farming areas of Buryatiya*

| Family class | Family size | Male workers | Livestock | | | | Acres arable |
			Horses	Cattle	Sheep/goats	Total	
Poor	4.8	1.8	3.4	17.2	3.2	23.8	—
Middle	5.8	1.7	12.6	59.7	41.4	113.7	—
Rich	7.0	1.7	312.8	193.2	738.2	1244.2	—

Source: Koz'min 1924, p. 12.

budget in this category is given for the 1920s in Table 6.3. This household was able to support itself and maintain or increase its herds despite the loss of live-stock to wolves. However, it was dependent on outside labour for the period of the hay harvest, and even so was unable to use its share of the common meadow to the full. This household can be compared with one in the 'poor' (*yaduu*) category (Table 6.4), which could only just provide enough meat to feed itself, and even then at less per head than in Household I. By killing animals for meat it reduced its herd to a size at which it could barely reproduce itself, and the household was therefore not able to sell animals for money. The household head was forced to go out hunting and to go for paid work, and by the very loss of time was unable to engage in agriculture and himself had to hire a worker to help with the hay-cutting. Despite this help the amount of hay obtained was only just enough to feed the animals. The household therefore was dependent on outside income.

Many of the families in Barguzin were poorer than this, according to my informants. They may have been underestimating their property in order to give the impression of a 'good' class background (i.e. poor), but if this is the case a large number of people, independent of one another, must have misinformed me. It seems more probable that their estimates of property were in broad out-lines true, but that their definition of 'independence' excluded help from relatives in production. Adoption of children, specifically for work, from other members of the '*-tang*' was very common. One old woman said that her father, who had a

Table 6.3. *Budget of a Buryat household before collectivisation (I)*

1 adult man, 1 adult woman, a baby adopted daughter.
This family made four migrations a year. They had a house at the summer settlement, a house and a *yurta* at the winter settlement, and another house and *yurta* at the pasture they used in spring and autumn. They had one cart, one horse-drawn rake, an iron plough, a harrow, a hay-cutter, a separator, a butter churn, three harnesses, and two saddles.

Working horses	3
Mares	1
Cattle	29 (7 milk cows, 6 barren cows, a bull, 7 one-year calves, 5 two-year calves, 3 three-year calves)
Sheep and goats	56
Arable land	4 *desyatina* (approx. 4.4 hectares), of which 3 were sown
Hay-fields	7 *desyatina* (7.7 hectares) *ütüg*
	10 *desyatina* (11.0 hectares) ordinary
For meat they killed	3 head of cattle (worth 60 rubles)
	10 head of sheep (worth 25 rubles)
	Wolves killed 2 horses, of which one was worth 150 rubles, and 2 cattle, worth 15 rubles each.
Their expenditure	buying working horse — 62 rubles
	hay — 5 rubles
	shoes, clothes — 20 rubles
	taxes — 40 rubles
	hire of hay-man — 26 rubles
	Total — 153 rubles
Their income	selling 1 horse — 40 rubles
	selling 2 cattle — 110 rubles
	Total — 150 rubles
Their production	30 *pood* (491 kg) millet
	8 *pood* (131 kg) potatoes
	300 bundles of hay from the *ütüg* and 15 bundles from the common hay-meadow, giving them 89 bundles per unit of livestock*

*See chapter 4, pp. 173—4.
Source: Koz'min 1924, pp. 34—8.

household consisting of himself, wife, one married son and two younger daughters in the early 1920s, could survive without going out for wage-labour with three milking cows and their calves, two horses, ten sheep and their lambs, and 4 *desyatina* (4.4 hectares) of arable fields. In a household with no arable land, ten milking cows plus calves, two horses, and twenty sheep with lambs were necessary for 'independent' survival. In Barguzin it was possible to earn good sums of money by hunting for sable during the intervals of farming work. In parts of Buryatiya near the towns men earned money by acting as carters.

Table 6.4. *Budget of a Buryat household before collectivisation (II)*

1 adult man, 1 adult woman, 1 boy of thirteen years (½ worker), 2 boys aged below six years, 1 baby girl.
This family had one house at the winter settlement, one *yurta* at summer pastures, and no other dwellings. They had one cart, one wooden plough, a scythe, a horse-drawn rake, one set of harness, and a saddle.

Working horses	2
Cattle	15 (4 milk cows, 2 barren cows, 4 one-year calves, 2 two-year calves, 3 three-year calves)
Sheep and goats	20
Arable fields	0.75 *desyatina* (0.8 hectares), but they did not sow at all
Hay-fields	1.5 *desyatina* (1.65 hectares) *ütüg* 6.5 *desyatina* (7.0 hectares) common hay-field
For meat they killed	3 head of cattle (worth 75 rubles) 5 head of sheep (worth 17 rubles)

Their expenditure	coarse flour	27 rubles
	hire of hay-man	25 rubles
	taxes	10 rubles
	other	10 rubles
	Total	72 rubles
Their income	sale of 200 squirrel pelts	22 rubles
	paid work	100 rubles
	Total	122 rubles
Their production	no grain	
	no potatoes	
	75 bundles of hay from the *ütüg* and 15 bundles from the common hay-field, giving them 50 bundles per unit of livestock*	

*See chapter 4, pp. 173–4.
Source: Koz'min 1924, pp. 34–8.

However, it was more common to acquire an outside income by doing seasonal labour for rich households.

One of the very richest men in Barguzin was B. Pasuyev, who had started as a poor man but, being a skilful hunter of sables, had managed to start up a business. He exchanged sable pelts for manufactured goods at the seasonal markets of Ulyun, Barguzin and Uro and then sold the goods to local Buryat farmers. By 1913 he had over 800 head of cattle, around 300 horses, and over 700 sheep. He sold over 100 head of calves every year, and in general from his livestock operations he had an annual income of over 4,000 rubles. He also had some arable land (10–12 *desyatina* of wheat-fields, on which he obtained a yield of 100–120 *pood* per *desyatina* – approximately 1,800–2,200 kg per hectare, much superior to present-day collective farms, see Table 4.7). He had a shop for the sale of manufactured goods, a water-mill, twenty-one houses, twenty barns and storage sheds, about thirty sheds for livestock, and many other farm buildings. He had twenty permanent labourers, not including seasonal workers. He also kept a number of Evenki sable-hunters indentured to him.[15]

According to Koz'min's data from the 1920s, around 30% of households in Barguzin had members who went out for paid labour.[16] Much of this wage-labour was concentrated in some rich farms. It thus appears that around half of the households were independent, neither hiring workers, nor being hired themselves. But in another sense no household was autonomous. This was because (a) there were essential processes of labour, such as the digging and maintenance of irrigation channels, fence-building, or house construction, which required large-scale communal work; (b) there were other tasks, such as herding, which could be done best by the reverse of communal work, i.e. by the selection of one representative to do the work of several households, and this also implies the interdependence of these families; and (c) there was a complex series of economic exchanges which took place at marriage and other points in the life-cycle which demanded at particular moments far greater outlays than any individual family could manage – this applied also to the richest people, since the expenses were correspondingly raised. All of these relations of interdependence existed primarily within the local kin-group ('-*tang*'), which indeed was to a great extent defined by them.

These kinds of economic interdependence were distinguished ideologically from wage-labour, which was considered demeaning and usually undertaken for non-kin. The type of wage-labour most in demand was hay-cutting, which took place in only a few weeks of the year. It was reckoned that the value of a day's work varied from 10 kopecks on an ordinary day to 1 ruble on a day when the demand for labour was high. The demand for other contractual labour was even more sporadic, and it coincided again with the times when everyone was busy (shearing time, lambing time, harvest). As a result, there were few jobs as permanent labourers, and almost all families of workers kept their own small-holding. Because paid work was available only when annual tasks came up, the household of workers never had time to cut their own hay and had to buy it later from the rich, who could ask high prices once the season was over. Sometimes poor families dispensed with their shares in the common hay-field altogether, 'letting' them to the rich or to neighbouring Russians in return for a cow and a small amount of hay. All of this led to the existence of a certain number of poverty-stricken households, caught in a vicious circle because they did not have the time at the right periods of the year to improve their own small-holdings. These were the people later to be classed by Soviet planners as *batraky* (wage-labourers) and seen, on occasion, as a 'class' which might serve to oppose the *kulaky* in the village. But the Barguzin Buryats told me that, while there were a few destitute families, extreme poverty was more often a stage, lasting from the initial setting up of the young household until the children were old enough to give substantial help in the farm. It should be remembered also that most payment for work was in animals, which could multiply.

Wage-labour of this kind should be distinguished from the forms of economic cooperation which occurred between kin. One of the commonest forms of this was the giving out of livestock for herding in exchange for use of the milk and wool and perhaps some of the young. This relation was so general, among all the pastoralist people of Central Asia at all periods, that it should not be seen as 'exploitation', requiring a separate explanation in the 'class' structure of each society, but simply as the fundamental mechanism by which labour was adapted to the existing herds. Vainshtein, writing about the Tuvinians, who had an economy similar to that of the Buryat, found that well over 70% of all households engaged in such relations.[17] Sometimes a household would simultaneously give out one kind of livestock, e.g. horses, and take in another, e.g. sheep. I have no numerical data on the frequency of this exchange among the Buryats, but my impression from Selenga and Barguzin informants was that many middling households engaged in it. Thus, it was not the case that only the rich gave out livestock, and only the poor took them in, as some Soviet writers have claimed,[18] although there must have been a tendency towards this.

A different version of this arrangement was universal at the summer pastures whatever the size of the herds. Each kind of livestock required different pastures, and therefore the members of the '-*tang*' amalgamated their herds, taking the horses to one area, the sheep to another, and the cattle to a third. Kinsmen who lived separately from one another in winter came together in summer precisely for this purpose. The products of the animals, especially meat if an animal was killed, were shared among the members of the summer camp. This is important because it means that there was an institution, based on agnatic kin relations, for the equalising of *consumption* of herding products, despite differences in holdings of livestock between individual families. Animals killed in the autumn for meat — much of which would be frozen to last through the winter — were slaughtered at a ritual known as *üüse*, and a certain amount of meat again had to be shared, uncooked, among neighbours and kin. This sharing in consumption of animal products was the reciprocal of the donation of labour outside the individual household to the care of the livestock pooled by the group as a whole. Calculations here were not made precisely. The duties of sharing meat and milk products, and of giving unpaid labour to help kinsmen, were considered sacred obligations to be carried out for their own sake. But in the long run, the two probably balanced one another out, despite the fact that they were very rarely calculated in direct relation to one another.

Indeed, it seemed to be the case that making a direct and one-off transaction ('you herd the cows for *x* months and you can take half of the milk and three calves') was something that occurred only among people who were not close kin. In the '-*tang*' group on the other hand the economic relations I have mentioned were only part of a lifetime's obligations in which 'debts' were not strictly recognised as such. This is the case with 'practical' kinship today. If a kinsman fell on bad times his relatives would give him a cow and there was no idea that he would be obliged to pay it back. But, I was told, if he was lazy and neglectful of his duties towards his kinsmen he would be angrily told off. A close kinsman who had bad luck would be given help through his life if he maintained his self-respect and that of his relatives, but if he did not play his part he would in the end be sent off to work for a rich man's household, where he could expect to earn a cow in one year.

The '*-tang*' or *khoton* had a religious identity. It had its own cult fire-place, its own spirit-protectors (*ezhid*) of the places which it used for field and pasture, and its own ancestor cult. Ancestors frequently 'became' the spirit-protectors of nearby mountains, trees, etc. and were thought to be responsible for good weather, rain, absence of disease and so on. At larger community festivals, both Lamaist and shamanist, the '*-tang*' acted as a single unit, led by its genealogically senior male in the patrilineal line. Contributions of meat and *arkhi* (milk vodka) were made by the group as a whole to these festivities.

To summarise, we can define three different levels at which the economic interdependence of households was manifest. (1) Wage-labour, which occurred between households of unequal wealth and status, and never between kin. (2) The adjustment of labour of individual households to the livestock in the community as a whole (and vice versa). This took place throughout the community, between equals and between non-equals, by means of specific agreements. Close kin were not involved. (3) Ideologically legitimated and long-term reciprocity between the members of the local group of close kin ('*-tang*').

I would argue that the '*-tang*' was a group whose significance was primarily economic, formed by the necessity for cooperation in pasturing in summer and for communal work of other kinds, in agriculture and construction, at other times of year. It was infused with a kinship ideology, but the secondary nature of this is shown by the fact that the '*-tang*' could be defined at various genealogical levels depending on the circumstances in which the '*-tang*' was required to operate. In Barguzin, indeed, the local group in the winter settlements was not constituted necessarily only of kin, but nevertheless certain activities normally associated with the '*-tang*' such as the distribution of meat and worship of local protector-spirits went on within it. Close agnatic kinship was associated in people's minds with long-term reciprocity. Therefore economic interaction which was defined in terms of contracts, i.e. arrangements which had a definite termination, were not seen in a kinship idiom. Indeed those contracts whose terms were clearly dictated by factors which overrode long-term mutual benefit — wage-labour whose conditions were determined by supply and demand in the economy of the district as a whole, or one-off trading deals — were never made with kin. Buryats said that they preferred not to work as wage-labourers for Buryats at all but to take jobs with Russians.

The obligation for reciprocity in large payments (e.g. brideprices and at

282

sacrifices) within the '*-tang*' was a check on wide economic differentiation between members of the group. But by the early twentieth century the emergence of outside and individual types of spending, the most important being education for the children of a single rich household, and the corresponding decrease in importance of brideprice payments, began to give rise to differentiation within the group (see Chapter 1 section 3). The situation in general can be summed up by saying that the '*-tang*' was brought into active existence for primarily economic purposes; its ideological/ritual practices were concerned above all with the taming of an anthropomorphised, but still inscrutable 'nature'.

3. Soviet kinship

Settlement and wealth

After total collectivisation in the early 1930s the kolkhozy were based on the existing winter settlements (*ulus*), but this state of affairs was transformed as soon as possible and now virtually no trace of the old villages remains. The first communes, such as the 'Arbijil', ancestor of the present Barguzin Karl Marx kolkhoz, were often able to obtain money from the Soviets to build themselves a new village, and the more privileged kolkhozy in each district during the 1930s were also reconstructed as compact villages instead of the scattered *ulus*. In these new villages all traces of the specifically Buryat traditions were removed: houses were constructed according to a model used in all collective farms, the size and distance between them being dictated by central planners. Thus the houses no longer faced south only, windows were put in all walls, and the old divisions into male/female/sacred/profane areas were condemned as 'unprogressive'. In the early days the old houses were taken apart log by log and rebuilt in the new kolkhoz or brigade centres, but since the 1960s there has been an extensive building programme and most kolkhozniks now live in recently constructed houses built to a more generous model. In one typical collective farm of the present day, of 152 households, sixty had houses giving them up to 5 square metres per person, sixty-four families had between 6 and 9 square metres per person, and twenty-eight families had 10 or more square metres per person.[19] This means that there are substantial differences between kolkhozniks in the amount of living space they have, even if the houses are more or less identical in type.

House-sites in collective farms are allocated by the kolkhoz committee or the brigadier, and it has been a deliberate policy to break down 'clan survivals' (*rodovyye perezhitki*) by putting relatives at some distance from one another. The great majority of kolkhozniks live in houses which they have built themselves and which they own. People in Selenga and Barguzin told me that they tried to live near relatives if they could, but that was not usually possible. Thus the '-*tang*' as a residential group has now more or less disappeared in the central villages of collective farms and brigades.

Each family has a wooden house, of which the front faces directly on to the road, with a large yard surrounding it on three sides. A gate large enough to take a cart leads from the road into the yard. This yard is the area which most Russian kolkhozniks cultivate intensively as their vegetable plot, but I never saw vegetables grown by Buryats, with the exception perhaps of a few potatoes. The yard is used for penning in the milk cows overnight, and it generally contains nothing but a cow-shed, a hole in the ground for frozen food storage, and some patchy grass. At the bottom of many of the yards, situated a regulation distance from the house, is the latrine, a deep hole with separate cubicles for men and women. Latrines are shared between families, and some people have to clamber over the fences of the yard to get to them. Also roaming in the yard is usually at least one large dog, a creature which is not a pet but bred for defending the livestock against thieves, wolves and bears.

All the winter houses which I saw are built on foundations which raise them off the ground and they have wooden floors. A door from the yard leads up a few steps to a porch or a closed-in veranda. From this one enters the house, which essentially is built as one room, but occasionally with partitions to create privacy. The cooking-stove, which also heats the house, is still usually to the right of the entrance and is made of brick faced with clay, with an enclosed chimney leading out over the roof. In large houses the stove is usually in the centre, so that all of the partitions can be heated from it. Fuel is scarce and even in winter the fire is allowed to go out overnight, so the task of the wife, who has to get wood and make up the fire in the early morning darkness of winter with perhaps 30° of frost outside, is a cold one. Water is fetched from a well which serves a street of houses.

The furniture is modern, and because there are not so many places where a Buryat kolkhoznik can buy it, fairly uniform. A particular carpet, depicting a stag in a glen, was hung on the wall behind the bed in almost every house.[20] There is electricity in the houses of the central village of every kolkhoz, but the supply is erratic and there is not enough for people to have electric fires. A gleaming nickel-plated electric samovar stands on the table, however, and most families have a radio and a sewing-machine. All these things are prized possessions. The old painted chests (*avtar*) in which traditional valuables used to be stored between festivals are kept in the veranda.

Buryat traditional beds, stools, felt rugs and low tables are nowhere to be seen. Only a handful of people still keep religious paintings and statues of deities openly. It may happen that the remaining, ever more scarce items of value of the old culture (women's decorations, silk gowns, painted chests, knives with silver sheaths, snuff-bottles of precious stone, silver bowls) will some day again come to be displayable items of wealth. Now, they are kept hidden, valued for the memory of the past, perhaps even signs of prestige and status in the past, but for this very reason almost anti-signs of status in the present. The important people in the kolkhoz and Party have larger houses, radiograms, cars or motor-cycles, expensive Soviet crockery, and items of elegant urban clothing. These are the things which form the currency of wealth today.

The winter house in the kolkhoz or brigade centre is the store and sign of wealth, but many kolkhozniks hardly live in it. The work of the farm is carried out elsewhere, on the pastures and fields, sometimes miles away (see Chapter 5 section 1).

In summer only officials and people in non-farming jobs (accountants, teachers, etc.) are to be found in the kolkhoz centre. Everyone else, including the schoolchildren, is out working on the fields and with the herds. Here we find the occasional reconstitution of the '*-tang*' kin-group, especially at festivals and weddings. Sometimes at field stations the communal open-air stoves are set up and kinsmen will join up with one another to share meat. In autumn the joint slaughtering and distribution of meat, *üüse*, is still the general practice. But at the present time the '*-tang*' group has no basis in the organisation of work in the kolkhoz. This is true even during the summer, when brigadiers assemble *ad hoc* work-gangs for hay-cutting and sheep-shearing rather than the regular units of the rest of the year. Kinsmen may try to join the same work-gang in the summer, but with the exception of the 'link' (*zveno*) teams which make a joint income, there is no economic reason behind this. There is no advantage for someone on

Drawing water from a well in the main street of Bayangol, summer 1967, Karl Marx kolkhoz, Barguzin.

piece-work, or paid a daily rate, in working with kinsmen. The desire to be together has the essentially social purpose of confirming and celebrating mutual solidarity, and since the kolkhozniks are mobile it is only more convenient but not necessary for them to *work* together.

There is a tendency for kinsmen to continue the old pattern of amalgamating their private livestock in summer for pasturing. But it is easier to amalgamate the livestock with neighbours, and these are usually now no longer kinsmen even in summer. Such neighbours would, however, be called by classificatory kin terms: 'older brother Lubsan', etc. The summer meetings of kinsmen are temporary, usually for some festival or ritual occasion. They are the culmination of the

Inside the home of a well-to-do member of Karl Marx kolkhoz, Barguzin, 1967.

regular visiting and feasting together which goes on all year. Most kolkhozniks I talked to saw their close relatives several times a week. They would go by horse-drawn light carts, taking gifts of food and drink with them. It is considered necessary to take some kind of present when visiting relatives. Usually they met at the house of the 'eldest' — the parents living with the heir (youngest son and his wife) — but there was also visiting between all close bilateral kin.

The '*-tang*' thus no longer has an economic base in *production* in either the collective or the private sphere. On the other hand, kin, defined in a loose way to include the occasional neighbour or friend, are still the focus of distribution and consumption. The reasons for the survival of the patrilineal and strictly defined '*-tang*' (it has become what is essentially a political element in kolkhoz life) will be discussed later.

Patriliny and the status of women

Within the family the most noticeable change since the 1920s is the greatly improved position of women. The social, economic, and political autonomy of women has affected personal relations within families and outside them, but, I would argue, has had curiously little effect on the patrilineal lineage as a kinship *concept*.

Patrilineal kinship groups used to dominate women as part of their general strategy of operation. Daughters were treated well until they were married off, usually without consultation with them, for as high a brideprice as possible. Incoming wives were kept in a subordinate position to ensure that they did not provide a focus for autonomy for their husbands as against the patrilineage as a whole. Their position only improved after the birth of sons. The aspects of the Buryat kinship system which were forbidden by law in the 1920s can be seen as the extreme results of such a strategy: marriages arranged for women against their will, marriages of pre-pubertal girls and boys, polygyny for the sake of acquiring male heirs, levirate. None of these were very common, and they disappeared rapidly after the Revolution. The payment of brideprice was also made illegal, and although it had been a general practice, it was, as we have seen, beginning to die out in any case. Buryat women were allowed to inherit all types of property equally with men. All of these laws were designed to improve the status of women, and gradually they did so.

The present-day situation of Buryat women has also changed dramatically in practical terms. No longer do they have to carry out the immensely laborious tasks of scraping, curing, softening and sewing leather, sewing clothes for the whole family, making winter boots, preparing felt, and making quilts, pillows, appliqué rugs, and leather bags and containers. The Buryat milk foods, which are time-consuming to make, are prepared much less often now than they used to be. Although the birth-rate is high, and the number of nursery places far from adequate, many women with children work in the kolkhoz. Employment for those in the 'general worker' category may be sporadic and badly paid, but women wish to have their own income. Specifically, they wish to have an income in rubles, since it is difficult to convert the products of the domestic economy into money in remote areas.

More important even than economic independence is the idea, which is an integral part of the Soviet value system, that women are equal to men and should have the same opportunities as them. This idea, it seemed to me, has been readily accepted by Buryat women and men, more so than, for example, in Central Asian nationalities. Though it is unfortunately impossible to treat this question adequately here, we could suggest that it is the imposition of a modern 'Soviet' division of labour between the sexes, and the structure of employment in rural areas, which result in women clustering in the more laborious or low-paid jobs, rather than any repressive treatment specific to Buryat cultural traditions. Buryat women in the rural population are as well educated, if not better educated, than men,[21] and if they predominate in the livestock sphere, they also predominate in the middle-range 'clean' jobs which are much sought after (secretaries, accountants, clerks, nurses, junior teachers). This indicates that, although the structure of employment is such that the 'clean' jobs are few and the livestock jobs are many, it is not Buryat ideas of what it is to be a woman as such which hinders them from advancement in the kolkhoz, at least to a certain level.[22] Women now usually have control of the household purse, whereas formerly it was Buryat men who were in charge of buying and selling. Large items are decided upon jointly. I was told that men now help their wives in certain household tasks: not washing clothes or cleaning the house, but cooking sometimes, and fetching the water from the well. I actually saw young boys, rather than men, fetching water, and I never saw either do the cooking. But however individual families arrange these matters, it is clear that in comparison to the past Buryat women now have much more economic independence, respect, and freedom to spend their time as they wish.

It is interesting therefore that the patrilineal kinship 'structure' remains in people's minds, even though its fangs have been pulled, as it were. All that is required for its maintenance is genealogical memory, and the persistence, in some form or another among men, of status differences according to genealogical seniority. It appears that the status of women is largely independent of this system, which now has completely different functions from those of the past (see Chapter 8).

Insofar as the reproduction of affinal relations between patrilineal groups retains some importance, it is necessary for women to cooperate by observing the rules of exogamy. In both Selenga and Barguzin the great majority of marriages of my informants were exogamous, and in Barguzin most marriages even today take place between the two large clans of Hengeldur and Shono (see Table 1.8). Buryats had always seen women as *passing between* patrilineal groups, thereby establishing their mutual relations. The previous domination of women by men was a function of the economic and political role of patrilineal groups in a society which has long since disappeared. Many women still pass between patri-lineages, but women in general have now created their own kind of kinship at another level.

The changing family

In the Selenga farm, the average size of the household of the people I visited was 5.9. Around 50% of these households consisted of a couple with their children living with the husband's mother, or his father, or with both of his parents. Perhaps because of the great loss of life in the Second World War, the proportion of these 'stem' families in which the father has died was higher than one would expect; thus 37% of all the families I interviewed consisted of a couple living with their children and the husband's mother. In only 6% of the households did a couple live with the wife's mother, and there were no cases of couples living with the wife's father. Only 12% of the households consisted of one generation, 37% were households of two generations, and the rest, about 50%, were families of three generations. In a few cases unmarried or widowed relatives also lived in the household. These data, which are not based on a large enough sample to be considered representative, can be compared with the material collected by Basayeva in the early 1960s in four Buryat farms of the Alar and Ol'khon districts.[23]

Two material factors are important in the setting up of new families independent of the parents: the house, and the private small-holding. Houses in the central village are owned privately (with the exception of a few good houses which go with official posts such as the Chairman, the chief technicians, etc.).[24] They can be passed on in inheritance and normally go, according to Buryat custom, to the youngest son. Older sons have to build themselves new houses, or else resign themselves to living in the more cramped quarters provided by the kolkhoz. Since around 50% of the young people leave the farm to work else-where, it is possible for most of the remaining sons to continue living with their parents, thus avoiding the great expense of building a new house.

Counteracting the tendency for a son to remain in the same house as his parents is the desire for a separate small-holding, which can only be obtained legally by the head of an independent household (see above, p. 269). Clearly this depends, however, on individual families establishing some kind of under-standing with the officials of the *sel'sovet*.

The present household economy in Buryat collective farms cannot be sum-marised as being of one 'type' because it depends on the subjective evaluation of the preferred way to manage such an economy. All three of the main factors which go towards making up the household economy — the size and composition of the small-holding, the amount of labour devoted to the small-holding, and the time given to (and hence, within limits, the amount earned from) the kolkhoz —

are matters on which individual decisions have to be taken. However, it does appear that there have been changed in the emphasis of these cumulative decisions over time as kolkhoz wages have risen and become more secure.

In the 1930s to the 1950s, when most collective farms in Buryatiya were poor, disorganised, and disheartened, the wages received by workers for their *trudodni* were not only insufficient for subsistence but they were also completely unpredictable. It was necessary to rely on the private small-holding. It is possible that the kolkhozy were in such a demoralised state that the Buryat government felt compelled to encourage the private sector in order to obtain any kind of increase in production. There were devastating losses of livestock during collectivisation. For whatever reasons, the Buryat government issued a decree in 1932 allowing kolkhozniks in livestock farming zones of Buryatiya a much larger small-holding than that legal in other parts of the USSR. According to this decree each household could keep three to four horses, eight to ten cows, and fifteen to twenty sheep, and they were allowed plots of 0.8–1.0 hectare.[25] In 1934 Buryat kolkhozniks were relieved of the onerous taxes in meat, milk, and butter imposed in other regions. Livestock was counted at the end of the year, after the autumn killing of animals for meat to last through the winter, and thus for much of the year a given household could quite legally keep a small-holding in excess of the limit. Furthermore, it is probable that adult animals only were counted. Thus, if we compare the small-holdings by kolkhozniks in this period with the pre-collectivisation household economy it seems that the Buryat Soviet limits established a ceiling at the level counted by people as 'poor' (*yaduu*), but at least sufficient to sustain life.

After the Second World War the limits on the small-holding were made more severe. Although the exact figures are not available, it is probable that they were about the same as they were in the 1970s: a 'vegetable plot' (the yard next to the house), a field of no more than 0.4 hectares (used by most kolkhozniks for hay and perhaps a few potatoes), five sheep with their lambs, five or six goats with their kids, up to six pigs with piglets, any number of chickens, and two cows with calves. Until the early 1970s this small-holding was taxed, at certain periods heavily so.

These restrictions could be partially circumvented by fictitious division of the household. We know from Basayeva's study of Alar and Ol'khon (west Buryatiya) something of the way in which joint families (e.g. officially separate households with a common budget) conducted their domestic economy. In one village (*ulus*) of sixty-two households in 1962, Basayeva found six cases in which households of close kin operated as a single economic unit. For example, Figure 6.1 shows a family consisting of three official households, each with their own winter house situated in one common yard. The cow-sheds and stores were held in common, and the livestock and plots of land allocated by the *sel'sovet* to three families were worked in common. In summer the whole group ate together, the women taking it in turns to cook, while another looked after all of the children. In winter each small family ate separately at home, but the food (potatoes and other vegetables, flour, salted fish) was kept in a common store and used by each family as they needed it. The money earned in the kolkhoz by the sons Andrei and Mikhail was put in a common purse which was managed by the mother. Guests were entertained in common. Only the private livestock were looked on as individual family property: the meat stored for winter was counted as belonging to each family, even if it was subsequently shared, and the money made by selling livestock was not put in the common purse. It went on buying furniture, clothes and decorative goods for the owner's family. The only item about which there was any ambiguity was the daughter-in-law's income as a teacher; it was felt that she could spend it on her own family, but in fact she herself often suggested using it for common group purposes.[26]

This example is interesting because it shows that, on a much reduced scale, divisions between communal and individual production and consumption characteristic of the '-*tang*' have been reproduced in Soviet conditions. The rationale behind the division in this case seems to have placed income from the kolkhoz and purchased 'Russian' foods, such as bread and salted fish, in the communal sphere, while retaining as private to the nuclear family what really mattered: the livestock and their products. It should be noted that the Buryat diet, like the Mongolian, is based almost entirely on meat of various kinds and a wide variety of milk products.

However, this kind of joint family is no longer typical even among west Buryat kolkhozniks and I did not come across any cases of this kind in Barguzin or Selenga — although this is not evidence that they did not exist; the many single women with children in the farms may try to retain such links. In the families which I visited there seemed if anything to be a reverse emphasis to that found by Basayeva: the income from the kolkhoz was kept privately, and the livestock was 'farmed out' among various relatives.

The proportion of the family budget from wage-earning in the kolkhoz is larger than it was in the 1940s to early 1960s. But since even in the late 1960s it was still not possible to buy adequate amounts of meat, potatoes, and milk products from the village shop, it was necessary even for the best-paid families to obtain their basic food from the domestic sector. Most households did their own

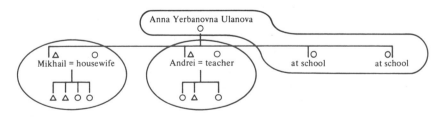

6.1. Relations between households operating as a single economic unit.

work in this private production, using the labour of children and elderly people as well as that of the mother and father. But most households farm the livestock out with relatives. Thus in one family in Barguzin in 1967, where the husband worked full-time in the kolkhoz, the wife was occupied with several small children and there were no other members of the household, only a cow for milk was kept with them. The wife's sister looked after their other livestock (sheep and pigs). I had the impression that privately owned sheep and goats were almost invariably herded by relatives or neighbours who had jobs as shepherds.

The budget of one Buryat household, where the husband worked as a machine-operator and the wife as an ordinary labourer was given by Dambayev, who made a study of his own farm in Barguzin (Table 6.5). In this household the income from the small-holding was 38% of the total income. Most of it was in the form of produce, and only 350 rubles was obtained in money. The small-holding covered the household's needs in milk, wool, potatoes and eggs, and almost all of its consumption of meat. The household's 'profit' was 1,266 rubles.

My own data indicate that many Buryat kolkhozniks can make a considerably greater 'profit' than Dambayev's machine-operator. Informants told me that a good milk cow was worth 500 rubles at 1967 prices, a one-year calf was worth 300 rubles, a fully grown pig 150 rubles, and a sheep 35–40 rubles. This means that a kolkhoznik with the full complement of livestock, not counting chickens and goats, would have around 3,000 rubles worth of animals.

One woman, Manidari, who was living alone with her five children, had the following small-holding on the Selenga Karl Marx kolkhoz in the summer of 1967:

2 cows (one was not a good milker and she was considering selling it): value 900 rubles

1 heifer (2-year-old, intended for killing in the autumn): value 300 rubles

2 pigs and 7 piglets (1 adult and 5 piglets intended for sale): value 500 rubles

12 sheep (3–4 of these would be killed each summer, and 1–2 in the spring; there would be 5–7 lambs born each year, and it was reckoned that a small family of four could feed themselves and have their flock reproduce itself if they kept 10–12 sheep, including lambs): value 350 rubles

potato plot: value of harvest 250 rubles

From this Manidari could reckon to make around 800 rubles cash from the sale of her cow and pigs, and she and her family and friends consumed about 1,350 rubles worth of mutton, beef, milk and potatoes from her small-holding. Thus, at a conservative estimate, which does not take account of chickens, goats, wool and *arkhi* (alcohol made from milk) which she may have produced, Manidari had a total income worth 2,150 rubles from her domestic economy.

It was clear that Manidari's small-holding was considered to be minimal. She had a rather small number of pigs, and these were the main commercial element in Buryat small-holdings; most Buryats do not eat pork or chicken for religious reasons, and some families raised substantial numbers of these for sale to

292

Table 6.5. *Family budget from Lenin kolkhoz, Barguzin, in 1967*

Income from the kolkhoz		Expenditure (expressed in retail prices)	
husband's pay (140 rubles × 12 months)	1,680 rubles	Food	
wife's pay (80 rubles × 12 months)	960 rubles	meat	600 rubles
extra pay (*dopolnitel' naya zarplata*)	200 rubles	milk	600 rubles
		bread	324 rubles
prizes	114 rubles	potatoes	216 rubles
		vegetables	22 rubles
		confectionery	114 rubles
Total from the kolkhoz	2,954 rubles	sugar	143 rubles
		salted fish	30 rubles
Income from the state		fresh fish	20 rubles
pensions and grants	– rubles	alcoholic drinks	160 rubles
child allowance	– rubles		
won in state lottery	20 rubles	Total expenditure on food	2,229 rubles
Total from the state	20 rubles		
Income from the small-holding (in retail prices)		Fodder (hay, straw, chaff, concentrates)	72 rubles
production of potatoes worth	240 rubles	Firewood	60 rubles
		Repair of house	– rubles
production of milk worth	600 rubles	Lighting	42 rubles
		Rent	– rubles
production of meat worth	560 rubles	Furniture	155 rubles
		Clothing	750 rubles
production of wool worth	48 rubles	Footwear	137 rubles
meat and eggs from chickens worth	48 rubles	Taxes	25 rubles
sale of vegetables	–	Fees for boarding-school and kindergarten	84 rubles
sale of livestock	300 rubles		
other income	50 rubles	Total	1,325 rubles
Total from the small-holding	1,846 rubles	Total expenditure of all items	3,554 rubles
Total income from all sources	4,820 rubles		

Source: Dambayev 1970, pp. 63–5.

Russians. The kolkhoz was 'not strict' about the number of pigs kept. Manidari also had a relatively small number of sheep. We can say this because, although she was at the legal limit, the animals were not actually counted until the winter when summer and autumn killings are over. Sheep are the animals par excellence which are killed for ritual occasions and given as gifts. Manidari said she had already killed four sheep that summer for guests, and another two would be absolutely necessary when some student nephews of hers came on a visit to the farm. Sheep were killed for these nephews regularly every year, and it was understood that they would 'do something' for their aunt when they got good jobs. It was also obligatory to kill a sheep for the visit of any 'important' relative, and since these visits could not be predicted a certain number of sheep were kept in reserve by most families.

Not all kolkhozniks kept to the legal limits of the small-holding: a reliable informant from the Dyren sovkhoz in Barguzin reported, without any surprise, one man as having sixty-five sheep, and Kerblay notes that in the Central Asian republics and the Caucasus the number of private animals may vastly exceed the norm: there were families in Turkmenistan with 100—200 sheep, and households in Kazakhstan with up to 220 head.[27]

In the farms I visited, if no relative was available, groups of neighbours paid a small sum, 1.50 rubles per month each, to a herdsman to take care of the private livestock; sheep were generally kept on distant pastures, where their numbers are less readily apparent. Cows, on the other hand, were taken out each day from the back-yards, where each family did their own milking morning and evening. In some collective farms the lack of grazing for cows near the settlement may limit the number of cattle which can be kept privately, but this was not the case in the two farms I visited. All the private animals grazed on kolkhoz land, and hay was obtainable from kolkhoz fields, as well as from the private plots. No one mentioned a shortage of fodder for privately owned livestock, although this is a severe problem in western parts of the USSR.

Thus only the availability of labour to manage the domestic economy, and the statutory limits set by the kolkhoz, prevent kolkhozniks from enlarging their holdings. The availability of labour depends above all on the women of the family, since it is they who do the most onerous tasks on a year-round basis (feeding and cleaning out the pigs, milking the cows, giving water and fodder, feeding the chickens). Hay is usually cut and transported by a group of relatives acting in turn for each family, and people told me that a widow or single woman would certainly be helped by her kinsmen in this. It is thus a matter of choice whether a woman works in the kolkhoz and keeps a smaller domestic economy, or whether she stays at home and keeps a larger one. Soviet authors like to maintain that the officials and better-qualified workers in farms place less emphasis on the private small-holding than uneducated 'backward' kolkhozniks.[28]

There is some truth in this, but the matter is not so simple. Specialists and officials tend to be married to women who are also well-qualified (doctors, teachers, etc.) and who can therefore earn good salaries if work is available. Officials also can obtain for their wives the prized 'light' work of the farm (librarian, accountant, telephonist, etc.). However, there are few of these jobs, and according to my data more farm officials than kolkhozniks had wives who stayed at home as housewives. This was the case even if there were grandparents in the household who could look after the children. The brigadier's wife, who stays at home and watches from her window the workers trudging to the fields, is the subject of a reproachful Buryat folk-song. All of this suggests that among families of officials there is wide variation in the amount of emphasis on the domestic economy. Wädekin's material, however, suggests that *on average* these families have larger small-holdings than ordinary kolkhozniks in the USSR as a whole, since officials are able to use their larger salaries and more advantageous bargaining positions to support them (e.g. in obtaining fodder in regions where this is scarce, in getting workers to 'help' with onerous tasks, and so on).[29] Khan and Ghai, on the other hand, found a perfect negative correlation between income from the private plot and total household income from the combination of kolkhoz and outside employment.[30] In Buryatiya where there is almost no rural employment outside the kolkhoz, people with low-paid farm jobs almost invariably keep the full complement of private livestock. This is the case even if the wife also goes out to work in the kolkhoz, and we may suppose that it is the case because the husband's pay (if there is a husband) is not sufficient to keep up the flow of exchanges in which the family is engaged.

It is interesting that, in the Selenga farm at least, kolkhozniks were allowed to possess larger small-holdings than employees (*sluzhashchiye*) of other organisations who worked in the village. We can see here the preferential treatment given by the kolkhoz management to 'its' workers, part of the general reciprocity between management and productive labour.

Probably the group least likely to emphasise the domestic economy is the category of well-paid skilled workers (machine-operators, *traktorists*, drivers, etc.). On the whole these tend to be younger people; they are mobile, and many of them are not Buryat but Russian (see Table 1.4) and therefore outside the reciprocal exchange structure constituted by the wider Buryat kinship system.

But such reciprocity operates also between households and the farm itself. The statutory limits on the small-holding vary from kolkhoz to kolkhoz. Reading between the lines of Gurevich's book on the activities of rural Soviets in Buryatiya it seems that in many farms small-holdings gradually increase in size, with the tacit agreement of the management, until for some reason there is a crack-down. This can be very severe. In the 'Kommunizm' kolkhoz near Ulan-Ude in 1960 the *sel'sovet* 'recommended' the general meeting of kolkhozniks to change their statutes so as to set the limits at 0.25 hectares of land, one cow with a calf below nine months, three sheep, one pig and one chicken.[31] However, the result may not be so disastrous to the domestic economy as first appears to be the case. At these 'correction' meetings of the kolkhozniks they agreed unanimously to renounce their 'illegal' animals and give them up to the kolkhoz. In fact, looking more closely, we see that the extra animals are *sold* to the kolkhoz (a regular practice anyway, if a household does not have enough labour to look after a herd which has multiplied). The 'consciousness raising' effort of the *sel'sovet* may end by being quite profitable to the kolkhozniks, depending on the price they are able to get from the farm.

There is thus a reciprocal flow of livestock and agricultural products between the farm and the households. It should be noted that sometimes the state also takes a hand in acquiring products from domestic producers, but in this case it is

295

difficult to talk of 'reciprocity' except in a most indirect sense. The procedure is known as a 'socialist obligation' and is carried out by the *sel'sovet*. For example:

We, inhabitants of the village of Kizhina of the Kizhina *somsovet*, having engaged in the national movement for the fulfilment of the seven-year plan, promise for 1961 to sell voluntarily to the state livestock products from each household in the following amounts:
   meat − 20 kg from each household with cattle
   milk − 60 litres from each milk cow
   eggs − 15 per hen
   wool − 2.5 kg from each sheep[32]

The problem with this from the point of view of the household is that state prices in the early 1960s were very low. It is not known for certain if such campaigns still continue in Buryatiya. What is clear is that they must have had a severe effect, as did the pressure to sell to the kolkhoz, on the ability of a household to provide its own subsistence. The disadvantage would be greatest for those, such as low-paid employees of the *sel'sovet*, who could not expect wages 'in kind' from the kolkhoz.

In view of all these fluctuations in production and income of the household, it has in the past made undeniable sense for the family to expand its close kinship ties as a safety net. So long as basic subsistence foods are not *reliably* available in rural shops, to be bought with kolkhoz money wages, this will continue to be true.

My data from both Selenga and Barguzin indicate that these kinship links are bilateral, not patrilineal. They are, however, conceptualised as kinship links, and not simply ties between friends, neighbours, or work-mates. This network, kept up by a multitude of helpful acts, surrounds every household. The 'independence' of the household is in fact an illusion. It would be impossible to maintain oneself as a respectable member of the Buryat kolkhoz community without such links. Apart from subsistence, and economic obligations at festivals, every household requires outside labour in the right place at the right time, often for short periods. This involves frequent movements of people between households during the year. For example, a young woman teacher, married to an electrician, has her older sister's two sons living with her during the school terms since the sister is a milkmaid living far from the kolkhoz centre. At hay-making time, the boys, the teacher and her husband and her sister all go off to stay with the grandparents (i.e. the teacher's mother and father). The milkmaid sister provides meat and dairy products to the teacher throughout the year.

In another case, the wife of a kolkhoz agronomist was brought up, together with her three siblings, by her father's sister, her own father having died young. She and her husband and children visit this aunt at least once a year, even though the aunt lives in Irkutsk *oblast'*. Her two brothers work in a factory in Ulan-Ude, and these relatives are visited even more often. They provide a reason for going to the capital (this woman was much more smartly dressed than most of the kolkhozniks). Living with this woman in the kolkhoz for the school terms was the daughter of a cousin of her sister's husband. The aunt in Irkutsk *oblast'* had seven children of her own, besides the four adopted children, and relations were kept up with all of them, though less so with those living in the country than with those who had moved to towns.

In a third example, a shepherdess, a widow, lives with her mother out on the pastures. Her ten-year-old son lives in the kolkhoz centre with a distant relative. Meanwhile, her married daughter's children have come to stay for the summer, 'for the good air'. One of these children lives permanently with the widow to help with work. The shepherdess takes care of her relatives' private sheep.

It can be seen from these examples that looking after the children alone involves many households in complex living arrangements: on the one hand working parents may live far from the kolkhoz centre where the school is, and on the other children are felt to need 'good air', and also their labour is useful out on the pastures, so they usually move out to the countryside during the summer and winter holidays.

Why are kin preferred to work-mates in making these arrangements? One reason is that production teams contain people essentially in the same situation as one another, while kin tend to be spread out among a variety of jobs and places. The complementarity, which is an essential feature of mutual help links, is easier to achieve with kin. More important than this perhaps is the trust placed in kin, a trust which is re-affirmed yearly at festivals and rituals (see Chapter 8). Work-mates, on the other hand, as we saw earlier tend to be either in competition with one another for scarce resources, or in relations of domination and subordination within the team. The pre-collectivisation Buryat cultural distinction between 'wage-labour' and work with and for kin seems to be maintained today.

Kinship links activated for these practical reasons are bilateral and informal; in fact, they appear to operate through women rather more than through men. This is partly because the arrangements for care of children play such a large part in them, and partly because domestic economic transfers are involved. As has been mentioned, it is women who now manage the household purse rather than men: women not only do most of the home-based work in domestic production, but their increased social status and ability to earn for themselves makes it possible for them to be involved in complicated arrangements almost independently of their husbands. Women have their own small pony-carts as means of transport. I frequently came across women in the farms who were living temporarily separated from either their husbands or their children. The complex settlement patterns and movements still associated with a primarily herding farm economy only reinforce this tendency.

This means that the practical kinship ties we have been discussing cannot be identified with the '*-tang*', the local segment of a patrilineage. It will be suggested in Chapter 7 that the '*-tang*' groups are still sometimes important in the farm, but their functions tend to be political rather than economic. More precisely, they constitute interest groups related to men in dominant positions in the kolkhoz. Some kinship mechanisms, such as adoption, however, operate in both 'practical' and 'political' kinship. Kin expect to be involved in both of these kinds of relationship. It was made clear on several occasions that, far from people resenting obligations they were placed under, they would feel *insulted* if for any reason they were not asked to help.

In summary, we see that the desire to qualify for a small-holding, and the rise in kolkhoz wages available to individuals, have each in their own way encouraged a tendency for the family to divide into the smallest possible household units. Such small households are however highly vulnerable. Several factors make it necessary for them to engage in outside relations of mutual help. (1) Domestic production, with such a tiny labour force available in the official household, requires frequent transfers of people between households at different times of year. (2) The fact that the private small-holding is subject to forced sales to the kolkhoz and to the state, while the village shops do not reliably stock subsistence foods, means that each household must have a network of kin on whom it can rely in times of need. The tendency is to spread such networks widely, spanning the distinct spheres of kolkhoz centre/countryside production units (*otara, ferma*), and kolkhoz/town, in order to benefit from complementary situations in the economy. (3) The limitations on accumulation and saving have created a relative emphasis on distribution and exchange among present generations, as opposed to inheritance between generations. The flow of distribution, maintained by festivals (see Chapter 8) and the wedding celebrations, takes place along the lines of kin ties already activated in mutual help. (4) In 'making a career' inside the kolkhoz it is virtually essential to have trusted people (usually kin) in complementary positions in the division of labour to oneself (this is discussed in detail in Chapter 7).

'Kinship' among contemporary Buryats thus comes to have three aspects defined by the use to which it is put: (a) practical kinship, established bilaterally by households in relations of mutual help; (b) local segments of the patrilineage, used by men in prominent positions to strengthen their capacity for effective operation in the kolkhoz; (c) the patrilineal lineage and clan structure, which establishes a Buryat ethnic identity vis-à-vis the state.

Even though these categories may overlap, particularly at festivals and weddings, where all three aspects of kinship are called into play, it is worth separating them for the purpose of analysis. This enables us to say, for example, that the change in the status of women since the Revolution, which is apparent in the operation of practical kinship, has not affected the conceptual structure and persistence of the patrilineage. The extent to which the three categories I have outlined are perceived by Buryats is not entirely clear. But it seems to me that one main distinction, at least, is made by them, and this is the categorical differentiation between practical kinship and the patrilineage. Women, who

were busily engaged in operating in the former sphere, citing very distant classificatory kin links to people they were involved with, frequently said that they did
not know anything about the patrilineage, it was not their affair, and I would
have to wait until their husband or father came home to find out about it. Of
course many women, particularly of the older generation, were expert in citing
long patrilineal genealogies. But my impression was that, even though the same
kin terms are used throughout, people did separate lineal kinship from the practical kind. Patrilineal kinship, as will be seen in Chapter 8, has an ideological,
even semi-religious, value, while practical kinship arises directly in the operation
of the domestic economy and the fragmentation of tasks in the kolkhoz. In the
fact that relations of mutual help are established with kin or people treated as
kin, rather than simply with friends, as might be the case in Russian collective
farms, we may see the persistence of Buryat cultural attitudes. But the selection
of kin to be involved has shifted from the local core of patrikin (pre-
collectivisation) to a far-flung network of bilateral kin (post-collectivisation),
and here an important influence is the present independence and mobility of
women.

7

Politics in the collective farm

1. The use of labour as a 'political' resource

This chapter explores the evidence for, and implications of, some simple propositions. The farm until 1969 was a bounded community and even now it is difficult to leave once registered there. People avoid working in the jobs which are exhausting, badly paid, and pointless. Training or education is required to obtain the better jobs and there is widespread desire to acquire these, but, because farms are so little mechanised and there are quotas on the numbers of specialists, there are at least in some places too many people with training for the jobs available. Jobs are allocated by officials. The administrators can only retain their positions if they can persuade people to work in the very jobs which are avoided. Workers, on the other hand, cannot take refuge in a simple accumulation of private productive resources — which had been the case before collectivisation — because this is forbidden by law. They are forced to 'realise' their wealth, either wages or productive assets, in other ways, one of which is the obtaining of a better job, or the means to a better job (training). A complex bargaining between officials and workers ensues.

The 'vertical' links thus set up, however transient, reinforce the conflict apparent in the division of labour between workers in different low-paid jobs. People in these jobs make separate individual negotiations with officials. However, when people give up in the competition for better jobs, a certain solidarity, based on the work-group, may appear. Paradoxically, from the Soviet point of view, this solidarity is most likely to emerge among the least 'progressive' people on the farm.

At the end of Chapter 6 I said that the scarce factor in producing 'manipulable resources' is labour. This needs to be demonstrated, and perhaps qualified, in view of the statistics which show that many people on collective farms simply do not come out to work. Let us look at the cases of our two Buryat collective farms.

The Selenga Karl Marx kolkhoz in 1966 had a total population of 1,724, comprising 369 households. Of this population, 740 were children up to the age of twelve, and a further 198 were adolescents aged between twelve and sixteen. The other categories not eligible for work were 'pensioners', aged between sixty and sixty-five for men, and between fifty-five and sixty for women (42 people), and 'old people' aged over sixty-five for men and over sixty for women (128 people). This leaves a possible working population of 616 adults. Of these, 524 were registered for work in the kolkhoz, and the other 92 lived on the farm but did not work in it. There were rather more women workers registered (270) than men (254).

In the Barguzin farm, at the beginning of 1974, there were 2,126 people, of whom 1,027 were children below the age of sixteen. Of the adults, 685 (that is, 382 men and 303 women) were registered workers. If we assume that the proportion of pensioners and old people to the total was approximately the same in Barguzin as in Selenga, roughly 10%, then it can be estimated that around 200 adults of working age living on the farm were not registered as workers. The Chairman of the farm explicitly stated that the great majority of those not working were housewives looking after their children at home.

In the Barguzin farm, although around 200 people were not registered for work, a large number of children, pensioners, and old people gave help at busy times of year. For example, in June 1973, the month of the hay harvest, fifteen men and twenty women over retirement age came out to work, as well as sixty boys and forty-five girls under sixteen. Seventy-nine young people who were students over the age of sixteen also came out to work. The implication of this substantial drafting-in of labour from outside the pool of registered workers is that many of the latter must have stayed away. This is, of course, one of the busiest times of the year, and hay-making must be carried out for the private livestock sector as well as the communal. Thus, the Chairman's figures for labour contributed in 1973[1] hide the fact that about one-fifth of the registered workers must have stayed away during the busiest period of the year. The Karl Marx farm is no exception in this.

The busiest months of the year in [Buryat] collective farms are July, August and part of September. It is in exactly this period that the greatest number of urban workers and employees take part in farm work. In 1964, 1,400 workers were asked to contribute in July, 2,600 in August, and over 7,000 in September. But in fact, it would not have been necessary to call in these people at all if the adult kolkhozniks' labour had been properly used. Thus in 1963 to 1967 over 10% of the kolkhozniks in the Buryat ASSR took no part at all in communal work in June. In some years this number of kolkhozniks even exceeds the number of urban workers and students called out, and in many years it has more or less equalled it.[2]

As for the working year as a whole, there are some winter months when even larger numbers of registered kolkhozniks do not come out to work. Altogether this allows Ushnayev to make the statement that 23.2% of able-bodied adults in Barguzin did not do communal work in 1963, and 31.4% did not work in 1967.[3]

This fits with my data from the Karl Marx farm. The exact figures need not concern us. The point is that even if a large proportion of the non-workers are housewives with children, and even if some people cannot work because of illness, a fairly large number of able-bodied people in the farms just do not come out to work.[4]

Furthermore, the figures for people coming out to work in a given month say nothing about how much work-time was put in. A significant number of people work only one to five days a month (see Table 7.1).

The pattern so far set out — a fairly high proportion of unemployed kolkhozniks supplemented by a draft of outside labour at busy times of the year — could be explained perhaps by the seasonality of arable farming. One would expect this to be the case in the days before the large-scale mechanisation of agriculture, when many people were working as field-labourers. But, as we saw in the Selenga farm, by the mid-1960s the number of arable workers had dropped by nearly two-thirds. Ushnayev's study of Buryat labour resources states that, generally speaking, only half the arable labour force is unemployed during the winter for lack of work.[5] This would mean, if the Selenga farm's occupational distribution is typical, that we could expect only one-tenth of the total labour-force to be out of work in winter because of the seasonality of arable farming. Livestock work carries on throughout the year — indeed the winter is often the busiest time. Even if all building work stops because of winter frosts, the percentage of people unemployed because of seasonality still does not reach the figures given by Ushnayev for registered adults who do not work *at all* in winter (between 22.5% and 37.3% in the 'Pribaikalets' kolkhoz, see Table 7.1). And this is not to count the people who put in only a few days a month at all times of the year (around 10%, see Table 7.1).

In other words, the seasonality of arable production cannot explain the large number of people not working in winter — just as it fails to account for the fact that in the summer months, when arable jobs are at their busiest, and none of the livestock tasks falls off either, there is still a certain number of adults who fail to come out to work in the kolkhoz.

We may assume that it is the constant small tasks of the private small-holding (milking, feeding poultry and pigs, etc.) which keep many women occupied, especially since these jobs can much more easily be combined with looking after a large family than employment in the kolkhoz. It is less clear why men withdraw from the collective labour-force. In the summer they must mow, dry, and transport hay, shear the sheep, and prepare winter fodder for the private animals, and it is also during the summer that the majority of Buryat festivals and rituals occur (see Chapter 8). But, as we have noted, this cannot explain what appears to be a year-round shortfall in labour for the collective.

Finally, we may cite the existence of 'youth brigades' as evidence of the shortage of labour in the collective farm. These brigades consist of children in their last few years of school, i.e. aged from about fourteen to sixteen. In many

Table 7.1. *Degree of participation by workers in the 'Pribaikalets' kolkhoz in communal work in 1965 (as a percentage of the monthly total)*

	Percentage of registered workers contributing						
	No days	1–5 days	6–10 days	11–15 days	16–20 days	21–25 days	26–31 days
January	28.7	5.1	4.6	6.8	8.1	13.9	32.8
February	25.2	6.4	6.3	7.2	9.7	18.8	26.4
March	22.5	5.9	5.9	6.8	7.4	12.2	39.3
April	20.9	6.1	5.6	7.2	7.2	14.0	39.0
May	19.9	4.1	3.4	9.4	10.8	18.9	33.5
June	20.7	6.0	5.6	6.7	10.4	15.1	35.5
July	14.5	5.6	6.6	8.3	12.2	13.6	39.2
August	20.0	7.4	6.2	10.3	10.5	14.6	30.9
September	21.2	6.8	6.8	6.4	9.8	13.8	35.2
October	24.9	6.3	8.5	9.5	9.9	12.1	28.8
November	29.7	6.2	5.6	6.3	9.9	10.4	31.9
December	37.3	4.8	5.2	3.7	6.2	9.3	33.5

Source: Ushnayev 1969, p. 46.

farms the school brigades do not simply 'help with the harvest'; they carry out the real permanent work of the farm. Thus, in the Noyekhon kolkhoz in the Selenga district, a Buryat schoolgirl in her last year (tenth class) wrote in the local newspaper:

Our pupils' production brigade, consisting of thirteen people, achieved good results in the fattening-up of lambs . . . One of my classmates, S. Budazhapov, sheared 1,024 sheep and was recognised the champion of the district among young shearers. Our brigade sheared 20,000 sheep altogether . . . We obtained 15 tons of fodder. We organise *voskresniki* (Sunday labour-days) for the cleaning out and heating of the cattle-sheds. The classes at our school are in charge of (*shefstvuyut*) six *otaras* of sheep and five *gurtas* of cattle.

We contribute all of our strength to give real help to our parents. Last February, at the general Komsomol meeting, we took on the 'socialist obligation' to work during the summer quarter. We promise to fatten up 3,000 lambs, to shear 20,000 sheep, to prepare 2,000 centners of hay, to obtain 20,000 tons of bush fodder, and 2,000 centners of silage. We also will grow *kuuzika* [a fodder plant] and potatoes.[6]

It is not clear if the children are paid for this work, though readers will be glad to know that the shearers of 20,000 sheep were given a holiday in Moscow. Probably it is not pay which motivates the children to labour while their parents are otherwise engaged. School-leavers know that if they refuse to take part in such work the fact will be noted. If they wish to acquire good jobs, either inside the farm or outside it, they need good references.

The explanation is not so much that a pool of unemployed kolkhozniks exists because there is too little work to do, but the opposite: there exists a number of people who will not come out because there is too much work to do. This must be immediately qualified by explaining that the phenomenon affects some jobs only. It has already been shown how laborious, endless, and badly paid some jobs are in comparison to others. The Buryat material suggests that many people would rather not work at all than take on these jobs.

But it is not simply that people avoid doing certain work because they dislike it, or because they feel worthy of something better. The withdrawal of labour is also a weapon. In fact, it is the weapon which can cripple the kolkhoz and condemn the farm's officials to certain dismissal. Why else was it the first action of Tsydenov, the Chairman who put the Barguzin kolkhoz on its feet after the Kalinin merger, to go personally round each house in the endeavour to get people to come out to work?[7]

The power of this weapon is recognised by everyone. Indeed it is acknowledged to the extent that, for the officials, it has become the ghost in the machine. In Soviet terminology it becomes 'the violation of labour discipline', and in the last resort almost any accident or bungling can be blamed on it.

How do the kolkhozniks use this weapon? At the simplest level there is a kind of naive bargaining, which there is no reason to suppose has changed since the 1950s when the Russian novelist Soloukhin made his study of the village of Olepino:[8]

The brigadier comes uncertainly into the *izba* at the very moment when the family is drinking tea.

'So, well, Anna Ivanovna, let's see, well, basically, there's an order (*naryad*) to dig potatoes.'

'Oh you shameless one, hold your pocket wider! I was just thinking things were getting easier. And he asks me to dig his potatoes for him! Anyway, I've got my own patch still to do. Go away, go away — or else. I've said I won't go to work, and that means, I won't.'

The brigadier after this, however, doesn't go, but sits down on a bench, asks the husband for tobacco, and chats about this and that.

'Well, right then, Anna Ivanovna, I'm off. So the potatoes are behind the stables, they've got to be dug.'

'Don't ask any more, just don't ask, I'm not going, whatever you do.'

'Right, then we'll fine you five work-days', said the brigadier in an indifferent tone, though not even himself believing in this means of punishment.

'And what the devil do your work-days mean to me? Fine me fifty of them!' said the housewife, inspired.

'All right, if that's how you take it. But in the spring when you need your patch ploughed, you'll come to me for a horse, and I won't give it to you. Or you'll need a horse to get firewood in the winter.'

'Yes, you'll give it,' laughed the housewife. 'I'll slip you a half-litre, and you'll like it. As if I didn't know you!'

A contemporary example comes from Chita *oblast'*, a region where many Buryats live:

The use of labour as a 'political' resource

Fodder production is in full swing. The hay-meadows are full with machine-operators, schoolchildren, workers for the club, pensioners, housewives . . . Every division of the farm has set up its fodder team. But not long ago things were very different. Hay was gathered only by those specifically responsible for this. And how the work goes now — you just have to see! In a day, they fulfil two or three norms.

What is the reason for these changes for the good? Firstly, guaranteed payment for work in fodder gathering has been introduced, and secondly, we give out fodder for the private livestock of all those who come out to work in the kolkhoz meadows . . .

N. Starchikov, machine-operator, 'Victory' kolkhoz, Chita *oblast'*[9]

This kind of bargaining, from all counts, is so widespread as to be simply the way things work. The need of the brigade leaders and officials is obvious. The gain to the kolkhozniks is a multitude of semi-legal trade-offs, bits of extra pay, the use of kolkhoz equipment, scarce materials (building materials, spare parts, transport, and so on).

There is no need to describe such transactions in detail, but two areas of 'exchange' between the farm and the kolkhozniks are important enough to deserve special mention. These are firstly the marketing of the workers' domestic produce, and secondly the building of their private houses. The necessity for this kind of 'realisation' arises because of the legal limits on private property in the means of production.

A certain amount — though as I have argued in Chapter 4, not a very large amount in Buryatiya — of the kolkhozniks' private produce is 'realised' as money (or goods bought with money) at the kolkhoz market. The difficulty here, where the nearest market is hundreds of kilometres away, is how to get the goods there, and how to keep the costs of marketing down far enough to make the proposition worth while. The first necessity is to obtain permission from the brigadier for absence from work and authorisation to go to the town — perhaps a bottle of vodka, or attendance at a 'voluntary' *subbotnik* might be required. The next problem is transport. In slack periods, the kolkhoz may provide a lorry, and in fact this is the only possibility for moving cumbersome goods such as potatoes or livestock. Most often, Kerblay concludes,

un accord tacite intervient entre le kolkhoz et les kolkhoziens: le camion du kolkhoz transportera toutes les femmes au marché du chef-lieu, mais le lendemain elles seront toutes au travail pour faire les foins. Dans un grand nombre de kolkhoz il est d'usage d'accorder aux paysans de s'absenter à tour de rôle de façon à maintenir un nombre constant de kolkhoziens disponibles pour les travaux collectifs; ceux qui partent se chargent de vendre les produits (lait et denrées perissables) de leurs voisins.[10]

The brigadier treads a tightrope between losing work because his peasants are absent at market, or antagonising them altogether by keeping them at home when perishable goods have to be marketed. Kerblay, quoting a Soviet source, mentions a brigadier who was forced to pay 28,000 rubles in compensation for allowing his workers to go to market when the harvest was due.[11] On the other hand, especially when the farm is itself struggling, it cannot afford to let the peasant produce go to waste.

As mentioned in Chapter 4 section 3, there is evidence that only a certain amount of private produce is destined for sale. Much of it is disposed of through non-market channels. It appears that here too the kolkhoz management helps its workers. In the pre-collectivisation period there was a barter exchange between Buryats, who produced meat, milk, wool, and leather, and neighbouring Russians, who produced grain, potatoes, and baked goods such as bread and cakes (see p. 29). Today, in the Barguzin Karl Marx farm, bread is obtained from the nearby Russian settlement at Yubileinyi and distributed among the kolkhozniks in return for meat. Many Buryat collective farms, where vegetable growing has never been developed, also obtain cabbages, carrots, and cucumbers from Russian villages.[12] During the Second World War Buryat leather gloves and footwear were taken to Russian villages as presents, or for sale, and it is probable that this continues in some places.

The kolkhozniks need help with transforming at least some part of their produce into money, but they also desire to convert their produce into the limited number of things which are durable and inheritable. The most important of these is houses. The building of private houses was especially important during the 1950s and early 1960s. The element of bargaining with the kolkhoz came from two things: firstly that sites in the new villages were allotted strictly by the officials,[13] and secondly, that the collective farms would lend people money, materials, and transport for building. In the Buryat ethnographer Tugutov's detailed account of the removal of the Zagustai kolkhoz from a place called Arbuzova to a new site called Tokhoi, we find that the first kolkhozniks to be allowed to build houses were the people who were active administrators and workers, not just anyone who wanted to move.[14]

This brief discussion of the 'transactional value', as it were, of labour in the kolkhoz, raises much more complex issues. The first concerns the kolkhozniks' attitudes to what they receive for their labour — that is, the whole range of their cultural values, some of which may be only very indirectly related to the public kolkhoz sphere. And yet we need to keep these in mind, because it is in terms of these ideas — for example about types of status, respect, wealth, and dishonour — that people conduct their lives and make decisions. The second issue is concerned with the kolkhozniks' relation to labour itself — labour is not of course seen as undifferentiated, but as composed of many types of work which have different value. This applies not only to the crucial distinction between urban jobs, which are dominated by Russian cultural values, and rural work, which is still influenced by Buryat ideas in these farms. It also applies to valuations of the 'hierarchy' of rural labouring or technical jobs themselves.

Some people do not share the Soviet idea of a career. In effect, they have given up as far as Soviet status ranking is concerned, seeing themselves as attributed with a low position (on both nationality and occupational grounds) with which they do not agree. These are old people, especially the religious, who are totally indifferent to concepts of work of an ideological kind — for example, the idea that more productive or mechanised work is somehow 'better'. There are young people, who might have subscribed to this ideology, but who have failed to leave the kolkhoz and failed to get training within it — the dispirited youth who hang about in the kolkhoz centre, working only when they absolutely have to.

Buryats had no word in the pre-Soviet period for the concept of work as a general category. This is not surprising if we remember that in the pre-collectivised economy there were no production groups organised as separate entities distinct from the households and local kin-groups. It is true that there was a word, *barlag*, for someone who was a worker of a general kind, but this was essentially a negative concept ('slave', 'servant', as in the saying *bayan khün malai barlag, ügytei khün khüei barlag* — 'a rich man is a slave to his livestock, a man with nothing is a slave to other people'), and it was not possible to generalise this word in the positive sense of 'worker' in socialism. The various words for work native to the Buryat language were either specific to particular tasks (*khoni*

Boys at the war memorial, Bayangol, Barguzin, 1967.

307

haakha — to milk sheep, *khoni kharakha* — to pasture sheep, etc.), or else they have somewhat negative undertones. *Üile*, for example, meant 'activity in relation to something' (e.g. *khonin üile* — 'sheep work'), but it also had the secondary meaning of 'fate' or 'misfortune', as in *üile boloo* — 'a misfortune has occurred'. The word *khüdelmeri*, 'labour', has its root in *khüdel*, 'movement', 'shifting about', which in Buryat culture is considered undignified. Elders and respected people such as high lamas remain still, and if they move do so in a slow and dignified way. The word *azhal*, 'task' or 'job', originally had the meaning of 'outside work', i.e. done for someone else, but not in one's own household (where the specific terms would be used).

In present-day Buryat, *üile* has become the root of *üilberi* ('industry'), while *khüdelmerchin*, is a 'labourer' and an *azhalchin* is a 'worker'. For a Buryat of the older generation to say 'I am a *khüdelmerchin*' is definitely to start talking the official political language. People would prefer to say 'I am a shepherd (*malchin*)' or 'I am a driver (*shofyor*)', and it is probable that kolkhozniks still think in terms of specific occupations, rather than of 'labour' in general. This is what we would expect, given the greatly increased division of labour (one might almost say discontinuity of labour) since collectivisation (see Chapter 4 section 2).

For most people, the possibility of changing jobs (i.e. 'moving upwards', or being demoted) is the dominating reality of Soviet working life, and the idea that things are better 'further up' is essential to a continuing belief in the worth of Soviet society. The conceptual conflict between the two ways of 'moving up' is described in the next section. One way is via the Party, where it can be a political advantage to have a humble origin. The other way consists in the very acquisition of a training and a speciality, if not for oneself, then for one's children. The second of these two alternatives has only really arisen for kolkhozniks since the war, when rural technical occupations started to become widespread. Up until then, the Party alternative was dominant, as the Buryat adaptation of a traditional blessing indicates. In the pre-revolutionary period, a young couple getting married would be blessed with the following words:

> Sergede uyakha moritoi baygaarai
> Sergete oskokho khübüütei baygaarai

> May you have (many) horses to tie to the tethering-post
> May you have (many) sons to enter the army

In the Soviet period, this has been altered to:

> Sergede uyakha moritoi baygaarai
> Ts.K. -da khüdelkhe khübüütei baygaarai

> May you have (many) horses to tie to the tethering-post
> May you have (many) sons to work in the Party Central Committee.[15]

The 'political' issue of who has which jobs is a matter of ceaseless manoeuvring for everyone. But the reasons behind individual strategies vary from the kolkhozniks' point of view. Thus, in bargaining between the workers and the farm officials over work, the 'counters' they are using, i.e. jobs, range in value from the hated to the positively desired, and there is no universally accepted valuation because people differ in their inclinations and concerns.

But what is general is the fact of the tacit bargaining, the most common type being: I will work in this job for a time if it is understood that later I can move to that one (or go for training, etc.). Thus, looking at the biographies of the Buryat kolkhozniks, we find that there is a great deal of job-switching.

When this phenomenon extends to movements of workers between farms — which it often does — it becomes that much written-about Soviet 'problem' of the 'fluctuation of cadres' (*tekuchost' kadrov*). Kolkhozniks have always been allowed to move from farm to farm if the two managements agree, and there is therefore a tendency for a flow out of unsuccessful farms into the more prosperous ones. This is a possibility especially for trained workers of which there is a shortage: the receiving kolkhoz will always accept applications, and the unsuccessful kolkhoz may find it difficult to keep people who threaten to move to another farm. The prosperous Selenga farm had twenty-two applications for membership in 1967, all of which were accepted. There was no record of anyone leaving. In some Buryat farms the flow is considerable: for example, in just one year in the 'Kizhinginskiy' sovkhoz (1970), out of 710 workers, 119 either came into, or left, the farm, i.e. 16% of the workforce was on the move.[16]

The important point is that, whether the move is within the farm or outside it, the standard demand by the management is for labour within the first job, usually work of the hardest and most badly paid kind, before a request to move is granted. For young people who want training, this labour demand is formalised (it is called a *stazh*) — a combination of payment in advance for the privilege of education, and demonstration of worthiness of character. 'They get used to the bad food, and living in barracks', said the Party Secretary of the Selenga farm. After a *stazh* of two to three years, a young kolkhoznik who has not won a place in higher education in the open competition after leaving school can be put forward by the kolkhoz as their student. In this case he enters the institute without taking an entrance examination, his fees are paid by the kolkhoz, and he must return there to work in his 'speciality'.

Here is an example from the Barguzin Karl Marx farm in 1980.[17]

The girls of Sunduyev's brigade

The girls had driven the flock right to the edge of the *otara* and now they were taking refuge from the sun in the cabin of a homely jeep. They shook my hand and smiled shyly.

The girls had finished school at almost the same time, in 1977 and 1978. They tried to get into an institute, but they hadn't managed it the first time. So they came back to Bayangol and started to work in their home kolkhoz.

. . . The girls have been working on the *otara* since February. They had been sent to the *sakman* flocks, to help the well-known shepherd with his new-born lambs. They had to work hard, often at night. But they did not spare themselves.

309

. . . The young workers live far from home. During the *sakman* period they were allotted a house. But now that the sheep will be taken to summer pastures they will have to live in wagons. But they don't particularly complain. 'It's necessary!' they replied to my question.

. . . The young girls are members of the Komsomol.

. . . When the lambs have been separated off, and the shearing is over, the girls will be able to go for further education. Where? Two of them want to go to agricultural college, and three to medical college. But friendship will stay friendship. Not from loud words, or speeches, but from many days of difficult work done together.

In the Khrushchev period virtually all schoolchildren had to take part in such work as a part of the government's practical training schemes. They were unpopular with the regular workers because the children were inexperienced and often unenthusiastic. Now, such work is clearly undertaken as part of a career. How- ever, the Barguzin Karl Marx farm only financed two or three such student places per year. Virtually every family I visited prided itself on those children (or cousins, or nephews, etc.) who had managed to escape, who had managed to get education and 'move upwards'; but the official attitude to this was negative. A typical example of the official view is the following:

In a number of families [among the Bichur Buryats] we still find survivals of property-consciousness. In these families people strive only for personal success and they are indifferent to the social life, to the affairs of the kolkhoz or sovkohz. It is the children who suffer most of all from these survivals of a dangerous ideology. They are brought up to be egoists, attracted to an easy life, to light work. A characteristic of these people is fear of honest, systematic labour in the communal economy. For example, when I asked the question, 'Why don't you allow your daughter to work on the cattle *ferma*?' a woman from Altasha *ulus* [village] replied, 'It's enough that I and my husband have worked all our lives in the cattle sheds, but her, let her be a cultured (*intelligentnaya*) person, let her do some clean office-type of work.' The trouble is that these attitudes and 'theories' are spread among the backward elements in many villages and settlements.[18]

Randalov's conclusion is very misleading. The implication of his concluding sentence is that sentiments tainted with 'careerism' are not to be found among the more 'progressive' people, that is, the Party workers, officials, and specialists. In my experience this is completely untrue: I never met a family of the rural elite in which aspirations both for themselves and for their children, were not evident. It is particularly these people, who already have some stake in the Soviet career structure, who will do everything possible in order to get their children a higher education. It is also these people who tend to move most from job to job themselves.

But what of the 'backward elements'? Attitudes to labour (see also Chapter 4 section 2 and Chapter 5) here are a good deal more complicated than Randalov suggests. It is fairly clear which categories of people are meant by the expression 'backward elements': they are those with least education, the older people, those who take the smallest part in voluntary 'social' work, and those most inclined towards religion. In Buryat conditions, these people are to be found almost exclusively among the livestock workers and the unskilled manual labourers (*rasnorabochiye*).

However, it is important to realise that the pattern this suggests — that young people, especially young men, are able to avoid livestock work and manual labour and enter occupations where the opportunities for further training and a fuller 'soviet' social life are greater — is rapidly changing in many rural areas of Siberia. During the early 1960s, when there was an absolute lack of trained machine-operators in the farm, it was possible for most young men who had the school qualifications to acquire the training, and to get jobs in their speciality. This is no longer the case. In the Barguzin farm, the school headmaster told me that, already by 1967, occupational training (for tractor-drivers, electricians, cooks, joiners, etc.) had been discontinued, because there were no jobs available for the trainees in this farm. The present lack of opportunities on the farms is complemented by the *availability* of work for trained people in other parts of the Soviet economy. Thus, between 1965 and 1969, 3,600,000 agricultural workers were trained in mechanical skills, but of these only 244,000 found employment in farms.[19] This fact, on an all-Union scale, probably reflects a positive desire for urban life on the part of many of the trainees, but it remains true that in many of the more prosperous parts of Siberia there are working on farms more people trained for mechanical occupations than are able to get jobs of this kind.

An interesting series of studies of three regions of Yakutiya[20] sets out to discover not only how many young rural workers were trained and how many had jobs in their speciality, but also how many were able to get further education in the occupation they wanted, how many were happy with the jobs they did have, and how many were intending to change work in the near future.

The data were collected in 1976 in the Megino-Kangalasskii region, the Leninskii region (which is distant from any urban centre), and the Namskii region (which is close to the city of Yakutsk). The study showed that the less distant of these regions had adequate supplies of mechanised cadres, but the utterly bleak and remote Leninskii district had filled only 58% of its mechanised jobs. Nevertheless well over 18% of the young people doing manual work in the Leninskii district had training as machine-operators.[21] This is significant, because it indicates that skilled people are being put into manual jobs even in those districts where life is so unpleasant that there are not enough workers of any kind. In other words, part of the wastage of trained people can be attributed not only to lack of skilled jobs, but also to the positive need for unskilled labour in the farms. It is virtually certain that the farms in question are not adequately mechanised and cannot provide work for their quota of skilled employees.

There is a high level of dissatisfaction, according to the Yakut study, among young people working in unskilled jobs. There are many reasons. Many fewer

311

Table 7.2. *The attitude of school-leavers in Yakutiya to study and work, and the realisation of their plans (in percentages), 1976*

	Leninskii region		Megino-Kangalasskii region		Namskii region		Total	
	Boys	Girls	Boys	Girls	Boys	Girls	Boys	Girls
Plans on leaving school								
Further study	72	91	60	68	79	96	71	86
Work and study combined	6	4	3	5	4	4	4	4
Work	22	3	37	27	17	–	25	9
What actually happened								
Further study	32	31	18	17	17	32	25	27
Work and study combined	2	1	–	1	–	–	1	1
Work	57	62	70	67	71	69	63	65

Source: Argunov and Isakova 1977, p. 55.

than half of the school-leavers who wish for further training are able to get it (see Table 7.2). Among those who do get training, large numbers are unable to take the courses they planned to take, let alone the courses they would have preferred in an ideal world (see Table 7.3). And, most important of all, for those who get no higher education, *only about one in a hundred* of the children who got occupational training in their last years at school can find themselves jobs in these occupations when they leave (see Table 7.4). It is not surprising that the Barguzin Karl Marx kolkhoz simply discontinued such training facilities in the mid-1960s.

It is possible that young people in collective farms in particular feel a lack of point in continuing their studies unless they have some real hope of leaving the farm by this means. The Buryat sociologist Plishkina found in 1967–8 that the rural school in the Buryat village of Takhoi enrolled only nine young kolkhozniks for evening classes, but forty-eight workers from the *Sel'khoztekhnika* organisation (i.e. workers who already had some qualifications and desired to better them).[22] It is not that farm children do not know about opportunities, even children from the Even and Evenki nationalities, living in the remote taiga, are aware of, and in most cases positively would prefer, jobs in industry, in towns, or in the professions.[23]

The Yakut studies are based on a limited, and possibly unrepresentative, selection of young people working as machine-operators, manual workers, and milkmaids (see Figure 7.1), and we may wonder how frankly negative opinions would be expressed in a written questionnaire. Nevertheless, the data are interesting, and indicate that those with skilled jobs are dissatisfied for different reasons from the people doing predominantly manual work (milking, and the field-labourers, *raznorabochiye*). To summarise Figure 7.1: the unskilled workers are discontented primarily with the sheer physical labour, the working conditions, the attitude of the administrators towards them, and the lack of variety in the work. The study further shows that 35% of the milkmaids and 38% of the manual workers wished to leave the region, and their main reason for this was lack of opportunity for further training and education on the farms.[24] The skilled workers, on the other hand, were discontented primarily by the conditions of work. Fewer of them wished to move away (18.9%), and the reason in their case was not so much desire for education (only 9% of them, as opposed to 44% of the unskilled workers, give this reason), but desire for better pay and living conditions. The unskilled thus expressed a wish to make a 'vertical' change (i.e. to the different kinds of jobs obtainable by training), while the machine-

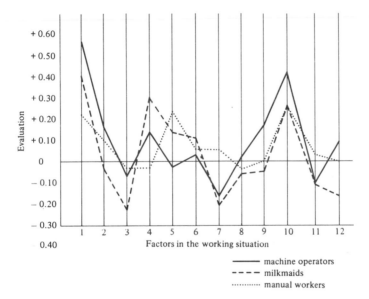

7.1. Evaluation of factors in the working situation by machine-operators, milk-maids and manual workers (*raznorabochiye*).

The factors were: (1) attitude to farm work; (2) necessity for use of native wits in the work; (3) the physical load of the work; (4) understanding of the meaning of the results of the work; (5) the pay; (6) the organisation of the work; (7) the working conditions; (8) the condition of machinery or equipment; (9) the possibilities of improving qualifications; (10) relations with work-mates; (11) the attitude of the administrators to the workers; (12) the variety of the work.

The study was carried out in January 1976 in sovkhozy of Megino-Kangalasskii, Namskii and Leninskii districts of Yakutiya. In total the three districts had 10,406 farm-workers, of which 3,824 were 'young people' (i.e. under thirty). The study covered 238 people by questionnaire: 120 machine-operators, 81 milkmaids, and 37 manual workers. There are now no kolkhozy in the Yakut ASSR.

Source: Kuz'mina 1977, pp. 23–36.

313

Table 7.3. *The structure of occupational interests of school-leavers from middle schools: ideal hopes, personal plans, and achieved reality, in percentages*

Occupations	Ideal				Personal plan				Actual behaviour			
	Rural		Urban		Rural		Urban		Rural		Urban	
	Boys	Girls	Boys	Girls	Boys	Girls	Boys	Girls	Boys	Girls	Boys	Girls
Technical	42	6	82	13	47	7	86	20	27	16	80	53
Agricultural	9	3	–	7	7	2	–	4	42	14	–	–
Finance, economics	–	2	–	7	–	3	–	–	–	4	7	–
Services*	–	2	–	7	–	2	–	20	–	2	–	29
Teaching (school)	9	35	–	13	13	41	–	24	5	30	–	–
Medicine	2	21	–	26	1	19	–	24	5	12	–	12
Culture and art	4	9	–	13	2	12	–	4	–	13	–	6
Law	4	9	4	7	5	6	–	–	–	–	–	–
Army and aviation	20	5	10	–	13	–	9	–	13	1	13	–
Other	–	3	–	–	2	4	–	–	3	8	–	–

*shop assistant, hair-dresser, waitress/waiter, etc.
Source: Argunov and Isakova 1977, p. 58.

Table 7.4. *Occupational training of schoolchildren in the ninth and tenth classes in the 1974–5 school year and work found by them in the Yakut ASSR*

	Driving and engine-maintenance		Work on tractors, combines and other agricultural machinery			
	General driver	Professional driver	Tractor-driver	Mechanic, machinist	Milking mechanic	Electrician
Number of schools in which training carried out	6	2	32	3	2	2
Number of schoolchildren training	438	83	2032	160	88	18
Number of those trained who managed to find work in the given occupation	—	1	248	16	16	2

Source: Argunov and Isakova 1977, p. 64, quoted from the Current Archives of the Ministry of Education of the Yakut ASSR.

operators were apparently more interested in a 'horizontal' move involving better material conditions within the same speciality. Furthermore, even those unskilled workers who expressed themselves as satisfied with their jobs were, in many cases, only happy for the time being: 57.3% of the 'contented' milkmaids intended to try to get other work in the farm within the next two or three years, and 58.5% of the 'indifferent' and 'discontented' milkmaids had the same aim![25]

It is because jobs are allocated by officials, because there is a limited quota of desirable positions, and because moves cannot be made without permission that the issue of who has what work becomes a 'political' one. It is not simply qualified workers but also trained professionals, especially women, who find themselves living in Siberian collective farms, but unable to do the work they have been educated for.[26] At the same time, many of the officials in influential jobs are relatively untrained people who rose to power through the Party. The question of the social relations between officials in this situation becomes crucial.

In this section I have suggested that some farm-workers do use the weapon of withdrawal of their labour, and that the price exacted by the kolkhozniks for their labour in unrewarding jobs — labour which is necessary if the management is to fulfil the plan and make a surplus — is paid by the officials either in help in the distribution of the proceeds of the private domestic economy, or in the allocation of jobs and training opportunities. In the next section I shall show that these two factors are closely connected in Buryat rural society. They are integrated by means of two 'unofficial' social structures: the Buryat kinship system, the present form of which, as we have seen, is to a great extent determined by this function, and the informal political system, which accretes around the formal structures of the kolkhoz, Party, and Soviets.

2. The Chairman and the Party Secretary: bases of their power

We now examine the three-cornered relations between the Chairman, the Party Secretary (*partorg*), and the *raion*. How do local power bases affect relations with the district authorities? These relations are much more complicated than is usually thought, in part because there is an essential difference between the kind of power exercised by the Chairman and that held by the Party Secretary.

The Party and Soviet committees parallel one another at the level of the farm and also at all succeeding higher levels up to the central government in Moscow.[27] The kolkhoz committee, on the other hand, where the farm is not involved in a major way in inter-farm enterprises, is not subordinate to any authority placed directly above it.

The farm is, however, subject to plan-orders for its produce from the Ministry of Agriculture which are administered by the *raion* Party committee (*raikom*) for all the farms in its district. It is also subject to policy decisions taken by the Party, and its activities may be checked or 'controlled' by the Party or the Soviets. Everyone *told* me that, of the three committees (farm, Party, Soviet) at the local level, the Party committee is the most important. Party members in all of the sections of the farm (brigades, the school, the Dom Kul'tury (cultural club)) must give monthly reports (*otchet*) of the work in their unit to the committee, which can order them to see that mistakes are rectified. But for various reasons which will become apparent later the farm Party committee may in some circumstances have less power than other institutions in the farm. But whatever the balance of power between the various committees, it is from this pool of officials that the farm is governed. Therefore it is essential to establish who are the people on the committees, and what are their relations with other members of the farm on the one hand, and with the *raion* committee members on the other.

I shall start here by looking at the relation between the kolkhoz and the *raion*, in particular the *raion* Party committee. Unfortunately, this crucial relationship is one about which very little is known except by those who live it out. The Soviet literature, so voluminous on innocuous topics such as the number of tractors in the district or the percentage of farm Chairmen with higher education, is almost silent on this subject. My informants in the Buryat kolkhozy were not very communicative either. The following is the outline of what they told me.

The Barguzin Karl Marx kolkhoz had a five-year plan (1970–5) divided into years. Negotiations with the *raion* can take place each year to change the plan, but after the beginning of any one year the plan is fixed. This used not to be the case and the *raion* sometimes used to increase the plan-orders if the farm was doing well during the year. The interest of the farm, of course, is to have a low plan, while the interest of the Ministry, operating through the *raion* agricultural administration, is to have a high plan. The plan is in theory suggested by the farm management committee, confirmed by the general meeting of kolkhozniks, and then sent to the Ministry in Ulan-Ude for final approval (*utverzhdeniye*). But in fact *raion*-level officials are present at all these meetings, and the implication from all that was said was that they took a prepared plan, based on previous ones, to the farm, where rather little bargaining was possible by this point, the plan having been prepared on the basis of instructions for the *raion* as a whole emanating from the Buryat ASSR-level (*oblast'* in other parts of the USSR) administration. Once confirmed, the plan must be fulfilled by the kolkhoz. One of the Secretaries of the *raikom* (First, Second or Third Secretaries) visited the farm once or twice a month to make an inspection, and if he found that the production for the plan was behind schedule he would scold (*rugat'*) the Chairman. If he made some positive suggestion, this would be made to the Party committee within the farm, and the members of this committee were then responsible for seeing that his recommendation was carried out. Their ability to do this must depend, to some extent, on their representation on other committees within the farm, and we shall discuss this below.

Meanwhile, let us look at the people involved in the kolkhoz–*raion* Party

317

committee relations in Barguzin. The first thing to note is that this farm had what to all appearances was a privileged relation with the *raion* since the First Secretary of the *raikom*, Viktor Rinchinovich Mangutov, had previously been Chairman of the Karl Marx and must have known the farm's problems and capabilities well. Furthermore, Viktor Mangutov was a native of Bayangol, the central village of the Karl Marx farm. However, the plan actually given to the Karl Marx seems to have been more difficult than that handed to other farms of the district. According to the 1974–5 Chairman of Karl Marx, the farm was 'not the largest' in the district, but the plan for meat, milk, and wool was considerably higher than that of the other farms (see Table 4.22). In his speech at the 1975 *raion* Party conference, Mangutov sharply criticised the Karl Marx for failing to meet its plan in milk and meat. Judging from this it appears that the kind of influence based on kinship which is so important *within* farms is not necessarily operative in the relation between the farm and the *raion*. In some regions of the USSR, such as Tadjikstan, where clan networks are effective over a wider area than they are in Buryatiya, efforts are made to break ties which might link all three levels (kolkhozniks–Chairman–*raion*) by installing 'foreign' kolkhoz Chairmen. In the farms I visited this was not done: even the drafted in Chairmen of the 1960s were local men with multiplex relations in the farm community. There are, in any case, good reasons why purely local-based strategies on the part of any farm are not likely to meet with much success in influencing the *raion* committee of the Party. For one thing, this committee (the *raikom*) consists of fifty-one members, most of whom work full-time in other jobs. Its executive committee, of nine members, has to direct and control the activities of a large number of diverse enterprises.[28] Among these, agricultural enterprises generally have low priority and collective farms in particular have tended to be least favoured, since they are not generally successful in terms of indicators and since they are not part of the state hierarchy.

It has been possible to establish the occupations of most of the members of the Barguzin *raion* Party committee in 1975 (Table 7.5). It appears that the committee consists very largely of the directors of enterprises in the district. Thus the kolkhoz Chairman who seeks to negotiate a low plan for his farm is in competition with the directors of other enterprises, most of whom sit on the *raikom*, and one or two of whom are members of the bureau or executive committee. The Chairman and Party Secretary of the Karl Marx kolkhoz were on the *raikom* in 1975, but so were the Chairman of the Ulyun kolkhoz, the Chairman of the 'Put' Lenina' kolkhoz, the Chairman of the 'Baikalets' kolkhoz, and the Director of the 'Barguzinskii' sovkhoz. The Karl Marx Chairman was not on the bureau, but the Chairman of the Ulyun kolkhoz and the Director of the 'Barguzinskii' sovkhoz were.

Another factor is that with the *raion* organisations for the first time we meet the issue of nationality. Most enterprises, as we have seen, are dominated clearly by one nationality rather than another: the Karl Marx kolkhoz is overwhelmingly

Buryat, while the Yubileiny lumber-station is almost wholly Russian, for example. But the *raikom*, to judge from the names of the members, had only seventeen Buryats as against thirty-four representatives of other nationalities, presumably mostly Russians. The bureau contained four Buryats and six Russians. Of the Secretaries, the First was a Buryat, and the Second and Third Russians.[29] It is difficult to say what effect the multinationality at the *raikom* level has on political life in the district, but it seems clear that strategies based on the existence of purely Buryat kinship relations must be ineffective at this level in most circumstances.

The three factors we have mentioned (the large number of enterprises under the *raikom*, the representation of enterprises on the *raikom* itself, and its multinationality) suggest that the primary role of the district Party committee must be in balancing the demands of the enterprises and nationalities against one another. To a great extent this 'balancing' must consist in coordinating the production of the different enterprises where these provide inputs for one another: the *Sel'khoztekhnika*, responsible for maintenance of agricultural machinery, must be given a plan which ensures that all the machinery in the various farms can be repaired; the central dairy must be given a plan which, in theory at least, could cope with the amount of milk and butter specified in the farm plans, and so on. Because of the centralised nature of planning in the USSR, only the district-level organisations (*raikom*, *raiispolkom*) actually have the information to organise such coordination. Individual enterprises do know about selected results in other individual enterprises, but they do not, officially, have information about inputs in the district, let alone the region, as a whole. If a kolkhoz is let down by 'its' supplier, e.g. of fodder concentrates, the Chairman's first action is to telephone the *raion* and ask the permanent staff to find him an alternative. It is true that individual enterprises do influence the supply situation in ways not planned by the *raikom*: for example, since suppliers have their next year's plan cut if they are left with unsold goods at the end of an accounting year, the receiving enterprise has an interest in buying up more than it needs in order to keep supplies flowing for the future (this may require some fiddling of the papers).[30] But such individual actions may create bottlenecks which only the *raion* can deal with.

Because of the difficulty of communications in Siberia — the miles of mountainous or boggy forest which separate farms from one another, the lack of roads *between* enterprises (as opposed to roads from each enterprise to the *raion* centre), the few telephones, even such apparently minor problems as the lack of telephone directories — a farm Chairman may have real difficulty in obtaining enough information to run his enterprise efficiently. Farms are often cut off for days even from the main road to the *raion*.

It is apparent, from the official speeches, that the *raion* Party conference provides virtually the only forum at which all heads of enterprises can communicate with one another. In particular, it is the only occasion on which managers can

Table 7.5. *The Barguzin raion committee of the Communist Party elected by the Party conference in November 1975*

Name	Likely nationality	Occupation (where known)
Arsen'yev, K.I.†	Rus	Director of Barguzin Agricultural Trade organisation (*selpromkhoz*); Director of Barguzin lumber-station (*lespromkhoz*)
Ayushiyev, Ts.Ts.	Bur	
Ayushiyev, Ts.A.* **	Bur	Director of govt dept responsible for agriculture
Bazarova, E.G.	Bur	
Batozhapov, B.O.	Bur	
Belikova, N.A.	Rus	
Bubeyeva, Ts.Kh.	Bur	From 'Ulyunskii' kolkhoz, winner of orders and medals
Bulakhova, N.N.	—	
Garmayev, V.Y.	Bur	Party Secretary in Karl Marx kolkhoz, Barguzin *raion*
Garmayev, Ts.B.**	Bur	Head of organisation sector of the *raikom* secretariat
Garmeyeva, K.G.	Bur	
Gagarin, V.A. * **	Rus	
Gatapov, S.L. * ** †	Bur	Chairman of 'Ulyunskii' kolkhoz at Ulyun, Barguzin *raion*
Gas'kov, G.G.	Rus	Secretary of the praesidium of the *raiispolkom*
Gongarov, B.G.	—	
Darmayev, B.Kh.	Bur	Harvester-operator, Karl Marx kolkhoz, Order of Lenin
Yerbanov, I.A. * **	Rus	Secretary of the *raikom*, i.e. Third Secretary
Zavarukhin, K.E.	Rus	Party Secretary in the Barguzin lumber-station (*lespromkhoz*)
Karpovich, S.I.	Rus	Director of the electric grid, northern section
Kozulin, N.N.**	Rus	Editor of *Barguzinskaya Pravda*
Kukhtik, Yu.G.**	Rus	Head of propaganda sector of the *raikom* secretariat
Kuchumov, V.S.	Rus	Head of *raion* society for the protection of nature
Lapushkov, A.A.	Rus	
Lubsanov, B.B.	Bur	Chairman of Karl Marx kolkhoz, Barguzin *raion*
Malykh, V.A.	Rus	
Makhov, V.Ya.* **	Rus	Second Secretary of the *raikom*
Mangutov, V.R.***†	Bur	First Secretary of the *raikom*
Men'shikov, G.I.	Rus	Director of the 'Put' Lenina' kolkhoz, Barguzin *raion*

Table 7.5. (*cont.*)

Name	Likely nationality	Occupation (where known)
Molonov, M.E.	Bur	
Myasnikov, A.V.	Rus	Head of 'Yubileinii' lumber-station
Nozovtsev, G.I.	Rus	Chairman of the 'Baikalets' kolkhoz, Barguzin *raion*
Nimayev, A.Sh.	Bur	Shepherd in 'Ulyunskii' kolkhoz, winner of order *Krasnoye Znamya*
Popov, V.N.	Rus	
Pozdnyakov, A.I.**	Rus	Secretary of the *aimak ispolkom*; Chairman of non-staff Party Commission
Pulyayevskiy, V.P.	Rus	
Revitskaya, V.V.	Rus	
Rusakova, I.A.	Rus	Head of MTF in 'Bodonskii' sovkhoz, Barguzin *raion*
Sankharova, Ts.D.	Bur	Kolkhoznik in Karl Marx, 'decorated with orders and medals'
Sokol'nikov, A.F.	Rus	Procurator of Barguzin *raion*
Stel'mashenko, M.P.	Rus	Chairman of Barguzin *raipo*, consumer union
Syshchuk, I.Ya.** †	Rus	Chairman of *aimispolkom*
Khmelyev, V.N.†		
Khundanov, P.V.	–	Head of *raion* agricultural–technical organisation (*selkhoztekhnika*)
Ushakov, A.F.* **	Rus	Director of the Baikal Water-Transport Bureau
Ukhov, V.M.	Rus	Bulldozer-driver, Hero of Socialist Labour
Fillipov, A.Kh.	Rus	
Filinov, V.N.* **	Rus	Chairman of the Barguzin People's Court
Tsyrempilova, A.T.	Bur	Chairman of Ulyun *sel'sovet*
Shelkovnikov, N.D.* †	Rus	Director of the 'Barguzinskii' sovkhoz
Shiretorova, D.Ch.* †	Bur	Chief doctor in Barguzin *raion* hospital
Shrager, B.Ya.	Rus	Director of the Gusikhin forestry station

Notes:
* Member of the bureau of the *raikom*
** Plenum of *raikom*
† Delegate to the 29th *oblast'* Party conference
Other delegates to the Party conference were as follows:
Boldogoyev, I.I., Belik, V.M. (Rus), Manzarov, P.T. (Rus), Narguleva, A.N. (Rus), Sangadiyeva, O.E. (Bur; shepherdess, Order of Lenin, in Karl Marx), Stepanova, T.E. (Rus), Stepanov, I.M. (Rus), Shalbanov, V.B.
Source: *Barguzinskaya Pravda*, 25 November 1975.

attempt to exert moral pressure on a defaulting enterprise by exposing its deficiencies publicly in front of the body of important people (*nachal'niki*) of the district. K.I. Arsen'yev, the Director of the Barguzin *lespromkhoz* (wood production enterprise), for example, took the opportunity of the 1975 Party conference to criticise the consumers' services organisation (*kombinat bytovogo obsluzhivaniya*) and the police (*militsiya*). The work of the former was almost non-existent, he said, so that it was impossible for the lumberjacks to get a hair-cut, while the police were completely failing to deal with illegality and crime on his lumber-station. Another delegate, the head of the water-transport organisation, said:

> Taking advantage of the presence of the head of 'Zabaikalles' [Trans-Baikal Wood Organisation], I would like to request the *raikom* to give careful attention to the reformulation of the state plans for our enterprise. We were unable to carry over one million tons of wood specified in our five-year plan, although we have been working, as is generally recognised, at full capacity. In the opinion of our collective our plans are too high and we cannot fulfil them with the productive base which we have. We do not have enough rafts . . . [31]

But although the head of water transport could say this in the presence of the head of 'Zabaikalles', the organisation overseeing all wood production in the area, it was already too late: this was the fourth year of the five-year plan. Only the *raikom* could have reformulated the plans, or organised the supply of more rafts earlier on. Only the Party, not the enterprises, has access to the vital special telephone network (*vertushka*) between different sections of the Party organisation which may have made contradictory or impossible orders.

Disputes of an ordinary kind between enterprises tend to be resolved at the level of the lowest common superior. Only if the enterprise involved is a very large and important one will the *obkom* rather than the *raikom* take charge.[32] However, in both *obkom* and *raikom* priorities between sectors, e.g. heavy industry as against light industry, wood production as against agriculture, are decided from above. From the point of view of the Party committees, these priorities appear as orders, and so it frequently occurs that the *raikom* will 'steal' from one enterprise to help another, or make an 'unfair' decision in favour of a heavy industry plant as against a struggling kolkhoz.

The monopoly of the means of communication by the Party not only supports control by the *raikom* over the enterprises, but also prevents the various discrete units (farms, etc.) from realising that they have a common problem in relation to the administration. Everything is presented as if they were simply in competition with one another. Even if it is realised that the phrase 'socialist competition' is often a hollow mockery, a figure of speech to cover the desperate plugging of gaps in production, the individual manager is nevertheless pleased to 'win'. It seems that he has 'won' against his neighbours; in fact, he has 'won' against all those obstacles created by the administration (conflicting indicators of success, switching of supplies to other enterprises, difficulty in obtaining *naryady* (orders for materials), inappropriate plans in the state procurement agencies, and so on).

Contrary to what one might suppose, the *obkom* (or the ASSR level of the Party in the Buryat case) does not always operate through the *raikom*. It occasionally intervenes directly in the work of enterprises. Consistent with this is the fact that delegates to the *obkom* are not simply chosen from the ranks of the *raikom*, but can be 'elected' directly from the local Party organs within enterprises. Thus in 1975 there were fifteen delegates from Barguzin to the *oblast'* Party conference, of whom seven, including the First Secretary, were also on the *raikom*, but eight were delegates from the lower level enterprise. Unfortunately, it has been impossible to find out the occupation of these non-*raikom* delegates with the exception of one, Ol'ga Sangadiyeva, a shepherdess from the Karl Marx kolkhoz. Such delegates usually play a passive role in the *obkom*, but their presence there establishes the principle that the *obkom* has a direct interest in enterprises.

The intention is that higher organs should be able to check that their subordinates are not executing policies wrongly at the lowest level. It is a recurring feature of Soviet imaginative literature that it is the highest Party officials who are closest somehow in spirit to the people. Intervening levels of bureaucrats are blamed for misrepresenting or distorting policy. Thus in one Buryat novel, the honest kolkhoz Chairman holds out against a *raikom* instruction to sow his crops by a certain date; although his refusal causes him much trouble, he gets a better harvest in the end 'to the glory of the working people' as recognised by the higher Party level.[33] Or, to shift the example one rung downwards, the brave shepherd fights for the kolkhoz by opposing a tyrannical and inefficient Chairman.[34] In these stories the wise representative of the people supports the underdog − the shepherd was upheld by the *raion* against his Chairman − because he is able to understand the full complexity of the situation without being drawn aside by local interests. But in real life, the chances of this happening, while better than nil, are not very great.

Let us look at the reasons. The effect of the situation just outlined is for all officials at any level to feel that they must have the confirmation of their superiors before taking any decision. In the sphere of personnel selection, for example, the *nomenklatura* system ensures that the *obkom* as well as the *raikom* has a hand in any appointment at the management of enterprise level.[35] Thus, in sacking a corrupt kolkhoz Chairman against the wishes of the *raikom*, the *obkom* would have to go back on a decision in which it had already taken part. This does sometimes happen, but generally, as far as we can see, only if the *obkom* had been given instructions from the republic level to carry out a policy of the type, 'Investigate corruption in your *oblast'* and demonstrate that you have taken action' (see Chapter 4 section 2).

The need for confirmation from above is not defined, and no one is certain as to the occasions when it may be dispensed with. For safety, local officials such as farm Chairmen may involve the *oblast'* Party on all kinds of matters. For example, in the Aga Buryat National Okrug, when two collective farms wished to build themselves cultural clubs, strictly an affair of the Soviets, the plan was taken up to the *oblast'* level of the Party. It is significant, also, that it was the farm managements which took the initiative, rather than the local Soviets, the reason clearly being that it was the farms which were providing the funds for the buildings.[36]

Even occasions of the individual's working life may be picked out and highlighted, given legitimacy by the attention of the higher levels of the Party, Soviets, and other organisations. Thus, for example, a milkmaid, Tsyndyma Togodoyeva of the Karl Marx kolkhoz in Aga, celebrated the twentieth anniversary of beginning work. She invited Party, Soviet, Komsomol, and collective farm dignitaries from the district to the 'red corner' (Party meeting-place) of her brigade.[37] Often on such occasions the officials do not attend, but they send messages which are read out. The private moment is made a social moment of public virtue by calling upon all the symbolic values of the Soviet cosmology; it would not be out of place on such an occasion to mention Soviet achievements in industry or space exploration.

The multiplicity of organisations which might be involved in any decision hides the actual moment and origin of action. A youth brigade working on the Baikal–Amur railway construction recently complained to the *raion* Komsomol that another team, which had been publicly disqualified from a 'socialist competition' for absenteeism, had nevertheless been awarded the winner's banner. But despite inquiries neither the head of the construction organisation, nor the Komsomol secretary, nor the Director of the Soviet, nor the Secretary of the *raikom* had any idea who had made the mistake.[38] 'Does it really matter?' was their attitude. 'We have more important things to think about.'

In normal times the entire *nachal'stvo* (leadership) of the district tends to be caught up in a web of mutually protective relations. Often this involves corruption. According to the émigré writer Zemstov it was standard in Azerbaijan in the early 1970s for lower officials (managers of enterprises, low-level Party functionaries) to pay protection money to the *raion* and *oblast'* Secretaries to ensure that they would be given warning of visits from police, auditors, or other 'control' organisations, and to deflect and squash awkward complaints.[39]

Yefimov, a Soviet journalist, mentions what he claims to be an even more widespread practice: the *raikom* deliberately involves the Chairman in minor illegal activities, for example the acquiring of 'left' (illegitimate) supplies, so that they can thereafter hold this over him as a threat and make sure he keeps quiet in the *raion* offices.[40] But since it is virtually impossible to live in the Soviet Union without contravening some regulation or other, we can deduce the same effect without supposing that the *raikom* deliberately sets out to achieve it. The Chairman is always vulnerable, and so, for that matter, are the *raikom* officials, but they are more open to attack from above than below.

324

The Chairman and the Party Secretary: bases of their power

This being said, it should be noted that the Party organs can be criticised in public, as it were 'from below'. At the 1975 Barguzin *raion* Party conference, K.I. Arsen'yev, speaking as the director of the Barguzin *lespromkhoz* (wood production enterprise), complained that the *raikom* officials did not come to the lumber camps, that they did not give lectures and political education classes (*beseda*) to the lumberjacks, and limited their activities to attendance at Party accounting and election meetings (*otchetno-vyborniye partiiniye sobraniya*). However, Arsen'yev was not simply the director of the *lespromkhoz*; he was also on the *oblast'* committee and held other important positions.[41] The 'criticism from below' was something of a fiction. In fact it was criticism from above.

As for organisations other than the Party, it is frequently the case that they have to endure criticisms and suggestions. Often these are made by ordinary Party members or delegates to Soviets, and this is one of the ways in which such bodies obtain information as to what should be done. But for the reasons we have mentioned, only if these suggestions are caught by the *raion* and taken up by it are they likely to be acted upon.

Within the *raion* Party organisation, while the First Secretary has primary responsibility for all the enterprises and other institutions in 'his' district, the Second Secretary is charged with relations with the *obkom*. The same pattern is true with regard to *obkom* Secretaries. It is the Second Secretary who is responsible for relations with the republic, and in view of what we have been saying this gives him more power, if less visibility, than the First Secretary. In the 'national' areas of the Soviet Union, the Second Secretary at *obkom* level is usually a Russian, sent down to work in the provinces.[42] The same, it appears from our data, may be the case at the lower level of the *raion* (see Table 7.5). Full-time Party *apparatchiks*, i.e. those working in the secretariats and as heads of departments, are often transferred from district to district and even, at *oblast'* level, to distant parts of the USSR. I met one Buryat Party official who was posted to an *oblast'* secretariat on the Black Sea coast.

For the individual enterprise not only are there few possibilities for solidarity with neighbouring farms, but the system has the effect that one is subject to a variety of pressures from different levels simultaneously. Besides the Party Secretary (*partorg*) of the local branch who is constantly at one's elbow, there is also the *raikom* staff who make visits several times a month, and the *obkom* may intervene on important matters. At the same time, the same three levels of the Soviet organisation (i.e. the *sel'sovet*, the *raiispolkom*, and the *obispolkom*) in their various roles (law, housing, the environment, culture, etc.) may make requests of an enterprise. Often the Party and the Soviets act together, both sending representatives to a meeting in the farm at which some policy from above is to be discussed and put into operation. Here we see clearly, as Hough has pointed out, that Soviet theory thinks quite deeply that a formal bureaucratic structure of the Weberian type, in which the decisions are made by the appropriate official and passed down by standard procedure through the hierarchy, is not the right method.[43] More than one person, and preferably more than one organisation, is required for each 'decision'. This is an aspect of the ideological emphasis on 'collective decision-making'. In practical terms it is the result of the formal political requirement of consensus despite the duplication of institutions at each level.

The management of the farm is thus involved in a complex series of relations in which the balance of power is weighted partly by the political capacities of the personalities involved (this will be discussed below) and partly by the demarcation of the economic and political roles of the organisations involved. Briefly, the Party is responsible for policy decisions over the whole range of socio-economic life, while the enterprises are responsible for the execution of these policies in the economy and the Soviets are responsible for the administration of the policies in social life. Since the *raion* Party also controls, as we have seen, allocation of resources between enterprises, this demarcation of responsibilities quite clearly places the *raion* Party in an overwhelmingly powerful position. But the possession by enterprises of material means, particularly 'manipulable resources' outside the planned budget, gives them in many circumstances an advantage over the Soviets. Enterprises such as farms produce resources; the Soviets on the other hand have a budget allotted to them for spending — not a very generous one given the wide range of activities they are supposed to engage in — and they are expected to obtain part of their finance from the 'surplus' resources of the enterprises themselves.[44] This places the Soviets in fact, if not in rhetoric, in a supplicatory relation to the enterprise managements.

The relation between the Chairman of the kolkhoz and the Party Secretary of the local branch is more problematic. Who is dominant at this level depends a great deal on personalities. However, certain constant features of the different bases of power of the two officials make it more likely that the Chairman will prevail. The Party Secretary is elected for three years, extendable for another two, and then, if the *raikom* puts him up again, for life (this was the case in the Barguzin Karl Marx). The Chairman is elected for three years, extendable for another three. This would appear to give the Party Secretary (*partorg*) the more unassailable position. But, in fact, biographies of these officials reveal that the *partorg* is removed from his job at least as frequently as the Chairman. The fact is that it is the Chairman who has the material resources and right to dispose of jobs which can allow him to build his own faction within the farm. The *partorg* can only request people to carry out his policies for ideological credit, with a vague threat of repercussions from the *raikom* if they refuse. The end of Stalinism has meant a definite weakening in the force of this threat.

To take a hypothetical case, what would happen if the Party Secretary put forward some policy *x* which the Chairman did not wish to carry out? If this policy is a direct order from the *raikom* the Chairman would in the end probably have to comply, since he would have no fall-back position at the higher level. However, if policy *x* was simply designed to reflect credit on the *partorg*, to demonstrate his enthusiasm and watchfulness, etc., there is every chance that it would fail. The Chairman might say to other influential people in the farm, 'What do you think of Comrade A. and his policy? We have elected him to serve our interests, and now he is putting forward this harmful policy . . . ' At the Party meeting the Chairman can use his faction to denounce the policy: 'We, as honest members of the Communist Party, do not agree with your proposal. We have entrusted you with a high position, and now you are acting against the interests of the working masses . . . ' To avert this possibility, the *partorg* may try to pretend that policy *x* is an order, but such a device is easily found out. In the last resort, either the Chairman or the *partorg* can appeal to the *raikom*. However, the Chairman is in a better position here too because of his local power base: the *raion* needs, for its own figures, the kolkhoz to be successful, and it may rely on farm resources for various district supplies which the Chairman could withhold. The Chairman has the possibility of using bribery, which the *partorg* has to a much lesser extent. And finally, although the *raion* is very influential in the election of kolkhoz Chairmen and most election meetings are formalities, nevertheless the removal of one Chairman and the installing of another does have to pass through the public meeting of kolkhozniks. The election or dismissal of the *partorg*, on the other hand, takes place in the closed circumstances of the Party.

Even internal Party activity can become dependent on the goodwill of enterprises at this local level. When a *raion* Komsomol branch in Alma-Ata proposed establishing a full-time activist to carry out security work in a section of the city it was necessary to make an agreement with the manager of a shoe factory, who would register and pay the young man in question although he would in fact be engaged in Komsomol work.[45] In Buryat collective farms the *partorg* cannot organise his own Party members in outlying settlements without the help of the kolkhoz in providing 'red corners', nor can he set up individual 'socialist obligations' among the workforce without the cooperation of the specialists, because only they have the detailed information about the capabilities of the workers.[46]

Within the Party there are so many spheres of activity that not all directives, even those upheld by several levels, can possibly be put into practice. The newspaper *Komsomol'skaya Pravda* quotes a case where enterprises were instructed to provide activists from among their Party members for social work; the instruction was signed by the *raion* Komsomol, the *raion* internal security branch, and the *raion* Soviet, but nothing happened for over a year and the same instruction was then issued again. A young Komsomol tried to put it into effect, but he was punished by the *raikom* Party Secretary, along with the other members who had failed to volunteer for the social work, for 'weak control' of his membership. The article implies that he was in fact punished for his independence and insistence. At this level 'the team of activists is a voluntary matter. We have no right to force anyone here. If they don't want to come out — well they don't.'[47]

The successful kolkhoz Chairman can be a much more powerful agent than his local Party colleague. We can picture his interaction with his district superiors as a series of forays and receptions. He makes forays to the *raion* Party office to negotiate plans, obtain supplies, and 'present himself' at district Party conferences. He holds receptions in his own *kontora* (farm office) for representatives of the Soviets or other enterprises which need his help or cooperation. When *raion* Party officials come down to the farm they are usually entertained at a banquet in the Chairman's house. Neither the foray nor the reception may be entirely what they seem. The idiom of hunting is used for the former (*ulovit* — to ensnare, or catch, as of fish), and the bait can be a valuable one. And the reception can involve more than one banquet tout simple: 'to feed' (*kormit*) is also the slang for bribery.

Tiktina, a school-teacher under the *sel'sovet* administration, makes it clear that the local Soviet in the 1960s was also subordinate to the kolkhoz. The kolkhoz 'provided us with transport for carrying firewood and building materials, on which we were absolutely dependent. The kolkhoz gave us electricity. The kolkhoz gave the teachers private plots of land and ploughed them with its horses or tractors.' The school paid for these services in labour: not just at harvest-time, but also during the year in tasks such as pulling out the roots of maize and turnips, weeding, or getting rid of marmots. The teachers worked as well as the children. Sometimes, if the kolkhoz was in a particularly difficult position, the teachers were given personal loads: they were allotted areas for weeding and harvesting. 'If we ask ourselves', Tiktina writes, 'what was the relationship between our school and the kolkhoz, this relation can most accurately be expressed by the word "dependency" (the school on the kolkhoz always, and the kolkhoz on the school in periods of labour crisis). This relation was the same everywhere, not just with us.'[48] Other institutions under the *sel'sovet* (the cultural club, the hospital, the sports organisations, the shops and canteens, etc.) are in essentially the same relation to the kolkhoz as the school.

Although the kolkhoz Chairman has the dominant position in execution of policies, nevertheless the Party retains control over the fundamental reality of the allocation of supplies and delivery plans. Therefore we can summarise the relations of power at the level of the district as a whole as: Party → enterprises → Soviets, while at the locality the pattern is more likely to be: enterprise → Party → *sel'sovet*.

These formulae do not take account of situational factors which might alter the relationship in particular places or times. In some state farms, the Chairman of the trade union (*profsoyuz*) can be important,[49] and in certain cases the *partorg* can use the Party's control over the distribution of diplomas, medals, and prizes to create an atmosphere in which people genuinely work for the ideological goals signified by these awards. Nor do these formulae take account of changes in Soviet government policy. These accorded more weight to the Soviets during the later 1960s, which may have been counterbalanced by the greater power given to the Party by the 1977 Constitution.[50] These policies probably had a greater effect at levels above that which we are discussing in detail. In the locality, the relation between the three organisations arises from the interplay of ideology, ambition and material conditions which have been described and which have not changed essentially in their distribution during the 1960s and 1970s.

Finally, we should return to the differences in formal management structure between the two farms I visited. The Selenga kolkhoz, with its 'lineal' structure of command, differed considerably from the Barguzin kolkhoz, which tended more towards a 'specialist' hierarchy of administration. The effect of this was to create a different relation between administrators and specialists in the two farms. Different styles of management were involved, as will be described in the following section. But the two cases also showed an interesting variation in the relation between the Chairman and the Party Secretary. In the Selenga farm, where the Chairman had a greater direct control over the kolkhozniks, not mediated by the specialists, his influence over the *partorg* was also correspondingly larger; in the Barguzin farm, the Chairman on both occasions when I visited was himself a specialist, *primus inter pares*, and while the power of these Chairmen had greater currency than that of the Selenga Chairman (i.e. they could more easily be taken on for jobs elsewhere), the control over the workers themselves was mediated and hence provided a less powerful base.

The position of Party Secretary is for those who want to integrate themselves within the system; the Chairmanship is for those who prefer to manipulate it. The *partorg* is powerful insofar as he is a link in the authority structure from above which provides ideological legitimacy. The base of Party power, if we take local and district levels as one, lies in the ambition of people to move up a career ladder within the system. The *partorg* is thus himself a resource of the system, while we could perhaps say that the Chairman tries to make use of resources. The Chairman's means, however, are limited to the sphere of his farm. His power lies in his brokerage of people and materials at this level, and he requires Party approval (*odobreniye*) to colour his activities with legitimacy. Thus, in dealing with the Chairman, people are renewing their present, as it were, while in engaging with the *partorg* they are making strategies for their future. The further up the hierarchy of the farm, the more education and wider horizons people have, the less they need be concerned with the material benefits the Chairman can provide. The lower in the hierarchy, the more likely people are to be caught as 'clients' of the Chairman or brigadiers. But given the general overlapping of functions of all organisations at the local level, it is not surprising to find, as we describe in section 3, that people at all levels in the farm become involved in both kolkhoz and Party-based unofficial networks.

3. Political life in two collective farms

The statutes of the kolkhoz state that the highest political organ in the farm is

329

the general meeting of kolkhozniks. The term for it in Russian, a term which is used also by Buryats, is *otchetno-vybornyye sobraniye* (report–election meeting), and this gives some idea of its function. It is linguistically differentiated from the meeting of the committee of the farm, which is called, again by both Russians and Buryats, *zasedaniye*. 'Meeting' in the former case has the idea of 'assembly', while in the latter case it means something in the nature of a 'working session'.

The general meeting of kolkhozniks in the Selenga Karl Marx farm in 1967 took 'decisions' (*resheniye*), but we should beware of interpreting this word literally. The general meeting held in February 1967, for example, took a 'decision' which consisted of one long speech, recounting successes of the previous year, giving details of deficiencies, and listing production plans for the forthcoming year. A Soviet informant said that such 'decisions' would be checked before the meeting with the *raikom*, and in the case of plans, they would have been agreed upon with the Ministry in the previous month. If a 'decision' is something which is purely internal to the farm, such as allocation of funds between different sectors, the matter will already have been discussed by the management committee, and in this case the *raikom* will most probably have been telephoned for its approval in advance of the meeting. However, on important political matters, i.e. central government policies affecting agriculture, the *raikom* may even draw up the agenda and the list of speakers, and outline what points should be made. Frequently, the *raikom* (Party) and the *raiispolkom* (Soviet) send representatives to the meeting.

In view of the involvement of the Party in farm affairs, we need not be surprised to find that kolkhoz general meetings are sometimes run by the farm *partorg* rather than by the Chairman. Thus the general meeting in the Selenga Karl Marx kolkhoz in February 1967 had the Party Secretary as Chairman of the meeting, and a woman who was on neither the kolkhoz nor the Party committee as secretary. The meeting was not of all farm members, but of representatives. There were 240 of these, for a membership of 524, and of the representatives 210 attended the meeting.

After the *otchet* (report) part of the meeting mentioned above, there was a section for ratification of requests (*zayavleniye*) to leave the farm (none) and enter it (twenty-two). All of the requests were accepted, by unanimous vote by show of hands.

After this, the meeting moved to discussion of problems in the farm. Many speakers complained about disorder in the cattle units and lack of discipline among the milkmaids in the special breeding station for cows. Unfortunately, I did not find out who made these complaints. But we can probably summarise the nature of such general meetings by saying that if 'decisions' are usually already made, the second half of the meeting does give the opportunity to farm members to express their opinions and dissatisfactions. There was no record, however, that the meeting put forward any concrete proposals for improving

330

matters. In all probability this would be the task of the management committee or the Party committee.

The result of this situation is that a farm Chairman does not necessarily feel that he has the true support of his members just because they have voted for some 'decision' at the general meeting. This would include his own election as Chairman of the farm. Thus, a farm Chairman recently wrote to the newspaper *Komsomol'skaya Pravda* as follows:

Thirty years ago, I, then being the head of a *raion* finance department, was sent to a kolkhoz as 'plenipotentiary'. I was two days in the farm, and on the third the kolkhozniks voted and I became their Chairman. I did not complain, I did not run to the *raion* channels, but I settled down to work. In those days this was normal. And today? You have to persuade a kolkhoznik to become a brigadier. As for the agronomist, sometimes you can't even 'nudge' him to go out and see the more distant fields. In the yard the cattle-sheds are wide open, the boards falling into the mud — in the village it is wedding time, or people are being given send-off parties for the army. The carpenters are off having a good time. My heart is breaking, because it is I personally who am responsible for the milk yields and the weight of the cattle. And so the *shabashnik* [private and therefore semi-legal handyman] became my best hope. My heart gets lighter when I see the speed with which he works . . .

But all the same I do not sleep at nights. I know well that I am acting illegally — I pay him far too much. Under my own eyes these outsiders come in and fiddle something together, and I look as though nothing is going on. Everything is quiet . . . The *resheniye* passed through the meeting, so that means the kolkhozniks as it were support me . . . but my conscience does not support me . . . [51]

The kolkhozniks' vote 'as it were' (*v rode by*) supports the Chairman, but the problem is that voting is usually by a show of hands and no one likes to appear uncooperative and hold things up. Since 1969, when the new kolkhoz master statutes were issued, it has been possible for the kolkhoz meeting to choose either open or secret voting procedures, but in the farms I visited voting was open.

The idea that the kolkhoz meeting does genuinely represent democracy is expressed as a serious concern in Soviet writings, for example in the press. Thus an article dated 1980 describes how a *raion* official goes down to a kolkhoz and upbraids an ordinary worker he meets in the street for having elected a young man as Chairman without the 'support' of the *raion*. Everything is described as though the kolkhoznik really personally wished to make this bold choice. But the same article goes on to describe how this *raion*, following Brezhnev's speech about cadres at the 26th Party Congress, maintained a pool of cadres for every post. It appears that the kolkhozniks at the general meeting do sometimes reject the candidature of the man put forward by the *raion* Party committee, but it is, simply from the procedural point of view, very difficult for them to vote in someone who is not on the *nomenklatura* list at all.[52] This means that the elected Chairman does not know that he really has the backing of the farm members simply from the fact of being elected, but he is constantly surrounded by the rhetoric of popular support. The same applies to other farm officials. In effect, if there is a lack of real support, an official has to deal with the problem himself.

Workers under the *sel'sovet* (e.g. teachers, officials of the cultural club) and Party propagandists have the task of explaining to the voters what the issue is, or who the candidates are. This is done more conscientiously in some farms than others. In fact, as Tiktina relates, elections (or any general meeting which requires the kolkhozniks to stop work) turn into a kind of festival:

Elections in the kolkhoz turned into a special kind of holiday; the monotonous life was broken; the general labour of the kolkhoz ceased (though the constant tasks necessarily continued); they brought in a travelling film-projector; they set up a buffet; the shop somehow obtained *defitsitniye* [normally unavailable] goods; there was dancing and music. People were interested least of all in whom they were electing to what position: as a rule both the kolkhozniks and the teachers year after year threw their papers into the urn without looking at them. After the elections there began in all the houses, offices, and school-buildings merry-making (*gulyanki*) — just like at any other festival . . . [53]

It is true that kolkhoz meetings give the opportunity for questioning. However, as the Party Secretary in Selenga informed me, activists are sent to meetings, even the smallest brigade gathering, with the express task of reporting who asks what questions. In the case of kolkhoz meetings these items of information are reported to the *raikom*. Thus there is strong pressure to use the question time as an opportunity for personal status building vis-à-vis the Party, in other words to ask 'good' questions, rather than awkward ones.

Real decisions are made, however, at the meetings of the management committee, the local Party committee, and the *sel'sovet* committee, and even more so in informal encounters between the officials of these bodies. Formal meetings of these committees take place once a month. Usually these regular meetings take the form of hearing reports given by brigadiers and heads of production teams on the progress of their section. A typical example was the meeting on 12 February 1967 of the management committee of the Selenga Karl Marx kolkhoz. The aim of this meeting was to assess results in livestock production for the months of December and January. Those present were the Chairman, the four brigadiers, the shepherdess Banzaraptsayeva (also on the Party committee), and the zoo technician Batorov, who was invited to attend, although he was not a member of the management committee. Matters of discipline were discussed, and it was decided to fine certain cattle-herders. Another kolkhoz management committee meeting on 14 March 1967 was attended by the Chairman, the Party Secretary, two brigadiers, the veterinarian, and Banzaraptsayeva and Zhambalova, both representatives of the Party Committee. This meeting was held to discuss a project for land reclamation put forward by an outside agency together with the farm's chief agronomist. The people who put forward the plan were not present at the meeting, but the project set out what work was to be done by each brigade and it was agreed without recorded discussion. These may seem small matters, but in sum they amount to the day-to-day running of the farm.

We know nothing about exactly how agreements are reached on such committees in collective farms. But it is clear that two factors are important, given the fact that other organisations, the Party and the *sel'sovet*, have the right to intervene on almost any topic. One factor is the membership of the farm committee and the degree to which it overlaps with Party and *sel'sovet* committees. The other is the personal following of individual officials within the farm community as a whole, including people who may not sit on any committee but have influence for other reasons.

I shall first discuss political strategies in a farm with the 'lineal' command structure, emphasising the role of kinship, since kin-based followings appear to be particularly important in this relatively traditional type of farm.

Political strategies in one 'lineal' command structure

If we look at the composition of the three main committees in the Selenga farm in 1967 it is evident that there was considerable overlap, although no single official was on all three (Table 7.6). The Party committee had an effective, though not decisive, presence on the kolkhoz committee (five out of fourteen members). The kolkhoz management, on the other hand, had an overwhelming representation on the Party committee (five out of eight members). Of course we know that the Party is in theory primarily concerned with seeing that the kolkhoz carries out policies ordered from above, that its members are bound to obey the Secretary, and that therefore its representation on any other committee is likely to be united. This would make a comparatively small number of people more effective. However, in this case I shall argue that the kolkhoz committee was the more powerful of the two: firstly because it numerically dominated the Party committee, and secondly because of the strong network of relations established around the kolkhoz Chairman, Dorzhiyev, who was himself on the Party committee.

In order to understand this network around the Chairman we need to look beyond the membership of committees to the elite of the farm as a whole. We note, first, that with the exception of Borkhodoyev, the veterinary specialist, and Batorov, the zoo technician, none of the main specialists of the farm were in any official position of importance; secondly, with one very important exception, Mariya Dymbrylovna, chief economist of the farm, none of the chief specialists were local people. The chief specialists were:

Dymbrylovna, Mariya N.	Chief economist	Local; from family important before collectivisation; father died or disappeared; brought up by kolkhoz Chairman Dorzhiyev

Table 7.6. Composition of committees in Karl Marx kolkhoz, Selenga district, 1967

Kolkhoz committee	Party committee	Sel'sovet committee
*Dorzhiyev, Zhamso Balzhinimaevich (Chairman; delegate to BASSR Supreme Soviet; delegate to USSR Supreme Soviet)	*Galsanov, Ts.Ts. (Secretary)	Pubayev, Budatseren Tsibikovich (Chairman)
Rinchinov, Tseretor Lobanovich (Vice-Chairman)	*Galsanov, A.N. (head of Dom Kul'tury)	Abiduyeva, E.T. (Secretary)
Batozhapov, Tserenzhap Tsyrenovich (Brigadier 1)	*Dorzhiyev, Zh.B. (Chairman of kolkhoz)	*Galsanov, A.N. (Vice-Chairman)
Munkhozhapov, Feodor Tsedensheyevich (Brigadier 3)	Batorov, Vasilii Yegorovich (zoo technician)	Rinchinov, Ts.L. (Vice-Chairman of kolkhoz)
Yakimov, Mikhail Akimfiyevich (Russian) (tractor-driver)	*Banzaraptsayeva, B.G. (shepherdess)	Bulgatov, B.Ts. (shepherd)
*Usov, Aleksey Timofeyevich (Russian) (mechanic)	*Usov, A.T. (mechanic)	
Tsybikov, Vladimir Baldanovich (Brigadier 2)	*Zhambalova, Pylzhit U. (head of MTF)	
Borkhodoyev, Trofim Markovich (veterinarian)	Vambuyev, Andrei (Secretary of Komsomol)	
*Galsanov, Tserendorzha Tsedendambayevich (Party Secretary)		
*Zhambalova, Pylzhit Ulzutuyevna (head of MTF)		
*Chagdurov, Feodor Lkhamozhapovich (head of MTF)		
*Banzaraptsayeva, Butit Garmazhapovna (shepherdess)		
*Tserenov, Badmazhap Shoibsonovich (Brigadier 4)		
*Batuyev, V.I. (Chairman of People's Control)		

*Party Committee members who are members of other committees.

334

Amagyrov, Pavel K.	Chief agronomist	From Irkutsk *oblast'*, married to woman from there; sent to farm by Ministry of Agriculture
Borkhodoyev, Trofim M.	Veterinarian	From Irkutsk *oblast'*, wife from Tunka region; sent to farm by Ministry of Agriculture
Yevreyev, B.O.	Chief book-keeper	From Barguzin district, wife also from Barguzin; sent to farm by Ministry of Agriculture
Batorov, V.E.	Chief zoo technician	From Irkutsk *oblast'*; married to local head doctor, sister of Mariya Dymbrylovna
Badmazhapov, L.L.	Chief engineer	From Zhida *raion*: wife also from there. Sent to farm by Ministry of Agriculture
Tupchinov, Yu.B.	Headmaster	From Noikhon; wife also not local; sent to the farm by Ministry of Education

Dymbrylovna was the only chief specialist who had emerged from the farm itself, but in a 'lineal' structure her job of planning economist is perhaps the most important of all (see Chapter 3). She is the adopted daughter of Dorzhiyev, the Chairman.

Several of the other specialists, although they seem to have arrived separately, were distantly related to one another. Amagyrov, Borkhodoyev, and Batorov were all from the Alagui clan in Irkutsk *oblast'*. This small group — which called one another *zemlyaki*, 'fellow-countrymen' — were closer to the centre of power in the kolkhoz than the other specialists. Through Batorov, who was married to another adopted daughter of the Chairman, they were linked to both kolkhoz and Party Committees (Batorov was on the Party committee). But the link was through Dorzhiyev, the Chairman, and otherwise the group would have been separated from the kin networks of the kolkhoz.

These specialists, isolated to some extent even from one another, can be contrasted with the group of officials in the farm who rose through the Party. These people, whose careers are given below, were local men. Although their Party careers had involved some moving around, most of their lives were spent in their own Selenga district.

The most important men in this category about whom I have information are:

RINCHINOV, TSERETOR LOBANOVICH. Vice-Chairman of the Selenga Karl Marx kolkhoz. He was born in 1920 at Zhargalantui, a neighbouring part of Selenga, where the 'Tel'man' kolkhoz now is. After eight years in the army, he worked in the Selenga *raikom* as a propagandist, and then went to the Party school in Ulan-Ude. From 1953 to 1956 he was the Second Secretary in the

Selenga *raikom*. Subsequently, he moved into the Soviet apparatus as Chairman of the Kizhinga *raiispolkom*. From 1959 to 1965 he was Chairman of the Tel'man kolkhoz, and in 1965 was moved to the Karl Marx as Vice-Chairman.

PUBAYEV, BUDATSEREN TSIBIKOVICH. Chairman of the *sel'sovet*. He was born in the Karl Marx kolkhoz at Tashir in 1924. He went into the army immediately after school. On leaving the army in 1944, he spent two years on the *raion* Komsomol committee in Selenginsk, and then from 1946 to 1948 was Party Secretary in the Karl Marx kolkhoz. From 1948 to 1950 he was Secretary of the Party in the Kalinin kolkhoz, in neighbouring Tamcha. He subsequently became a book-keeper in the Karl Marx farm, but was then appointed as Chairman of the *sel'sovet*.

NAMZHILOV, TSERENZHAP LHASARANOVICH. Party personnel official in Karl Marx kolkhoz. He was born in Tashir in 1911, and worked as a *komsomol* secretary in various parts of Buryatiya from 1930 to 1933. From 1933 to 1939 he was sent to Mongolia as an interpreter, and in 1939 returned to Ulan-Ude as head of a department in the NKVD (People's Commissariat of Internal Affairs, the secret police). He was in the army from 1939 to 1947, fighting mostly on the eastern front. From 1947 to 1954 he returned to internal security work in Tamcha, and then came to the Karl Marx kolkhoz 'on the Party line'. From 1959 to 1966 he was brigadier of the building brigade in the kolkhoz.

Unlike the alien specialists, these men were members of local lineages, and it appears that the use of agnatic kinship links was important in their mode of operation. The role of such officials — in propaganda, agitation, security, and supervision of Party orders — is to ensure the carrying out of higher level instructions in the local community, in other words to 'control' the community. Namzhilov was almost certainly still engaged in internal security work alongside his job as brigadier. It is said to be 'impossible to resign' from the KGB (or NKVD as it was known). From my materials it appears that these Party people carried out their work by establishing networks of influence, and that these networks were structured by the patrilineal kinship system — in particular by the local kin-group known as the '-*tang*'.

From the biographies of these people and others (for example, p. 350) it is apparent that at this local level officials of the Party are the same people as the 'line' officials of the farm: the same man can move from one kind of work to the other and back again several times in his career. In effect what we have is a relatively small corpus of people willing to take official jobs, and exerting their influence, whether the current job is a Party one or not, by means of locally based kinship strategies. Thus, although the formal system of committees in the farm makes it appear that there are three separate spheres of influence (the kolkhoz, the Party, and the *sel'sovet*), this may be largely illusory. In fact, in Selenga in the late 1960s there were two distinct groups among the farm's elite, the outsider specialists and the local officials. Among the latter, which committee a man sits on is less important than his position in a network of kin.

What are these 'networks' of kin, and how extensive are they? Let us look at the case of Tserenzhap Namzhilov, the official of the secret police (Figure 7.2). Although he was not on any of the three main committees of the farm, it is apparent that with his NKVD background he was an important figure locally. During his period at Tamcha he worked as head of the personnel department (*zaveduyushchii otdel kadrov*), i.e. in allocating jobs to trained personnel, obviously a crucial position, and it seems that he continued this work after he moved to the Karl Marx farm (he said only that he did 'Party work'). Himself of the Alagui clan, one of the largest in the locality, he married a woman of the princely Bayan-Kharanuud ('rich Kharanuud') clan. His mother also was a Kharanuud. He adopted the children of his brother Zhamso, who was killed in the war, and had two children of his own. In the farm, the three sons of his adopted son Kim lived nearby. His sister was married into the populous Tsybykdorzhi section of the Khatigan clan, the clan of the Party Secretary of the farm. These Khatigan brothers-in-law had good jobs in the farm, such as electrician and mechanic. His adopted daughter Mariya was married into the Yangut clan, the clan of the Chairman of the farm, Dorzhiyev. Her husband Buyantuyev had the very desirable job of head of the kolkhoz motor-park. This was an influential position, since the centralised structure of the farm required each brigade to apply to the central park for the vehicles, machines, and petrol they needed. Buyantuyev's goodwill was quite literally essential for any of the brigadiers to fulfil their production plans. Namzhilov's own current job as brigadier of the building brigade was perhaps particularly dependent on the availability of transport.

Namzhilov also had extensive kin relations through his wife (Figure 7.3). The extent of affinal kin connections recognised by people in the farm appears to have been as wide as that of one's own agnatic kin for the simple reason that people were known in groups, i.e. the local section of the patrilineage ('*-tang*'). Thus, for example, at Namzhilov's daughter Nadya's wedding all the members of her mother's agnatic group, including kin of the category *nagatsa* three generations distant, were invited. Her own relatively distant affinal kin (mother's father's sisters and their children) were also invited to the wedding. It is significant, however, that when she was giving the genealogy she did not mention these people by name, nor were their descendants listed. This is not because she did not know them, but because they ceased, on marriage, to be part of the agnatic group. The same principle was evident in the genealogy given to me by Namzhilov himself: he did not mention his kin through his sister, his adopted daughter Mariya, or his father's brother's son's daughter Balonsinimya. All of these people, however close to him they might have been in personal relations, were not members of his '*-tang*'. These parts of his genealogy were filled in by myself from information given by Mariya. Thus it is evident from these genealogies that

7.2. Genealogy of Tserenzhap Namzhilov, official in security and head of the building brigade in Karl Marx farm, Selenga, 1967.

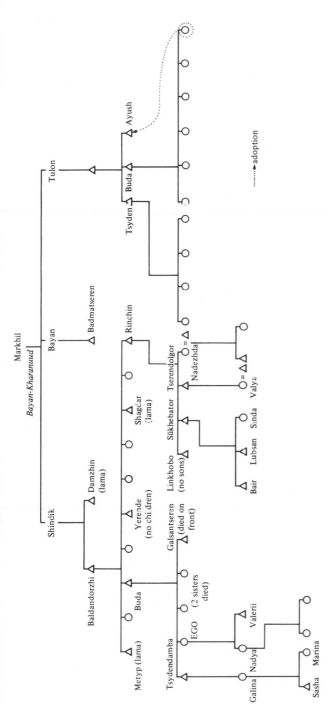

7.3. Genealogy of Dolzon Baldanovna Budayevna, wife of Tserenzhap Namzhilov, given 30 May 1967.

patriliny continues to operate as the cognitive principle of ordering kin relations, and this is despite the fact that in the Soviet period such agnatic kin-groups no longer function as units of residence and production. The kin relations actually most important in practical life, such as the link between Namzhilov and his son-in-law Buyantuyev, are not necessarily patrilineal, but it is by means of an existing patrilineal structure that they are defined.

A patrilineal classificatory kinship system of the Buryat type is capable of almost infinite extension, since it is possible to construct genealogies by which all Buryats are related to one another. In the pre-collectivisation kinship system the genealogies which people actually used differed between western and eastern Buryats, and in an article on this subject I related these differences to the functions of kinship in the organisation of production in the two areas (intensive agriculture in the case of the western Buryats, and extensive pastoralism in the case of the eastern Buryats).[54] In the kinship system of the present, the genealogies which are constructed depend, in their extent and 'shape', on a variety of adaptations to Soviet political economy.

Here it is necessary to make a distinction between several forms of kinship in the Soviet present of the Buryats. (1) Patrilineages which designate a place in Buryat society for every individual (see Chapter 8 section 1); (2) 'practical kinship, bilateral and with few generations depth, operated mostly by women (see Chapter 6); (3) the local descent group, traced to an ancestor about five generations back, called '-*tang*'; (4) agnatic links traced with important people in the wider society. The first two of these types are discussed elsewhere, but the latter two forms of kinship are directly relevant to political life in the farm.

In Chapter 3 I suggested that officials in the 'lineal' type of command structure attain their positions through personal social status, and I now wish to describe how this status is built up by means of kinship. The first type is manifest in the local networks conceptualised on the basis of the '-*tang*' (agnatic descendants of an ancestor between four and five generations distant from Ego). In practice these local descent groups are linked through marriage, and indeed the affinal relationships are crucial. I shall argue below that affinal kinship has come to be increasingly important in the Soviet period because it represents a difference of status between the two 'sides', and because, unlike agnatic kinship, affinal links are created with an element of choice.

The second form of kinship to be discussed in this chapter is manifest in extended genealogical operations, traced through the idea of patrilineal lineages and clans, which serve to link individuals or local descent groups with important personages outside the immediate circle of face-to-face relationships. Often such links are made with officials in the towns, and they bridge the rural—urban gap.

It is important to realise that, in contrast to the situation before collectivisation, none of these forms of kinship are based on productive units of the economy. Instead, their function is to 'deal with' the organisation of production as given by the Soviet system and outside people's control — in much the same way that kinship before collectivisation served to 'deal with' the exigencies of nature.

The greatly increased division and hierarchisation of labour of the Soviet period has made it necessary for the kinship system to represent individual interests. People now require, to a greater extent than before, to be able to choose which kin ties they wish to emphasise. At the same time, because of the lack until the late 1960s of state social security benefits, and because of the uncertainty of maintaining 'good' jobs in the kolkhoz, it has still been necessary to retain a basic network of unquestioned reliability. But those who wish to build up more substantial local networks — the aggressive, as opposed to defensive, version of local kinship, as it were — can do so by use of affinal links and other types of kinship-by-choice (adoption, serial marriage). It is these expanded '-*tang*' groups which give weight to claims of social status — and which, I suggest, are even necessary for officials of the farm to be able to perform the tasks of Chairman, brigadier, and so on, in the organisation of production.

At the same time, the second form of kinship, the widely ramified links with 'important people', is available for anyone who needs occasionally to bypass purely local officialdom, or who wishes simply to affirm in this way a more prestigious representation of himself or herself.

Let us look at an example of these kinds of kinship in operation. One typical example of the extended '-*tang*' was a section of the Kharanuud clan in the Selenga Karl Marx kolkhoz in the late 1960s. The head of the group was Batozhapov (age approximately 50), brigadier of the 1st brigade, and a member of the kolkhoz management committee. He had three younger brothers, all working in the kolkhoz at 'good' jobs: Dorzhitseren, a builder, another brother who was a tractor-driver in the 3rd brigade, and the youngest brother, Tsebukzhar, who was book-keeper to one of the tractor teams. There were also three sisters, two of whom were married to workers in the farm. The third lived in the nearby *raion* centre of Gusinoozersk. There were numerous offspring from all of these marriages. Batozhapov's father had died, but his mother, the *emegee* (grandmother) of the family, lived according to tradition with the youngest son, Tsebukzhar. Her younger brother, Bimba, also lived in Gusinoozersk. Batozhapov's patrilateral uncles and cousins in the kolkhoz were regularly visited. The group maintained close links with relatives of the *zee* category (classificatory sister's sons) who were 'doing well': Batozhapov's father's sister's daughter's sons, who had work in the Pedagogical Institute in Irkutsk and the Agricultural Institute in Ulan-Ude.

The members of the group living in the kolkhoz met one another almost every day. They tried to live as closely as possible to one another, although it had not been possible to build their houses actually adjacent. They met either at the house of the senior brother, Batozhapov, or where the grandmother lived, i.e. with the youngest brother, Tsebukzhar. Tsebukzhar said that the group frequently gave one another material help. The Kharanuud clan as a whole was not involved in this day-to-day reciprocity, but they felt themselves to be closer to one another than to members of other clans. On the occasion of a large wedding, all of the Kharanuud people living in the kolkhoz would be invited, as well as many from outside. At a smaller wedding only fifty or so of the Kharanuud would be invited.

The Kharanuud clan had several divisions in the kolkhoz and neighbouring areas, and they were sufficiently distant genealogically for marriage to be possible between them. Tsebukzhar had married a Kharanuud woman, Tselima (at first she said she did not remember her clan, so it may be that the marriage was felt to be slightly improper), and as a matter of curiosity I traced some of the affinal links which this marriage brought to the local kin-group. Tselima was one of sixteen children, all but four of whom had died in early childhood. Of the surviving brothers and sisters, one brother was killed in the war, and one sister had married a man living in Kyakhta town. The pride of the family was the second brother, Dugar, who was the editor of the Buryat-language newspaper *Buryaad Ünen* and was living in the ASSR capital of Ulan-Ude.

It is because Dugar appears in several genealogies that it is possible to see how really quite distant relationships are maintained by means of the extended patrilineal system. For example, one man who kept links with Dugar was Sanzha Lapilov, aged sixty in 1967, who was an ordinary meadow-worker (*lugovod*) and later a miller in the kolkhoz. Sanzha traced the link with Dugar by conceptualising three groups of Kharanuud people, each of them of five generations' depth, descended from three sons of Anda, who was consequently in the sixth generation ascending from himself. The relation with Dugar was, as Sanzha saw it, father's father's father's brother's son's son's son. In fact, the upper levels of this genealogy cannot have represented 'reality', because all of the extraneous people (e.g. women, men with no sons) were omitted in generations above that of Sanzha's own father.

The view that 'backward patriarchal relations' are maintained only among the people leading humble 'traditional' lives (shepherds, cattle-herders, etc.), which is frequently expressed by Soviet ethnographers,[55] is the reverse of the actual state of affairs. Shepherds and cattle-herders have rather few kin connections with officials, and their genealogies as volunteered to me were much less extensive than those of the ostensibly more progressive administrators. Only in very few cases did they extend further than five generations (from grandchildren of Ego to his/her grandparents) in depth, but commonly a wide range of bilateral kin in Ego's own generation was recognised. This is consistent with the use of kinship as a safety net by those who do not have ambitions of a political kind. It was interesting that in one or two of these families the patrilineal structure had almost completely disappeared: thus one shepherd, Lubsan Balzhinimayevich Ukhanayev, said that he belonged to the Ukhana-*tang*, and it emerged that Ukhana had five daughters (the descendants of whom were the -*tang*) and no sons at all (Figure 7.4). The members of the '-*tang*' in this case were related as *baza* (men married to sisters), a relationship of equality and intimacy. Men who are *baza* call one another by the informal *shi* and personal names, rather than *ta* and kinship terms.

In contrast with this modest variant of kinship, the construction of extended local kinship groupings can be seen on the one hand as strategic linkages made by people requiring the patronage of officials, and on the other hand as the deliberate creations of the big men themselves. These two kinds of manipulation of kinship are associated with a variety of deliberate kinship strategies, which, because they have 'political' aims beyond the reproduction of the kin-group itself, must allow the possibility of choice. The two most important of these strategies, and they are not unrelated to one another, are adoption, and the son-in-law/father-in-law relationship.

Adoption

Adoption in Buryat families no longer has the simple character of 'providing an heir' for the patriline which, by all accounts, was its main function before collectivisation. We find that today children are adopted by couples who already have their own offspring, including boys. Another intriguing fact is that most of the children who are adopted now are girls. In pre-collectivisation times by far the greatest number were boys.

One factor which Soviet writers sometimes use to explain the widespread adoption of recent decades is the very large number of Buryat men killed in the Second World War, their children thereby becoming orphans (and, we could add, the unknown number of people of both sexes who 'disappeared' in Stalinist times). Buryats fought as front-line troops on both the eastern and the western fronts, and literally every family among the kolkhozniks mentioned the names of men who had died. Epidemic diseases, particularly smallpox, were not controlled until some time after the war. It is thus true that there were many children of the immediate post-war period requiring care. But this does not explain

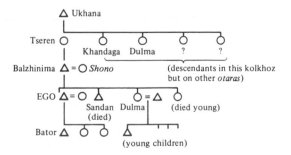

7.4. Genealogy of Lubsan Balzhinimayevich Ukhanayev, shepherd in 2nd *otara* of 3rd brigade, Karl Marx farm, Selenga, 1967. Question marks represent names I did not ask for, not names the informant had forgotten.

343

the pattern of adoption which I found in the collective farms: in the Selenga farm virtually every well-to-do family adopted, or brought up, children other than their own, and this has continued to be the case up to the 1960s—1970s, i.e. long after the problem of war orphans was over. In fact, even in wartime, only about half of the cases of adoption involved death of the natural parents. Children were *given* by arrangement, from one family to another.

Another explanation, brought forward by Vyatkina, the ethnographer of the Buryats from Leningrad, to explain the frequency of adoption among the Buryats concerns a belief that the adoption of outside children would prevent one's own children from becoming ill and dying.[56] She gives the example of one woman from the 'Krasniy Orongoy' kolkhoz who passionately tried to convince Vyatkina that all her children had suffered from various illnesses and finally died, until she adopted a daughter. Thereafter she had three children of her own, all of whom had survived, and she felt herself happy. However, in Buryat collective farms today the early death of children is becoming rare,[57] and it would be surprising if this belief, which incidentally was not mentioned to me, was the complete explanation of the practice of adoption. In particular, it does not explain the pattern of adoption among families in different positions in the division of labour in the farm.

In the farms I visited the great majority of the adopting parents already had children of their own (healthy, as far as I could tell). Vyatkina may have been closer to understanding the true reason for adoption today when she noted that the Chairman of the 'Tel'man' kolkhoz in Selenga district had adopted three children.[58] I would suggest that the primary reason for adoption is the desire to have a wide circle of kin, and in some cases the hope of acquiring control over labour resources in the abstract — that is, labour not for oneself, but embodied in positions in the division of labour which would function as complementary to one's own. In the case of adoption, this 'control' (for want of a better word) involves both the family from whom children are adopted, and later the children themselves. We would thus expect, as seems to be the case from my data, adoption to occur mainly into the families of men who are in the process of making careers as officials. Let us take the example of the Chairman of the Selenga Karl Marx kolkhoz, Zhamso Dorzhiyev.

Dorzhiyev is a member of the Yangut clan, but he comes from a junior branch — junior, that is, even in respect of that section of the Yangut which ended up in the Tashir area of Selenga (see Figure 7.5). Most of the Yanguts live to the west of Lake Baikal, and the senior line in Selenga, in the generation after the revolution, seems to have been headed by Dymbryl.[59] The fate of Dymbryl himself is not known (perhaps he was a *kulak*?), but he had four children, two boys and two girls, of whom Dorzhiyev adopted three (two girls and a boy). By this step Dorzhiyev was allying himself with a senior branch of his lineage, and relieving Dymbryl's brother, Dashnim, from the task of bringing up the children which would normally have fallen to him. If Dashnim's goodwill was earned in

344

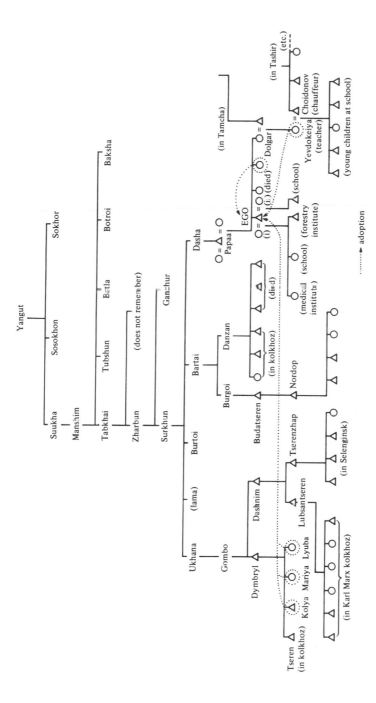

7.5. Genealogy of Zhamso Dorzhiyev, Chairman of Karl Marx kolkhoz, Selenga district. Given by Lyuba Dymbrylovna, 1 June 1967.

this way, this was later to Dorzhiyev's benefit, since Dashnim had numerous descendants who now work either in the kolkhoz or in the *raion* centre of Selenginsk. The eldest son of Dymbryl, Tseren, also works in the kolkhoz. The children adopted by Dorzhiyev were able to leave the farm for higher education and had very successful careers: the second son obtained a job as a publisher in Irkutsk, the older daughter Mariya became the chief planning economist of the kolkhoz, and the second daughter Lyuba went to medical school and subsequently became the head doctor in the hospital in the farm.

Dorzhiyev also had four children of his own. They also had or were likely to have successful careers. By his first wife he had a son, who was at forestry technical institute in 1967, a daughter at medical school in Ulan-Ude, and a daughter in the upper classes of secondary school. His second wife bore him a son, who was aged twelve in 1967. Also part of the Dorzhiyev household were his mother and a middle-aged sister who had not married. Apart from all these people, Dorzhiyev had also adopted another girl, Yevdokeiya, the daughter of his third sister. When I visited the farm Yevdokeiya had married and left home. She was married to a driver, a job with good pay, but she described herself as somewhat above this, as one of the local intelligentsia — which was true: she was a most educated and interesting woman with a wide knowledge of Buryat oral literature.

Dorzhiyev thus became the centre of a formidable network of kin. All of his adopted children, Kolya, Mariya, Lyuba, and Yevdokeiya, had higher education, and his own children were proceeding along the same path. Dorzhiyev, himself, as far as I know, had little education. It is significant that all of the children in Dorzhiyev's household had Russian names.

The Chairman's immediate kin thus provided him with people placed in the division of labour in complementary positions to himself: his adopted daughter was in the key job of planning economist (see Chapter 3 for importance of this position), his son-in-law was the chief zoo technician in a farm renowned for its livestock production, and his other daughters were usefully placed in the hospital and the school respectively. Other slightly more distant relatives provided representatives in the productive units of the farm: his agnatic kin, the children of Lubsantseren, Nordop, and Danzan, and his distant cousin Tseren, were all in the farm, and the numerous siblings, five brothers and some sisters, of his son-in-law Choidonov were also in 'good' jobs in the kolkhoz.

It is possible that this pattern of accretion of kin is a transformation, appropriate to the Soviet situation, of pre-revolutionary traditions. Certainly it was common in Buryat villages, long after the revolution, to continue to call kolkhoz or Soviet officials by the terms for traditional Buryat leaders. Tsydendambayev, a Buryat novelist, mentions the Chairman of a *sel'sovet* who was known as the *zaisan* (from the Chinese *tsai-hsiang*), a title used all over Mongolia for the chief of a clan.[60] In a novel which appears to be an accurate representation of Buryat speech, officials in general are called *noyon* (Bur. 'lord'). Although one of the *noyon*s was actually unlike anything seen before in the village — she was a woman Soviet official — attitudes to traditional leaders seem to have persisted along with the word. 'Who would ever have thought I would live to see the day when I would have to accept a woman *noyon* . . . but better not ask her about my troubles, if she's a *noyon* that means she's short-tempered, and everyone knows an angry *noyon* is dangerous . . . '[61] Today, kolkhozniks tend to use Russian rather than Buryat terms for official positions.

It is possible that the existence in Buryat culture of agnatically structured kinship groups may provide one explanation of the continued desire among Buryats to have very large families (see also Chapter 1 section 6). The birth-rates among Buryats are significantly higher than those of the RSFSR as a whole,[62] and are similar to those found in the Central Asian republics of the USSR. The peoples of these republics, Uzbeks, Turkoman, Tadjiks, Kazakhs, etc., also retain patrilineal kinship structures of a kind similar to the Buryat. It appears that such structures are used in economic, and perhaps especially political, manoeuvring complementary to the Soviet organisation of society. Among the Buryats heads of lineages are clearly recognised and the indices of seniority within them are renewed each year at the *tsagaalgan* ceremony (see Chapter 8). The lack of such structures of authority in Russian kinship may go some way towards explaining why Russian kolkhozniks, in similar economic and political conditions of Soviet organisation, do not tend to have such large families. Among Russians, the *rod*, a group of related households of the '*-tang*' type through which control could be exercised by means of an agnatic structure of authority, has ceased to exist, and there have been no clans for some centuries. Thus, while it is still true that the crucial resource in Russian kolkhozy is labour — as I believe in all Soviet collective farms — Russians would not turn in the first place to *kinship* as a means of gaining control over labour or establishing ethnic identity.

The son-in-law/father-in-law relationship

This relationship is voluntary in a sense that the relation with the son is not. Through the twentieth century this voluntary aspect has become more important in Buryat kinship as marriage has ceased to be initiated by lineage elders of the senior generation.

The son-in-law/father-in-law relationship also implies a distinct status difference, arising not only from the difference in generation but also from the precedence accorded to the givers of wives over the receivers (see Chapter 1 section 4). It is the combination of status difference with individual choice which makes this relation significant. Thus, other kinship relations which have only one of these characteristics, for example, the relation between mother's brother and sister's son (*nagatsa/zee*) which implies status difference but is not voluntary, are not equally important in present-day Buryat kinship.

From what has been said above it is apparent that, although Buryat women now have the opportunity to take up political careers, in general it is still the case that relations between men dominate this type of strategy. In fact, relatively few women have important positions in kolkhoz or *raion* committees.[63]

In the pre-collectivisation period the son-in-law was seen in popular culture as equivalent to a servant, especially if he lived with his father-in-law:

Khürgen khübüün
Khülhenshe khün khoyor adli

The son-in-law and
The hired worker are similar.

Khürgen khübüün tuhaa üzüülkhe
Khürin ükher khüsöö kharuulkha

The son-in-law is useful to you,
The brown ox brings you brute strength.[64]

This attitude seems to continue, but now the son-in-law himself has some say in where his 'usefulness' is to be placed. It must be the case in present Soviet society that it is not so much the father-in-law who chooses his son-in-law (although he still has a strong influence on his daughter) as the reverse: an ambitious young man will seek marriage with the daughter of an important man.

It is not, of course, possible for me to impute motives in the cases of the marriages on which I have field-work data. The limited conversations I had with the people involved would make such interpretation on my part invidious. Nevertheless, in the purely factual terms of who married whom and the political positions of the people involved in a whole series of cases, it is possible to see certain patterns.

As an example, let us take the case of Budatseren Pubayev, if only for the reason that we have already mentioned his career in the Party (see p. 336). Pubayev left the army in 1944, before the war ended, and went to the Selenga district as a Secretary in the *raion* Komsomol. At this point, his future father-in-law, Babasa Tsedenov, was chairman in the Selenga Karl Marx kolkhoz. Pubayev married Tsedenov's daughter, Natasha, in 1945, and shortly afterwards became Party Secretary in his father-in-law's farm. Tsedenov was moved to the Kalinin kolkhoz in 1946 (when Dorzhiyev took over in Karl Marx), and a year or so later, Pubayev was nominated Party Secretary in Kalinin too. For reasons unknown, Pubayev was removed from that position in 1950 and returned to the Karl Marx in the relatively lowly position of book-keeper. Subsequently, he became Chairman of the *sel'sovet* in the Karl Marx, a position which as we have seen is a weak one in relation to the kolkhoz management. Pubayev, however, retained his close links with his father-in-law, now retired from the Chairmanship of Kalinin, and used to make visits to that kolkhoz at least every month, and also sent his children there for extended visits. From these facts, it does look as though Pubayev rose through the initial patronage of his father-in-law Tsedenov, and for a number of years the two worked together as Chairman of the kolkhoz and Party Secretary respectively. As we have seen, and Hough also confirms, the

348

holders of these offices in a collective farm are likely to work in tandem. It is quite probable that Pubayev's demotion in 1950 coincided with the retirement of his father-in-law as Chairman.

It would be tedious to recount other cases of politically significant father-in-law/son-in-law relationships in detail. In any case, I do not have enough data to make any numerically based conclusion. However, the material suggests that there is a pattern to such affinal relations in respect of the jobs fulfilled by the people concerned: the son-in-law does not work for his father-in-law directly, i.e. he does not take a lower position within any of the 'lineal' hierarchies. Rather the son-in-law is placed in some position which is complementary to that of the father-in-law, usually a position vital to the father-in-law's concerns but over which he would otherwise have only precarious control. For example:

Father-in-law	*Son-in-law*
Dorzhiyev, Chairman of kolkhoz	Batorov, chief zoo technician, responsible to Ministry of Agriculture
Namzhilov, head of building brigade	Buyantuyev, head of transport section
Tsedenov, Chairman of kolkhoz	Pubayev, Party Secretary of kolkhoz

Virtually all of the political leaders in Buryat kolkhozy with whose biographies I became acquainted held their positions with extreme insecurity of tenure. Dorzhiyev, who held the job of Chairman of the Selenga Karl Marx for twenty years, was very exceptional in this respect — but even he was ousted in the period between my two visits to Buryatiya (1967 to 1974). In order to have any control over jobs at the enterprise level — including one's own job if one is, say, a kolkhoz Chairman — it is necessary to be able to exert influence at the *raion* level. As we have seen, the acquiring of such influence is an uncertain, even risky, business, and it would probably be true to say that most local officials lack such influence for most of the time. Hence, the political aspect of the relation with the father-in-law cannot be seen as anything permanent or secure, since either of the two parties to the relationship is likely to be switched into some other position with no possible redress. The relation, from the subjective point of view, represents simply a possibility of political alliance, which it may, or may not, be possible to exploit at any one time.

This can be seen from looking at the vagaries of the career of a typical local official. The account translated below was given to me in written form by the man concerned. When I asked him for details of his life history he replied that it was 'too complicated', and I imagined that this was the end of the matter. However, the next day he came round with a carefully typed 'autobiography'. Synge Darmayev was a pensioner in the Barguzin Karl Marx farm by the time I visited the kolkhoz in 1974. He lived with his wife and an ancient 'aunt', who had been married to one of the pioneers of the revolutionary movement in Barguzin.

This 'aunt' must have been a fairly distant relative: at any rate, when I asked her for a genealogy beginning with the most senior ancestor she remembered, instead of tracing the ancestors down to herself she started with the founder of the Butuma-Shono clan and then without faltering filled in every single name in the branches senior to her own; this meant that, after an hour, we had still not come to her own section, still less that of Synge, who must have come from some other, junior branch. I remember being both surprised and irritated by this, and after I had asked her about her own branch, which was five generations distant, as it turned out, from the people she had been describing in such detail, I gave up taking genealogies on that occasion. This was a mistake, because it means that I have no genealogical data on Synge's family. However, I mention this moment of bad ethnographic practice because it does illustrate two things: firstly, the truly amazing ramifications of kin which Buryat kolkhozniks remember, and secondly, the *ordering* of genealogical memory by seniority in the male line. This latter point may perhaps be correlated with the tendency to forget lines junior to Ego's own, as can be seen from consulting the various genealogies given in this chapter.

Autobiography
I, Synge Sanzhiyevich Darmayev, who was born on 1 September 1911 in the *ulus* of Karlik, Barguzin district, Buryat ASSR, in the family of a middling-rich peasant. Up to the age of ten I grew up with my parents. In 1921 I went to the Karalik school from which I graduated in 1925.

From the time of leaving school, right up to 1931, I worked in my father's household. Then I entered the kolkhoz 'Urzhil' in the Bayangol *sel'sovet*.

From May 1931 to March 1932 I worked as an accountant in the 'Urzhil' kolkhoz. From March 1932 to May 1932 I was the Chairman of the 'Urzhil' kolkhoz. From 1932 to April 1939 I worked as an accountant in the Karl Marx kolkhoz, Bayangol *sel'sovet*. From April 1939 until November 1939 I was the Chairman of the Bayangol *sel'sovet*.

From November 1939 to April 1940 I was Chairman of the auditing commission of the Karl Marx kolkhoz.

From April 1940 to July 1940 I was Secretary of the Komsomol committee in the Karl Marx kolkhoz. From July 1940 to November 1940 I worked as Director of the Kuitun machine—tractor station. From November 1940 to August 1941 I was Chairman of the Karl Marx kolkhoz. From August 1941 to February 1945 I served in the ranks of the Soviet army, and from August 1941 to February 1942 I served as an officer (*v komande*) of the evacuation hospital in Ulan-Ude. From February 1942 to March 1943, by the fault of the investigatory officials of the Ministry of State Security (MGB) of the Buryat ASSR, I was in an internal (*vnutrennaya*) prison in Ulan-Ude. Subsequently the charge was dropped and I was rehabilitated, was not excluded from the ranks of the Party, and bore no legal responsibility for what had happened. From March to July 1943 I served in the 67th Artillery Regiment at Olovyannaya Station in Chita *oblast'*. From June 1943 to February 1945 I was one of a special group for obtaining food provisions for the partisan groups working behind German lines in the Belorussian partisan movement.

After demobilisation from the Soviet army I returned to my home kolkhoz, and I worked from February 1945 to February 1948 as a book-keeper in the Karl Marx kolkhoz. From February 1948 to November 1948 I was the Vice-Chairman of the kolkhoz, and then, from February 1948 to January 1951 I was elected Chairman of the Karl Marx kolkhoz. From January 1951 to April 1951 I worked as an ordinary kolkhoznik. From April 1951 to December 1955 I was an accountant in the kolkhoz. From December 1955 to July 1961 I was the Party Secretary in the kolkhoz. From July 1961 to the present [July 1967] I have been the planning-economist of the Karl Marx kolkhoz. I have been a member of the Communist Party since 1940. I entered the Komsomol in 1931. I have the following honours:

1. The order 'Znak Pocheta' (Sign of Honour).
2. The medal 'Za Pobedu nad Germaniyei v Velikoi Otechestvennoi voyne 1941—5 gg' (For the Victory over Germany in the Great Patriotic War 1941—5).
3. The medal 'Za Osvoyeniye Tselinnykh i Zalezhnykh Zemel' (For the Opening up of Virgin and Fallow Lands).
4. Jubilee medal '20 let Pobedy v Velikoi Otechestvennoi voyne 1941—5 gg' (20th Anniversary of the Victory in the Great Patriotic War).
5. The medal 'Za Doblestnyy trud v Velikoi Otechestvennoi voyne 1941—5 gg' (For Valiant Labour in the Great Patriotic War).
6. The medal 'Za Doblestnyy trud v oznamenovaniye 100-letiya V.I. Lenina' (For Valiant Labour in Commemoration of the 100th anniversary of V.I. Lenin).
7. The medal '50 let Vooruzhennykh Sil SSSR' (50 years of the Armed Forces of the USSR).
8. Two Honourable Diplomas (*pochetnyye gramoty*) of the Praesidium of the Supreme Soviet of the Buryat ASSR, 1948 and 1961.
9. Three Diplomas of the Barguzin *raion* committee of the Communist Party and the *aimispolkom*.

My family position is: my wife is Dulma Muzhanova Lamuyeva, born in 1917, and my daughter is Svetlana Syngeyevna **Darmayeva**, born in 1957.

27 December 1974, Bayangol.

Darmayev's autobiography shows the extreme insecurity of an official's life: things go well for a time and it appears that a career is being made by moving up the rungs of the ladder (book-keeper, Vice-Chairman, Chairman), but there is the ever-present possibility of some fall right down the snake to the bottom ('I worked as an ordinary kolkhoznik'). From Dymbrenov's history is it possible to infer that the reason for Darmayev's downfall was non-fulfilment of the livestock products quotas in the 1950 plan. Darmayev was replaced by Ochirov, who was moved from the Ulyun *kolkhoz im. Kirova* to become Chairman of Karl Marx, but as we know (see Chapter 4 section 1) within three years Ochirov had been severely criticised for mishandling the amalgamation with the *kolkhoz im. Kalinina* and was replaced himself in 1954.[65]

To summarise this section on political strategies in a kolkhoz with the 'lineal' type of command structure: kinship ties appear to provide officials with a group of people on whom they can rely while in office, but it may be even more important that kinsmen also provide a safety network on the occasion of a downfall. The latter function of kinship is necessary for everyone, while the former applies only to the ambitious and enterprising. The establishing of a kin network for an official is perhaps necessary, but not sufficient. In particular, as

351

we have seen, kinship relations are not much help in either establishing or renewing ties with the *raion*. Since it is the *raion* which is responsible for the appointment and dismissal of officials, we have to look for some other strategies by which people seek to influence these decisions.

I shall argue that there are three main avenues for advancement which can be analytically distinguished from kinship strategies — though in practice they tend to work in conjunction with them. These are: (a) getting oneself into a position where one is able to do hard work which is recognised (the recognition is essential); (b) the building of 'political capital' by means of 'social work' (*obshchestvennaya rabota*); and (c) the acquiring of educational or technical qualifications. The last of these modes of advancement is noticeably more prominent in farms of the 'specialist' type, such as the Barguzin Karl Marx kolkhoz, and I shall therefore briefly describe the official political structure of this farm before returning to a discussion of the strategies of operation within it.

Political strategies in the 'specialist' command structure

If we look at the membership of the three important committees in the Barguzin farm in 1974–5 (Table 7.7) we notice immediately several significant differences from the Selenga kolkhoz. In Barguzin the kolkhoz committee and the Party committee overlapped in membership (in 1974) just as they did in the Selenga farm. In Barguzin, however, the Party committee was considerably larger. Party and Soviet committees also overlapped in membership; this in fact is the case right through the hierarchy of the USSR, and in this respect the kolkhoz can be seen as a microcosm of Soviet society as a whole.

In theory, the fact that the Party committee is supposed to be more unanimous than the kolkhoz committee should give the Party the upper hand. This should be especially the case in a farm such as Barguzin Karl Marx, where Party representation on the kolkhoz committee is in a majority (in Selenga it was in a minority). However, the tendency towards formal domination by the Party is counteracted by the interest group of the Chairman, as we saw from the Selenga farm. In Barguzin, however, the Chairman is surrounded by the chief specialists, all of whom are represented on the kolkhoz committee. As already pointed out, the Chairman not only has less formal control over specialists than he does over his brigadiers, but he also may be challenged by their possession of specialist knowledge. The Chairman is thus perhaps in a weaker position in a 'specialist' farm than he is in a 'lineal' farm — although a great deal depends on personality. The Chairman *can* make life impossible for specialists (or anyone) on the farm if he does not get on well with them, for example by refusing to grant their requests, failing to distribute firewood and other things to them, and so on. On the other hand, Chairmen may come and go, while the specialists remain. This is what happened in the Barguzin Karl Marx kolkhoz. The Chairman in 1974–5,

Table 7.7. *Composition of committees in Karl Marx kolkhoz, Barguzin district, 1974*

Kolkhoz committee	Party committee	Sel'sovet committee
*Lubsanov, Bato Budayevich (Chairman; delegate to *raikom*)	*Garmayev, Vasilii Yenkhoyev (Secretary; delegate to *raikom*)	Timunova, Galina Semenova (Chairwoman)
*Montoyev, Buda Gatapovich (Vice-Chairman)	*Lubsanov, Bato Budayevich (Chairman of kolkhoz)	Lubsanova (Secretary)
*Garmayev, Vasilii Yenkhoyev (Party Secretary; delegate to *raikom*)	*Montoyev, Buda Gatapovich (Vice-Chairman of kolkhoz)	Radnayeva Sabkhandayev (driver)
*Chimidtserenov (chief engineer; head of People's Control)	*Chimidtserenov (chief engineer; head of People's Control)	*Radnayev, Dygvid (Secretary of Komsomol)
*Rinchinov, Bator Ayusheyevich (chief zoo technician)	*Radnayev, Anatolii Khaptagayevich (OTF 3 Brigadier)	*Radnayev, Anatolii Khaptagayevich (OTF 3 Brigadier)
*Garmayev, B-M.Ts. (chief agronomist)	*Garmayev, B-M.Ts. (chief agronomist)	Badmayev (head of *Dom Kul'tur*)
Dorzheyev, Batorzhargal Shadopovich (chief veterinarian)	Bubeyev (MTF 1 Brigadier)	
Rinchinov, Vladimir Batozhapovich (chief economist)	Sangadiyeva, Ol'ga (shepherdess; delegate to *obkom*)	
Tsydipov, Solbon Shairopovich (chief accountant)	*Rinchinov, Bator Ayusheyevich (chief zoo technician)	
	*Radnayev, Dygvid (Secretary of Komsomol)	

*Party Committee members who are members of other committees.

Bato Budayevich Lubsanov, was no longer in his post in 1980, but several of the chief specialists were still in place.

In the Barguzin kolkhoz, the *sel'sovet*, headed by Galina Tumunova, a pleasant middle-aged woman who did not belong to the Party, seems to have been more active than the *sel'sovet* in Selenga. This may have been partly the result of central government instructions to increase activity of the Soviets around 1970 (the Barguzin material refers to 1974–5, whereas I was in Selenga in 1967). However, it is more likely that the Barguzin farm was lucky enough simply to have an enthusiastic person who agreed to take the job. It is not the case that all people in responsible positions are urged to join the Party. The Party is supposed to provide 'leading cadres', and this does imply that there are and should be others who hold a variety of opinions. In the Barguzin farm people were pleased to be able to emphasise to me that a non-Party woman (*bezpartiinaya*) was in an important position. In fact, she could perhaps better play her role as caring social worker and general tidier-up of messes (this seems to be the main function of the local Soviets) as a non-Party member. The fact that women were important in the *sel'sovet* in both kolkhozy is also not an accident. Women in public life are allowed a greater emphasis on emotions, on charm, and the human aspect of problems than are men.

Under Lubsanov, the quiet and serious Chairman and a graduate veterinarian, and Tumunova the Barguzin kolkhoz seemed a distinctly more 'modern' place than the Karl Marx in Selenga. Let us look now at the ways in which people attain prominence in the farm other than strategies involving the Buryat kinship system.

The recognition of 'hard work'

In a collective farm, because of the use of numerical indicators and the piece-work system, it is easy to measure the 'work' of one kolkhoznik against another (indeed this is one of the main reasons for using such a system). The Party Secretary in Barguzin told me that he saw it as one of the main duties of his office to look out for people who were working well, who volunteered for hard jobs, and showed initiative in tasks which the management regarded as important. These people's photographs appear on the 'honour board' outside the kolkhoz committee room, articles are written about them in the local newspaper, and, on the recommendation of the primary Party cell, the *raion* or even the ASSR authorities may award them a diploma or medal. Work-teams, brigades, and also the kolkhoz itself can be awarded such insignia too.

What do these signs of 'hard work' (or war service in the case of military medals) bring to the holders? Orders and medals used to confer extensive privileges, but the nature of these, and also the number given out, has varied at different times in Soviet history. A 'Hero of Socialist Labour' meant far more in the pre-war period than it did later, for example. From 1930 until 1947 the following three orders brought a string of advantages: the Order of Lenin, the

Red Banner of Labour, and the military medal of the Red Star. The advantages included:[66]

(1) The number of years' labour required to attain full pension rights was reduced by one third;
(2) Each holder was entitled to a subsidy of 30 rubles a month (with an extra 25 rubles for a second order or more);
(3) In the event of unemployment, the holder was entitled to priority in job placement;
(4) The children of holders were accepted into higher educational institutions (*VUZy*) on the same favourable terms as the children of ordinary workers (as opposed to children with white collar backgrounds);
(5) Holders were entitled to free bus and tram tickets.

Large numbers of medals, including civilian ones such as the Order of Lenin, were given during the war. The only title to retain some exclusivity in this period was the 'Hero of Socialist Labour', which was awarded to only twelve persons in two-and-a-half years during the war. But in the post-war years, it too acquired a mass character, being awarded to 17,704 persons between 1946 and 1957.[67] During the early period many of these awards were associated with large cash grants. Thus, in the Barguzin Karl Marx farm during the war, the farm itself was awarded a Diploma of the First Degree, carrying with it a prize of a car and 10,000 rubles, and the pig unit in the farm obtained a Diploma of the Second Degree, with a prize of 5,000 rubles. Individual kolkhozniks received medals such as the Small Gold Medal of the All-Union Economic Exhibition or the medal 'For Outstanding Labour'. These must have carried money prizes with them, because we read in Dymbrenov's history of the farm that these very same people later donated huge sums of their personal money to the War Fund. For example, D. Linkhoyev, who obtained the medal 'For Outstanding Labour', donated 30,000 rubles to the War Fund.[68] It is not really possible that he could have earned this money simply from wages. At this time the average kolkhoznik worked 200 labour-days a year in the Karl Marx farm, and even someone who worked very hard indeed, 700 labour-days a year, could earn only 2,000 rubles and 54 poods of grain.[69] If we recall some of the procedures by which 'donations' were made to the War Fund,[70] one is tempted to conclude that what the state gave with one hand, it took away with the other.

In decrees of December 1947 and July 1951 most of the material advantages associated with awards were removed. Khrushchev, furthermore, greatly reduced the number of decorations given out. He forbade the making of awards for long service, rather than for concrete achievements. The next important shift in policy was introduced by Brezhnev in 1967, when 'Heroes of Socialist Labour' were suddenly granted a whole series of benefits: priority in housing, extra room, reduced rent, free transport, free sojourn at a rest home, etc. The lesser medals, orders and diplomas, however, remained as simply honorary distinctions.

At the collective farms the medal-holders had a completely different kind of

355

career from the Party officials. This does not mean to say that people with decorations were not frequently members of the Party, nor that Party officials were devoid of honorary awards. But the typical medal-holder was a hard worker in a definite job, someone with extraordinarily good milking figures or a diligent tractor-driver. These people were often mentioned in the newspapers, their medals and decorations attached to their names like titled ('Honoured Shepherd of the Buryat ASSR So-and-So'), and therefore we have no difficulty in finding out who they are. What emerges is that the medal-holders *per se* almost never have positions of real power. Sometimes they are deputies to the *sel'sovet*, sometimes they are Party members, or even delegates to Party conferences, but very rarely do they sit on the executive committees of any of these organisations. In other words, they do not have careers in politics.

As an example, we can cite an elderly woman from the Selenga farm called Butyd Batuyeva, 'senior shepherdess' and the holder of many diplomas and awards. She was a delegate to the 22nd Party Conference and had been given at one stage the prize of a 'Moskvich' car — the only kolkhoznik to have such a valuable possession in 1967. But she was not on any committee. It is noticeable that many of these outstanding workers are women, though not exclusively so. To a great extent the privileges to be gained from being a medal-holder depend on the personality of the man or woman concerned. These days, I was told, even the statutory advantages do not automatically follow from holding a decoration. But if someone pushes himself forward, declaring on every occasion, *Ya ordenonosets!* ('I am an award-holder'), he can expect to obtain advantages ranging from the relatively trivial — first place in queues, free cinema tickets — to the comparatively significant — representation at Party conferences or congresses of the Soviet. Some of these devoted workers push for every advantage, and some get taken up by the authorities, as we saw for example with Voinovich's satirical account of the celebrity milkmaid (see Chapter 5 section 1). They give lectures, conduct newspaper interviews, and even have books written about them. A shepherdess in the Barguzin Karl Marx farm, Sh.L. Tsyrempilova, was the subject of a small book in Buryat describing her herding and breeding techniques.[71] A very few manage to convert recognition as workers into political influence: one such person was Ol'ga Sangadiyeva, a shepherdess in the Barguzin Karl Marx, who was holder of the Order of Lenin (one of the highest decorations in the Soviet Union) and the Sign of Honour. She was on the kolkhoz Party committee, a delegate to the *raion* Party conference in 1975, and a delegate to the ASSR (*oblast'*) Party conference in the following year. But many lead very modest lives and simply get on with the job. As far as I could judge, the diplomas and medals are awarded impartially, for work done, assessed on the standard criteria for the particular job, e.g. for a shepherd the number of lambs and weight of wool per 100 sheep.

For many jobs (e.g. milkmaid) these figures are presented to the authorities not by the worker himself or herself but by the team-leader (see Chapter 5 section 1), and it is therefore necessary to have the goodwill of one's immediate boss if one is to hope for recognition. But even more risky than this is the material situation of the worker in the job (see pp. 233–58). It is known that every farm has its carefully fostered production teams, just as every *raion* has, or tries to have, its model kolkhoz. It is much more difficult to become a recognised 'vanguard' worker if one belongs to a disadvantaged, or even just an ordinary, team. Other workers on the team, with no such ambitions, often greatly resent people who try to excel, since good results encourage the authorities to raise the norms for the job.[72]

As important as advantageous material conditions of production are the transmission of skills and a devoted attitude to work. But 'work' here is defined in a particular way. It refers to attaining the indicators for the job (100 lambs from 100 ewes, for example), not to native Buryat concepts of accomplishing the task well (see Chapter 5 section 1 for discussion of this point). A 'devoted attitude to work' thus in effect means a particular attitude to the Soviet organisation of production, a trust in the higher and more general advantages of attaining the indicators as contrasted with the evidence of one's own eyes. This is why so much Soviet writing on agriculture also now stresses the worker's *honesty* and *initiative*, i.e. care for the task as a whole, not simply the indicators. But nevertheless, it is in fact the indicators which are used to assess workers. Thus we find in collective farms, alongside the agnatic kinship groups which have already been discussed, 'dynasties' of workers who have cultivated the necessary attitudes and techniques. Such 'dynasties' are much encouraged by the authorities. On occasion they are composed of kin, but just as often they are not. It is not therefore surprising to find that Tsyrempilova's famous shepherding team in the Barguzin Karl Marx farm consisted of herself, her husband, her daughter, and the unrelated Ol'ga Sangadiyeva (the holder of the order of Lenin mentioned above). Tsyrempilova had taken Sangadiyeva under her wing as a young girl and taught her the methods of sheep-farming in a crack production team together with Ol'ga's daughter, Raisa. That was during the late 1960s. By 1975, Ol'ga Sangadiyeva was already training young people in the same techniques, and we find that Dusya Badmayeva, who was appointed at such an early age to be 'senior shepherdess' of another team, was one of her trainees.[73] By 1975, Dusya herself had been awarded the decoration 'Valiant Labour' by the central committee of the Komsomol and she was a *sel'sovet* and *oblast'* Komsomol delegate.

In a sense the medals and diplomas which are the signs of hard work are not so much goals of individual kolkhozniks as the results of conditions already created. We have seen how little ordinary workers are in control of their conditions of production. One had the feeling in the kolkhoz that it was almost known in advance who would be decorated. Certainly the honour board, with its row of tattered photographs, had no names attached to the portraits, and its abandoned air may have owed as much to the lack of information conveyed as to the Siberian winds.

Politics in the collective farm

What can we conclude from this discussion of the insignia of hard work? People who are prepared to toil in the collective economy and according to its criteria of success are rewarded in a relatively impartial way, but whether they turn this to any political advantage is largely a matter of personal ambition — which, by itself, in many cases would make use of some other strategy. A Soviet friend told me that most people who work in an average but honest way can expect to end up with one or two 'honourable diplomas'. These are of use in everyday life when people need to demonstrate social reliability, for example when making complaints to the bureaucracy, or when they become involved in law suits, or when they need testimonials of good character. But real devotion and some expertise is required to obtain the high honours such as 'Hero of Socialist Labour'. Even so, not all of these people are motivated towards political activity — it is not everyone who wants to become involved in lengthy political meetings, committee work, and political intrigue. Yet for others, these activities are like a drug, as one informant said, and these people cannot bear to be left out of decision-making procedures, the checking of other people's work, making 'responsible' reports on slackers, or left bereft of the latest Party news. The 'visible hard work' strategy is certainly one way into the local political arena. But few, it may be said, try to consolidate their position by taking political courses, attending Party schools, and becoming agitators and propagandists in a serious way. This is already another kind of activity altogether, and one which may be pursued without the initial back-breaking toil of the front-line worker.

Party and other committees are carefully weighted in composition. There has to be a certain proportion of ordinary workers on each committee, as opposed to the 'line' officials and Party bureaucrats who make up the majority. This is true even of committees at the *oblast'* and republic level. It appears that it is the order- and medal-holders who are used to make up these numbers. They are living evidence of 'grass-roots' participation (see, for example, composition of Barguzin *raion* Party conference, Table 7.5). Every one of the 'ordinary workers' on the *raikom* was a laureate of some high award. But not a single one of them was a member of either of the two inner circles of the *raikom*, the bureau and the plenum. The prize-winning workers become themselves like emblems of the Workers' State; their chests shining with medals and decorations, they attend congresses, listen to speeches, and vote for prepared lists of candidates. But the control, even in local politics, tends to lie in other hands.

The creation of 'political capital'

The list of official posts, for which Party approval must be granted before personnel changes can be made, is the Party's *nomenklatura*. In the case of a *raion* this would include positions such as Chairman of a collective farm, officials of the *sel'sovet*, director of a forestry production enterprise, etc. The word *nomenklatura* applies also to the people who are listed for such jobs. But in order to try to guarantee that the Party organs pay attention to other personnel, each Party organisation is given a second list of positions, the *uchetnaya nomenklatura* (the 'reporting' list). The Party committee's confirmation is not required when changes are made in positions on its *uchetnaya nomenklatura*, but it must be informed of any changes in them. As Hough says, 'The purpose of this list is to keep each Party organ acquainted with a secondary group of officials in the area, so that it can "study these people attentively", "follow their growth", and "create a reserve fund from which to promote new officials".'[74] People do not necessarily know if they are on this list.

Below the *uchetnaya nomenklatura* are the people who have ambitions, the 'activists' and 'agitators'. Most of them are members of the Party, but some may pursue more limited political careers through the Soviets. At the real grass-roots level are those people who are searching for recognition as politically reliable workers, or who genuinely feel responsibility for their community and identify the only structure by which this can be expressed with the Party and its activists. Several people said to me: 'There are many things which should be changed in our society, but the only way to do this is by joining the Party, by making the Party *better*.'

In the Barguzin Karl Marx kolkhoz in 1975 there were 119 members of the Party and 10 candidate members (out of a total population of 2,126).[75] The kolkhoz Party organisation was divided into eight brigade organisations, each with its own Secretary. The Komsomol had 135 members, with a committee of nine. After the age of twenty-eight people are eligible to apply to join the Party. The agitators, who are often also lower officials such as brigadiers or heads of production teams, are required to give a report (*otchet*) each month to the Party committee, listing the problems of their unit, who is working well, who badly, who is 'unreliable', who attends religious ceremonies, even problems of people's personal lives. Some Party activists are given a lecturing brief, i.e. several papers on political subjects which they should read in various units of the farm (*putevka politinformatora*). They note the reaction to the lecture and report on 'positive' as well as 'negative' questions from the audience. About once a month there is a 'Day of the Lecturer' (*den' lektora*), when someone is sent from the *raikom* to give a talk on more weighty political subjects (international politics, the latest plenum, Brezhnev's visit to Mongolia, etc.). Members of the Party are expected to join in 'voluntary' labour, to organise activities at the cultural club, to run local newssheets, etc. All of this is called 'social work' (*obshchestvennaya rabota*), and as a rule it is not paid. Members of the Party can easily find virtually every evening taken up with activities of this kind.

Party members and young people who are members of Komsomol are also frequently asked to take on particularly arduous jobs of ordinary farmwork. One milkmaid told me that because she was a Party member she was asked to take on one especially decrepit group of cows which none of the other women would agree to touch. She had made a success of this job and in a year the cows were giving as much milk as the others. Thus, although such tasks are sometimes simply allocated with production in mind, they are also frequently 'social work' in themselves — an example to others, and a step towards expansion of the 'political capital' of the worker.

It should be noted that volunteering for such a task, or even simply agreeing to take it on, can reverse the negative 'political capital' incurred by making some mistake. In other words, this kind of work is the obverse of the liability to which all Soviet citizens are subject. The local newspapers often report on stories of this type: 'He was careless and lazy and was dismissed as brigadier, . . . but then he changed his attitude, and by his honest work as a cowhand proved . . . ' It is the Party which directs people to such jobs, which takes note of their achievements, and which informs the newspaper if the experiment is a success.

Sociological studies of the 'social work' undertaken by young people in various rural occupations indicate that administrators and specialists take on most such tasks and stockmen least. Party members do more 'social work' than Komsomol members, and the latter do more than people who have no connection with the Party.[76]

In the Barguzin Karl Marx kolkhoz, besides the Party itself, there were a variety of other organisations which came under the *sel'sovet*, but which in effect carried out Party activities:

(1) The Women's Soviet (*zhensovet*) consisting of five activists, whose task was encouraging women to work, combating slackness and drunkenness;

(2) The People's Militia (*narodnaya druzhina*), consisting of thirty activists, whose task was to make checks on villages, work-places, the clubs, etc., searching for cases of illegality, thieving, drunkenness, fighting, broken equipment, littered streets, etc.;

(3) The People's Court (*tovarishchestvennyi sud*), consisting of seven people, who made judgements in cases of illegality;

(4) The People's Control (*narodnyi kontrol'*), with twenty-one members, whose job was to check illegalities and inefficiencies in production (see discussion in Chapter 2 section 4);

(5) The *agitbrigad*, consisting of from seven to fifteen people, who were responsible for putting on propaganda-type lectures, plays, and concerts.

Work on any of these committees counts as 'social work' and can be used to create a reputation for reliability and enthusiasm in the eyes of the Party. The expression 'morally stable' (*moral'no ustoichiv*) is used in recommendations for people who prove themselves in this way.

Another type of 'social work' is acting as course organiser (*kursant*) for political-military studies after school hours. It is reported that inexperienced social workers avoid this task for fear of getting things wrong, the danger of shipwreck (*proval*) in the turbulent waters of current policy.[77] A safer and widespread form of 'social work' in the kolkhoz is to give talks on the farm internal radio, which in the Barguzin case operated once a week from the local post office.

'Social work' is perhaps necessary, but not sufficient, if one wishes to attain a position of political influence. The people who work for the *sel'sovet* in their regular jobs are liable to be used as drones in the sphere of 'social work' because it is considered to be part of the job of the *sel'sovet* to undertake such (frequently boring and time-consuming) tasks for 'their' kolkhoz. Thus Tiktina, the school-teacher, explained, admittedly from a jaundiced point of view:

The kolkhoz, basically, disposed of our time: its task was to squeeze out of us as many man-hours as possible for weeding, harvesting, maize-planting, etc. And the kolkhoz *partorg* 'allotted' the teachers, even non-Party members, to 'agit-sections' in the brigades and work-teams. He ordered the teachers by *prikaz* (command), on the authority of the *raikom*, to: give lectures, conduct political information classes, read newspapers to the kolkhozniks, conduct propaganda on agrotechnical subjects and recent production experience, edit and publish kolkhoz, brigade and work-team news bulletins, etc. The kolkhoz organisation used not the school itself, but the teachers, as putters-into-action of the Party policies, as privates in the ideological army of the Party.
For us to have created our own Party organisation in the school would have required the presence of only three Communist Party members, but, strangely enough, they are only rarely found in schools. I suspect that it was more convenient, both for the kolkhoz and the *raikom*, to have the communists in schools subordinate to the Party organisation of the kolkhoz: it allowed them to strengthen the dependency of the school on the kolkhoz, i.e. the school's subordination to the tasks of the Party in respect of collective agriculture.[78]

Activity in 'social work' does not even guarantee membership of the Party. Individuals write *zayavleniye* (applications) to join the Party, but long before this their work and character will have been assessed, and it is clear that their position in the division of labour is taken into account. The Party has guidelines for the composition of its membership (percentage of ordinary kolkhozniks, officials, intelligentsia, etc.). In effect individuals are asked to join the Party, and just as some categories are encouraged to join, others may have difficulties put in their way.[79]

The Party sometimes intervenes in decisions of the kolkhoz committee about transfer and dismissal of personnel. To take one case from the Karl Marx farm in Barguzin: in 1975 the kolkhoz management decided to dismiss the brigadier of OTF 1, Viktor Badmayev. However, the *partorg* asked the Chairman to delay carrying out this decision until he had asked the opinion of the Party members under Badmayev. A meeting was called of the communists in Badmayev's brigade. He was criticised strongly for his undemanding attitude and his leniency towards undisciplined workers, but it was also recognised that he himself was energetic and able to get on good personal terms with people. The Party members recognised themselves at fault for failing to help Badmayev carry out his work. The meeting decided to delay the dismissal of the brigadier, especially since there had been many changes of leadership in the farm and this was felt to be harmful. A short article was written on this episode in the local newspaper by another brigadier in the kolkhoz, M. Dabayev from OTF 2, the moral of the story being the correctness of involving ordinary Party members in decision-making.[80] In effect the demonstration of 'moral integrity' (*printsipial'nost'*) and 'trustworthiness' (*doveriye*) in the context of the various organisations concerned with 'social work' often means reporting critically on one's colleagues. Such report-making is standard in Soviet life because morality is inextricably involved with work. People providing such reports as part of their 'social work' are able to see this activity as helpful to the people reported upon.

Reporting on other people's conduct as a general practice should be distinguished from the deliberately defamatory report, which Russians call *donos*, which has the aim of incrimination of a political kind. This latter kind of report is a political move. It is weighed up and debated at a meeting (e.g. of the *raikom* if the report is to them) at which the accused has a chance to defend himself. People take sides on such occasions, and therefore such reports are not usually written unless the writer knows he can rally support on his side.

In cases concerning children the overseeing role is formalised. The 'social educator' (*obshchestvennyi vospital'*), usually a woman, is appointed to look after and oversee the care of 'difficult' children and adolescents. For example, a 'social educator' was appointed to Sasha Sobolev, a boy living in the lumber-station village of Yubileinyi, adjacent to the Karl Marx kolkhoz. Sasha, aged fifteen, left home and wandered about for weeks on end. To quote the local newspaper:

he stole personal property, and his mother, afraid of the consequences, burnt some of the goods and together with Sasha's sister re-sewed the stolen clothes so that they would be unrecognisable. The mother was fined and criticised by the 'commission for juvenile affairs'. In March of this year [1980] Sasha appeared before the People's Court. The members of the court took a humanitarian attitude, took all the circumstances into account, and gave the boy the opportunity to continue at school, to live with his mother and step-father, and the sentence (two years deprivation of freedom) was suspended on condition he fulfilled the order (*prigovor*). This was the time when the boy could have grown close to his family again, but the parents continued to get drunk and engage in debauchery, and again left the boy unattended. In sum, Sasha started to steal again, and now is under investigation.

Sasha and five other boys were allocated 'social educators', people such as librarians, personnel managers, chemists and architects, all of them women. Several of these people had been awarded diplomas by the Party.[81]

This kind of 'social work' is not usually associated with making a career, but it is necessary to do some kind of 'social work' in order to make a career. Some people carry out their tasks with honest and loving care, others treat them as a formality to be 'got through'. In either case, the expressed aim is to provide an institution for the social concern for individuals.

In Yefimov's somewhat cynical view, the road to advancement by this means is in contradiction with a straightforward concern for one's work because the allocation of the more important tasks in 'social work' — by which advancement is attained — is so tied to control and careerism.

One need not think that the higher officials are in ignorance of the underhand dealings of their subjects . . . These people are moved up a little, or, for a more careful trial of their governability, they are transferred for a time to work in the local Party committee (*mestkom*), the *partkom*, or the bureau of the Komsomol (these people are called OOR — *osvobozhdennyye obshchestvennyye rabotniki*, i.e. social workers freed from other work). 'In the Leningrad optical-mechanical works, for example, almost 90% of people who were moved to management jobs alternated or combined their work with "social work" . . . In the country as a whole, sociologists note that in eighty cases out of a hundred "social work" is the most important step in the further advancement of the career of a leader.' (*Leningradskaya Pravda*, 17 Dec. 1975). Thus, up the ladder 'master → head of section → head of sector (*tsekh*) → director of enterprise → head of *glavk* → official in the Ministry' there moves a bustling crowd of former mechanics, plumbers, technicians, and assemblers; and the professional engineer, who is inclined to reflection and analysis, is squeezed out to some backwater where his diploma and knowledge are completely unnecessary.[82]

Although the post of Chairman of a collective farm is not a particularly high one in the terms Yefimov is discussing, it is nevertheless worth noting that all the Chairmen in Buryatiya on whose careers I have some information spent some period working for the Party as an OOR. This was their 'political capital'.

Educational qualifications

In Selenga, as we saw, the people with higher education, the specialists, were on the whole excluded from political positions of power: Party and kolkhoz 'line' officials made wide use of genealogical ties — an essentially non-literate, let alone educated, mode — in establishing their positions of influence. We should now look at the question of whether this should be seen merely as a phase in Soviet rural history and whether the system replacing it, as exemplified by the Barguzin farm in the 1970s, is in fact radically different.

In Selenga, the main effect of education was to remove people from the farm altogether and to place them in an urban, more 'cultured' — as the Buryats saw it — context. I am here making a distinction between 'education' and 'training'. There were many people on the farm who had trained as mechanics, tractor-drivers, book-keepers, etc. This meant that they had been given permission by the kolkhoz to leave for short courses, or they had attended evening classes, or they had studied in their spare time and taken the necessary examinations. These people remained on the kolkhoz, and they were able to get higher pay after obtaining training qualifications. However, a certain proportion of young people, perhaps even as much as 50%, left the farm either to go into the army, or to get full-time higher education in the towns. These people seldom returned.

The army is the non-privileged way out of the farm. To leave for higher education, on the other hand, is the ambition of all those who desire a life which is not only urban but also has high status, is well-paid, and above all is 'cultured'. Soldiers demobilised from the army form the backbone of the small Buryat 'urban proletariat', working in the factories of Ulan-Ude and the engineering works in the towns along the Trans-Siberian Railway.[83] This life in itself is considered to be more 'cultured' than that on the farm, as was pointed out to me many times, and I was taken to meet families of railway workers where the daughter played the violin, the son was at an institute of higher education, and so on. However, our task is not to describe this life in itself, but to assess its significance for the kolkhozniks living in the forests and steppes of Buryatiya.

High status and education is linked with the notion of being 'cultured' (*kul'turnyi*) — jokes were made about Khrushchev for his lack of culture, and I was assured that the Soviet Union would never have such a leader again. A direct parallel with this on the local level was the way people talked about Dorzhiyev in 1974—5 after his dismissal from his position as Chairman of the Selenga kolkhoz. Had I not noticed the 'low cultural level' in his farm, they asked. (This, in fact, was the reason given for refusing me permission to re-visit this kolkhoz in the 1970s.) The word *kul'turyni* has rather different connotations in Russian from its English equivalent 'cultured'. It has associations with a nexus of ideas which Soviet ideology ties together: scientific, productive, correct, true, communist. Its opposite *neku'turyni* (vulgar) is linked with the ideas 'unscientific' and 'uncultured'.[84]

This association of ideas has become an axiom of public culture in the USSR by means of the educational process. That this has penetrated as far as our Buryat kolkhozy can be seen from the following excerpt from an essay written by a schoolgirl in the Lenin kolkhoz in Barguzin district on the theme 'What has the study of [correct] social behaviour (*obshchestvovedeniye*) at school taught me?': 'To build communism means to have a powerful technology, to raise productivity of labour, and to attain abundance in everything. To build communism is first of all to prepare oneself for communist labour, to work perseveringly on oneself, to raise one's level of culture, to produce in oneself a scientific world-view.'[85]

This association of ideas is important because it implies that there is no way of being 'cultured' without at the same time being 'scientific', i.e. advanced in techniques and knowledge in the Russian, definitely not traditional Lamaist Buryat, mode. This means that public social status is even more directly connected with education in the Soviet Union than it is in Western Europe, where there are several other ways of establishing status or culture, unconnected with educational qualifications.

The objection might be raised that in the Soviet Union the Party hierarchy constitutes a set of positions of high status which may be attained almost without education of any kind. In practice, of course, this has been true in the past. The internal 'Party schools' which train Party cadres are not seen in the same category as 'secular' education. The latter in the Soviet Union, although it might appear to be very ideologically oriented, is understood by unreflective Soviet people to be simply 'the world of learning', the true facts about nature, history, languages, etc. — which is the same attitude that unreflective people have towards education everywhere. 'Education' *per se* has a validation outside Soviet culture altogether, but this is not the case with 'Party schooling' — even though the latter is maintained to be the distillation of all that is 'best' in education. Everyone, since Khrushchev, has some inkling that the 'Party line', which constitutes the body of what is taught at Party schools, has an institutional rather than an intellectual character, if only for the simple reason that people in their own lifetimes have seen doctrines rise and fall.

What cannot have escaped the attention of even the dullest of farm-workers is that not merely did the theories change, but with them changed the political fortunes of those propagating them. Party teaching could not be seen as anything but conditional. This is not so to the same extent with 'secular' education. 'Secular education' is carried out in institutions which are separate from, if not independent of, Party organisation. Even if the material taught in schools is in fact ideologically selected, it is never presented as if this were the case. It is presented as 'knowledge' in some absolute sense, and associated with this, for reasons which will be discussed below, is the fact that academic diplomas and degrees do confer a certain immunity — not total — from the vagaries of political life.

From within, however, from the school-teacher's point of view, there is an interior questioning of the nature of what they teach.

The official version of social and humane sciences was doubted by only a few (the more enlightened and thoughtful) teachers, only in the sanctuary of unofficial conversation (with trusted friends). I was trusted, and I was often the recipient of these doubts — when we visited one another, when we went looking for mushrooms, or went fishing . . . There was a lot of time for conversation, but the criticism was mostly concrete and on particular subjects, and did not touch upon fundamental problems of structure and ideology. The same thing was true of the older schoolchildren with whom I became close.[86]

Whether the teacher believes in himself or not, the ideal of true knowledge is socially upheld. When codified in certificates and degrees this ideal acquires a transactional value. The force of the idea of the association of status with education is so strong that there is a remarkable tendency to acquire 'scientific' qualifications *ex post facto*. In other words, although it is not in fact necessary to have higher education in order to progress in the Party, a man who has already acquired a high position may use it in order to obtain for himself a degree, doctorate, or other academic distinction. This phenomenon is called by Yanov the 'migration to academe':

By the 'migration to academe' I mean the acquisition of academic degrees on a massive scale by the Party and state functionaries . . . Today it is considered unseemly if, for example, the vice-chairman of a city Soviet executive committee, or a provincial Party secretary (but not the first secretary), or a Central Committee instructor is not a candidate of sciences. The Central Committee's departmental consultants and department heads are now often doctors of sciences or academicians.

365

But what is the objective basis of this migration to academe? It is certainly not that these functionaries have suddenly felt an irresistible passion for knowledge: academic titles have not yet kept anyone from maintaining his ignorance in all its purity. But in the USSR these titles confer the only status that offers guarantees of lifetime privileges.

The cases of Shafarevich, Sakharov, and Levich — academicians who are in open opposition to authority and have still not been deprived of their privileges as academicians — are striking evidence of the fact that these privileges are not a dead letter but a living political reality.[87]

What Yanov is implying, and goes on to say more explicitly, is that academic titles and degrees confer a more *permanent* kind of status in Soviet society than official posts themselves. This is true not only of the high levels of which Yanov is writing, but also of the local situation even in remote districts of Siberia. In other words, the relation between political office and academic titles can be seen as a structural feature of Soviet society in general.

In the Khrushchev period there was a strong reaction against the association of education with social prestige. As Khrushchev said:

If a boy or girl does not study well . . . and fails to get into a college, the parents . . . frighten him by saying that . . . he will have to work in a factory as a common labourer. Physical work becomes a thing to frighten children with . . . Such views are an insult to the working people of socialist society. Such an incorrect situation . . . can no longer be tolerated. In socialist society work must be valued by its usefulness, must be stimulated not only by its remuneration, but also by the high respect of our Soviet public.[88]

Khrushchev's idea was to replace some of the time spent in education with vocational training, but this was organisationally not a success and was virtually abandoned in most schools by 1966. In the 1980s there is still an idea that general education should be linked with practical work,[89] but this is more an attempt to fit children for the various jobs they will encounter than a policy which aims to change social values themselves.

Bourdieu has written extensively on the role of education in society, and although he was addressing himself primarily to modernisation in a capitalist world, it may be helpful to consider some of his conclusions in relation to the rural Soviet material. Bourdieu's arguments about education have two strands. One concerns the establishment, by general education, of *objectified* relations of power for the first time, unhampered by the need constantly to reproduce power relations by means of personal influence and patronage, which was characteristic of societies in the era before education became general.

Academic qualifications, like money, have a conventional fixed value which, being guaranteed by law, is freed from local limitations (in contrast to scholastically uncertified cultural capital) and temporal fluctuations: the cultural capital which they in a sense guarantee once and for all does not constantly need to be proved. The objectification accomplished by academic degrees and diplomas, and, in a more general way, by all forms of credentials, is inseparable from the objectification which the law guarantees by defining *permanent positions* which are distinct from the biological individuals holding them, and may be occupied by agents who are biologically different but interchangeable in terms of the qualifications required.

He continues:

Relations of power and domination no longer exist directly between individuals; they are set up in pure objectivity between institutions, i.e. between socially guaranteed qualifications and socially defined positions, and through them, between the social mechanisms which produce and guarantee both the social value of the qualifications and the positions and also the distribution of these social attributes among biological individuals.[90]

Materials from the rural Soviet Union indicate that this state, whereby 'relations of power are set up in pure objectivity between institutions', is far from being realised in contemporary provincial society. Let us look first at the role of the school in the Karl Marx farm and its relations first with the kolkhoz and secondly with other educational, military, or productive institutions.

The school in Bayangol is large and well-equipped and the kolkhoz is rightly proud of it. Re-built between 1967 and 1974, the new school was by far the largest building in Bayangol village and was situated in a central position at the intersection of the two main streets. It was the largest middle school in the entire Barguzin district, having 764 pupils in 1974, one hundred boarders, fifty-seven teachers, and eleven classes (one of them preparatory) starting from the age of seven. The school was one of the elite establishments of the republic specialising in foreign-language teaching.[91] In this case the language was English, and children of about thirteen or fourteen were capable of holding simple conversations in English with me. The senior classes were reportedly reading a novel by Iris Murdoch. All teaching in the school was in Russian or English from the first class, although Buryat had to be used in explanation for the three first years. By the fifth class, i.e. age twelve, children were competent in Russian, and by the ninth or tenth class they were fluent. The subjects taught were: Russian, English and Buryat languages, mathematics, history of the middle ages, history of the USSR, recent international history, biology, zoology, chemistry, physics, astronomy, botany, geography, and literature, Russian and foreign. Curricula in all these subjects are standard throughout the Soviet Union. In the final year it was possible to learn 'machine-handling', i.e. tractor-driving and car mechanics, and girls were also given courses in cooking, sewing, and running a household.

A distinction is made between scientific subjects, which can be taught by any qualified teachers, and subjects with political implications (history, literature, etc.). The latter subjects may only be taught by people whose political credentials have been checked and confirmed by the *raikom*.[92]

Not all children in the kolkhoz attend the main school in Bayangol for their full school career. About 250 children whose parents lived in the brigade settlements of Kharasun, Urzhil, Soyol, and Ina, attended primary schools (*nachal'nyye shkoly*) providing the first three classes in these places. Subsequently, they transferred to the Bayangol middle school. About two-thirds of all pupils stayed for the full ten-year course.

At the end of their school careers in Bayangol, if children had obtained the ten-year school-leaving certificate they could take the competitive examinations for VUZy (*vysshiye uchebnyye zavedeniya* – higher educational establishments). The competition for VUZ places was strong – about 500 applied every year in the Barguzin district for around 100 places. All of this seems to conform with the ideal of the 'meritocratic' institution. However, the relations with other institutions – higher and special educational establishments, the kolkhoz and other work places – was far from straightforward. Two categories of children were able to obtain VUZ entrance without taking the competitive examination: those who had done exceptionally well at school and been awarded a gold or silver medal, and those who went to work in the kolkhoz and were subsequently recommended for higher education at the farm's expense. I did not find out what proportion of the total number of candidates was taken up by these two categories in Barguzin, but estimates have been made that 'production candidates' were 23% of the intake of VUZy in the USSR as a whole in 1973, having been a rather larger proportion of the whole during the Khrushchev era of relative 'democratisation'.[93] It is possible that in a collective farm the proportion of 'production candidates' would be higher than in the population in general. As for the medal-winners I was told by the school director in Selenga that medals were awarded on the basis of character and good behaviour as well as academic performance. Thus, although a certain proportion of school-leavers could be said to pass into higher education simply via the competitive examinations, those exempted, either by being awarded medals or by proceeding through the 'production' channel, were dependent on the goodwill of either the school director or the farm committee for their chances of success.

The same applies to children applying for places at training or technical schools (*srednyye spetsial'nyye uchebnyye zavedniya*). These schools cater for children who have given up general education after eight classes, at the age of about fifteen, and they teach a range of subjects, among which the students specialise in training for jobs such as: electrician, telephonist, book-keeper, builder, driver, librarian, economist, or mechanic. In the USSR as a whole rather few (one in forty approximately) of the students at these establishments are sent by enterprises as 'production candidates'.[94] However, about one-third of all the students carry on with their jobs at the same time, i.e. they go to evening classes or take correspondence courses.[95] Since all students, whether at VUZy or at technical schools, require a reference from the Party and/or their place of work, the *kharakteristika*, we can be fairly certain that a close watch is kept on the courses which young kolkhozniks take in their spare time. That special permission is required in order to leave work for a full-time course can be seen from the following account of a young shepherd, Vasya Ochirov, from the Barguzin Karl Marx farm. He was a lazy youth according to the local newspaper, and 'therefore the kolkhoz *rukovodstvo* [leadership] paid no attention to his frequent applications to go on a course for drivers'.[96] He then turned to Dusya Badmayeva, a senior shepherdess on good terms with the authorities. She talked to him and saw that he was a person who might have a 'real calling' for being a driver, and she persuaded the farm leadership of his worth. They sent Ochirov on the course, but he simply went off for a month and reappeared in the kolkhoz with no qualification. Dusya attacked him strongly, 'sharp, hurtful words were spoken to him'. This had an effect. He went back on the course, and the experience, it seems, changed much in his attitudes. We see that although there is no evidence that the kolkhoz was supporting him while on the course, and one might imagine that the episode had no relevance for anyone except Ochirov himself, it is nevertheless clear that even relatively unimportant educational opportunities are controlled by the authorities very closely.

Finally, there is the issue of parental influence in the selection of children for VUZ entrance. I have no evidence of my own on this subject, but it is well-known that this is an extremely common occurrence in the USSR. Khrushchev complained of it several times: 'frequently it is not enough to pass the examinations to enter college. Great influence of the parents also plays a part here. With good reason, one rather widely hears young people entering college saying that after they themselves pass the contest, a contest among the parents begins — and it often decides the whole matter'.[97]

There is evidence that in some parts of the Soviet Union the competition for places in academic institutions is so intense that bribery has become widespread. This creates the necessity for establishing a fund of money for the purposes of paying for a child's education, even though grants are given to all students except the children of the well-off (the top 10—20% incomes):

In every VUZ in Azerbaijan a certain number of places were taken out of the competition and sold . . . The rector of the Azerbaijan Pedagogical Institute *imeni* Lenina took this pay 'in kind': they used to bring sheep, bottles of cognac, honey and fruit to his dacha.

There is a long-standing custom in the villages of Azerbaijan: when a child is born they set aside a pot for savings and put money in it; the child will grow up, enter an institute, and be a scholar . . .

The prices of bribes for entering institutes grow from year to year: in 1972 in Azerbaijan they were: medical institute — 30,000 rubles, university — 20—25,000 rubles, institute of foreign languages — 10,000 rubles, institute of economics — up to 35,000 rubles. The people who enter? The children of heads of enterprises, the future heads of enterprises themselves.[98]

Despite the discovery of this situation in Azerbaijan in 1972, the bribery did not stop. The Central Committee official responsible for science and education, Trapeznikov, took the decision, according to Zemtsov, not to expel the 29% of students who had entered VUZy illegitimately, but to dismiss the professors involved. The result was that subsequent bribery prices were even higher: there was more risk involved.[99]

Even if bribery is not involved in Buryatiya, it is still the case that groups of relatives establish funds to pay for the higher education of their children. Student grants are insufficient to cover the cost of living, and most children have also to be supported by their parents. At the point of leaving the farm parental influence with the Chairman used to play an important role.

Access to higher education is thus not simply a matter of an 'objectified' relation between institutions, in this case the school or the kolkhoz and the training school or college. Similarly, graduates leaving college with identical degrees have far from equivalent possibilities open to them. This cannot simply be attributed to the domination of 'pure' academic values by Communist Party ideology, giving an advantage to ideological activists. It is due rather to the specific institutional organisation of Soviet society, which varies of course from place to place. Thus in the western cities of Russia, where labour moves fairly freely in certain professions (construction work, engineering, geology), the holding of a qualification may confer something like the 'conventional, fixed value' envisaged by Bourdieu. But in rural districts (and probably in some urban professions too) movement is still circumscribed, cadres are allocated to jobs, and the Party *nomenklatura* and *uchetnaya nomenklatura* operates precisely to control the free convertibility of qualifications into official position. Thus, certainly for rural areas, Bourdieu's analogy between 'cultural capital' (educational qualifications) and money is definitely misleading − that is, if 'money' is understood in the western capitalist sense (a medium of exchange, a common measure of value, usage determined by demand and supply).

However, if the analogy is made between 'educational wealth' and *Soviet* money, the comparison becomes a more useful one. This is because in the Soviet Union both education *and money* are limited in their usage by the social status of the holder. Because of the existence of special shops and distribution organisations serving only the members of particular groups (the army, the KGB, the Party officials, etc.) it is not the case that one and the same sum of money buys the same amount or the same things for everyone. Usually the special shops sell imported and scarce goods in general demand. Often the distribution points operate by counters (*talony*), not ordinary money. The system does not operate within the locality, but certainly exists at *raion* level.[100]

Polanyi long ago observed that where economies are organised differently from the capitalist one, 'money' itself takes on different characteristics.[101] The 'different characteristics' of rubles and their relation to wealth of other kinds in Buryat communities will be discussed in the next chapter, but here we need emphasise only the fundamental importance of the fact that money has a socially relative value, as has education, in the Soviet Union. This springs from the circumstance, which was underlined in Chapter 3, that the division of labour

370

giving rise to social positions is bureaucratically determined — or, as I expressed this for economic institutions such as the kolkhoz, the productive and administrative hierarchies are one and the same thing.[102]

Because the division of labour is the deepest source of inequality, it follows that the focal point of the conflict of interests in society is not so much the distribution of rewards for labour — as we have seen, these (medals and prizes) confer only a relatively sterile 'honour' which is not readily convertible into alteration of political status — as the distribution of labour itself. This is why the disposable surplus in material wealth is used by management to procure labour, and by workers to negotiate better jobs for themselves and their children. Thus competition for (as Rudolf Bahro puts it) 'the appropriation of activities favourable to self-development, for appropriate positions in the multi-dimensional system of social division of labour'[103] becomes the driving force of economic life in Soviet society. In the earlier phase of Buryat history our studies show that this competition was conducted in terms of manipulation of kinship values, visible 'hard work', and advancement by 'social work', in which the ostensible value is the image of being 'responsible for others'. In the modern phase the previous operations still continue, but now competition focusses on access to education not only for itself but also as the value in terms of which position in the division of labour may be allotted. In other words, education now mediates the relation between those with power and those who seek power, but is itself to some degree subordinate to earlier political strategies which have not lost their value and therefore reproduce themselves.

For those at the bottom of the hierarchy, there may be a conflict not only between different means of advancement but between different values. As a subject acted upon by the forces of Soviet society, with few resources, few alternatives, and encumbered with the weight of strategies already pursued, for example by parents, the kolkhoznik with the old-fashioned way may find that he or she had in all good faith made a tactical mistake. Who can predict, from the wilds of the collective farm, when there will be a crack-down on nepotism? Increasingly, as higher positions in the hierarchy are attained, people find themselves in a position to make choices, to distribute their resources, as the good herdsman did in the economy of the past. But it is only at the very height of Soviet society that the relative weight of different values (political reliability, activism in society, education) and the relations between them are defined.

The conflicts may be apparent even within one family. A visitor to Buryatiya in 1971 told me he had met a party official who complained that he did not know where he stood with his children. His daughter insisted on attending a school in which the language of instruction was Buryat, despite the lessening in career prospects this entailed, and criticised her father for the numerous Russicisms in his language. She said that he was no longer a 'real Buryat'. His sons, on the other hand, went to an English-medium school, and complained that their father did not know English or German and was insufficiently aware of international culture. It is true that this incident took place in Ulan-Ude, not in a distant kolkhoz, but as we have seen kolkhoz schools such as the Bayangol secondary school do sometimes have foreign languages as the medium of instruction, with a consequent widening in the horizons of the pupils, and this may lead to a conflict with their actual career prospects, especially if they have to stay in the farm.

Bourdieu is right to insist that an educational degree is a value which can be translated into material advantages, but it is precisely because this cannot be done freely (freely, that is, on the analogy he draws with the market) that, in the Soviet Union, degrees and academic titles come to have an aura attached to them which is beyond the simple attribution of 'knowledge'. In fact, as we saw, in the case of those degrees acquired *ex post facto* by high officials, academic ability may hardly be required at all. First it is necessary to have power, then legitimacy and security.

Thus, to return again to the collective farms, we must conclude that there are political operations directed towards the acquiring of education, but these involve factors we have not yet defined: on the one hand, it is not quite enough simply to be a 'good worker' in order to persuade the kolkhoz or Party to give one's child a permission note to leave; on the other hand, devoted work in the Party and Soviets is not sufficient either. Kinship networks may support people who already have educational opportunities, but we cannot advance them as a serious explanation of negotiations towards obtaining higher education in general, even if they are used in some cases. In order to complete this picture of kolkhoz socio-political organisation (including among other things the pattern of granting of educational opportunities), it is now necessary to draw into the discussion two elements which have emerged as important in previous chapters: (a) the creation and distribution of material resources surplus to the production plan, and (b) the syncretic conjuncture of Buryat with Soviet cultural values. This latter is disclosed not at kolkhoz meetings but rather at the cycle of festivals and rituals which establish unofficial as well as official social positions. It is primarily on the occasion of these festivals that material resources are transformed into 'gifts', which can thus mark status and open up the promise of future reciprocity.

8

Ritual and identity

1. Changes in ritual in the Soviet period: the interlocking of 'Buryat' with 'Soviet' consciousness

The economic life of Buryat herdsmen and farmers was always ordered in relation to ritual which accompanied the seasonal tasks of the year.[1] Sometimes the tasks themselves determined when the rituals would take place (for example, when it was decided to go on a hunting expedition offerings would be made to the spirit-owner of the forest), but in the case of the largest and most important rituals it was the ceremonial calendar itself which ordered the conceptual sequence and coordination of productive activities. Similarly, we could say that the social groups conducting rituals were sometimes productive groups (the household, the local kin-group '-*tang*'), but on more important occasions they were those larger, socially constructed groups which made possible reciprocity (or alternatively negative reciprocity — enmity) between productive groups, i.e. sections of clans and patrilineages.

The 'traditional'[2] religion of the Buryat was shamanism, that is the worship of a host of deities, ancestor spirits, and supernatural beings thought to be present in mountains, trees, rivers, cliffs, marshes, animals, etc., the relation with these being mediated by the shaman, who could talk with them, travel to their abodes, and even embody them in his own person. By the eighteenth century this religious system was being overlaid among eastern Buryats by Lamaism, the form of Buddhism current among the Tibetans and Mongols. In response to the great success of the Lamaist missionaries, the Russian Tsarist government encouraged the activity of Orthodox priests in order to secure the loyalties of the Buryat population on the Empire's frontier. Orthodox missionaries were more effective among the western than the eastern Buryats, but on both sides of Lake Baikal shamanist traditions continued to exist, emerging with particular strength in times of trouble and hardship.

The most large-scale 'shamanist'[3] ritual was the *tailgan*, the massive sacrifice of livestock by a patrilineal lineage to its ancestors and spirits of the locality. The calendar of *tailgans*, performed throughout the summer months, was already being altered during the nineteenth century among western Buryats to coincide with saints' days of the Orthodox calendar.[4] Among Lamaist eastern Buryats *tailgans* were replaced by similar rituals, though often without blood sacrifices, at *tailgan* sites, now re-named *oboo*. These rituals took place according to the Lamaist calendar. In both cases, Buryats used to time their economic activities in relation to the ritual dates. Thus, for example, the wheat harvest was carried out after the sacrifice to Saint Nikolai, and the manes and tails of horses were cut — this involved the selection of breeding stallions whose manes were not cut — on the eve of Easter Day.[5]

This ritual regulation of agricultural time has been shattered by the commandeering of production by the Soviet state. Tasks in livestock herding and agriculture now have an order superimposed on the simply productive by the convulsive sequence of special campaigns, accounting periods, and 'socialist competitions'. It is only by chance or good fortune that these could appear as anything but arbitrary in relation to the process of production in any given farm, since the timing of campaigns is decided centrally and the farms have their own natural conditions of production which vary from place to place. Punctuating this often agitated sequence is the series of public festivals of the Soviet year. These, which occur on 23 February, 8 March, 22 April, 1 and 2 May, 9 May, 7 and 8 November, and 5 December, commemorate political and military events which are quite unrelated to natural and productive cycles. But, they do frequently regulate the timing of 'socialist competitions' in agriculture. The ordering of time by the Soviet state can in itself be seen as ritual.

We cannot agree with certain Soviet ethnographers that this new ritual is in every sphere coming to take the place of the previous system rooted in early Buryat culture.[6] Both Lamaist and Orthodox missionaries in their time attempted to suppress 'shamanist' activities, and neither were totally successful. The lamas were forced to adopt 'shamanist' deities and ritual sites as their own, thus creating localised forms of folk-Lamaism. What the Soviet ritual has replaced is the organised, 'high', forms of Orthodoxy and Buddhism, both of which were foreign in origin and language (i.e. Russian and Tibetan) and which were promulgated by means of a socio-political hierarchy which has now disappeared.

Unacknowledged, and often opposed, by the Soviet authorities, the ritual of Buryat folk culture has continued everywhere. There is no single kolkhoz or sovkhoz in Buryatiya where *only* Soviet rituals are celebrated. But the nature of Buryat ritual has been transformed, not only in the periodicity, form, and content of the ceremonies, but also in the social groups involved in conducting it. Furthermore, just as Buryat 'shamanist' ritual was to a great extent fused with Lamaism in the past,[7] the complex of Buryat culture, which contains 'shamanist', Buddhist and syncretic fusions of both elements, is now — in a fragmentary way — being linked with Soviet ritual. The integration is fragmented mainly because of the rejection by Soviet ideology and practice of any social action, whether spontaneous and anarchic or ritualised, which seems to be, through its cultural rationalisation, *other* and therefore outside Soviet control. In fact, as some Buryat ethnographers have realised,[8] their national rituals are mostly far from being unpredictable or anti-Soviet and seek on the contrary to deal with the predicament of what it is to live to good purpose in Soviet society. These writers have urged that Buryat rituals be 'turned into' new Soviet festivals (for example, that the *tsagaalgan* ritual should 'become' the *den' zhivotnovodov* — the Day of Livestock Workers). But this general project is, in my view, unrealisable for reasons which were discussed in earlier parts of this book and which go beyond the simple rejection by Party ideology of the 'other': Soviet 'culture' constitutes itself as something definite, active, and in a constant process of change, and yet it is relatively impervious to the desires and intentions of ordinary workers because it is defined and redefined only by its higher levels. For Buryat kolkhozniks it is in effect something as arbitrary as nature, which requires to be 'understood' and 'acted upon' just as nature always did. Soviet festivals are institutionalised as part of Soviet culture. One might suppose that they could represent any of those intentions which people might have as units of Soviet-constituted society. But, because of the relatively introverted substance of Soviet culture, which repeats itself but does not reflect on its own nature, such festivals can never be concerned with one important matter, the relation between Soviet culture itself and the rest of reality. The bridging of this gap is now the most important function of specifically Buryat ritual, which is thus about Soviet culture but not part of it.

In this chapter I shall discuss the implications of four arguments: (1) In the Soviet period there has been a tendency even in Buryat ritual for the social groups involved to change from kinship groups ('-*tang*' and lineage) to productive groups of the kolkhoz. (2) Within rituals, the differential social status marked by such things as seating arrangements or the distribution of ranked pieces of meat is beginning to take account of the various ladders of prestige mentioned in Chapter 7 section 3 (Soviet insignia, Party work, etc.) in combination with the traditional distinctions of age, sex, and genealogical seniority. (3) The shift in social basis from kinship groups to kolkhoz groups, while very incomplete, has not resulted in a decline of ritual itself but it has been accompanied (again not invariably by any means) by a general erosion of the religious basis for ritual. (4) The specifically ritual practitioners, shamans and some lamas, exploit the differences between Buryat and Soviet consciousness, and other schisms in society, like those between people who labour and those who 'do not work'. Whereas formerly they were the holders of laboriously acquired and complex 'traditions', they are now *bricoleurs* of the here and now, the people who attempt to make sense of the disjunction between local or personal problems and a social system which claims to be able to solve them, but which itself, although this is only half-recognised, presents people regularly with the new dilemma of having to act 'in the interests of society' when their own concerns are frequently quite different.

375

Ritual and identity

Buryat and Soviet festivals and their interrelationship

I shall not discuss here in any detail the specifically Soviet rituals such as the 'Day of Livestock Workers' or the 'Day of the Shepherd', the 'Day of the Machine-Operator' or the 'Day of the Teacher'. This is partly because the holding of such rituals is far from being as widespread as Soviet literature pretends.[9] And it is partly because where such rituals are held they approximate very closely to the model of the general meeting of kolkhozniks, which has already been described. As the Buryat ethnographer T.M. Mikhailov remarks:

we cannot claim that our performance of rituals is altogether successful. Firstly, festivals of a social character such as the festivals of songs, the harvest, the Day of the Livestock Worker, and others, are carried out in most cases as a meeting, usually with long and boring speeches, with the taking on of some obligation, and with a little mild criticism. This type of festival does not really raise the spirits of the participants, and does not arouse aesthetic and other satisfaction ... [10]

At the 'Day of the Shepherd' in the Barguzin Karl Marx kolkhoz, production figures are read out by the heads of livestock production units, and prizes are awarded to some kolkhozniks, diplomas (*gramota*) to others, and yet others are chided by name for inefficiency or lack of dedication. Sometimes a special exhibition of achievements is organised in the cultural club, sometimes there is an evening concert of songs and dances. The order of the day (*povestka dnya*) is decided by the kolkhoz management committee and the *sel'sovet*, and the success of the occasion from the point of view of the participation and involvement of the kolkhozniks depends entirely on the enthusiasm of the activists in organisations such as the *agitbrigad*. In the Selenga kolkhoz, the *sel'sovet* was run by a pleasant, but meek and vague, lady who did not give the impression that she would organise anything unless specifically told to. There was no mention in this kolkhoz of any 'Days' for workers. In the Barguzin Karl Marx kolkhoz the *sel'sovet* was clearly a more active institution, but at the same time run by people of a more didactic temperament. In this farm they celebrated the 'Day of the Shepherd' and the 'Day of the Machine-Operator'. But what about the 'Day of the Milker', the 'Day of the Pig-Keeper', or the 'Day of the General Worker (*raznorabochii*)'? This question is not entirely rhetorical. As Christopher Binns remarks in his interesting paper on Soviet ritual, the theory is that these 'Days' should give recognition to labour of every type:

Whatever the ministerial aims, these days should not be seen just as morale and productivity stimuli. For the first time virtually all groups of workers have an opportunity to express their identity and interests and be the centre of national attention. They display a similar democratisation to that occurring in life-cycle ceremonies: recognition should be accorded to all types of work, however unromantic, for the part they play in the life of society.[11]

But in fact, even in an ideologically well-organised farm such as the Barguzin Karl Marx, ceremonial 'Days' are only celebrated for certain groups of workers, two groups among the many which exist in the farm. Furthermore, these two groups are not the least recognised in the kolkhoz. If we take the pay-scales of this kolkhoz as a rough indication of the value attached to different types of work, shepherds and machine-operators come out as about average: in 1973 they earned between 130 and 170 rubles a month, while the general workers earned 90 rubles and the builders earned up to 240 rubles. In effect, since the kolkhoz specialised in sheep-farming and was perennially in difficulty with arable farming (the primary task of machine-operators), we should perhaps return to the idea of seeing these celebratory 'Days' as deliberate stimuli to production — similar to 'socialist competition' in function. The intention, somewhere along the line, may also be democratic, but the practice is not.

The Soviet public rituals, the anniversary of the October Revolution, May Day, Women's Day, etc., are celebrated everywhere, unlike the 'Days' for particular groups of workers. By 'celebrated everywhere' I mean that these occasions are public holidays. In towns and cities, depending on the occasion, military parades, speeches, presentations, laying of wreaths, taking of solemn oaths, etc., are organised by the Party and the Soviets. However, collective farms lack the means to provide special facilities for all of these occasions, and the 'celebration' is often reduced to yet another ceremonial meeting (*torzhestvennoye sobraniye*), and in some cases is not marked at all in the official sphere. People can choose whether to attend the meeting, or simply spend the time at home having a rest. Generally, the members of organisations such as the Party, Komsomol, and the *sessiya* of the *sel'sovet* will feel obliged to attend. But what always does happen on these public holidays is a great proliferation of parties, banquets, dances and drinking sessions. Usually a banquet will be organised by the kolkhoz for the 'top people' (*verkhushka*), which will be of a more or less official kind, and accompanied by speeches and toasts. On Women's Day (8 March) there is generally a dance, at which women can ask men to dance rather than the other way round. Women also ask other women to dance, and in my experience the men often retire to another place to drink, leaving women to enjoy Women's Day somewhat on their own. In any case, at all of these festivals a great deal is drunk, and normal working life is suspended in the aftermath as people gradually sober up. Sometimes it is decided to celebrate a public holiday in a more 'mass' and 'cultured' (*kul'turnyi*) way, as was the case with the 1 May festival in Barguzin Karl Marx in 1963.[12]

What has been the fate of specifically Buryat rituals and festivities? The most important of these, in the sense that all rural Buryats take part in them, are *tsagaalgan*, the festival of the New Year in the lunar cycle of twelve months, which occurs usually in February; and *suur-kharbaan*, a festival of archery and other national sports, which takes place in the summer. Of life-cycle ceremonies the most important are *milaagod*, a festival in which a child, or group of siblings, honours his relatives; the cluster of ceremonies accompanying a wedding; *zheloruulga*, carried out every twelve years for personal success and happiness; and the funeral rituals. Of religious rituals the main categories still existing are: (1) *tailgan*, sacrifices conducted by a community to ancestor-spirits or spirit-masters of localities; (2) *oboo takhikha*, offerings and prayers at ritual cairns (*oboo*) inhabited by spirits and deities of localities; (3) rituals (*duhaalga, serzhem*) conducted at a sacred spring (*arshan*) or the site of a shaman's burial or sacred boundary post (*barisa*); (4) *khereg, mürel, zahal*, shamanist rituals conducted on behalf of an individual or family for some particular purpose (request for fertility, for success in some endeavour); (5) sacrifice to the fire-spirit of the household (*gal gulamta*); (6) *maani*, Lamaist rituals for the souls of the ancestors; (7) offerings to protector-deities of the family at Lamaist monasteries; (8) astrology and divination.

To make an analysis of all Buryat rituals and festivals, even simply those celebrated in one kolkhoz, would require a separate work. Here, since my purpose is to show how the present political-economic situation of Buryat kolkhozniks has an effect on ritual, there is no need to describe a large number of examples: the general tendencies I noted earlier are present in *any* ritual. Therefore I shall discuss in some detail only three types of ritual: *tsagaalgan* and *suur-kharbaan* festivals, wedding ceremonies, and certain 'shamanist' rites.

The *tsagaalgan* and *suur-kharbaan* festivals have come to be the main communal festivals of the winter and summer respectively. I do not know if this was always the case, in that, while the *tsagaalgan* has always been tied to the idea of the 'New Year', it is not clear whether the *suur-kharbaan* was celebrated at any particular time of year. Both of these festivals were formerly very Lama-icised, and the *suur-kharbaan* used to be celebrated at Lamaist *oboo*s, and at monastery services (*khural*) in honour of Maidari (Sanskrit Maitreya), the next Buddha to appear in this world.[13] Today, all collective farm workers in Buryatiya celebrate these two festivals, the *tsagaalgan* occurring at the time when livestock first begin to give milk and the *suur-kharbaan* taking place in July after early summer tasks of sowing and sheep-shearing are over, and just before the laborious enterprise of hay-harvest begins.

Of these two festivals, the *tsagaalgan* has retained its social base in the Buryat kinship system and remains a largely religious event, while the *suur-kharbaan* is based on work-groups of the kolkhoz and has become entirely secular.

The *tsagaalgan* is not recognised or organised by any Soviet institution.[14] As a festival its roots go far back into the past of the Mongolian people (the date on which it takes place coincides with the 'Chinese' New Year, which is celebrated all over Eastern Asia). In Mongolia and Buryatiya this festival is associated with the approaching end of winter, the birth of young livestock, and the availability of milk products. Milk products are called *sagaan edeen* ('white food'), and the Buryats when offering one another cream, yoghurt, *kumiss* (mare's milk), etc., say *Sagaalagty*, which means 'Please take some white food', but since whiteness and milk are associated with purity and good this phrase is also a kind of blessing. The name *tsagaalgan* (also pronounced *sagaalgan*) is derived from this complex of ideas.

Changes in ritual in the Soviet period

In Lamaism the *tsagaalgan* festival is associated with the defeat of 'heretical teachings' and the triumph of the 'true belief'. In the monasteries on New Year's Eve the lamas used to burn rubbish, symbolising people's sins of the past year, and then conduct a service (*khural*) dedicated to the protector of the faith, Lhame. After the New Year there were fifteen days of services in honour of the victory of Buddhism over the six propagators of heresies. The victory was accomplished by means of miracles of the Buddha, which at the same time brought about the complete realisation of human capacities and the transformation of the souls of the ancestors into a state of bliss.[15] It is this complex of ideas, which integrates a deeply felt moment of the productive cycle with the upholding of the faith, the rejection of heresies, the absolution from sin, and above all, the responsibility of everyone in their world for the well-being of the souls of their dead relatives, which has survived best of all the onslaught of atheist propaganda. This is not surprising — the *tsagaalgan* might almost have been designed with this in mind.[16] At any rate, despite the fact that there are now no monasteries within hundreds of kilometres of Barguzin, and very few lamas ever visit the distant valley, the festival has remained intact.

It is carried out as follows: in the more religious families on the eve of the New Year the Lamaist religious paintings, which are kept rolled up for the rest of the year, are revealed and hung up for worship (*burkhan delgeelge*). The paintings are done on canvas, sewn with a wide silk border, and are simple versions (though artistically no less powerful) of the *thanka*s to be found in Mongolia, Tibet, Nepal and Bhutan.[17] Lamps of oil are burned before the paintings and metal statues, incense (*khüzhe*) is burnt, and small prayer-wheels are turned. Prayers are said, or read from books, in honour of the dead kin, especially patrilineal ancestors. This is done by old people in most rural families. In some parts of Buryatiya people organise a pilgrimage to a monastery for this religious part of the festival, but I did not hear of this in Barguzin.

The rest of the festival, which goes on for several days, is a celebration of present kinship. On New Year's Day itself the young, particularly boys, must honour their senior relatives (*zolgokho*). Everyone dresses in their best clothes, and often national Buryat clothes are worn on this day. The juniors, one by one, must present all of their senior relatives with 'white food', however token the amount. White or blue silk scarves of a ritual kind (*khadag*) are presented to the most honoured as a sign of respect. Children honour their parents first, and then, strictly following the rules of genealogical seniority, all the rest of their relatives. In the case of more distant kin there is some argument as to the order: in particular, since women are now also honoured, it is not clear whether a senior woman should be paid her respects before a junior man, or vice versa. After the immediate family, or all those kin invited for the feast, the boys and men go in groups to visit kinsmen in other houses. The senior of the lineage must be visited first, and then the other kin in order afterwards. In fact, nowadays, all neighbours are visited as well as kin. On the second and third days of *tsagaalgan* young people go to visit kin living in other villages. There are feasts and parties every day of the festival, races, games and songs. According to some Soviet writers, *tsagaalgan* is the occasion for drunken bouts and 'disorder',[18] but I did not hear of this in Barguzin.

Tsagaalgan was, and perhaps still is, the occasion on which it is publicly defined who is one's kin. When I asked a kolkhoznik what was his kin-group, he replied that it was all the people he visited at *tsagaalgan*, 'all the West Barbinsho', all the people who lived on this left bank of the Ina. This indicates that the 'kin' were conceptualised as a group, a minor lineage (see Chapter 1 section 4). According to the same man this group was also the exogamous unit of the lineage. This view of kinship, which maintains the idea of the kin as a local group — and which today would incorporate people living in the neighbourhood and related through women — coexists with a stricter patrilineal reckoning 'by rule', in which kin are kin wherever they live, links through women do not count, and exogamy is reckoned by number of generations (it is forbidden, again according to the same man, to marry a woman related closer than nine generations in the male line). It seems that the *tsagaalgan* maintains both the first, more practical and less ideological, version of kinship as well as the latter, which is the focus of the rituals for ancestors. It is a deeply felt celebration, in which every single person's place is recognised by criteria which are quite distinct from the divisions of Soviet society. One man told me that when he was young, he used simply to enjoy *tsagaalgan* as a wonderful good time with all his family, but as he got older it became also a nostalgic occasion as he remembered all the past festivals, the changes in people's lives, and the kin who had died.

Unlike *tsagaalgan*, which was always reckoned to be a religious festival, *suur-kharbaan* was seized on by the atheist activists soon after the Revolution as a suitable case for secularisation. The *suur-kharbaan* was originally a ritualised archery competition, accompanied by other Buryat sports such as wrestling (*bükhe barildaan*) and horse racing (*mori urildaan*) which took place at the Lamaist territorial *oboo* festivals. Already by 1922, a conference of the Buryat–Mongol Autonomous *oblast'* of the RSFSR and the Far Eastern Republic set out to unify the rules of competition, establishing categories of events, and popularising these among the people.[19] Some international sports such as athletics were added to the three main Buryat competitions. During the 1920s and 1930s the *suur-kharbaan* was given a political direction (*politicheskaya napravlennost'*)[20] aimed at combating Lamaist influences. It began to be celebrated as a festival of labour achievements, at which the productive achievements of the kolkhoz, sovkhoz, or *raion* were proclaimed. The front-line workers (*peredoviki*) were awarded prizes. All of this is still the case today: the *suur-kharbaan* is a combination, to use the analogy with school, of sports day and prizegiving.

Early after the Revolution the Soviet leaders had the idea of holding *suur-kharbaan* festivals on a wider scale, and in 1924 there was the first all-BMASSR *suur-kharbaan* as a 'national' jubilee. Since then, this festival has been held every

380

year on the first Sunday in July as a commemoration of the founding of the Buryat republic. It takes place in the stadium of the capital, Ulan-Ude. Smaller versions are held simultaneously in kolkhozy and *raion* centres. In these district *suur-kharbaan*s the contestants are teams from brigades, kolkhozy, sovkhozy or the *raion*. In the largest festivals sportsmen from Yakutiya, Tuva and Khakassiya also take part, and games from these nationalities are included among the events. In the local versions Russians, Tatars and any other people living in the vicinity take part along with Buryats. Mikhailov complains that the *suur-kharbaan* is in danger of becoming one of those festivals which lose all national characteristics, and he noted that it is already becoming less celebrated by the 'mass' than it used to be.[21] Perhaps he meant that it is being professionalised as a serious sporting event, for which people have to be trained and equipped.[22]

The *suur-kharbaan* used to take different forms among the various groups of Buryats. In the east it was associated with Lamaism, and the cult of the *oboo*, but in the west it was a more local affair, which took place at the home of some wealthy family. In Barguzin the local variant was called *bai-kharbaan*. All of the competitions were very ritualised, and the details of the construction of bows for archery, the targets, the ritualised cries to encourage or discourage arrows, the eulogies to the winners, the grouping of lineage elders which greeted the jockeys in horse races, the songs sung to the horses themselves, etc., were different from place to place.[23] To some extent these local variations have remained in the *suur-kharbaan* when held at the kolkhoz level, but two factors increase standardisation: the political role of the *suur-kharbaan* as a national festival of all Buryats, and the tendency to use the *suur-kharbaan* as an arena for international and professionalised sport. There are also material difficulties in the way of continuing the traditional forms of sport: the complex Buryat bows, made of bone, sinew, and wood, are almost unavailable – people have to use simple metal bows manufactured in Russia – and horses for racing are also becoming rare, since individuals cannot own them and not all farms have a herd. I should say, however, that from my own materials it is clear that the forces for standardisation have far from completely taken over: in both Selenga and Barguzin the summer *suur-kharbaan* in the kolkhoz was something which everyone looked forward to and expected to take part in, local people improvised the *yörööl*s (eulogies), and horse herds were kept in both kolkhozy with amblers, geldings and stallions specially set aside for racing purposes.

The social basis for competition has, however, definitively changed. The village (*ulus*) of patrilineal kin is no longer the unit which competes, even though, as we have seen, such kin-groups still exist in the kolkhozy. People compete as individuals and as members of work-teams. Since the old rituals were based on the participation of kin-groups and the organising presence of lineage elders, they have been largely dropped. The eulogies, which used to honour the owner-spirits (*ezhed*) of the locality and ancestors (often these were the same), or in the Lamaist version, the clan aristocracy and famous lamas, have been simplified and fragmented. Soviet 'ancestors', such as Lenin, now take these very places in the eulogies.

If the social and economic base for the *suur-kharbaan* has changed – it is the kolkhoz which now organises and pays for the festival – this does not mean that the summer in Buryatiya is now empty of occasions for the gathering of kinship groups or the holding of religious rituals in honour of ancestors and local spirits. The *tailgan* sacrifices still continue in many places, and among the western Buryats, where the link between ancestors and the cult of locality spirits was always stronger than in the east, they are still held in nearly every kolkhoz. Participation in many places is strictly by lineage membership, and the resources for the sacrifice as a rule come from the domestic economy. People sometimes travel from afar to attend their home *tailgan*.[24] Each household may be required to make a contribution of meat, milk foods or drink, even if no member attends the *tailgan*.[25] I shall return to the question of the present form of *tailgan*s later, but meanwhile we should note that the balance between this kind of sacrifice and the *suur-kharbaan* has completely changed. The *suur-kharbaan* used to be a relatively small and localised event, without great expenditure of resources on food and drink, while the *tailgan* sacrifices were often huge affairs, with mass slaughterings of sheep and horses, and participation of hundreds of kinsmen who would travel from distant places, even across Lake Baikal, to attend.[26] The exception to this was in very Lama-icised areas, where *suur-kharbaan* and other similar festivals at large *oboo*s (ritual cairns) under the patronage of –and often financed partly by – the Buddhist church, had already replaced *tailgan*s before the Revolution. Today, the *tailgan* is characteristically a small affair, with no more than around fifty participants, and only a few animals given in sacrifice.[27] It is disapproved of by the Soviet authorities. To attend a *tailgan* is the negative equivalent of building political capital by 'social work' (*obshchestvennaya rabota*). The *suur-kharbaan*, on the other hand, is already part of Soviet life, and to take part in its organisation *is* 'social work'. The *tailgan* is hidden from the authorities, furtive, and an occasion for drinking and fighting; the *suur-kharbaan* is a presentation of oneself in an officially defined role and in every sense public: the names of the 'front-line workers' are announced by loud-speaker, the names of the winners of sporting events are published in the press. A rich kolkhoz can hold a large and splendid *suur-kharbaan*. Officials from other farms and enterprises, the Party and Soviet bosses from the *raion*, patrons and influential people can be invited to have a good time. This is one of the occasions on which the 'manipulable resources' of the kolkhoz can be put to good account.

2. Wedding ritual and cycles of reciprocity

It is in the changes in Buryat wedding ritual, which was so clearly a formal definition of social, economic, and political relations in the pre-collectivisation period, that we can see revealed the conflicting impulses of rural Buryat society today. In the 1920s and early 1930s many progressive Buryats rejected the wedding ritual altogether, even refusing dowries and gifts for setting up house, on the grounds that this was part of the past.[28] However, by the mid-1950s, as Basayeva remarks, 'The development of wedding ritual went in two directions. On the one hand, we can see an ever greater recreation of many elements of the traditional wedding ritual, and on the other the construction of new forms of wedding festivity, Komsomol or youth weddings.'[29]

This section analyses weddings of Buryat kolkhozniks as they were described to me and then gives material related to the exchange of 'gifts' which takes place on these occasions. The weddings of the 1960s and 1970s retained the essential Buryat *form* — and this is true even of the Komsomol type — but the social groups involved and the people appointed to key positions, such as the match-makers, are in the process of change.

The decision as to what ritual to include in the wedding is made from the point of view of confused, or opposed, ideological positions. The series of rituals constituting a wedding, which is almost never simply a family affair, makes sense from the practical aspect of participation in the cycle of reciprocity within the community, but because the socio-economic elements on which this cycle is built are not explicitly recognised, the ideological rationalisation of why the wedding is to be as it is comes from elsewhere. It is constructed anew with each wedding, grasped piecemeal from the available folk-lore and opinions, and in most cases only with difficulty accommodated to any ideological notion in the community of strict 'tradition' or radical 'progressiveness'.

This will only become clear if we look at some weddings in more detail. Since the extremely complex pre-revolutionary Buryat wedding ritual has already been described in several publications,[30] I shall not give another account of it here (in fact two accounts would be necessary since there were differences between Selenga and Barguzin). I shall first give an outline of what the present-day Selenga Buryats *call* the 'traditional' wedding, as it is celebrated today, noting the points where it differs from the pre-revolutionary practice, and then I shall mention the differences which exist in respect of marriage between the various social groups in the kolkhoz.

The most essential point in which a present-day marriage differs from the pre-revolutionary version is that brideprice (*aduu-baril* — 'presentation of horses') is no longer paid in the vast majority of cases. However, the 'traditional' payment of dowry (*zahal* — 'special outfit' or trousseau) is still made, consisting of hallowed jewellery and ornaments, if the family still has these, and a range of clothes, crockery, linen, and furniture for the bride in her new status. Besides this, the young couple are given further large presents (livestock, furniture) in the category of *enzhe* ('inheritance'), and these come from both the groom's and the bride's sides.[31] The *zahal* is what a young woman is entitled to from her natal group, and its payment signifies that she has separated from them, but the *enzhe* given to a woman is a voluntary present, indicating that she has worked in her parents' household and deserves some of its resources (for discussion see Chapter 1 section 4). A man, however, receives his inheritance by right. The *enzhe* need not be paid, in either case, at the time of the marriage itself, but it seems from my informants' accounts that it is in fact either paid or *announced* at the wedding. This, I suppose, is because the wedding is the occasion when wealth is displayed, and the exchanges between the two sides to the marriage are made known. Besides the *zahal* and the *enzhe* the wedding rituals provide the occasion for extensive gift-giving between the bride's kin and the groom's kin (i.e. not to the young couple). These gifts (*beleg* or *khariu*) vary from the merely token to valuable and expensive items (gold watches, etc.) and being unlike the brideprice and dowry ideologically neutral in Soviet terms, they provide a catch-all category for the various transfers which take place between the two 'sides'. It is possible that in some places a *de facto* brideprice is hidden in this category. However this was not the case in Selenga or Barguzin, where the brideprice has disappeared.

Thus we can summarise the differences between the present wedding exchanges and those of the past as follows: the brideprice was by definition paid by agnatic kinship groups to one another in exchange for women. The dowry (*zahal*) valuables, passing from mother to daughter, were transferred from the women attached to one agnatic group to the women attached to another. This automatic tying of the material exchanges at marriage to patrilineal kinship groups no longer in fact exists (even if people talk as though it does): the *enzhe*, it is true, is still paid by close kin, but the *zahal* now includes items given by neighbours and other non-kin 'on the bride's side', and the flexible category of *beleg* ('gifts') allows exchanges to take place between social groups of several different kinds. While the brideprice used to be agreed upon in advance by contract, the present wedding exchanges are given both by contract and as people wish and this allows a last-minute expansion in competitive gift-giving.

The 'value' implications of the change from brideprice to dowry are very interesting. As mentioned in Chapter 1 section 4, the brideprice was essentially a political contract, a kind of tribute in a sense, and it was something to be got out of if possible. In the late nineteenth century, the non-fulfilment of brideprice contracts was the source of endless litigation and accusations of cheating among the Buryat.[32] To give a large dowry, on the other hand, was a matter of honour. Brideprice became less important, even before the Revolution, as genealogically defined lineages grew more and more distinct from the administrative/political lineages, which had been defined after the Speransky reforms in the early nineteenth century.[33] By the end of the nineteenth century this dowry, it appears, was often larger than the brideprice, i.e. the brideprice was used to cover expenses *towards* the dowry, which exceeded it in value and also included different items (jewellery, etc.) as opposed to cattle and money.[34] The political function of lineages began to erode with the establishment of territorial administration at the beginning of the twentieth century, and entirely disappeared after collectivisation; it has been replaced by Soviet institutions. The dowry and reciprocal gift-giving, with their connotations of honour, have remained.

The categories of the pre-revolutionary wedding rituals demonstrate the political and economic importance of marriage. There were seven main sequences, each of which contained numerous smaller rituals: (1) the agreement between representatives of the kin-groups that a marriage should take place between them; (2) the betrothal, which was at the same time a definite agreement on the amount of the brideprice; (3) the visit of the bridegroom to his future wife's kin-group and the payment of brideprice; (4) the farewell celebration of the bride among her own kin and the accumulation of the dowry; (5) the fetching of the bride by the groom's kin-group, the bridal journey and the laying-out of the dowry; (6) the marriage itself, which took place among the groom's kin; (7) the return of the bride for a visit to her kin-group – this lasted a month or two and one of its purposes was the collection of presents.

The contemporary 'traditional' wedding among Selenga Buryat kolkhozniks takes place as follows. Sequences (1) and (2) are now combined. Choice of marriage partners is now made by young people themselves, but as we saw in Chapter 1 section 4 (Table 1.8) the great majority of marriages are still exogamous. It seems that, if marriages can no longer be arranged by the older generation, they can still sometimes be prevented. I was earnestly told about an unfortunate pair who had met in Ulan-Ude at work, and being outside their local communities did not know the genealogies properly (this was disgraceful, it was implied by my old lady informant), but after they had decided to get married the matter was gone into. It was discovered that they were only nine generations distant, an eleven generation exogamy rule was invoked and the marriage was stopped. Until the 1930s in Barguzin brides and grooms were sometimes married without ever having seen one another.[35]

It is the responsibility of the bridegroom to make inquiries about the genealogical status of the girl he wishes to marry. A particularly 'traditional' family will also consult a lama about the suitability of the marriage from the astrological point of view. It is thought that some years in the twelve-year cycle 'go together' and will make a good marriage, while others do not.[36] Nowadays, if people hold this belief they rationalise it in terms of people's characters, which are determined by the year they are born in. Since not only the years, but also the months and hours in the day are counted by the same twelve-animal cycle, and other astrological facts about the bride and groom can be added to the forecast, the lamas actually have enough conflicting data to allow a certain leeway in their predictions, and it is to be doubted whether the lama's intervention these days is more than a ritual gesture on the part of the parents.

The bridegroom or his father chooses a respected man (*khudain türüü*) and woman (*khudagyn türüü*) from amongst their agnatic kin as match-makers. These people must have had successful lives and happy and fruitful marriages. Often they are officials of the kolkhoz. They become responsible for the conduct of the betrothal, which now combines the initial agreement between the two sides, symbolised by an exchange of belts or ritual scarves (*behe* or *khadag andaldakha*), and the betrothal itself. The groom's father, with his male match-maker, and a few other respected male kinsmen, set out to the prospective bride's home to ask for her in marriage. The bride herself should not be present, and if she is at home when the betrothal party arrives, she hides away. The negotiations start with a ritual conversation which is supposed to deceive the girl's family as to what this visit is about. The groom's match-maker says that he has come in search of a lost animal, 'A black god, a white god, we think it has joined your herds.' 'What kind of animal?' ask the bride's side. By now, the girl's parents, whom she may not have told, especially if the young man is someone she met while away from the kolkhoz, realise what is being asked and begin to size up the proposition. If they do not want the marriage, they say, '*Orson boroo zogsodog, Irsen ailshan mordodog*' ('Rain comes and then stops, Guests come and then ride away'), a ritual couplet which is not as rude in Buryat as it sounds in English. If the proposal is accepted, the groom's side must offer *arkhi* (spirits distilled from milk) or vodka, and the bride's side reciprocates by offering a *töölei* (a cooked sheep's or horse's head) to the groom's match-maker. Even in the most attenuated form of modern wedding, even if the young couple have already registered their marriage somewhere far away from home, this visit from the groom's side still occurs and spirits must be offered to the bride's parents.[37]

The *töölei* head is placed with its nose facing towards the *khudain türüü*, who must then eat small pieces of meat from five places in order (in the direction of the sun, see Figure 8.1a). Then he hands the head back to his host. The head is taken away and a hole cut in the centre of the skull and a rib is inserted in the hole (Figure 8.1b). Coming back with the head, the bride's representative sings the following song:

> Let's put out to green pasture
> The quiet, gentle horse,
> Let's offer a family festival
> To the respected lord and official.[38]

a

b

khudain türüü   *khudain türüü*

8.1. *Töölei* head offering to respected guests.

386

The guest offered the *töölei* must eat the brain and the rib, and then he must put some money down on the plate and hand it back to his host. If he does not put down money it is a great insult to the father of the girl.

After this they get down to the matter of arranging the wedding. They decide on a date, and on the number of people who will be invited to the marriage itself. In former days, the brideprice would have been negotiated at this point. Now, the exchange of 'presents' and the amount of dowry and *enzhe* are not exactly negotiated, but efforts are made to discover approximately what will be given so that one will be able to give as much, if not more. The exchange of belts marks the definite agreement to hold the wedding. According to my Selenga informants the exchange of belts is still an obligatory part of the betrothal, but in other parts of Buryatiya it is disappearing or sometimes takes place later, when the bride is taken to the groom's house.[39] After a general feast, at which at least the *töölei* animal has had to be killed, the bride's side gives presents (shirts, dresses, decorated scarves) to the groom's match-makers before they leave.

The rituals associated with the bringing of the brideprice (in Barguzin, apparently, it used to be fetched) are now either abandoned, or incorporated in the taking away of the bride.

The bride's farewell (*basagani naadan*) feast is still given. In the old days this used to take place about two months before the wedding: all of the bride's patrilateral kin, and people of her mother's agnatic group (*nagatsa*), were invited to a large feast by her parents. The bridegroom and his kin were not invited. After the feast, the bride, accompanied by her father's brother (*abaga*) or other senior male kinsman and some girl-friends, went to visit every house of her group. She was entertained, given presents towards the dowry or *enzhe*, and took part in a series of festivities which went on right through the months until the wedding itself. These evening parties were primarily for young people, and it is apparent from the literature that there was every chance that the bride would not end up as a virgin.[40] Today this round of parties is somewhat shortened, but otherwise it is essentially unchanged. There was much laughter and shouts of 'No, no!' when I asked if the bridegroom could attend. Basayeva, however, notes that among the Alar Buryats the groom is sometimes present.[41] The bride takes a filled cup which she offered to each relative (*pokhal barikha*), who, as he or she accepted the cup named his present and gave the bride a blessing (*yörööl*).

On the day of the marriage itself, a group — this time including the bridegroom himself — comes to fetch the bride. They again bring *arkhi* or vodka as their offering to the bride's family. The bride sings songs of lament and farewell. A sacrifice is made to the fire (*gal taikha*) and local spirits of the bride's kin. Among the Barguzin Buryats the bridegroom should bring a sheep, which he kills himself for the sacrifice. Small pieces of cooked meat are offered to the fire, and the bride's relatives address the fire saying, '*Altan möngö, aduu mal irnem*', which can be loosely translated as, 'We ask for money and horse herds.' After this, in the past and still sometimes today, the bride prays to the family deity

387

(*burkhan*), and a senior representative of her side prays to the spirits of the locality.

The bride is dressed usually in national costume, a dark-blue silk Mongolian-style gown (*degel*), with silver ornaments, ear-rings, and necklaces. In Barguzin the bride's face is covered with a shawl, so she cannot see, but this was not mentioned to me in Selenga. The agreed number of guests from the bride's side gather together and prepare to set out to go to the groom's village. Even if he lives almost next door, the idea of the journey is still preserved. Usually from 70 to 100 people, but sometimes up to 200 or 250, are invited from the bride's side — all of them kin except for one or two girl-friends of the bride. Her appointed match-makers go with her, but her parents, especially her mother, usually stay at home.

The bride's train sets out in specially ordered cars and lorries. Sometimes the bride herself, accompanied by young men of her kin, rides on a specially decorated horse. The dowry, large pieces of furniture as well as boxes of crockery and clothes, goes in a trailer pulled by a tractor. The guests ride alongside in their little carts.

On the way a small group of elders including the match-makers from the groom's side is waiting to receive them. They make a fire at a scenic place in the steppe, lay a table with food, and again offer *arkhi* or vodka. Here there is another ritual conversation, carried on between the match-makers of each side, full of jokes and innuendo. It goes something along these lines:[42]

Local people [groom's side] : Who are you?
Guests: We have come from far away. We have lost a bullock and are looking for him. Has a bullock strayed into your herd?
Local people: Yes, yes. He came yesterday. And what colour is your bullock?
Guests: He is grey.
Local people: And has he got horns or not?
Guests: He has no horns, he's a fat lively one.
Local people: Yes! Just getting ready to butt, isn't he?
Guests: He's ours! That's the one. So this is where he's got to!
Local people: There is nothing more to say.
Guests: Do you have some *arkhi* here?
Local people: Yes we do. We have a huge amount. Get down from your horses and accept our humble offering.
Guests: We cannot refuse . . .

After a small party on the way, the wedding train moves to the groom's house, where all of his kinsmen and guests are waiting to receive him. The bride herself is offered milk, 'to purify her'. A ritual tethering-post (*serge*) is erected outside the bridegroom's house. The *serge* in some districts had carvings indicating the wealth and status of the owner, and one is set up for each son as he marries.

The dowry, both *zahal* and *enzhe*, is unloaded and put in a special small house near the main one, as though the young couple were going to live there. Beds, tables, sideboards are set out, and a table is laid with vodka and sweets.

Presents from the groom's side to the young couple are added to the show. A queue is formed to inspect the dowry. As each guest comes in he throws money on the table (about 5 rubles) and drinks a glass of *arkhi*.

Before the wedding feast there is an offering (*khayalga*) to the fire. In the old days, the bride threw fat into the fire to make it burn up, at the same time making obeisance to the groom's father and all of his senior male relatives in turn. She then joined hands with the groom, they knelt on a felt rug (*shirdeg*), and prayed to the groom's family deity (*burkhan*).[43] This in essence was the rite of marriage, i.e. the receiving of the bride into the groom's lineage. The obeisance to senior males is supposed to have been discontinued because of its overtones of female subservience, but — although my informants rather skated over this point — it seems that some reduced version of it still does occur in 'traditional' weddings. All of the guests do still make a libation to the fire, dipping the fourth finger of their right hand in *arkhi* and flipping it against their thumb to sprinkle drops on the fire. Old people also make libations to the spirits of the locality (*ezhed*) and ancestors, requesting in long speeches (*yörööl*) timely rain, fertility and wealth. The bride is given a speech of admonition about how to treat the fire, the symbol of the continuity of her husband's lineage: sharp and dirty things must not be thrown on it, the fire-tongs must not be thrown on the floor, and so on. She is instructed to behave respectfully towards her father-in-law, not to speak loudly in his presence, and to obey her mother-in-law.

This is the point in the wedding when lineage traditions are remembered. Even in weddings which are not entirely 'traditional', in that the very same, standardised blessings are replaced with new improvisations, the content still refers to the lineage and only the references to 'religious' elements (*ezhed* and other spirits) are left out. Tugutov gives one example of a new blessing:[44]

> She and he,
> Making the happiness of fertility
> Have created a new family,
> On a sacred time and year,
> On a sunny happy day,
> When the grass is fresh and 'blue',
> The young ones are gathered together,
> The wedding is prepared,
> And having untied the halter, watered the horse,
> I invite you, 'Please come!'
> The ten older brothers go before,
> Follow the four younger brothers,
> Our great lineage (*üg*) of Ukhaasai
> Opens wide the skirts of its gown
> To receive its offspring . . .

According to Vyatkina, it was at this point that, among the Selenga Buryats, the sister's sons (*zee*) would be required to name their mother's brothers (*nagatsa*) in three ascending generations; those who could name also the *nagatsa* relatives of their father and father's father were greatly respected, especially if they could name six or nine generations.[45] It went without saying that any self-respecting Buryat could name his own patrilineal ancestors. Buryats said, 'A man who forgets his lineage will be eaten by fire even if he is on water. A man who forgets the sky will be bitten by a dog even if he is on a camel.'[46]

After this there is a large feast, at which, in some weddings at least, the bride and groom sit together and are offered cooked neck of mutton. This they must eat in turn, not using a knife, but using only their lips and teeth (for some reason this custom was mentioned with embarrassed laughter, but no explanation was given). The seating for the feast is strictly by age and seniority in the lineage, not by riches or position in the kolkhoz. The men sit along the top of the table, facing north, and in order of descending age they are placed down the western side; the women, starting with the oldest, sit from the north-eastern corner, along the eastern side, and along the bottom of the table at the south. In most weddings there is a separate table for all the young people, including the bride and groom. According to Basayeva, the western Buryats divide the guests not by age and sex but by kin-group, the bride's side sitting in one half of the room and the groom's kin opposite them. In this variant, the married couple sit in the position of honour in the middle at the main table.[47] The Barguzin Buryats also sit in this way, with the kin on either side seated by genealogical seniority. The number of guests on each side should be equal. If it was agreed at the betrothal ceremony that the bride's side should bring one hundred guests and only seventy-five arrive, my informants told me that this would constitute a great insult to the groom's kin. It is traditional to exchange witty repartee between the two sides. The meat at the feast is divided into named sections (the *tö̈lei* – head, the *dala* – shoulder, etc.), and it should be allocated among the guests by the represen-tative (*zahul*)[48] of the groom's lineage. If the wrong pieces of meat are given to a particular kinsman or affine this is considered a great insult – even a fighting matter.

After the feast a round of presents (*beleg* or *khariu*) is given to the bride's kin from the groom's side, starting with her main representatives, the match-makers. They give shirts to the men, dresses or cloth to the women, scarves or perfume to the younger people. Reciprocal presents are given from the bride's side to the groom's parents and match-makers, with appropriate speeches.

As the bride's kinsmen prepare to go away they are given a crate of vodka and sweets 'for the road'. The young wife now stays with her new kin. Her group leaves, but on the way they stop by a stream or on a hill, open the crate of vodka and discuss the wedding – was it a good one, were they given good treat-ment, equal to the presents they brought? If the answer is positive, then it is thought that the marriage will be happy; if not, it is a bad omen for the future. The bride's kin then proceed to her home to tell her parents how the wedding went. Here, there is a further party.

At the groom's house feasting and dancing continue through the night. Some

390

weddings go on for days, moving from house to house of the groom's kin, and the bride's people do not go away immediately.

After the wedding the bride and groom usually live in the same house as the husband's parents for a time, until it is possible to build a new house for them. Houses are built between sowing time and the hay-harvest. The rest of the year people are too busy, or the weather is too cold. All the groom's kinsmen and some neighbours help to build the house in these summer evenings. Arrangements are made with the kolkhoz for transport of the logs and for specialist carpenters to construct windows. No payment is made to the kin, but the husband's father gives a large feast for everyone who took part.

The bride is taken back home to her parents by her husband two or three months after the wedding. In some areas of Buryatiya she may stay for some months, but in Selenga this visit (*ailshaluulkha*) lasts only a week or two. From her husband's kin she takes vodka, sweets, and presents to her family. Then she should visit all of her kin, taking presents to each one, giving the sweets to the children in each house. When she is taken back to her husband by her parents, she must take presents from her side of cooked meat (a sheep is killed and she must take the chest, the most respected part, to her parents-in-law). She takes sweets for the children of her husband's kin, but on no account should she take vodka. This visit is one occasion on which presents which had been announced at the wedding but not actually given by her kin are handed over. This is particularly likely if she is already pregnant, and the presents in this case (e.g. livestock) are seen as gifts to the unborn child. In some parts of Buryatiya the groom and some of his friends also take part in the visit to the bride's kin (*ailshaluulkha*). Basayeva mentions a wedding in Alar in 1964 at which, the young wife's kin already knowing about the visit in advance, six houses of her kin prepared feasts, each one killing a sheep, so as to be able to present a *töölei* to the groom. On his side each guest brought and presented a ritual vessel of *arkhi* or vodka (*zorig*), and belts were exchanged between the two sides.[49] In another western Buryat wedding of the 1960s, the entire series of rituals (betrothal, the bride's feast and collection of the dowry, the giving of presents to the groom's kin, and the wedding itself) were all compressed into the final visit of the bride and groom to her father's house. All of this occurred after the couple had been married, in the legal sense, for six months — but nevertheless it was felt that some enaction of the main rituals should occur in however sketchy a form.

In Selenga, however, the legal marriage, i.e. registration at the *sel'sovet*, almost always took place after the wedding, sometimes years later, when there were already several children (see Chapter 1 section 3).

Some version of the 'traditional' wedding which I have described was the predominant form in Selenga in the 1960s. In the three years before my visit to the Karl Marx kolkhoz in 1967 there had been only one or two weddings of the 'Komsomol' type. All other weddings, around fifteen a year, had been 'traditional', according to the secretary of the *sel'sovet*.

In Barguzin it appears that a slightly larger number of weddings are of the 'Komsomol' type, which I shall describe later, but this does not at all mean that the material expenses, the number of guests invited, or the amount of gift-giving is reduced. Let us look now at the expenses involved in a wedding. According to Basayeva in the 1940s and 1950s weddings were relatively modest, but during the 1960s they became increasingly extravagant, a 'negative tendency' (*otritsatel'naya tendentsiya*) in the view of the Soviet authorities.[50] As Basayeva says,

At such weddings there is an unhealthy rivalry between the kinsmen of the young pair, rivalry as to which side invites more guests, kills more sheep, offers more drink. Each side tries to overwhelm the other. They invite all the kinsmen of the bride and groom, not only those living in the same village but also people from other, distant villages, and even from far towns and other districts.[51]

A wedding is a large expense not only for the immediate kin of the marrying couple but even for distant kin and neighbours who live close by, since at several points (the *basaganai naadan*, the visit for betrothal, and the visit of the bride's kin to the groom's) the guests expect to be entertained in many houses. Consequently, each of these separate ceremonies may go on for days.

In recent years the generosity of wedding gifts has come to be seen as a demonstration of the good standard of living of the giver. People as it were compete with one another to give more expensive presents, and it is not only the families of the bride and groom which are involved, but all the kinsmen on both sides too . . . Often wedding presents consist of the entire furnishings of a house (sometimes even imported goods), fridges, vacuum cleaners, washing machines, suits, clothes, livestock, etc. Besides presents to the young couple, there are gifts to be given to the match-makers, to all guests, and almost every kinsman in the village feels he has to give a reception . . . It is particularly difficult to afford all this, people say, when there are several weddings in one summer (it is at this season that most weddings are held).[52]

Often many gifts are duplicated and the recipients give away, or sell, the surplus.

Table 8.1 gives the approximate expenses of a modest wedding in Barguzin (the bridegroom was a zoo technician and an official of the Komsomol) in 1967. We see that the amount spent on either side, around 2,500 rubles, is about equal, and that it is equivalent to a year's salary for a prosperous skilled worker. In fact it seems to me that on balance the bride's side bears greater expenses in most weddings, particularly if the Selenga custom of donating money when viewing the dowry also exists in Barguzin (I did not check this fact). In the only other wedding where I asked in detail about the presents which had been given (the marriage of the chief veterinarian of the Barguzin Karl Marx kolkhoz), it was clear that the bride's side had provided the greater share of the presents.

This implies that there has been a change from a brideprice system to a dowry system among the Buryat in the Soviet period. We can relate this to several factors already discussed: (1) the prohibition by law of brideprice payments in

Table 8.1. *Gifts at a kolkhoz wedding, 1967 (rubles)*

Bridegroom's side		Bride's side	
200	presents	250	two sheep, vodka, etc. at
100	money gifts		Feast 2 (bride's fare-
35	one sheep (live) given		well)
	by grandfather	100	presents at Feast 2
70	*töölei* and meat taken to	700	bride's clothing
	bride's house for	800	furniture
	Feast 1 (betrothal)	100	bedding, linen
100	vodka and presents for	550	cow and calf (live) given by
	Feast 1		father
500	six sheep, vodka, cakes,	110	small presents and money
	etc. for Feast 3		at Feast 3
	wedding at bride-		―――
	groom's house	2,610	
1,000	two cows (live) given by	―――	
	grandfather and		
	mother		
105	three sheep (live) given		
	by relatives		
250	money gifts at Feast 3		
100	expenditure on house		
―――			
2,460			

the 1920s as 'degrading to women' — but it should be noted that brideprice was already less frequent among the Buryat before this time; (2) the continuing value placed on having sons, rather than daughters, which has only been accentuated by the division of labour in the kolkhoz between men and women, according to which women are concentrated in the less well-paid jobs, and, if they are quali-fied, find it difficult to get appropriate employment as against qualified men; (3) the tendency for the more prosperous men, kolkhoz officials and to a lesser extent the specialists to keep their wives at home as housewives 'who do not have to work'; (4) the number of strategic marriages, in which an ambitious young man marries the daughter of a well-placed official, and the official attempts to acquire useful sons-in-law; and (5) the prestige which attaches in dowry-type gift-giving to donating more than the other side — in this case the bride's father is required to outdo the groom's side. All of this is consistent with a hierarchical society, in which high status women are valued not so much for their economic contribution to the household as for their value in terms of pres-tige, and they also have to be maintained. We would consequently expect to find this pattern — strategic marriages and predominance of dowry — in the prosperous official stratum of rural society rather than among the ordinary kolkhozniks.

393

Ritual and identity

Field-work data from Selenga and Barguzin in 1967 make it clear that marriage choices are influenced by occupation in the kolkhoz. There is a clear stratification between four groups: officials and specialists, teachers, skilled workers, and ordinary kolkhozniks. The separation out of teachers, virtually all of whom marry one another, may be because they tend not to be local and are sent to the farm from other areas. The category of skilled workers contains many Russians, especially in mechanical types of work, and since there is virtually no inter-marriage between Russians and Buryats in this stratum of society, this factor may create a somewhat artificial division between skilled and other workers. Some of the data are given in Table 1.4. What is clear from this register and my own field material is the gulf which separates the officials from the unskilled workers. Not a single official or specialist was married to a spouse giving their occupation as 'kolkhoznik' (i.e. general worker), nor even to the more skilled categories of 'shepherd', 'milker' or 'driver'.

As far as I can tell from my limited data, dowry is less likely to predominate over other gifts among ordinary workers. One or two shepherds and milkmaids said they had married without having a wedding at all (admittedly this was during the poverty-stricken 1940s and 1950s). In a very poor family the role of gifts given from the bride's side would, in any case, be very different since they, and the wife's labour in the small-holding, would be essential for the new family's subsistence. The kinds of gifts given are utilitarian (chairs, a bed, ordinary cutlery and crockery) as opposed to objects of display (gold-painted crockery and electrical gadgetry in houses where there is barely enough current for a low-watt light bulb). For the badly paid labourer in the kolkhoz the most important thing is to live in some kind of household. The head of a household can receive a plot and a cow from the kolkhoz, but it is difficult, unless he has someone living with him (or her) to manage a small-holding and a job in the farm at the same time.

The official ceiling on land and livestock ownership by any one household has the effect that wealth is either consumed — in gargantuan festivities of the wedding type — or transformed into property of a type on which there is no legal limit, consumer and display goods. Buryat life-cycle ceremonies have become ritually simpler in recent years but materially more complex and more extravagant as people become more prosperous. The calculation and discussion on the way home from the wedding shows that people make this conversion of wages or products into gifts within a system of *reciprocity* existing in temporal sequence: thus, speaking about a western Buryat equivalent of the *milaagod* ritual (see below), one Buryat woman from Ekhirit-Bulagat *raion* said in 1965: 'Everyone does the same, and so you have to have a *milaagod* too, because if you don't take part you lose out. If you give a festival you have to recoup the losses — they bring presents to you later in your turn.'[53] The very word for a gift in the Barguzin dialect, *güilga*, is their version of the Buryat literary word, which means 'request'.[54]

Money, in Buryat kolkhoz society, appears to have not only an economic function, but also a symbolic one. It is notable that money, often a token amount, is handed over at important rituals of the life-cycle: at the *milaagod*, at the betrothal, at the viewing of the dowry, and at funerals. A more profound study than I have been able to make would be necessary in order to understand this completely. It may be relevant that at this time uses of money were limited for the kolkhoznik. Until recently local shops held little that was desired, opportunities to visit the capital city were restricted, and luxury goods were in short supply (*defitsitnyye*) and obtainable not by money alone, if by money at all. It was reported to me in Barguzin in 1975 that many kolkhozniks have savings accounts of money which they cannot spend – in the same way, we might add, that they have stores of livestock, valuables, *khadag* (ritual silk scarves), and other items. Just as a sheep can have two meanings, as a utilitarian animal and as a symbolic beast (*khaluun chanartai* – hot, as opposed to the goat, which is *khuiten chanartai* – cold), the Buryats are able to give a double value to money. It is a more or less neutral means of exchange, and at the same time it can be made into a gift, with what precise significance we do not know, but in which the insistent 'how much' aspect of money becomes irrelevant.

What is the nature of these social groups which enter the cycle of reciprocal exchange? Firstly we note that since many of the ritual gifts are announced by the giver as he or she pronounces a *yörööl* (blessing), there is a moment of individualisation in respect of particular objects. But secondly, there is constant mention, both in the literature and in the conversation of my informants, of 'the bride's side' and 'the groom's side'. What are these groups?

We should note the important fact that the Buryat classificatory kinship terminology (Figure 8.2) and the concept of exogamy have both survived. In other words, with very few exceptions, Buryat men still do not marry women whom they classify as *üyeelenüüd* (F's B's D, etc.) or *zeenser* (F's Z's D, etc.). It was stated earlier that the main function of brideprice was to legitimise children in a patrilineal descent group. Brideprice is no longer paid. An interesting question therefore arises as to how the exogamous groups are now defined.

In pre-revolutionary times, as I was told by both Selenga and Barguzin Buryats, it was considered the utmost disgrace for a girl to bear an illegitimate child. It was an unspeakable insult to her own kinsmen, and rather than let them know the truth girls sometimes even disappeared for a time, bore the child in the forest, and killed it (but see Chapter 1 section 6). Now this is no longer the case. An unmarried girl with a baby is accepted all the sooner because she is known to be fertile. In these cases the husband accepts paternity of the child. If the girl for some reason does not get married immediately, perhaps because she wishes to go away to study or work, her parents accept the child as their own. If she marries later, the child may be taken back and brought up in her new family. In other words, children may grow up knowing that they 'belong' to two agnatic groups. The same is true in cases of divorce. One shepherdess told me that her father, who came from the west Barbinsho lineage of the Hengeldur clan in Barguzin,

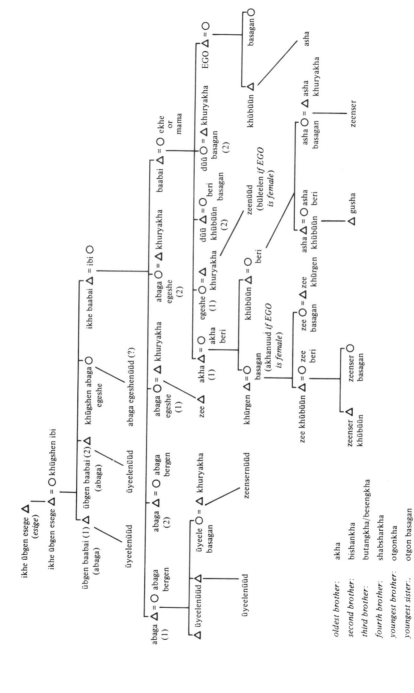

oldest brother: akha
second brother: bishankha
third brother: butangkha/besengkha
fourth brother: shabsharkha
youngest brother: otgonkha
youngest sister: otgon basagan

a   Consanguineal kin

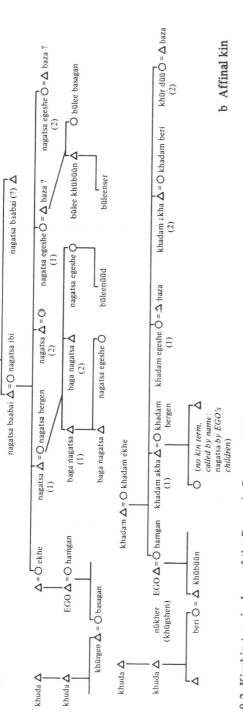

b Affinal kin

8.2. Kinship terminology of the Barguzin Buryats, 1967.

(1) = older; (2) = younger
-nuud/-nüüd = suffix denoting plural collective
-ser/-sar = suffix denoting younger generation
akha = older brothers (collective); older agnates
baza = reciprocal males married to women of a lineage; females married to males of a lineage
bülee = reciprocal (cf. üyeele), the children of sisters, male and female
düü = younger brothers and sisters (collective)
khuda = reciprocal child's spouse's parent
khügshen = old person

khür düü = collective wife's younger sisters, nieces in male line
khürgen = daughter's husband (khürgekhe means 'to accompany', 'to send', 'to reach', 'to attain')
khuryakhe = collective husbands of older and younger sisters (khuryakha means 'to collect, gather together, accumulate')
üyeele = reciprocal male parallel cousins, children of brothers, male and female
zee = collective all descendants of women of EGO's lineage, reciprocal with nagatsa, all males of mother's lineage

üyeeld = BrSoCh; FaFaYoBrSoCh; FaBrSoCh   üyinchir = BrSoSoCh; FaFaFaYoBrSoSoCh; etc.
hayaald = BrSoSoCh; FaFaFaYoBrSoSoCh   hayinchir = BrSoSoSoCh

The Barguzin kinship terminology is essentially similar to the Khalkha Mongol, see Vreeland 1957, pp. 58–9. However, there are the following differences: the Buryats of Barguzin no longer differentiate between üyeeleniiid and agnates of different generations; thus the Khalkha series no longer exists among the Buryats. On the other hand, the Barguzin system makes a distinction which the Khalkha ignores: between khuryakha (sister's husband) and khürgen (daughter's husband). In Khalkha these are both khürgen. The Buryats also seem to have a more elaborate list of terms for distinguishing older and younger among siblings than do the Khalkha.

Note the use of senior terms (e.g. egeshe 'older sister') for younger sisters and daughters in the mother's brothers' lineage (nagatsa).

had divorced her mother when she (Ego) was very young. Her mother had subsequently married a man from the Bayandai lineage who had brought her up and whose name she took, and now she counted both Barbinsho and Bayandai as her kin. In cases of adoption too, as we saw (Chapter 7 section 3), the family of origin is not forgotten, even though the adopted child takes a family name and 'patronymic' from its adopted father. In all such situations of doubtful or dual paternity, it appears that exogamy is counted for both sides. This was certainly the case for the shepherdess mentioned above: she could marry into neither Barbinsho nor Bayandai lineages. In effect, what we are seeing is an expansion of the extent of exogamy. Brideprice as the means par excellence of establishing legitimacy has been replaced by a variety of links which are recognised as agnatic kinship. Exogamy, particularly if it is reckoned not 'by rule' of number of generations, but by broad kinship groupings, is equivalent to the definition of those kin who are expected to play a role on one's own 'side' at weddings.

In the 'traditional' wedding it is still groups conceptualised as patrilineages which take part, and it was expressly stated to me that position in the kolkhoz does not necessarily play a part in allocating the most respected roles (matchmakers, and the *zahul* 'master of ceremonies'). The wedding in this case, like the *tsagaalgan*, is a ritual which operates in a relation of counterpoint with the hierarchy of the kolkhoz. However, as we shall see below, officials often try to dominate weddings. When kolkhozniks give their genealogies they are normally concerned with two separate interests, the circle of local kin, and the tracing of links with prominent people; these individual interests to a great extent define the genealogies themselves. In the case of the wedding, where prestige attaches to having as many guests as possible, there is an attempt to involve everyone of a given named lineage. In other words, the group brought into play is not ego-centred (this is demonstrated by, amongst other things, the relatively minor role which the actual parents of the marrying couple play, as opposed to lineage seniors).

However, there are two means by which the differentiation which is so marked in the kolkhoz by the division of labour now affects the social groups concerned in a wedding (and hence in the cycle of reciprocity). The first of these is the traditional ritual of the *milaagod*. This is a festival which is given once in the life of every child, in some places shortly after birth, in others during the teens, with the aim of thanking the kin who gave it life. This is the explanation which was given to me in Barguzin. Some presents are given to the child, but the main point of the ritual is the giving of gifts from the child (in fact from its parents) to a circle of kin whom they invite. Since, as people in Barguzin said, one cannot get married without having previously held a *milaagod*, it seems reasonable to assume that at least one of the functions of this ritual is the engagement of suitable kin in the cycle of reciprocity prior to the major expense of the wedding. In other words, those given expensive presents at the *milaagod* are expected later to make generous contributions at the wedding. This interpretation is supported by the complaints of Soviet observers that the *milaagod* too is becoming increasingly extravagant.[55] It is clear that if anyone wished to involve the kolkhoz officials in the cycle of reciprocity, the *milaagod* is as good an opportunity as any. There are two large clans in Bayangol, three smaller ones, and five clans of minimal size. Since kin on both parents' sides are invited to the *milaagod* there is a good chance of catching one or two of the farm bosses in the kinship net.

The second way in which kolkhoz-based differentiation is introduced is not 'traditional'. It is simply to invite kolkhoz officials, as opposed to kin elders, to play the part of master of ceremonies and match-maker. The literature from all over Buryatiya suggests that rather than a clear dividing line between the 'traditional' and the 'Komsomol' wedding, there is more of a continuum, in which the average types of weddings are those in which overt religious ritual is avoided.

Let us look at some examples. It is significant that it was an orphan, Roza B., who was given a Komsomol wedding in the Selenga Karl Marx kolkhoz in 1962. In the words of a local writer this is what happened:

Roza B. is an orphan. In 1961, after finishing school, she was sent by the Komsomol, together with twenty-two other Komsomol members, to the Karl Marx kolkhoz. They sent her to work in the village of Shuluta, in a calf-breeding unit. Here she soon mastered her new job and recommended herself as a good 'social worker' (*obshchestvennitsa*). The Komsomols of her unit chose her as their representative in the Komsomol organisation.

Her wedding took place in 1962 and the Party Secretary asked a girl member of the kolkhoz to organise it. The wedding took place in the 'culture centre' (*kul'tbaz*). The whole complex brigade, of which the calf-breeding unit was a part, participated.

Just as the wedding was beginning, the old woman in whose house Roza was living refused to let her go, demanding that the traditional ceremony *takhil tabikha* [sacrifice to the fire-spirit and other local deities] should take place, with offerings from her as foster-mother to her own ancestral deity. The Komsomol organiser explained that the new Komsomol wedding does not include the *takhil* ceremony. Then the landlady asked that, if only for the sake of propriety, she be asked for Roza's hand in marriage. 'You see, Roza has no parents, and I've got so used to her, she's like my own daughter', she begged.

At this wedding there were many traditional elements too, which gave it an emotional character. For example, the bridegroom Boris invited his distant kinsman, a great expert in ancient rituals, to come from the 'Selenginskii' sovkhoz. It was this man who, respecting the old traditions, gave the young couple their blessing. After him, the Komsomol organiser gave a speech. The wedding in Shuluta was very lively. There were many songs, laughter, and jokes.[56]

The stricter types of Komsomol wedding take on the character of all Soviet rural ceremonial, in other words, almost as though people can think of no other 'Soviet' way of doing things, they become like meetings. For example, in the wedding of the agronomist Darizhab Dashnimaev and the school-teacher Tsybegmit Dondokova in the 22nd Party Congress collective farm in Aga district in 1968:

399

The Party committee, the kolkhoz management, the *ispolkom* of the *sel'sovet*, the committee of the local Komsomol, and the parents of Tsybegmit and Darizhab agreed to their proposal [to have a Komsomol wedding].

The Commission, set up for this purpose from representatives of the community, addressed themselves carefully to their honoured task. Together with the young people they delimited the circle of people to be invited to the ceremony. They decided together on the day of the wedding, the hour it should start, and they set up a detailed plan of the proceedings: which foods to prepare, how to lay the table, who to play the music, and so on.

And so the day of the wedding arrived . . . The spacious hall of the *Dom Kul'tury* was festively decorated. On the stage was a long table, covered with red velvet. The electric light was burning. Silence. A ceremonial atmosphere. At the table sat the Chairman of the executive committee of the *sel'sovet*, the Party Secretary, the Chairman of the kolkhoz, the Director of the school, the secretary of Komsomol, and the parents of the young couple.

The Chairman of the *sel'sovet* asked the young couple to come forward and sign the official marriage act. They came forward, exchanged rings, and were given the good wishes of the Chairman as he shook their hands. The couple were now married. It was the Party Secretary who offered the first toast, and he was followed by each of the people sitting at the table and then many others.[57] Although this wedding subsequently turned into a cheerful party, with traditional *yörööl* (eulogies) from the old people, the 'Komsomol' part approximated closely to other Soviet rituals described earlier.

Although a Komsomol wedding is supposed to avoid massive exchanges of goods, we find that Buryats cannot do so. When the officials become as it were match-makers, they organise the collection of presents, and here the collection is based not on kinship groups but on the political and economic units of socialist society. Thus, in the wedding of Dashilai B. from the 'Mir' kolkhoz with Zinaida H. from 'Red Tori' kolkhoz, the two collective farms themselves took on the roles of wedding participants. Zinaida's kolkhoz gave her valuable presents, and Dashilai's kolkhoz gave him equally expensive things. Furthermore, the Tori Komsomol organisation and the teachers of the local school also participated in the gift-giving. These institutions agreed together what to give, also consulting friends of the young couple, and together they provided the entire furnishings of the new home (wardrobes, sideboard, cupboards, and all domestic equipment) and other valuable things (a gold watch, suits and dresses). The kinsmen on either side also gave presents, but the ethnographer remarks that only close relatives participated, and that the presents were individual ones.[58] In other words, the role of the competing 'sides' at the wedding passed from the wider kin-groups to the wider work-groups to which the marrying couple belonged. At the same time the 'exchange' function of gift-giving almost disappeared: each kolkhoz gave presents to its own member, not to the 'other side'.

The officials, for their part, sometimes make use in their perennial quest — the pursuit of labour — of the general striving to give. Thus the Secretary of the

Komsomol in one kolkhoz asked every member of his organisation how they as a group could contribute to the wedding of one of their number, due to marry soon. 'We could bring a contribution each from home', someone suggested. Someone else proposed borrowing money from the kolkhoz. But the Komsomol Secretary decided on a third plan: they would hold a *subbotnik* (voluntary work-day) and pay for the present with the money earned. 'This will be the most expensive and most memorable present of all', said the Komsomol members, as they agreed. Each young kolkhoznik 'experienced an inner agitation as he prepared for the family festival of his colleague. The *subbotnik* brought the young people together, they experienced the beauty of the brotherhood of labour in the best sense of these words.'[59]

Thus, in Buryat weddings, as in the *tsagaalgan* and *suur-kharbaan* festivals, we see a range of ceremonial activity which varies according to the degree of engagement with the kolkhoz—Soviet—Party structure. At one extreme — perhaps the majority of cases — the wedding is acted out as it were in contradistinction to the kolkhoz. A different structure, in which meaning and value reside in concepts of kinship, is activated in the break between organised work and organised work, in the period called 'holiday', when people wear special clothes and hear again the half-forgotten prayers and blessings which used to be at the heart of Buryat culture. This kinship structure, although it is dormant in ordinary working life, is unlikely to disappear totally, because each occasion on which it is brought into activity includes the promise of a future such occasion: a return must be made to every gift. If 'holiday' is opposed to 'work' in people's minds, so the reciprocity and certainty of kinship (by *being born* one is the member of a group) is opposed to the uncertainty and arbitrariness of the allocation of work.

At the other extreme, the wedding is aligned with the potential structure of competition and solidarity in the Soviet system itself. As we have shown earlier, the Soviet ideology (e.g. of 'socialist competition' or 'emulation') poses one team against another, one kolkhoz against another. At the same time, it proclaims the interdependence of such units, and encourages this by ever increasing specialisation of production tasks. The higher levels of the Buryat genealogical structure used to have primarily administrative-political functions, but as I showed in Chapter 1 sections 1 and 4 they were being superseded by Tsarist governmental units even before the Revolution and have now been replaced entirely by Soviet institutions. It seems that, as the Soviet administrative units are becoming social units too — in the sense that workers identify with them and their interests — they are beginning to take their place even in that heartland of traditional values, marriage. Buryat weddings are occasions for both competition and solidarity — perhaps primarily competition. Marriage — what more suitable metaphor? — is an entirely appropriate occasion for the mutual gestures of social units with means at their disposal, the 'manipulable resources' discussed earlier.

401

3. Religion: shamans as the *bricoleurs* of the Soviet world

Let us begin with the evidence of religious activity which I found in Karl Marx collective farm in Barguzin.[60] As can be seen from Map 3, there are five or so religious sites within the territory of the farm.

(1) A small Lamaist *muukhan*[61] among the trees on the hills above Bayangol. This used to be a small *khiid*, Lamaist temple, with religious paintings, statues, and lamps kept inside, and with one lama in attendance to carry out services and prayers. No one else was allowed to enter. The *khiid* is now destroyed, and people only remember this as a religious site. I visited the place in the winter of 1975 and there was no sign of religious activity. It is a very beautiful place, with tall rock outcrops, bushy, twisted pine-trees, and a view over the whole valley of Bayangol. I talked about this place with an old man, father of the chief engineer of the farm, and the Chairman, Lubsanov. The two disagreed on every point, quite politely, but it was clear to me from my reading of the extensive literature on Buryat religion that the Chairman either was ignorant of the traditions or was, perhaps out of habit, just saying whatever came into his head that he thought would please a visitor. The old man firmly put him right, and the Chairman excused himself by saying that he came from a different village, Ulyun, and did not know the traditions of Bayangol. The old man was much moved by this conversation and at one point could not refrain from tears. It seemed that it was unbearable to him that such traditions were now 'forgotten'.

(2) There is a small shamanist *oboo* (ritual cairn of stones) on the hill overlooking the River Ina, which forms the southern boundary of the kolkhoz with the territory of the lumber-station at Chilir (Yubileinii).

(3) There is a larger shamanist *oboo* at Tasarkhai, which used to be the main *ulus* (winter settlement) before the kolkhoz centre was moved to its present site, Bayangol.

(4) There is a Lamaist site at Khadagshan, near the village of Urzhil.

(5) At Shinagolzhin, on the Kuitun steppes to the north of the kolkhoz, there is a shamanist site, the burial place of an ancestral line of shamans (*aranga*). This consists of a large tree, in which a deep hole has been cut for the disposal of the shamans' ashes. It is considered a sacred place: women used to be forbidden to approach, and people were not allowed to cut wood, dig the earth, or collect wild fruits or nuts in the vicinity. Men still make small offerings at this place to the shamans' souls, which are at the same time the spirits of the locality (*ezhed*). They put money in the hole in the tree, and tie cloth strips and rags to its branches.

Throughout the valley of Barguzin, and indeed all over Buryatiya, there are numberless variants on these types of ritual site. Many are simultaneously shamanist and Lamaist places of worship. In the Barguzin valley itself, the main *oboo*, to which people come from far and wide, is at Baragkhan hill, where there was also a Lamaist monastery. In the north of the valley (see Map 2) are numerous springs, each with spirit-owners which are currently still worshipped. Lamaists sometimes say that these springs are the residence of *luus*, dragons.

If an *oboo* is shamanist it is called 'black' (*khara oboo*); if it is Lamaist it is known as 'white' (*tsagaan oboo*). The difference consists in the fact that shamans recognise and 'deal with' demons and evil spirits (*chitgur, adkha*, etc.), the bringers of misfortune, while lamas are concerned with the perfection of human spiritual capacities. For the lamas, misfortune arises from human sin, incorrect acts, and lack of faith in the religion, and this misfortune can be averted by prayers, making offerings, and divination (so as to know in advance what actions would bring bad luck). This explanation as reported by an old kolkhoznik is certainly somewhat simplified, but it does indicate one fact, which has been reported by Buryat ethnographers for other areas,[62] that the old division amongst the shamans themselves between 'black' — those concerned with evil

Ritual site where offerings are made to local deities, Selenga, 1967.

spirits and sorcery between living people — and 'white' — those concerned with bringing prosperity and fertility — has been transferred to the distinction between shamanism and Lamaism.[63]

In the minds of some of the old people of Barguzin there is an idea of cyclical time: shamanism had been driven out by Lamaism, and Lamaism had been driven out by communists, but shortly, they said, the time of shamanism would come again. This can perhaps be associated with the early-twentieth-century view of shamanism as connected with evil forces, which were swept away by the enlightenment of Lamaism. In the genealogies, shamans were mentioned in the father's father's father's generation, also also in the father's father's generation, but no closer to Ego. In two families, the middle-aged informants said that their grandparents had been shamanists, while their parents were Lamaists.

Shamans (*böö*) were much more common than shamanesses (*udgan*). The latter created only trouble and mischief, setting people against one another, while some shamans were good people, much respected, who gave protection from all evil. There were from one to five shamans in every village.

We know from many sources (see below) that shamanism continues today. Nevertheless, among the Barguzin people there is a general theory that *real* shamanism died out with the disappearance of the *naigur*,[64] who fled to Irkutsk *oblast'*, driven out by the lamas (see Chapter 1 section 6). He (some people said 'she') was 'black' (*khara*) and ill-intentioned. If he dropped in on someone and they did not give him food and presents, tobacco and vodka, all kinds of misfortune might occur. The *naigur* was embittered, because he/she was born of a mother with no other children, and when the mother died he/she was cruelly treated by a mother-in-law. After this sad childhood, the *naigur* did only harm to people.

However, living at the same time as the *naigur* was a good shaman called Tülkhesen, the great-grandfather in the male line of Bator Lambriyevich Erdeniyev (aged seventy-eight in 1967). Tülkhesen lived to be eighty, and people everywhere respected him for his powers of removing evil spirits from patients who were ill. People came from far and wide to consult him. When the lamas denounced shamanism, Tülkhesen behaved with great dignity. The great lama was too proud to come to him, so Tülkhesen went to the lama and they had a conversation. The lama said, 'You are a good helpful man, and we shall not kill you.' Nevertheless, Tülkhesen also fled and took refuge in Irkutsk *oblast'*. He said to his children 'I am the last shaman of my lineage', and since that time no more shamans appeared among his descendants in Barguzin.

People became shamans either by inheritance of the power (*udkha*) or by learning the skill from another shaman. Each of the main clans had their shamans, whose special *udkha* enabled them to perform different kinds of magic with the aid of their wild-animal spirit helpers. Many shamans 'wasted time' by competing with one another; they would take on the bodily form of their animal-spirits and have fights (snake against bear, wild goat against eagle, etc.). The winner of such a competition would be invited by people to cure them. The loser would not be invited and would occupy himself with attacking the 'good' shamans by magical means. A powerful shaman was known by his mastery of language: his ability to improvise on the theme of the known invocations, to move people and convince them that evil was banished.

In the childhood of Bator Erdeniyev shamans were paid at the following rates: 15 kopecks, plus a share of the meat, if a sheep were sacrificed to mollify a spirit, 9 kopecks for a *türge* purifying ritual,[65] and 6 kopecks for the 'cleansing' of a house of demons (*chitgur*) by juniper smoke with the use of a *yëdo*.[66]

Shamans in Barguzin now take part in two kinds of community ritual. The first is at the ritual cairn (*oboo takhikha*),[67] a ceremony which takes place in summer only. Men — women are not permitted to attend — come from everywhere around, and a sacrifice of male sheep, *zööhe* (cream), and *arkhi* (milk vodka) is made to the spirits of the locality and nature (*baidalin ezhed*).

The second type of ceremony is the *tailgan* sacrifice. This, unlike the *oboo takhikha*, is usually strictly confined to kin of one clan or lineage. There used to be up to fifteen *tailgans* a year to different kinds of spirits and deities, some of which women and children were allowed to attend, but it is impossible to say how many *tailgans* occur in Barguzin today. Valerii Basayev described to me one *tailgan* of the Hengeldur Buura lineage, dedicated to an old woman spirit called Tirdai. The men of the lineage each paid a share (*khubi*) of the animals to be sacrificed, sixty horses and two sheep. This *tailgan* took place every year, at night, and it was one of those which women could not attend: this was because it was thought that women, coming as wives from strange clans, had themselves brought evil spirits (*dakhabre*) which were to be exorcised by means of the sacrifice to Tirdai who had control of them. The Buura lineage had its own spot on a hill for its *tailgans*: two huge stones, 3 metres high and 10 metres in diameter. Below this, from east to west, the groups of kin, divisions of the lineage, arranged themselves in a long line, each building a fire before its place. There were around twenty such groups, ordered by seniority from the west. Each group had its elder as a representative. Before each group was a vessel filled with *arkhi*. The shaman, who came from the senior line, Mayngan-*tang*, consecrated the sacrificial animals with *yëdo* and libations of vodka. He then chanted the prayer to the ancestors, the spirits of the locality, and to Tirdai herself. The animals were sacrificed by slitting the chest and pulling out the aorta, and the blood was drained from the rib-cage into buckets. The meat was divided into the number of shares of those contributing, but the bones were burnt, and the heads, lungs and wind-pipe of at least some of the sacrificial animals were left propped on sticks pointing in the direction of Tirdai. From each group, every man in turn went up to the sacred stones and walked three times round them, making a libation upwards to the spirits as he did so. Some of the meat and all of the vodka was consumed at this *tailgan*. The rest of the meat was taken home to eat. This *tailgan*, which was reported to have occurred 'in the past', coincides in most details with the *tailgan* described by Tugutov for the present-day Yangut Buryats,[68] and so we may assume that those *tailgans* which still take place in Barguzin would take this form.

To take part in a *tailgan* used to be considered an honour: it showed that a man had a family and was part of the lineage. The *tailgan*, even when women were allowed to attend, was a masculine affair, and those held in summer were followed by archery, wrestling, and horse racing. The contestants were the representatives of their patrilineal kinship groups.

Let us now consider the role of shamanism in relation to Soviet life among the Buryats today. The most detailed description of the series of *tailgans* carried out by Buryats before the Revolution is that of the western Buryat Yangut clan, who celebrated eleven *tailgans* regularly each summer, and others on occasion.[69] It is significant that, writing of the 1960s, Tugutov describes these very same Yangut Buryats as holding fourteen *tailgans* — all of the ones mentioned by Manzhigeyev for the pre-revolutionary period plus two which Manzhigeyev may have described under some other heading.[70] In addition, by the 1960s, the Yanguts had created a new *tailgan* in memory of the last shaman of the Tarasa line, a man called Yegor Fedotov. This man 'kept up with the spirit of the times': when his spirit entered the shaman in his trance, he said:

> At the age of six
> The books arranged in six rows
> I fluently read,
> I wrote faultlessly.
> At the age of seven
> The books arranged in seven rows,
> I was fluent in reading,
> I wrote perfectly.
> I am Egor Fedotov,
> I am gentle as a foal,
> I am Egor with a mild temper.
> My yellow boots made of sandal-wood
> Do not wear out;
> Being born young,
> I do not become old.[71]

This gives us a series of fifteen *tailgans* celebrated every year. What was the intention of these festivals? The first five, to the spirits of the mountain peaks (*khushuunai*), the majestic earth and the severe hills (*khan daida khatuu uulad*), the blue stones (*khükhe shuluunai*), the cold springs (*khüiten bulagai*), and the waters (*uhanai*), were requests to local spirits and ancestors for belevolent control of nature: the keeping away of drought, early frosts, flooding rivers, disease, animal predators, etc. The sixth and eighth *tailgans*, to the Ardai ancestors and the bull ancestor, were requests for fertility. The ninth sacrifice, to the girls of the Khori lineage, was concerned with protection from female spirits, and the seventh, tenth, eleventh, twelfth, thirteenth and fourteenth *tailgans* were again concerned with nature: they were addressed to the spirits of the rocks (*khabsagain*), the severe mountains again, to the cliffs (*khahii*), the manured hay-fields (*ütügei*), the steep slopes which must be climbed on foot (*kheltegein*), and the low-lying settlement (*huudaliin*). All of these *tailgan*s are traditional, in the sense that they were also celebrated in the pre-revolutionary period. In the fact that they continue today at all we can perceive the ever-present fear of environmental and economic disaster. *Tailgan*s were held in increased numbers in Bokhan district during the droughts of the 1960s.[72] As I described in Chapter 4 sections 3 and 4, the chances of environmental misfortune in many areas of Buryatiya, including Barguzin, have actually increased during the period of collectivisation because of over-use of pastures, mismanagement of the 'Virgin Lands' campaign, neglect of protective planting of trees, and so on. In pre-collectivisation times a farmer could remove his flocks from over-pastured land; in the collective farm he has to follow the itinerary set out for him. Since natural misfortunes happen *in any case*, and since the planning of production is invariably described by officials as *in general* beneficial, as good *in the long term*, or valuable for society *as a whole*, the relation between techniques of production and environmental degradation is not perceived by the traditionally minded: the spirits, which always were responsible, are still so, but they have become more capricious. The fault is ascribed to the waning of belief and to godlessness among the people themselves.

In most regions there are many fewer *tailgan*s today than previously, but nevertheless the ethnographic literature describes several new *tailgan*s which have emerged in the Soviet period, or old ones which have acquired a new importance. There are four rituals which are most frequently mentioned. (1) A *tailgan* to the deities of war (*khara moriton*, Azhiral *bükhe*, Khan Shargai, etc. – Buryats in different regions prayed to different spirits). In Barguzin, one informant mentioned a huge *tailgan*, at which 470 people participated, the whole of the 221st regiment, before setting out to the front in the last war. The deity was the spirit-owner of the island of Ol'khon in Lake Baikal, otherwise known as Zhamtsaran by Lamaists. This was 'dirty work' (*chernaya rabota*), he said, and no women were allowed. In another account, western Buryats carried out *tailgan*s to the Ulei spirits, of which there were apparently 366. They went to the front with the Buryat soldiers, fought alongside, and some of them died. Now there are only about 126 Ulei spirits left.[73] Individual families, kin-groups, and whole villages still carry out sacrifices to various deities of war when their sons depart for military service.[74] (2) A *tailgan* to spirits of learning. Usually this sacrifice is made to *Erlen khanai besheeshenüüd* (the scribes of Erlen Khan, the king of the underworld), but possibly the new *tailgan* among the Yanguts to Yegor Fedotov, mentioned above, may also be concerned with education. This *tailgan* is carried out when people leave the village for higher education, or even when children start school. It is carried out at night, with the killing of a black sheep, and obligatory drinking of vodka.[75] (3) A *tailgan* to the spirit of the livestock-sheds (*khüren ezhen*), who is called Khükhkheer Sagaan Noyon. This is a sacrifice of milk products, carried out at night, with the aim of averting cattle disease. It is significant that this ritual is carried out by work-teams of the kolkhoz, and on occasion even conducted by the brigadier himself or the zoo technician.[76] (4) A *tailgan* to various new deities of communism itself. An example of this is the new deity of the Kabansk *aimak*, the communist Uhan-Khaalyuud ('water-otters'), a god, or perhaps a group of gods,[77] which lives in Lake Baikal and is the metamorphosis of the Parisian communards who were defeated in 1871. They took refuge in Lake Baikal, underwent metamorphosis into otters, and now, if sacrifices are made to them, they give help with the fulfilling of the plan (in this case, with the plan for fish). Sacrifices are made both by individuals and by the collectivity at the end of May and beginning of June when the fishing season starts.[78]

*Tailgan*s are now attended by many fewer people than they were in the past.[79] It is also apparent that whereas the social basis of attendance used to be only the patrilineal lineage, it now also may comprise kolkhoz/sovkhoz groups in the case of certain rituals. However, the general basis for taking part is still the kinship group. The Buryat ethnographer Tugutov describes the senior elder anxiously counting which kin-groups had sent representatives.[80] Mikhailov, the Buryat expert on shamanism, mentions the fact that in certain parts of Buryatiya each kin-group is supposed to make a contribution and receive its share (*khubi*) of the sacrificial meat, even if it does not send a representative to the ritual itself. For example, in one *tailgan* there were only forty participants, but the meat was divided into seventy-seven shares and taken back to the households which had made a contribution.[81] In parts of west Buryatiya it is still normal for every household to participate, sending a male representative and providing a bowl of milk vodka and money to buy the sacrificial animals. In these areas (Bokhan, and others) there are up to ten *tailgan*s every year, and the — perhaps slightly shocked — ethnographer noted that the rituals took place in the brigade centres of various kolkhozy — places with a shop, a club, radio, electricity, and even in some cases a telephone.[82] Since it is mentioned in his field-notes that a contribution and representative were sent from various named *ail* (households) living in different villages but all descended from 'one father', we may conclude that the social basis of these remarkably persistent rituals is still in most cases the patrilineage. As with wedding rituals, even if non-kin, for example neighbours, do take part, the idiom of the *tailgan* — the arrangement of the participants, the idea of representation of each line within the lineage, the enumerating by the officiating shaman or elder of patrilineal ancestors who are at the same time spirits of the locality — is a kinship one. Zhukovskaya, an ethnographer with wide field experience of Buryat and Mongolian shamanism, attributes the survival of religion very largely to the continued importance of kinship in Buryatiya.[83]

Unlike the annual festivals, which are either Soviet in ideological orientation (*suur-kharbaan*) or Lamaist (*tsaalgan*), and unlike the wedding rituals, which have a structure within which an ideological sliding-scale from the deeply 'traditional' to the 'Komsomol' can be accommodated, the *tailgan*s are always at variance with, perhaps even in opposition to, the social system created by the kolkhoz. This is the case even with those *tailgan*s, such as the sacrifice to the spirit of the cattle-sheds, which are conducted not on the basis of kin-groups but by production units of the kolkhoz itself. In these *tailgan*s, although the social unit involved is a Soviet one, and the expressed aim is the benefit of the kolkhoz community, the relations invoked with other such units is not the Soviet ideal of a hierarchical organic solidarity but the real tensions of competition and frustration which arise within the farm. These as it were 'modern' *tailgan*s have as their focus crucial points of compulsion, desire and uncertainty in rural Soviet life which are concealed, and therefore unsatisfied, by the official ideology. The existence of rituals in connection with entering the Red Army, which is an overwhelmingly Russian-dominated organisation,[84] with success in education, and with fulfilling the production plan, is to be expected. That these rituals arise in connection with Soviet life, and not *merely* as 'survivals' of a dying Buryat religiosity, is clearly shown by the fact that Russians or Ukrainians who happen to belong to the production teams in Buryat kolkhozy also may take part in them. In the Lenin kolkhoz in Bokhan district, for example, the head of an OTF, a Belorussian called Olin, conducted the *tailgan* to the *ezhen* of the livestock pens in the name of the kolkhoz, although he said he was 'not a shamanist'.[85] As we showed in Chapter 3, such teams in collective farms are frustrated in their stated purpose by the very system of the division of labour which creates them. Even in farms where it is not, the system is still claimed to be rational and efficient. The *tailgan*s invoke an ideology which is in opposition to the Soviet one if only because, by its very existence, it admits the fallibility of the Soviet explanation.

Shamans do not even try to be efficient, trustworthy, or morally irreproachable. They do not preserve traditions consciously, no longer wear the complicated shaman costume and, on their own admission, most of them cannot achieve a genuine trance state. Although it is known that in the 1920s, when socialist ideals were sweeping through the Buryat villages, there was a 'shaman's charter', by which lower prices were to be charged to the poor,[86] it is doubtful whether this has any force today. Shamans are not in the business of purveying ethics, but remedies. In this they are unlike lamas, who try to set an example of moral conduct by their own lives. Shamans are separate even from the morality of the patrilineage — there is no necessity to have a shaman officiate at the *tailgan*. Rather, shamans are irresponsible, unexpected, and sly, since after all everything they say comes from the spirits, not from themselves. Shamans are the ones who can make fun of Soviet reality, improvise, and cast things in a new light.

For many people, educated in atheism in Soviet schools and contemptuous of the trickery of shamans, this being 'something else' is all that the *tailgan* provides. The same is true in medicine, when people who say they are non-believers consult shamans about their illnesses. One woman who travelled all the way from Bilchir to Ulan-Ude to consult a shamaness in 1960 said, 'My baby was in hospital for a long time — nothing got better: I consulted the lamas — nothing got better; who knows, maybe the shaman will help.'[87] Many of the people who attend *tailgan*s are too uncertain of the value of their own culture, too generally despondent, to believe consistently in the cosmology of spirits. In respect of some of the people who attend *tailgan*s I see no reason to distrust Mikhailov, himself a Buryat and an ethnographer of wide experience, when he writes: 'These days among "believers" there is no complex of ideas, no defined system of rituals and sacrifices, but only fragmented, vague images, illusions, and thoughts, haphazardly called into being by events.'[88] Mikhailov mentions one *tailgan* which he attended in 1965 at which almost the entire male population of the village was present, including young herdsmen and machine-operators, but, talking with these people and observing the way in which they carried out the ritual, he came to the conclusion that only one-third of them were 'active believers' (*aktivno veruyushchiye*). These were people, mostly middle-aged, who knew the ritual and invocations to the local deity well, who performed them with particular feelings of responsibility and reverence. The others at the *tailgan* included some who said they were not believers, who simply wished to have a good time and enjoy themselves 'in a Buryat way'. The neighbouring Russian village was celebrating their *troitsa* festival, and both places had just finished the spring sowings of the fields. 'The Russians have got their festival today. They have given it a new name ("Russian birch-tree" festival). Why shouldn't we Buryats have a festival of our own? It doesn't matter what you call it — "the May festival" or "Sunday rest", whatever you like. In fact, we are just enjoying ourselves, and only the old men are really praying', they said. They performed the shamanist ritual simply out of respect for the believers and the elders.[89] Perhaps it makes no sense, without a much more sophisticated ethnographic analysis, to make a distinction between 'active believers' and those who simply carry out ritual — a distinction which is after all present in any community of people taking part in a religious event — and we should perhaps simply conclude, given the alien presence of Mikhailov himself, that only one-third were prepared to declare themselves publicly as believers.

The very fact that Soviet citizens who have some stake in the official social organisation have to deny religious involvement is important. There are many Buryats in the kolkhozy, perhaps particularly those of the revolutionary generation and the youngest generation, who are convinced atheists (this I say from having talked to some of them myself). 'Shamans' — or people discovered to have received remuneration for carrying out shamanist rituals — were prosecuted and imprisoned during the 1950s. All of this makes it almost impossible for us to talk with any conviction about the true state of belief among Buryat kolkhozniks. We know only that many people *take part* but say they do not believe, and conversely that some people who actively propagandise against religious practices are psychologically involved at some level. One man, a school-teacher, and we know that teachers must carry out atheist propaganda, said to me, with a grin of excitement, 'We are all shamans, we can all do it', (he meant 'we can all enter the shaman's state of trance'). Maybe he was joking, maybe not.

The emergence of new spirits, such as the Uhan-Khaalyuud, who give success in fulfilling the production plan shows that the faculty for creative symbolis-ation in the Buryat shamanist idiom is still in existence – if only fitfully, and not everywhere. The idea of the Uhan-Khaalyuud conforms in every respect to the concepts of spirits in 'traditional' Buryat shamanism, and the very fact of the intervention of new spirits is characteristic of this religious system: the Uhan-Khaalyuud (the Paris communards) are the representatives of an idea ('communism'), they are located in the mythical past, their power derives from vengeance for persecution (of the *naigur* mentioned earlier), they are 'embodied' as animals (water-otters, which do inhabit Lake Baikal), and they are understood to be the 'spirit-owners' of a locality (in this case Lake Baikal) which is crucially important in its natural manifestations – storms, currents, depths – for the given endeavour, the fulfilling of their plan by the fishermen. It is impossible to document here the implications of this way of thinking, and the reader if interested should consult the literature on Buryat shamanism,[90] but it is clear that this mental construction is utterly at variance with the Soviet ethic of how properly to go about fulfilling the plan for fish.

Even if we leave aside the question of the sense in which it can be said that present-day Buryats believe in spirits such as the Uhan-Khaalyuud, nevertheless the participation in *tailgan* sacrifices on a kinship basis – even if not all *tailgan*s are organised on this principle – has certain implications: there must be a view of the social world, redeemable in the face of the multiple Soviet divisions into production teams, the educated and uneducated, the holders of office and the *raznorabochiye* ('general workers'), the 'progressive' and the 'backward', which sees people as related to one another by virtue of a single idea. Patrilineages, as concepts, are divisible down to the last individual, but they are all divisible in the same way. In the absence, in present Buryat society, of any political or econ-omic advantage to the holding of a senior genealogical position, the pure prin-ciple of segmentation and fusion is all that is left. One division becomes equiv-alent to another in a way which never was the case when social privilege was attached to genealogical position.

There is one *tailgan* which specifically celebrates nothing other than the patri-lineage itself and its reproduction. This is the *ug tailgan* (literally, the 'root', 'genealogy' or 'ancestor' *tailgan*), and among the Baikal–Kudarin Buryats it was celebrated in the late 1960s every year or once every two to three years. In 1969 there was an *ug tailgan* in Korsakovo village of the Kaban *aimak* at which there were numerous blood sacrifices and plentiful provision of alcohol. The *tailgan* was in honour of the ancestors of the Segen and Khaital lineages, and not a single male of these groups was allowed to be absent.[91]

The idea of the qualitatively different status created by marriage has, on the other hand, been emphasised in the Soviet period. This was demonstrated symbolically in the wedding rituals by the repeated giving of non-equivalent items from one side to the other: the groom's side always gives *arkhi* (milk vodka) and the bride's side always gives cooked meat. It is shown practically by the continued, perhaps increasing, importance of the father-in-law/son-in-law relations in politico-economic strategies, where each side deliberately appears to choose affines in kolkhoz positions complementary to its own.

In the idiom of the patrilineage, on the other hand, everyone is equivalent: *akha* ('older brother/sister') in relation to some and *düü* ('younger brother/ sister') in relation to others – including those who are ancestors and those who are yet to be born.

In the patrilineage there are many fathers (*baabai*). The same word is used for one's own father at home and all grandfathers stretching back to the bull ancestor of all western Buryats. Bukha-noyon-baabai. I would suggest in brief that the continued vitality of the Buryat kinship terminology, even if we leave aside kin-based activities of a regular kind such as the *tailgan*s and the *tsagaalgan*, demonstrate that cognitively the Buryat concept of 'father' is one which has echoes back through time, and that this must influence the Buryat development of a personal identity. I am not arguing for the 'extension of sentiments', since quite apart from other theoretical considerations I consider sentiments here to be unknowable in the same way that beliefs are unknowable. But it is a fact that the conceptual map of the kinship terminology, which is reproduced by every Ego, and which constitutes the Ego-centred topology of the ideal patrilineal system, is still the means by which the Buryats define their initial social place in the world. This is the classificatory background against which there take place such characteristic activities of contemporary Buryat kinship as the marked respect and deference shown to seniors and the aged, the 'lending' of children for long periods (sometimes several years) to kin, and the extremely indulgent and tender behaviour towards infants – noted with some disapproval from a Soviet point of view by the Buryat ethnographer Basayeva.[92] The patrilineal classification of the social world may 'determine' nothing in people's feelings, but it cannot be for nothing that it continues to exist.

In fact, the affectual aspects of Buryat kinship may exist in opposition to the actual practices of Soviet society (not necessarily to the ideology), just as the mental classification of society by patrilineal kinship stands in contrast to the idea of the Soviet division of labour. I say this because Buryat affective relations towards the very old and the very young appear to be so different from those practised by people who are 'getting on' in Soviet society. Instead of 'bringing children up' with some conscious instilling of ideas of duty, etc., the kolkhoz-niks regard all childish behaviour with indulgence; many kolkhoz people prefer keeping their children at home rather than sending them to the kindergarten. And instead of treating old people with affectionate condescension, they offer them real deference and respect. In the Buryat kinship system old people do not slip into the state of being 'past it'. On the contrary, their power increases — however frail they may be physically or mentally — as they approach the state where they will be more powerful still, as ancestors.[93]

Within the patrilineage all men of approximately the same generation, whether they are siblings who have grown up in the same house or far distant cousins, call one another *akha* ('older brother') or *düü* ('younger brother') and expect help and support from one another. It is not specified in conversation how close or distant the genealogical relationship is. 'And of course when I'm over there I always go to see my younger brother (*minii düü*)', someone would say. 'Is that your real brother?' I once inquired. 'Of course he is my real brother.' 'The son of your father?' I persisted. 'Ah no, he is a distant relative. Do you really want me to tell you how we are related? Well, he is my father's father's uncle's . . . [a long explanation] but it is all the same, we are very close to one another and I am always very glad to see him. All the time he was training at the Institute I used to take him meat . . . '

Similarly, women in the patrilineage are all sisters, *egeshe* ('older sister') or *düü* ('younger sister'). It is this boundary, between the women whom it is unthinkable to marry, because they are sisters and in a sense equals, and the

A shepherd and his granddaughter.

women who belong to outsiders with whom negotiations — which bring into question one's own status — may be conducted, that exogamy exists to preserve. Thus, if we ask why exogamy, even a genealogically defined rule of exogamy, still exists in Buryat society when patrilineages have long ceased to have any direct political or economic function, it seems that the answer must lie in the preservation by almost all Buryats of the *idea* of the brotherhood and sisterhood of kinship. It is my impression that this ideal of relations within one's own generation of kin — as also with the very young and very old — is almost consciously held back from the Soviet world of superiors and subordinates and negotiated relations. But in the absence of the Soviet organisation it would not exist in the form it does. (I would like to specify that it is the ideal which is reserved and segregated, rather than the actuality of material and other exchanges between kin. As was discussed in Chapter 7, individuals do make use of agnatic, along with other, kin links in forming Ego-centred networks in the kolkhoz which are of vital practical importance to them.)

It could be said that it is the ideal of kinship which is represented in ritual, at the *tsagaalgan* and at the *tailgans*. Both of these occasions are seen, by Soviet writers and probably by most Buryats too, as irredeemably a-Soviet.[94] The Buryat ideal of kinship is irreconcilable with and stands opposed to the system of values which maintains that the members of the Communist Party are the 'best people', but it is not at all irreconcilable with what is left of the shamanist world view. The latter is not necessarily at all disposed to challenge Soviet power, but instead strives to deal with it. Mikhailov wrote:

From conversations with Buryat shamans which I carried out in 1960–3 I was able to distinguish a particular shamanist ideology. Everything which occurs in the world, they maintain, is the doing of supernatural forces. The October socialist revolution, Soviet power, the building of Communism, etc., all this is the will of the gods. The Communists are their emissaries to the earth. Lenin, Sverdlov, Kalinin — in a word all the main figures of the CP USSR and the Soviet state — are also deities, which, together with the sky-gods (*tengri*) and 'kings of nature' (*khat*), hold meetings in the other world and decide about matters which are important to living people. The shamanist religion thus helps Soviet power.[95]

But shamans have been persecuted, and they are still liable to punishments of various kinds, particularly if it can be proved that they take no part in kolkhoz work (cf. the laws on 'parasitism', Chapter 3). Whatever the shamans may have said to Mikhailov about Lenin and Sverdlov being gods, in fact shamans are defined as anti-Soviet by their activities. The act of shamanising is held by the authorities to be mere charlatanism, the making use of people's sufferings and ignorance. It is significant, however, that the more shamans are punished, the more authority they come to have in the eyes of the local people:

It is difficult to determine the extent of shamanist survivals and this is partly to be explained by the fact that shamanist rituals today are being put a stop to. In various places there have been purely administrative struggles by the local

414

organs against shamans, and this has done harm instead of good. In the eyes of the believers these forbidden rituals become secret and more attractive. And this to a significant degree strengthens the existing shamanist survivals and the authority of the shamans themselves. It seems that this must be the reason why more shamanist survivals exist in Kurumkan in the Barguzin district, where the ritual of worship at the shaman's graves (*böögiin shandal*) was stopped, than elsewhere.[96]

To the extent that the ideal of Buryat patriliny is manifest at *tailgans* and other shamanist rituals, and the latter are carried out in secrecy and despite the condemnation of the authorities, there comes to be an association between the deepest identity of 'being Buryat' with the officially forbidden.

The local authorities, who are Buryats, are placed in a contradictory position. While they would deny to Soviet and especially Russian officials placed above them any personal involvement in shamanist rituals, to a complete outsider they might well reveal pride in local traditions. Thus, when three ethnographers visited a sovkhoz in the Barguzin valley in 1978, it was the Party Secretary who not only showed them the site of sacred springs (*arshan*), but also made an offering there himself. The cliffs above the spring, and the *arshan* itself, were held to be inhabited by master-spirits (*ezhed*) of the locality, and the surrounding trees were hung with scarves and scraps of cloth, both Mongolian and silk *khadag* and expensive Russian head-scarves. A box for offerings hung on a tree, and it was the official who placed a little meat, bread and money in the box and made a libation (*khayalga*). Nearby was a birch-tree, hung with clusters of sheep's shoulder-blades, which are used by Buryats and Mongolians in divination rituals, and the ground was strewn with vodka bottles. Far from the Party Secretary being, as it were, caught *in flagrante delicto* by members of his farm who perceived his little rite of devotion, a milkmaid shouted after him, as he was setting out for the *arshan*, 'Since you are going up there, say a prayer for me too!'[97]

How general is Buryat shamanism, and what are the material conditions in which it exists? The data we have are fragmentary, far more so than the phenomenon itself, but it is worth noting a few facts. (1) Shamanism is not purely a rural phenomenon. In the 1960s there were at least one well-known shamaness and a noted lama-cum-shaman in the industrial city of Ulan-Ude.[98] (2) The fee for a shaman's services is quite substantial. In the early 1960s, when the average kolkhoznik's monthly wage was around 70 rubles, a shamaness from Ivolga, between Selenga and Ulan-Ude, asked at least 10 rubles plus a half-litre of vodka per seance.[99] (3) Since the destruction of the monasteries in the 1930s, the number of shamans far exceeds that of lamas, even in areas which were formerly Buddhist. Thus in Tunka in the early 1960s there were only five wandering lamas, while there were at least thirteen shamans known to the authorities.[100] At around the same time, in just one kolkhoz in Tunka the *raion* Party Secretary reported that five shamans and two diviners had 'appeared' and were diverting the youth of the kolkhoz from their work.[101] (4) The majority of shamanist rituals carried out for individuals are exorcisms of spirits in the case of illness or depression (*hanaanda abagtakhadaa*, 'to be taken in the mind'), and for fertility, successful childbirth, and fortune in education and the army.[102] (5) Shamans are consulted not only by Buryats, but also by Russians and people of other nation- alities. One shaman, Tsimzhit Batorov, made his main living from conducting rituals for the Orthodox Russians living at the station of Slyudnyak on the Trans-Siberian railway.[103] (6) Lamas and shamans, who used to be in competition with one another for control of the Buryat 'congregation', are now cooperating. The lamas of the only monastery in Buryatiya, at Ivolga, send patients to the shamaness who lives nearby, and she loyally attends all the *khurals* (services) at the Lamaist temple.[104] Mikhailov describes several people who were both lamas and shamans at the same time. They were called *dzhochi*.[105]

These facts attest to the dependence of shamanism on the Soviet social sys- tem itself. Before the Revolution, Buddhism was fast gaining ground among the Buryats, and shamanism, it appears, was losing it. Shamanism was at a particu- larly low ebb in the 1920s, the very period of the Buddhist reform movement and the attempt to make a creative fusion between Buddhist philosophy and socialism.[106] But since that time Lamaism in the 'high' or institutionalised sense has become much weaker among the rural population, and although we must attribute this primarily to the loss of the material and political base of the monasteries, it is also true that the hierarchical structure of the Lamaist organis- ation of ideas was similar to, rather than complementary to, the structure inside the Party, and for this reason was not in a position to provide a rationality which could 'deal with' this kind of system. A Buryat Lamaist monastery was an auth- oritarian organisation, highly graded according to the vows and educational degrees which the lamas had taken, and containing within itself a fairly rigid division of labour. Life within the monastery was strictly regulated in sequences of time, and, even in the period of revolutionary renaissance, the lower ranks of lamas were instructed what to think according to doctrine. The lay public were issued with didactic tracts on matters such as behaviour towards seniors, marriage rules, attitudes to be taken in misfortune, and many other moral points.[107] Even though the Reform movement substituted a different, and perhaps more varied set of doctrines, it was still the case that only those at the head of the organis- ation, in particular the Khambo-Lama, Agvan Dorzhiyev, decided what the new teachings were to be, and for the ordinary lamas they appeared institutionally as dogma. Furthermore, they claimed to be the truth. Since I have argued that the Party ideology has, in a similar way, the problem of proclaiming infallibility when, for all kinds of reasons, the proclamation alone is not enough, we can see why Buryat kolkhozniks would not have recourse to a system with such a parallel stance in attempting to come to terms with Soviet life.

Shamanism, on the other hand, is fluid, undogmatic, secret and transient. Its practitioners need have little personal authority, since it is as vehicles for the spirits and ancestors that they have power. To take part in shamanist rituals does not require a personal commitment of belief, as we see from the fact that

416

Russian 'Orthodox' believers consult shamans. It is quite possible to go to a shaman for various kinds of problems and at the same time think of oneself as a Buddhist or even an atheist. The very particularity of the shamanist spirits, the fact that the people in the next kolkhoz will sacrifice to different ones, the lack of commandments or any kind of ethical precepts, conforms to the requirements of the almost schizogenic identity which many Buryats must have. Shamanism demands nothing (as Buddhism, for example, does, even in the form of the most elementary precepts) which must be taken into the rest of life as a personal commitment.

But it is perhaps most important that shamanist thought provides – perhaps even consists of – an explanation of suffering. The spirits are powerful because they are people who once suffered and must exact vengeance on the living; they reproduce the misfortune they themselves experienced. In this view, suffering or misfortune, refracted into a thousand particular forms, continues to exist through time as something which, in the form of spirits, must constantly be 'made up for' and compensated for, by prayers and sacrifices. All that in Soviet ideology should never happen, all that is explained away as a 'mistake', or a 'shortcoming', or a 'deviation', is in Buryat shamanism only what is to be expected by the living – that is by the sons and daughters of the ancestors who have suffered. By insisting only on positive values, such as the values of labour and productivity, the Soviet ideology reproduces the conditions in which shamanism, or something functionally similar, must continue to exist. It is not merely, as some Soviet ethnographers admit, that ill-judged over-emphasis on these values in practical life – as when kolkhoz Chairmen feel themselves justified in refusing transport to hospital to ill people 'who might be working'[108] – encourages shamanism, although it does. It is also that Soviet social and cultural organisation provides no locus for reflection on itself. As was shown in Chapter 4 sections 3 and 4, the system of collectivised farming places some kolkhozy in successful and others in extremely difficult positions. Of the two farms I visited, the more ideologically 'progressive' was in by far the worse situation. Blame is fastened to *individuals*, who may suffer disastrous consequences (see Chapter 3). Denying that there is anything to be explained, the Soviet ideology only makes inevitable the existence of other constructions of meaning, even if they be defensive and fragile, as in the case of Buryat shamanism today.

4. Lamaism and visions of the future

Lamaism in Buryatiya today is almost entirely a kind of floating ideology – its institutional supports have been reduced almost to nothing – but nevertheless in looking at what remains of it, and how it relates to Soviet life, we can pull together many of the themes of this book. We might say that before the Revolution Lamaism found expression in two broad streams of religiosity: the formal ceremonial of the monasteries, and the informal family and local rituals. Because

417

the institution of the church was largely destroyed, these two have been both weakened and split apart. Folk Lamaism is being reincorporated into shamanist practice. What remains to a surprising extent is not Buddhist ethics, but a Buddhist view of time and the 'future'. The view is both pessimistic and Messianic.

A brief description of Buryat Lamaism

The Buryat Lamaist church is part of the reformed 'yellow hat' sect of Mahayana Buddhism, which spread from Tibet to Mongolia in the seventeenth and eighteenth centuries and to Buryatiya in the eighteenth and nineteenth centuries. By the beginning of this century the church had rich landed monasteries in all areas where Buryats lived,[109] with the partial exception of the region to the north and west of Lake Baikal. The Selenga district had many monasteries, and even remote Barguzin had one. The church as a whole was loyal to Tsarism, in fact the Tsar was considered a reincarnation of the White Tara goddess, but during the Civil War it began to divide into radically different movements. One of these was the attempt, headed by a lama of the Kizhina *datsan* (monastery), to set up an independent Buryat theocratic state. Meanwhile the head of the church, the Bandido-Khambo Lama, travelled in 1919 to Omsk to offer support (of a spiritual kind!) to Kolchak. In the same year the Cossack ataman Semenov, who was half Russian and half Buryat, attempted to set up a 'Pan-Mongolian State', headed by a lama reincarnation, Neisse-Gegeen. At this period rumours were rife among the Buddhist laity about the coming war in which soldiers of the mythical country Shambala would fight against the destroyers of the faith, and the coming of the next Buddha, Maidari (Maitreya), who would defend the 'khan of the three kingdoms', the head of the theocratic state.[110]

However, even before the Revolution another tendency had appeared in Buryat Buddhism, one which was to predominate during the 1920s and 1930s. This was the 'reform' (or the 'renewal', *obnovlencheskoye*) movement, which, influenced by Western oriental studies and populist writings in Russia, called for a return to the original teachings of the Buddha and to the way of life of the early monks. The Buryat leaders of this movement, some of whom were intellectuals rather than clergy, denounced the later Lamaist church as decadent, concerned in a mindless way with rituals and amassing wealth. The most radical of the reform leaders, the 'Nirvanist-Independents', headed by the former ruling prince of the Khori Buryats, Vambotsyrenov, rejected the whole ritual aspect of Lamaism. Only the philosophy and ethics of Buddhism could form a suitable basis for Buryat religion and preserve it in the face of social change and technical and scientific progress. Less radical reform leaders, such as Agvan Dorzheyev, head of the church in the 1920s, did not reject the entire Lamaist cult of deities, but they also maintained that the low cultural level of the lamas detracted from the authority of the church. This 'Reform' movement argued that Buddhism is

418

not a religion, nor Buddha a god, though gods were admissible for the unsophisticated. Buddha was a thinker and practitioner of an ethical system which is fully consistent with communism. Indeed, Lenin was seen as another teacher in the same spirit (sometimes he was seen as a reincarnation of the Buddha).[111] Some of the first communes in Buryatiya were in fact set up by lamas belonging to this movement.[112] However, by the mid-1920s, the 'Nirvanist-Independents' and the 'Reform' movements were virulently opposed by a large section of the Lamaist establishment, the 'Conservatives'. The church was split into three opposed factions, of which the 'Reform' movement was politically dominant, since it had the support of the Buryat Nationalist (later the Buryat Soviet) government in the 1920s.

By the end of the decade the inconsistencies between the ideologies of Bolshevism and reformed Buddhism were apparent, and the 'left' turn in Soviet politics ended the half-hearted support given to the 'Reform' movement. The 'Reform' leaders were dispersed,[113] and the church was left in open opposition to the Soviet government. The extent of support for the church can be seen from the fact that in 1927 the Anin *datsan* alone received three times as much from its parishioners as the entire income of the Khori Soviet – and there were six *datsans* (monasteries) in the Khori district.[114] Church lands were confiscated and redistributed. The church reacted by conducting rituals for the destruction of the Soviet state,[115] and later by supporting open fighting. By the end of the 1930s every single monastery in Buryatiya was closed, most lamas dispersed to live in villages, and some killed or imprisoned.

Two monasteries, the Ivolga *datsan*, in the Buryat ASSR, and the Aga *datsan*, in the Aga Buryat National Okrug, were re-opened in 1946 with a small staff of lamas, and these are the institutional base of the church today. In 1916 there had been some thirty-six monasteries and 16,000 lamas[116] in Buryatiya, but in the 1960s there were probably no more than 100 official lamas. Kalmuykia and Tuva, which had been strongly Buddhist regions before the Revolution, now have no monasteries. Lamas in these areas are subordinate to the Buryat church.

The present church professes Buddhism of the 'Reform' movement. This also is the teaching which is found in the countryside; other currents within Lamaism, such as tantrist sects or the discovery of 'living Buddhas' (*khubilgan*) have become illegitimate.[117] Documents composed by the 'Reform' leaders of the 1920s, such as the 'Twenty-three vows of Lamaism', are occasionally found in Buryat villages. The official lamas, who take an oath of loyalty to the Soviet state, encourage 'kolkhoznik-believers' to increase productivity and so on,[118] but nothing can really disguise the fact that Buddhism is fundamentally in opposition to Soviet thinking. Even if Buryat history, in which it was the Lamaist church which put up the only serious opposition to the Soviet state, were not enough to show this, it can be seen from the Buddhist ideology itself. However, all available evidence suggests that most Buryat rural 'believers' do not perceive this as an opposition.

419

Ritual and identity

Mahayana Buddhism in the form known to Buryats teaches that everything, both the material and spiritual, is void (Bur. *khooson shanar*, the essence of vacuum).[119] The essence can transform itself into specific worldly forms, which are real from the point of view of earthly, conditional understanding, but unreal from the point of view of the transcendental dharma. This idea opens the way for all kinds of deities and spiritual powers, helpful in meeting the difficulties of this life, but it strongly suggests that the best way is not to care for this life in itself at all. Good deeds are valued insofar as they lead to a superior re-birth, but the aim is not so much a good reincarnation in this world as birth in the Western paradise of Sukhavadi, or escape from rebirth altogether. This view does not so much contradict Soviet materialism and humanism as encompass and transcend it. All scientific progress was foreseen by ancient teachings ('a fiery snake will encircle the earth' – this means railways), but in any case it is a mere transitory moment in the immense, cyclical passing of the *kalpas*. Each *kalpa* (Bur. *galab*, aeon) is divided into four epochs: destruction, emptiness, foundation, and regeneration. In this last epoch, in which we now live, people's lives will become shorter and shorter as sins are accumulated. Buddhas appear – the fourth was Sakyamuni, the next will be Maidari (Maitreya) – and after the arrival of another 995, the world will again begin to enter the stage of destruction.[120]

Lamaism today

The Lamaist church in Buryatiya today is organised along the lines of a Soviet, as though no other model were available. Thus it operates under a government regulation of 1946,[121] its highest organ is the congress (*s'yezd*) of all believers, which elects an executive committee of five members and two candidate members, and the latter body (*sovet datsana*) elects the head of the monastery. Each of the two *datsans* has its own internal rules (*vnutrennaya rasporyadka*) and is required to give annual accounts (*uchet*) of its financial affairs. Lamas are allowed to own no private property. The monasteries are financed entirely by the believers: direct contributions made at services, collections, payments made to lamas for conducting rituals, and the proceeds from the sale of offerings (clothing, butter, meat, etc.). The income is placed into two funds (*dzhas*): the monastery fund and the lamas' fund. The latter pays each lama a wage of 80 rubles a month.[122] In 1958 the Ivolga *datsan* received 82,000 rubles, and in 1962 its offerings amounted to 120,000 rubles and it also acquired a car. A study in 1965 estimated that 5,000 people visited the monastery for temple services every year.[123]

The Ivolga *datsan* has seven religious buildings,[124] and these are surrounded by the small wooden houses of the lamas. Outside the *datsan* fence is a village consisting of the houses of lamas' relatives and other religious people, such as women who have taken Buddhist vows.

420

The *datsan* conducts six main services (*khural*) a year,[125] the same as in the pre-war period. The only large ritual now dropped from the calendar is the tantric dance called *tsam*, which had the aim of purifying the given place from 'powers opposed to religion'. The dance, in which every movement was heavy with the symbolism of fear, ended with the metaphoric destruction of the enemies of the faith: a gigantic pyramid of paper and dough (*sor*) was taken outside the boundaries of the *datsan* and burnt. In the 1920s and 1930s the *sor* used to be carried in the direction of the nearest office of the Soviet.[126] The *tsam* was one of the most popular rituals,[127] but now the two best-attended services are *tsagaan sar* in winter (see section 1 above) and 'Maidari' in summer. The former commemorates the souls of dead ancestors, and the latter heralds the arrival of the next Buddha.

Because the monasteries are distant from most collective farms, people cannot attend them easily. It is significant that the purpose for which individuals go, apart from services, is reported to be most commonly for the marking of the passage of time: every nine years from birth is the *mengyn zahal* ritual, and every twelve years, at the beginning of the next twelve-year animal cycle, is the *zhelei orolto* ceremony.[128] People who call themselves 'non-believers' go to the monastery to pray for recovery from illness, for remembrance of the dead, or for solace from unhappiness.[129]

Let us see what has happened to Lamaism in the countryside, without institutional supports. Lamas used to conduct or be otherwise involved in numerous

Lama standing in front of a temple in the Ivolga *datsan*, 1967.

421

Buryat life-cycle rituals (ritual purification of infants, name-giving, first hair-cutting, invocation of the personal guardian-spirit (*sakhiusan*), betrothal, marriage, death, and the leading away of the soul). They now perform only the last two of these rituals with any frequency. Lamas used to conduct the cer-emonies at *oboo*, ritual sites found near every village, and also at *arshan*, sacred springs, and other places where spirits were thought to reside. Now, although the rituals continue, it is almost never lamas who conduct them. Lamas used to cure illnesses, set bones, carry out purification rites, pray for success in particular ventures, foretell the future, give astrological advice, and interpret omens. Most of these activities are still known in Buryat villages, but they are practised to a far smaller extent than before the war, and usually it is not official lamas but a variety of ex-lamas, soothsayers, and quacks whom the kolkhozniks have recourse to.

Relatively few people admit to being 'believers' in Buddhism. In 1897 over 80% of eastern Buryats said they were Buddhists.[130] In the late 1960s, around 30% of families had members who were believers in Tunka and Barguzin, and around 10% kept religious statues (*burkhan*). Of the 'believers' 70% were aged over sixty, but only 1% were under thirty;[131] another study showed that 48% of the 'believers' were over sixty, but only 0.3% were aged under thirty.[132]

The most popular and mass ritual of Lamaism outside the *datsan*, the *oboo* ceremony, has virtually passed out of the hands of the lamas. This festival used to unite religion and politics: the ruling prince (*zaisan*) ordered it to be con-ducted for the success and well-being of his domain. It was known all through the Mongol world from early times.

An *oboo* cairn is usually made of earth and stones, with brushwood and flags fluttering from the top. Around the foot lie stones engraved and painted with prayers in Tibetan, coins, bottles, and bones. Most *oboo* sites were thought to be inhabited by spirits of nature, or ancestors; in fact they were originally very similar, if not identical, to the sites of *tailgan* sacrifices, but the spirits were subsequently given Lamaist names and blood sacrifices were forbidden. By the eighteenth century, the Lamaist church was hastening to acquire these popular cults for their own. There are still numerous *oboo* in every district, and people of different patrilineages assess their relative importance differently according to the allegiance given to the various spirits.[133] In Barguzin, the head lama of the *datsan* and the ruling prince 'systematised' the *oboos* at the end of the nine-teenth century and gave their support to the five they considered most import-ant,[134] but in the 1960s people were still mentioning up to nine *oboos* grouped by threes, or fours and fives, these being ritual figures for the numbers of certain kinds of spirits held to be contactable at these *oboos*.[135] The main *oboo* in Barguzin is generally agreed to be Baragkhan mountain, and the Lamaists even moved their *datsan* there at the end of the nineteenth century.

Oboo cults are concerned with nature, particularly rain, and in Barguzin, wind. In the post-war period they have almost lost their Lamaist disguise.

Informants of the 1960s said that the spirit of the Baragkhan *oboo* was a shaman, Solbon Khashkhi Noyon, who 'lives' on the mountain with a large household, cattle, and two servants, an Evenk and a one-eyed Russian.[136] At one point Solbon was given a Lamaist name, but this was not the one he was currently known by. Shamanists conducted their sacrifices at the foot of the hill. The 'rules' of shamanist ritual were approximately observed, since women, for example, were forbidden to attend sacrifices, but the Lamaist ones, such as rule forbidding the taking of life, were often ignored. An informant in Barguzin in 1975 explicitly said that sheep were taken to Lamaist *oboos* and *muukhan* for sacrifice, together with cream (*zööhei*) and spirits (*arkhi*), and that the sheep were killed and eaten on the spot. The meat was unsalted, the bones left behind, and the extra meat taken home, just as in a shamanist sacrifice.

The specifically Lamaist ritual at the *oboo* consists of reading by a lama of a Tibetan text *solchit* ('prayers and sacrifices') or *serzhem* ('offering of the golden drink' — i.e. spirits). The text consists of passages invoking the names of deities of nature, listed in hierarchical order, interspersed with prayers requesting them to accept the offerings of the congregation. Such Tibetan texts were composed by the lamas for 'shamanist' deities, such as the ancestor-spirit Bukha Noyon, which had been transformed into Lamaist gods.[137] When the lama gives a signal, the people start to walk clockwise round the *oboo*, making libations of tea, vodka, and milk, after which they drink what is left.[138]

The congregation at the *oboo* is very heterogeneous: the *oboo* at Ubukhe in Barguzin is worshipped by Evenki and Buryats, shamanists and Lamaists, even Russians and people of other nationalities.[139] In the Karl Marx collective, an old man said, 'Everyone can come. It is connected with the village (*ulus*), not the lineage (*omog*). We all have to worship nature.' However, Zhukovskaya reports that in some parts of Buryatiya only members of the given patrilineage participate in the *oboo* ritual and others attend only as observers.[140] *Oboo* ceremonies take place only in summer and particularly at one short period of the year, after sowing and before the move to summer pastures.

Virtually no one understands the Tibetan text. What remain important for the people are the place, the remembrance of sacred mountains and rivers — the aesthetic contemplation of nature — and the goal of the prayers, timely rain, warm sun, fertility. We need not be surprised that it is reported that there is a massive pilgrimage of 'non-believers' to the *oboo* festivities. After the religious ritual there are usually sports and games. People consider attendance at such festivals part of Buryat tradition, and many claim that the religious aspect is unimportant to them. The pure enjoyment part of *oboo* festivals has become so predominant that some deeply religious people refuse to attend on the grounds that a part of the congregation is simply using religion as a pretext for drinking and fun.[141]

Has Lamaism then completely lost its influential and distinctive role in village life, outside the monasteries? This would be true were it not for three factors:

the relation between Lamaism and national sentiment, the link between kinship and other social groups and the remaining church organisation, and the hold which Lamaism still has over funeral ritual. It is impossible to give an adequate account of these three important and complex matters here, but I will give a brief indication of their significance.

The relation between Lamaism and national feeling in rural parts of Buryatiya is not, as far as we can tell, anti-Soviet, though it may be anti-Russian; in all probability the kolkhozniks know very little about the historical role of the church in promoting political nationalism, theocratism, etc., since Buryat school textbooks mention these events only sketchily. It is rather a positive identification of certain 'Lamaist' ways of thinking, such as cyclical counting of time, and some quite minor rituals, for example the widespread habit of offering *khadag* (silk scarves), or the giving of Tibetan names to Buryat children, with 'being Buryat'. Specifically 'Buryat' styles of painting, for example, are derived from Lamaist iconography. There is nothing necessarily 'Buddhist' about this at all — the iconographic style is used to paint portraits of Lenin or mechanised harvesting. The identification with Lamaist religion comes about mainly because the people who are repositories of 'Buryat traditions' also tend to be religious. The old men in the villages who organise local rituals, for example at the building of a new house, or *tsagaalgan*, insist on including religious elements which might otherwise be left out, and their advice is followed because of the deep respect in which Buryats hold their elders. These old people tend to be close friends with *datsan* lamas visiting the kolkhoz; often they are themselves former lamas.

This leads us to the relation between the organised church and the community. Before the war, each monastery had its 'parish' which provided tithes collected by the local administration; in the early years after the Revolution this was even done by the Soviets. The 'parish' was originally a kinship unit, a patrilineal clan or lineage, and later became the territory associated with that unit. These relations remain, in other words each 'parish' still organises collections and support for the church, although this is now not for its own monastery but for its 'own' lamas within one of the two central monasteries. Worshippers from Barguzin, or some area within Barguzin, stay in the houses of 'their' lamas when they visit the monastery, and they invite these lamas to the village to conduct rituals. The network of former lamas, now living as ordinary kolkhozniks in the villages, is kept alive in that it is these people who organise donations to the monastery, see that annual rituals are performed in their locality, and get together artisans to do artistic or practical work for the *datsan*. One-day services (*nege üder münkhelkhe*) in the monastery are organised and paid for by the 'activists' of each *raion*. In 1969 the Doichid *khural* was provided by the Kyakhta *raion*, the Gandan Shünserme *khural* by the Mukhorshibir and Zakamen *aimaks*.[142] As there are so few official lamas, and they are not allowed to make journeys outside the monastery of more than ten days' length, the requests for religious services are often passed on to ex-lamas in the villages as substitutes.

The two requests most frequently made are for *maani* prayers, said annually in the autumn on behalf of the whole village (see below, p. 426), and for funerals. Soviet writers particularly regret the influence of lamaism in the ritual of death, and see this as a result of slackness on the part of officials: 'The managers of collective and state farms do not take measures to organise the funerals of their former workers in a real Soviet way, and essentially they just hand the whole thing over to the lamaist clergy.'[143] In the farms I visited it appeared that, even if lamas or shamans were not invited to conduct funerals, the form such rituals took was almost always the religious form, because no other way of adequately paying respect to the dead was known. In Selenga all funerals were 'Lamaist', while in Barguzin they were both 'Lamaist' and 'shamanist'.[144] In areas of Buryatiya where kin traditions are most strong, for example the Baikal-Kudarin *aimak*, people are buried in lineage cemeteries, or they were in the 1950s.[145]

In the Selenga collective farm young children were given different death rituals from adults, possibly because it was considered that they had not yet acquired souls. There was a separate children's cemetery, where coffins, open at the top, were laid on the ground so that wild animals and birds could eat the flesh. It is considered a good sign if the bones are bare after a few days. I came across this place by accident, and clearly it was considered something I should not have seen.

Adults in this farm were usually buried, although sometimes the lama would order that the corpse should be cremated on a pyre in the forest. The body after death was dressed in ordinary clothes (the lamas were against putting on fine clothes, placing objects in the grave, killing the dead man's horse, and other shamanist rituals). The face was obligatorily covered with a white cloth, and the body taken if possible out of the house to a shed. The body was laid out for three days, but people avoided it. At the time appointed by a lama, the corpse was taken out to the graveyard by a roundabout route. Only a few close relatives accompanied the body. In winter a fire had to be made to warm the ground to dig the grave. At the grave a lama read prayers, but not, my informants said, in the case of young people. Grain was scattered in the grave. On the way back a fire of *argal* (dried dung) was lit, and those who had been at the burial placed their hands in the smoke, having washed them first, and then they drank milk. This purification ritual was followed by a large feast, attended by large numbers of relatives, including people from far away. They served *buuz* (Buryat meat dumplings), mutton broth with noodles, tea, biscuits, sugar, and sweets, but not vodka (this was considered a bad Russian habit). Tugutov mentions, though my informants did not tell me this, that the bereaved family sometimes used to give out tea and money (1—5 rubles) to the kinsmen who attended. No presents are given *to* the family, although close relatives help them prepare the feast.[146] However, in some Lamaist areas people sent gifts of animals and money to the bereaved family to help them pay for lamas' assistance. The lamas were essential (a) for divining the direction in which the spirit of the deceased should depart, (b) for praying for a good reincarnation, (c) for accompanying the spirit out of the body in the proper direction, (d) for the rituals on the forty-ninth day after the burial, when the soul is considered to be removed finally to the world of the Buddha, or to be reincarnated. According to strict Lamaist views prayers should be said during the whole forty-nine days, during which the soul hovered uneasily, without a resting place.

In Buryatiya the Lamaist funeral ceremony purifies the corpse from the activity of the evil spirit (*totkhor*); the soul should be kept, by means of ritual, in the body until it is accompanied out by the lama, while the *totkhor* must be prevented from entering. It is supposed that the lama can conduct the soul into a representation (*minchzhan*), a drawing of the dead person on a piece of paper, which is placed among the folds of the clothing on the corpse. Offerings are made to the *totkhor*, otherwise it might appear in the guise of the dead person to threaten the living, and separate offerings of food are made to the soul in the *minchzhan*. This bit of paper is burnt on the forty-ninth day, and five pyramids of ash and clay (*sasa*) are placed on the grave. This signifies that the soul has united with the five Dkhyani buddhas.[147] A more sophisticated explanation of the *totkhor* is that there are several of these, and that they are personifications of sins (selfishness, anger, passion, etc.).[148]

The second ritual of popular Buddhism which is still frequently performed is the collective invocation called *maani* or *sangaril-maani*. These rituals are held by one household on behalf of the whole village and they are usually attended by all the believers of the vicinity. The constantly muttered prayers, which continue ceaselessly for as long as three days and nights, the darkness and fervent atmosphere give rise to what Zhukovskaya calls a 'collective hypnosis'.[149] A *sangaril* ritual may be held for various reasons (for success in having children, for a long life without disease, for a good rebirth) and in honour of several Lamaist deities (Sakyamuni, Aryabala, Nogoon Dara Ekhe, and Tsagaan Dara Ekhe).[150] But the most widespread ritual is the *zangaril* to Aryabala, the Mongol version of Avalokiteshvara, with the aim of helping the soul of a dead person to attain nirvana. An ordained lama should be invited to conduct the ritual, but often the villagers have to make do with their own resources. The reason why a lama is required is because Aryabala is an *idam* (Tib. *yi dam*, tutelary protector spirit) and only a consecrated person, i.e. a lama, is able to invoke the spirit and convey to it the wishes of the congregation. By the third night of constant recitation of prayers the people present reach a state of religious ecstasy and the image of the deity appears to them too. As Zhukovskaya remarks, this ritual is one of the practices of folk Lamaism most similar to shamanism.[151]

Belief in reincarnation of the soul is one of the few Buddhist doctrines which seems to have survived widely. Rural Buryats have a saying, 'A human being dies and a cow is born, a cow dies and a human being is born.'[152] To this day it happens that parents inspect the bodies of their newly born children for birth-marks or other signs which would indicate who was the ancestor whose soul has been re-born in the infant.

Some kolkhozniks of the older generation still wear an amulet generally called a *guu*, but known among the Barguzin Buryats as *ürel süme* (for women, literally 'round temple') and *ürel ger* (for men, literally 'round house').[153] The amulet was in the form of a small box or packet, worn on a thread round the neck, and it contained grass seeds. It was believed that if, just before death, one opened the amulet and ate the seeds, one's soul would be re-born on earth as a human or in heaven.

There was also a belief in a personal protector deity (*sakius*), and the eth-nographer Gerasimova reports that while the concept has survived, the ritual associated with it has changed.[154] Certain of the Lamaist deities were protectors, and the name of the appropriate deity had to be divined by a lama for the indi-vidual. Buryat women used to wear a locket containing a drawing of the deity and a prayer written on paper — the prayer was to be taken out and recited before death. These lockets are no longer worn, but the idea of a personal pro-tector is still handed down from generation to generation in the male line, the head of the family having responsibility for making offerings to it. Writing in the late 1970s, Gerasimova reports that people no longer hold rituals in honour of the *sakius* in their homes, but prefer to send the head of the family to collective rituals at the *datsan* when the occasion of a service to that deity occurs. It is also common for religious families to order a service to be held in the *datsan* on their behalf. Gerasimova remarks that this gives the impression that religious activity is on the increase, because more people visit the *datsan*, but in fact it is an indication of the dying-out of religious practice in the countryside.[155] The idea of a personal protector deity which can be inherited in the male line is interest-ing because it is so similar to the concept of ancestral shamanist powers or spirits (*onggod*, literally 'vessels' for spirits)[156] which has existed among the Mongols and Buryats from ancient times. The family protector deity is of course known throughout Tibet and northern India. In the Buryat case Zhukovskaya reports that it coexists in competition, as it were, with the *onggod* in the religious section of the population; the *onggod* are 'fed' (i.e. given offerings) in secret, so as not to annoy the *sakius* protector deity.[157]

It is interesting to consider which aspects of Buddhism have not survived in the Buryat population. Gerasimova suggests that religious morality and doctrine have proved less strong than ritual. Even people who claim to be believers no longer value the Buddhist notions of good and evil, of the meaning of human life, and of the ways of achieving true happiness. They do not believe in with-drawal from activity, the negation of passions, and contemplation as the path to serenity, and they no longer hold that personal *happiness* will result from devotion to the Buddha, the church, and 'belief' itself. In Gerasimova's view, it is the instrumental aspect of Lamaist practice which has survived for the very reason that people are involved in the world and have problems which appear to them insurmountable.[158] It is difficult to tell whether the ideal of ascetic withdrawal was ever very strong among the Buryat laity (though we must remember what a high proportion of the male population was in orders before the 1930s), but there seems no reason to doubt Gerasimova's assessment of the situation today. We are, however, left with the intriguing fact of the survival of the idea of reincarnation and a concern with time and the future, as materials discussed below will indicate.

The openly expounded ideology of Buryat Lamaism today has taken on much from Soviet values and ethics, which negate Buddhist ideals of withdrawal from this world. One of the current texts describes the teaching of Buddha as 'the experience of a community of labour', as the 'song of the greatness of labour, the song of the victory of humanity, the song of severe joy (*surovoi radosti*)'. The Bandido Khambo-Lama in 1969, Zhambal Dorzhi Gomboyev, said to his congregation:

In the name of the increasing of the wealth of our great Homeland, you, kolkhoznik-believers, multiply your herds, raise their productivity in collective and state farms, increase their quantity and quality, bring up good children, and produce worthy builders of communist society, struggle against amorality and with various charlatans of the Buddhist-Lamaist faith, disclose their illegal activities mercilessly, lead them to pure water, struggle with hooliganism, with drunkards, and with deserters from social labour.[159]

Such attitudes have penetrated to the ordinary people. A middle-aged woman said to a student at the Chita Teachers' Training College in the early 1970s, 'Lamas wish harm to no one. They pray to the good spirits so that everything should be all right, so that there should be peace, calm, and order, so that the young should respect their elders, so that they should believe in the Buddhas, so that everything should be all right.' A man attending the *Tsagaansar* at the Aga *datsan* said, 'On earth, people are in charge, in the heavens, the Buddhas are in charge. But when people make a mess of their lives, the Buddhas come to them. There have always been Buddhas; there will be more, and we should wait for them. We should address them very tenderly and respectfully, just as we address Marx and Lenin, as we glorify our leaders.'[160]

But however much some people respect the lamas, there is little evidence that anyone really thinks they have power to change Soviet society here and now. In many circles, particularly among young technocrats, lamas are despised and disliked. They are a rejected part of the Buryat heritage, serving only to spoil the chances of the progressive-minded by their dangerous and ridiculous activities. In places where the Party is vigilant, even unwitting contact with Lamaist activity draws public censure from the officials, and this causes believers to hide their religious practice even from members of their own family, or to conduct it at a distance (for example by ordering services in the *datsan* rather than carrying them out at home).

We can summarise this section by saying that Lamaism has lost much, if not all, of its political and economic hold on Buryat life. The great *oboo* festivals have turned into disorganised, largely 'shamanistic', occasions, the *tsam* has been stopped altogether, and the revenues of the two remaining monasteries are relatively small. Even Buddhist ethics have been turned on their heads. However, Lamaism retains a claim on people by the persistence of its organisation of time. This starts indeed within the life of the individual: Buryats traditionally count the beginning of life with conception and say that a child is already a year old when it is born. After this, years are counted from the new year (*tsagaalgan*) irrespective of the month of birth. Thus a baby born on the eve of *tsagaalgan* is counted two years old on the second day of its life.[161] People I met in the collective farms thought that a person's character depended on the year of birth in the twelve-year animal cycle.

The annual productive cycle in the farms has become less distinctively marked by Lamaism than it used to be, but some important ritual time periods still influence people's activities (no killing of domestic animals in the fourth month of Buddha's birth, festivities and enjoyment in the fifth month, village *maani* rituals with the return to winter dwellings in the autumn). Most striking is the *tsagaalgan* (New Year) festival which has, among other aspects, an economic calendrical significance. Buryat collective farms are in the habit, although the accounting year officially ends at the beginning of January, of doing their reckoning with the kolkhozniks, giving out shares, work-day payments and bonuses, on the eve of *tsagaalgan* in mid-February.[162] But the most striking survival of Lamaist attitudes is in the concept of time in the long term, the idea of 'ages' which will reappear. It is to this which we now turn.

Time and the future

Sociological studies carried out among Buryats and Kalmyks show that belief in the imminent arrival of the fifth Buddha, Maidari, is widely and sincerely held.[163] The Maidari *khural* is the most splendid and massively attended at the monasteries. A carriage with a statue of the coming Buddha, and the horse made of wood which is harnessed to it, symbolise the powers which should hasten the arrival. Each person tries to make a personal appeal, not simply by throwing money as the statue proceeds around the *datsan*, but by touching the horse and reins. When the procession makes its 'great standings' at each corner of the *datsan*, the fanaticism of the worshippers reaches its peak. They start to jump up and down on the ground near the holy horse, incoherently muttering, 'We are waiting for you, Maidari! We are waiting, hoping that you will not disappoint us ... we shall not forget you ... no, we shall not forget!'

429

The coming is described in various tracts. This is how the coming of Maidari was represented among the Kalmyks:

A pock-marked old man with an iron stick will appear from the south-west. Fire will flash from his mouth. When this person comes people will be so frightened that they will become like the fluff caught on wild grasses. Human blood will flow to ankle-height . . . The time will come when women will manage affairs. Cattle will get more expensive. One measure of flour will cost 1,000 kopecks . . . The Russian will have the honoured place in the *yurta*, but the *gelyung* (lama) will stay by the door. The first offerings will be made not to God but to the Russian. A child born yesterday will go to its neighbour for fire today. People will shrink to elbow height. Horses will become the size of hares. Then, on a white horse, coming down from the sky, Maidari will appear. And the sinful will stay here, but the sinless, holding to the hairs of the white horse, will fly away and be saved. And for them will begin a new, heavenly life.[164]

A study carried out in 1967 showed that 26% of adult Kalmyks believed in the coming of the next Buddha; among Buryats the figure was higher: of 536 people questioned, 45.7% said that they believed in this event, including 10% who were young people.[165]

The coming of Maidari is associated with the mythical country of Shambala, protector of religion. Inquiries among Buryat kolkhozniks in 1970 showed that they almost all could talk in detail about the coming 'Shambala War'. One old man said:

People will become enemies of one another, they will dislike one another and try to destroy one another, and thus gradually the Shambala War will start. A sea of blood will flow, the whole earth will be covered in it. Only true Lamaists will stay alive unbloodied, and then only those who follow the lamas in everything and are devoted to them both in days of terrible trial, and in days of happy prosperity . . . [After the war] people will believe in God — everyone as one. God will answer them with the same love . . . No one will govern (*upravlyat'*) the people. Society itself will accurately and harmoniously organise a well-shaped order of life, which will be agreeable and necessary to God . . . If people all, as one, believe in the heart of the Lamaist church, then there will be no war . . .

Some people thought that Eregdyn-Dagbo-khan, ruler of Shambala, would kill all human beings 'as they only cause harm'. 'Most punishment of all will be meted out to those who betrayed the Lamaist faith.' Some of the kolkhozniks associated the threat of the Shambala War with the coming atomic war.[166]

The cult of Maidari is not new, that is, it is not peculiar to the Soviet period, nor to the Buryats as distinct from Mongolians, Tibetans, and other followers of Lamaism.[167] But it is interesting that it, of all the Lamaist ideology, seems to have survived best in Soviet Buryatiya. The quotations show that it has become intermingled with ideas derived from Christianity (the love of God) and from communism ('Society itself will . . . harmoniously organise'). It is clearly associated with a feeling of threat to a traditional way of life, a feeling of living in a period of decline, which will be superseded by an age of uncomplicated harmony. This pessimism as to the present world is *not* specific to Buryat Soviet society, and I do not think that it would be justified to read into the persistence of the Maidari cult a greater dissatisfaction with this world now than existed among Buryats of earlier generations. What is interesting, however, is the particular content given to the current versions of the myth.

Descriptions of the Maidari cult in the pre-revolutionary period show that the central concern was the mortality of humans and animals. A story was recorded among the Buryats in which Sakyamuni, the fourth Buddha, and Maidari, the coming Buddha, quarrelled as to which of them should govern the world. They decided that the matter would be settled by seeing which could grow a flower faster in a pot. They sat down, each with a seed in a pot in front of them. Maidari's flower grew faster, but he fell asleep and Sakyamuni stole his flower. Maidari was angry, and said: 'Govern this world, but may your people be as deceitful as you are, and may they live only to the age of sixty, and animals only to the age of forty.'[168] In the age to be ushered in by Maidari people would live for a thousand years, and they would be huge and strong. This was 'confirmed' by the enormous size of the statues of Maidari kept in the *datsan*s of Buryatiya, so large that special temples had to be built for them.

The concern with longevity has been replaced by the idea of the society which governs itself, where *upravlyat' lyud'mi niko ne budet* (no one will govern the people). It used, perhaps, to be the communists who put forward this idea. Perhaps its power as a utopian ideal will die with the revolutionary generation, the old people who are now the main participants in the Maidari cult.

At any rate, it would seem to be too simple to see Soviet ideology as merely replacing Lamaist or shamanist thinking. What has occurred is a much more complex cross-cutting of ideas, in which Soviet elements and ideals enter into folk structures — ways of thinking which survive even though their previous strong institutional supports in society have virtually disappeared. In this, we should not forget that Soviet ideology itself has changed since the time of the Revolution. The ideal of communism, of the harmonious and equal brotherhood of man, is now rarely spoken of as actually impending. The early measures in collective farms which began to put this particular ideal into practice (equal pay for all, the collective division of income by the work-day system, payment in kind rather than in money, even the experiments with education by work-experience of the Khrushchev period) have all, one by one, been dropped. The present model of 'developed socialism' is rather different. But, paradoxically, an ideal of communism is to be found where one would least expect it, in the Messianic prophecies of the oldest generation.

We cannot doubt that the great majority of Buryats would claim not to be 'believers'. All sociological studies carried out by Soviet ethnographers indicate that the people who do admit to being 'believers' are clearly correlated with criteria of age, sex, occupation, education and distance from urban centres (that is, 'believers' are older, more likely to be women, more likely to work in livestock production, have less education, and live in more remote areas, than those who say they are indifferent or antagonistic to religion).[169] But it is significant that, as we saw with shamanism, large numbers of people who are 'not believers' take part in Lamaist rituals, and that, in the 1950s at least (comparable data are not available for more recent years), the frequency of such 'unreligious' religious rituals appeared to be on the increase:

The collective Lamaist ritual *maani* in this or that village was formerly held only once a year, and, for example, in the Khori *aimak* it was not known at all. Now it is carried out every quarter, and in the 'Communism' kolkhoz of Ivolga *aimak* it is carried out on the thirtieth day of every month according to the Buddhist calendar. In many cases the rite for the *sakius* is attached to the *maani* ceremony, another thing that used not to happen. Formerly, the *sakius* rite was conducted by each family at home, but now, adapting to new conditions, it is done collectively. This means that everyone, independent of whether he takes part in the collection of means for *maani*, contributes his *khandib* offering of money, from 50 to 200 rubles, and gives it directly to the lama. The same thing happened in the Karl Marx collective farm in Khori *aimak*.

Formerly, the Lamaist clergy felt it was its duty to oppose drunkenness, but now they encourage this sin. In 1958 in the Khori *aimak* at an *oboo* ceremony they collected offerings of about 10,000 rubles, over 90 litres of vodka, and 50 kilos of meat.[170]

One thing which is interesting about this is the new, collective, basis of such activities. It is clear that, as in the shamanist *tailgan* sacrifice, it is felt that everyone should take part, at least in the material offerings. A religious attitude matters less. 'At the *oboo* they get drunk, at the *maani* they get drunk', sighed one old man. 'It was never like that when I was young.'[171] The community involved in these festivities is not the kinship group, nor the circle of 'believers', but the collective farm village. 'It's our kind of May Day (*mayevka*)', as one kolkhoznik said. In other words, in all the complexity of Buryat religious activity, one thing is clear: the contents of Soviet ideology and the units of Soviet society are making their appearance in a light totally unforeseen by the architects of the planned society, and with what consequences for the future it is very difficult to tell.

Conclusion

The Soviet collective farm is an economic institution; nevertheless, within it and between it and the district agricultural authorities rights over people are more important than rights over materials. The kolkhoz consists of a hierarchy of productive and administrative estates, but as systematically as possible the surplus product is removed from each unit in order to fulfil an obligatory delivery plan. At the same time, there is a legal and fairly strictly enforced limitation on the amount of productive property which individuals are allowed to own and to pass on in inheritance. It is these two conditions which ensure the fundamental importance of direct rights over people, and because of this, whenever disposable property is acquired it tends to be used towards the same end, that is, it is converted into rights of one kind or another over people.

Rights over people are held by virtue of position in the division of labour which is at the same time a hierarchy of management. In other words, economic and 'political' functions are not separate. There are no *economic* classes in the collective farm, but rather there are status groups, denoted by terms such as *nomenklatura* (people designated for high-level administrative posts), 'trained cadres', 'specialists', 'the rural intelligentsia', 'the ordinary kolkhoznik', etc. Broadly speaking, we could divide the kolkhoz community into four status groups: the management, the specialists, the intelligentsia (teachers, doctors, librarians, etc.), and the workers, but in fact each of these is sub-divided by virtue of its own intricate hierarchy, reaching down to the very lowest positions in the farm. Even tiny production units consist of, for example, a head shepherd, a second and a third shepherd, so no kolkhoznik considers himself outside the all-encompassing hierarchy. The head shepherd may feel he is, and in fact may be, part of 'the management'. Since rights and *de facto* powers accrue to positions in the hierarchy (or related to it in the case of illegitimate roles), the ultimate interest of individuals lies in improving his or her position in the hierarchical division of labour.

In this structure rights are held in parallel by office-holders of the kolkhoz on the one hand, and office-holders in the Party on the other. The bases of power in the two cases are different. The kolkhoz officials have rights and capacities by

433

virtue of their control of the process of production, that is, their rights in the administration of the means of production, including labour. The Party officials, on the other hand, are vested with authority from above, from the centralised hierarchy responsible for policy-making. Their authority in the local community today is primarily moral, and in practical life is considerably outweighed by the powers of the enterprise management. However, because the Party as a whole is in charge of job placements at higher levels, and because it indirectly regulates the entry into status groups (recruitment to higher education and assessment of political reliability), it is the Party which has control of 'careers': movements in time up and down the hierarchy. In other words, the Party has control of people's future, while the kolkhoz can only reproduce their present.

This book is concerned with the Buryat kolkhozniks' reactions to this state of affairs, both in understanding Soviet society and in activity within it. The kolkhoz itself is not simply an organisation. It is constituted on the basis of *ideologically* formulated statutes and instructions. There are inconsistencies in the ideology itself, and this gives rise to instructions or stated aims which are either contradictory or confusing – the confusion being compounded by actual difficulties of production, mistakes in higher-level planning, and adverse price structures, which are quite outside the farmers' control. The nature of the information made available to collective farmers and the narrow range of acceptable public explanations of failure, both of which tend to focus on *individual* circumstances, leave rifts and disjunctions in local understanding which shamans and fortune-tellers attempt to fill in.

Since collectivisation Buryat society has undergone a complete transformation, even the structure of the family reflecting socio-political changes at higher levels. Furthermore, the Buryats, as compared with other oriental minorities of the Soviet Union, have a revolutionary tradition: it was during an *internal* Buryat civil war in the 1930s that the powerful Lamaist church, combined with the remnants of anti-Soviet resistance, was suppressed by the government, by force. Not that the Buryats would have done this on their own initiative, but nevertheless there was a 'revolutionary' section in the Buryat population, which arose anew with succeeding generations.[1] The vast majority of Buryats today, if the people I met are representative, would agree with general Soviet values were they to be asked – and yet there are activities and beliefs which are quite specifically 'Buryat' in a Buryat collective farm. To ask what can possibly have survived if social organisation and 'ideology' have changed would be to put the wrong question. Relatively few Buryat institutions and cultural conceptions have in fact disappeared; most of them exist, transformed, within Soviet society – or, if we restrict the referent of 'Soviet society' to officially sanctioned institutions, it would be correct to say that Buryat social and cultural forms subsist either within 'Soviet society' or in contradistinction to it, having in both cases undergone a metamorphosis determined by the social 'environmental niche' they have found.

434

Conclusion

Let us take the case of ritualised exchange, which finds its place in the political economy of the farm. In the practice of production, the multitudinous instructions do not prevent the creation of non-legitimate resources in both materials and people. The farm itself, and the individuals and groups within it, create what I have called 'manipulable resources', consisting of products and money. Because it is illegal to accumulate or invest these, they are transformed by means of the system of public festivals and the network of private exchange, into rights over people who are placed in relations of reciprocity by the giving of gifts. At the same time as the farm inevitably creates such resources because it is an institution of production which can never exactly conform to the plan, the farm's social organisation requires the deployment of such resources. Some farms, or sections of farms, make a financial loss or fall behind in the obligatory deliveries, but these failures can be covered by normal economic means (e.g. State Bank loans, negotiation of a lower plan). 'Manipulable resources' are used because the officials' continued hold on their position demands that they get the kolkhozniks to work for them, and because the workers, for their part, are dependent on the officials for a range of benefits of utmost necessity (varying from firewood in winter to permission for children to leave the kolkhoz for further education). Jobs in the farm are very unequal in pay and conditions of work. It is not possible to move from one job to another without permission from the officials, and yet we find that kolkhozniks frequently change jobs. It is perhaps to this end, the attempt to find an acceptable position in the division of labour, that 'manipulable resources' are most frequently employed.

The practical working of the farm, which implies the existence of non-legitimised resources, also creates and maintains socio-economic roles concerned with their management, transfer and disposal, the 'left' occupations of the *perekupshchik*, 'middleman', and the *spekulant*. It should be noted that contradictions in central planning also require the existence of illegitimate roles, such as the *tolkach*, 'pusher', who obtains inputs and ensures the sale of kolkhoz products to state organisations, for purely legitimate ends. However, in Buryat farms which are remote from markets, the former roles are reduced to a minimum, and the redistribution of 'manipulable resources' is largely an internal affair, only minimally mediated by ruble currency. The strength of the Buryat 'gift economy' is such that money can enter it as an object — that is, it has the symbolic value of being a precious thing, like all gifts, and in this mode it is not counted up as currency. Individuals, of course, can use money in both its market and its limited symbolic sense. The Buryats are thus no exception to the many other societies with 'gift economies': it is not the nature of the objects which are transferred as gifts which determines the relation, but rather the cultural conception of what is implied by the exchange.

In point of fact, both the nature of the objects and the concepts of reciprocity, have changed since collectivisation. We can trace their transformations much further back in history than the Soviet period, and this series of changes

435

has implications for the theory of 'the gift'. Natasha Zhukovskaya has rightly emphasised the importance in Mongolian culture of the gift and counter-gift (*podarok-otdarok*) and she makes the point that it has never simply performed one social function but has always had a 'scale of meanings'.[2] In a summary of a longer paper unfortunately unavailable to me, she suggests that in Mongol culture the *podarok-otdarok* is a means of social communication in the following contexts: (1) within the patrilineal kin-group or between affines, when the gift functions not only as a material exchange but also as a symbol of warmth of kin ties; (2) as a marker of 'symbolic brotherhood' between unrelated people, who, with the exchange of gifts, become ritual comrades of equal standing (Mong. Bur. *anda*); (3) between political non-equals, for example serf and lord, when the serf gives a nominal gift as a sign of subservience and the senior replies with a gift, often of some economic importance; (4) the gift to the guest in one's home, to the complete outsider, which one could perhaps interpret as a sign of honour and self-respect, as participation in the 'generous society'. All of these types are true 'gifts' in the sense that the honour lies with giving, not receiving, and that acceptance of a gift implies acceptance of the obligation to reciprocate. But they are unlike one another and this differentiation of gifts, which I suspect must occur in most if not all societies, renders the classical theory which simply opposes 'the gift' to the 'commodity transaction', inappropriate in this case, and perhaps wrong in general.[3] There are categories of exchange among Buryats, furthermore, which lie between 'the gift' and 'the commodity transaction', for example the autumn meat distribution *üüse*, in that no particular honour attaches to giving and yet there is an obligation to reciprocate in some way at an unspecified time in the future. But my concern is not to criticise the 'gift'/'commodity transaction' dichotomy, but rather to establish the categories of ritualised exchange in Mongolian and Buryat culture and examine the ways in which they have changed.

The materials from this book, and from earlier periods, show that the categories themselves, as concepts, have changed less than their social content. In other words, the categories have been applied to new relationships, while retaining a core of meaning. For example, the category *anda*, which during the Mongol Empire and subsequent periods, perhaps into the Ch'ing Dynasty, was used for ritual brothers, who exchanged gifts as a sign of their promise to support one another, was by the nineteenth century being used for exchange marriage (a brother and a sister for a brother and a sister), which negated the status difference between the affinal sides. *Anda* denoting ritual brotherhood fell into disuse; the institution itself seems to have disappeared. The idea of establishing equality between patrilineally unrelated and therefore qualitatively different people remained.[4]

This makes one suspect that it is incorrect to derive categories of exchange directly from particular social relationships, in the way that Zhukovskaya and others have done.[5] I would suggest, rather, that there are concepts, embedded in cultures — such as, for example, our idea of 'charity' — which may change their social function and their referent while retaining their sense.[6]

Let us look at the Buryat material on exchanges from this point of view. Mongolian and Buryat society became increasingly stratified during the seventeenth to nineteenth centuries. The Selenga Buryat law codes of the period 1775–1841 mention seven grades among civil and Cossack leaders and twenty-nine grades among lamas, each with their own distinguishing signs of dress and rank.[7] Patrilineal lineages, as we have seen, were internally constituted or seniors and juniors; as the Selenga Buryats said, 'However long stirrups are, they never reach the ground, however good a junior (*düü*) is, he can never reach a senior (*akha*)'.[8] There were therefore few categories of ritual exchange between equals, but rather exchanges expressing the idea of giving upwards (from the Mongolian root *bari-* 'to offer, to bear') or giving downwards (trom the Mongolian root *kesig-* 'favours'), or establishing equality between previous unequals (from the Mongolian root *anda*). There were, of course, terms for buying, selling, barter, giving and transferring, which implied no status differences, but these were not used in the ritual context we are discussing.

Words deriving from the root *bari-* 'to offer upwards' had an interesting fate in Buryat. According to Kowalewski's Mongolian dictionary published in 1844 the word *barilga* was used for offerings, for brideprice, and for fees to senior people for some service (e.g. to lamas).[9] Baldayev mentions *baril*, *barilga*, and *aduu bariuur* as terms used by Buryats for presents given upwards and for brideprice. But, he continues, these terms began to be employed for payments made to the clan senior for some misdemeanour. Subsequently, *barilga* in this sense was replaced by *edilge*, with the meaning 'bribe', or with *yala*, for customary payments made for crimes, such as bride-theft, or manslaughter.[10] The term for brideprice became *basaganai aduun* 'horses (paid for) the bride' or *basagain khudaldaan*, literally 'the bride's price', which had negative implications, since the word *khudaldaan* 'price' derives from *khudal*, meaning 'lie, falsehood'. As we have seen this payment is now never made. *Barilga* is now used for 'takings' or 'catch', and *baril* now has the separate sense of 'offerings', and more rarely 'bribe'. Another word from the same root, *barisa*, is used colloquially for offerings and gifts upwards. The word, since the nineteenth century at least, has been used also for the site where sacrifices and offerings are made to local spirits.[11]

The word *kesig* (Bur. *khesheg*), which was formerly used in formations such as *kesigle-* 'to give presents, to confer favours', for example by a prince to his subjects, is now rarely used for gifts between people because of the religious connotations of the word. *Kesig* has the meaning 'blessed', 'fortunate', and it is part of honorific vocabulary, now thought to be inappropriate to socialist society.[12] *Khesheg* is still used in very restricted senses for particular gifts, such as the present made by the bride to her parents when she returns home after marriage to collect her *enzhe*. More commonly it is now used in high-flown language for *impersonal* gifts, e.g. *ünder urgasyn khesheg* 'the fruits (i.e. blessing) of the lofty harvest'.[13]

These examples show that there has been a process of transferral of Mongolian—Buryat cultural concepts, with relatively minor changes in sense, from one social context to another, as society has been transformed. This contrasts with the process identified in Eastern Europe, where *social* change has been more gradual, in particular as regards rural communities: 'the trend of change . . . consisted of absorbing new cultural elements into the existing social structure'.[14] In the Buryat case, old 'cultural elements' have been diversified, split apart, and ramified in order to make sense of the drastic actual transformation of economy and society.

We see this in Buryat kinship organisation. Kinship is in a sense independent of Soviet institutions because the latter do not specify the forms by which human groups may reproduce themselves in kinship structures. Nevertheless, if the kinship 'system' as a conceptual structure is independent of Soviet institutions, the practical organisation of kinship, for example in relation to the administrative-economic household (Russ. *dvor*), is entirely bound up with Soviet reality. We thus have to separate out diverse actualisations of kinship, not all of which may be conceptually distinct to the Buryats themselves. The same kinship terminology is used for patrilineal clans and lineages, for variants of everyday kinship, including 'semi-kin' (relations through adoption, divorce, illegitimacy, etc.), or for clusters of local kin, linked by *ad hoc* ties, built up by influential individuals. But in fact these are separate phenomena.

The admittedly fluctuating and intermittent resurrection of traditional groups on the basis of the cognitive structure of the lineage might be seen simply as a 'survival' of the past. Such structures are latent, and they appear as groups only at rituals such as the *tailgan* sacrifice to ancestors and spirits of nature, and even on these occasions the number of people from the 'structure' who are absent usually exceeds those who are present. Nevertheless, the fact that all families may have to send contributions to these sacrifices, and the fact that the kin positions of those who do not attend is noted, indicates that the 'structure' is potentially realisable. But why does it exist, why is it not simply forgotten? It functions, I think, as a positive counterpart to the embodiment of the Soviet ideology in the collective farm. Like the hierarchy of the farm and the Party it is a system for the control of people rather than things. To the specialised division of labour and manifest inequality of the farm it counterposes a common humanity of all those who are born as Buryats. Nothing is left of the economic or political advantages which used to be tied to genealogical position. All that remains today is the fact of having a position, that is, the 'being related' to other people. To the arbitrariness of being allotted to one task after another, or the precarious construction of a career, it counterposes simply absolute status, a security which does not disappear even after death, since the system is defined by reference to ancestors. In the Soviet ideology all striving is directed towards the future, a future which is defined as superior to the present and doubly superior to the past — the 'bright future', *svetloye budushchee*, of communism. In the Buryat kinship system the most senior lines are those which go back deepest and furthest into the recesses of time, to the period of Genghis Khan, to the Tibetan kings, to the ancient Indian sages. In this system nothing is expected of the future except a recurrence of the past, and the duty of each generation is to reproduce what was given to oneself.

If to the Buryat kolkhoznik the world of work, despite all efforts to influence it, appears as arbitrary and inflexible in contrast to the sphere of patrilineal kinship, which is the realm of humanity, this is the opposite of what many people may feel in Europe, including Russia, where individuals become themselves as human beings at work and with friends made at work, and experience the circle of kin, whom they have not chosen, as arbitrary and restricting. Perhaps this change will take place in rural Buryatiya too, but it has not yet done so. The patrilineal kinship system is not what it *was* — a set of genealogical positions adjusted to constitute a political-administrative structure — and yet what it *is* cannot be understood by itself alone, but only in relation to Soviet society.

The same is true, *a fortiori*, of contemporary shamanist practice. Shamanism continues in its intersticial way as a result of alienation from, or misunderstanding of, utilitarian, 'scientific' ideology, which appears at the local level to be without adequate explanation for failure and success, and which moreover contains no possibility of reflection upon itself. The more specific the prescriptions, the greater the inevitable, mysterious gulf between themselves and reality. Shamanist thought patterns, as we have seen, make connections between past events and the present disasters, between humanity and nature (ancestors who 'became' locality spirits), between misfortune and revenge. The pattern of such connections has changed relatively little in the last fifty years, but the close relation between present-day shamanist *activities* and Soviet life is shown by the concerns (education, entering the army, fulfilling the plan, the health of the collective livestock) which form the content of contemporary rituals. The capacity of the shamanist mode — the as-it-were ecstatic trance — for invention, for poking fun, for uncovering hidden meanings, also makes it perhaps inevitably the focus for a counter-culture, where Buryats, not 'believers' at all, go to enjoy themselves. This can become a kind of ethnicity — not an exclusive pitting of Buryats against Russians and others, since Russians not infrequently attend Buryat rituals, but certainly a festive activity which gains its point from being different from Soviet rituals. The furthest extension of this process occurs when devoutly religious Buryats refuse to attend the *tailgan* sacrifices and *oboo* ceremonies on the grounds that they have become disrespectful, wild and drunken. In these circumstances the shamanist or folk-Lamaist core of the ritual becomes completely eroded, and even on the occasion of the activities themselves becomes the subject for cynical humour.

Nevertheless, shamanism is perhaps surprisingly stronger today than folk

Conclusion

Lamaism, which used to overwhelmingly dominate Buryat religious life in the areas I visited. At the time of the Revolution over 10% of the entire Buryat population were lamas, and we cannot but be amazed at the speed with which Buddhist ideas in general seem to have disappeared in rural areas. The one exception is significant: the Lamaist church, though formally tiny in numbers, has retained control of the rites of death. In so doing it has contributed to the maintenance of the idea of individual reincarnation and cyclical time. Needless to say, this is at odds with the Soviet theories of gradual, unilinear progress and development. However, Buddhist theory is not clearly incompatible with Marxist dialectics and the 'class struggle' — at least insofar as these ideas were understood by Buryat farmers. The idea of the war of the righteous country Shambala against the infidels seems to have gained popularity among Buryats and Mongols at around the same time as revolutionary ideas were spreading among them. As noted earlier, the Mongolian leader Sukhe-Bator actually merged these two concepts in the revolutionary soldiers' songs of 1921. Even in the 1960s–1970s, joined with the utopia of the early revolutionaries, the 'bright future' of communism, we find belief in the messianic idea of the coming of the next Buddha, Maidari, who will put an end to the terrible war of Shambala and usher in the age of prosperity and long life, when society will order itself without rulers.

Both shamanism and Lamaism are supported as institutions by the continued existence of the Buryat extended patrilineal kinship system. Participation at sacrifices is based on divisions of the lineage, and the Lamaist church also collects its 'dues' by means of the old semi-territorial 'clans' (Russ. *rod*) which used to form the parishes of the monasteries. The existence of religion at all cannot be explained only by social and economic factors — it must have its own, more mysterious reasons for existence — but such factors can account for the pattern religion assumes in society. In this case, as we have seen, the form taken by kinship is itself dependent on the institutions of Soviet society.

Contemporary Buryat religion is characterised by a divorce between folk practices and the higher philosophical traditions (i.e. of Buddhism), which now only exist among a few individuals of the urban intelligentsia. This separation was caused by the destruction of the monasteries, which formerly encompassed the whole range of religious practitioners and beliefs, from the most crude to the most sophisticated. Folk religion, without its connection with the scholarly and metaphysical traditions, is held by many people in low esteem, even though they may have recourse to it in moments of extremity. It is maintained by the tight relations which among rural people still are thought to link kinship groups, the ancestors, the locality spirits, the weather, and fortune in agriculture. Each district has its own myriad sites for offerings, 'inhabited' trees and mountains, dangerous genies, revengeful spirits of the dead, just as it has its own dialect, its own repertoire of songs, proverbs and sayings.

This specific pattern is maintained by two features of Soviet society: the static, restricted, and endogamous community of the collective or state farm, which has communications links with the district and republic centres rather than 'horizontal' links with other farms in other areas;[15] and the lack of general explanations for failure, as opposed to attributions of individual responsibility and blame. This latter, given the limited capacity allowed to individuals actually to take responsibility, contributes to a sense of powerlessness and reproduces the need for familiar local remedies.

In the decades with which this book is concerned, the 1960s and 1970s, Buryat kolkhozniks continued to explain many aspects of the Soviet world to a great extent by their own patterns of thought. Rather than the insertion of a Buryat native content into Soviet modes of explanation, we find the reverse: the phenomena of the Soviet world appear, disconnected from their theoretical origins, structured by a Buryat consciousness. Those Buryat social institutions which exist are wholly adapted to Soviet circumstances, but this is not recognised and they continue to be explained as though there had been no break with the past. In this, the nature of rural economic organisation has probably played an important part, since it has preserved intact the Buryat communities of the remote countryside, and even the exodus of up to 50% of the younger generation has not, given the extremely high birth-rate, had the effect of destroying them.

From this situation we can see revealed a central contradiction. Soviet values as we saw in Chapter 2 discourage individualism and individualistic activity. But the communal values, inherent in the working of a collective farm, have the effect of supporting parochialism and local ties. As we have seen, on some occasions such as the wedding ritual or the *suur-kharbaan* games, units of the collective farm even take over the functions of the earlier kin groups. More common, however, is a dual and parallel maintenance of two different kinds of communal group, purely Soviet on the one hand, and 'Buryat' (or more correctly Buryat–Soviet) on the other. This has lent support to those aspects of folk religion, whether shamanist or Lamaist, which are tied to a communalist ideology. The attribution of individual blame for failures in the Soviet system leads people to have recourse to group support from the alternative 'Buryat' system. Yet, as Soviet sociologists and ethnographers have amply demonstrated, it is processes leading to greater personal individualisation, such as higher education and mobility,[16] which break the communal networks in which folk ritualism thrives.

Now that the links between the farm, the educational system, and the city are becoming more open we may expect to see the inturned social relations I have been describing replaced by new ties, of a different kind, linking the Buryat farmers with Soviet society at large. This will be a new kind of society, with new demands made on individual capacities for flexibility and choice. Perhaps in these circumstances there will be a renewal of interest in those aspects of Buddhism concerned with the internal spiritual resources of the individual.[17]

Therefore, we should perhaps understand the life of Buryat collective farmers, described in this book, as an intermediate stage. Behind them lies the period of semi-feudal political organisation, lacking the basic amenities of economic security, universal education, and health care; behind them also is the unrealised hope of national independence. This book has shown the Buryats as integrated into an all-USSR economic and political structure, but one which, at the level of the collective farm, has served to maintain some of the very features of Buryat culture which it was hoped to eliminate. There is nothing surprising in this. As detailed sociological studies of Western societies have shown, the exclusively 'modern' society, dominated entirely by utility, calculation and science, exists nowhere. What I have tried to analyse in this book is the specific ways in which the Soviet political economy has maintained and yet transformed the 'traditions' of one of its ethnic minorities. One of the conclusions is that we cannot identify 'traditions' with culture, as if this were divorced from 'real' economic life. Although the Soviet government made a radical reorganisation of production, this has not eliminated those 'traditions' concerned with economic practice and understanding. If this book maintains therefore that rural Buryats are 'traditional' in some deep sense, this should not be misread as understating the complexity or capacity for simultaneous 'modernity' of their society. Like most if not all of the minorities in the USSR, the Buryats have shown potentialities for internal variation and differentiation for as long as their history has been known.

UPDATE

9

The collective farms after Socialism (1996)

With the demise of the Soviet regime in the early 1990s the old structure of automatic credits, planned inputs, and designated purchasers disappeared. The collectives are now self-financing economic units. Their dilemma is that they have to operate exposed to the harsh vagaries of price, without, however, having the benefits of a market. Farms are faced with low prices and low demand for their products from the poverty-stricken population but also with high taxes and high prices for their inputs, such as petrol, fertilisers, machinery, and spare parts. There is a general absence of marketing organisations. Farms themselves have to bear the costs of transporting, storing, and selling their produce. Small traders in the countryside have mostly failed, as the costs of transport from distant farms cannot be covered by the sale of goods. Not to put too fine a point on it, what this means is that virtually all collective farms operate in a state of bankruptcy. This chapter is about economic life under such conditions.

In a more anthropological idiom we can imagine the change as a radical reduction in vertical flows – of products flowing "upward" to the state and subsidies and inputs going "downward" to the farms. As a local reporter put it: "This is the time of horizontal links and deals. You to me, me to you, we to him, and him to us."[1] As the essence of the Soviet system was to strictly regulate such lateral flows (Verdery 1996), collectives and individuals have little publicly legitimate experience to help them along, so activities previously seen as illegal or informal have come to the fore. Inside the collectives the members now receive no money coming "down" to them in wages. Here at the fundaments there has been no alternative to the turn to a domestic economy, which has however developed a multifarious character. It is at the same time an intensification of subsistence for the household, the invention or honing of skills in order to engage in exchange, and the expansion of "lateral" foraging over the whole area of reachable resources.

In Soviet times, as was shown in earlier chapters, the main players of the political economy as officially conceived – the state, the collectives, and the

444

households – were always interwoven with other nonofficial relationships, of patronage, kinship, black markets, rural-urban reciprocities, and so forth. This whole sphere used to be kept in the background, partly because much of it was illegal, and partly because the main income of both collectives and households did regularly come from the official system of "vertical" redistribution. It is part of Russia's tragedy that the new capitalism itself has had to be created from within such an ambiguous space, publicly immoral and yet at the same time "domestic" and subject to domestic morality. In present circumstances, when ruthless profiteering, monopolies, and rackets thrive in provincial Russian cities, it is interesting that cultural differences seem to be emerging. In Russian cities, according to one sociologist, kin and close friends are now often kept out of business, because it is assumed that economic activity is pitilessly self-interested and also highly risky, so one may well "take one's partners down with one."[2] By contrast, in rural Buryatiya (and it appears among many Asian parts of Russia) kinship and other personal ties are extensively used in economic relations to evoke the qualities of trust, honesty, and reliability. This may mean that the quality of the business that goes on within such networks is different (a topic which requires further research); at the same time, it produces social hiatuses, because outside the personal network mistrust reigns supreme. If there are "kin" (*rodnya*), there are also "nonkin"; if there are "fellow countrymen" (*zemlyaki*), there are also "aliens," and of the latter categories nothing much is expected, and no quarter is given. Thus, a space is created for avid foraging, cheating, and appropriation. All this requires us to look carefully at this evanescent and eventful terrain of reciprocity/dis-reciprocity so as to understand its range, its gulfs, and its limits.

Yet it will be argued that these "horizontal" relations, necessary as they are to survival, cannot tell the whole story. They are not sufficient, for at every level the new political economy is producing overarching, hierarchical rights. This is not just the remnant of the Soviet welfare state, which has shrunk, though its bare bones remain. It is a new structure of vertical money flows and hierarchically overlapping control of land. Moreover, the culture of Buryats, and perhaps of Russians too, provides expectations that things will be this way, that even as a single person one is part of a larger, higher, governing, social whole. This expectation is so strong that it affects the way in which people conduct even the subsistence economy. Far from seeking "freedom" on tiny, separate holdings, there is resistance to the idea and practise of autonomy.

Inevitably, the collectives, as they are changing, are influenced by these interests. I shall argue that economic circumstances, politics, and cultural concerns are interacting in volatile ways, creating different types of collective and producing two branching paths along which rural societies look as though they may diverge: shareholders' collectives and collectives based on contracts with smallholders. This is always supposing the potential conflict between the two does not just result in muddle and stagnation. The present chapter tries to give an account of the current situation over a wide range of topics, however, and does not limit itself to presenting an argument. It first lays out the types of collective now present in the agricultural scene, discussing their dilemmas in coping with the unsustainable inheritance of Soviet times and the current recession. The chapter then takes the perspective of people's domestic economic tactics and problematises the notion of "household subsistence." Returning again to the collectives, the next section deals with strategies of farm directors in the regional economy. This introduces the subject of the political dynamics of the reforms. The idea of "shares" of land and other means of production is central to the reformist goal of creating private property, and it has been used throughout Russia and elsewhere in Eastern Europe. In Buryatiya, however, it looks unlikely that individual private property in land will develop, since shares in practise are not freely negotiable and not disposable to outsiders. Rather, they are combined into "insiders' collectives" (in the helpful phrase suggested by Konstantinov 1997), and dividends are distributed (on the same basis as the shares themselves) according to sociopolitical status. This contrasts with the contract system, which designates a functional, economic role for each household.

The agricultural landscape

The reform policy of the early 1990s aimed to end the system of collectivised agriculture and replace it with private farms. When Buryatiya acted on these reforms in 1992–3, the districts initially varied in their response. A few disbanded the collectives altogether and tried to organise a multitude of "private" farms of varying size. But in subsequent years the small farms have almost all joined up again into collectives.[3] With the infrastructure centralised (roads, housing, or electricity supplies), with large-scale arable production unmanageable by households, and with general unfamiliarity with taking independent decisions, most soon decided that collective organisation was better. So the pattern seen today in Selenga and Barguzin, neither of which did much initial disbanding, is now characteristic of the whole Republic.[4] In the course of this chapter I shall try to explain why collectives are seen as necessary by rural people.

It is noticeable that the collectives of Selenga retain a rhetorically Soviet aura, as can be seen from their names, while those of more reform-minded Barguzin are named after places. Capitalist types of farm, such as the joint-stock company, are few and far between in Buryatiya.[5] Other parts of Russia may have established larger numbers of business firm–like farms, including curious hybrids such as the Memory of Lenin, Ltd. (Konstantinov 1997). Selenga District (*raion*), however, whose collectives in 1996 are listed here, seems resolutely socialist in spirit:[6]

446

Collective Farms (*kolkhoz*):	Bestuzhevskii[7]
	im. XX Parts'yezda (Named
	after the 20th Party Congress)
	im. Karla Marksa (Named after
	Karl Marx)
	im. Lenina (Named after Lenin)
	Erdem (Science)
Union of Peasant Farms (OKKh):	im Kirova (Named after Kirov)
United Peasant Farm (SKKh):	Selenginskoye
Association of Peasant Farms (AKKh):	Oblepikhovoi
Association of Collective Peasant	
Farms (AKKKh):	Zhargalanta

These nine farms cover most of the agricultural land of the district, though there are also two small "subsisidary farms" at Tsaidam and Temnik attached to an electricity station and a mine, respectively. The district also contains 13 sizable industrial enterprises (mining, brickmaking, manufacture of electrical equipment, etc.), most of which are based at the administrative centre at Gusino-ozersk. Several other factories and mines have recently closed down. The preeminent enterprise of the whole district, the "patron" plant under which many smaller businesses shelter, is the electricity power station (GRES) at Gusino-ozersk. In theory there are also 104 private (also called "peasant") farms in the Selenga district, i.e., small farms administratively outside the collectives and licensed to operate separate economies. Yet only four of them operate as farmers, the rest having closed or turned to trade. The only private farm set up at Tashir, out of land belonging to the Karl Marx, has failed altogether and exists only "on paper," as local people say.

In the Barguzin district there are 6 collectives (1996):

State Farms (*sovkhoz*)	Chitkanskii
	Barguzinski
Collective Farms (*kolkhoz*)	Khilganaiskii
	Ulyunskii
Unions of Peasant Farms (OKKh)	Bayangol (the former Karl Marx
	Collective)
	Bodonskoye

There are 32 private farmers in the district, and their names (Hope, Progress, Source, Golden Spring, Renaissance, Union, Dawn, and Labour) indicate something of the inspiration with which they were set up. As in Selenga, however, the great majority of them no longer operate as farmers. In this region there is less industry than in Selenga, and there is no "great patron" firm.

Generally in Buryatiya, the collectives are centred at the same main villages as in Soviet times, and these villages are also the centres of subdistricts (R. *selo*, B. *somon*), which are the bases for local government and educational, medical, and cultural services. The governmental administrative boundaries of the former districts and subdistricts have remained unchanged, as far as I can tell. The former Selsoviet at subdistrict level is now called the Local Administration (*mestnaya administratsiya*), and it operates with an appointed leader (*glava*) under the District Administration (*raionnaya administratsiya*). The Communist Party has lost all power locally, though it was revived after a brief ban and now engages in such activities as celebrating Lenin's birthday and largely fruitless propaganda. Thus, the troika of local power in Soviet days (the Chairman of the collective, the Party Secretary, and the Head of the Soviet) has now been replaced by a twosome, the Chair of the collective, who is now more frequently than in Soviet times a woman, and the Head of the Local Administration. These two do not always see eye to eye.

As for the internal organisation of the collectives, the terms suggesting they are different types are something of an illusion. The collectives are now free to establish their own statutes (*ustav*)[8] and to organise themselves as they see fit. In practise this seems to depend greatly on the preferences of the Chair (*predsedatel'*). Whatever they are termed, most of the farms have come to operate more or less as they did in Soviet days. The former Karl Marx Collective at Bayangol, for example, is officially a new-sounding Union of Peasant Farms (OKKh), but actually it operates like a sadly reduced version of its old self, with the members grouped in specialised brigades under a management committee as before (MTF, OTF, KTF, Agricultural Brigades, etc., see p. 138). In 1992–3 it had divided into three large peasant farms based on the three main villages, Bayangol, Karasun, and Urzhil. By 1996, however, the three had come together again under the Bayangol collective, though the latter continues to be known as a Union of Peasant Farms.

The main ostensible difference from the 1960–70s, when work teams were *ordered* what to do according to a plan, is that now in farms like Bayangol they have *contracts* with the farm to produce according to a plan. Contracts operate much like the orders of old when the work team is engaged in barely profitable production like livestock herding (Humphrey 1989), but teams now have more leeway for independent action, such as taking out a contract outside the collective, if they produce goods that are in demand. The OKKh Bodonskii and the Barguzinskii State Farm operate in an even more traditional manner, with orders (*naryad*), competitions between workers (now renamed from "socialist" to "economic" competitions), posted lists of duties, published indicators, and categorisation of workers by status (senior, 2nd, and 3rd shepherds, and so forth). Meanwhile, the Chitkan State Farm, which sounds from its name as though it would be a traditional Soviet-type farm, has virtually collapsed and at the same time has become bizarrely democratic. For example, the members vote on who should be allowed to do the spring ploughing and sowing. This is an indication of the desperate straits these farmers are in: spring sowing is a valued job because of the opportunity it offers to steal the grain. At a meeting in April 1995 several men were voted as suitable for the ploughing, but no one was voted as trustworthy enough for the sowing.[9]

The agricultural landscape

Kotz and Weir (1997) have argued that the reforms of the Soviet system have been a revolution from above. Buryatiya gives evidence of this, though we can also see how Moscow policies ground to a halt. It was certainly in response to central government directives that general meetings were held in all collectives in 1992–3 to determine their future, yet the members mostly voted against the spirit of the reforms. The meetings were intended to dissolve the old farms and create new ones fitted to operate in market conditions. At this point the leadership of almost all farms was changed and new Directors/Chairs were voted in, mostly a younger generation of people experienced in the old system. Most farms, in fact, chose to reconstitute one of the traditional types, as can be seen from tables, and yet this adherence to the old Soviet forms was claimed by local directors as brave local resistance against the overpowering state! Though no one likes admitting this, since the rhetoric is one of democracy (as it was even in Soviet times, see pp. 331–2), there is also evidence of pressure from Buryat government officials in these crucial meetings. Moscow wanted privatisation, but the Republic-level government in Ulan-Ude was dominated by former Communists, as were the Raion-level administrations. So it is significant that many farms took their decisions by unanimous vote, always a suspicious sign. Buryats have often said to me, "People are used to doing what their bosses tell them to do." In fact, the villagers' support for disbanding collectives was patchy in 1992–3 and has gone virtually to zero since then.

So small private farms set up in the early 1990s were not the result of popular pressure. The first private farms were established by officials as showpieces, to demonstrate that reform policy was being followed. Loans, machinery, insurance, and complex bureaucratic documentation were required even for the smallest private farm. Usually, it was friends of the government or the collective managers themselves who were given these opportunities. The first well-funded farms have fared better than later volunteers, who had little help, but even the first farms have failed in many places (as, e.g., in both Bayangol and Selenga). This period is now spoken of as the "privatisation campaign" and has passed into history like so many Soviet campaigns before it.

The old apparatus of control is now so weak that leaders can no longer operate by orders plain and simple. Not only has the Party lost power, but the Auditing Commission and the People's Control (see Chapter 2) have disappeared, as far as I can tell. With their demise the "rebuke," the "severe reprimand," and the whole intrusive, moralizing of Soviet times (p. 111) have lost their force. It is true that the work record (*trudovaya knizhka*) survives and is still used for assessing pay rates, pensions, allocating "shares," and when trying to get a new job. But, for the increasing numbers of villagers who in effect have no job, it is becoming correspondingly irrelevant. The discourse confronting the individual with the state is undergoing a metamorphosis. In Soviet times to "cause a loss to the state," to "disobey a command," and "to alter a set norm" were specified as punishable violations (*narusheniye*).[10] Now, people quite openly cause a loss to the state by not paying taxes, and they obey commands as they see fit. There are farms, like the Barguzinskii State Farm, where the Director operates by orders and has revived the workday (*trudoden'*; see p. 220), but people told me: "No-one wants to work for the *trudoden'*. You need to know what you will get for your work. We'd prefer to give up on the collective altogether." As we shall see, this is not the whole story, because the Barguzinskii State Farm is the most successful farm in the district and the only one to make a profit. The main point here, however, is that, if people obey orders, they do so out of choice, not because of state-induced fear. More generally, we could say that the command system is giving way to one based on contract, or, to put it another way, the discourse of orders is intermixed with the discourse of the agreement (*dogovor*). The actual situation, however, is that people flout both orders and contracts, unless their interests or needs compel them to fulfill them. The principles of any kind of government-determined social order are vitiated by the confusion and abeyance of the legal system,[11] with the result that it is personal power and economic clout confronted with family interests that form the turbulent arena of practise.

At the same time, there is strong social pressure to "stand together" and live like other people. This is why the few remaining private farmers are often robbed and attacked and why there is support for the new statutes, which make it impossible for anyone to leave the farm without the agreement of all other members.

Whatever the type of farm voted for in 1992–3, one of Yeltsin's edicts in 1991 was to have far-reaching effects. This was the decision that social services, such as providing housing, repairs and maintenance, electricity, central heating, road repairs, transport, kindergartens, libraries, medical services, clubs and sports, etc., were to be transferred from the jurisdiction of collectives to that of local government (the former Soviets). The transfer is by no means complete. The main reason for the delay is that the whole notion of the *kollektiv* involves social responsibility as well as economic coordination. Collectives take pride in providing services, just as the members expect it of them. Local administrations, on the other hand, have been inadequately funded and staffed to take over, and the result has been that services handed over often faced closure. Directors are faced with complex decisions: on the one hand, it is extraordinarily difficult for them to obtain the resources to provide the services, but, on the other, their general bargain with the workers, or a feeling of responsibility, or their own strategies of power and "ownership" may compel them to try to continue. An old-school Director of an agricultural research station, which still maintains a large housing stock and various other services, was preoccupied with this subject.

I will never give up my houses, unless they make me. Just the other day, a young family came to see me, and I want to give them a house and help them. Of course, they'll have to work well, or I'll throw them out! Well, I

450

gave up just one of my houses, to a local school which burned down; you can see I had to do that. I didn't even charge them for it – oh, they thanked me a lot. But all this caring for people is a terrible headache. I'm supposed to run the station, but I spend my whole time with their problems, getting medicines, firewood for them, presents for them, all that stuff.

It is remarkable that the Soviet revolutionary goal of abolishing privilege based on private property ended up nevertheless with such clear notions of property founded on leadership. The sense of "mineness" referred to by the Director is puzzling in relation to existing theories of property, and it will be investigated further in the next chapter. Meanwhile, it is evident that the provision of social services can be used in intricate political negotiations, in which the popularity of the socialist "providing" morality is pitted against the new realities of paying taxes and making profits. In 1995 an article about the Barguzin fish factory noted:

With mass poverty, the fish factory cannot simply close off the central heating, because this would be simply to abandon the workers to dying out in the Siberian winter. A ton of coal costs 150,000 rubles, and to fully cover the costs of heating for each inhabitant over the 1994–5 winter we need 1,500,000 rubles.

But here is the paradox. The fish factory covers the social sphere, but at the same time tax is taken from it in order to pay for this same social support. The local administration and the higher bosses know about this situation, but they either cannot, or do not want, to alter the funding priorities. Leaving things as they are is simpler. Today, the fish factory is the enteprise most capable of paying taxes in the whole district. Furthermore, the authorities take out 93 kopecks per ruble without blinking an eye. Can the government really not see that such a policy can lead only to ending production altogether?

The Director of the factory said that when he went to see the President of the Republic to discuss this matter, the President was surprised that he was not asking for money. "How come, don't you need money?" The Director replied, "We need money, but we don't need sops (*podachki*). We can make money ourselves, only you please create the conditions in which we can work normally."[12]

In 1997 this fish factory had closed down. A few of the more traditional farms, such as the OKKh Bodonskii, continue to provide a skeleton of social services, and virtually all farms give some of them (subsidised housing maintenance, firewood, transport, petrol); though in some farms whether this should be regarded as giving or "having them taken" is a moot point. The Selenga Karl Marx continues to run a surprising number of services, but in the Bayangol farm the spacious kindergarten is now a ruin, and the public dining room, the museum, the sports complex, the library, the hotel, and the resthome have closed. The issue of services is an important point of difference between the farms which envisage themselves as communal wholes and those which do not. This also has wider implications, for it reflects the understanding of what constitutes the moral community. As I have argued elsewhere (Humphrey 1995,

1997), the end of the *assumption* that collectives would provide community security from childhood to old age is an enormous social turning point. My research suggests that the break with the past has occurred everywhere. Crucially,
in 1992–3 the newly voted-in directors in all types of collective took the opportunity to economise by divesting themselves of "useless" workers (the weak,
the ill, the alcoholics, the women coping alone with large families). This marks
the end of the collective as the primary unit of rural society and a "total social
institution" (Clarke 1992). Nevertheless, the existence of collectives at all reflects the continued value given to communality, as will be discussed in the
next chapter.

Collectives today continue to take general votes on the sort of farm they
wish to be. They still discuss whether to disband or not and how to best combine the various constituent units. These formal arrangements, however, are not
the real reasons for the great differences between them. Most of all, the collectives differ quite simply in whether they work or not. It goes without saying
that virtually all of them are bankrupt, but on the foundation of bankruptcy, as
it were, some carry out the ploughing, sowing, shearing, hay cutting, and all the
rest of it, while others are wastelands of weed-covered fields, broken fences,
skeletal cattle, and despairing people. Distance from markets, assets, and links
to the state are part of the explanation; also some farms in Buryatiya have recently been designated as *goskhoz* (state enterprises) and given subsidies for
particular types of production.[13] But individuals too make a difference, or,
rather, the ability of some leaders to plan strategically and fit together the diverse "actants" of the agricultural landscape, not just the workers but the
weather, the politicians, the exhausted land, information about prices, and so
forth.

A word is in order about private, also known as "individual" or peasant,
farms. Privatised farms (*ferma*) consist of small groups of some one to seven
families, with their own commercial economies independent from collectives.
They lease land from the Administration and also hold licenses to trade. Con-
fusingly, they are also known as peasant farms (*krestyanskoye khozyaistvo*), but
they are in fact different from the peasant farms that exist inside collectives like
the OKKh and AKKh. The latter are the brigades contracted to produce for the
collective from the latter's publicly owned herds and lands, and they are not
licensed to operate independently. They are not supposed to trade, for example.
On many farms, no one really cares these days whether such production teams
are called by old labels (OTF 1, etc.) or by the new term *peasant farm*. It is
important, however, that readers distinguish both of these types from the
usad'ba, the tiny smallholding based on the so-called private plot of Soviet
times.[14] These smallholdings are kept by virtually every household in the countryside, as they provide the basic livelihood needed in the absence of money.
Membership of a collective guarantees the right to land for subsistence, but the
numerous people who live on the farm, though not members of it, also have

452

plots on a more informal basis.[15] In many areas these plots have become the most active element in the economy, and in Russia as a whole they are thought to provide 50% of the food produced.[16] The term *private plot* is somewhat misleading, however, since the plots were always allocated by the collective and still are so today. Today, vegetable plots by people's houses are never taken away if they are in use, but hay plots can become an issue because they compete with the collective for land. There are cases, like that of a retired schoolteacher, not a member, who wrote an angry letter to the local newspaper accusing the Director of the farm of capriciousness. "I have worked my entire life educating your children, and now you deny me enough hay-land to feed my two cows," she wrote.[17]

So to summarise, there are three kinds of farms which are called peasant, or private, both in the literature and by the people themselves, but they differ from one another: (1) the privatised commercial farms; (2) the contract brigades within collectives; and (3) the newly important smallholdings. Lying behind the confusion of naming there is perhaps an unspoken distinction dividing the old and well-known from any of the newly formed enterprises. People do not know what to call them because they are not sure what they really are or might become.

The Soviet heritage: A densely populated countryside

In the Preface I wrote that the Soviet collective farms preserved a way of life that was not sustainable (i.e., not sustainable given the existing agricultural mode of production). There are two main aspects to this, both relating to a shortage of usable land. The first concerns the ecology of livestock production. The Soviet-era collectives multiplied vastly unbalanced herds. In particular they maintained far too many sheep for the fodder available, and the total system of agriculture had a disastrous effect on the ecology. *Karl Marx Collective* mentioned the threat apparent in the 1970s, but it has now become clear that by 1993 the great majority of pastures in the Barguzin valley were ruined (Gomboev et al. 1996, 124–40). The herds of improved, nonnative breeds had to be stall-fed for most of the year. Therefore, generally in Buryatiya lands were ploughed up to provide not only wheat for human consumption but also fodder crops, and the expansion of agriculture on unsuitable lands caused wind and water erosion. It was soon clear that this type of extensive agriculture required fallow and rotation, taking out further land from the stock of available pasture, with the result that the vast flocks had to feed on an ever smaller resource (see also Humphrey and Sneath 1997).

The second aspect of unsustainability relates to the human population. Collective farms supported an expanding populace, with overmanning in almost all sectors, so many people became used to spending months of the year with hardly any work to do. Others were employed in the numerous services run by the farm (librarians, cooks, accountants, nurses, and so forth). Now many of these jobs have gone. Even local experts used to Soviet-type overmanning say that the rural population is around twice the level that the land can sustain using available techniques of farming.

Let us look at livestock production first. In 1996 it was finally revealed to me what I had suspected before: the vast flocks of the Selenga Karl Marx Collective, its pride and raison d'être in Soviet times, were dependent on hay and grazing from Mongolia. Sheep were trucked to the border in early summer and grazed on Mongolian lands by Karl Marx herders till autumn. Hay-making teams from Selenga also simply went to Mongolia and cut what they needed. As people used to say at the time (now they are somewhat ashamed of the ditty):

Kuritsa ne ptitsa   A chicken is not a bird
Mongoliya ne zagranitsa   Mongolia is not abroad

Hidden because the ideology was that settled Russian-type farming can develop endlessly, mobile pastoralism in fact sustained the prize-winning collective (for discussion, see Humphrey and Sneath, in press). After Mongolia became independent of Soviet domination, in 1990, this arrangement was no longer possible, which is one reason for the dramatic reduction in numbers of sheep in recent years.

Buryats today have a vague consciousness of prerevolutionary times, when sheep were outnumbered by cattle, and they have a completely nonsentimental attitude to the disappearance of the flocks. "It was so easy to get rid of those sheep," people said, "they were sold, killed, given away. Some just died of neglect." Prices are so low that a sheep is worth only a few bottles of vodka.[18] The pride of the farm became a sector that has to be subsidized by other activities. The main reason is that buying prices do not cover the cost of production. Furthermore, there has been a drastic fall in demand for local wool in Buryat factories, which now buy higher-quality Australian wool on the world market for lower prices. A former official in the Ministry of Agriculture told me:

We made a big mistake in going down the road of keeping so many sheep. The fine wool breeds are good for making high-quality wool fabric, but we cannot farm them at this standard and we have allowed them to interbreed with rough-wooled sheep. Also, we cannot make them productive enough: if they gave 5 kg of wool per sheep, instead of 2–3 kg as now, they would be economic even at present prices. The farmers cannot raise their wool prices because the factories would pass this on to retail prices. There are just not enough buyers, and there is competition from cheap wool clothing imported from China.

Table 9.1 shows the result. Though all such figures are suspect, we get the general picture. Along with the drastic fall in sheep numbers, the other main

454

Table 9.1. *Livestock numbers in Iroi subdistrict, location of Karl Marx Collective, Selenga district (608 households in 1996)*

	Cattle	(incl. cows)	Sheep	Horses	Pigs
1966 (collective)	3,118	945	44,522	458	300
1996 (collective)	1,300	450	5,000[a]	110	70
1996 (private)[b]	1,669	685	1,746	79	856

Notes:
a. People gave me various figures for the number of sheep in the farm, ranging from 5,000 to 8,000. The more "pro-collective" the person, the higher the figure they gave. The figure of 5,000 was given by the head of the Trade Union.
b. Owned privately by members of the farm and nonmember villagers of the *somon* (locality), not including private farmers.

types of livestock have also declined:[19] in 1966 there must have been at least 1,000 cattle and 1,800 sheep additionally on the household plots. So the small rise in numbers of privately owned stock in the last five years, particularly of cattle, has not compensated for the losses of collective animals. In the Barguzin farm the same overall pattern is seen in table 9.2.[20] The difference between the two farms is that in Bayangol (Barguzin) the households have substantially more private cattle (3.9 as opposed to 2.7 per household). This may seem trivial, but it is vitally important. Village life now revolves around cattle, because they are the only livestock with which villagers can hope to get money, by selling meat (Meshcheryakov 1996, 54).

In both districts the reduction in collectively owned livestock, as of mid-1997, showed no sign of ending. The acreage of fields ploughed up for food grain and animal fodder crops has also been declining each year.[21] Hay meadow land is much less than in the Soviet heyday.[22] One positive result is

Table 9.2. *Livestock numbers in Bayangol subdistrict, including former Karl Marx Collective, Barguzin district (912 households in 1996)*

	Cattle	(incl. cows)	Sheep	Horses	Pigs
1974 (collective)	3,149	1,129	30,223	?	251
1990 (collective)	3,400	900	24,000	700	?
1996 (collective)	954	?	5,000	550	70
1996 (private)[a]	3,555	1,931	2,151	113	811

Note:
a. This does not include the livestock owned by private farmers. According to figures provided by the district (*raion*) administration, private farmers keep very small herds in Barguzin, ranging from a maximum of 45 cattle and 25 sheep to a more usual 5–7 cattle and 2–3 pigs per farm. Some private farmers have no livestock. In Bayangol there are 13 registered private farmers, of whom only 3 really work as farmers.

that the pastures are recovering. But with fewer productive resources, how are the people to live?

The population living in rural Selenga and Barguzin has remained more or less constant since the time I wrote *Karl Marx Collective.*[23] Perhaps surprisingly, the agricultural disaster of the last five years has not caused a huge net outflow of population.[24] This broad observation, however, hides some negative facts. The birthrate has gone down since the 1980s, and the deathrate has risen. There has been an increase in serious diseases such as tuberculosis, polio, gonorrhea, and syphilis, especially in the small towns.[25] Most critical for economic life was an outflow of young, energetic people in the early 1990s. "All the best young people have gone," said the economist of the Bayangol farm.[26] There is still some out-migration from disorganised collectives, but the population remains stable in the more successful farms like the Barguzinskii State Farm. In general, out-migration is slowing down, not only because it is more difficult than ever to get a residence permit for a city but also because there is little work there. In fact, industry and services in local towns like Gusinoozersk or Barguzin were still cutting jobs in 1997. Thus, as local officials in Barguzin explained, while rural towns lose enterprising people to the capital city, there has also been some in-migration to the countryside of older people and those who have lost hope. Unemployed factory workers, former builders of the BAM (the railway to the north of Lake Baikal), failed petty traders – such people are going back to where they were born, because at least there they can hope to attach themselves to relatives, get a cow, and stay alive.

In sum, rural areas contain many older people but also the less educated of the school leavers who cannot obtain work elsewhere. This demographic situation has import with regard to the more general problem found in many postsocialist economies, which is that agriculture cannot be rationalised while industry and services are cutting back.

So the question remains: how can these people make a living in a productive way? They cannot obtain employment in the collectives, because the latter are virtually all bankrupt, and none of them pay wages in money. As it is, between a quarter and a third of the households living in each collective are not working members. Tashir, the village which is headquarters of the Selenga Karl Marx collective, has 490 to 500 households,[27] of which 320 are members of the farm, another 20 are nonmembers who work on contract for the farm, and the rest make do from their plots, pensions, and some occasional work in building, sheep shearing or hay cutting (paid not in money but in kind). The situation is similar elsewhere. The Director of the State Farm at Baragkhan near Barguzin told me that, even though working members have been reduced from 500 to 300, around 160 of the latter "don't work, except for seasonal jobs." She has eliminated two of the four sheepherding brigades. She said she would be delighted if 250 or so "extra" families moved away, because she felt unable to help them. Most of them have no intention of leaving, however, because there

456

is nowhere for them to go. Local administrators have various marvellous ideas about how to deal with this situation in the future. Only a few years ago it would have been possible for an enterprising person to obtain a loan and set up as a private farmer or a trader. But in the present crisis it is almost impossible to get a loan. There is only one option: live on the subsidary plot and, if you cannot get one of your own, squeeze into the household of a relative who has one.

Problematising "household subsistence"

Here I would like to switch perspectives, from that of the collectives as wholes to that of the villagers. Although I have not yet described the intricacies of the working of the collectives, households and families are irreducibly more basic to rural life. If you ask people about changes in the last few years, the household economy is what they mention first: "Prices have gone up, and we do not get any pay. Meat and milk, we live on that." Belonging to collectives now is not a matter of compulsion, as in the past, but a matter of choice. Arguably, it is combinations of households which now *in practise* establish the form the collectives take. This is quite different from the Soviet situation, when standardised collectives and state farms corralled the households into pre-set brigades and production teams.

As in Soviet times, families register as "households" (*dvor*) as soon as possible, usually at marriage, in order to qualify for a vegetable plot and hay meadows (*usad'ba*). Young couples can do this even if they are in fact living at home with the parents. The notion of household membership is quite problematic, since a young couple may work their *usad'ba* independently but pool resources with a wider kin group for certain purposes. At the same time, family members may regularly leave for a period to earn money in towns yet return for crucial periods such as the hay making. This coming and going, and the fact that a household usually has at least two houses, at summer and winter pastures, confuses any clear picture of a set number of people living in a single residence. In fact, when asked the question, "How many members are there in your farm?" herders often found it impossible to answer.[28] It will be argued here, however, that a contextually defined group maintaining a common economy and based on kinship, which we may call a "domestic production" group, is crucial to the present economic situation. I hope that the way this operates and the concepts involved will become clear through examples given later and a further discussion in the next chapter.

If one wanders into a Buryat collective farm these days at first sight things look little different from the 1960s. The wooden houses, the brick stoves, the fences of rough-hewn poles, the little "summer houses" and privies in the yards, the carts and sledges bowling along the roads – all seem unchanged. Then one notices the improvements of late Soviet times: an asphalted road, an electric pump where there used to be a well (p. 285), a new club building. A closer look reveals the changes of post-Soviet times. The main one is that the backyards, which used to be dusty areas where the cows returned at night, are now packed with carefully tended rows of potatoes. Many people also grow carrots, cabbages, and onions, and some have raised beds and greenhouses with tomatoes, cucumbers, and other delicate plants. Pigs no longer run free but are fattened in closed sheds. All is surrounded by a high and tightly locked fence. This is the main part of the *usad'ba,* the primary source of the food of the household.

If all this can be kept going, together with a couple of cows, a pig, and a few sheep, the household can live quite well, as people told me. Whatever Medegma said (p. xvii), it is hard work, and it mostly falls on women. In late Soviet times, when people received money wages, they could buy bread, meat, vegetables, and conserves, and crucially they could get hay and feed for their animals from the collective. Now, after rising at 5:00 A.M. to milk the cows, women bake their own bread, and the day is filled with work (weeding, watering, planting, digging, processing meat and milk products, gathering mushrooms and berries, cleaning, sorting and preserving vegetables, cooking, fetching water for the livestock). Besides the food needed from day to day, each household has its stores, locked in a shed or kept under the floorboards. These are the essential products set aside for the long months of winter: tens of jars of salted cabbage, sacks of potatoes and flour, frozen and salted meat, bottled fruits, marinated mushrooms and tomatoes. There are some people who cannot manage all this.[29] But for others there is satisfaction in the flourishing gardens, a kind of pleasure in surviving so well, in working so hard, in managing things for oneself in such difficult circumstances.

The second part of the *usad'ba* is the hayfield (B. *büüse*), usually allocated some distance from the village. A huge store of hay is essential for feeding the cattle and sheep over the long Siberian winter. Without hay the animals would die, and the family would be without meat – and food is considered not a human meal without meat. All collectives restrict the size of household hayfields, as hay is the most precious resource for their own herds.[30] Hay land is "land" par excellence for Buryat villagers. If they are asked, "How much land do you have?" they forget the vegetable plots and pastures and reply about the number of hectares of hay meadow they have access to. Many families have "ancestral haylands" (*büüse*), meaning that their parents and grandparents worked there before them right through Soviet times. There is a strong feeling among villagers that rights accrue through working and knowing the land.[31]

The equation hay equals meat is central to villagers' calculations. The collectives generally allocate two hectares of hay meadow to each household (*dvor*),[32] but this feeds only two cattle, and therefore many families have to glean extra hay wherever they can – on roadsides, in bogs, under trees, and so forth. All hay has to be cut during a short period in July and August. This is exhausting, mosquito-ridden work, which demands the utmost of the household's resources. The children, the old people, and near kin take part. Furthermore, the hay equals meat equation is enshrined in long-standing reciprocity between kin in the village and town. In the last few years this relation has taken on a new urgency, as so many people in the towns are almost without income (sacked, put on unpaid leave, or simply working without pay). City relatives thus often depend greatly on their villager kin, and they come out each summer to take part in the hay making to "work for their winter meat" (*zarabatyvat' sebye üüse*). From the point of view of the city folk this is like a hardworking summer holiday – "We get out to the clean air, our children get exercise," they say – but for the villagers it is one more crucial and difficult task to organise. More people have to be housed and fed, and plans must be made for the storage, transport, and guarding of the hay. If the hay is ruined by rain or dried out by drought, it means problems for the little smallholding. Fires or theft are a disaster. While all this is going on, it is during these very days in the year that there is also pressure from the collective to take part in its hay making.

A household with three milking cows is already "rich." Poor households have no livestock, and the family may live for months mainly on potatoes. Yet gathering, fishing, and hunting have become essential not just for these people but for everyone. Newspapers publish regular information on where various berries, nuts, and mushrooms are to be found. But more common is for small kin groups to "have" their own places in the forest. These are generally avoided by others, if they are known, but often they are kept secret. In Selenga the forests are vast, with enough resources for all, but in sparsely wooded areas or those near towns there have been fights over stray infringement of foraging places. It is perhaps also in the spirit of foraging that people search for temporary jobs: loading, a spell as a night watchman, building, dismantling, a trade run to the city, all may bring in resources and, with luck, even money.

In an economy of barter each product is precious. Its value comes not just from its potential immediate use in subsistence but from its capacity to draw in other goods by exchange. A calculating eye is cast over the animals for their potential. A sheep may be designated to exchange for a few bags of oats or fodder concentrate to feed the pig. In the prosperous valley of Tunka people said: "See that cow? It's a T.V. See that pig? It's a video. In autumn we'll slaughter another piglet – that will be a 'Dandy'" (Mescheryakov 1996, 55).[33] Money is often a means of exchange in these transactions (the cow, e.g., is taken to the nearest large town to sell for money to buy other goods), and money is greatly desired for its instant convertability into many different things, but no one saves money. Massive inflation is too recent a memory for that. Indeed, in 1992 many people lost huge sums which had been carefully hoarded over the Soviet years. Money as a substance is regarded with suspicion (there are special machines to check the validity of dollar notes at most banks and stores). The rationale now is more or less immediate transactability, and this involves an extraordinarily complex set of conflicting calculations. The notion of "subsistence" is therefore problematic not only because there is no universal human level of need (Sahlins 1965), and because even in one culture subsistence may be practised "richly" (with meat, cream, butter, bread) or "poorly" (with potatoes and bran), but also because no household produces all it requires. Subsistence therefore always involves an incoming and outgoing of products from the household, all of which have alternative uses, and, furthermore, intangible things (skills, promises, charm, threats) enter into the transaction of products. A family may, for example, fatten an extra sheep, and in an instant its designated purpose of acquiring money to buy shoes for the children might be changed to providing a banquet for a visiting relative. And this could be a most satisfactory outcome, because in the meantime the mother's charm alone had enabled her to elicit (*vyprosit'*) the shoes from some cousins, while only good things could now be expected from the visiting relative.

Work in the collective is part of these domestic calculations. There are two essential goods that households in Buryatiya do not produce themselves. One is concentrated fodder. This is required by cattle, sheep, and pigs – only horses can live on hay alone through the winter. The second is flour to make bread and noodles. The simplest solution is to do some work in the collective. In practise, for very many people, "work" is no longer a career or a calling but is a strategic value, since time spent for the collective must be subtracted from that spent on the smallholding. For many people this going out for a bit of work is different from the "having a job" or "being a calf herder" in Soviet times, impelled as it now is by the irregular contingencies of bringing quite definite products into the household. For most people work is so irregular and so infrequently paid with money that labour is conceptually entered into a wider system of barter and reciprocity. These days it is having a source for fodder or wheat, etc., which compels people to work, and this is one of the first things villagers mention when addressing *why there must be collective farms.*

In his study of Buryats in the Tunka Valley, Meshcheryakov (1996, 55) observed that villagers are buying luxuries (prestige goods, things for pleasure), even though they lack basic household utensils and means of transport. He attributes this to the "habitude produced by the Soviet regime that the population would be supplied with the means of production 'from above,' while the task of the people themselves is the organisation of leisure according to their own ideas," and he notes wryly that, if the people of Tunka go for TVs and videos, at least this is better than alcohol (which is a serious problem in many parts of rural Buryatiya). The point to emphasise here is that Meshcheryakov rightly describes a resistance to totally autonomous subsistence by households. Villagers expect not only lateral reciprocity with kin and neighbours but also vertical inputs from the farm and the state. With regard to the collectives, I suggest, this reflects not just attitudes engrained in Soviet times but also rational understanding of production in the absence of a functioning market. Just those items expected from above (fodder concentrates, grains) are those arable products which can best be produced on the scale and with the technology available to collectives rather than households.

More broadly, the reason people want collective farms to continue is not just economies of scale, nor the fact that there are not enough tractors to go round the households anyway, but that the Russian state has failed so catastrophically.[34] It has failed to do one of the few things a state must do, which is to ensure that its money functions throughout the economy. In these circumstances people are attached to collectives because they are the only thing that looks like a functioning intermediate institution and stand in for what is almost a nonfunctioning state at the village level. It is true that district governments now publish their budgets and look as though they have money, but its actual destination is a mystery (nobody seems to have it!). In this situation, and with the abeyance of law, to want the dissolution of collectives would be to vote for anarchy. In the next chapter I shall describe how actually turning the collective into a "ministate" is one solution now being proposed. In that case the household is likely to be locked into local power structures even more than it is today.

Changes in the meaning of domestic production

Some people speak bravely of domestic self-reliance. Picture the small town of Barguzin, where women track across the main square before dawn with their cows, where the carved windows are still painted white, the statue of Lenin gleams and has fresh flowers beneath it, where a few Russians have started to keep goats to make ends meet. A Buryat woman's job as a secretary has long since ceased to provide her with an identity, and she focuses on an inward view of her domestic economy:

If we lived in another state we would be so rich, with all our possibilities and our love of work. We have lived a good life. We regret nothing, we are sad only for our children. We live for our children. My economy [*khozyaistvo*] is just for that. My son is twenty-four, but I send everything over to him and it will go on like that until I die. I never buy foreign products and I tell my children not to. Why buy foreign things when ours are better? I don't even buy things from Irkutsk. I only eat my own. I kill two pigs for spring and two for autumn, and we cut a calf for the winter too. The earth is good here, and we live like this.

What is difficult for us to imagine is the dashing of expectations. There are no expectations of the law, or that politicians or police will keep to their word, or that money will keep its value, or that you can trust a stranger. But till recently there were expectations that electricity would be free, children would be taken to school, heating or winter fuel would be provided, pensions, grants, and wages would be paid, houses would be maintained, and land, fodder, and tractors would be there to use. People are affronted that they themselves have to find petrol, pay for electricity, mend the roof, run here and there to arrange

461

everything. They feel abandoned. Without a money income they are conscious that the main avenue out of the farm into a better life – higher education for the children – is blocked off. They cannot pay the fees and bribes required to enter an institute. A tangle of hindrances prevents even the most energetic people from developing the domestic smallholding into a small business: if you are dependent on the collective for fodder, this limits the number of cattle you can keep; you cannot bypass the collective by getting a loan because no banks give loans these days; public transport to market has become prohibitively expensive; and, finally, you cannot personally sell at the market without having a special license to trade as well as certificates about sanitary arrangements, storage, and so forth. Many people told me, "No one is going to help us." Hemmed in, tied down by the constant work in the *usad'ba,* which cannot be left for a single day, some burst into angry despair, like this man who wrote to the Selenga newspaper:[35]

We have achieved "liberation." But from whom, and from what? This article is written by a hereditary peasant [*krestyanin*]. Why do peasants so humbly accept not being paid? Life is worse now than in the Great Patriotic War [the Second World War]. In Soviet times we lived well – so well that we fell asleep and didn't notice that we were living like slaves. They fed and clothed the slaves to make them work. Now they make us work, but don't feed or clothe us.

We are still asleep and don't see that our votes are bought at a cheap price. We are deceived, and we vote in the deceivers to be Presidents and Mayors. We are made to give up our products almost free, and we are pleased. But some people have started things up again, clubs, kindergartens, medical centres, and so forth, and some places even pay wages. Russia will rise again, and other countries will respect us.

But the Democrats don't want any of that. We peasants are just sitting waiting till our beloved President signs a law allowing foreigners to buy land. Then we'll have to labour for Uncle Sam and eat foreign delicacies like Bush's chicken-legs. Meanwhile, simply so as not to die, we go into self-exploitation, on our own little farms. And we'll get fodder from the collectives still remaining. What beauty!

Let me tell you some truths.
1. If we allow land to be sold and liquidate the collectives, where will we get fodder? Even now, everyone, even the private farmers, gets it from there. So we cannot do without the "agro-gulag." You must have good grain to produce anything else.
2. God help us if the city comes to the countryside. They won't come with a respectful bow but to requisition; they'll take everything without paying.
3. Peasants should remember that in bad times it was the peasants who died of famine, not the city people.

We sell 1 kilo of live weight of beef for 4,000 rubles, but to produce it costs 7,000. We are not allowed into the bazaars and markets.[36] Life has become unbearable.

I met an old woman in Bayangol who said, referring to Moscow politicians: "Sometimes I'd like to kill someone. They have destroyed everything dear to me!" and she spat, upon which the leader of the Local Administration, a reform-minded man, looked embarrassed and laughed uneasily. All of this is a reminder, if such be needed, that in times of radical upheaval basic social forms like the *dvor* (household) do not disappear, but they lose their doxic, taken-for-granted character and become questionable objects about which people agonise; thus, it is that the domestic unit, which was formerly a haven of familial security, can be reimagined, at least by some people, as the place of self-exploitation.

Survival strategies in some wider contexts

The immediate context for the domestic economy is the subdistrict and the collective, which dominates it. Although all inhabitants are given equal amounts of hay meadow and vegetable plots more or less as they require, the position held in the collective (or not held, in the case of those who have left or been excluded) has a greater influence on the domestic economy than ever before. Of course, in Soviet times some jobs were definitely much more advantageous than others as regards *private* economic possibilities (see Chapters 5 and 7). But in the 1960s through the mid-1980s strategies were directed more toward obtaining a better job in the *public* sphere, which provided the main income. Now the situation is reversed, and it is not just pay but, more important, the intrinsic "appropriation possibilities" of the job which are turned to benefit the domestic economy.

The main point here is that the household smallholding has become the centre of gravity of local economies. Chayanov pointed out that "self-exploitation" hits some peasants at certain stages of the family cycle far harder than others and that they would all want Buicks, tractors, and radios if they could get them. But he did not dwell on the fact that there are people who cannot manage at all: they are too old, sick, drunken, or despairing. They might have had to sell their last cow, or it might have died.[37] Even subsidised fodder, wheat, and so forth has to be paid for somehow. Yet some people are desperately poor, hardly able to feed themselves by borrowing or earning some food by working for others or foraging.

A Buryat friend told me that he overheard a conversation among some secretaries as he was taking notes in a collective farm office in 1993. "The drivers do so well," said one girl, "because they can use the kolkhoz vehicles to earn money for themselves." "So do the shepherds, stockmen, and milkers," said another, "they just take the animals or sell them." "Nurses too," said a third, "with their medicines." "Yes, it's just us who have got nothing to take," replied the first girl, looking searchingly round the office.

Generally anything in public is liable to be taken: fuel, machinery oil, fertiliser, cattle feed, windows, pipes, grain and milk, baths and beds from the closed resthome, not just mail from letterboxes but also the letterboxes themselves. The abandoned *otara*s in the collectives have been stripped bare and some completely removed log by log to build a house somewhere else. In the cattle sheds women milk in the dark, because the lightbulbs have been taken. All this is silently, sometimes even explicitly, accepted by the farm officials, because people are not paid for the work they do[38] and because they know that things that were once free now have to be paid for. A saying quoted by Jacob Rigi (1997), *"Vsye vokrug kolkhoznoye, vsye vokrug moye"* (Everything around belongs to the collective, everything around belongs to me), conjures up the sense of the collective as a common resource, coextensive with an ironic definition of *mine* – ironic, because so many Soviet slogans encouraged the *kolkhozniks* to identify in heroic mode with the collective.

To analyse the situation, I think it is possible to point to three different foraging practises. In the first, each job (herding, driving, sowing seed, nursing) involves the conditions for certain limited resources to be appropriated, and this is now silently almost accepted as part of the job by the officials. In the second, summed up by the saying just quoted (Rigi), the whole arena of the collective is seen as no one's (or everyone's): if no colleague is using a thing, why not take it? The third case is different, more clearly regarded as theft because it involves individuals. I met several people who used to keep chickens but gave up after they were stolen. The few "private farmers" are regularly subject to attack.[39] Visitors with a vehicle, such as myself, may wake up in the morning to find the petrol gone or some part stolen. Here, the shifting boundary of us/not us is moved to define a space in which theft is possible, because the targets are enemies or defined as outside the moral universe of the villagers. Actually, there is nothing new about any of this. Peasants spoke of *dobychniye* (loot-giving) jobs and *zakhvat* (seizure) in Soviet times (Kovalev 1996, 109). The extent of foraging has historically gone in waves, and its strength in late Soviet times has carried over into the present. This has definite effects in relation to the reforms, since the idea of "getting it for free" inhibits people from undertaking anything for which they have to pay.

I recognise that, in using the word *foraging* here, I am glossing over the distinction between a normal, self-reproducing practise and a harmful one brought about by exceptional and desperate circumstances. This glossing over, however, is not mine alone: the Soviet state itself often pushed the economy over the boundary of what was self-reproducible (as with massive sheep flocks). Similarly today, illegal hunting is damaging wildlife. People know this, and they complain about both environmental destruction and crime, but the problem is that there are many areas where the rules which people do observe have little to say, and the government's short experiments have not helped either – for example, Gorbachev's abandoned attempt to criminalise distilling alcohol, which is now widely derided. In such cases it is just not clear where to draw the moral boundary. As people hear of great conglomerates stripping the forests, they shrug at local plunder, recognising it as a strategy they themselves might have to employ sometime.

Now it seems that the things seen as "waiting to be taken" have already gone. Many farm leaders have strengthened discipline, and they have set up communal facilities, like Buddhist prayer houses, which the people themselves have asked for. There comes a time when even the remains of collective productive property seem worth preserving if anything at all is to be expected from the farm at harvest time. This point, it should be said, varies in different places. In the disastrous Chitkan State Farm, where no one would trust anyone else to do the spring sowing, people in 1996 were still breaking down the collective's fences to enable their own cows to graze on the wheat fields.[40] In Bayangol, on the other hand, households even collected 100 cattle to help the *kolkhoz,* and a teacher paid one million rubles toward the spring sowing.[41] In most farms foraging has settled down to a sustainable, minimal flow. Now, a highly important form of income from above is state benefits, all the more so as the recipients are mostly the very people who have no work and cannot prosper from advantageous work positions in the collective.

The poorest households survive only because of subsidies of one kind or another: pensions, child benefit, invalid benefit, grants to veterans, grants to mothers of large families, and so forth.[42] The local newspapers are full of articles about when these should be paid, where they can be claimed, why they have been delayed, and who is responsible for paying them. Evidently, the authorities make it difficult to obtain many kinds of grants, while others, such as pensions, can be delayed for months in the whole Republic and indeed in the whole of Russia.[43] Yet great numbers of people depend only on such subsidies for their money income. One man said to me seriously, "It is better to have two live grandparents than to have two cows."

The dependence on pensions and state incomes has now been described in a few publications (Meshcheryakov 1996a–b; Clarke, Ashwin, and Borisov 1997; Panarin 1997). On payday supplicants for loans home in on the old person, who has become so important.[44] It is difficult to refuse, as everyone knows that the money is received, and in any case the borrowers are often kin. Borrowers may be people who themselves expect some money income (from trade, from an invalid grant, or other kin whose pension has not yet arrived). Otherwise, they offer services, like stacking wood for the old person or help with hay cutting. Pension day is a focal point in the entire village micro-economy, and the regularity of the payment is especially important, as it enables people to calculate, forecast, manipulate, and so forth.[45] For example, a teacher who had not received wages for three months was forced to live by trading vodka. "You give it on credit, and then on pension day you go round the whole village and collect. The youth buy on credit, but you have to get the money from the grannies. It's embarrassing for them and they pay up" (Meshcheryakov 1996b, 167). The pensions, however, can simply not arrive, which is a calamity not just for the named recipient. When I was sitting in the Chairman's office in the Karl Marx Collective in Selenga an old man came in. There was no need for him to explain. He sat in dignified silence. It was really to me that the Chairman explained: "The pensions are three months' late. I have nothing to give him but flour." He shepherded the old man gently to the door and called to the accountant to write him a chitty for a bag of flour.

It is not only the poor and helpless who depend on pensions. The main reason for this is that farms are generally not paid in money when they sell their products, so *any* cash income is rare and uncertain. The chief engineer of the Bayangol collective said to me angrily, "I am a healthy working man, and for money I have to go to my aunt for her pension." In the Selenga farm Valya, the head of the Trade Union, laughed heartily when she saw me making notes of the wages in theory paid to members: "I get far more than the Chairman from my benefits as a mother of seven children."

Some households are sent money by children working in the cities. At the edge of the village of Bayangol there is a row of new houses built privately by families and kin, and the means for such large expenses probably comes from outside the village. Still, some relatively prosperous villagers have too large a household economy to do all the work themselves. The wife of a former Chairman of the Bayangol collective told me that she had eight cows, plus their calves, that she paid a woman to do the milking, and that her husband had acquired a small wheat field with a colleague who had a tractor, and they also employed a worker. I should point out that this is not the language generally used by villagers. The notion of private paid employment is too redolent of capitalist exploitation. The poor person "helps" (*pomogayet*) the richer one, and vice versa. Such an expression is not necessarily a euphemism. Everything depends on who is helping whom. In fact, the motivation to give without any foreseeable return coexists with extraordinary mistrust in Buryat society. A logic of "ours" and "not ours" governs the distinction between helping someone and paying them. The language of help (*pomoshch'*) is pervasive partly because most people in the village are related but perhaps more because it holds at bay the coming into being of "capitalism," of the presence of employers and employees.

The pay workers receive from the collective has long since departed from standard rates, and it seems to depend on a mixture of bargaining and the whim of the Chair. Workers are paid mostly in butter and flour. In theory this is reckoned by inscrutible money rates for the job per month.[46] In practise, given the seasonality of tasks and the sporadic habits of the workers, they are usually paid by the workday (*trudoden'*). Some of this is given in advance and the rest at harvest (if there is any spare harvest). Even this arrangement varies if the worker's family seems to need it. The Chairman of the Selenga Karl Marx told me, "We give 10 bags of flour for a full year's work,[47] less if fewer days are put in, and if someone has a large family, we give extra." In some farms contracts specify a specific amount of pay for a given amount of product. Hay making is a time of extreme pressure which gives the workers an edge over the Chairman for a change. In Karl Marx in late July 1996 seven brigades were organised. The grass was at its peak. One day went by, no one came out, then another; by the third day the officials were running round distractedly – the grass was beginning to lose its juiciness. It emerged that the workers were demanding 10 boxes of cigarettes per head. Somehow these were found, and the work went ahead.

At the same time, many collectives give members allocations, subsidised or free fodder, fertiliser, transport, winter fuel, payment of electricity bills and road tax, etc., which far exceed the value of the wages.[48] Nonmembers living on the farm also benefit from many of these subsidies. In fact, most people cannot pay and live in debt to the collective. Besides this, the collective makes allocations of clothing, sugar, tea, and vodka. Acquired by the Chair, sent "down" to the brigadiers, and then divided among the workers, these are part recompense for not paying wages. At festivities such as weddings, the lunar New Year (*sagaalgan*), Women's Day, and so forth, further gifts are given – sausages, butter, sweets, money, champagne, whatever is available. All this reinforces vertical, personalised relations. From the people's point of view these good things are expected, but it is not possible to rely on them, and one does not know what they will actually be. From the collective's point of view we have to ask: how does a bankrupt organisation pay for them?

The collective in the regional economy

The collective, and in particular its Chair, is still the mediator between the productive economy and that of the district and the Republic. Unsuccessful farms have even less leeway than they did in Soviet times. They are held in the vice of barter contracts with the Products Corporation, a state organisation which is part of the Ministry of Agriculture. This works as follows. All farms have massive debts. Therefore, they cannot afford to start off the cycle of production, the spring sowings, which require purchase of petrol, oil, and spare parts as a minimum. The Chair acquires these necessities by negotiating "commodity credit" with the Products Corporation, repayable by means of the harvest, wool, and other products later in the year. The Corporation gives the farm a list of the goods it may obtain at specified prices at given firms. It charges 30% interest, its selling prices are high, and its buying prices are lower than market prices, but the collectives have no alternative: no one else will give them credit. If collectives are so unlucky with the weather, or so badly organised, that they cannot produce more than the contracted harvest, they must pay up *all their grain.*[49] This means that next year they have to barter with the Corporation for seeds too, contracting at high prices for something they themselves produce.[50] This whole practise is explicitly seen as a matter of state control by the Corporation. Barter gives the collectives less freedom of action than money. An official told me: "We have to feed the army and the hospitals, don't we? If we gave money credit to the collectives, they would just squander it. This way, we know more or less what the state will receive."

A Chair of one farm told me her excitement when she read in a newspaper of a promise given by Yeltsin before the presidential elections. His edict promised to cut farm debts and give credits in *money.*

It would have been heaven for us! If only we had money, we could also sell normally, to other people for money. I went to the District Administration and waved the paper under their noses. But they said the money for the credits had not arrived. And we don't know if they have annulled our debts or not. We are still paying them off at 180 million a month.

These are the vertical dependencies of debt which tie the collectives to the state, just as most of the households are in debt to the collective. In Soviet times the farms were also in debt,[51] but now collectives are ordered to pay back credits before allocating funds to wages. The relation with the Products Corporation was described to me as "monopolistic exploitation," though of course, without it, many collectives would simply have to close down. The Buryat republic is heavily in debt to Moscow on account of the Products Corporation operation.

The long-term endebtedness of the farms conditions many strategies, since, if a collective were to show a positive balance on its account, the money would automatically be deducted to pay off debts and to pay taxes. It is best, I was told, to have *nothing* in one's bank account. This is one important reason for the prevalence of barter. Outstanding credits/debts can be kept away from the eyes of tax inspectors. At the same time, nonpayment of money wages enables the collective not to pay social insurance, pensions, etc. "Frankly," said one Chairman, "I never pay taxes." In effect, the bankruptcy of the farms is a tacit agreement by the administration to keep agriculture going at all.

Nevertheless, relatively successful farms are visibly different from failing ones. I was amazed, when driving across the Kuitun uplands, to pass from the weed-filled, unploughed, barren territory of the Bayangol OKKh to the vast acres of neatly ploughed, green-growing, newly fenced land of another farm. This turned out to be the Lenin Collective Farm at Baragkhan,[52] which is headed by a young, active Chairwoman. Her farm has grain products left over above the contract with the Corporation, giving her a certain amount of "manipulable resources." We can see this success as partly a matter of internal efficiency and partly due to external factors. The Chairwoman and everyone else ascribed it mainly to the knowledgeable and active Head Agronomist and his two brigadiers, who put in place a well-planned rotation of

468

crops and efficiently manage the sorting of high-quality seed.[53] Also, as in Soviet times (see Chapters 5 and 7), the collective depended on attracting the members to work well by making sure payments were regular, rather than sporadic handouts. The Chairwoman herself was the pivot with the outside world, and she described her life as a constant struggle to dispose of her manipulable resources.

Last year I spent weeks going round by car, trying to sell my extra grain. No one wants grain, though they'd buy flour. We need a flour mill, and I tried to get credit to build one last year, but I was refused. The collectives should get together to have a common mill, but they cannot agree; no-one will cooperate with anyone else these days. One thing I can do is exchange grain for milk with the State Breeding Union. They can get the grain milled and sell the flour for money. We do have a dairy to make butter, but we can't sell it, nor store it properly, so it spoils. As for livestock, it used to be profitable for us to buy it from the householders because I could then sell wool and skins to Chinese traders at the Ulan-Ude market. But the government has cut out the Chinese by raising customs taxes[54] and now there is a monopoly: we have to sell to the Fine Fabric Factory. They pay us in sugar, flour, cloth and curtains, but they give terribly low prices. And we don't even want half the things we get. Last year I got a load of trousers to give out to the members – at 75,000 per pair, far too expensive, I'll never do that again!

This account shows the importance of local processing to raise the value of farm products and enhance local autonomy.[55] The Karl Marx Collective in Selenga relies on its dairy to make butter and cream, which is at least more salable than milk. To operate the dairy, however, it relies on the school. How so? The school is funded by the District Administration, which also provides it liberally with coal for heating. The school itself is now a mini-economy, with its own farm for subsistence, and the Head Teacher said proudly, using the language of "help": "The school now gives help to the farm. For all those years of Soviet power it used to be the other way round. Now they can't run their dairy without our coal for the furnace.[56] And the poor families could not support their children were it not for our boarding-school and school meals." The products of the dairy are one of the main items of wages for the workers, an important gift of help to units inside the farm like the kindergarten and a crucial item for outside sales and payments for services.[57] The collective also reciprocates by looking after the school's pigs for free.

The reader may be wondering: how is it that the school has extra coal? It is clear that, as in Soviet times, much depends on particular relations between leaders of institutions and wealthholders (officials or patrons) outside. Beyond the mutuality of the farm, it is generally a free-for-all. Cosy allocations to friends are still possible from state budgets, as with the coal, but between enterprises they have given way to the most antagonistic forms of barter. Thus, barter deals are usually not the regular, trust-based, almost ritual exchanges found in some long-standing exchange economies (Humphrey 1993). They are negotiated anew each time, so that each side is free to take account of sudden exigencies of price.[58] The people involved usually know one another, but this does not soften the bargaining or lessen the arguments. I was told that this makes negotiations very stressful. "You don't know where you are, you can't plan, you feel humiliated by the weak bargaining position of agriculture," a Chairman said to me.

It is not surprising that directors are trying to form mutually supportive cartels, especially vis-à-vis the great monopolistic factories and government ministries. Thus, the Selenga Karl Marx is among a small group of Buryat collectives organised into the Golden Fleece association, which has negotiated higher wool prices with the monopolistic Fine-Fabric Factory, the only remaining cloth manufacturer in Buryatiya. The factory pays the farm for the wool with good-quality foreign shoes, suits, and coats; fuel and oil; and recently two tons of sugar. The Golden Fleece also operates as a rotating credit association: members pay regular fees, and they can then request largish sums in money. The Fine-Fabric Factory is run by a famous Soviet woman director. She is close to government circles and has recently turned the formerly state-run factory into a limited company. This company is part of the Motom group, one of the two great private consortiums in Buryatiya.

If some strategies involve directors forming protective associations, others depend on kinship links with government patrons. It turned out that the young Chairwoman of Baragkhan benefitted from such patronage. "She's doing well partly because of her Agronomist," I was told by one jealous fellow director. "But the main reason is that she comes from a large kin group and she has a 'roof' [*krysha*], two influential uncles in central government. When we wait for an audience with the President, she goes in before me!" Furthermore, the Baragkhan farm had a regular arrangement whereby it bartered its meat to the aircraft factory near Ulan-Ude. This very beneficial agreement had been set up in Soviet times as the *sheftsvo* (leadership) of the factory in order to "help the small place" (see p. 144), but clearly its continuation must have been authorised by the government. The farm received regular supplies of petrol, spare parts, and building materials from the factory, thus lessening its dependence on the Products Corporation and enabling the farm to operate with its own manipulable resources.

Thus, kinship is only one of the strategies of social recognition for making contacts and softening negotiations. Old schoolmates, a common birthplace, mutual friends – all kinds of links are sought in order to create some reassurance (not always justified) that the deal will be honourable. Indeed, it is difficult to imagine a deal in the rural areas where some such tie is not invoked. The Directors of collectives act personally and have given up using agents (*brokery*) because "such people just line their own pockets." The great patron firms and state institutions have special departments to organise barter. The electricity station (GRES) at Gusino-ozersk, for example, is paid mainly in products, though it tries to insist on money. (It puts pressure on enterprises, sometimes even on whole districts, by switching off the current for a time, but to no avail.) Therefore, it has to pay for its inputs, chiefly coal, with goods. I know a director who paid her electricity bill one quarter in 1996 with 10,000 saplings, having spent hours persuading the Director ("I know him well, the louse") to accept them. One can imagine these unfortunate trees circulating, being received by miners as "wages," for example, and then passing through the domestic exchange circuits until they reach someone who wants them. This whole situation is aggravating to people, requiring them to work endlessly at acquiring information, selling, buying, exchanging, and above all caring for their networks of relations. A crunch came in early 1997 with the attempt to pay pensions too in goods, which was hotly resisted by the pensioners. It is easy to see that the pension funds are in a difficult situation: money is received late from above, while most firms seem to pay their pension dues in products. But these are often not things even the most amenable pensioner would accept. "We have to dispose of bricks and metals," complained the pension fund director (*Krasnaya Selenga,* 31 January 1997, 2). At the same time, it is all too evident why pensioners insist on money and resolutely oppose the issue of cheque-books entitling them to goods purchasable at special shops. So, hidden behind all "personal" negotiations, both vertical and horizontal, is the unequal access to money and to the goods with greatest exchange value, and this is producing a new disturbing weighting in relationships. Collectives, with their huge costs and relatively low value products, are not in a good position.

The collectives rise and fall by means of deals, but it is highly significant that the Local Administration does not always help them. This is because numbers of administrators, at local and district levels, are sympathetic to the reforms and would rather see the collectives split up into private farms. In general administrators are nominated to their posts, not elected, and a flood of young officials were appointed during the last few years under the aegis of Yeltsin's success. These are graduates of business training courses – the former Higher Party Schools in the main cities were turned into Management Training Centres, I was informed. Now these young administrators are at odds with certain of the officials who have clung to power from Soviet times,[59] and some of them certainly seem to despise the "old-fashioned" Chairmen of the collectives. Politics thus enters the economic area. "You ask for a loan, and they ask you who you voted for in the Russian Presidential elections," said one villager in disgust. Loans are still very occasionally being given to groups wishing to set up private farms, taking a chunk of collective land and possibly even bypassing agreement by the collective management. Here we reach the thorny issue of the politics of land, since all land distribution is now in the hand of the administration. And at this point, at last, I am able to outline my ideas on the two different paths which it seems farming may take.

471

The collective farms after Socialism (1996)

Two possible paths in the organisation of agriculture

In brief, it seems that collectives may develop in two directions. They may turn into centres which organise and service small subfarms on a contractual basis. Or they may become unified cooperatives, from which shareholders receive dividends. Neither of these scenarios is in place at present. It is quite possible that the current disorganised stalemate – mostly a shrunken version of the old Soviet system – may continue for some time, as the politics of moving to anything else is stymied. Nevertheless, let me explain the signs of what may be the future.

First it is necessary to explain the idea of shares. The reform has taken the line of privatising farming by dividing all useful land into shares, called *pai* in Russian (for the history of *pai,* see p. 94). Land shares are to be envisaged as real estate (*nedvizhimost'*), say the reformers, but in "the first stage" they are still state property and cannot be sold. The "second stage," when shares will be collective and individual property, has not been reached because, as of the end of 1996, the Land Codex of Russia had still not been confirmed. Nevertheless, administrations have to varying degrees obeyed land reforms initiated in 1990 and continuing up to the Presidential edict of March 1996 by dividing the land and other collective property into shares. In Barguzin district the people eligible for land shares were those working up to 1991, who were divided into three statuses: collective farmers, pensioners, and state employees. By 1995 the total land of the district had been divided to give a notional "on paper" amount for each eligible individual. The actual land, however, was handed over to collectives and the few private farmers.

Now the land shares have an existence at several levels, from the purely theoretical to the real. In some districts, like Selenga, the shares consist only of calculations in the district administration, and they have not been "given out" to people. Other places, like Bayangol, have gone further down the road of reform by allocating shares to individuals in the form of certificates. Collective farmers got the best category land, the pensioners the next, and each individual got a specific amount according to length of service and salary over the last five years. State employees like teachers have not been allocated shares. Nevertheless, the bosses always being exceptions, the Local Administrator told me he "had" 3.5 hectares of arable field, 2.8 of hay meadow, and 7 of pasture (he also has shares in the machinery and buildings). This land is notional, however, and he does not know where it is. He leases (*arend*) his land shares into the collective at Bayangol, and in theory he should receive in return a dividend in the form of products. As everyone leases their shares into the collective and the dividends seem remarkably like the fodder, straw, and grain that the collective gives out anyway, on the surface everything seems to operate as if the shares did not exist. And in Selenga district they do not exist. On the other hand, in Barguzin district, in principle (which is to say "legally," though the status of the

472

law is uncertain), all collectives operate on the basis of shares. Whatever the type of farm (state farm, collective farm, OKKh, etc.) the idea is that the resident Soviet-era workers have shares in the whole and give them back in return for a dividend; meanwhile, they can work in the farm or not as they choose.

In practise, even a progressive OKKh, like the Bayangol, will not in the foreseeable future make an actual division of land into plots corresponding to shares. "How could I possibly do that?" said a manager. "Some land is so hopeless and far away. It would be all-out war in the village. And anyway, people don't want it, most of them would have no idea how to manage." Therefore, as the collectives continue to operate on the basis of wages and contracts, the most "advanced" form, according to reformers, now practised is when an enterprising group "takes out" their shares from the unwieldy whole and sets up a smaller, profitable organisation, also on the basis of shares.

Let us now look at some ethnographic examples, to see how people are understanding and operating within this system. It will be seen that the "share" scenario is coexisting both with old work teams operating under plans and with contract-holding work teams. To understand the situation it needs to be appreciated that the domestic smallholdings are increasingly being elided with collective production teams, whether operating on a share or a contract basis. Of course, the correct practise used to be to maintain a strict separation, but now certain resources of the collective are being sucked out and mingled with the subunits, whether these are families or larger groups.

The first example is an "old-fashioned" shepherding camp operating under plans in the Selenga Karl Marx Collective. Dorzhi and his wife, Oyuna, are both shepherds, and together they form a work team. Their domestic group consists of themselves, Dorzhi's parents, and three children. They take care of 250 rams for the collective, using two bases, at summer and winter pastures. The rams are kept in sheds during winter, grazed in early summer, shorn, then sent out to flocks of ewes in midsummer to "get to work," then gathered together again and fattened in autumn. Dorzhi's production indicators according to plan are the survival rates of the flock, the cut of wool, and the good organisation of the insemination. For achieving the planned indicators, he is paid in kind during the year – in flour, butter, and vodka – by the collective. If he fails, the farm may take away the flock and give it to someone else.

In July 1996 I visited Dorzhi at his summer base (*stoyanka, otara*), a spacious old wooden house in the steppes. Oyuna was out gathering berries with the children. Half of the house had collapsed and was in ruins,[60] but Dorzhi's side, consisting of one large room, had a wood-burning stove, electricity, a TV, and a fridge. In the dark recesses were pails with milk, a harness, and other equipment. There was a transformer (to lower the long-distance current to a usable level), but it had to be hidden away for fear of theft every time Dorzhi left the house. A broken motorbike was in the shed. Dorzhi told me he relied on his horse, and, that if he had not owned a horse of his own, the collective would have given him one. The sheep were grazing in a large fenced field, which Dorzhi surveyed with binoculars.

Along with this collective economy Dorzhi and Oyuna have their own small-holding in the central village, consisting of a vegetable plot, five cattle, ten sheep, and two pigs. These were kept at his own house (i.e., the third house used by the household). His parents, Oyuna, and the children take turns looking after the *usad'ba*. His livestock are herded along with all the privately owned stock of the village, the cattle near a small lake, and the sheep on the hills. The villagers take turns providing men as herders.

Dorzhi told me that he never received enough flour from the collective to sell any. His only money income comes from occasional sales of his butter wages and from selling his own livestock in Gusino-ozersk or Ulan-Ude. It was a difficult life, he said, moving so often, guarding against theft, and fattening an animal for three years only to receive such a small sum when it was sold. But, as we left his camp, another *kolkhoz* member commented sourly: "It's all so easy for him. He is privileged, look at that fence. He can just sit and watch TV if he wants. On other *otara*s there is no fence and no water, the shepherd has to work constantly to give the sheep water and salt and prevent them from getting mixed up with other flocks. That is hard work, but it is no better paid."

The second example is a shepherding camp on contract, and it demonstrates the elision of collective and domestic economies in Bayangol. In the Selenga collective, only 20 out of 340 workers are on contracts, but in Bayangol all workers in production are on contracts. Dulma is the head of a sheep *otara* camp. She has 150 ewes from the collective, and she also keeps her own 50 sheep, 20 cattle, and 4 pigs at the *otara*, where she stays all year round. The household is large, including a husband and eight children in their teens and twenties. All of them live in the two-roomed house, with beds separated by curtains.

Dulma's contract only seems to specify giving a specified amount of wool from the ewes to the collective each summer. She was silent about who took possession of the lambs.[61] Otherwise, she seems to take and give remarkably little from the collective. "Once upon a time they paid me 20 rams," she said. "But since then, nothing. They did not even give us any hay last year." She and her daughters milk the cows morning and night by hand and use most of the milk themselves – they make butter and alcohol. If there is any milk left over, it is given to the pigs. She finds it difficult to sell either meat or milk, partly because she lives miles from the village, let alone any town, and partly because no one can afford to buy. Sometimes a trader comes round to barter flour, sugar, and clothing for meat, and in summer Dulma aims to sell a few sheep to a known person in the local town. She also barters sheep for hay, because even with all hands the family cannot cut enough for the collective flock. Except at hay-making and shearing time, however, there is not enough work for the whole family. When I visited in mid-July, four or five sons were playing cards, the husband (a huge Russian, recently released from prison) was drunk, two strapping daughters were listlessly preparing some food, the youngest son rode in from herding the sheep. I asked Dulma why she stayed in the collective: "Two reasons," she replied. "To keep livestock and feed the family, and to qualify for a pension." She was expecting to leave the collective next year, as her husband had been injured in an accident and would qualify for a pension early. Leaving the collective would mean no more than handing back the 150 ewes and perhaps returning to the family house in the village. Her one wish, her golden dream, was that her children would find work and set themselves up in life.

The third ethnographic example is of a brigade with contracts, a nascent business. Andrei, a 40-year-old Buryat, was head of an arable production team at the Bayangol farm. When I visited in the summer of 1996 they were engaged in hay cutting. A raggle-taggle group – young boys, old men, a few adults – had built a huge hay shelter in the marshes where they were temporarily living. Inside its dark, spacious, sweet-smelling interior, some young boys were sheltering from the heat and mosquitoes, but they leapt out when I arrived to show me how they could harness and ride the oxen, which would pull the cutter and the rake. There were also some tractors on the scene ("A Belarus, that's a foreign mark for us now"). To economise on petrol, tractors were not used except when a cart got bogged down in the marsh. Nearby flowed the rushing River Barguzin, and some other boys arrived with five huge fish.

"I have a contract," Andrei told me, "to cut two wagonloads for the collective, and then the rest is for us." The brigade has some arable fields, and it also has some 95 cattle on lease (*arend*) from the collective. It turned out that the hay cut "for the collective" is in fact just what is sufficient for this herd. They do not produce any hay which the central collective management could use (e.g., in supplying a shepherd camp like Dulma's). The collective, however, meanwhile supplies the brigade with tractors and other machinery, the petrol, oil, transport, and so forth, and, of course, the land. Andrei said that by autumn villagers who had not cut much hay themselves would be ordering his hay. They would pay by barter. Come the winter, of course he would raise his prices.

Tolui, the Head of the Bayangol Administration, who was present during my visit, is reform minded. "Only 1.5% of the villagers are entrepreneurial like Andrei," he said. "But if we could get six or seven teams going like this, then things would take off." Tolui tried to prompt Andrei to admit to a desire to take over the production unit as his own private enterprise: "It's all the same, the *kolkhoz*'s hay or yours, isn't it?" But Andrei disagreed. "No, those two stacks are for the collective, and that other stack is for the butter factory; we concluded a contract with them yesterday; the rest will be ours." Tolui said that next year Andrei would probably "take out his shares" and set up an independent peasant farm, but Andrei looked doubtful; the advantages of staying in look fairly clear.

The fourth ethnographic example is of a privatised herding farm in the spirit of familial collectivism. In 1993 Olga and Dondup, both Buryats, set up a private livestock farm with three other families, separating off from the Kurumkanskii Collective Farm in the north of the Barguzin valley.[62] The new farm was called *Hubishal* ("Revolution" in Buryat). They took their shares of land and machinery from the collective (including two tractors, a plough, and a haycutter) but started off with only their own private livestock – 5–6 cows, 6 other cattle, 200 sheep, and 4 pigs. They migrated winter and summer between the same pastures and used the same hay meadows they had previously used in the collective. Olga could not say how much land they had.

The farm, consisting of four families, was spoken of by Olga as one family, linked by agnatic and affinal ties. When she was asked why this particular group of people had gotten together to set up the farm, she replied without hesitation, "Because *this is our family.*" In other words, the sense of family (*sem'ya*) came before the idea of what would be an appropriate set of people to make a farm. Interestingly, she saw the farm as a collective. "We started a new *kolkhoz,*" she said, "Well, a peasant farm, or whatever they call it, a little *kolkhoz.*" Olga's farm was far too poor to sell anything. She was almost expecting it to fail and said that if she could return to the collective her life would certainly be easier.

The fifth example is of a leased arable farm: not quite separated from the collective. Katya is a middle-aged Buryat woman, formerly a brigadier in Bayangol, who has set up her own peasant farm called *Ekaterina,* named after herself. In March 1996 she obtained a loan of 380,000 million rubles ($76,000) through the good offices of her husband's sister.[63] This enabled her to lease a total of 380 hectares, including 180 hectares of good wheat land, from the collective. She also leased tractors from the Bayangol OKKh for five years. The farm has fourteen members, not related by kinship, including a commercial agent and an accountant. Katya, however, is the only one who has taken the step of "taking her shares" and leaving the collective. Her colleagues are more timidly waiting to see if the new farm will work out. They live in the village of Bayangol and come out each day to work on Katya's farm, which is near the wheat fields. Their wives and families remain at home looking after the smallholdings and only come out to *Ekaterina* for holidays and festivities. "This is the velvet approach to reform," Tolui told me earnestly. "We should not force people into these associations. Let them decide whether to put their own shares and livestock into the farm. The worst thing about the Communist Party is that it told people what to do."

To understand the economics behind this, it must be repeated that only the grain-growing sectors of collectives are profitable. Katya has rented around one quarter of the wheat land of the collective (her own shares are quite small). Her second-in-command is a former Chief Economist of the Karl Marx Collective. As she herself is a former brigadier, it can be seen that in this case a group of former collective officials have taken the opportunity to set up what may become a flourishing medium-sized farm, even though this must detract from the resources remaining to the OKKh Bayangol. Katya pays off the lease for the collective by a contract to supply the farm with produce; anything produced over that belongs to her and her colleagues and will have to go largely toward paying off the initial loan.[64]

The sixth, and final, example is of a village which may separate off as a share-based collective. Soyol is a small village of 217 inhabitants located inside the Bayangol collective. It had been categorised as "without a future" (*neperspektivnyi*) under the Soviet policy of economies of scale, therefore deprived of services, and its people were expected to leave (for an account of such villages on Sakhalin, see Grant 1995). The policy has changed, however, and the President of the Republic even visited to show his support for reviving small villages in the all-Russian "Programme of Rebirth of the Village."

The leader of the village is Volodya, a Buryat, aged 30, who is still a brigadier in the *kolkhoz*. He is intending to set up a new share-based farm enterprise, using the land shares of all the people in the village. Of the 67 families, around 50 will provide workers, while the rest are pensioners, who will only give in their shares. The workers and director will be paid agreed-upon wages, while the surplus income will be divided among the shareholders. The farm will have a mainly livestock specialisation, with cattle, pigs, etc., taken as shares out of the Bayangol collective. The main problem at the moment is the machinery: for one thing the Bayangol has little left to lease, while "taking out" the shares in machinery involves also taking on the collective's debts.[65] So Volodya is intending somehow to acquire tractors by getting a loan. The club, school, and clinic will be financed by the Administration, while the collective has promised an initial loan to finance the electricity and a furnace. At the moment the village, like most parts of Bayangol, has no power; it has only enough electricity for lights, because the collective has not paid its bills.

This new collective may seem a highly problematic enterprise, but the village has a patron. This is a famous wrestler, an Olympic champion, and widely popular Buryat hero, who was born in the village.[66] He has promised to help his people with gifts of vehicles and petrol and use of his influence. "He came from here," I was told, "So he is obliged to help. He has great authority in the Republic. Volodya is his relative through his mother, and this way Volodya got interested in commerce, looked around and saw other people making money, and thought 'Why not us too?'" Furthermore, the wrestler comes from the main clan of the village and knows how to perform a ritual for success to the spirit of the clan, which inhabits a local mountain. All this, even the Local Administrator felt, is a promising basis on which to start.

Of these six examples the first is prevalent in all unreformed areas, while the

477

second is the most widespread type elsewhere. As yet, only Olga's farm was in fact completely separate from the collective, and it is likely that this farm has not survived. This reminds us that it is unlikely that the smallholdings will simply become little private farms belonging to individuals.[67] This is a matter of culture and principle, not just economic fact. It arises because people still tend to see themselves as specialised workers within organisations rather than as undifferentiated peasants, a tendency which was strengthened in the later Soviet years, since I wrote *Karl Marx Collective* (see discussion pp. 230–2).

Furthermore, for the villagers land is not property in the sense of giving exclusive rights and rights of disposal. Unlike most of Eastern Europe, Buryatiya had almost no experience with individual private property in land and then only certain types of land (p. 29). Not only is land attached to communities, but this land is special, ancestral, full of significance, and not an abstract value exchangeable for other land. Today, though in principle it is possible to alienate land shares outside the area, the District Administration forbids it. It is true that many villagers have privatised their houses and vegetable plots, but it is not anticipated that outsiders will buy them.[68] In general, there is a widespread fear, even terror, of any alien people "getting control of our ancestral land," and it was several times said to me that "they" would immediately force the locals to become "hired workers" and "slaves."[69] It is interesting that similar fears have appeared in Hungary after the end of the socialist regime despite the individual peasant farm tradition there (Hann 1996; Lampland 1995). This suggests that socialist practises created their own collectivist values, which in Hungary are now in tension with the earlier, more individualist peasant traditions and with the new legal reforms (Hann 1996, 45). In Buryatiya the early collectives strengthened what was already a communal tradition of land ownership (see Chapter 10), and the struggles over collectivisation concerned the pooling of livestock, not land. Therefore, all the variants now in existence involve commonly held land (i.e., pooled land shares).

The issue is whether to lease out collective land, livestock, etc., to large numbers of semi-independent producers with a centralised management, as in the contract variant, or establish more corporate units in which a smaller proportion of people will work while most will simply give in their shares and hope to receive a dividend. In practise, there are problems with the operation of either ideal type. Seen optimistically, the contract scenario leaves each producer free to develop the domestic smallholding along with the collective task, contributing a limited product to the collective, and the sum of these incoming products allows the centre in turn to help each small production node. Newspapers extoll the virtues of the Belogorod Region in Russia, where this ideal appears to be unfolding.[70] But Belogorod is one of those fertile regions where the small, mixed farm is viable. In Buryatiya, however, contracts are only popular with the few people who already have substantial smallholdings. This is because unforeseen disasters may prevent a weak herder from fulfilling his or her side of the contract and because there is no mechanism to force the collective to observe its part of the contract. So, as with Dulma, many people take out contracts only really to make use of the collective property on the side. In fact, the share as a general idea is closer to peoples' way of thinking than contracts. The *share* (R. *pai,* B. *khubi*) or portion (R. *dolya*) is part of indigenous language, while the *contract* (*kontrakt*) is a foreign (European) term. A tractorist told me he stayed in the collective because otherwise "my portion," his tractor, would be taken away and, with this tractor, his living.

The problems with the share scenario are more with the way it is being implemented than with the concept. Collectives have a tendency simply to turn existing specialised brigades into share-based farms. From the perspective of a manager this looks efficient, but ordinary villagers dislike it. Such an organisation requires reciprocity and trust *between* the specialised units, yet the whole idea of shareholding is for mutual benefit *within* units. In 1993 a herder, who had been set up as a private farmer with a livestock specialisation in Argada and whose shares in arable land had been given in to a new agrarian enterprise, said, "I know with iron certitude (*zhelezno*) that though they may give me a minimum of fodder, I'll never see a cent of their profits."[71] The problem here is not just the need to integrate complementary production, the necessary transfer of arable products (fodder) to herders and to a lesser extent vice versa (animal fertiliser), as the centralised collectives had done. It is also the moral requirement of evening-out income, when the arable sector is profitable while the livestock one is loss making. For some managers the moral issue seems to take a secondary place to making profits at all, and they ignore widespread mistrust between various *kollektivs*.

The go-ahead young woman Chair of the Lenin Collective Farm at Baragkhan told me that she intended to implement the share system. Her plan has a distinctly authoritarian ring to it, and it certainly goes against any hope of seeing the shares as individual private property. Individuals' shares will all be put into the brigades, she said, which would become specialised farms, and furthermore the shares will rise and fall in size according to how well the shareholders work. Slackers and nonworkers would have their shares, consequently their dividends, cut. This idea reminds us of the extent to which in reality shares are a matter of sociopolitical status. Pensioners anyway have smaller shares than workers (not to speak of the state employees in Bayangol, young people, and those whose registration papers were not in order in 1991, who do not have shares at all). The Baragkhan plan would subvert the share itself to the time-honoured and deeply felt value of "hard work." The point is that this conforms to villagers' moral tenets and ideas about social worth. A whole crowd nodded their approval when the young Chair spoke of her plan: as a strong leader, she would maintain discipline and see that all workers got their fair share! This is far indeed from the new reformist ideology, which is that managers will "have to negotiate a new relationship with the people, persuading each babushka that it would be to her advantage to put her shares in to their farm. Directors are not accustomed to bowing to old women, but it must be done, or she'll give her share elsewhere."[72] As things are, of course, in a place like Baragkhan the old woman has no choice: the collective is the only landholder in the area.

Nevertheless, the real politics of the wider situation is that, if someone has an outside patron, like Katya through her husband's sister and Volodya with the famous wrestler, they can bypass the collective farm managers, take out a chunk of shares, and set up on a more independent basis. The question then arises of the basis on which these new farms will operate. The hesitancy of Katya's workers to join her is an indication of how crucial is this question. Katya's farm, which is "individualistic" even in its name, contrasts with the clan-based all-inclusive unit of the village of Soyol. The economic relation with the patron is also vital to the eventual profile of the farm. The wrestler's duty was evidently to the village of Soyol as a whole, whereas Katya had obtained a personal loan to herself. This suggests that within the category of share-based farm there may emerge two different types: one with a general engagement of most shareholders in production, salaries paid to the leaders, and relatively egalitarian distribution of dividends; the other, like Katya's *Ekaterina,* a type in which a few director-shareholders take all the profits (see Kaneff 1996).

It is very significant, however, that *Ekaterina* is spoken of in terms of shares and colleagues, not employer and workers. We are reminded here of what is happening in Inner Mongolia (China), where in the past ten years herders' land has been physically divided into plots and poor people without livestock have leased their plots to rich neighbours. Frequently, the original title holders then take jobs as hired herders on what used to be their land. Outsiders from other parts of China are also able to take out these leases, with the result that Mongolian pasture is gradually passing into the hands of Han Chinese, who use it mostly for agriculture. As a result, both ethnically and within the community there is a marked land-based economic differentiation (Humphrey and Sneath, in press). This is a process which was already in train before the socialist period in Inner Mongolia (Sneath, in press) and, of course, is found also in other parts of the world. The Buryats are all too aware of it, saw a first glimpse of it in the first wave of officials' privatisation, and now dislike and resist it. In their case it is true that there are no floods of hungry Chinese anxious to take their land, but internal differentiation along employer/employee lines is a real possibility, and it is being encouraged by certain reform-minded officials (see Chapter 10). "How could I take paid work with a kinsman or neighbour? That would be shameful," is what the villagers say. This is why the men working with Katya are so carefully called colleagues (*tovarishchi*) and potential shareholders. Inequality is acceptable, but only if mediated by a larger whole to which loyalty is owed by all. This is similar to the situation of working domestically for kin, which may also be unequal but is disguised by the trope of "helping."

I have identified two main issues here: the extent to which relatively freely negotiated contracts with collectives will support the domestic smallholdings, a scenario in which success/failure will depend on *economic* performance; and the extent to which collectives will emphasise the concept of the share, which subordinates individuals to the whole and then allocates income according to the *social* basis on which the collective is set up. Both collective forms envisage the domestic smallholding as incomplete. Furthermore, they imply a notion of centrality which has an ideological character. Even the contract scenario should not be seen simply as a functional exchange of material goods between productive units and the servicing centre, for the incompleteness of the units is ideational as well as material. "How can you live without a plan?" said one driver to me.

To conclude, it seems that resistance to privatisation is due to several factors: cultural unfamiliarity and indigenous/Soviet values, economic rationality in respect of the complementarity of arable and livestock production in Buryatiya, well-advised prudence given the failure of earlier private farming attempts and previous waves of "anti-kulak" jealousy, and resistance to direct, economic differentiation ("exploitation") in the village. It is evident that the share reform will not turn into agrarian capitalism in the near future, since shares are not transactable in an open land market. This means that, for all the lateral deals and survival strategies, some form of insiders' collective will be present. Such farms will be much influenced by the kind of society that constitutes the inside. What are the identities, cultural imaginings, and understandings of land and space that look as though they may influence the forms taken by new kinds of farms? It is to this subject that I turn in the next chapter.

10

Rural culture and visions of the future

In the last chapter it was shown that collectives can no longer be taken for granted, and here I move on to the question of how they are being reimagined. Collectives are being retained on the basis not of Soviet blueprints but local loyalties, and this is reinforced by *ad hoc* rules such as that members cannot leave the community to set up as private farmers without the agreement of everyone else. Attached to local relations, people also search for patrons above, for a more powerful source of funds. Quite simply, money means power these days. The result is a funding pyramid which we can imagine standing on the base of the physical landscape of villages, roads, fields, and pastures organised in Soviet times – a precarious pyramid, because there is always the possibility of disaggregation and collapse to the foundations of the tiny, barely solvent plots. All of this must apply over much of rural Russia. But in Buryatiya, it will be suggested, the pyramid scenario is a post-Soviet construction which also happens to provide a congenial ground for emergent indigenous concepts of the polity. Elsewhere in Russia a number of other factors, such as strengthening in the rule of law, greater viability of small, independent mixed farms, and particularly the advent of private property in land, may take agrarian developments in a different direction, but in Buryat areas a hierarchical type of "insiders' collective" is likely to prevail, at least in the medium term. Buryat indigenous plans are couched in a hybrid mixture of categories: native notions of leadership jostle with Soviet concepts and ideas gleaned from globalised management-speak. If social institutions always must have an imaginary dimension (Castoriadis 1997, 156–60), here we see the struggle to achieve the imaginary in a context of uncertainty.

The political, the religious, the genealogical, and the personal are all intertwined in Buryat thinking. We need to discover how these are imagined in order to understand the social nature of the "communities" (the insiders) in which collectives are being reformed. It is somewhat arbitrary to begin with any of these aspects. But, as religious ideas are so important in establishing ties to land, I shall start with a description of the present cult of ancestors in the Selenga Karl Marx. Here we shall see that religious cults exist at many levels, there being both wide, inclusive rituals and small, exclusive ones. It will be argued that these cults offer a *conceptual model* of a shareholding hierarchy. In the conclusion to *Karl Marx Collective* (p. 438) I suggested that rituals like the *tailagan* sacrifice used to present a counterpart to the Soviet ideology embodied in the collectives: "To the arbitrariness of being allotted one task after another, or to the precarious structure of a career, it [the sacrifice ritual] counterposes simply absolute status . . . defined by reference to ancestors." Now it seems that this certitude of kin-based identity is coming to invade the space left by the almost extinct Soviet ideology; not directly – collectives are not being taken over by kin groups – but as a set of ideas and values that underlie the polities imagined for the future.

People told me that patrilineal clans (R. *rody,* B. *yahan, esege*) have become more important to them than they were in Soviet times. Clans do not usually coincide with either production groups or the multifarious "horizontal" networks of reciprocity. So why should people still call upon the patrilineal genealogies in the 1990s? They still serve to delimit exogamy in marriage relations.[1] They also provide lines to famous historical predecessors (see p. xviii). In some areas of Buryatiya it is said that clans are used politically to form blocs of votes.[2] Most germane to my argument here, they conceptually locate the quasimythical "ancestor" who, by becoming a spirit inhabiting the land, gives a rationale for local cults. These ancestors constitute unquestionable ties to the land, provide rallying points for groups, delimit status (seniority-juniority), and activate quite substantial economic exchange (at any rate "giving" and "taking") in one vertical structure. The chapter will explain the implications of this idea in several stages, starting with a description of the burgeoning of ancestral rituals in the 1990s.

Territory, kinship, and ritual

When I visited the Karl Marx collective in Selenga in summer 1996, practically the first place I was taken to see was Emege-Eezhiin Mörgöliin Gazar (the Worshiping Place of Woman-Mother). "Woman-Mother" is one of three ancestresses who became spirits of the locality (*ezhed;* see p. 415) and are now worshipped by their patrilineal descendants.[3] Located far away up a twisting track to the west of Tashir, the site is a broad south-facing meadow at the edge of a forest. It consists of two magnificent pine trees on which ribbons (*seternuud*) and wind-horse flags (*khii mori*) are tied by worshippers, a cupboard-like shrine into which the spirit descends,[4] a prayer sign in Tibetan, eight large tables for offerings, a huge cauldron, an incense burner, and many long trestle tables and benches for the feasting. Hundreds of empty vodka bottles lie in heaps under the trees. The whole site is surrounded by a white thread, tied at about waist height from tree to tree. Entering this sacred place, my Buryat companions

483

stood near the shrine and made circular libations of milk and vodka around themselves and then prayed silently.

The collective helped with the construction of the new worshipping place and provides transport for people to get to the ceremonies. Milking brigade no. 1 is responsible for the thick creamy tea, which is consumed in gallons. Clearly, official disapproval of such religious activities (pp. 414–5) is a thing of the past. My guides, Lyuba, the head of the Trade Union and the Chairman's right-hand, and Purbo, the Chairman's father-in-law, were happy at the beauty and order of this place, at the large numbers who come (200 to 300 people attend the summer rites),[5] the wealth of the offerings and feast (30 to 40 rams, buckets of cream and yoghurt, cauldrons of tea, heaps of sweets and cakes, vodka as much as all can drink), and the joyful dancing and singing which go on late into the night. The provisions are collected by the organisers from the villagers, and every three years each family should provide a *töölei* (see p. 386), the head of a ram ritually prepared for offering to the Mother.

Who are the organisers? The Mother is considered to be an ancestor of the Atagan clan, and in particular the local patrilineage Maamai-*tang,* the descendants of Maamai some four or five generations back.[6] These are the people who organise and *must* come to the ritual. Many of the Atagan travel from distant regions, even the capital. Several other clans are also present in the Iroi Valley, and the Emege-Eezhi rites are also local festivities to which all Buryats of Tashir are welcome (though the Russians, Chinese, and Tatars do not attend).[7] The meat is cut into named and graded pieces, laid on the tables in order, and then distributed by Atagan elders to all those present according to their status (this is done by age, rather than by sex or genealogical position). Such relative inclusiveness concords with the purpose of the rites, which is to call down the Mother's blessing for the prosperity of the whole community, and with the fact that, though local people say the cult is "really shamanist," the prayers are conducted by the Buddhist lama of Tashir. Emege-Eezhi is said to have been a shamaness, whose grave is at the worshipping place.[8] The shamanic focus on genealogical exclusiveness and particular sites (Humphrey 1995) has been overlaid recently, however, by the inclusiveness of Buddhist ritual practise.[9] Indeed, by building monasteries with territorial, rather than kin-based, congregations, the Buddhist Church was a prime mover in establishing social relations founded on locality in Buryatiya (Galdanova 1992, 143).

Clanship, place, and religion link people in extraordinarily complex patterns. On the one hand, practises establish the spiritual importance of particular places, but, on the other, genealogical and mythic relations spread far and wide. Just as the clans themselves have areas of denser home settlement but also branches scattered in different districts and regions (Hamayon 1990), the systems of sacred sites also exist at anything from the family to the regional level. The lability of the kinship idiom is evident also from the fact that the ancestor of the mountain cults may appear as a warrior or ruler, and in this case several different clans come together to worship at the same site.

Thus, not only are there the two other Mothers, but three male "Kings" (*Khan*) also preside over the dominating mountains of the area, each having its own ritual cairn (*oboo;* see pp. 422–3) as the site for worship. The Khan spirits, who are both ancestors and "rulers," extend their influence far beyond the region from which their mountains can even be distantly glimpsed. Burin Khan is the name of the massive mountain dominating the area of the Karl Marx Collective and its presiding spirit, and he is one of the three Khans of Ar-Khalkh (northern Mongolia).[10] Locally, Burin Khan has other links, since not only did he "have adventures" and "meet" other mountain spirits at various places which were pointed out to me, but he is also said to have a wife and son, who are also spirits with *oboo*s on smaller mountains. Besides this, in the Iroi Valley there are several small, secret *oboo*s for other patrilineal groups (*-tang*), there are springs whose "master" is worshipped, and there are sacred trees and stony outcrops where spirits dwell and people go to make offerings. Some of these spirits, such as the Kharuukha Eezhi (one of the three Mothers, inhabiting a darkly wooded low hill), are said to be vengeful. They insist that every scrap of food and drink taken to the site must be consumed on the spot and not taken away and that all worshippers behave with the utmost circumspection and politeness, moving slowly and thinking "only good thoughts." Misfortunes, called "punishment," will happen to anyone infringing these rules.

Here we see the definition of places and occasions for the drawing together of small patrilineal kinship groups and at the same time a mythic expansion, which links local sacred sites with others outside the Iroi Valley (one of the Mothers is in the nearby Noyokhon subdistrict, while one of the Kings is in Mongolia, and the other is outside Buryatiya in Chita Oblast). In principle, none of this privileges the particular community that is the collective farm. Indeed, the genealogies stretch back to times long before there were collectives. Yet one of the newly active cults, Emege-Eezhi, in effect takes Tashir (i.e., the central village of the collective) as its sphere of operation. This can be seen in the role of the Woman-Mother at the marriages of outside women to local men. The Woman-Mother is the master (*ezhin*) of the land. The parents of an incoming bride should come to the shrine before the marriage and beg: "We intend to give our daughter to your lands, can we have your permission?" and the girl herself should bow and request the approval of the spirit to live there.[11]

This situation of course is defined by gender, since comparable rites are not performed by men. Men are supposed just to "be there." They, on the other hand, may have to ask permission to leave. I did not hear of this in Selenga, but in Barguzin a young man told me: "The ancestor-spirit does not like his young men to go away. You should go to the shrine, explain why you need to leave, and promise to return." The idea of the approval of spirits for women coming in and men going out thus maintains the concept of groups of men attached to localities and binds the inhabitants together as recipients of the blessing of prosperity.[12] The members of such groups confirm their attachment at the lunar New Year rituals of *tsagaalgan* (see pp. 378–9, 429),[13] when the young people go round to all the houses of their seniors to give greetings, and when the winter rites of Emege-Eezhi are held.

The vengeful spirits, the forbidding of the removal of the offerings from the sacred site, and the fact that people's everyday misfortunes are explained as infringements of rules established by spirits all serve to promote recognition of ties between kin groups and territories. Newly active shamans, both in the cities and the villages, pressurise people to discover their ancestors and those ancestors' birthplaces if they do not know them. Shamans cannot remove the causes of misfortunes (the anger of spirits) unless they have this information (Humphrey 1996). All this seems to induce a feeling of submission among the people, as if prosperity and its obverse, misfortune, were the result of conduct in respect of an unseen spiritual order. This affects everyday activities,[14] and the collective itself is an actor in at least one annual ritual. The Chairman of the Selenga Karl Marx told me that spiritually "strong people" (*silniye lyudy*), including a lama, are sent each year to pray for rain after the spring sowings. In 1995 they were sent on horseback up to an *oboo* on a mountain at the source of the River Temnik; the snow was so deep and the path so dangerous that one horse fell to its death.

One cannot forget the local spirits as one goes through the day. It is obligatory to recognise them by making token offerings at every main meal and every single drinking occasion. When a bottle of vodka is opened, each person should make a libation to the spirits before drinking by flicking a few drops in the air; this was a "custom" in Soviet times, but now it has become a more elaborate rite, for which people from different areas observe different rules (e.g., in a house, which direction the libation should be made, which finger to use, how many spirits to honour, whether to wear a hat or not). The point is that people acknowledge the presence of master-spirits wherever they are. Travelling in Buryatiya includes numberless stops at wayside *oboo*s and shrines, a host of these having arisen since Soviet times. This includes boundary-*oboo*s at the frontier of each district (*raion*) and subdistrict. Inside the collective, the stopping to make libations of vodka becomes even more frequent, as local people know the invisible denizens of each sacred grove and spring, and one is supposed to acknowledge them even if passing at some distance. The constant libations, apart from imparting an alcoholic haze to all journeys, remind the traveller of her dependency and luck, and they fix in the mind the idea of boundaries and centres, of spirit territories, whose masters expect contributions.

Though this is a general set of ideas, it is not everywhere that villagers have built a mass cult site like that of Emege-Eezhi. Perhaps it is an accident, though I think not, that the people of the strongly traditional Karl Marx Collective at Selenga have established a more or less common cult, while in the more dispersed OKKh at Bayangol there was no such general festivity. In Bayangol people travel to a variety of ritual sites.[15] The spacious Rest Home of the Bayangol collective, with its nearby sacred site at a beautiful birch grove with a clear, bubbling spring, could have provided a place of general worship.[16] But the Rest Home was closed and vandalised in 1996, and the Sacred Grove was visited by small parties and single worshippers.

What does seem to be generally true in Buryatiya is the importance in such rituals of the small patrilineal group, which Sydenova (1992) calls the patronymic group, as it is named after its founding ancestor (with the suffix *-tang*). This group mirrors in miniature the structure of the wider clan in which an apical ancestor represents the whole. But, before I return to this subject, let me first address the question of the kind of society maintained by the collective itself.

What kind of community does the collective maintain?

The significant point here, and one reason why the imagination is often strongly invested in them, is that most collectives are struggling to be far more than economic institutions. Meetings of collectives are often both political and definitional, since they concern the reorganisation of the farm, voting in of leaders, and admission and resignation of members.[17] Even in the current economic crisis the Selenga Karl Marx just about manages to maintain the following services: a large new club (called the House of Culture), including a theatre, disco, and museum; a trade union; a Buddhist prayer house;[18] a hotel;[19] a dairy; a bakery; a central heating plant;[20] and a rest home[21] next to a sacred spring. Besides this, the collective maintains public wells, local roads and bridges, and the electricity supplies. The village of Tashir also has services on the budget of the Administration, but these cannot function without further help from the collective: a kindergarten,[22] a high school,[23] a specialist music school,[24] a library,[25] a Veterans' Association, and a hospital.[26] In sum, the collective either provides or is intricately involved with the institutions constituting a whole way of life, including the aesthetic and religious. But they can no longer be taken for granted (Chap. 9). Many villagers say that they are only now coming to realise the benefits of the Soviet regime, summarised as "culture" (*kul'tura;* see Anderson 1996), for it is all of these things that they regard as the components of "normal" life, just as it is crumbling before their eyes.

Now the benefits of these services are certainly unequally distributed: some, like the hospital or the Buddhist prayer house, are open to all, while others are for collective farm members only (the rest home), others benefit mainly officials (the central heating plant), and yet others have to be paid for, and so many people cannot afford them (film shows at the club). Unequal distribution was always the case, however, also during Soviet times.[27] People expect it and even support it, provided that the grounds for access is legitimately based on values they defend: devotion to work, official position, age, or "being a native of the place." Even the current exclusion of certain workers from the collective is explained away by the same criteria ("they are lazy," "they don't really come from here," etc.). In fact, there is little regret for the old Communist rhetoric of incorporation of everyone on an egalitarian basis. An acceptance and even approval of inequality is in the air. Now I do not mean by this *economic* inequality created by buying and selling and generally by market conditions, for this is regarded as illegitimate.[28] The inequality people accept is seen by them as inborn, a matter of different abilities and dispositions.

This, too, is founded on kinship concepts. "The eight clans here, they have their characteristics," said the Local Administrator in Bayangol. "We have to take them into account when working with the people. The Tsegeenuud – people of this clan cannot be leaders. The Shono – they can be leaders. Some people are born in ne'er-do-well families. This information has been passed on from generation to generation; there are no explanations, but there is something in it." Even stronger is the "difference" attributed to *-tang* patronymic groups (pp. 291, 297, 336). In the village they are known by nicknames, so the Badmayev-*tang* may be called Dalai-*tang* (wide, broad, generous people); another group are the Untakhai-*tang* (sleepy, lazy ones); yet another are the Bagaga-*tang* (the shitty ones; i.e., with lots of children who leave a mess). Such names perpetuate the sense of a village composed of "naturally" different kinds of people. This is not seriously at odds with Soviet practise, despite the teaching that institutions and services should provide "a normal life" for all, since in fact access was never the same to everyone. "The collective used to be 'one family,' but now there is discrimination," some complain, but others retort, "It never was a family of equals."[29]

Now, access to collective services has shrunk drastically. The solution is to cut back, eliminate some herding units, shut down a kindergarten, close the club, use kerosine instead of coal, but not to dismantle the whole. Significantly, the services are not excluded from the orbit of spiritual influences: economic decline and social malaise have spiritual as well as mundane causes. Thus, in Tory (Tunka) there was a Buddhist consecration ritual of the local school in 1994, when it was felt that an inexplicable wickedness and aggression had affected the children.[30] Also, in July 1995 the House of Culture was given a purification to "cleanse the evil that has accumulated around it," manifested by "worsening in the circumstances of life" in the village and the recent death of several local youths. Money was collected from each family in the village to pay lamas to conduct these rites (Zhukovskaya 1997, 98–9).[31] These incidents show that, for all the inequality and personalisation of access, the services represent community well-being as a whole: they are the responsibility as well as the source of benefit for the people.

Before I return to this point, let me briefly relate the analysis so far to that of other postsocialist regions and countries; this may enable us to see how far socialist structures and practise, as opposed to regional differences, are the key to current developments.

The Buryat situation compared

The great differences in economies, cultures, and political traditions in the former socialist world are evident and seem certain to widen. Nevertheless, certain similarities between the Buryat situation and findings of Kaneff (Bulgaria), Lampland (Hungary), and Pine (Poland), for example, are striking, which suggests that the operation of "socialism" did generate certain characteristic postsocialist dilemmas.

Thus, Kaneff (1996) describes the tension in a Bulgarian village between two different types of collective. There is the communitarian Progress, in which a large membership, mostly of old people, pays the wages and production costs of workers who then distribute the fodder, harvest, etc., at the end of the season, while the households keep individual plots; and there is the smaller, profit-oriented Talpa 95, in which three active workers take all the income and pay the shareholders only a rent for the use of their land. Kaneff rightly points to the political and moral attitudes lying behind the support for one or another of these collectives. This theme is developed further in the work of Pine (1996), who shows how in the more industrialised regions of rural Poland the idea of "duty" linked the workers with the state. The socialist state had done what a state ought to do; people said, "We have worked for the state, and we therefore have rights and can expect our dues from the state." The crisis of postsocialism for such workers was that "unworthy" people, people who had no sense of duty, like the Gorale of the southern mountains, were able to achieve instant economic success through entrepreneurship rather than labour. The same theme is echoed by Stewart (1997) for Hungary, where the Gypsies contrast their own inventive, "make-a-quick-profit" mentality with the laborious work of "the peasants," i.e., everyone else. All of this literature contrasts, to make an outrageous simplification, the idea that labour creates value and gives rights with the idea of making a profit through "market" operations. The reforms, in many eyes, have led to the gypsification of society.

The same contrast is present in rural Buryatiya, despite the fact that there are few examples of profit making and entrepreneurial success in the villages. People know about moneymaking "outside," in the capital city or in trading between Russia, China, and Mongolia. Their children go off to train, join the army, or get jobs wherever they can. Even in the villages, former officials have set up profit-oriented farms in many places, while Chairmen of collectives talk of "business plans." This raises issues like those illuminatingly discussed by Lampland (1995), who argues that it was the socialist regime, with its commoditization and time budgeting, that developed attitudes of calculation, utilitarianism, and economism among Hungarian peasants which spread into the domestic economies. To some extent Lampland's ideas apply also in Russia, where "self-accounting," for example, was an idea present in collectives from Brezhnevian times (p. 237) and was further promoted by Gorbachev through the policy of promoting family contract teams (Humphrey 1989). Where Lampland's terminology is questionable, however, is her suggestion that these attitudes are "capitalist" (1995, 17), which means that she has to backtrack somewhat to explain why so many Hungarian villagers have been resistant to actual capitalist relations in the 1990s – and, of course capitalism itself has changed from a labour-based to an increasingly international, fragmented process, with dispersed manufacturing, as Bridger and Pine (1998) point out. The Buryat case suggests that a few former officials of collectives, who were used to both organising production and making deals, were enabled to set out on the moneymaking path during the privatisation campaign, and some of them profited from it. But everyone else was stuck. For them there is totting-up of course, but calculation and economism are buried in the politics of relations, of dealing with *someone,* not anyone. Domestic economies still adhere to a rather loose reciprocity, encompassing lazy or incompetent kin without too much complaint. Most Buryat villagers would agree with the contradiction of values so starkly put by Lampland's Hungarians (1995, 349): "The activities of hard work and the machinations of moneymakers inhabit two separate worlds, and cannot be bridged." They would prefer not to have to spend so much of their energies on moneymaking deals on the side.[32]

Nevertheless, we can see two important differences between Buryatiya and Eastern Europe. First, the presence of calculative attitudes in the domestic economies, if not absent in Buryatiya, seems to be indissolubly tied in with far more widespread personal reciprocities with kin and absence of time budgeting. As compared with European Russia (Bridger 1996), the family is stronger, and women have more willing support from its members in all the tasks to be done. Second, there is the existence in Buryatiya of an indigenous model for territorially based, communal, hierarchical shareholding, which does not exist as far as I know in Eastern Europe. Both of these characteristics of the Buryat situation are related to the presence, and indeed the resurgence, of a variety of kinship images and associated ideologies and practises which are slatted over one another to form a dense, though not always coherent, matrix.

I should now, in fairness, present an alternative view, describing a Buryat village as almost disintegrated. According to Panarin (1997), based on his work in the village of Tory in the Tunka Valley, the Buryats lost most of their culture during Soviet times, and family life came to be separate from and even opposed collective life. In the 1990s there is a move to revive "traditions" in the form of the kin-based economy. The problem is, however, that these small farms cannot exist independently of the collective. They take much of their income from it, yet they are acquiring independent viability more slowly than the collective is weakening (or being "thieved away"). The likelihood is that the collective will collapse and with it many of the households. Kinship and ritual will not be able to prevent this, because, although they are effective in "mutual help," they are also used by local leaders in mobilising support for their attempts to control resources, which creates enmities. Criminality has grown, and this indicates the weakness of ritual in preserving morality and the brevity of its effects in compensating people for the hardships of daily life. Panarin indicates two further threats to the survival of Tory as a community. One is the numerical preponderance of those who live off vertical resources (pensioners, state employees) or who work in the loss-making livestock sphere. All these people are oriented toward dependency on the state and constitute a "force of inertia," because they do not accept the principle of making an independent livelihood. Finally, there is the threat of intergenerational cultural breakdown. The culture of the young people of Tory is partly Russo-Soviet and partly attracted by international films, videos, etc., both of which are far from their indigenous culture and from the real everyday life of the village. Young people are therefore oriented to globalised city culture, and many of them are unlikely to take part in the process of adaption of the village to the new times.

This is a serious analysis, and it is certainly true that a cold eye would see signs of similar phenomena even in a relatively strong collective like the Selenga Karl Marx. For example, the remote hamlet of Udunga, where Dorzhiev (see pp. 334–5) had built a magnificent milk production base, was now almost without work, without a school, abandoned by young families, and inhabited mostly by disheartened pensioners.[33] But I would like to suggest nevertheless that the main problem is not how one sees the facts, nor even the undoubted differences between Buryat districts, but that Panarin limits what he takes as indigenous culture to kinship and ritual, so the existence and operation of collectives is not part of it.

A broader approach is seen in the interesting work of Konstantinov (1997) among the Evenki of the Kola Peninsula. He argues that there are three competing ideological stances among Evenki reindeer-herders: "privatism," "*sovkhoism*" (support for the former all-caring state farms), and "pre-Sovietism" (idealisation of pre-Soviet ethnic and kinship traditions, such as the caring for the unemployed by rich Sami families within the traditional settlement called *pogost*). Konstantinov suggests that the weakness of individual initiative (privatism) does not mean support for *sovhoism,* since the cooperatives, which are the state farms' successors, are largely seen as prey, a "fertile basis for informal activities" (1997, 18). The brigades are becoming *pogost*-like settlements, but they, too, do not seek autonomy. Konstantinov makes some acute observations on the importance of the search for patrons and the notion of the "insiders' collective." Yet he does not explain, except by the difficulty the herders have with accounting, why the herders decided to leave marketing of their meat to the cooperative, even though this meant they received a lower price:

491

There is not only reluctance to strike out as private herders (this is considered madness), but even to let go of the skirts of the ex-sovkhoz on a brigade level. Contact with outside reality, especially the Western one represented by Polarica [the main patron in the region], is felt to have to be mediated by superiors of the administration. (1997, 17)

Even in Panarin's village of Tory, where the abject collective was raided right, left, and centre, a parallel study found that the vast majority of the villagers would prefer to work in a collective farm to any other type.[34]

In my view, at least in the Buryat case, such attitudes can be explained if "culture" includes the *habitus* developed during Soviet times, if it includes the collectives, the search for patrons, and the "superiors of the administration" too. In other words, the political economy is not extrinsic but integral to the cultural phenomena we are trying to explain. The tendency to preserve some form of insider-based collective is found in so many radically different environments and economies of the postsocialist world that, while granting the economic difficulties of going it alone in such decisions, we should also acknowledge that *socialist political culture* is still influential. By this I do not just mean *sovkho-ism* (nostalgia for collectives) but more general political attitudes and collectivist values engendered by the socialist experience. The matter is highly complex, since it is only now, when their achievements are almost overwhelmed, that many people recognise these values. Socialist political culture certainly clashed with some indigenous cultures, but it is a little noticed fact that it accorded rather well with others. I would hazard a guess that Evenkis preserve very little of it (Fondahl 1998) and stay in collectives mainly for pragmatic and prudential reasons. On the other hand, the hierarchical, commandist, allocative principles of Soviet culture, as well as its grandiose and heroic character (which so often flew in the face of reality), accorded rather well with aspects of Mongolian and Buryat indigenous culture. In other words, Buryats might prefer a pyramidal collective form not only for economic reasons. I approach this subject by first turning to an example which exemplifies such ideas in contemporary Buryat thinking.

"The State of Bayangol"

The literature on postsocialist societies is in universal agreement on the confused presence of diverse ideological stances which confront one another, "creating an unresolved state of tense ambivalence" (Konstantinov 1997, 15), and Buryatiya is no exception. What follows is one such stance, which, though it might not find universal approval in the district, is rather influential, since it is espoused by powerful local administrators and farm leaders of a reformist bent. What is interesting about this is that it is both market-oriented and also a strong statement of political ideas which invoke categories and values of historical Buryat culture. At the same time, there is a strong breath of Sovietism about the

492

idea. Badmaev, a high District (*raion*) Administrator for Barguzin, and Tolui, the Local Administrator for Bayangol, mentioned earlier, explained to me their plans for creating "*Shtat* Bayangol" (the State of Bayangol).

"If we just wait for things to happen," said Badmaev, "we shall continue to decline economically. The district government must take action to put a new system of relations in practise. You know that the Kuitun arable lands are shared now by three collectives, Ulyun, Khilganai, and Bayangol. My plan is to establish a massive grain enterprise over the whole of Kuitun, and it definitely would be profitable because we have experienced agronomists who understand the soils and rotation systems for this high tableland. This enterprise will be linked with small livestock units in the lower lands surrounding the Kuitun. They will have shares in the enterprise."

"You know in the United States there is the State of Texas, the State of Colorado, and so on? The State of Bayangol will be like that, a political subject in its own right. It will have its own government and militia and be able to raise its own taxes; not only will it have its machine-tractor park but also all services, including repair worshops, transport, petrol station, food processing, dormitories, a hotel, a mill, a bakery, everything. We will give them power (*vlast'*) and their own budget. There will be a Governor who will be both the representative of the population and the executive in charge of self-government (*samoupravleniye*)."

"The basis will be the Land Codex and land shares (*pai*) distributed to the whole population, to the pensioners, teachers too, all of them. They will give their shares to the enterprise and receive grain, straw, fodder, and so forth as their dividend. You know this is already starting to happen, in Karasun, Urzhil, and the Bodonskii State Farm. The advantages here will be the concentration of technology, reduced transport costs, unified storage, and processing of grains, and this will revive the economy, give more work to the people, and make the district self-sufficient in grain. If we divide off the arable part, then all the livestock units will be left. We cannot live like Chinese peasants, each on our 12 hectares, each the master of the backyard; already the people are pushing beyond the *dvor'ya*. We shall go for middling sized farms, 100 head of cattle or so, like a big *kulak* economy. This means that we have to change the psychological attitude to wage labour. In Soviet times we thought of the *batrak* (labourer) as a type of slave. But here the workers and everyone else will consist of kinsmen, brothers and sisters, and we will educate them about the usefulness of seasonal jobs."

Here Tolui broke in on the conversation: "If we look to history the *darga* (B. 'boss') was always surrounded by seasonal workers – *hulumsha,* they were called. The master employed them in summer and gave them enough to live on through the year, their *üüse* meat for winter, their clothes, and so on, because they did not have their own livestock. In April, when all their food was finished, there was *tolgoi gargaha* (B. 'put out head'), which meant they came and

493

stood at their gates silently – their Buryat conscience would not allow them to ask for food – and the people going past gave them charity (*podachki*). They were waiting for the "green doctor," the grass, to appear, and then they would be hired again. That is how feudal things were here. Now we'll come to this again, because this kind of people exists among us, the *hulumsha*. They don't work, run around the village, get drunk, violate discipline, and steal, but the instance of history shows that they can be transformed into workers."

Badmaev then resumed: "This is the realisation of the principle of the self-supporting, self-regulating governmental system. Moscow is promoting this policy, but the Buryat Republic has not taken it to the people. At present all the power stops at the district (*raion*) level; it is blocked there by conservatives. But the logical process is to take it right to the people at the local level, so we can say to them, 'We gave you power, so why don't you use it, why don't you work for yourselves?' They'll find out for themselves what is profitable, they'll make their own business plans, and the *raion* will stand back and just help them with marketing and training. At present we administrators receive all the blows from above for failures and nothing but demands for resources from below. So we must carry forward the principle of self-development to the villages, and I am convinced it is immanent, brewing. For me, as a new person, I think this is a revolutionary thing, but it is not simple, because we'll have to explain it, propagandize, give support . . . there are difficulties."

This conversation was interrupted by the arrival of 48 workers from the Butter Factory, who had come to receive their land shares. They were to receive 2.7 hectares of hay meadow, 3.5 of arable land, and 8 of pasture. These shares would be handed over to the factory, which itself operated a farm it seems, and in return the shareholders would hope for dividends in butter. "So you see, the process is under way," said Tolui.

The implementation of the State of Bayangol was evidently held up by the status quo in Barguzin district: the reluctance of other *raion* administrators to hand over power, the existing structure of collectives, and the tendency for units of production and exchange to appear at lower levels (the Butter Factory, the arable brigade within a collective, etc.). Nevertheless, the idea of a State based on shareholding is significant, because what is happening here is the diversion of the reformist economic idea of shares away from a purely capitalist trajectory and its re-creation as the basis for a total institution in the local political economy. This is not seen as, and could not be, simply a re-creation of the early twentieth century, prerevolutionary situation. With all its emphasis on kin-based membership and resurrection of the *kulak* and *hulumsha* (incidentally, I was told the *hulumsha* was often the son-in-law of the *kulak*), the plan is intended as a powerful interception in the harsh contemporary conditions of Buryatiya.

The concept of *Shtat* Bayangol has Soviet aspects (the initiative from above, the rhetoric of discipline, the emphasis on economic development). At the same time, the State here, in my view, relates to the ancient and very widespread

494

Shares (khubi) in the cultural practises of Mongolian peoples

practise in Mongolian cultures of rule through "shares" (*khubi*).[35] The medieval practise – as opposed, say, to European feudalism – was that an individual had *unconditional* rights to a share and also owed service as a matter of course, by virtue of membership in the polity.[36] It is not possible here to give an adequate explanation of why this practise has surfaced again and again in inner Asian history. Its functionality in relation to mobile pastoralism must be one aspect (Sneath, in press), and another, in the case of the Buryats, is related to their positional status in the Tsarist and Soviet regimes. Today, although it is reappearing in a world inhabited by commercial discourses, the shareholding polity does not seem to explicitly contest them. Indeed, it may colour itself in the foreign guise of the business plan; nevertheless, it subverts one-dimensional rationality in an inseparable whole of the political, economic, ritual, and psychological.

Shares (khubi) in the cultural practises of Mongolian peoples

Khubi means share, lot, portion, part, feudal appanage, share of familial inheritance, and also fate or destiny. Chingghis Khan's divisions of his state, the *ulus* or "people," were appanages allotted to his sons, nephews, wives, and other subrulers in the imperial family (Jagchid and Hyer 1979, 252). Kinship and politics were inseparable in this medieval state. Inclusiveness was produced by the oath of loyalty to a senior, while independent contractual agreements between equal individuals were weak. A similar principle operating in various local contexts appeared in later history, especially among the Buryats, where rule by clan-based aristocrats lasted into the twentieth century.[37] The Buryats were governed by indirect rule under their own chosen leaders and by means of clans (*rody*), which were the tax-paying units. The local community, the scattered homesteads of a river valley (p. 273), was called both *ulus* (in Mongolian the whole nation) and *ail* (in Mongolian the domestic group), which suggests the relative, fractal nature of social concepts. Essentially, the smallest group (*-tang*) was seen as a microcosm of the whole (Sydenova 1992, 13).

By the nineteenth century shares (*khubi*) in Buryatiya came to operate at the level of allotments of hay and arable land to each family on the basis of their membership in a clan. Pasture was common to the whole group, while livestock was owned by each family. Such land distributions were made by a meeting of the whole community in some places, in others by a chosen leader, and among the great widespread tribe of the Khori by the hierarchy of genealogically senior "princes" and "lords." The principle, however, was the same everywhere: the people had a right to a portion of the land of a whole subpolity by virtue of birth into a given clan-community, while the community as a whole was responsible for paying taxes to the state.

The principle of the share was relative, so the amount one received changed during one's lifetime. In general, land was allotted according to the number of

495

sons in the domestic group and the size of the herds. Aristocrats and seniors generally had superior land, however, and if they cleared an arable field they were not required to give it back for reallotment unless the line died out (p. 29). The idea of the relativity of relations also applied in kinship, in which one was always senior to someone else, junior to another, and similarly a person's kinship status changed through time.

Shares also worked in other institutional settings in which other kinds of property were at issue. Thus, in Buddhist monasteries the Khori Buryat law of 1851 states that, while some of the laypeople's donations should be set aside for the upkeep of the monastery (food and housing for the lamas, the purchase of holy books, etc.):

The order of distribution of income not set aside for the monastery should accord with the ritual of religious services in conformance with the hierarchical divisions, namely: the Head of Lama should receive seven shares; the Shiretu six; the Latsab, Tsorzhi and Shanzotba five; the Zasak, Da, Nansu and Soiban four; the Geik, Umzaat, and Nirba three; the Takhilchi, Duganchi, Zhama and Soiban two; and the lamas without posts or the title of Khuvarag, one. (Tsibikova 1992, 93)

In Inner Mongolia (China) the start of collectivisation saw the emergence of cooperatives also using a share principle. Here the distribution of livestock, rather than hay and agricultural land, was the issue. Sneath (in press) reports that the stock acquired by Producers' Cooperatives set up in the late 1950s was considered as the shares of the herders, so the original owner received a proportion of the produce equal to the number of animals he submitted. This system was not particularly opposed by the Mongols, and it was not detrimental to the interests of the wealthy families. The owner got a large proportion of the produce of his animal shares, but the actual herding was done by ordinary herdsmen who had taken jobs in the cooperative. Sneath comments:

In effect, as an arrangement, it was remarkably similar to the traditional *süreg* method of leasing animals. It provided poor pastoralists with access to livestock they did not own, and the livestock owner with an income from animals that he did not have the domestic labour to herd himself. Each family retained the ownership and management of some livestock for "subsistence," and although the exact number of animals that could be kept in this way is not mentioned, it was said to be related to what the family concerned could herd.

What did arouse intense hostility throughout the Mongol world was the commune, which ironed out all differences and insisted on keeping everyone equal.

In all three cases the late-nineteenth-century Buryat farmers, the Buddhist lamas, and the Inner Mongolian herders, there is a social "whole" within which a certain asset (land, donations, livestock, produce) is allocated according to a notion of shares. Membership in the given group confers enough resources for life, but above that the system of shares is not egalitarian. The social hierarchy in terms of which shares are allotted is different in these three examples

496

(kinship status, religious seniority, wealth), and in no case are shares equal. The concordance of this principle with that of the classic collective farm, in which the status of given types of labour was the crucial value, is evident.

In a wider context the operative political idea was that of a community, rather than an individual, relation with the state. Thus, it was the Buryat community which was responsible for tax in the nineteenth century.[38] The Tsarist state dealt with such communities through the intermediary of their leaders, who were elders of the clans. Clans as fiscal units were fixed early in the nineteenth century and, despite the expanding and mobile population, remained remarkably conservative. As a result, taxes might have to be collected from clan members scattered elsewhere, or people moved and changed their clans. The inertia of Tsarist administration fitted remarkably well, however, with Buryat concepts, for in indigenous views the clan's relation to its land was essentially sacred.[39] Within the community land was allotted and reallocated in nonpermanent rights of use (with the increasing exception of the aristocrats), but the ownership of the whole was constant and structured by the patriline of the titular clan. This was validated on the one hand by sacrifices to land spirit-ancestors, and on the other it was politically confirmed by the joint payment of dues to the state via the clan elders. Far-flung clan members would make offerings to the spirits of their new lands, but they considered the original clan territory in some sense "theirs" too and would return to attend ritual sacrifices (*tailagan*).

Sacrifice and sharing

This sacred relation of clan-polities to land is the reason for the centrality of sacrifices to land spirits (ancestors) in cultural practises of the Mongolian peoples. From the earliest Mongol history there are accounts which show the role of sacrifice in determining who is a member of the community or not, i.e., the political importance of sacrifice. For example, in the thirteenth century *Secret History of the Mongols,* Hö'elun, mother of the future Chingghis Khan, is cheated of her share of the fortune (*kesig*) of the sacrificial meat and wines offered to the ancestral land masters by the Taichi'ud clan.[40] Hö'elun arrived late, was left without her share, told her destiny was to eat only what happened to be around, and abandoned by the rest of the clan to bring up her sons alone. This famous event, the cause of the future Chingghis Khan's hard childhood, is often interpreted merely as a familial quarrel sparked off by the death of Hö'elun's husband and Chingghis's father, Yesügei. But the fact that Yesügei had gathered the Mongol clans together and that the lineages involved, Yesügei's (the genealogically senior) and the Taichi'ud (the junior but suddenly more powerful), had both provided Khans of the Mongol *ulus* in previous generations, shows that greater political issues were at stake (Even and Pop 1994, 263).

One might think that such an ancient account would have nothing to do with contemporary Buryatiya were it not that there are records of such sacrifices to

497

land spirits throughout Mongolian history and that the same term *kesig* (*khesheg,* fortune, blessing; pp. 437–8) is used to this day across the region. As for the Buryat practise in the nineteenth century, attendance at the *tailagan* sacrifice was regarded as obligatory, and to get one's portion (*khubi*) of sacred meat was a matter of the honour of the family. Not to attend was not only to break with ancestral tradition but also risked offending the spirits and therefore causing misfortune. In some cases unequal shares were contributed,[41] though everyone clearly ate their fill at such feasts. Nevertheless, it is evident that what is consumed at sacrifices cannot be "equal." This is because the animals sacrificed, horses and sheep in the Buryat case, consist of symbolically disparately valued parts.[42] All Inner Asian cultures seem to make elaborate categorisations of limbs and organs, and in sacrifices these are separately listed and commended to the spirits then distributed to people of appropriate status. In fact, the same is true of the familial meal when an animal is killed (which is always somewhat ritualised and always something of a festivity). A rib cannot be "the same" as stomach fat: people know the different taste, consistency, deliciousness, and *significance* of each type of meat. The meat is never served out in individual portions but is placed on a large common platter. The host first offers appropriate parts to his guests according to their status, and then people help themselves.

What the sacrifice instantiates is the idea of the insider polity, with a hierarchy which is legitimate because it is collective. This idea contrasts with individual, uncontrollable inequality, the frightening alternative which has flooded in since the collapse of Communism.

The person and identity

This cryptic remark can perhaps be explained by the fact that the idea of sharing in a whole is essential to the concept of the person (the socially recognised idea of the individual). The person in Buryat culture has several kinds of essential identity (which we might call "souls"), only one of which ceases to exist at death. Another part of the person may become a spirit inhabiting the natural world (a cliff, a tree, a mountain), while another may be reborn in subsequent generations (see Humphrey 1996, for further discussion).[43] Such ideas attached people both to specific places and to previous generations by directly felt ties (one may oneself be the reincarnation of a great-grandmother; one's well-remembered deceased uncle might have his spirit inhabiting a rock). The person is not a single, separate unit but is understood as a part, like a bone in a skeleton,[44] or in the case of *oboo* rituals (and this is my own expression) like a molecule in an organism which self-reproduces through the generations. Perhaps it is for this reason that when Buryats are exposed to individualist ideas they often alter them; for example, the Buddhist idea of *karma,* classically referring to individual moral actions, is interestingly overlaid in Buryat thought by "collective *karma*" (Galdanova 1992, 156; Urbanayeva 1997).[45]

The leader

Mobility and relativity were also intrinsic to such concepts, as the Buryat philosopher Morokhoyeva observes (1992), and this corresponded to the Mongol-Buryat transhumant economic existence with herds. In such a way of life there were two culturally recognised means of having knowledge, an interior seeing, which accompanied one everywhere, and an external surveying, which became more complete the more comprehensive one's movements were. This is why the archetypal hero of Mongolian and Buryat epics has two types of helper, unifying the idea of knowledge in one term, the *mergen,* the wise thinker, and the *mergen,* the keen-eyed, unfailing archer. Morokhoyeva (1992, 95) writes that, if all things should be seen from all points of view and also known "within," then the individual experiences each object as a microcosm within a macrocosm. She further comments that the person, comprehending the world as a relatively placed, mobile observer, must also take into account where the observer is and the self's sited perception of the world. This site is given by kinship, in which one's position changes through life by one's own actions and as others marry and have children around one (a "stable instability"). The worship of the ancestors is the essential act in which the individual gets his "face," his place in the social categorisation of the world. In this context one's *khubi* (share, destiny) is both inevitable, unconditional, relative, and immediate (specific in time). We may conclude from this that the *khubi* defines the person as not separable from the whole. As Morokhoyeva notes (1992, 97), *khubi* on no account represents a part taken out and distanced, for which there is another Buryat word, *tahag,* from the verb *taha,* "to break off."

The relation of such ideas to identity is exemplified in an account given to me in 1996. A man from Bayangol said that his uncle had recently died. As he lay ill, the old man asked, "Who am I?" He wanted to be reminded and reassured of his place in the world. The family asked a young man, a genealogical expert, to help them. He sat for three days by the bedside, explaining every last link, and the old man died at peace.

The leader

The social whole of which the person is a part is a speculative entity, in the sense that it can be represented by various icons and symbolic (or real) personifications of the wholeness. The founding ancestor, the Khan, the mythical hero, the mountain spirit, the leader, are all possible personifications, and they are often conflated. If the social whole seen in this way can be a tiny group, it can also be a large agglomerate or a nation, as we see from Hamayon's discussion (1996) of the mythic epic hero as the focus for contemporary Buryat nationalism. I would like now to turn briefly to another of the Mongol peoples, the Kalmyk, to integrate some of the themes discussed in this chapter.

Like the Buryats, the Kalmyks are a Buddhist offshoot from Mongolia who have lived in Russian surroundings for centuries, and today many relations link

499

the two peoples.[46] The Kalmyks have recently elected a charismatic young native President, Kirsan Ilyumzhinov, and his devotees are warmly invited to Buryatiya to tell of his creation of a newly inspirational Eurasian kind of state. His enormous popularity among Kalmyks has survived all criticisms in the Russian press of his high-handed rule, suppression of opposition, and business misdoings. This example illustrates the way in which the notion of the leader-focussed polity (a heroic, magnified variant as compared with the workaday State of Bayangol) is integrated with indigenous culture and Soviet experience to produce a nation as an actor in the post-Soviet political arena.

After a period of bureaucratic rule between 1989–93, which provoked only apathy among the Kalmyks, Ilyumzhinov, a young and handsome millionaire, was elected President in April 1993. The source of his funds is shrouded in mystery, but, with his degree in Japanese, his contacts with the Pope and the Dalai Lama, and his headship of the International Chess Federation, he puts his wealth to spectacular global use. The Kalmyk author Guchinova explains why the Kalmyks, who, like the Buryats, are one of the poorest peoples of Russia, support Ilyumzhinov (1996, 300):

Today, like other nations of the former USSR, the Kalmyks lack deep feelings of personal initiative and responsibility, and sometimes have a wrong conception of freedom. Political life, the value of personal freedom, the habit not to expect everything, good and bad, from the government are still alien to many Kalmyks. They tend to identify their destiny with supreme state power.

Guchinova explains this mentality partly by the Kalmyk experience of deportation and dispersal under the Soviets.[47] The leader therefore has the responsibility of rallying and unifying the people. "As a consequence," Guchinova writes, "authoritarianism is perceived not only as a desirable but even as an inevitable form of government" (1996, 301). It became habitual for Kalmyks to show respectfulness to their superiors. Opposition as a mode of social behaviour is not approved. The political sympathies of the majority of the people are oriented not toward parties and their programs but toward specific persons.

Ilyumzhinov's election campaign made direct reference to the first model of a state for the Kalmyks, the Kalmyk Khanate within the Russian Empire. He proclaimed, "The people need a khan, then I'll be that khan," as a pleasantry, but Guchinova observes that the khan-exemplar in fact guides him as he assumes personal responsibility for all victories, failures, and prosperity of his people, makes much of his ancestry, and settles quarrels between clans. In popular verses he is even perceived as granted by God, not unlike Chingghis Khan:

Sent by God, sweet envoy!
The grandson of the most worthy of the sons.
Today you are not only a great man,
But the hope of the whole Kalmykia!

(Guchinova 1996, 303)

500

Like the khan, his actions and appraisal are unpredictable, and his selection of personnel works through ties of kinship or friendship (Guchinova 1996, 302). Another Kalmyk devotee of Ilyumzhinov describes how he exemplifies the qualities of the epic hero Jangar and how he has introduced studies of this epic into all schools, along with the Kalmyk native version of chess. Interestingly, pupils are encouraged to play chess collectively ("a collective training of the mind, spirit and will towards life and victory" [Mukayeva 1997, 47]), an initiative which has been taken up by Buryats.[48] The concept stressed in these Kalmyk publications, and approvingly supported by some Buryat intellectuals, is the idea of the nation as an earthly union of its peoples ruled by the Spirit to conduct a "wise life." The Spirit "derives from centuries of indigenous culture." This idea is startling in the post-Soviet context, in which generations have been taught that the material mode of life determines consciousness. In sum, the new Kalmyk state is an exemplar not only of the personal leadership–based state but also of the idea of the leader as the channel of inspiration and morality, which the people receive and carry out.

In Ilyumzhinov the fabulously wealthy patron, the patri-kin-based hierarchy, the epic hero, the emphasis on collectivity, and the idea of the model-exemplar whom others should follow in miniature, are brought together. This may seem very distant from the Buryat collective farms. The recent election of the famous singer Kobzon as the Aga Buryat deputy to the Moscow Duma, however, is similar in some ways. Kobzon is far from being a native of Aga, but he is extremely rich, an international figure, a patron of culture, and influential in Moscow government and Mafia circles.[49] The proposed collective at Soyol is even more like a minuscule version of the Kalmyk-type polity, with its supranational, global hero (the Olympic wrestler), the patron who knows how to make money in the capitalist world, the inclusive collectivity, the rituals to clan ancestors, the respect for religion and the land spirit. Enquiring further, I discovered that, although each rural Buryat community may not have found an economic patron, they do each take pride in a similar glorious, representative figure of their own: a five-star general here, a well-known actor there, a famous surgeon, and so forth. These stars are called *kumir naroda,* which is one of those Soviet expressions that is difficult to translate into English. Literally, "idol of the people," *kumir* is one worthy of respect, devotion, and love, while *narod* connotes the populace, faithful, devout, brave, simple, honest, and all-enduring (Ries 1997, 28).[50] These iconic figures alive today recall, in an ideational sense, the ancestors so carefully recalled in the genealogies (since they will be the famous ancestors of future generations), and they function to represent the real, day-to-day identities which Buryats use when meeting one another: "I come from such-and-such a village where X [a famous name] comes from. . . ."[51]

I hope it is clear that I am not suggesting the appearance of some archaic *system* (Oriental Despotism or the Asiatic Mode of Production!) in the Russian hinterlands. It is more a question here of diverse, but sometimes overlapping, discourses and practises, which may in the future take a number of forms. In pointing out that villagers and collectives take part in sacrificial cults that maintain ties to land, create insiders and outsiders, and channel "fortune" to the people and that, at the same time, they exist in a harsh, de-ideologized, globalised world in which patronage and inspiration are at a premium, I am doing no more than suggesting a parallel; a reconfiguration in which religious practises that used to be antithetical to state-dominated practical life are now part of it.

Conclusion

It is time now to draw the threads together. In the previous chapter I concluded that rural Buryats will keep collectives of some kind if they possibly can and that these look as though they will be founded either on the principle of the contract or that of shareholders in a collectivity. The contract is an idea weakly emphasized in indigenous culture, and it depends for its implementation on a functioning system of law. Buryats are generally a highly educated people and familiar with European culture in its Russian variant, so handling contracts would present no problem in the abstract, but the actual situation is that the law of contracts does not function and people have to rely on personal trust for contracts to be fulfilled. If collectives are to be retained, this situation immediately places the shareholding option in the forefront, as such an institution is founded on mutual trust within preexisting social relations that delimit a person's status and access to shares. An example of this was seen in the Baragkhan State Farm, where local people approved of the young woman Director's plans to implement shareholding on the basis of work contributions largely because they trusted her to distribute dividends fairly.

This chapter has attempted to describe the cultural ideas within which hierarchical shareholding has its place. It was shown that religious cults express the inhabitants' sense of their ownership of land and that these cults may reflect the divisiveness or cohesiveness of the communities. A shamanic cult in the Selenga Karl Marx collective was Buddhicised and thus made inclusive of all Buryat villagers, while no such development occurred in the more divided OKKh Bayangol. Ancestral cults do not, however, exactly coincide with economic or political groupings and movements. Rather, they provide exemplary notions which people may actively use in other contexts (or, indeed, which they may ignore, against social pressure). For example, there is the notion of submission (to the will of the unseen ancestral spirit) and the idea of accepting one social place defined by distribution at the sacrifices. It is interesting that the Emege-Eezhi cult in Tashir defines hierarchy by age, rather than by genealogical status or gender, and this is a case of adapting the principle to the contemporary value of communitarian inclusiveness. As was shown earlier, the village services founded by the socialist regime are included in the sphere of spiritual influence, aided by the notion of *collective* accumulation of *karma.*

The ancestor spirit is the owner, or master (*ezhen*), of the land, a term related to the verb *ezhele,* "to rule." Here we can see how different are indigenous from European concepts of property. Yet they accord rather well with the Soviet practise, in which all productive property belonged to the state and yet was clearly felt to "be mine" by directors at various points in the hierarchy. I suggest that ownership and rulership could coincide in such cases, because the idea of the ruler was both representative and executive. In the State of Bayangol the Governor is both to represent all the people – i.e., to stand for the idea of the whole community – and to rule this community. In such a collective the Director is right to think that everything is his or hers. And at the same time the people are right to think that the Director is "theirs," i.e., that they can call on him or her personally to answer their needs, as I saw in the office of the Chairman of the Karl Marx Collective in Selenga, where a line of petitioners came endlessly, one after another. The still surviving (in some places) totality of the community is seen by the fact that the collective actually supports all inhabitants, not just working members, and petitioners for flour include pensioners and mothers whose benefits should actually come from the state. In fact, the collective often still acts like a substitute for the state, and where it does not, it is felt that it should do so. It is therefore not surprising that plans in rural areas include the establishing of new, mega-collectives as small self-governing "states" and that kinship, shares, power (*vlast'*), and hierarchy are their basis.

Most of Buryatiya cannot go the way of the heroic polity, if only for the prosaic reason that there are not enough patrons. As I have also shown, there are also tendencies toward subdivision and use of contracts which employ different principles from that of the hierarchical polity. If the monopolistic Products Corporation and state subsidies for chosen farms are important in keeping the collectives going as integral wholes, independent barter contracts taken out by production units between one another create another set of relations based on the self-interest of either side. Such relations are said to be stressful. Kinship networks and associations are employed where possible just because of the prevailing mistrust. It is not clear that collectives will be able to overcome a tendency found in many places to narrow cooperation to the smallest units of trust, the *-tang* groups of families known by their nicknames. In some areas (e.g., Chitkan) collectives have almost ground to a halt for lack of wider social confidence, whereas in others the members are making contributions into them, to ensure their survival.

Since funds are the lifeblood of power, it is probable that the Republic government will continue to direct its attention upward to Moscow, from whence come the vital credits. Like enactments below, the recent "high" negotiations of extraordinary transfers for Buryatiya were conducted personally between the President of the Republic, Potapov, and Chernomyrdin and Yeltsin. In such funding flows agriculture has a weak bargaining position: it is difficult to see how the price scissors that depress agricultural production can be changed. Therefore, a sober assessment has to be that the agricultural, and especially the livestock economy, will continue to operate with utmost difficulty and at a loss as far as the monetised economy goes.

Nevertheless, despite this contradictory picture, I submit that the political inclinations of most rural Buryats may be akin to those in Kalmykia. As it is, they explain what might look to outsiders like economic events, such as the setting up and closing down of privatised farms, not by economic motivations but entirely politically. "If they had not been pushed forward by the politicians, there would be no private farmers," say the people of Tory (Manzanova 1997). In fact, this is not just an opinion – the people of Tory are probably right: Russia has been since Soviet times, and still is in places like Buryatiya, a country where it is power, more than economic interests, that initiates and rules. Thus, it is a crucial fact about the famous wrestler who is patron of the village of Soyol that he is "very influential in government circles."

It is also important that the patron is a wrestler and that a sportsman can be glorious – a *kumir*. Perhaps this is where the Mongolian cultures meet and interlock with the global culture seen on TV. The "manly games" always had a ritualised, supernatural significance; as part of the *oboo* festivals, they were the enactment of virile strength that gave evidence of the flourishing of the people (see Hamayon 1996, on the close relation between the manly games and the epic hero). Even now, in hard times, rural collectives and city firms make large donations to support wrestling prizes and tournaments. In autumn 1996 the collective at Baragkhan was host to an all-Republic contest for which the main prize was donated by a former wrestler called Tsyrenov. Tsyrenov's biography exemplifies the parallels I am drawing: born in Baragkhan, he achieved glory in the Moscow Olympics in 1980; then, after a spell as a trainer, he became Chief Engineer in a collective farm in Irkutsk Oblast; after a short period in the Party bureaucracy he was elected, in 1987, Chairman of the Lenin Collective Farm in Baragkhan. Succeeded there by the young woman Chair mentioned earlier, he has moved to work for Arig Us, which is one of the two great capitalist conglomerates in Buryatiya and sells oil throughout Siberia. Arig Us is the financial sponsor for the games.[52]

In the abstract this story could have been a disaster. Is there anywhere else an ex-wrestler would seem a natural choice to manage a huge farm with hundreds of workers? But the logic of the Buryat situation is different. The wrestler-Chairman-patron is one of the reasons why the Lenin farmworkers have done so well: it is not just the efficient agronomist and not just the energetic, well-connected young Chair; it is the sense of being part of something inspired and worthy, connected to Power and Money, and resting on sacred territory.[53]

A Buryat writer has recently suggested that Buryats face three options: as-

504

similation into Russian/European culture, retiring into their villages to "quietly die out," or creating a new society based "not only on re-creation of past values and symbols, not only on the cleansing of individual and collective *karma,* but also on the renaissance of the Clear Light of *dharma* in consciousness" (Urbanayeva 1997, 13). The words were written by an urban intellectual, but they are echoed in rural newspapers[54] and, less pretentiously, in what people say. There are real struggles of Buryat people to transcend the mere struggle for existence and to achieve spiritual values. It is remarkable that at the end of 1996 contributions were made by practically every institution – state, private, and collective – in the valley of Barguzin, and from countless individuals, to fund a celebration in memory of Soodei Lama at the refurbished district monastery.[55] Carefully listed in the local paper (the Lenin collective at Baragkhan gave four tons of grain to pay painters, the Murgunskii collective gave 3 litres of sour cream and 20 litres of milk, the residents of Bayangol gave 325,000 rubles, the school at Bayangol gave two sheep, etc.), the whole valley by its generosity would "plant fruitful seeds in its *karma* and create the preconditions for Soodei Lama to be reborn again with us here."[56] Soodei Lama had the supernatural ability to tell the future, and to this day his predictions are handed down by word of mouth. It seems to me that we cannot understand Buryat rural life without taking into account such phenomena. Here I am not suggesting, as I did in the example of Tsyrenov and the Baragkhan farm, that there is a direct connection between a *kumir* and a collective or any particular group. Rather, Soodei Lama is an example of the principle of the great man "whom Buryats gave to the world,"[57] an outward, non-self-referential projection of greatness necessary to sustain the aura of the *kumir* concept as such.

A sober assessment of present trends in the Buryat countryside would predict that nothing will change very fast; that there will be a gradual decline of rural population as the rest of the economy starts to improve; that the regions near towns will see the emergence of economic classes based on land possession, because land will come to have value even if it cannot be formally privately owned; and that far distant villages may be abandoned altogether (like Udunga in the Selenga Karl Marx Collective). But it is also possible that in many places successful collective farms will survive, or be created, on the basis of village communities. In these cases the idea of hierarchical shareholding, which entails an inspirational representation of the collectivity, may well be the one that is chosen as a model.

Notes

The following abbreviations are used in the Notes and References.

AN SSSR	Akademiya Nauk of the USSR
BF	Buryatskii Filial
BION	Buryatskii Institut Obshchestvennykh Nauk
BKI	Buryatskoye Knizhnoye Izdatel'stvo
BKNII	Buryatskii Kompleksnyi Nauchno-Issledovatel'skii Institut
B-MASSR	Buryat-Mongol ASSR
B-MKI	Buryat-Mongolskoye Knizhnoye Izdatel'stvo
B-MNIIK	Buryat-Mongolskii Nauchno-Issledovatel'skii Institut Kul'tury
BNKh	Buryaadai Nomoi Kheblel
HRAF	Human Relations Area Files
Izd.	Izdatel'stvo
KNIIFE	Kalmytskii Nauchno-Issledovatel'skii Institut Istorii, Filologii i Ekonomiki
Min. Pros.	Ministerstvo Prosveshcheniya
SO	Sibirskoye Otdeleniye
VSORGO	Vostochno-Sibirskoye Otdeleniye Russkogo Geograficheskogo Obshchestva
YF	Yakutskii Filial
YKI	Yakustoye Knizhnoye Izdatel'stvo

Introduction

1 I follow McAuley in using the term 'state' to refer to the Soviets, Ministries and Communist Party as one structure. Mary McAuley, *Politics and the Soviet Union*, Penguin, Harmondsworth, 1977, p. 209.

2 For example, G. Klaus, *Kibernetika i obshchestvo* (Cybernetics and society), Moscow, 1967; also works by A.M. Rumyantsev, V.A. Trapeznikov, A.M. Yeremin, and others.

3 A.D. Elyakov, 'Printsip iyerarkhichnosti v upravlenii sotsialisticheskom obshchestvom' (The principle of hierarchy in the government of socialist society), MSS p. 56.

4 For comparable studies see: C.M. Hann, *Tázlár: a Village in Hungary*, Cambridge University Press, Cambridge, 1980; S.F. Moore and B.G. Meyerhoff (eds.), *Symbol and Politics in Communal Ideology*, Cornell University Press, Ithaca and London, 1975. A descriptive account of comparable col-

506

lective farms is given in S. Rimsky-Korsakoff Dyer, *Soviet Dungan Kolkhozes in the Kirghiz SSR and the Kazakh SSR*, Oriental Monograph Series no. 25, ANU, Canberra, 1979.

5   V.I. Lenin, *Pol'niye sobraniye sochinenii* (Full collected works), Moscow, vol. 36, p. 171.

6   The 'command model' of Soviet society was dominant in political sociology until recently. It conceptualised Soviet society as totalitarian (albeit without terror since the Stalinist period), even social change being imposed unwanted by the constituents. This model is discussed in detail and challenged by Hough, who proposes instead a modified pluralist view of Soviet society and advocates a comparative approach (Jerry F. Hough, *The Soviet Union and Social Science Theory*, Harvard University Press, Cambridge, Mass., 1977). Other sociological models are discussed by David Lane, *The End of Inequality? Stratification under State Socialism*, Penguin, Harmondsworth, 1971a, and M. Matthews, *Class and Society in Soviet Russia*, Allen Lane, London, 1972.

7   Max Gluckman, *The Ideas in Barotse Jurisprudence*, Manchester University Press, Manchester, 1972, pp. 75—112.

8   But I.A. Asalkhanov documents in many of his works the beginnings of 'non-industrial capitalism' among Buryats in the late nineteenth century, particularly among those living near the towns. I.A. Asalkhanov, 'Vliyaniye vklyucheniya buryatii v sostav rossii na khozyaistvennoye i obshchestvennoye razvitye buryat' (The influence of the inclusion of Buryatia in Russia on the economic and social development of the Buryats), *Trudy BKNII SO AN SSSR* (Ulan-Ude), 1, 1959, pp. 21—38.

9   The *buluk* usually contained several clans or lineages; for further discussion see Chapter 1 section 4. I.A. Asalkhanov, 'O buryatskikh rodakh v XIX veke' (On Buryat clans in the nineteenth century), *Etnograficheskii Sbornik* (Ulan-Ude), 1, 1960a, pp. 68—81.

10   Max Gluckman 1972, p. 92.

11   Leszek Kolakowski, 'Permanent and transitory aspects of Marxism', in Leszek Kolakowski, *Marxism and Beyond*, Paladin, London, 1971, pp. 191—2.

12   *Ibid.*, p. 182.

13   Maurice Bloch, 'Symbol, song and dance, or is religion an extreme form of traditional authority', *European Journal of Sociology* (Paris), 1974.

14   Jack Goody, *Death, Property and the Ancestors*, Stanford University Press, Stanford, 1962, p. 286.

15   Meyer Fortes, *The Web of Kinship among the Tallensi*, Oxford University Press, London, 1949, p. 305.

16   A.M. Emel'yanov (ed.), *Osnovy ekonomiki i upravleniya sel'skokhozyaistvennym proizvodstvom* (The foundations of economics and management in agricultural production), Ekonomika, Moscow, 1977, p. 74.

17   *Ibid.*, p. 77.

18   *Ibid.*, p. 75.

19   N.S. Tonayevskaya, *Rabochiye sovkhozov zapadnoi sibiri (1959—1965gg)* (Workers of the state farms of western Siberia 1959—1965), Nauka, Novosibirsk, 1978, p. 17.

20   For example, by splitting up unwieldy and over-large state farms, by price reforms, by supply of machinery, etc.

21   Emel'yanov 1977, pp. 75—6.

22 Tonayevskaya 1978, pp. 65—7. In 1930 the state farms of western Siberia had 13,100 permanent workers, 15,100 seasonal workers, and 12,800 temporary workers. By 1965 there were 530,000 permanent workers, and 34,800 seasonal and temporary workers.

23 *Ibid.*, p. 61. Cadres in state farms of the USSR are shown in the table. For a comparison with Buryat farms in the same period, see Chapter 4. By 1975 the numbers of chief specialists and ordinary specialists in Buryat state farms and collective farms were about equal per farm.

Personnel (%)	1950	1959	1965
Workers	91	95	94
Agronomists, zoo technicians, veterinarians, engineer-technicians	4	3	3
White-collar workers	3	1	2
Lower service personnel and guards	2	1	1

24 For example, by training of specialists and sending them to work in state farms, or by transforming collective farms into state farms.

25 Azizur Rahman Khan and Dharam Ghai, *Collective Agriculture and Rural Development in Soviet Central Asia*, Macmillan, London, 1979.

26 *Ibid.*, pp. 96—101; the Central Asia figures are for 1973, those for the USSR and for Buryatiya are for 1976.

27 I am grateful to Philip Lineton for unpublished information on the Khanti fishing kolkhoz. He visited this farm in 1975 and 1978.

28 The Central Asian output of cotton per hectare was the highest in the world in 1976 and exceeded that of the USA and China (Khan and Ghai 1979, p. 63). According to Lineton, the Khanti fishermen pulled in staggering netfuls of fish every time they checked their nets; the main work was in getting the fish back to the village.

29 The Ivolga *datsan* consists of several temples, stupas, and shrines, surrounded by the houses of the lamas. When I visited it, most of the lamas were elderly. Although they were prosperous from donations by believers, and many were building themselves new houses, few young men wanted to join them. By 1975 the attitude towards Buddhism on the part of the authorities, while remaining repressive towards unofficial activities — an important Buddhist leader, not an official lama, was imprisoned in that year — was more tolerant to the monastery itself, and several Buryat boys had been allowed to study at the religious school recently opened in Ulan-Bator. According to students in Ulan-Bator, there were many applicants for these places. Other Buryats had been sent to Ulan-Bator to study oriental theology from the academic point of view.

30 D.Ts. Urtyubayev, 'Molochnaya pishcha barguzinskikh buryat' (The milk foods of the Barguzin Buryat), *Etnograficheskii Sbornik* (Ulan-Ude), 2, 1961, pp. 137—40.

31 G.E. Dambayev, 'Sovremennoye zhilishche barguzinskikh buryat' (Contemporary dwellings of the Barguzin Buryats), *Etnograficheskii Sbornik* (Ulan-Ude), 5, 1969, pp. 11—15.

32   I.E. Tugutov, *Material'naya kul'tura buryat* (The material culture of the Buryats), BKI, Ulan-Ude, 1958. This book is primarily on the Selenga district.

33   E.R. Radnayev, 'Barguzinskii govor' (The Barguzin dialect), in Ts.B. Tsydendambayev and I.D. Burayev (eds.), *Issledovaniye Buryatskikh govorov* (The study of Buryat dialects), vol. 1, BKI, Ulan-Ude, 1965, pp. 71–106.

34   S.P. Baldayev, *Buryaad aradai duunuud* (Buryat folk songs), vol. 1, 1961, vol. 2, 1965, vol. 3, 1970, BNKh, Ulan-Ude, 1961–70.

35   Ts.B. Tsydendambayev, *Buryatskiye istoricheskiye khroniki i rodoslovnyye* (Buryat historical chronicles and genealogies), BKI, Ulan-Ude, 1972.

1 The Buryats and their surroundings

1   This point is disputed among Soviet archaeologists and physical anthropologists; see A.P. Okladnikov, *Yakutia, Before its Incorporation in the Russian State*, ed. H.M. Michael, Arctic Institute of America, no. 8, McGill–Queen's University Press, Montreal, 1970, and A.P. Okladnikov, *Ocherki iz istorii zapadnykh buryat-mongolov* (Sketches from the history of the western Buryat–Mongols), Leningrad, 1937.

2   The census figures for 1959 and 1970 are shown in the table.

	1959	1970	Difference
Number of Buryat population	135,789	178,660	+42,871
% of Buryat population in total of Buryat ASSR	20%	22%	+2%
Number of working (*zanyatogo*) Buryat population	51,941	65,859	+13,918
% of working Buryat population in working population of Buryat ASSR	18%	18%	0

Source: V.V. Belikov, 'Izmeneniye sotsial'no-klassovoi struktury naseleniya buryatii (1923–1970). (Changes in the social class structure of the population of Buryatiya, 1923–1970), in D.D. Lubsanov (ed.), *Iz opyta konkretno-sotsiologicheskikh issledovanii* (From the experience of concrete sociological investigations), BION, BKI, Ulan-Ude, 1974a, p. 144.

3   Jews and Chinese settled in Trans-Baikaliya during the nineteenth and early twentieth centuries primarily as traders.

4   The Tatars of Buryatiya, who live in small groups of from ten to twenty families scattered among the villages of the republic, are presumably Crimean Tatars, exiled from their homeland. I did not meet any Tatars, although they were living in both Selenga and Barguzin collective farms.

5   M.G. Levin and L.P. Potapov (eds.), *Narody Sibirii* (Peoples of Siberia), AN SSSR, Moscow–Leningrad, 1956, p. 224.

6   In the Aga National Okrug, with a population of 557,860 in 1970, there were representatives of sixteen nationalities. Buryats were 50.2% of the total, Russians 43.9%, and the others 5.9%. The great majority of the

population (79.2%) was rural. In the Ust'-Ordynsk National Okrug, Russians were 51.8% of the population, Buryats 34%, Ukrainians 7.4% and Tatars and others 5.1%.

7 See Owen Lattimore, *The Mongols of Manchuria*, John Day Company, New York, 1934, and K.M. Gerasimova *Obnovlencheskoye dvizheniye buryatskogo lamaistkogo dukhovenstva* (The reform/renewal movement of the Buryat Lamaist clergy), BKI, Ulan-Ude, 1964, p. 139. In 1929 about 2,000 households of Aga Buryats tried to emigrate to Barga, for example.

8 Robert A. Rupen, *Mongols of the Twentieth Century*, vol. 1, Indiana University Publications Uralic and Altaic Series no. 37 part 1, Mouton, The Hague, 1964, p. 33.

9 A.B. Tivanenko and V.G. Mitypov, *V taige za Baikalom* (In the taiga forest beyond Lake Baikal), BKI, Ulan-Ude, 1974, p. 29.

10 Rupen 1964, p. 33.

11 *Ibid.*, p. 33; Tivanenko and Mitypov 1974, p. 28.

12 Quoted in Rupen 1964, p. 33.

13 V.A. Tugolukov and A.S. Shubin, 'Kolkhoznoye stroitel'stvo u evenkov severnoi Buryatii i ego vliyaniye na ikh byt i kul'turu' (Collectivisation among the Evenki of northern Buryatiya and its influence on their way of life and culture), *Etnograficheskii Sbornik* (Ulan-Ude), 5, 1969, pp. 42—64.

14 M.G. Voskoboinikov, 'Evenki severnoi Buryatii' (Evenki of northern Buryatiya), *Etnograficheskii Sbornik* (Ulan-Ude), 1, 1960, p. 96.

15 I.V. Vlasova, 'Poseleniya Zabaikal'ya' (The settlements of Trans-Baikaliya) in I.V. Makovetskii (ed.), *Byt i isskustvo russkogo naseleniya vostochnoi Sibiri* (The way of life and art of the Russian population of eastern Siberia), vol. 2, *Trans-Baikaliya*, Nauka, Novosibirsk, 1975, pp. 21—2.

16 *Ibid.*, p. 22.

17 Owen Lattimore, 'Inner Asian frontiers: Chinese and Russian margins of expansion' in *Studies in Frontier History, Collected Papers 1928—58*, Oxford University Press, London, 1962, pp. 134—64.

18 Georgii Vinogradov, 'Zamechaniya o govorakh Tunkinskogo kraya' (Remarks on the ways of speech of Tunka district), *Buryatovedcheskii Sbornik*, 2, 1926, p. 21.

19 *Ütüg*, Buryat word for irrigated, fertilised hay-meadow.

20 See Sevyan Vainshtein, *Nomads of South Siberia*, Cambridge University Press, Cambridge, 1980, pp. 145—61.

21 N.V. Kim, 'Iz istoriya zemledeliya u buryat v kontse XVIII i pervoi polovine XIX veka' (From the history of agriculture among the Buryat at the end of the eighteenth and the first half of the nineteenth centuries), *Trudy BION* (Ulan-Ude), 5, 1967, p. 124.

22 Vlasova 1975, pp. 24—5.

23 I.A. Asalkhanov, 'Dorevolyutsionnyye sistemy zemledeliya u buryat' (Pre-revolutionary systems of agriculture among the Buryat), in V.I. Boiko *et al.* (eds.), *Rabochii klass i krest'yanstvo natsional'nykh raionov sibiri* (The working class and peasantry of national regions of Siberia), Nauka, Novosibirsk, 1974.

24 Vlasova 1975, pp. 25—6.

25 F.F. Bolonov, 'Ob izmeneniyakh v bytu i kul'ture russkogo (semeiskogo) naseleniya buryatii' (On the changes in way of life and culture of the Russian (Semeiskii) population of Buryatiya), *Etnograficheskii Sbornik* (Ulan-Ude), 5, 1969, pp. 29—30

26 T.M. Mikhailov, 'Vliyaniye lamaizma i khristiyanstva na shamanizm buryat' (The influence of Lamaism and Christianity on the shamanism of the Buryat), in I.S. Vdovin (ed.), *Khristianstvo i lamaizm u korennogo naseleniya sibiri*, Nauka, Leningrad, 1979, p. 138.

27 *Ibid.*, p. 129.

28 P.T. Khaptayev, 'Aimachnoye i antiaimachnoye dvizheniya' (The *aimak* and anti-*aimak* movements), *Trudy BKNII SO AN ASSR*, 10, 1962, pp. 99—107. Unfortunately it is impossible to give a full historical account of the politics of this period here.

29 In 1966 there were thirty-six monasteries (*datsan*) in Buryatiya, with a population of over 16,000 lamas, including trainees. Mikhailov, 1979, pp. 128—9.

30 Gerasimova 1964, pp. 152—4.

31 For discussion of this point see Alastair McAuley, *Economic Welfare in the Soviet Union*, George Allen and Unwin/University of Wisconsin Press, Madison, 1979, p. 36.

32 Belikov 1974a, p. 144.

33 McAuley 1979, pp. 35 and 40.

34 Vlasova 1975, p. 27.

35 For example the sovkhoz 'Kizhinginskii' in Buryat ASSR, which in 1971 had a national composition of: 75% Buryats, 18% Russians, 4% Tatars, and 3% other nationalities. V.V. Belikov, 'Sotsial'no-professional'nyi sostav rabotnikov sovkhoza "Kizhinginskii" ' (The socio-professional composition of the workforce of the 'Kizhinga' sovkhoz), *Etnograficheskii Sbornik* (Ulan-Ude), 6, 1974b, p. 148.

36 E.G. Loseva, 'Ob etnicheskikh protsessakh u buryat' (On ethnic processes among the Buryat), *Trudy BION*, 20, 1973, pp. 156—7.

37 Bolonov 1969, pp. 38—9. Of course, within any given farm wages are determined without reference to nationality.

38 A.D. Zhalsarayev, 'Nekotoriye predvaritel'nyye itogi issledovaniya natsional'nogo samosoznaniya podrostkov v natsional'no-smeshannykh sem'yakh' (Some preliminary results of the study of the national consciousness of adolescents in nationally mixed families), *Etnograficheskii Sbornik* (Ulan-Ude), 6, 1974, p. 132.

39 The table at the top of p. 449 shows mixed marriages in Ulan-Ude in 1970 by nationality of husband and wife

40 Loseva 1973, p. 158.

41 Zhalsarayev 1974, p. 134.

42 *Ibid.*, p. 135.

43 G.I. Voronin (ed.), *Buryatskaya ASSR administrativno-territorial'noye deleniye na 1 aprelya 1977 goda* (The Buryat ASSR, administrative-territorial divisions, on 1 April 1977), BKI, Ulan-Ude, 1977, p. 28.

44 Tivanenko and Mitypov 1974, p. 132.

45 Hugh Brody, personal communication.

46 Loseva 1973, p. 158.

47 *Ibid.*, p. 160. There were only two divorces out of sixty-nine mixed marriages involving Buryats in the Aga National Okrug.

48 *Ibid.*, p. 160. Kolkhozniks, soldiers, medical workers, and housewives made few mixed marriages.

49 *Ibid.*, p. 160.

50 Data provided by the Party Secretary of Karl Marx kolkhoz, Selenga *aimak*, 1967.

511

Men	Women	Percentage of mixed marriages
Buryat	Russian	27.2
Russian	Buryat	3.0
Buryat	Ukrainian	2.0
Buryat	Belorussian	0.8
Russian	Ukrainian	13.4
Ukrainian	Russian	7.4
Russian	Jewish	3.0
Jewish	Russian	8.0
Russian	Tatar	1.4
Tatar	Russian	5.2
Russian	Belorussian	1.2
Belorussian	Russian	4.4
Russian	Mordvinian	2.2
Mordvinian	Russian	1.2

Source: Zhalsarayev 1974, p. 132.

51 Data provided by the Chairman of Karl Marx kolkhoz, Barguzin *aimak*, 1975. This material on age structure in the two farms can be compared with that given by Ushnayev for the kolkhoz population of the Buryat ASSR as a whole in 1967, as shown in the table.

Age	% of total
0—5 years	15.4
6—15 years	30.2
16—49 years	35.9
50—59 years	7.9
60 years and over	10.6

Source: F.M. Ushnayev, *Trudovyye resursy kolkhozov buryatskoi ASSR i ikh ispol'zovaniye* (Labour resources of the collective farms of the Buryat ASSR and their use), BKI, Ulan-Ude, 1969, p. 25.

52 The 'working age' is between sixteen and sixty for men, and between sixteen and fifty-five for women. After this age kolkhozniks are entitled to go on pension.

53 Cf. K.D. Basayeva, *Preobrazovaniye v semeino-brachnykh otnosheniyakh buryat* (Transformations in the family and marriage relations of the Buryat), BKI, Ulan-Ude, 1974a, p. 50.

54 I do not have data on births and deaths for the Barguzin Bayangol *sel'sovet*.

55 Contraceptives available in the Soviet Union in rural areas do not include the pill for women. Several kolkhozniks told me that it was formerly considered a great shame to bear a child before marriage. The following story from Barguzin illustrates this: 'When the day came that he should marry the pregnant bride, Sagan went up to his future wife, and in a flash pulled her off her horse and put her between his legs. By this act he purified his

bride from the shame and the child could be a full member of his lineage. The Barguzin Buryats think an unmarried young man should not marry a pregnant girl. Such a marriage would be a disgrace and humiliation; anyone could ask him, "Who is your mate for lying with your wife?" Pregnant girls are usually married off to widowers or divorced men.' S.P. Baldayev, *Rodoslovnyye predaniya i legendy buryat* (Genealogical stories and legends of the Buryat), part 1, *Bulagaty i Ekhirity* (Bulagats and Ekhirits), AN SSSR BION, BKI, Ulan-Ude, 1970, p. 199.

56   In the Ust'-Ordynsk National Okrug around 1970, Loseva found that 37.2% of her sample of 363 people had lived all their lives in the same villages. In the Aga National Okrug of 435 people the following percentages had lived in the same place:

From birth	35%
Less than 20 years	13.7%
Less than 10 years	12.1%
1–5 years	39.2%

Loseva 1973, p. 158.

57   This is a general process in the rural USSR and much less marked in Buryatiya than in parts of central and northern Russia. In Buryatiya, there was a mass movement to repopulate the countryside with males in 1954–6, when 7,500 people settled in rural areas, either 'by the call of the Party', or by their own initiative. Ushnayev 1969, p. 20.

58   The study was conducted in the Okrug capital, the small town of Aginskoye, and in two collective farms.

59   Loseva 1973, p. 158.

60   Members of the Party are in duty bound to take work if they are ordered to do so, and this fact is often used in collective farms to fill unpopular jobs (see Chapter 7 section 3).

61   The working population was distributed by age-group in 1967 as shown in the table.

Age-group	USSR 1959	Kolkhoz population of Buryat ASSR 1959	Kolkhoz population of Buryat ASSR 1967
16–19	13.2	15.0	15.7
20–29	31.0	30.0	18.9
30–39	24.4	21.5	31.2
40–49	19.5	20.8	21.2
50–54	3.2	9.9	9.3
55–59	2.7	2.8	3.7
Total	100.0	100.0	100.0

Source: Ushnayev 1969, p. 22.

62   Caroline Humphrey, 'The uses of genealogy: a historical study of the nomadic and sedentarised Buryat', in *Pastoral Production and Society*. Ed. by L'Equipe écologie et anthropologie des sociétés pastorales, Cambridge University Press/Editions de la Maison des Sciences de l'Homme, Cambridge–Paris, 1979b.

63   G.N. Rumyantsev, *Barguzinskiye letopisi* (Barguzin chronicles), B-MKI, Ulan-Ude, 1956.

64 'Sokrashchennaya istoriya Barguzinskikh buryat s prisovokupleniyem dokumentov', in Rumyantsev 1956, pp. 40–52. In Buryat and Russian.

65 Rumyantsev 1956, p. 95. The other historical details on Barguzin in this paragraph are also derived from the *Barguzinskiye letopisi*.

66 G.E. Dambayev, *Iz proshlogo i nastoyashchego barguzinkikh buryat* (From the past and the present of the Barguzin Buryat), BKI, Ulan-Ude, 1970, pp. 42–3.

67 *Ibid.*, p. 42.

68 Rumyantsev 1956, p. 90.

69 E.R. Radnayev, 'Barguzinskii govor' (The Barguzin dialect), in Ts.B. Tsydendambayev and I.D. Burayev (eds.), *Issledovaniye Buryatskikh govorov* (The study of Buryat dialects), vol. 1, BKI, Ulan-Ude, 1965, p. 78.

70 According to the most common version given by Barguzin informants.

71 S.P. Baldayev, 'Materialy o buryatskikh plemanakh i rodakh' (Materials on Buryat tribes and kin-groups), *Etnograficheskii Sbornik* (Ulan-Ude), 2, 1961b, pp. 131–2.

72 Baldayev 1970, p. 276.

73 N.P. Yegunov, *Kolonial'naya politika tsarizma i pervyi etap natsional'nogo dvizheniya v buryatii v epokhu imperializma* (The colonial policies of Tsarism and the first stage of the national movement in Buryatiya in the imperialist period), BKI, Ulan-Ude, 1963.

74 I.M. Manzhigeyev, *Yangutskii buryatskii rod* (The Yangut Buryat lineage), BKI, Ulan-Ude, 1960, p. 51.

75 S.P. Baldayev, *Buryatskiye svadebnyye obryady* (Buryat wedding rituals), BKI, Ulan-Ude, 1959, pp. 10–11.

76 K.M. Cheremisov, *Buryatsko-Russkii slovar'* (Buryat–Russian Dictionary), Sovetskaya Entsiklopediya, Moscow, 1973, p. 88.

77 Baldayev 1959, p. 21.

78 *Ibid.*, pp. 8–9.

79 Manzhigeyev 1960, p. 59.

80 Baldayev 1970, p. 197.

81 *Ibid.*, pp. 221 and 285.

82 See Humphrey 1979b, on the use of this device in Mongolian kinship.

83 Rupen 1964, p. 162.

84 *Ibid.*, p. 187.

85 N.R. Mangutov, *Agrarnyye preobrazovaniya v sovetskoi buryatii (1917–1933gg.)* (Agrarian transformations in Soviet Buryatiya, 1917–1933), Academy of Sciences, BKNII, Ulan-Ude, 1960.

86 Khaptayev 1962.

87 It was not the case that only the poorest people entered the first collectives. They were dominated to begin with by intellectuals, or by people who had been given some training, usually by the Bolsheviks. The founder of the Barguzin Karl Marx collective farm, for example, was Buda Sangadiin, who had been sent on a course in Leningrad, and then set up the farm, initially as a commune, on the instruction of the Party. Of the sixteen founder members, several were *srednyaks* (middling peasants), and even when the farm grew larger a few years later, around three-quarters of the ninety or so members were *srednyaks*. An early history of the farm gives several cases of families quarrelling bitterly over attitudes to the farm. N.P. Yegunov, 'K istorii organizatsii odnogo iz pervykh zhivotnovod-cheskikh kolkhozov BMASSR' (Towards a history of one of the first live-

stock collective farms of the Buryat-Mongol ASSR), *Zapiski B-MNIIK* (Ulan-Ude), 16, 1952, pp. 63–93.

88 Radnayev 1965, p. 75.
89 A.I. Vostrikov and N.N. Poppe, *Letopis' barguzinskikh buryat, teksty i issledovaniya* (Chronicle of the Barguzin Buryats, texts and investigations), Trudy Instituta Vostokovedeinya 8, AN SSSR, Moscow–Leningrad, 1935, p. 10.
90 *Ibid.*, p. 13.
91 *Ibid.*, p. 49.
92 V.P. Buyantuyev, *Barguzinskaya dolina* (The Barguzin valley), BKI, Ulan-Ude, 1959, pp. 11–12. Gold is mined at Novomeiskikh in the Ikat mountains, but very few Buryats take part in this operation and little is known about it.
93 *Ibid.*, pp. 14–15.
94 *Ibid.*, p. 10.
95 Rumyantsev 1956, pp. 48–9.
96 Buyantuyev 1959, p. 54.
97 *Ibid.*, p. 24.
98 I.A. Romashev, 'Byt i sotsial'nyye bolezni ol'khonskikh buryat' (The way of life and the social diseases of the Ol'khon Buryats), *Severnaya Aziya* (Moscow), 4 (22), 1928.
99 K.D. Basayeva, *Sem'ya i brak u buryat* (Family and marriage among the Buryat), Nauka, Novosibirsk, 1980, p. 59.
100 'Khaluunda huukha khübüütei bolooroi, khadamda oshokho basagatai bolooroi.' *Ibid.*, p. 59.
101 'Khoimoroor düüren khübüütei, khüreegeer düüren maltai bolooroi.' *Ibid.*, p. 59.
102 'Khün boloo, seeree garaa.' *Ibid.*, p. 62.
103 V.P. Makhatov, *Stranitsy iz zhizni buryat kudarinskoi stepi* (Episodes from the life of Buryats of the Kudarin Steppe), BKI, Ulan-Ude, 1964, pp. 44–51; Yu.B. Randalov, *Sotsialisticheskiye preobrazovaniya khozyaistva, byta, i kul'tury buryatskogo ulusa za gody sovetskoi vlasti* (The socialist transformation of the economy, way of life, and culture of the Buryat *ulus* in the years of Soviet power), BKI, Ulan-Ude, 1967, pp. 54–5; P. Kuz'menko, 'Bor'ba za ozdorovleniye buryatskikh mass' (Struggle for the health of the Buryat masses), *Zhizn' Buryatii*, 10, 1927, p. 14.
104 Basayeva 1980, pp. 64–6. In the Irkutsk *oblast'* Buryat boys up to the age of fourteen were 29% of the total male population, while among Russian peasants they were 36.7% of the total male population. Girls up to the age of twelve were 28.4% and 33.7% of the total of women respectively.
105 Romashev 1928, p. 97. Another doctor working in a nearby district found 42.7% of Buryat men to have syphilis. Romashev's study was carried out among 1,116 people of a total population of 2,042.
106 The word for 'bone' (*yahan*) is also a term for the patrilineage. Even today the ritual bone (*shata semgeen*, 'tube marrow bone') is important at festivities. The marrow can contain a soul. At weddings Buryat men try to break this bone with one chop of their hand, a paradoxical custom, since the marrow bone is a symbol of fertility. K.V. Vyatkina, *Mongoly Mongol'skoi Narodnoi Respubliki* (Mongols of the Mongolian People's Republic). Trudy Instituta Etnografii AN SSSR, vol. 9, Moscow, 1960, p. 230.

107 At times of misfortune, Buryats used to come back to the place of burying their afterbirth and conduct a private ritual. In many parts of Buryatiya, the *milaagod* ritual, described later in this book, was thought of as a thanksgiving to the old women officients at the burying of the afterbirth. Basayeva 1980, pp. 79—80.

108 See C. Humphrey (forthcoming), *Magical Drawings in the Religion of the Buryats*, Cambridge University Press, Cambridge.

109 A.M. Pesterev, 'Polovoi byt buryat' (The sexual life of the Buryat), *Zhizn' Buryatii*, 4, 1930, pp. 89—98.

110 *Ibid.* The onset of puberty among girls was usually between the ages of fourteen and seventeen.

111 Rich families married their sons early, sometimes even between the ages of nine and twelve, more often at fifteen or sixteen. The reason for early marriage was the acquiring of a daughter-in-law as a worker, and the brides in these cases were almost always considerably older that the grooms. Most girls were married between the ages of seventeen and twenty-one, shortly after puberty.

112 *Ibid.*, p. 63.

113 *Buryatskaya ASSR za 50 let — statisticheskii sbornik* (The Buryat ASSR after 50 years — a statistical collection), BKI, Ulan-Ude, 1967, p. 78.

114 Visitors are still kept away from the maternity homes in Buryat farms.

115 The Barguzin Karl Marx farm had one kindergarten at Bayangol with seventy places, and one at Urzhil with forty-five places. A further kindergarten with thirty places was planned for Soyol. Twenty-five of the children at the Bayangol school were boarders, visiting their parents only on Sundays. The fees were 13.50 rubles a month, reduced to half in the case of families with over five children. The children learnt Russian language, arithmetic, drawing, sculpture, sewing, and music. Non-boarders stayed at school between 8 in the morning and 6.30 in the evening. The Bayangol school had a staff of fourteen. However, there were places for only about a quarter of the children of the village.

116 It seemed to me that the people pointed out to me as successful workers almost always had large families.

2 Ideology and instructions for collective farms

1 V.A. Peshekhonov, *Rol' gosudarstva v ekonomicheskom razvitii kolkhozov* (The role of the state in the economic development of collective farms), Izd. Leningradskogo Universiteta, Leningrad, 1980, pp. 39—40.

2 Alec Nove, *The Soviet Economy*, George Allen and Unwin, London, 1961, p. 40.

3 *Ustav kolkhoza buryatskoy ASSR* (Collective farm statutes of Buryat ASSR), Soviet of Ministers of the Buryat ASSR, Ulan-Ude, 1970.

4 A.P. Chubarov (ed.), *Spravochnik predsedatelya kolkhoza* (Directory for the Chairman of a collective farm), Kolos, Moscow, 1972.

5 See for example M. Ellman, *Planning Problems in the USSR: the Contribution of Mathematical Economics to their Solution, 1960—1971*, Cambridge University Press, Cambridge, 1973.

6 V.N. Kosinskii and G.F. Mikhailik, *Formirovaniye kolkhoznykh fondov i ikh ispol'zovaniye* (The formation of funds in collective farms and their use), Kolos, Moscow, 1977, pp. 114—15. The first 'provisional statutes' of

the collective farm were adopted in February 1935 by the 2nd All-Union Congress of Kolkhoznik-Udarniks. It replaced the 'provisional statutes' of agricultural communes, which had been in use up to that time. The 1935 'provisional statutes' remained in force until 1969, but certain of their paragraphs were altered by resolutions (*postanovleniya*) of the Soviet of Ministers of the USSR and the Central Committee of the Communist Party between these dates. An account of these changes is to be found in V.F. Nemtsov (ed.), *Organizatsiya i planirovaniye proizvodstva v kolkhozakh i sovkhozakh* (The organisation and planning of production in state and collective farms), Vysshaya Shkola, Moscow, 1978, pp. 26—31. The most important of them from our point of view are: (1) membership of the collective farm is now voluntary, whereas previously all children of kolkhoz members automatically joined at age sixteen unless they were given permission to go elsewhere; (2) kolkhoz members have guaranteed pay at a basic minimum level; (3) kolkhoz members now are paid pensions on retirement.

7   Various regions of the USSR are allowed to alter the number and type of animals kept in the private small-holdings of the kolkhoz members. However, these exceptions are not decided by the regions themselves but by the Ministry of Agriculture in Moscow. See Chubarov 1972, pp. 618—25.

8   Kosinskii and Mikhailik 1977.

9   *Pod znamenem marksizma* (Under the banner of Marxism), 7—8, 1943, p 65, quoted in Nove 1961, p. 268.

10 Nove 1961, p. 273.

11 Karl Marx, *Capital*, vol. 1, 8, quoted in R. Freedman (ed.), *Marx on Economics*, Penguin, Harmondsworth, 1976, p. 67.

12 *Ibid.*, p. 68.

13 Sh. Suleimanov, *Vosproizvodstvo i ispol'zovaniye proizvodstvennykh fondov v kolkhozakh* (The reproduction and use of the productive funds in collective farms), Uzbekistan, Tashkent, 1975, pp. 20—1.

14 *Ibid.*, p. 21.

15 *Ibid.*, p. 22.

16 V.I. Isayev, *Vyravnivaniye i ratsional'noye ispol'zovaniya dokhodov kolkhozov* (The equalising and rational use of the incomes of collective farms), Kolos, Moscow, 1977, p. 17.

17 *Ibid.*, p. 23.

18 Nemtsov 1978, pp. 74—5.

19 N.F. Panchenko and V.A. Lomakhin, *Nakopleniye v kolkhozakh* (Accumulation in collective farms), Kolos, Moscow, 1976, pp. 38—9. Nemtsov explains this by means of a distinction, derived from Marx, between 'material wear and tear' and 'moral wear and tear', the latter concept (*moral'nyi iznos*) accounting for the growth in the productivity of labour and the appearance of new, more productive machines. Nemtsov 1978, p. 73.

20 Kosinskii and Mikhailik 1977, p. 18.

21 *Ibid.*, pp. 19—20.

22 Nemtsov, however, indicates the difficulty of using this concept in agriculture, since many items such as productive cattle have to appear in *both* 'circulation' and 'basic' funds; calves appear first in the circulation fund and then are transferred to the basic fund when they become productive cattle. Nemtsov 1978, pp. 67—8.

23 Kosinskii and Mikhailik 1977, p. 22.
24 *Ibid.*, pp. 24—5.
25 *Leningradskaya Pravda*, 4 February 1976, p. 2.
26 Kosinskii and Mikhailik 1977, pp. 61—2.
27 Karl Marx, *Capital*, vol. 1, 6, quoted in Freedman 1976, p. 34.
28 Karl Marx, *Capital*, vol. 1, 1, quoted in Freedman 1976, p. 31.
29 Kosinskii and Mikhailik 1977, p. 72.
30 *Ibid.*, p. 75.
31 *Ibid.*, pp. 57—8.
32 Isayev 1977, p. 18.
33 Kosinskii and Mikhailik 1977, p. 47.
34 Chubarov 1972, pp. 248—51.
35 Kosinskii and Mikhailik 1977, pp. 51—2.
36 *Ibid.*, p. 32.
37 Peshekhonov 1980, pp. 35—6.
38 *Ibid.*, pp. 36—8.
39 *Ibid.*, p. 38.
40 This is stated in all of the textbooks cited in this chapter. See Peshekhonov
    1980, pp. 44—59 for argument. The textbooks cite Lenin's article 'On
    cooperation', which states that if cooperatives are set up on communally
    owned land, work under the control of state power directed by the work-
    ing class, and coordinate their activities with other truly socialist enter-
    prises, their development will create the necessary conditions for the build-
    ing of socialism. V.I. Lenin, *Pol'niye sobraniye sochinenii* (Full collected
    works), Moscow, vol. 45, p. 375. V.V. Kuibyshev, *Lenin i kooperatziya*
    (Lenin and cooperation), Moscow, 1925, p. 3.
41 Peshekhonov 1980, p. 62.
42 *Ibid.*, p. 63.
43 *Ibid.*, pp. 65—6.
44 S.I. Semin, P.I. Gusev, and N.P. Pisarenko, *Razvitiye sotsialisticheskikh
    proizvodstvennykh otnoshenii vi sel'skom khozyaistve* (The development
    of socialist productive relations in agriculture), Moscow, 1977, p. 108.
45 Chubarov 1972, pp. 141—2.
46 *Ibid.*, pp. 142—60.
47 *Ibid.*, p. 141.
48 *Ibid.*, p. 141.
49 *Ibid.*, pp. 161—4.
50 Kosinskii and Mikhailik 1977, p. 55. See also A.P. Dolotov and S.N.
    Seleznev, *Tovarno-denezhnyye otnosheniya v kolkhoznom proizvodstve*
    (Commodity-monetary relations in collective farm production), Ekon-
    omika, Moscow, 1978; M.K. Vasyukin and A.S. Davydov, *Gosudarstvenyye
    zakupki kolkhoznoi produktsii: ekonomicheskii analiz* (State purchases of
    collective farm production: an economic analysis), Ekonomika, Moscow,
    1978.
51 Isayev 1977, p. 138.
52 Nove 1961, p. 38. The *Directory for the Kolkhoz Chairman* states that the
    kolkhoz is now responsible only for transportation to the frontier of its
    own *oblast'*. The *Directory for the Chairman of a Collective Farm* (1972)
    states that the *zagotoviteli* should help the kolkhoz with transport and
    production according to their contract. But it is not made clear how, or in
    what amounts, this help should be forthcoming. Chubarov 1972, pp. 162—3.

53 Nove 1961, p. 137.
54 V.V. Novozhilov, 'Problems of planned pricing and the reform of industrial management', in A. Nove and D.M. Nuti (eds.), *Socialist Economics*, Penguin, Harmondsworth, 1972, pp. 388–9.
55 Isayev 1977, p. 143.
56 Novozhilov 1972, p. 379.
57 Isayev 1977, p. 150.
58 *Ibid.*, p. 137.
59 *Ibid.*, p. 157.
60 Nove 1961, pp. 227–8.
61 I use the word 'political' here to refer to the exercise of power, both formally and informally, not simply to the functioning of political institutions.
62 P.A. Kal'm, N.A. Pilichev, and F.V. Zinov'yev, *Osnovy nauchnoi organizatsii upravleniya v kolkhozakh i sovkhozakh* (The foundations of the scientific organisation of management in collective and state farms), Kolos, Moscow, 1977.
63 P.A. Kal'm *et al.* 1977, p. 61.
64 Vaskhnil G.M. Lozy, *Osnovy nauchnogo upravleniya* (The foundations of scientific management), 3rd edn, Ekonomika, Moscow, 1977, p. 143.
65 Kal'm *et al.* 1977, p. 116.
66 Lozy 1977, pp. 122–9.
67 Kal'm *et al.* 1977, p. 16.
68 *Ibid.*, p. 16.
69 V.I. Lenin, *Pol'niye sobraniye sochinenii* (Full collected works), Moscow, vol. 36, p. 200.
70 *Ibid.*, vol. 36, p. 206.
71 *Ibid.*, vol. 39, pp. 428–9.
72 Kal'm *et al.* 1977, p. 125.
73 *Ibid.*, p. 118.
74 *Ibid.*, p. 131.
75 *Ibid.*, p. 28.
76 *Ibid.*, p. 28.
77 M.I. Kalinin, quoted in *ibid.*, p. 119.
78 *Ibid.*, p. 38.
79 *Ustav kolkhoza buryatskoi ASSR*, p. 11.
80 Kal'm *et al.* 1977, p. 208.
81 *Pamyatka uchastnika sorevnovaniya za kommunisticheskii trud* (Record book for a competition for communist labour), Michnevskaya tipografiya, 1960s.
82 Chubarov 1972, p. 625.
83 Kal'm *et al.* 1977, p. 205.
84 *Ibid.*, p. 208.
85 Bato Semenov, *Narodnyy kontrol' v deystvii* (People's Control in action), Soviet of Ministers of Buryat ASSR, Ulan-Ude, 1967, p. 8.
86 *Ibid.*, pp. 8–9.
87 *Ibid.*, pp. 58–60.
88 *Ibid.*, pp. 62–3.
89 *Ibid.*, p. 68.
90 Chubarov 1972, pp. 512–13, and pp. 599–617.

519

3 The hierarchy of rights held in practice

1 See for example V.V. Belikov, 'Ismeneniye sotsial'no-klassovoi struktury naseleniya buryatii (1923—1970)' (Changes in the social class structure of the population of Buryatiya, 1923—1970), in D.D. Lubsanov (ed.), *Iz opyta konkretno-sotsiologicheskikh issledovanii* (From the experience of concrete sociological investigations), BION, BKI, Ulan-Ude, 1974a. He gives the following classes: state workers, employees, collective farm workers, individual peasants, and others. This is the standard Soviet approach to the study of 'social structure'.

2 Charles Bettelheim, 'State property and socialism', *Economy and Society*, 2 (4), 1970; *La Lutte des classes en URSS*, Maspero-Seuil, Paris, 1974; and *The Transition to Socialist Economy*, trs. Brian Pearce, The Harvester Press, London, 1975.

3 Yu.V. Arutyunyan, 'Experience of a socio-ethnic survey relating to the Tatar ASSR', in Yu. Bromley (ed.), *Soviet Ethnology and Anthropology Today*, Mouton, The Hague, 1974. See also Murray Yanowitch, *Social and Economic Inequality in the Soviet Union*, Martin Robertson, London, 1977, chapter 1, 'Soviet conceptions of social structure', which discusses various Soviet sociological classifications of socio-occupational groups. The idea of a hierarchy within what were previously regarded as undifferentiated strata ('the working class', 'the intelligentsia', etc.) is now accepted, and there are conflicting views of the worker-intelligentsia boundary itself, but as Yanowitch remarks, 'The political dimensions of stratification and inequalities in the distribution of power — unlike economic and cultural inequalities — remain largely ignored' (p. 20).

4 B. Malinowski, *Crime and Custom in Savage Society*, Kegan Paul, Trench and Trubner, London, 1926, pp. 20—1.

5 Max Gluckman, *The Ideas in Barotse Jurisprudence*, Manchester University Press, Manchester, 1972, pp. 166—7.

6 Certain categories of people, such as exiles, do not have voting rights.

7 P.I. Bartanov, 'Ukrepleniye kolkhozov i sovkhozov Buryatskoi ASSR rukovodyashchimi kadrami i spetsialistami v gody semiletki (1959—1965 gg)' (The strengthening of the collective and state farms of the Buryat ASSR with managerial cadres and specialists in the seven-year period 1959—65), in Z.N. Tsydypova (ed.), *Nekotoriye voprosy podgotovki kadrov i kommunisticheskogo vospitaniya trudyashchikhsya v buryatskoi partorganizatsii* (Some questions concerning the training of cadres and the communist education of the workers in the Buryat Party organisation), Min. Pros. RSFSR, Ulan-Ude, 1972, p. 10.

8 The principle is shown by the fact that higher fines should be imposed on officials than on ordinary workers if they break certain laws, e.g. the law as to forest fires (*Vedomosti verkhovnogo soveta SSSR*, 23, 1971, p. 329). But in Buryatiya in the period we are considering the Chairman of the kolkhoz or Director of a sovkhoz was commonly not brought to book, since it was *through* the management that the People's Control and other organisations exercised discipline. If the Chairman was punished this usually was only a token, as we see from the following typical cases: 'Already at the beginning of 1964 the *oblast'* committee of the People's Control had decided to check how the management of the Okino-

Klyuchevskii sovkhoz was carrying out the *postanovleniye* about developing pig production. A series of faults was discovered. Although definite measures were taken in the sovkhoz, still it was found that pigs were dying. Therefore in 1966 the Bichur *raion* committee of the People's Control carried out a further check and found that in five months 640 pigs, including 423 piglets, had died in the 4th sector of the farm, that the loss incurred by the deaths was 4,200 rubles and that there was a further deficit of 18,000 rubles which would have been received for the sale of the pork. Furthermore, it appeared that the head of the pig production *ferma* had killed and sold privately the meat of 90 piglets. The committee dismissed the head of the *ferma* and submitted his case to the prosecuting organs. The Director of the sovkhoz had the brigadier of the complex brigade brought to responsibility, together with other workers responsible for the loss, and they were charged the value of the pigs lost.' 'The same committee found that in another farm, the *Pobeda* [Victory], the management had been negligent in carrying out the *postanovleniye* and many pigs had been lost. The committee recommended that the value of the pigs should be sought from individuals responsible, including the Chairman of the kolkhoz, who was fined 100 rubles.' B. Semenov, *Narodnyi kontrol' v deistvii* (People's Control in action), Soviet of Ministers of Buryat ASSR, Ulan-Ude, 1967, p. 51.

9   Feder Abramov, *Vokrug da okolo*, Posev, Frankfurt am Main, 1962 (trans. *The Dodgers*, Flegon Press, London, 1963).

10 According to the minutes of meeting which I saw of the Selenga farm, attendance at *pravleniye* meetings was limited usually to the members who had direct business there, even if this meant that there was not a quorum by official standards. The Chairman was always present. Other people could be invited to attend if the matter being discussed concerned them. In this farm the specialists were *invited* to attend but did not have the right to be present. In many farms the Chairman spends the greater part of his time in such meetings, see I.M. Slepenkov and B.V. Knyazev, *Rural Youth Today*, Oriental Research Partners, Newtonville, Mass., 1976, p. 57, who say that farm Chairmen in Krasnodar region spend up to 76% of their time in meetings.

11 A.P. Chubarov (ed.), *Spravochnik predsedatelya kolkhoza* (Directory for the Chairman of a collective farm), Kolos, Moscow, 1972, p. 44.

12 *Ibid.*, pp. 50–1.

13 Brigadiers have significantly fewer qualifications than Chairmen or specialists, and they rarely rise above this position in the hierarchy.

14 I.E. Tugutov, *Material'naya kul'tura buryat* (The material culture of the Buryats), BKI, Ulan-Ude, 1958, pp. 78–9.

15 *Krasnaya Selenga*, 25 May 1967.

16 It should be noted, however, that this attitude has recently changed (1981), see Introduction.

17 In Buryat farms the official household head is quite frequently a woman, even when the husband is alive.

18 *Ustav kolkhoza buryatskoy ASSR* (Collective farm statutes of Buryat ASSR), Soviet of Ministers of the Buryat ASSR, Ulan-Ude, 1970.

19 *Komsomol'skaya Pravda*, 9 June 1981, p. 2.

20 *Trud*, 3 March 1972, p. 2. However, the general rule that workers may not

be dismissed by employers without the agreement of the trade union does not apply to collective farms, *Rahva Hääl*, 26 April 1972, p. 4.

21 In practice a worker can apply to the Party and/or the *sel'sovet* for help, since the responsibilities of both of these bodies are very wide. Clearly workers who take an active part in these organisations have a better chance of obtaining help.

22 The *pravleniye* was overstepping its legal rights. According to the Statutes a worker may only be fined up to one-third of his monthly pay, unless it is proved that there are aggravating circumstances.

23 This rule was frequently broken.

24 *Komsomol'skaya Pravda*, 2 June 1981, p. 2.

25 This, the *trudovaya kommissiya po zarplatu*, was elected at the general meeting, and consisted of eighteen members, one from each profession. The Chairman did not sit on it, but the Vice-Chairman did. It operates by majority open vote. This may have been one of the most genuinely democratic organisations in the farm, and does not seem to have been subject to outside authority; see F.M. Ushnayev, 'Denezhnaya oplata trude v kolkhoz imeni Karla Marksa Selenginskogo aimaka Buryatskoi ASSR' (Money wages in the Karl Marx collective farm of Selenga district of the Buryat ASSR) in O.V. Makeyev (ed.), *Voprosy razvitiya narodnogo khozyaistva buryatskoi ASSR* (Questions of the development of the economy of the Buryat ASSR), Ulan-Ude, 1961a, who wrote a disapproving article about the high pay and low work-norms in this collective farm.

26 G.I. Gorokhov (ed.), *Zemleustroistvo kolkhozov i sovkhozov* (The system of land tenure in collective and state farms), Urozhai, Kiev, 1977, pp. 12–16.

4 The collective farm economy

1 *Narodnoye khozyaistvo buryatskoi ASSR v devyatoi pyatiletke – statisticheskii sbornik* (The economy of the Buryat ASSR in the 9th five-year plan – a statistical collection), BKI, Ulan-Ude, 1976, p. 53.

2 Hough suggests that, in practice, the autonomous republic and the *krai* are similar in importance to the *oblast'*, the difference in terminology being associated with the desire to give recognition to various nationality groups. Jerry F. Hough, *The Soviet Prefects: the Local Party Organs in Industrial Decision-Making*, Harvard University Press, Cambridge, Mass., 1969, pp. 8–9.

3 A Party cell was organised in Karalik on 13 January 1921 by Dima Lutunov and Rinchin Tubchinov. By March the cell had forty-five members, all of them Buryat. This was one of the first and strongest Party organisations among Buryats.

4 See for example Caroline Humphrey, 'The uses of genealogy: a historical study of the nomadic and sedentarised Buryat', in *Pastoral Production and Society*, ed. L'Equipe écologie et anthropologie des sociétés pastorales, Maison des Sciences de l'Homme/Cambridge University Press, Cambridge–Paris, 1979b.

5 N.P. Yegunov, 'K istorii organizatsii odnogo iz pervykh zhivotnovodcheskikh kolkhozov B-MASSR' (Towards a history of the first livestock collective farms of the Buryat-Mongol ASSR), *Zapiski B-MNIIK* (Ulan-Ude), 16, 1952, pp. 75–6.

6   S. Patkanov, *Statisticheskiya dannyya, pokazyvayushchiya plemennoy sostav naseleniya Sibiri* (Statistical data showing the tribal composition of the population of Siberia), vol. 3, *Irkutsk Gub., Zabaykal'sk, Amur, Yakutsk., Primorsk., i.o. Sakhalin*, Zapiski Imperatorskogo Russkago Geograficheskogo Obshchestva po otdeleniyu statistiki, vol. 11, no. 3, St Petersburg, 1912, pp. 550 *et seq.*

7   Yu.B. Randalov, *Sotsialisticheskiye preobrazovaniya khozyaistva, byta, i kul'tury buryatskogo ulusa za gody sovetskoi vlasti* (The socialist transformation of the economy, way of life, and culture of the Buryat *ulus* in the years of Soviet power), BKI, Ulan-Ude, 1967, pp. 91–4.

8   Patkanov 1912, p. 550.

9   Yegunov 1952, pp. 82–3.

10   V. Tyushev, 'Leningradskaya mnogotirazhnaya gazeta "Skorokhodovskiy Rabochiy" kak istochnik po istorii kolkhoznogo dvizheniya v buryatii' (The Leningrad wide-circulation newspaper 'The Skorokhod Worker' as a source for the history of the collective farm movement in Buryatiya), *Buryat-Mongol'skiy Gosudarskvennyy Pedagogicheskii Institut im. Dorzhi Banzarova Uchenyye Zapiski* (Ulan-Ude), 14, 1958, pp. 138–9.

11   Basile H. Kerblay, *Les marchés paysans en URSS*, Mouton, Paris, 1968, pp. 120–1.

12   Tovarishchestvo po obrabotki zemli: literally the association for working the soil, an early form of cooperative in which the farmers shared access to machinery but continued to hold land separately.

13   Kerblay 1968, p. 129.

14   Tyushev 1958, p. 141.

15   *Ibid.*, p. 142.

16   *Ibid.*, p. 142.

17   Hough 1969, pp. 190–7.

18   V.G. Dymbrenov, *Kolkhoz imeni Karla Marksa*, BKI, Ulan-Ude, 1961, p. 25.

19   *Ibid.*, p. 24.

20   A.G. Yandanov, *Povysheniye kul'turno-teknicheskogo urovnya kolkhoznogo krest'yanstva buryatii* (The raising of the cultural-technological level of the collective farm peasantry of Buryatiya), BKI, Ulan-Ude, 1975, p. 40.

21   *Ibid.*, p. 41.

22   *Ibid.*, p. 39.

23   *Ibid.*, p. 46.

24   *Ibid.*, p. 47.

25   Dymbrenov 1961, pp. 28–32.

26   *Ibid.*, p. 46.

27   *Ibid.*, p. 49.

28   *Ibid.*

29   A.A. Chernoyarova, 'Trudovyye resursy severa buryatii, ikh formirovaniye i zanyatost' (Labour resources of North Buryatiya, their formation and employment), in P.R. Buyantuyev (ed.), *Voprosy ispol'zovaniya trudovykh resursov Buryatskoi ASSR* (Questions of the use of labour resources of the Buryat ASSR), BKI, Ulan-Ude, 1967, p. 51.

30   Charles Bettelheim, *The Transition to Socialist Economy*, trans. Brian Pearce, The Harvester Press, London, 1975, pp. 46–50.

31   Ts. Zhamtsarano, 'O pravosoznaniye Buryat' (On the law-consciousness of the Buryat), *Sibirskiye Voprosy* (St Petersburg), 2, 1906, p. 117.

32 See, for example, B. Malinowski, *Argonauts of the Western Pacific*, E.P. Dutton and Co., London, 1922, chapters 11 and 12; Marshall Salins, *Stone Age Economics*, Tavistock Publications, London, 1974, last chapter.

33 Dymbrenov 1961, pp. 49–50.

34 G.I. Voronin (ed.), *Buryatskaya ASSR administrativno-territorial'noye deleniye*, 3rd edn, BKI, Ulan-Ude, 1977, p. 118.

35 Collective farms used to be the constituent members of an all-Union Soviet (the *sovet kolkhozov*), which had branches at national, republic, and regional levels. This body had a primarily consultative function, dealing with letters of complaint (e.g. on the way kolkhoz elections were run). The *sovet kolkhozov* was never able to make any changes itself however, and it was disbanded in 1952 (see Yu.V. Zaitsev, 'Iz istorii razvitiya vnutrikolkhoznoi demokratii v pervyye poslevoyennyye gody (1946–1950 gg)' (From the history of intra-kolkhoz democracy in the first post war years, 1946–1950), in N.Ya. Gushchin (ed.), *Obshchestvenno-politicheskaya zhizn' sovetskoi sibirskoi derevni* (Socio-political life of the Soviet Siberian village), Nauka, Novosibirsk, 1974, pp. 117–19. By 1971 it was reconstituted. The all-Union *sovet* meets only once every five years. The *raion sovet* meets four times a year. A.P. Chubarov (ed.), *Spravochnik predsedatelya kolkhoza* (Directory for the Chairman of a collective farm), Kolos, Moscow, 1972, pp. 21–8.

36 F.M. Ushnayev, *Trudovyye resursy kolkhozov buryatskoi ASSR i ikh ispol'zovaniye* (Labour resources of the collective farms of the Buryat ASSR and their use), BKI, Ulan-Ude, 1969, p. 20.

37 P.I. Bartanov, 'Ukrepleniye kolkhozov i sovkhozov Buryatskoi ASSR rukovodyashchimi kadrami i spetsialistami v gody semiletki (1959–1965 gg)' (The strengthening of the collective and state farms of the Buryat ASSR with managerial cadres and specialists in the seven-year period 1959–65), in Z.N. Tsydypov (ed.), *Nekotoriye voprosy podgotovki kadrov i kommunisticheskogo vospitaniya trudyashchikhsya v buryatskoi partorganizatsii* (Some questions concerning the training of cadres and the communist education of the workers in the Buryat Party organisation), Min. Pros. RSFSR, Ulan-Ude, 1972, pp. 9–10.

38 See discussion of agrarian industrial enterprises in A. Yanov, *Detente After Brezhnev: the Domestic Roots of Soviet Foreign Policy*, Institute of International Studies, University of California, Berkeley, 1977. However, these do not as yet exist in any significant numbers in Buryatiya.

39 V.F. Nemtsov (ed.), *Organizatsiya i planirovaniye proizvodstva i kolkhozh i sovkhozakh* (The organisation and planning of production in state and collective farms), Vysshaya Shkola, Moscow, 1978, p. 41.

40 Buryat collective farms never seem to have operated independently of further unifying organisations. The machine–tractor stations supervised a 'group' (*kust*) of kolkhozy which had its own Chairman, senior to each of the farm Chairmen taken separately. In the 1930s collective farms were members of another organisation, *Burkolkhozsoyuz* ('the Union of Buryat Collective Farms'), but little is known about its functions. See Yandanov 1975, pp. 40–7.

41 For discussion of this see Robert F. Miller, 'The politics of policy implementation in the USSR: Soviet policies on agricultural integration', *Soviet Studies*, 32 (2), April 1980, pp. 171–94.

42 V.A. Peshekhonov, *Rol' gosudarstva v ekonomicheskom razvitii kolkhozov* (The role of the state in the economic development of collective farms), Izd. Leningradskogo Universiteta, Leningrad, 1980, p. 39.
43 Nemstov 1978, p. 39.
44 Yanov 1977, p. 37.
45 Miller 1980, p. 190. See Miller's discussion of the role of the Estonia First Secretary in attempting to introduce a new system of agricultural integration on *territorial* lines.
46 Hough 1969, p. 136.
47 Personal communication.
48 Yegunov 1952, pp. 63—93.
49 Dymbrenov 1961, pp. 34—60.
50 There were of course sanctions for the carrying out of government campaigns, such as spot checks by government commissions. Nevertheless it was possible simply to ignore general instructions, especially if the district Party organisation was not insistent. It was considerably easier to evade instructions of the Soviets on such matters as education and housing than it was to ignore production plans.
51 Zaitsev 1974, p. 114.
52 Vladimir Soloukhin, *Izbrannyye proizvedeniya (Kaplya rosy)* (Selected works ('Drops of dew')), vol. 1, Khudozhestvennaya Literatura, Moscow, 1974, pp. 423—5.
53 Zaitsev 1974, p 117 (my italics).
54 *Ibid.*, p. 117, quotes archives indicating that in Novosibirsk *oblast'* after the war when inquiries were carried out, 27% of the kolkhoz Chairmen were said by the kolkhozniks to have worked badly, 68.5% were said to have worked satisfactorily, and only 4.5% were said to have worked well.
55 *Ibid.*, p. 119. See also Alec Nove, *The Soviet Economic System*, Allen and Unwin, London, 1977, p. 143.
56 Zaitsev 1974, p. 118.
57 *Ibid.*, p. 119.
58 Hough 1969, p. 128.
59 Dymbrenov 1961, p. 25.
60 *Barguzinskaya Pravda*, 21 June 1967.
61 An article entitled 'For a centner of added weight in the summer', *Barguzinskaya Pravda*, 21 June 1967.
62 *Barguzinskaya Pravda*, 21 June 1967.
63 Dymbrenov 1961, pp. 52—3.
64 *Krasnaya Selenga*, 25 May 1967, p. 1. However, the Karl Marx fell behind during the succeeding thirteen years. In 1980 it was announced that the farm had only milked 1,797 kg per cow. *Krasnaya Selenga*, 10 January 1980.
65 *Barguzinskaya Pravda*, 20 November 1975.
66 It is not unknown for a 'socialist competition' or 'socialist obligation' target to be set at the level of the plan, but this, if discovered, is considered to be an example of dishonesty and Party workers are chastised by their superiors for not noticing that it has happened.
67 *Barguzinskaya Pravda*, 24 June 1980, p. 3.
68 Satirised in the novel by V.N. Voinovich, *Zhizn' i neobychainyye priklyucheniya soldata Ivana Chonkina* (The life and amazing exploits of the soldier Ivan Chonkin), YMCA Press, Paris, 1975, pp. 126—7.

69 This had changed by 1981. 'Competition', not however called 'socialist', includes the private sector. See account of a competition for private production of milk, *Komsomol'skaya Pravda*, 17 March 1981, p. 1.

70 *Komsomol'skaya Pravda*, 7 April 1981, p. 2.

71 Dymbrenov 1961, p. 53.

72 *Narodnoye khozyaistvo buryatskoi ASSR — statisticheskii sbornik* (The economy of the Buryat ASSR — a statistical collection), BKI, Ulan-Ude, 1963, pp. 36—7, and *Narodnoye khozyaistvo buryatskoi ASSR* 1976, p. 68.

73 *Buryatskaya ASSR za 50 let — statisticheskii sbornik* (The Buryat ASSR after 50 years — a statistical collection), BKI, Ulan-Ude, 1967, p. 34; *Narodnoye khozyaistvo buryatskoi ASSR* 1976, pp. 55 and 59—60.

74 *Buryatskaya ASSR za 50 let*, p. 30; *Narodnoye khozyaistvo buryatskoi ASSR* 1976, pp. 82—3.

75 In 1940 the hay harvest was 45,500 tons; in 1962 it was 106,000 tons; and in 1973 it was 131,000 tons, from sown meadows.

76 Ts.B. Galdanov, *Ekonomicheskiye problemy intensifikatsii sel'skogo khozyaistva buryatskoi ASSR* (Economic problems of the intensification of agriculture in the Buryat ASSR), BKI, Ulan-Ude, 1969, p. 37.

77 *Buryatskaya ASSR za 50 let*, p. 36; *Narodnoye khozyaistvo buryatskoi ASSR* 1976, pp. 82—3.

78 Galdanov 1969, p. 25.

79 See Chapter 1, p. 33.

80 Galdanov 1969, p. 37.

81 R.A. Medvedyev and Zh.A. Medvedyev, *Khrushchev, the Years in Power*, Oxford University Press, London, 1977, pp. 125—8.

82 *Buryatskaya ASSR za 50 let*, p. 37; *Narodnoye khozyaistvo buryatskoi ASSR* 1976, p. 84.

83 Ts.B. Galdanov, 'Dostignutyi uroven' i osnovnyye napravleniya razvitiya sel'skogo khozaistva bur. ASSR' (The achieved level and main directions of the development of agriculture in the Buryat ASSR), *Trudy otdel ekon. issled. BF SO AN SSR* (Ulan-Ude), 3 (7), 1970, pp. 28—31.

84 Galdanov 1969, p. 33.

85 *Ibid.*, p. 30.

86 *Ibid.*, pp. 38—9.

87 No data are available after 1976, and even the data for that year may well be an estimate, since the statistics themselves were published in the same year.

88 Galdanov 1970, p. 37.

89 Information from kolkhozniks in Karl Marx kolkhoz, Barguzin, 1975.

90 Galdanov 1970, p. 25.

91 B.A. Ayushiyev and G.M. Radnayev, 'Razmeshcheniya proizvodstva i potrebleniya pishchevykh produktov v buryatskoi ASSR' (The coordination of the production and consumption of food products in the Buryat ASSR), *Krayevedcheskii sbornik* (Ulan-Ude), 6, 1961, p. 55.

92 Galdanov 1970, p. 25.

93 *Narodnoye khozyaistvo buryatskoi ASSR* 1976, p. 54.

94 Galdanov 1970, p. 163.

95 D.G. Bazheyev, 'Osvoyeniye tselinnykh zemel' v Buryatskoi ASSR (1954—1958 gg)' (The appropriation of virgin lands in the Buryat ASSR 1954—1958), in I.A. Asalkhanov (ed.), *Issledovaniya i materialy po istorii buryatii*, Trudy BION, vol. 5, BKI, Ulan-Ude, 1968, p. 165.

96   Medvedyev and Medvedyev 1977, pp. 119–20.
97   O.V. Makeyev and A.D. Ivanov, 'Vodnaya i vetrovaya eroziya pochv v buryatskoi ASSR i zonal'nyye osobennosti protiverozionnykh meropri-yatii' (Water and wind erosion of soils in the Buryat ASSR and zonal particularities of anti-erosion measures), *Krayevedcheskii Sbornik* (Ulan-Ude), 6, 1961, p. 20.
98   *Ibid.*, p. 21.
99   *Ibid.*, p. 21.
100 I.A. Asalkhanov, 'Dorevolyutsionyye sistemy zemledeliya u buryat' (Pre-revolutionary systems of agriculture among the Buryat), in V.I. Boiko *et al.* (eds.), *Rabochii klass i krest'yanstvo natsional'nykh raionov sibiri* (The working class and peasantry of national regions of Siberia), Nauka, Novosi-birsk, 1974, p. 130. The Buryats west of Lake Baikal kept around 50% of their fields fallow at any one time. The Trans-Baikal Buryats kept only 20–30% fallow, the rest being either in current use or *zalezh* (long-period fallow).
101 *Ibid.*, p. 131.
102 Medvedyev and Medvedyev 1977, p. 165.
103 *Narodnoye khozyaistvo buryatskoi ASSR* 1963, p. 39.
104 *Narodnoye khozyaistvo buryatskoi ASSR* 1976, pp. 54 and 68.
105 Newspaper articles suggest, however, that there are problems of main-tenance of farm machinery.
106 *Narodnoye khozyaistvo buryatskoi ASSR* 1963, p. 32; *Narodnoye khoz-yaistvo buryatskoi ASSR* 1976, p. 74.
107 *Narodnoye khozyaistvo buryatskoi ASSR* 1963, p. 33.
108 *Narodnoye khozyaistvo buryatskoi ASSR* 1976, p. 73.
109 *Ibid.*, p. 72.
110 *Ibid.*, p. 31.
111 Makeyev and Ivanov 1961, p. 41.
112 *Narodnoye khozyaistvo buryatskoi ASSR* 1976, p. 100.
113 F.M. Ushnayev, 'Sotsial'nyye izmeneniya truda krest'yan pri sotsializme' (Social changes in the work of peasants in socialism), *Trudy otd. ekon. issled. BF SO AN SSSR*, 1 (5), 1961b, p. 13.
114 B.A. Ayushiyev (ed.), *Ekonomicheskiye problemy prigorodnogo sel'skogo khozyaistva buryatskoi ASSR* (Economic problems of agriculture in the suburban areas of the Buryat ASSR), BKI, Ulan-Ude, 1973, pp. 81–2.
115 *Ibid.*, p. 82.
116 *Ibid.*, p. 82.
117 Ushnayev 1969.
118 With natural mating the shepherds can tell if the ewes have conceived by observing the behaviour of rams towards them subsequent to the first attempts at mating. This is not the case with artificial insemination, and there is a loss of fertility since shepherds are unable to tell until it is too late whether a given ewe has conceived or not.
119 Ayushiyev and Radnayev 1961, pp. 59–61.
120 Galdanov 1970, p. 28.
121 V.N. Deryugina, *Proizvodstvennyye tipy kolkhozov i sovkhozov buryatskoi ASSR* (Productive types of collective and state farms of the Buryat ASSR), BKI, Ulan-Ude, 1968, p. 84.
122 *Ibid.*, p. 98.
123 M.K. Vasyukin and A.S. Davydov, *Gosudarstvennyye zakupki kolkhoznoi*

produktsii: ekonomicheskii analiz (State purchases of collective farm production: an economic analysis), Ekonomika, Moscow, 1978, p. 68.
124   *Ibid.*, p. 73. This information refers to the period 1971–4.
125   *Ibid.*, pp. 68–9. Galdanov 1969, p. 71 says: 'In 1966 in collective farms the total product per man-day in agriculture was 75% higher than in live-stock production. And in the last five years (1962–66) the productivity of labour per man-day rose by 87% in agriculture, while it only rose by 8.1% in livestock production, and at the same time wages for livestock workers rose by 34%.' This 34%, however, represents in the great majority of farms simply the introduction of a minimum wage.
126   Galdanov 1969, p. 73 cites the case of two collective farms in Selenga district. The Karl Marx kolkhoz, one of the farms I visited in 1967, gave more fodder per cow and also paid higher wages to its milkmaids than the Erdem kolkhoz, but it made a profit rather than a loss.

kolkhoz im. Karla Marksa	cost of maintaining one cow per year	295.8 rubles
	milk per cow per year	1,883 kg
	cost of production of one centner of milk	15.4 rubles
	profit per cow	+13.0 rubles
Kolkhoz 'Erdem'	cost of maintaining one cow per year	260.1 rubles
	milk per cow per year	1,329 kg
	cost of production of one centner of milk	18.9 rubles
	loss per cow	−22.0 rubles

127   Vasyukin and Davydov 1978, p. 81.
128   *Ibid.*, p. 82.
129   *Ibid.*, pp. 71–8.
130   *Pravda*, 24 November 1980, p. 2.
131   M.T. Buruyev, *Spetsializatsiya khozyaistv skotovodcheskikh zony buryatskoi ASSR* (Specialisation of enterprises in the cattle-farming zones of the Buryat ASSR), BKI, Ulan-Ude, 1974, p. 56.
132   *Narodnoye khozyaistvo buryatskoi ASSR* 1976, p. 106.
133   *Ibid.*, pp. 114–17.
134   Galdanov 1969, p. 53.
135   Ushnayev 1969, p. 57. The figures given for Buryatiya by Ushnayev are for males only. Women tend to work fewer days a year than men if they are in casual/manual jobs (*raznorabochiye*), but a few women in livestock jobs work longer hours than the average (see discussion in Chapter 5). For comparison it is worth noting that the USSR average number of days worked by a kolkhoznik (male and female) was 247.9 in 1976, but in some prosperous cotton-producing collective farms in Central Asia it was as low as 142.6 man-days. Azizur Rahman Khan and Dharam Ghai, *Collective Agriculture and Rural Development in Soviet Central Asia*, Macmillan, London, 1979, p. 97.
136   Andrei Amalrik, *Involuntary Journey to Siberia*, Collins and Harvill Press, London, 1970, p. 167.
137   *Ibid.*, p. 171.
138   D.D. Nimayev, 'Istoriko-etnograficheskiye issledovaniya v buryatii v

1977 g' (Historical-ethnographic studies in Buryatiya in 1977), in *Polevyye Issledovaniya Instituta Etnografii*, Nauka, Moscow, 1979, p. 76.

139 F.M. Ushnayev, 'Rabochee vremya i uroven' zhizni kolkhoznikov' (Working time and the standard of living of collective farmers), *Trudy Buryatskogo instituta ON AN SSSR* (Ulan-Ude), 11, 1968, p. 152.

140 Chimit Tsydendambayev, *Buryatskiye uzory* (Buryat decorations), Sovetskaya Rossiya, Moscow, 1970, pp. 9—12.

141 *Ibid.*, p. 12.

142 Amalrik 1970, p. 249.

143 B.S. Gurevich, *Obshchiye sobraniya (skhody) grazhdan v buryatii* (General meetings (*skhody*) of citizens in Buryatiya), BKI, Ulan-Ude, 1963, p. 24.

144 *Ibid.*, p. 25.

145 See, for example, 'Dolg pered polem' (Our duty to the fields), *Pravda*, 24 Nov. 1980, p. 2.

146 *Narodnoye khozyaistvo buryatskoi ASSR — statisticheskii sbornik* (The economy of the Buryat ASSR — a statistical collection), BKI, Ulan-Ude, 1953, was published in an edition of 5,000, which is small by Soviet standards.

147 *Pravda*, 24 Nov. 1980, p. 2; *Barguzinskaya Pravda*, 19 July 1980, pp. 1 and 3.

148 See discussion of the variation in local statistics in section 4 of this chapter.

149 D.D. Lubsanov, *Gazeta 'Pravda Buryatii' i eyë chitateli* (The newspaper 'Pravda Buryatii' and its readers), BKI, Ulan-Ude, 1971, p. 47. It is true that, as the author says, the fact that many of the readers of the paper are urban dwellers may affect interest in agriculture. However, in support of the view that it is the redundancy of the information, rather than the topic of agriculture itself, which turns readers away, we may cite the fact that the most popular article on agriculture for both urban and rural readers was one in which a milkmaid wrote to complain that the prizes in the 'socialist competition' in which she was engaged were unfairly distributed.

150 *Pravda*, 24 Nov. 1980, p. 2.

151 Personal communication.

152 S.K. Kazakov, *Praktikum po bukhgalterskomu uchetu v sovkhozakh i kolkhozakh* (Textbook for accounting methods in state and collective farms), Statistika, Moscow, 1973, p. 25.

153 *Ibid.*, p. 50.

154 *Sovetskaya Kirgiziya*, 15 July 1973, p. 4.

155 Dora Tiktina, *A Rural Secondary School in the Ukraine, 1948—1962* (in Russian), Soviet Institution Series no. 2, Soviet and East European Research Centre, Hebrew University of Jerusalem, 1978, p. 88.

156 *Ibid.*, pp. 104—10.

157 *Ibid.*, p. 106.

158 *Buryatskaya ASSR za 50 let*, p. 37.

159 *Krasnaya Selenga*, 25 May 1967, p. 2.

160 Kazakov 1973, p. 26.

161 Galdanov 1969, p. 37.

162 Dymbrenov 1961, p. 50.

163 *Barguzinskaya Pravda*, 29 Nov. 1975, p. 2.

164 *Ibid.*, 25 Nov. 1975, p. 5.

165 *Ibid.*, 19 July 1980, p. 1.

166 *Ibid.*, 26 June 1980, p. 2.

167 *Ibid.*, 13 Dec. 1975, p. 1.
168 *Ibid.*, 13 Dec. 1975, p. 1.
169 *Ibid.*, 19 July 1980, p. 3.
170 K.V. Vyatkina, *Ocherki kul'tury i byta buryat* (Studies in the culture and way of life of the Buryat), Nauka, Leningrad, 1969, p. 168.
171 *Barguzinskaya Pravda*, 19 July 1980, p. 1.
172 V.N. Kosinskii and G.F. Mikhailik, *Formirovaniye kolkhoznykh fondov i ikh ispol'sovaniye* (The formation of funds in collective farms and their use), Kolos, Moscow, 1977, pp. 54—9.
173 Mervyn Matthews, *Privilege in the Soviet Union, a Study of Elite Life-Styles under Communism*, George Allen and Unwin, London, 1978, pp. 93—4. It is now proposed that this should change and kolkhozy be allowed to distribute their own bonuses and prizes, *Pravda*, 24 Nov. 1980, p. 3.
174 Kerblay 1968, p. 292. Kerblay is quoting from *Izvestiya*, 22 October 1960.
175 Kerblay 1968, p. 282. He quotes A.G. Charichina, *Rol' zheleznykh dorog v razvitii sel'skogokhozyaistva* (The role of the railways in the development of agriculture), Moscow, 1958, p. 92.
176 Kerblay 1968, pp. 282—3.
177 *Ibid.*, p. 369.
178 P.B. Pleshakov (ed.), *Ocherki istorii potrebitel'skoi kooperatsii v Buryatii, 1923—1973*, BKI, Ulan-Ude, p. 142.
179 Kerblay 1968, p. 298.
180 Fedor Abramov, *Vokrug da Okolo*, Posev, Frankfurt/Main, 1962. This study of a Russian collective farm in the 1950s was originally published in the Soviet Union, in the journal *Neva* (5 May 1962), but it was later criticised.
181 Dymbrenov 1961, p. 42.
182 N.Z. Prozorov, 'Oplata truda v kolkhozakh buryatii' (Payment for labour in the collective farms of Buryatiya) in P.R. Buyantuyev (ed.), *Voprosy ispol'zovaniya trudovykh resursov bur ASSR* (Questions of the use of labour resources in the Buryat ASSR), BKI, Ulan-Ude, 1967, p. 113.
183 A. Katsnenlinboigen, 'Coloured markets in the Soviet Union', *Soviet Studies*, 29 (1), January 1977, pp. 62—85.
184 Galdanov 1969.
185 Nove 1977, p. 139.
186 Tiktina 1978, pp. 88—90.
187 Igor' Yefimov, *Bez burzhuyev* (Without the bourgeoisie), Posev, Frankfurt am Main, 1979, p. 208.
188 *Sel'skaya Zhizn'* (Rural life), 4 March 1973, p. 3.
189 *Sovetskaya Yustitsiya* (Soviet justice), 3, 1973, pp. 8—10.
190 *Pravda*, 25 Feb. 1972, p. 3.
191 *Komsomol'skaya Pravda*, 16 Jan. 1971, p. 2.
192 *Ibid.*, 2 June 1981, p. 2.

5 The division of labour

1 G.L. Sanzhiyev and Yu.B. Randalov, 'Ob izmenenii sotsial'noi struktury sel'skogo naseleniya buryatii' (On changes in the social structure of the rural population of Buryatiya), in D.D. Lubsanov (ed.), *Iz opyta konkretno-sotsiologicheskikh issledovanii* (From the experience of concrete sociological investigations), Trudy, BION 11, BKI, Ulan-Ude, 1968, pp. 41—4.

2 See K.V. Vyatkina, *Ocherki kul'tury i byta buryat* (Studies in the culture and way of life of the Buryat), Nauka, Leningrad, 1969, p. 167. For comparison with a Buryat sovkhoz see V.V. Belikov, 'Sotsial'no-professional'nyi sostav rabotnikov sovkhoza "Kizhinginskii" ' (The socio-professional composition of the workforce of the 'Kizhinga' sovkhoz), *Etnograficheskii Sbornik* (Ulan-Ude), 6, 1974b, p. 145.

3 F.M. Ushnayev, *Trudovyye resursy kolkhozov buryatskoi ASSR i ikh ispol'zovaniye* (Labour resources of the collective farms of the Buryat ASSR and their use), BKI, Ulan-Ude, 1969, p. 39.

4 Sanzhiyev and Randalov 1968, p. 43.

5 *Ibid.*, p. 44.

6 *Ibid.*, p. 44.

7 *Ibid.*, p. 45.

8 The Chairman of the Selenga farm saw the central administrative core of the kolkhoz slightly differently from Sanzhiyev and Randalov. He limited the list to seventeen people, only one of whom was a woman: Chairman (1), Vice-Chairman (1), chief accountant (1), assistant accountant (1), planner economist (1), book-keepers (3), cashier (1), head storemen (3), brigadiers (5).

9 Yu.B. Randalov, *Sotsialisticheskiye preobrazovaniya khozyaistva, byta, i kul'tury buryatskogo ulusa za gody sovetskoi vlasti* (The socialist transformation of the economy, way of life, and culture of the Buryat *ulus* in the years of Soviet power), BKI, Ulan-Ude, 1967, pp. 59–66; V.P. Tyushev, 'Iz istorii kolkhoza Zagustaiskogo somona' (From the history of the kolkhoz in Zagustai *somon*), *Ucheniye Zapiski B.-M. Pedinstituta* (Ulan-Ude), 1, 1947, pp. 24–5. The early collective farms were based on the Buryat kinship group called *khoton*.

10 D.G. Dugarov, *Khadyn azhalsha khünüüd* (Working people of the mountains), in Buryat, BNKh, Ulan-Ude, 1968, pp. 17–18.

11 G.Ts. Molonov, 'Sravnitel'nyi analiz uchebnykh interesov shkol'nikov goroda i sela' (Comparative analysis of the school interests of urban and rural pupils), in D.D. Lubsanov (ed.), *Iz optya konkretno-sotsiologicheskikh issledovanii* (From the experience of concrete sociological investigations), BION, BKI, Ulan-Ude, 1974, pp. 136–8.

12 *Barguzinskaya Pravda*, 25 Nov. 1975, p. 4.

13 Traditionally goats were used to keep the sheep warm after autumn shearing. However, sheep are now shorn only once a year in summer.

14 Vyatkina 1969, p. 167.

15 The Barguzin Karl Marx farm had a different division of the flocks in its advanced units, see V.P. Kotlykova and E.M. Erenprais, *Khonin bürihöö – khur'ga* (A lamb from every sheep), in Buryat, BNKh, Ulan-Ude, 1963. In fact the complicated division of the flocks in the Selenga farm was largely for accounting purposes and the sheep were not actually divided in this way on the pastures.

16 Ushnayev 1969, p. 72.

17 The working day is shorter, *ibid.*, p. 73.

18 Dugarov 1968, p. 20.

19 F.M. Ushnayev, 'Denezhnaya oplata truda v kolkhoz imeni Karla Marksa Selenginskogo aimaka Buryatskoi ASSR' (Money wages in the Karl Marx collective farm of Selenga district of the Buryat ASSR), in O.V. Makeyev (ed.), *Voprosy razvitiya narodnogo khozyaistva buryatskoi ASSR* (Ques-

tions of the development of the economy of the Buryat ASSR), BKI, Ulan-Ude, 1961a, pp. 110—23. The shepherds were paid 80% of the basic wage in advance each month, and the remaining 20% at the end of the year if the planned amount was produced.

20　N.S. Prozorov, 'Oplata truda v kolkhozakh buryatii' (Payment for labour in the collective farms of Buryatiya), in P.R. Buyantuyev (ed.), *Voprosy ispol'zovaniya trudovykh resursov bur ASSR* (Questions of the use of labour resources in the Buryat ASSR), BKI, Ulan-Ude, 1967, p. 113. Prozorov states that at least 25% of pay from the kolkhoz to livestock workers is 'in kind', usually in lambs.

21　Kolkhozniks also have the opportunity to buy products from the farm at reduced prices.

22　For a discussion of 'traditional' Buryat use of space in the domestic dwelling, see C. Waddington (C. Humphrey) 'Simvolicheskii aspekt v razvitii buryatskogo zhilishcha' (The symbolic aspect in the evolution of Buryat dwellings), *Etnicheskaya istoriya i sovremennoye natsional'noye razvitiye narodov mira*, IE AN SSSR, Moscow, 1967. For the very similar Mongolian use of space, see C. Humphrey, 'Inside a Mongolian tent', *New Society*, 31 October 1974a.

23　Randalov 1967, p. 107.

24　Dugarov 1968, p. 17.

25　*Ibid.*, p. 19.

26　*Komsomol'skaya Pravda*, 15 May 1981, p. 2.

27　*Komsomol'skaya Pravda*, 8 March 1981, p. 2, and 17 April 1981, p. 2.

28　*Barguzinskaya Pravda*, 22 Nov. 1975, p. 2.

29　One old man in Barguzin remembered the following months. For the full list see D. Banzarov, *Chernaya Vera* (The black faith), reprinted in *Sobraniye sochinenii*, AN SSSR, Moscow, 1955. *Khusa hara* (the month of the ram, January); *Yekhe ulaan* (big red, February); *Besege ulaan* (small red, March); *Khagdanai* (last year's grass, April); May — forgotten; *Khün hara* (month of the man, June); July, August, September, October, November — forgotten; *Buga hara* (month of the stag, December). It is significant that the Buryat months were remembered by reference to the Russian months, and that the beginning of the year was seen as January, not the beginning of the oriental lunar calendar.

30　Everyone in both Selenga and Barguzin knew the animal cycle of years and could relate them to the European calendar, e.g. from *bara* (tiger) year which was 1962 to *ükher* (ox) year which was 1973. These years were used by farm people to designate people's fortunes and personalities according to the sign under which they were born. Thus one woman said that her daughter had been born in the year of the snake (*mogoi*) and she expected her to have a difficult and sour character, but in fact she was sweet-tempered, just as though she had been born in the year of the horse. The animal years are still used by many people to assess whether couples will suit one another as marriage partners.

31　See note 20 above.

32　This policy is no longer in force, see Introduction.

33　*Sel'skaya Zhizn'*, 3 June 1973, p. 2.

34　Ushnayev 1969, pp. 65—7.

35　*Ibid.*, p. 67.

36　B.A. Ayushiyev (ed.), *Ekonomicheskiye problemy prigorodnogo sel'skogo khozyaistva buryatskoi ASSR* (Economic problems of agriculture in the suburban areas of the Buryat ASSR), BKI, Ulan-Ude, 1973, p. 74.

37 *Ibid.*, p. 77.
38 V.N. Voinovich, *Zhizn' i neobychainyye priklyucheniya soldata Ivana Chonkina* (The life and amazing exploits of the soldier Ivan Chonkin), YMCA Press, Paris, 1975, pp. 151—2.
39 *Barguzinskaya Pravda*, 2 Dec. 1975, p. 3.
40 *Ibid.*, 13 Dec. 1975, pp. 1—2.
41 *Komsomol'skaya Pravda*, 11 Feb. 1981, p. 2.
42 *Ibid.*, 18 March 1981, p. 2.
43 Ushnayev 1969, p. 71.
44 *Ibid.*, p. 71.
45 *Komsomol'skaya Pravda*, 18 March 1981, p. 2.
46 Ushnayev 1961a, p. 120.
47 *Ibid.*
48 *Ibid.*, p. 116.
49 Ushnayev 1969, p. 76.
50 P.I. Bartanov, 'Ukrepleniye kolkhozov i sovkhozov Buryatskoi ASSR rukovodyashchimi kadrami i spetsialistami v gody semiletki (1959—1965 gg)' (The strengthening of the collective and state farms of the Buryat ASSR with managerial cadres and specialists during the seven-year period 1959—65), in Z.N. Tsydypova (ed.), *Nekotoriye voprosy podgotovki kadrov i kommunisticheskogo vospitaniya trudyashchikhsya v buryatskoi partorganizatsii* (Some questions concerning the training of cadres and the communist education of the workers in the Buryat Party organisation), Min. Pros. RSFSR, Ulan-Ude, 1972, p. 15.
51 *Komsomol'skaya Pravda*, 6 May 1981, p. 2.
52 Sanzhiyev and Randalov 1968, p. 44.
53 Randalov 1967, p. 83.
54 *Ibid.*, p. 82.
55 *Barguzinskaya Pravda*, 20 Nov. 1975, p. 3.
56 *Ibid.*, 2 Dec. 1975, p. 2.
57 In 1975 the Karl Marx kolkhoz in Barguzin organised a centralised distribution of fodder to all of the distant production points. This was to be carried out by a specially constituted team of drivers. The Vice-Chairman of the kolkhoz was appointed to 'control' the operation and see that there were no illegalities by the drivers.
58 *Barguzinskaya Pravda*, 21 June 1967, p. 2.
59 Ts.B. Galdanov, *Ekonomicheskiye problemy intensifikatsii sel'skogo khozyaistva buryatskoi ASSR* (Economic problems of the intensification of agriculture in the Buryat ASSR), BKI, Ulan-Ude, 1969, p. 59.
60 *Barguzinskaya Pravda*, 5 June 1980, p. 3.
61 Sechin Jagchid and Paul Hyer, *Mongolia's Culture and Society*, West View Press, Dawson, Folkestone, 1979, p. 137.
62 Ushnayev 1961a, p. 118.
63 *Ibid.*, p. 114.
64 If the wage figures for the Karl Marx kolkhoz, Barguzin (Table 5.2) are compared with those given by Wädekin as all-Union averages for collective farms in 1968—9 it appears that the Karl Marx paid tractor-drivers and shepherds more than average, and drivers less.

Although we have no data for the Buryat ASSR on the changes in wage

Average USSR wages for 'top jobs' in collective farms grouped by gross income per square hectare of agricultural land, 1969 (rubles per month)

	I	II	III
Kolkhoz Chairman	155	183	256
Deputy kolkhoz Chairman	108	126	183
Chief accountant	104	121	165
Planner economist	99	101	135
Agronomist	97	104	118
Zoo technician	95	99	114
Engineer	77	73	108
Brigadier (agriculture)	76	83	115
Brigadier (livestock)	68	72	101

Source: K.-E. Wädekin, 'Income distribution in Soviet agriculture', *Soviet Studies*, 27 (1), January 1975, p. 23.

Pay for one man-day of various groups of workers in collective farms of the Tatar ASSR between 1966 and 1976

	1966		1976	
Category of worker	r. per man-day	% of lowest wage	r. per man-day	% of lowest wage
Chairman of kolkhoz	7.51	414.9	9.45	308.8
Chief specialists	5.61	300.0	6.71	219.3
Agronomists (lesser)	5.21	287.9	5.00	163.4
Zoo technicians (lesser)	4.90	270.7	4.93	161.1
Veterinarians	2.51	138.7	3.60	117.6
Engineers/technicians	4.32	238.7	4.70	153.6
Brigadiers	3.43	190.0	4.67	152.6
Heads of *fermy*	2.95	163.0	4.25	139.0
Tractor-drivers/combiners	4.02	220.0	5.56	181.7
Drivers	3.35	185.7	4.70	153.6
Milkmaids	2.41	133.2	3.98	130.0
Stockmen, shepherds	2.39	132.0	3.86	126.1
Pigmen	2.55	140.3	3.90	124.2
General manual workers	1.81	100.0	3.06	100.0

Source: V.V. Dyukov, *Osnovnyye napravleniya sovershenstvovaniya raspredeleniya po trudu v kolkhozakh* (Basic directions in the improvement of wage distribution in collective farms), Izd. Kazansk. Universiteta, Kazan, 1979, p. 88.

differentials in the past few years, the table from the Tatar ASSR shows that the general policy has been in the direction of raising the wages of the lowest paid in relation to those of the other groups.

65 Ushnayev 1961a, p. 116. This was an exceptionally high wage and was

criticised by Ushnayev as being abnormal. The figure of ten times the wage of the lowest worker may have included bonuses. Bonuses for farm Chairmen are paid for various 'success indicators', and the prevailing idea is that they should be kept relatively low, especially once performance has improved and they have 'served their purpose' (see Robert C. Stuart, 'Managerial incentives in Soviet collective agriculture', *Soviet Studies*, 22 (4), April 1971a, pp. 539—55).

66 Ushnayev 1961a, p. 116.
67 *Ibid.*, p. 121.
68 Dyukov 1979, pp. 91—3.
69 Prozorov 1967, pp. 110—11.
70 Recent publications have stressed the desirability of introducing a single tariff system for all wages in collective farms, including the Chairman's and specialists' incomes. Dyukov 1979, p. 83.
71 Andras Hegedüs, *Socialism and Bureaucracy*, Allison and Busby, London, 1976, p. 177; Hegedüs, *The Structure of Socialist Society*, Constable, London, 1977, p. 136; Rudolf Bahro, 'The alternative in Eastern Europe', *New Left Review*, 106, Nov.—Dec. 1977, pp. 10—13.
72 *Komsomol'skaya Pravda*, 31 July 1981, p. 2.
73 For example, in exhortations to agricultural workers to use initiative in 'struggling for the realisation' of the perspectives of the development of his farm, and instructions to administrators not to be too rule-bound and to do away with the 'narrow framework defined by various instructions'. *Pravda*, 24 Nov. 1980, p. 2.

6 Domestic production and changes in the Soviet Buryat family

1 N.R. Mangutov, *Agrarnyye preobrazovaniya v sovetskoi buryatii (1917—1933 gg.)* (Agrarian transformations in Soviet Buryatiya, 1917—1933), Academy of Sciences, BKNII, Ulan-Ude, 1960, p. 95. The shares were supposed to be allotted on the basis of the number of adult members (*yedok*) in the household, but in fact most Buryat livestock communities continued throughout the 1920s to allot shares whose size was determined by the number of livestock owned, pp. 154—9.
2 *Ibid.*, p. 159. Poor people, even though they needed hay-land, sometimes refused to take shares from the expropriated monasteries, p. 101.
3 Yu.B. Randalov, *Sotsialisticheskiye preobrazovaniya kohzyaistva, byta, i kul'tury buryatskogo ulusa za gody Sovetskoi vlasti* (The socialist transformation of the economy, way of life, and culture of the Buryat *ulus* in the years of Soviet power), BKI, Ulan-Ude, 1967, p. 138.
4 Tax on privately owned cattle and horses was abolished in 1972 (*Vedomosti Verkhovnogo Soveta SSSR*, 40, 1971, p. 535).
     In the Taimyr Peninsula, inhabited by Dolgans and Nganasans, the traditional keeping of domesticated reindeer for meat and milk has almost ceased in both the kolkhoz and the private small-holding. The culling of wild reindeer has now taken over from intensive deer-herding in the kolkhoz, and this pursuit is incompatible with the breeding and training of domestic deer by households (this was primarily men's work). Now, the men work in the public sphere for wages, and the women also work in the kolkhoz, but at their traditional task of sewing items of clothing and footwear from reindeer skin, and the household small-holding is reduced to a

minimum. Only a few domesticated deer are kept, mainly for transport. G.N. Gracheva, 'Izmeneniya v khozyaistve i bytu naseleniya pos. Ust'-Avam za poslednyye gody' (Changes in the economy and way of life of the population of the village of Ust'-Avam in recent years), *Kratkoye soderzhaniye dokladov godichnoi nauchnoi sessii instituta etnografii AN SSSR 1974–76*, Nauka, Leningrad, 1977, pp. 107–9.

5 Mervyn Matthews, 'Top incomes in the USSR; towards a definition of the Soviet elite', in *Economic Aspects of Life in the USSR*, Colloquium 1975, Brussels, 1975, pp. 132–3.

6 Stephen P. Dunn, 'Structure and functions of the Soviet rural family', in James R. Millar (ed.), *The Soviet Rural Community*, University of Illinois, Urbana, 1971, pp. 342–3.

7 C. Humphrey, 'Women, taboo and the suppression of attention', in Shirley Ardener (ed.), *Defining Females, the Nature of Women in Society*, Croom Helm, London, 1978.

8 Randalov 1967, p. 29.

9 *Ibid*.

10 M.N. Khangalov, *Sobraniye sochinenii v 3-kh tomakh* (Collected works in 3 volumes), BKI, Ulan-Ude, 1958–60, vol. 1, p. 192.

In Barguzin, an informant told me that the formula was: *dörvön büdüün* ('the four fat ones'), consisting of *nege mori, nege ükher, nege chüü*, and *nege ineen* ('one horse, one ox, one ? and one cow'). In fact, the amount paid varied from kin-group to kin-group, did not necessarily include the four 'fat ones', and often did include other items.

11 K.D. Basayeva, *Sem'ya i brak u buryat vtoraya polovina XIX–nachalo XX veka* (Family and marriage among the Buryat – second half of the nineteenth and beginning of the twentieth centuries), Nauka, Novosibirsk, 1980, pp. 139–41.

12 Basayeva 1980, p. 135.

13 Humphrey 1978.

14 N.N. Koz'min, *Ocherki skotovodcheskogo khozyaistva v Burrespublike* (Studies of the livestock economy in the Buryat republic), vol. 1, Gos. Planovaya Kommissiya, B-MASSR, Verkhneudinsk, 1924, p. 12. These studies were carried out in 1922 in the Kizhinga region, which lies somewhere between Selenga and Barguzin in its economic characteristics.

15 G.E. Dambayev, *Iz proshlogo i nastoyashchego barguzinskikh buryat* (From the past and the present of the Barguzin Buryat), BKI, Ulan-Ude, 1970, pp. 30–1.

16 Koz'min 1924, p. 13. Mangutov shows that in Buryatiya as a whole in 1929, 56.9% of the 'proletariat' went out to work in other households for some part of the year, as did 40.6% of the 'half-proletarian' families, 17.6% of the simple commodity producers, and 6.5% of the 'small capitalists'. Even families of the 'proletarian' category took in labour for 6.9 days a year on average, and the highest class of small capitalists took in labour for 104.6 days a year. Mangutov 1960, pp. 141–2.

17 Sevyan Vainshtein, *Nomads of South Siberia: the Pastoral Economies of Tuva*, Cambridge University Press, Cambridge, 1980, pp. 20–31.

18 L.P. Potapov, 'Ocherki narodnogo byta tuvintsev' (Studies of the way of life of the Tuvinians), *Trudy Tuvinskoi Kompleksnoi Ekspeditsii Instituta Etnografii AN SSSR*, vol. 1, ed. L.P. Potapov, Moscow–Leningrad, 1960, pp. 122–3.

19 A.A. Plishkina, *Povysheniye kul'turnogo urovnya i ulushcheniye uslovii byta sel'skogo naseleniya buryatii (1959–70)* (The raising of the cultural level and the improvement of the conditions of life of the rural inhabitants of Buryatiya 1959–70), BKI, Ulan-Ude, 1975, pp. 26–8.
20 Basayeva 1980, pp. 141–2. Skin carpets were an obligatory part of the traditional dowry, and they were hung over the bed.
21 Plishkina 1975, p. 38. According to the 1970 census, including other nationalities besides Buryat, the educational levels of rural dwelling men and women were as shown in the table.

	Total population	Higher finished	Higher unfinished	Middle technical	Middle general	Middle unfinished	Primary	None	No reply
Both боллоп	341,130	7,114	2,021	17,978	18,694	72,556	123,049	98,324	664
Men	161,097	3,601	950	6,786	9,900	38,358	65,970	35,288	244
Women	180,033	3,513	1,071	11,192	8,794	34,198	57,879	62,966	420

22 Robert C. Stuart, 'Structural change and the quality of Soviet collective farm management, 1952–1966' in James R. Millar (ed,), *The Soviet Rural Community*, University of Illinois, Urbana, 1971b, p. 30. Women reached brigadier status in 10–20% of cases in RSFSR collective farms, but Chairman level in only about 2% of cases in the 1950s and 1960s.
23 K.D. Basayeva, *Preobrazovaniya v semeino-brachnykh otnosheniyakh buryat* (Transformations in the family and marriage relations of the Buryat), BKI, Ulan-Ude, 1974a.
24 Plishkina 1975, p. 26.
25 Randalov 1967, p. 74.
26 Basayeva 1974a, pp. 52–5.
27 Basile H. Kerblay, *Les Marchés paysans en URSS*, Mouton, Paris, 1968, p. 306.
28 For example Plishkina 1975, p. 24.
29 Karl-Eugen Wädekin, 'Income distribution in Soviet agriculture', *Soviet Studies*, 27 (1), January 1975. See the whole article for analysis of the position of officials.
30 Azizur Rahman Khan and Dharam Ghai, *Collective Agriculture and Rural Development in Soviet Central Asia*, Macmillan, London, 1979, pp. 98–9.
31 B.S. Gurevich, *Obshchiye sobraniya (skhody) grazhdan v buryatii* (General meetings (*skhody*) of citizens in Buryatiya), BKI, Ulan-Ude, 1963, p. 32.
32 *Ibid.*, p. 17.

7 Politics in the collective farm

1 The Chairman of the farm gave me the following figures for people coming out to work on average per month in 1973:

January	600
February	617
March	630
April	656

May	700
June	770
July	774
August	775
September	717
October	650
November	600
December	552

2 F.M. Ushnayev, *Trudovyye resursy kolkhozov buryatskoi ASSR i ikh ispol'zovaniye* (Labour resources of the collective farms of the Buryat ASSR and their use), BKI, Ulan-Ude, 1969, p. 49.

3 *Ibid.*, p. 44. Barguzin was the worst district of Buryatiya in this respect. In the Ulan-Ude *raion*, for example, only 2.3% of kolkhozniks did not come out to work in 1963, and 7.3% stayed away in 1967. Most of these non-workers were women. In Barguzin, the figure for male kolkhozniks who did not work in 1967 was 10.1%, and in the Tunka *raion* it was 11.5% of able-bodied men.

4 In the Barguzin Karl Marx kolkhoz, only five men and one woman were prevented from coming to work by illness in June 1973.

5 Ushnayev 1969, p. 48.

6 *Krasnaya Selenga*, 18 March 1980, p. 3.

7 V.G. Dymbrenov, *Kolkhoz imeni Karla Marksa*, BKI, Ulan-Ude, 1961, p. 49.

8 Vladimir Soloukhin, *Izbrannyye proizvedeniya (Kaplya rosy)* (Selected works ('Drops of dew')), vol. 1, Khudozhestvennaya Literatura, Moscow, 1974, p. 426.

9 *Komsomol'skaya Pravda*, 18 July 1981, p. 2.

10 Basile H. Kerblay, *Les Marchés paysans en URSS*, Mouton, Paris, 1968, p. 330.

11 *Ibid.*, p. 330. Kerblay here is quoting Efim Dorosh, 'Derevenskiy dnevnik', *Literaturnaya Moskva*, Moscow, 1956, pp. 549 and 626.

12 Yu.B. Randalov, *Sotsialisticheskiye preobrazovaniya khozyaistva, byta i kul'tury buryatskogo ulusa za gody Sovetskoi vlasti* (The socialist transformation of the economy, way of life, and culture of the Buryat *ulus* in the years of Soviet power), BKI, Ulan-Ude, 1967, p. 112.

13 I.E. Tugutov, *Material'naya kul'tura buryat* (The material culture of the Buryats), BKI, Ulan-Ude, 1958, p. 79.

14 *Ibid.*, p. 80. The people who were first allowed to build houses in the new settlement were: (1) a brigadier, (2) a fitter-mechanic, (3) a post-office official, (4) a shepherd, (5) a harvester-operator, (6) an ordinary kolkhoznik, (7) a saddler, (8) the brigadier of the tractor team, (9) the head of the cattle-breeding unit, (10) a kolkhoznik, (11) the brigadier of another tractor team, (12) the father of no. 11, (13) the head of the meat-cattle unit, (14) the book-keeper of the tractor team, (15) a stockman. This list shows the dominance of agricultural−mechanical work in the kolkhoz status hierarchy. Some of the people listed as simply 'kolkhoznik' turn out to have influential connections (e.g. no. 10 whose son was the head of the school, or no. 6 whose son was a tractor-driver and who was himself a joiner who built several of the important kolkhoz buildings and was a communist. Before collectivisation he had lived in a felt tent).

15 T.M. Boldonova, 'Traditsionnyye pesni khorinskikh buryat, po materialam

fol'klornoy ekspeditsii 1957 g' (The traditional songs of the Khori Buryat, from the materials of the 1957 folklore expedition), *Kratkiye Soobsh-cheniya BKNII SO AN SSSR* (Ulan-Ude), 1, 1959, p. 139.

16 V.V. Belikov, 'Sotsial'no-professional'nyi sostav rabotnikov sovkhoza "Kizhinginskii" ', (The socio-professional composition of the workforce of the 'Kizhinga' sovkhoz), *Etnograficheskii Sbornik*, Ulan-Ude, 6, 1974b, p. 148.

17 *Barguzinskaya Pravda*, 24 June 1980, p. 3.

18 Randalov 1967, pp. 140—1.

19 I.M. Slepenkov and B.V. Knyazev, *Rural Youth Today*, trs. James Riorden, Oriental Research Partners, Newtonville, Mass., 1976, p. 54.

20 V.I. Boiko (ed.), *Sel'skaya molodezh' yakutii, sotsial'naya mobil'nost', otnosheniye k trudu, professional'naya orientatsiya* (The rural youth of Yakutiya, its social mobility, attitude to work, and professional orien-tation), AN SSSR SO YF, YKI, Yakutsk, 1977.

21 R.A. Kuz'mina, 'Nekotoriye aspekty otnosheniya k trudu molodykh rabochikh sovkhozov' (Some aspects of the attitude to work of young workers in state farms), in Boiko 1977, p. 35.

22 A.A. Plishkina, *Povysheniye kul'turnogo urovnya i ulushcheniye uslovii byta sel'skogo naseleniya buryatii (1959—70)* (The raising of the cultural level and the improvement of the conditions of life of the rural inhabitants of Buryatiya 1959—70), BKI, Ulan-Ude, 1975, p. 80.

23 N.V. Vasil'yev, 'Kharakter i tendentsii sotsial'no-professional'nykh pere-meshchenii evenskoi i evenkiiskoi molodezhi', in Boiko 1977, pp. 38—42.

24 Kuz'mina 1977, p. 38.

25 *Ibid.*, p. 32.

26 In the collective farms I met several women who were qualified as doctors, medical assistants, librarians, etc., but who were unable to get jobs in these professions. The majority of them were working in less good jobs (cashier, milkmaid), and spoke as though these were somewhat off and on affairs. Thus it should not be imagined that the lack of places for trained people is limited to tractor-drivers, electricians, etc. I have no figures, but it is poss-ible that the problem is just as severe for the 'higher' professions in rural districts.

27 See Mary McAuley, *Politics and the Soviet Union*, Penguin Books, Har-mondsworth, 1977, pp. 272—6 on the structure and mode of operation of the Party from primary to *obkom* levels, pp. 198—9 on the relationship between Party and Soviets at upper levels, and pp. 209—11 on overlapping personnel in the two structures.

28 The *raikom* (district Party committee) in Barguzin had at least the follow-ing enterprises and organisations under its control, each of which would have at least one primary Party organisation within it. All communists belong first to such a primary organisation and are 'elected' from this to higher bodies. In Barguzin *raion* there were: an agricultural production organisation (*selpromkhoz*), several wood production organisations (*les-promkhozy*), three kolkhozy, three sovkhozy, branches of the main Ministries, an agricultural—technical organisation (*selkhoztekhnika*), the Baikal Water-Transport Company, a *raion* hospital, a newspaper (*Barguzin-skaya Pravda*), a People's Court, a consumers' cooperative (*raipo*), the Soviet organisation's executive committee (*raiispolkom*), a society for the protection of nature, the headquarters of the northern section of the

electric grid, several fishing collectives, a bread-making factory, a fish products factory (*rybkombinat*), a dairy products factory (*maslozavoda*), many secondary schools, a meat products factory (*myasokombinat*), a food factory (*pishchekombinat*), a building organisation (SMU), and other building organisations (*PMK*, *Irkutsklesstroi*, and the Barguzin *MSO*), mixed forest and furs products organisations (*mekhleskhozy*), etc.

29 In the Aga National Okrug in 1970 64.5% of deputies to the *okrug* Soviet were Buryats, although Buryats were over 70% of the population. B.Sh. Shagdarov and Zh.D. Dorzhiyev, *Aga stepnaya* (Steppeland Aga), BKI, Ulan-Ude, 1971, p. 30.

30 Igor' Yefimov, *Bez burzhuyev* (Without the bourgeoisie), Posev, Frankfurt am Main, 1979, pp. 217—20.

31 *Barguzinskaya Pravda*, 25 Nov. 1975, p. 4.

32 Jerry F. Hough, *The Soviet Prefects*, Harvard University Press, Cambridge, Mass., 1969, p. 32.

33 *Istoriya Buryatskoi Sovetskoi Literatury*, BKI, Ulan-Ude, 1967, pp. 286—7.

34 *Ibid.*, p. 292.

35 The *obkom* checks decisions made by the *raikom* as to appointments on its *nomenklatura*. Some posts are on the *nomenklatura* of the *raikom* and the *obkom* simultaneously. See Hough 1969, p. 115.

36 Zh. Dorzhiyev and B. Shagdarov, *V stepi aginskoi* (In the Aga Steppe), Sovetskaya Rossiya, Moscow, 1967, p. 5.

37 Shagdarov and Dorzhiyev 1971, p. 99.

38 *Komsomol'skaya Pravda*, 17 Sept. 1981, p. 2.

39 Il'ya Zemtsov, *Partiya ili Mafiya?* (Party or Mafia?), Les Editeurs Réunis, Paris, 1976, pp. 26—7.

40 Yefimov 1979, p. 138. Yefimov quotes from *Leningradskaya Pravda*, 17 June 1974, on this point. 'Once he [the Chairman] has sinned to the "left", he will conduct himself in the *raion* quieter than water, lower than grass, and you can never expect him now to stand up to his superiors with any kind of criticism. He is afraid: what if suddenly they turn nasty and instead of acting as "saviours" decide to call in the procurator?'

41 *Barguzinskaya Pravda*, 25 Nov. 1975, p. 4.

42 Robert F. Miller, 'The politics of policy implementation in the USSR: Soviet policies on agricultural integration', *Soviet Studies*, 32 (2), April 1980.

43 Hough 1969, pp. 97—9.

44 Dora Tiktina, *A Rural Secondary School in the Ukraine, 1948—1962* (in Russian), Soviet Institution Series no. 2, Soviet and East European Research Centre, Hebrew University of Jerusalem, 1978, p. 24. See also B.S. Gurevich, *Obshchiye sobraniya (skhody) grazhdan v buryatii* (General meetings (*skhody*) of citizens in Buryatiya), BKI, Ulan-Ude, 1963, p. 60, where it is described how a Buryat *sel'sovet* obtains finance from individual households by voluntary 'self-taxation' (*samo-oblozheniye*).

45 *Komsomol'skaya Pravda*, 17 September 1981, p. 2.

46 M.M. Gas'kov, *Sotsialisticheskoye sorevnovaniye v kolkhozaleh i sovkhozakh buryatii* (Socialist competition in collective farms and state farms of Buryatiya), BKI, Ulan-Ude, 1970, pp. 29 and 39.

47 *Komsomol'skaya Pravda*, 17 Sept. 1981, p. 2.

48 Tiktina 1978, pp. 60—1.

49 The trade union organisation, which has branches at each enterprise and a

committee with an executive bureau at the *raion* level, seems to be more active in state farms than in collective farms. The trade union discusses such matters as: security of tenure of jobs, safety at work, the introduction of new machinery, the uncovering of people who 'violate labour discipline', the organisation of 'socialist competition', and educational work among kolkhozniks. Articles in the Selenga local newspaper complained that the trade unions were being insufficiently active. In one farm the trade union had only held two meetings in the past year. *Krasnaya Selenga*, 17 July 1980, p. 2. The trade union does however have financial resources, and it can help workers with loans in domestic crises, such as payments for funerals, visits to sick relatives, help for the children of someone hurt at work, and so on.

50 For a discussion of the changes of the 1977 constitution with particular reference to the notion of 'advanced socialist society', declared in that constitution to have been achieved, see Marie Lavigne, 'Advanced socialist society', *Economy and Society*, 7 (4), Nov. 1978. Lavigne makes the point that the achievement of 'advanced socialism' does not indicate a turning-point in Soviet society, nor a real alteration in the relations between the Party and the Soviets, but rather a change perceived in the general continuity of development in respect of three factors: the management of economic units, the relation between technical progress and the socialist economic system, and the mode of adaptation to a modified external environment.

51 *Komsomol'skaya Pravda*, 16 May 1981, p. 2.

52 Yu.V. Zaitsev, 'Iz istorii razvitiya vnutrikolkhoznoi demokratii v pervyye poslevoyennyye gody (1946—1950 gg)' (From the history of intra-kolkhoz democracy in the first post-war years, 1946—1950), in N.Ya. Gushchin (ed.), *Obshchestvenno-politicheskaya zhizn' sovetskoi sibirskoi derevni* (Socio-political life of the Soviet Siberian village), Nauka, Novosibirsk, 1974, p. 117. In many kolkhozy, despite the higher instructions to activate kolkhoz democracy in the immediate post-war years, the *raikom* could insist on holding meetings for as many times as it took for the kolkhozniks to vote the *raikom*'s candidate into office, even when it was clear how unpopular he was.

53 Tiktina 1978, p. 14.

54 C. Humphrey, 'The uses of genealogy: a historical study of the nomadic and sedentarised Buryat', in *Pastoral Production and Society*, edited by L'Equipe écologie et anthropologie des sociétés pastorales, Cambridge University Press/Editions de la Maison des Sciences de l'Homme, Cambridge and Paris, 1979b.

55 Randalov 1967, p. 140.

56 K.V. Vyatkina, *Ocherki kul'tury i byta buryat* (Studies in the culture and way of life of the Buryat), Nauka, Leningrad, 1969, p. 191.

57 K.D. Basayeva, *Preobrazovaniya v semeino-brachnykh otnosheniyakh buryat* (Transformations in the family and marriage relations of the Buryat), BKI, Ulan-Ude, 1974a, p. 75. Basayeva quotes material from the Alar (western Buryat) *sel'sovet*, where, of 220 children in 1959, only 7 died before reaching the age of one year, and in 1961, of 216 children born, only 5 died in the subsequent year.

In the Selenga Karl Marx kolkhoz, there were 95 births registered in the *sel'sovet* in 1966 (of which 71 were Buryat and 24 Russian). There were 24 deaths in the same year, but none of them according to the Secretary of the *sel'sovet* were young people. However, when visiting the children's graveyard in early summer 1967, I saw a few recent children's graves.

58 Vyatkina 1969, p. 191.
59 S.P. Baldayev, *Rodoslovnyye predaniya i legendy Buryat* (Genealogical stories and legends of the Buryat), vol. 1, BKI, Ulan-Ude, 1970, p. 158.
60 Chimit Tsydendambayev, *Buryatskiye uzory* (Buryat decorations), Sovet-skaya Russiya, Moscow, 1970, pp. 133–40.
61 *Ibid.*, p. 56.
62 *Narodnoye kohzyaistvo buryatskoi ASSR v devyatoi pyatiletke – statis-ticheskii sbornik* (The economy of the Buryat ASSR in the 9th five-year plan – a statistical collection), BKI, Ulan-Ude, 1976, p. 9. In 1975 the RSFSR birth-rate was 15.7 per 1,000 population, the death rate was 9.8, and the natural increase was 5.9; in the same year in Buryat ASSR, the birth-rate was 20.7 per 1,000, the death-rate was 8.8, and the natural increase was 11.9. Since over half the population of the Buryat ASSR is Russian, and Buryats have larger families than Russians, we may assume that these rates would be even higher if Buryats only were singled out.
63 C. Humphrey, 'Do women labour in a worker's state?', *Cambridge Anthro-pology*, 5 (2), 1979a.
64 I.N. Madason (ed.), *Buryat aradai on'hon khoshoo ügenüüd* (Buryat folk proverbs and sayings), BNKh, Ulan-Ude, 1960, p. 135.
65 Dymbrenov 1961, p. 49.
66 The full list of advantages is given in Mervyn Matthews, *Privilege in the Soviet Union: a Study of Elite Life-Styles under Communism*, George Allen and Unwin, London, 1978, p. 120.
67 *Ibid.*
68 Dymbrenov 1961, pp. 33, 35, 37.
69 *Ibid.*, p. 45.
70 Fedor Abramov, *Pryasliny* (Verandas), Lenizdat, Leningrad, 1978, pp. 27–9.
71 V.P. Kotlykova and R.M. Erenprais, *Khonin bürihöö – khur'ga* (A lamb from every sheep), BNKh, Ulan-Ude, 1963.
72 Yefimov 1979, pp. 29–33. 'Everywhere the workers consciously and deliberately try to work below their capacity, so as not to give the admin-istration the possibility of increasing their work-norms. Everywhere they hold back those people who, because of inexperience or vanity, try to move forward as *peredoviki* (workers of the vanguard). These people are surrounded by silent ill-will, general criticism, which is not outweighed by diplomas of honour, *gramoty*, and medals.'
73 *Barguzinskaya Pravda*, 22 Nov. 1975, p. 3.
74 Hough 1969, p. 116.
75 This population figure does not include people living in the *sel'sovet* who are not members of the kolkhoz, but who are eligible to join the local Party (e.g. teachers, doctors, nurses, shop-workers, etc.).
76 Slepenkov and Knyazev 1976, pp. 62 and 64.
77 I.P. Kisilev, 'Obshchestvenno-politicheskaya aktivnost' kak pedagogi-cheskoye sredstvo vospitaniya patriotizma' (Socio-political activism as a pedagogical means for the development of patriotism), in R.G. Yanovskii *et al.* (eds.), *Voyenno-patrioticheskoye vospitaniye molodezhi v sovre-mennykh usloviyakh* (The military-patriotic education of youth in con-temporary conditions), AN SSSR, Novosibirsk, 1975, p. 165.

78 Tiktina 1978, p. 25. This account refers to the 1950s and 1960s.
79 See McAuley 1977, pp. 287—90, for discussion of this point.
80 *Barguzinskaya Pravda*, 22 Nov. 1975, p. 2.
81 *Ibid.*, 19 July 1980, p. 4.
82 Yefimov 1979, pp. 169—71.
83 P.T. Khaptayev, 'Formirovaniye i razvitiye rabochego klassa v natsional'-nykh raionakh sibiri' (The formation and development of the working class in national districts of Siberia), in A.P. Okladnikov (ed.), *Rabochii klass i krest'yanstvo natsional'nykh raionov sibiri* (The working class and the peasantry of national districts of Siberia), Nauka, Novosibirsk, 1974, p. 22. In 1959, of 37,098 Buryats and Yakuts in the BASSR and YASSR who were classified as 'workers', only 7,614 worked in industry and 3,110 in transport. Most of the 'workers' were agricultural labourers in sovkhozy.
84 'Later, in Gujerat, Kosygin began a lecture on socialism and industrialis-ation to Fernandes. He spoke of the global trend towards big industries. "See how all the multinationals are developing", he is reported to have said. "Talk of small industries was 'vulgar' ", said Kosygin criticising the Janata Party's economic policy. This angered Fernandes, who objected to Kosygin's language. Immediately Kosygin apologised, saying that he only meant that the Janata Party's policy was unscientific, and since the Russian word for vulgar was the same, his interpreter had translated it as vulgar. With that ended socialist Fernandes' lessons in Soviet socialism.' *Economic and Political Weekly*, April 1979.
85 G.E. Dambayev, *Iz proshlogo i nastoyashchego barguzinskikh buryat* (From the past and the present of the Barguzin Buryat), BKI, Ulan-Ude, 1970, pp. 89—90.
86 Tiktina 1978, pp. 62—3 and 38.
87 A. Yanov, *Detente after Brezhnev*, Institute of International Studies, University of California, Berkeley, 1977, p. 9.
88 N.Z. Khrushchev, quoted in Nigel Grant, *Soviet Education*, 4th edn, Penguin Books, Harmondsworth, 1979, p. 114.
89 Grant 1979, p. 117. Pupils now do five days of production practice in the fifth, sixth, and seventh classes, and twenty-two days in the ninth class.
90 Pierre Bourdieu, *Outline of a Theory of Practice*, Cambridge University Press, Cambridge, 1977, pp. 187—8.
91 The others were:
        in Kurumkan — a Spanish language school
        in Tunka and Oka — French language schools
        in Zakamensk — a German language school
        in Selenga — an English language school
    In 'Buryat language schools', it is possible to take classes one to seven in the Buryat language.
92 Tiktina 1978, pp. 96—7.
93 Matthews 1978, p. 117.
94 *Narodnoye obrazovaniye i kul'tura v SSSR, statisticheskii sbornik* (Education and culture in the USSR — a statistical collection), Statistika, Moscow, 1977, p. 175.
95 *Ibid.*, p. 175. In 1975, of a total of 1,403,900 pupils in middle special schools, 896,100 were day students, 152,600 were evening students, and 355,200 studied by correspondence course.
96 *Barguzinskaya Pravda*, 22 Nov. 1975, p. 3.

97 *Pravda*, 21 Sept. 1958, quoted in David Lane, *Politics and Society in the USSR*, Weidenfeld and Nicolson, London, p. 505.

98 Zemtsov 1976, pp. 141—2.

99 *Ibid.*, p. 142.

100 A. Katsnenlinboigen, 'Colored markets in the Soviet Union', *Soviet Studies*, 29 (1), January 1977.

101 Quoted in George Dalton (ed.), *Tribal and Peasant Economies*, University of Texas Press, Austin and London, 1967, p. 256.

102 'The "socialist" industrial director . . . is necessarily first and foremost a bureaucratic person. How he stands with his party district leadership, or even with the local leadership, etc. is not only just as important as the economic success that he achieves together with his collective, and cannot only in many cases make up for failure, it can even predetermine the "economic" success that our system is sometimes ascribed.' Bahro 1977, p. 222.

103 Rudolf Bahro, 'The alternative in Eastern Europe', *New Left Review*, 106, Nov.—Dec. 1977, p. 212.

8 Ritual and identity

1 For an account of this see I.M. Manzhigeyev, *Yangutskii buryatskii rod* (The Yangut Buryat lineage), BKI, Ulan-Ude, 1960, pp. 181—205.

2 T.M. Mikhailov, the Buryat ethnographer, has written a detailed history of Buryat shamanism in which he suggests that the first religion of the tribes in the Baikal area was totemism and animism. This evolved into shamanism very early, between 3000 and 1000 BC. T.M. Mikhailov, *Iz istorii buryatskogo shamanizm* (From the history of Buryat shamanism), Nauka, Novosibirsk, 1980b. Other Soviet writers, however, date the development of shamanism much later, see C. Humphrey, 'Theories of North Asian shamanism', in Ernest Gellner (ed.), *Soviet and Western Anthropology*, Duckworth, London, 1979.

3 I use the word 'shamanist' in this chapter to denote the folk religious system in which shamans played an important part, but it is not necessarily the case that shamans played a role in all of the rituals described. At the *tailgan*, for example, shamans were not present.

4 T.M. Mikhailov, 'Vliyaniye lamaizma i khristianstva na shamanizm buryat' (The influence of Lamaism and Christianity on the shamanism of the Buryat), in I.S. Vdovin (ed.), *Khristianstvo i lamaizm u korennogo naseleniya sibiri* (Christianity and Lamaism in the native population of Siberia), Nauka, Leningrad, 1979, p. 139.

5 *Ibid.*, p. 140.

6 See Yu.B. Randalov, *Sotsialisticheskiye preobrazovaniya khozyaistva, byta i kul'tury buryatskogo ulusa za gody sovetskoi vlasti* (The socialist transformation of the economy, way of life, and culture of the Buryat *ulus* in the years of Soviet power), BKI, Ulan-Ude, 1967, pp. 146—68.

7 N.L. Zhukovskaya, 'Modernizatsiya shamanstva v usloviyakh rasprostraneniya buddizma u mongolov i ikh sosedei' (The modernisation of shamanism in the conditions of the spread of Buddhism among the Mongols and their neighbours), *Etnograficheskii Sbornik* (Ulan-Ude), 5, 1969a, pp. 175—9.

8 B.D. Tsibikov, 'Tsagalgan', in A.P. Okladnikov and D.D. Lubsanov (eds.),

544

Voprosy preodoleniya perezhitkov proshlogo v bytu i soznanii lyudei i stanovleniya novykh obychayev, obryadov i traditsii u narodov sibiri (Questions of the overcoming of survivals of the past in the way of life and understanding of people and the establishing of new customs, rituals and traditions among the peoples of Siberia), BION, Ulan-Ude, 1969, p. 49.

9   T.M. Mikhailov, 'Ob obychayakh i traditsiyakh buryat v sovremennyi period' (On the customs and traditions of the Buryat in the contemporary period), *Etnograficheskii Sbornik* (Ulan-Ude), 4, 1965a, p. 12. Mikhailov mentions that attempts have been made to hold the *tsagaalgan* ritual purified from all religious Lamaist elements, but that these have remained attempts.

10 *Ibid.*, p. 11.

11 Christopher A.P. Binns, 'The changing face of power: revolution and accommodation in the development of the Soviet ceremonial system', *Man*, 14 (4), Dec. 1979, and 15 (1), March 1980, p. 181.

12 'The kolkhozniks were invited to the festival in the tar stadium on one hot clear summer's day. The ceremonial meeting was opened by the Party Secretary, who warmly congratulated those present. The Chairman of the kolkhoz described the significance of the international festival of solidarity of labour, spoke about the success of our country in economic and cultural progress and external political affairs, and then gave the results and tasks of the kolkhoz, mentioned the brigades and teams which had distinguished themselves, and individual kolkhozniks. The front-line workers and people in the vanguard were given money prizes, valuable presents and honourable diplomas. After the ceremonial meeting there began an amateur concert, which became in fact a mass improvisation by the kolkhozniks. Then there were mass sports: gymnastics, volley-ball, rifle shooting, archery, national wrestling, and horse races, which greatly interested the workers. The kolkhozniks were served with hot dishes . . . and the evening ended late.' Yu.B. Randalov, 'K voprosu o formirovanii novykh obshchestvennykh prazdnikov v buryatskikh kolkhoznykh ulusakh' (On the question of the formation of new social festivals in Buryat collective farm villages), *Etnograficheskii Sbornik* (Ulan-Ude), 5 (1969), p. 21.

13 In the 1920s the *suur-kharbaan* was detached from its Lamaist associations, taken up by the Komsomol, and then deliberately staged beside the monasteries to deflect the believers from their worship. The Maidari ritual (see Chapter 8 section 4) was copied but in Soviet form. Thus, instead of the statue of Maidari pulled on a decorated cart, the Komsomols had an emblem with the hammer and sickle and the five-cornered star. To drown the sound of the monastery drums they had an orchestra, playing revolutionary marches. According to reports, the congregation, gathered for the Buddhist festival, was simply diverted to the Soviet festival, mainly by the attraction of sports and games and the demonstration of new technology, such as a Fordson tractor. Zh. Dorzhiyev and B. Shagdarov, *V stepi aginskoi* (In the Aga Steppe), Sovetskaya Rossiya, Moscow, 1967, pp. 41–2.

14 Tsibikov 1969, p. 41. Among some groups of western Buryats the festival has completely disappeared and the Russian *maslenitsa* festival takes its place.

15 G. Tsybikov, 'Tsagalgan' (Buryat new year festival), *Buryatiyevedeniye* (Verkhneudinsk), 3–4, 1927, p. 71.

16 The lama missionaries in Siberia appear to have made use of some local rituals deliberately, while fiercely denouncing others.

17 The range of deities worshipped in Buryatiya is somewhat different from Tibet.

18 I.E. Tugutov, 'Obshchesvennyye igry buryat' (Communal games of the Buryat), *Etnograficheskii Sbornik* (Ulan-Ude), 2, 1961, pp. 62—3; U.-Zh.Sh. Dondukov and B.-N. Tsyrenov, 'Bai', *Etnograficheskii Sbornik* (Ulan-Ude), 1, 1960, pp. 130—2; Tsibikov 1969, p. 39.

19 B.D. Sandanov, 'Surkharban — massovyi sportivnyi prazdnik buryatskogo naroda' (Surkharban — a mass sports festival of the Buryat people), in Okladnikov and Lubsanov 1969, p. 43.

20 *Ibid.*, p. 44.

21 Mikhailov 1965a, p. 11.

22 This is advocated for example by Sandanov 1969.

23 Tugutov 1961, pp. 62—3; Dondukov and Tsyrenov 1960, pp. 130—2.

24 T.M. Mikhailov, 'Perezhitki dolamaistskikh verovanii v buryatskoi ASSR' (Survivals of pre-Lamaist beliefs in the Buryat ASSR), in T.M. Mikhailov (ed.), *Sovremenniye problemy buddizma, shamanizma i pravoslaviya* (Contemporary problems of Buddhism, shamanism, and Orthodox Christianity), BFION, Ulan-Ude, 1980a, p. 53.

25 T.M. Mikhailov, 'O sovremennom sostoyaniye shamanstva v Sibiri' (On the contemporary situation of shamanism in Siberia), in L.E. Eliasov (ed.), *Kritika ideologii lamaizma i shamanizma*, BKI, Ulan-Ude, 1965b, p. 91.

26 S.P. Baldayev, *Rodoslovnyye predaniya i legendy buryat* (Genealogical myths and legends of the Buryat), part 1, *Bulagaty i Ekhirity* (Bulagats and Ekhirits), AN SSSR BION, Ulan-Ude, 1970, pp. 198, 48—9; I.E. Tugutov, 'The tailagan as a principal shamanistic ritual of the Buryats', in V. Dioszegi and M. Hoppal (eds.), *Shamanism in Siberia*, Akademiai Kiado, Budapest, 1978, pp. 278—9.

27 Mikhailov 1965b, p. 91.

28 Sybzhit Tupchinova, aged 67 in 1967, and wife of the famous Bolshevik leader and founder-member of the Communist Party in Bayangol, Rinchin Tupchinov, is an example of someone who married without a wedding.

29 K.D. Basayeva, *Preobrazovaniya v semeino-brachnykh otnosheniyakh buryat* (Transformations in the family and marriage relations of the Buryat), BKI, Ulan-Ude, 1974a, p. 99.

30 S.P. Baldayev, *Buryatskiye svadebnyye obryady* (Buryat wedding rituals), BKI, Ulan-Ude, 1959; Basayeva 1974a; K.D. Basayeva, *Sem'ya i brak u buryat (vtoraya polovina XIX — nachalo XX veka)* (Family and marriage among the Buryat — second half of the nineteenth and beginning of the twentieth centuries), Nauka, Novosibirsk, 1980; L. Linkhovoin, *Zametki o dorevolyutsionnom byte aginskikh buryat* (Notes on the pre-revolutionary way of life of the Aga Buryat), BKI, Ulan-Ude, 1972; Manzhigeyev 1960.

31 My informants from Selenga and Barguzin occasionally called the endowment given to the son on marriage *enzhe* as well as using this word for the endowment of the daughter. However, the latter is the usual meaning of the term.

32 Basayeva 1980, p. 135.

33 *Ibid.*, p. 133.

34 A.F. Trebukhovskii, *Svad'ba balaganskikh buryat v proshlom i nastoya-*

shchem (The wedding of the Balagansk Buryat in the past and the present), Verkhneudinsk, 1929, p. 10, and Basayeva 1980, p. 138.

35 An old man from Barguzin said that the bridegroom would sometimes go on a formal visit to inspect the prospective bride (*basagan üzekhe*) and had the right to refuse to marry her if he did not like her. The bride had no such right.

36 In Selenga they said that the horse year (1954) produces people of 'soft' character, who should marry someone from a 'hard' year, e.g. the snake (1953), the leopard, or the monkey years. Such beliefs were less prevalent in Barguzin, which is further from Mongolia and less influenced by Lamaism.

37 Basayeva 1974a, p. 101. The Buryat ethnographer Tugutov describes Selenga Buryat weddings of the 1950s as marked at each point by ritual offerings of vodka: (1) at the betrothal, (2) when the groom comes to take the bride and her girl friends refuse to allow him to take her until they are offered vodka or *arkhi*, (3) when the bride's side 'recognise' the lost animal as the groom, and signal this fact by sipping *arkhi*, saying 'Yes, it's ours, a very capricious one', etc., (4) during the marriage itself, when the bride's match-makers are offered vodka, which they refuse until more is added, and then all guests from the bride's side are given vodka and money. I.E. Tugutov, *Material'naya kul'tura buryat* (The material culture of the Buryats), BKI, Ulan-Ude, 1958, pp. 181–3.

38 *Nomkhon, nomkhon morigoo*
    Nogoodoni tabiya
    Noyon tüshimel tandan'
    Ain zugaa ürgeye.

39 Basayeva 1974a, p. 102.

40 B.E. Petri, *Vnutrirodovyye otnosheniya u severnykh buryat* (Intra-clan relations among the northern Buryat), Irkutsk, 1925, p. 43.

41 Basayeva 1974a, p. 103.

42 Baldayev 1959, p. 117.

43 This ritual is called *basagan mürgekhe* (obeisance of the bride) by the Barguzin Buryats. When praying, the Buryats used to kneel, to place their palms together above the head, in front of the face, and at the chest. The family deity's representation was placed in the north-west corner of the *yurta* on an altar (*burkhan shiree*).

44 I.E. Tugutov, 'Stanovleniye novykh semeinykh obryadov' (The establishing of new family rituals), *Etnograficheskii Sbornik* (Ulan-Ude), 4, 1965, pp. 19–20. Buryats and Mongols call grass which is green and juicy 'blue'.

45 Vyatkina 1969, p. 52.

46 *Ugaa martahan khüye uhan deerhee gal edikhe,*
    Tengriyee martahan khüye temeen deerhee nokhoi zuukha.
    T.M. Mikhailov, 'O shamanskom fol'klor buryat' (On the shamanist folklore of the Buryat), in A.I. Ulanov (ed.), *Buryatskii fol'klor*, BION, Ulan-Ude, 1970, p. 73.

47 Basayeva 1974a, p. 105.

48 This could be a Buryatisation of the Russian *esaul*, or it might be *zahal* from the verb *zahakha*, to correct, set right.

49 Basayeva 1974a, pp. 106–7.

50 *Ibid.*, p. 107.

51 *Ibid.*, p. 108.

52 Randalov 1967, p. 145. Mikhailov 1965a, p. 13, mentions a wedding in Ulyun in Barguzin in 1963 at which the young couple were given commodes, sideboards, chests of drawers, a bed, several sets of bedclothes, five tables, two complete table settings, a suit of clothes, dresses, seven samovars, two radios, two clocks and several head of cattle, not including smaller gifts.

53 Basayeva 1974a, p. 83. Tugutov (1965, p. 35), mentions that the word used for the presents taken home from the *milaagod*, usually meat, was *garguu*, which has two meanings: exceptional, and fertile or prolific in giving birth. Sometimes in Barguzin this ceremony used to occur in expectation of giving birth, the 'egg *milaagod*' *ündege milaaga*.

54 Radnayev, 1965, p. 86.

55 Tugutov 1965, p. 35; Basayeva 1974a, p. 83.

56 Tugutov 1965, pp. 23—5.

57 Tugutov 1965, pp. 27—8.

58 Tugutov 1965, p. 29.

59 A *subbotnik*, however, is normally not paid labour.

60 This material was obtained from conversations with a few people and should not be regarded as exhaustive.

61 *Muukhan* — a Barguzin variant of *buumkhan* from the Tibetan *bum-k'ang*, a shrine erected in commemoration of a lama.

62 Mikhailov 1965b, p. 97.

63 Mikhailov mentions that there is near Bayangol a stone, shaped like a lying bull, which is worshipped. It is called *bukha shuluun* (bull stone) and is probably connected with the shamanist cult of Bukha Noyon, mythical bull ancestor of the Ekhirit and Bulagat tribes, and hence ancestor of the Hengeldur and Shono clans who form the majority of the Bayangol population. This stone was not mentioned to me by the kolkhozniks, but it is possible that it was transformed into an *oboo* under Lamaist influence and was in fact one of the *oboos* just mentioned. Mikhailov 1980a, p. 56.

64 *Naigur* usually means an ecstatic religious movement among young shamanists, who go from village to village in a crowd, singing, shaking from head to foot, and wailing. I.A. Manzhigeyev, *Buryatskiye shamanisticheskiye i doshamanisticheskiye terminy* (Buryat shamanist and pre-shamanist terms), Nauka, Moscow, 1978, p. 59.

65 *Türge* are branches of birch, which are put into the ground in a row at the *tailgan* sacrifice. Wooden pails with milk (*sagaan*) and milk vodka (*arkhi*) are placed by each birch branch, according to the number of families taking part in the sacrifice. The *türge* has more or less the same significance as lighting a candle before an icon for an orthodox believer. I do not know exactly what ritual the informant meant. Manzhigeyev 1978, p.73.

66 *Yëdo*, also known as *zhodoo*, a piece of pine bark, lit to provide a cleansing smoke.

67 *Oboo*, means 'heap or cairn'. The word *oboo* is used in Lamaism for the stone equivalent of the shamanists' *sheree*, a heap of bones formed on a stone altar by the remains of sacrificed animals at the *tailgan*. See discussion in section 4 on *oboo*. The Barguzin informant said an *oboo* could be at a tree or stone in the steppe, which makes the shamanist origin of these sites even clearer. They are held to be inhabited by spirits of the locality.

68 Tugutov 1978, pp. 267—80.

69 Manzhigeyev 1960, pp. 189—95.
70 *Tailgans* which separated the rituals for individual spirits were conducted in the later period, and this is why the number of *tailgans* increased.
71 Tugutov 1978, p. 278.
72 Manzhigeyev 1961, p. 18.
73 T.M. Mikhailov, 'O perezhitkakh shamanizma u buryat' (On the survivals of shamanism among the Buryat), *Etnograficheskii Sbornik* (Ulan-Ude), 3, 1962, p. 90.
74 Mikhailov 1965b, pp. 92—3.
75 Manzhigeyev 1978, p. 104. This existed before the Revolution, but has become more important.
76 I.A. Manzhigeyev, 'Prichiny sushchestvovaniya shamanisticheskikh pere-zhitkov i sposoby preodoleniya ikh' (Reasons for the existence of survivals of shamanism and means of overcoming them), *Etnograficheskii Sbornik* (Ulan-Ude), 3, 1962, p. 81.
77 The Buryat shamanists had various other deities which were the personifications of the power of water itself for good and evil, the Uhan-Khad (the 'water kings'). Myths associated with them were different from the ones about the Uhan-Khaalyuud.
78 Mikhailov 1965b, pp. 92—3.
79 Mikhailov 1962, p. 89.
80 Tugutov 1978, p. 271.
81 T.M. Mikhailov, 'O metodike izucheniya sovremennogo sostoyaniya sham-anizma' (On the methodology of studying the contemporary state of shamanism), in D.D. Lubsanov 1968, p. 119.
82 T.M. Mikhailov notes from 1963 expedition to Bokhan *raion*. Archives of Buryat filial of AN SSSR, no. 3082.
83 Zhukovskaya 1969b, p. 234.
84 Helene Carrère d'Encausse, *L'Empire eclatée*, Flammarion, Paris, 1978, p. 167. She also makes the point that the Red Army is an instrument of de-nationalism for small ethnic groups, because of its Russian ambiance. This is perhaps something which concerns the families of Buryats sending their sons away.
85 Manzhigeyev 1962, p. 81.
86 During the shaman's initiation ceremony, he was asked:

Kholoin khünde	To the far away person
Ükhereer oshkhuush?	Will you travel by ox?
Ööryn khünde	To your own person
Ulaan ybagaar oshkhuush?	Will you go on foot?

The shaman replied, 'I shall.'

Bayan khünde	From the rich person
Yuhen müngehöö	Nine kopecks
Ülüü abkhysh?	No more will you take?
Ügytek khünhee	From the needy person
Gurban müngenhöö	Three kopecks
Ülüü münge obkhysy?	No more will you take?

The shaman replied 'I will not take more.' T.M. Mikhailov, 'O shaman-skom fol'klor buryat' (On the shamanist folklore of the Buryat), in Ulanov 1970, p. 75.
87 *Ibid.*, p. 84.
88 Mikhailov 1965b, p. 89.

89 Mikhailov 1968, p. 119.
90 See T.M. Mikhailov and P.P. Khoroshikh, *Buryatskii shamanizm, ukazatel' literatury (1774–1971 gg)* (Buryat shamanism, bibliography 1774–1971), BKI, Ulan-Ude, 1973.
91 T.M. Mikhailov, 'Shamanskiye perezhitki i nekotoryye voprosy byta i kul'tura naradov Sibirii' (Shamanist survivals and some questions of the way of life and culture of the peoples of Siberia), in Belousov 1971, p. 63.
92 Basayeva 1974a, p. 77. Old men, in particular, says Basayeva, give way to a child's every whim. The old people say, *ükher bolokhodo ukhaa orokho*, 'when he becomes big [literally, an ox] then sense will come.'
93 Manzhigeyev 1962, pp. 83–4.
94 *Ibid.*, p. 82.
95 Mikhailov 1965b, pp. 102–3.
96 Manzhigeyev 1962, p. 80.
97 Personal communication.
98 Mikhailov 1965b, p. 93.
99 Manzhigeyev 1962, p. 82.
100 *Ibid.*, p. 84.
101 Mikhailov 1968, p. 122.
102 Mikhailov 1965b, p. 103.
103 Manzhigeyev 1962, p. 82. This shaman threatened atheistic-minded inhabitants of the village with the magical word *zhadkhadkham*, 'I cast a spell on you.'
104 *Ibid.*, p. 84. Manshigeyev reports that all religions present a 'united front'; he makes the point that this demonstrates not their strength but their weakness. However, T.M. Mikhailov recounts that he met a shaman in 1973, who said that, instead of the usual dreams of the beginning shaman, he had had to undergo an examination in his dream. The examining board gave him three questions, one on shamanism, one on Lamaism, and one on general religion of the Buryat. He passed the examination with top marks, and thereafter considered himself qualified to practise as a shaman. Mikhailov 1979, p. 134.
105 Mikhailov 1979, p. 133. This is not a new phenomenon since the existence of *dzhochi* is reported from 1923. The *dzhochi* had shaman's equipment (the headgear, *maikhabshi*, the drum, *khese*, the drumstick, *toibur*, the horse-stick, *unagan hor'bo*, the whip, *tashuur*, and the iron tube, *kholbogo*); at the same time he had lama's equipment (the hat, the *khadag* ritual scarf, the dagger, *purbu*, the musical instrument, *khur*, the offering bowls, etc.). Mikhailov reports the existence of other shamans who became lamas, but continued to shamanise. Present shamans and unofficial lamas have very little of the traditional equipment. The drum is almost the only item retained by shamans, and even this is sometimes dispensed with. *Ongons*, the models or pictures made of the ancestor and locality spirits, have also largely disappeared, it seems from the literature. However, informants' views of this differed: some said that no one kept *ongons* any more, while others said that they were kept by old people, but hidden.
106 *Ibid.*, p. 146. Mikhailov describes the rise of a new syncretic cult 'Maidarism' in the 1920s. Although Maidari is a deity of the Buddhist pantheon (see section 4 below) this cult spread among the shamanist western Buryats and was characterised by simplified rituals to shamanist, Orthodox and Buddhist deities, requiring only small offerings. This cult must have

been related to, though not identical with, the popularity of Maidari, the coming Buddha, among the more purely Lamaist eastern Buryats.

107 K.M. Gerasimova, *Lamaizm i natsional'no-kolonial'naya politika tsarizma v zabaikal'ye v XIX i nachale XX vekov* (Lamaism and the national-colonial politics of Tsarism in Trans-Baikal in the nineteenth and beginning of the twentieth centuries), B-MNIIK, Ulan-Ude, 1957, pp. 93—104.

108 Mikhailov 1971, p. 68.

109 In 1893 there were 15,000 Buryat lamas, about 10% of the entire Buryat population. Not all of these were official lamas. A Tsarist government resolution of 1853 had limited the number of official lamas to 285, with the intention of suppressing pro-Mongolian feeling in its border population — a concern which was to remain with the Soviet government. The official lamas received their own land shares, the size depending on their rank in the monastery. Each monastery also had its own land. The *datsan* at Gusino-ozersk in Selenga district, for example, had 1,500 *desyatinas* (1,650 hectares). About one third of the total number of lamas lived not at the monasteries but with the general population. A.K. Kochetov, *Lamaizm*, Nauka, Moscow, 1973, p. 48.

110 *Ibid.*, pp. 124—5.

111 K.M. Gerasimova, *Obnovlencheskoye dvizheniye buryatskogo lamaistkogo dukhovenstva* (The reform/revival movement of the Buryat Lamaist clergy), BKI, Ulan-Ude, 1964, pp. 155—73.

112 *Ibid.*, p. 88.

113 For a description of the fate of these leaders see Robert A. Rupen, *Mongols of the Twentieth Century*, vol. 1, Indiana University Publications Uralic and Altaic Series no. 37 part 1, Mouton, The Hague, 1964, pp. 45—7, 103—11, 201—3.

114 R.E. Pubayev, 'Perezhitki lamaizma v bytu i soznanii buryatskogo sel'skogo naseleniya' (Survivals of Lamaism in the way of life and understanding of the Buryat rural population), in Okladnikov and Lubsanov 1969, p. 137.

115 Kochetov 1973, p. 177. At the Aga *datsan* they built a new *suburgan* shrine, the 'concentration of the strength of the lamas', and buried inside it 100,000 steel needles, which at the moment of the outbreak of war would turn into the Shambala army to fight against destroyers of the faith.

116 Mikhailov 1979, p. 129.

117 Pubayev 1969, pp. 138—45.

118 Kochetov 1973, p. 185.

119 Pubayev 1969, p. 139.

120 Kochetov 1973, p. 126.

121 R.E. Pubayev, 'Zadachi nauchno-ateisticheskoi propagandy po preodoleniya perezhitkov lamaizma i shamanizma' (Tasks of scientific-atheist propaganda in overcoming the survivals of Lamaism and shamanism), in L.E. Eliasov (ed.), *Kritika ideologii lamaizma i shamanizma* (Criticism of the ideologies of Lamaism and shamanism), BKI, Ulan-Ude, 1965, p. 10.

122 Kochetov 1973, p. 181.

123 Pubayev 1965, p. 14.

124 *Ibid.*

125 Pubayev 1969, p. 140.

126 Kochetov 1973, pp. 170—1.

127 *Ibid.*, pp. 152—3.

128 Zh.D. Dorzhiyev, 'K voprosu ob obychayakh i obrayadakh aginskikh buryat' (On the question of the customs and ceremonies of the Aga Buryat), in Okladnikov and Lubsanov 1969, p. 167.

129 Pubayev 1969, pp. 144—5.

130 Mikhailov 1979, p. 129.

131 Pubayev 1965, p. 17.

132 A.D. Takhanov, 'O preodolenii perezhitkov proshlogo v bytu i soznanii sredi nasleniya Tunkinskogo aimaka' (On the overcoming of survivals of the past in the way of life and understanding of the population of Tunka district), in Okladnikov and Lubzanov 1969, p. 132.

133 Described in detail by K.M. Gerasimova, 'Kul't obo kak dopolnitel'nyi material dlya izucheniya etnicheskikh protsessov v Buryatii' (The oboo cult as additional material for the study of ethnic processes among the Buryat), *Etnograficheskii Sbornik* (Ulan-Ude), 5, 1969a.

134 *Ibid.*, p. 136.

135 The deities are called 'Mongols' (i.e. ancestral inhabitants of the region), 'Sabdaks' (from the Tibetan term for locality spirits), and 'Khans' (i.e. owner 'lords' of the vicinity). *Ibid.*, p. 136.

136 *Ibid.*, pp. 137—8.

137 A.D. Urzhanov, 'Ob odnom sanaginskom spiske "serzhema" Bukha-Noionu na tibetskom yazyke' (On a Sanaginsk text, the 'serzhem' of Bukha-Noion in Tibetan), *Trudy BION* (Ulan-Ude), 12, 1969, pp. 129—33.

138 Zhukovskaya 1969b, p. 228.

139 Gerasimova 1969a, p. 139.

140 Zhukovskaya 1969b, p. 230.

141 K.M. Gerasimova, 'Izmeneniya v bytovoi obryadnosti lamaizma v sovre-mennykh usloviyakh' (Changes in the practical ritual of Lamaism in contemporary conditions), in Mikhailov 1980a, p. 23.

142 V.B. Tsybikzhapov, 'Sovremennaya tserkovnaya organizatsiya lamaizma v Buryatii' (Contemporary church organisation of Lamaism in Buryatiya), in A.A. Belousov (ed.), *Voprosy preodoleniya perezhitkov lamaizma, shamanizma i staroobryadchestva* (Questions of the overcoming of the survivals of Lamaism, shamanism, and 'Old Believer' orthodoxy), BKI, Ulan-Ude, 1971, p. 77.

143 Pubayev 1965, p. 19.

144 The shamanist burial ritual was carried out in 1958 for the father, a teacher, of Dorzhi Zhambal, former Chairman of the Bayangol *sel'sovet*. The body was dressed in good clothes and taken out of the house immediately (not left for seven days and taken out on a horse, as would have been the case for a shaman). No coffin was made. The body was taken to be burnt at a spot in a wood, where other cremations had taken place. All male relatives of the Buura lineage were present and some friends from work, but no women. Tobacco and other things for smoking were put with the corpse, which was burnt without delay. Those present drank vodka while it burnt, and some speeches were made about the dead man's life and achievements. On the way home a gate was built with a small fire between the posts and all those present had to cross it for purification. There was a big feast, at which women could be present, afterwards. On the third day afterwards a few male relatives went to see that the corpse had burnt entirely, collected the bones and buried them. On the fortieth day there was a memorial dinner at home for close kinsmen and women

(possibly Russian influence, since orthodox wakes end on the fortieth day after death).

145 Tugutov 1958, p. 186.
146 *Ibid.*
147 Gerasimova 1969a, p. 118.
148 K.M. Gerasimova, 'Lamaistskaya transformatsiya animisticheskikh predstavlenii' (The Lamaist transformation of animist conceptions), in B.V. Semichev (ed.), *Materialy po istorii i filologii tsentral'noi azii* (Ulan-Ude), 4, 1970, p. 35.
149 Zhukovskaya 1969b, p. 231.
150 Sakyamuni (Sanskrit Ćakyamuni, the last Buddha); Aryabala or Ariyabalo (Sanskrit Aryabala, he of the noble powers, popular name for Sanskrit Avalokiteĉvara, the most famous of the Bodhisattvas. He was portrayed among Buryats as having six arms, see V.V. Ptitsyn, *Selenginskaya Dauriya, ocherki zabaikal'skago kraya* (Selenginsk Dauriya, studies of Trans-Baikaliya), St Peterburg, 1896, p. 25); Nogoon Dara Ekhe and Tsagaan Dara Ekhe (Green Tara Mother and White Tara Mother, from Sanskrit Tārā, star, usually explained as saviouress, the most popular goddess of late Lamaism, bringing family happiness).
151 Zhukovskaya 1969b, p. 231.
152 *Ibid.*, p. 238.
153 I.E. Tugutov, 'V Baragkhanskom sel'skom muzee' (In the Baragkhan Rural Museum), *Sovetskaya Etnografiya*, 2, 1960, pp. 178—9.
154 Gerasimova 1980, pp. 18—19.
155 *Ibid.*, p. 27.
156 See C. Humphrey, *Magical Drawings in the Religion of the Buryats*, Cambridge University Press, Cambridge (forthcoming).
157 Zhukovskaya 1969b, p. 230.
158 Gerasimova 1980, p. 28.
159 Kochetov 1973, p. 185.
160 *Ibid.*
161 Linkhovoin 1972, p. 79.
162 Takhanov 1969, p. 137.
163 Kochetov 1973, p. 187.
164 *Altkhna Zyayarlig*, a Kalmuck publication quoted in Kochetov 1973, p. 187.
165 K.A. Nadneyeva, *Kritika nekotorykh nravstvennykh doktrin lamaizma* (Criticism of some moral doctrines of Lamaism), 1969, p. 12, quoted in Kochetov 1973, p. 190.
166 Kochetov 1973, pp. 188—9.
167 The Maidari cult was increasing in importance in Nepal, Tibet and Mongolia during the 1920s. In Mongolia new monasteries were founded at the beginning of the century in honour of Maidari, and in Nepal a Mongolian lama had erected a statue of Maitreya with the legs not in the usual lotus position but on the ground, indicating that the deity was prepared to arrive. Nicholas Roerich reported that in Mongolia in 1924 the clergy were expecting the arrival of Maitreya Buddha in 1936. In Buryat and Mongol conceptions Shambala is a place of learning. The original idea was that this was mystical knowledge, attained through the third eye by the use of mystical forces. But the Buryat version was 'modernised', to quote Roerich: 'Another highly intelligent Buryat, one of the Mongolian leaders,

told us how a Buryat lama reached Shambala after many difficulties . . . As this lama, returning home from Shambala, passed a very narrow subterranean passage, he met two men carrying, with utmost difficulties, a thoroughbred sheep needed for some scientific experiments, which are being made in this remarkable valley' (Nicholas Roerich, *The Heart of Asia*, New Era Library, New York, 1929, p. 142). Shambala was invoked by the Mongolian troops in the 1921 Revolution who sang: 'The war of Northern Shambala! Let us die in this war, To be reborn again As Knights of the Ruler of Shambala!' (*ibid.*, p. 143).

In the early decades of this century a Maidari cult appeared even among the western Buryat shamanists. A shaman called Ünkhei started this movement, which included in its pantheon Buddhist shamanist deities and Orthodox saints. The ritual included reading from a text, as in Lamaism, and sacrifices as in shamanism. Its attraction partly lay in the fact that it was cheaper than ordinary shamanism; instead of tubs of vodka and whole sheep 'Maidarism' demanded only small goblets and pieces of meat. Mikhailov 1979, pp. 146−7.

168 N.L. Zhukovskaya, *Lamaizm i ranniye formy religii* (Lamaism and early forms of religion), Nauka, Moscow, 1977, p. 105.

169 Eliasov 1965.

170 N.A. Mironov, 'Soderzhaniye i nekotoryye formy i metody antireligioznoi propagandy' (The content and some forms and methods of antireligious propaganda), in *Protif religioznykh perezhitkov*, BKI, Ulan-Ude, 1960, p. 40.

171 *Ibid.*, p. 41.

Conclusion

1 It has unfortunately been impossible to make an adequate analysis of Buryat political history in this book. The early nationalist and socialist leaders of the revolutionary period were succeeded by Bolsheviks, such as Sangadiin of Barguzin, in the late 1920s. These were succeeded by a different kind of leader, based on Party position, in the 1930s.

2 N.L. Zhukovskaya, 'Iz istorii dukhovnoi kul'tury mongolov ("podarok-otdarok" i ego mesto v sisteme tsennostei)' (From the history of Mongolian spiritual culture − the 'gift and counter-gift' and its place in the system of values), in V.I. Vasil'yev and G.P. Vasil'yeva (eds.), *Vsesoyuznaya konferentsiya 'Etnokul'turnyye protsessy v sovremennom mire'* (All-union conference 'Ethnocultural processes in the contemporary world'), AN SSSR, Elista, 1981, pp. 145−6.

3 See C.A. Gregory, 'Gifts to men and gifts to god: gift exchange and capital accumulation in contemporary Papua', *Man*, 15 (4), 1980, pp. 626−52.

4 It will be remembered that each patrilineage is supposed to have its own spiritual qualities, deriving we must suppose from the accumulated and recycled qualities of the ancestors. Buryats call people from lineages other than their own *khari*, 'foreign', while patrilineal kinsmen are called *khaluun*, literally 'warm'.

5 Zhukovskaya 1981, pp. 145−6 is doing the same as Malinowski did in his analysis of the kula and other transactions in Trobriand society, or Marshall Sahlins (*Stone Age Economics*, Tavistock Publications, London, 1974, pp. 196−204) in a more abstract version.

6 I am here adopting the distinction made for example by Skinner between the sense of a word, the nature and range of the criteria by which a word is standardly employed, and its range of reference, that is, given an understanding of the sense of the word, the relating of the word to the world. Quentin Skinner, 'Language and social change', in Leonard Michaels and Christopher Ricks (eds.), *The State of the Language*, University of California Press, London, 1980, pp. 564–6.

7 B.D. Tsibikov, *Obychnoye pravo selenginskikh buryat* (The customary law of the Selenga Buryat), BKI, Ulan-Ude, 1970, pp. 78–9, 82–5.

8 I.E. Tugutov, *Material'naya kul'tura buryat* (The material culture of the Buryats), BKI, Ulan-Ude, 1958, p. 43.

9 J.E. Kowalewski, *Dictionnaire Mongol–Russe–Français*, 3 vols. Universitetskaya Tipografiya, Kazan, 1844, vol. 2, p. 1102.

10 S.P. Baldayev, *Buryatskiye svadebnyye obryady* (Buryat wedding rituals), BKI, Ulan-Ude, 1959, p. 21.

11 The word *barisa* was current in the Barguzin Karl Marx farm in this sense in the 1970s and there were evidently some such sites in the vicinity.

12 Mongolian and Buryat used to have a special vocabulary for addressing honoured people. It was rigorously excised from the written language in the 1920s and 1930s.

13 K.M. Cheremisov, *Buryaad-orod slovar'* (Buryat–Russian dictionary), Sovetskaya Entsiklopediya, Moscow, 1973, pp. 654–5.

14 Joseph Obreski, *The Changing Peasantry of Eastern Europe*, Schenkman Publishing Co., Cambridge, Mass., 1976, p. 37.

15 Zhukovskaya has written about the Buryats: 'And thus, it is particularly territorial-kinship ties which most of all preserve traditions from oblivion.' 'People who for one reason or another are torn from their accustomed social sphere are more inclined to depart from tradition. Usually this applies to young people going to Ulan-Ude or to other cities for education, and finding themselves on their return for work not in their home village but in another place. Traditions are upheld by collective consciousness. The cross-cutting distribution of the population, moving for its own ends, leads to a natural dismemberment of family-kin collectives. Finding themselves away from kin-groups and their traditions, these people lead lives in accordance with the rules, customs and traditions of a new collective. The necessity of governing themselves in their activities not by the opinion of kin, but by their own healthy sense and experience, has the effect of individualising their consciousness.' N.L. Zhukovskaya, 'Sovremennyi lamaizm (na materialakh buryatskoi ASSR)' (Contemporary Lamaism, on the basis of materials from Buryat ASSR), *Mysl'* (Moscow), 1969b, p. 234.

16 I believe that this conclusion is justified, on the basis of work such as that of Zhukovskaya (*ibid.*) or that of T.M. Mikhailov, even though the question is more complicated in detail. Certain authors have tried to maintain the classical 'early Bolshevik' position that individualism of consciousness is a 'survival' of pre-collectivised economic practice, for example, from a Buryat novel: ' "I do not believe in your commune!" flared the old man. "Brother and brother cannot live under one roof. And here you are talking about strangers . . . and everything in common? I don't believe it. I'll believe in your commune when some bright chap invents a rake which will rake away from oneself and collect it all in one heap. But till then, while rakes work in the old way, towards oneself . . . remember my words, you'll

never build your commune." ' (V.Ts. Naidakov, A.B. Soktoyev and G.O. Tudenov, *Rol' literatury i isskustva v bor'be s perezhitkami proshlogo* (The role of literature and art in the struggle with survivals of the past), BKI, Ulan-Ude, 1968, p. 127). But to identify this individualism, which can in fact coexist with recognition of higher collective rights, with the differentiation and personalisation of individual values and goals, is to make a methodological mistake (see discussion in the Introduction).

17　There is some evidence that this is already the case in the capital city of Ulan-Ude and elsewhere in the Soviet Union, where there is growing interest in yoga, techniques of meditation, Buddhist theories of perception and consciousness, etc. Unfortunately we know little about these developments.

9　The collective farms after Socialism

1　Mikhail Zhvanetskii 'Kak vyzhit'?' *Vechernii Ulan-Ude,* 17 Sept. 1997, p. 16.
2　I am endebted to Alena Ledenova for this observation.
3　This happened in the Dzhida and Ivolga districts. The re-amalgamation was difficult, as the livestock and machinery had all been divided up. Unfortunately, I do not know more about the process of recollectivisation.
4　Bair Gomboyev, Vice-Chairman in the State Committee for Ecology, Buryatiya, personal communication.
5　There is one joint-stock company (*aktsionernoye obshchesvo*) in Kurumkan District, along with one state farm, six collective farms, and two OKKh.
6　As in the Preface, I use the term *collective* for all types of large joint enterprise. OKKh is *ob'yedinaniya krestyanskikh khozyaisv;* SKKh is *sovmestnoye krestyanskoye khozyaistvo;* AKKh is *assosiyatsiya krestyanskikh khosyaistv;* and AKKKh is *assosiyatsiya kollektivnykh krestyanskikh khosyaistv.*
7　Named after a famous nineteenth-century Decembrist rebel against Tsarism, a traditional Soviet hero.
8　The new statutes of the Karl Marx Collective in Selenga, established in 1993, state that the farm is self-financed, has its own independent bank balance, and is a "juridical person" (i.e., licensed to trade on its own account). The economic base of the farm is its rights to use its land, and its main purpose is the increase in income of its members. Its tasks are listed as collective regulation of "interpeasant" relations, the introduction of effective economic forms and balanced technologies, and the collective protection of the rights and legal interests of the members. The members have the right to work in their speciality. The farm is managed by a Chairman and a 12-person Committee, both voted in for two years, and general meetings are to be held twice a year, with a quorum consisting of one-third of the members and two-thirds of the managing committee. The Chairman is allowed to make independent decisions on economic questions of up to 100,000 rubles in value.
9　*Barguzinskaya Pravda,* 21 April 1995, p. 1.
10　Luzhkov (1996, 166–8) gives an excellent example of how this operated in the late 1980s in his attempt to reform the provision of vegetables for the city of Moscow.
11　The laws about land, such as the Land Codex, were in abeyance in summer 1996, and a Presidential Edict of 7 March 1996 on the same subject had not been put into practise. The laws in any case are badly known. The Local Administrator of Barguzin told me that he was the only person in the area to subscribe to a newspaper which printed the new laws.

12 *Barguzinskaya Pravda* 17 March 1995, p. 2.

13 The Selenga Karl Marx Collective was recognised in 1995 as successful in breeding of high-quality livestock and given a subsidy to develop this work; it is not clear if this qualifies the farm as a *goskhoz.*

14 These were, and often still are, known as *podsobnoye khozyaisvo* (subsidiary economy), reflecting the continued importance given to the collective as the main economy.

15 See Hivon 1998, for an interesting discussion of how a similar system works in north Russia.

16 "Russia survey," *Economist,* 12 July 1997, p. 17.

17 *Barguzinskaya Pravda,* 4 Sept. 1996, p. 2.

18 In 1995 one kilo of live weight in sheep was worth around 3,000 rubles, while a bottle of vodka cost 10,000 rubles in rural Barguzin.

19 Only a few years ago the Selenga collective had 300 pigs, but it was unable to afford to feed them. Households also have difficulty in getting fodder for pigs, and the number in private ownership has been declining. Horse numbers are gradually rising, because the high cost of petrol forces people to use them for work and transport. They are also used for meat (though, unlike in Mongolia, their milk is not used).

20 In the Barguzin District as a whole the number of collectively owned cattle went down by 10,000 from 1990 to 1996, while the number in private hands rose only by 4,000 (*Barguzinskaya Pravda,* 31 Oct. 1996, p. 1).

21 The Karl Marx Collective in Selenga sowed 3,750 hectares of grain fields in 1996, as compared with 5,003 hectares in 1966, and it was expecting a harvest of around 40,000 centners of grain, as compared with 82,912 centners in 1966.

22 The Selenga Karl Marx had 2,800 hectares of hay meadows in 1996, as compared with 4,009 hectares in 1966. One thousand of the 2,800 hectares was given out to the households as part of their private economies.

23 The population of the Iroi *selsoviet* (site of the Selenga Karl Marx Collective) in 1967 was 2,483; in 1996 it was 2,103 (608 households). The main difference between the two periods is that household size has gone down from an average of 4.6 people in 1967 to 3.45 in 1996. In Bayangol *selsoviet* the population in 1996 was 3,042, consisting of 912 households living in five villages. Average household size reduced from 4.22 in 1975 to 3.3 in 1996.

24 In the Barguzin District the rural population went from 14,700 in 1985 to 14,600 in 1995, while in Selenga it changed from 20,400 to 18,800 in the same period. Since 1990 the population of the Iroi *selsoviet* has remained almost constant: 2,290 in 1990 and 2,103 in 1996.

25 *Barguzinskaya Pravda,* 29 March 1996, noted that cases of syphilis in the district had risen fourfold in a year. Buryatiya had 453 cases of syphilis per 100,000 population, a total of 4,700 in the Republic, in 1996 (*Ogni Kurumkana,* 21 Feb. 1997, p. 3). It has recently been decided that no one may be offered a job without first being tested for venereal diseases.

26 In 1995, 123 people left the Bayangol subdistrict, and in the same year there were 47 births and 28 deaths.

27 This is not counting those living in the outlying villages of Udunga and Ust'-Urma, which make up the 608 households of the Iroi subdistrict.

28 They responded with further questions, such as, "You mean the people staying here now?" or "Do you mean the official adult workers?" or "Do you mean our family or the whole group of families?"

29 Meshcheryakov (1996a) reports that many Buryats, whose indigenous economy is pastoralism, have only the most rough and ready methods for growing vegetables, even as compared with Muscovites like himself (who also depend on domestic production to some extent).

30 In Karl Marx Collective, Selenga, there is around 1,800 hectares of collective hayland, as compared with 1,000 used by the households.

31 In a few parts of Buryatiya, but not in Bayangol or Tashir, the *ütüg* (cleared, fertilised, and irrigated meadows, see pp. 273, 275) of pre-collective times are being restored.

32 In Bayangol three hectares were allocated. Much depends on the quality of the grass; three hectares in one place is equivalent to two in another.

33 Tunka is relatively prosperous mainly because it has a well-surfaced road and good access to the ports, railways, and towns along the south shore of Baikal. A "Dandy" is a computer game for children.

34 I am grateful to James Laidlaw for suggesting the point.

35 *Selenga,* 7 Feb. 1997, p. 2.

36 In Gusino-ozersk, district capital of Selenga, till recently it was difficult to buy milk because the town dairy had few suppliers of milk as it paid such abysmal prices. Seeing the queues, neighbouring plot holders began to disobey the sanitary regulations and sold unpasturized milk at markets. The district authorities reacted to this situation *not* by supporting the households by providing pasturizing facilities but by forming a group of collectives and enforcing a joint price agreement with the dairy. The collectives then made agreements with the individual sellers, paying them 50% of the price in money and the rest in fodder in autumn. As a result the position of collectives was strengthened, the "spontaneous" (*stikhiinoye*) milk was forced off the market, and the plot holders lost out (*Buryatiya,* 25 July 1997, pp. 2).

37 In the Selenga Karl Marx Collective in 1996 there were around 100 households out of 608 which had no livestock at all, and the Chairman told me that he gave emergency supplies to around 10 of them. In Bayangol *somon,* of 912 households 141 have no livestock.

38 I am grateful to Roberts Kilis for this observation, from his work in rural western Siberia (1997).

39 I never met anyone who spoke well of the private farmers, mainly because they were thought to be only out for personal (and absurd) enrichment – e.g., "He got a grant to buy machinery and he bought a Mercedes; think of it, on our roads!" For an interesting discussion of how villagers and private farmers exert social pressure on one another and thus help one another survive, however, see Hivon's account (1997) of north Russia.

40 In this farm the collective's sheep and pigs have gone altogether, seed corn and fertiliser were stolen to buy drink, the cows' milk yield went down by six times in one year because so much fodder had been stolen, and most work is done by hand because the machinery has been stolen (*Barguzinskaya Pravda,* 15 March 1996, p. 1).

41 *Barguzinskaya Pravda,* 21 April 1995, p. 1.

42 Unemployment benefit hardly exists in rural areas; as the former employer is obliged to pay into the unemployment fund, ways are found to get rid of workers without making them formally unemployed.

43 Pensions are paid in principle from funds contributed by employers, along with social insurance, employment, and medical insurance. Contributions to social funds took up around 40% of the wages bill, I was told, in the Selenga farm.

Yet, as most collectives do not pay wages they do not contribute to the pensions fund either. A republic like Buryatiya does not in any case cover its total pensions bill and relies on subventions from Moscow. Even when Moscow launches a campaign to cover the arrears in pensions, however, the local pension fund officials may refuse to pay out, claiming that the local dues have not been received.

44 Pensions can be quite small but with various extras which most people can claim for length of work, ill health, etc., they amount to about two-thirds the wage of a worker (e.g., fitter, secretary, or forester).

45 Roberts Kilis, personal communication.

46 People complain that collectives do not use market prices, but lower ones, to make these calculations.

47 Each bag contains 50 kilos of flour. "A full year's work" is a number of days which varies in different farms.

48 Taxes for hay land, house, and vegetable plot are paid to the administration, not the collective. Tax is around one-third of a month's wage for a manual labourer. It can be paid in produce.

49 In the case of unfulfilled contracts the Corporation could demand other goods, such as livestock, but normally it gives a "prolongation" of the contract: the farm may pay later without interest.

50 The Chief Economist of Bayangol told me that the Corporation buys at 1,000 rubles per kilogram of grain in the fall and sells seed grain at 1,600 rubles in spring.

51 The former Chairman of Karl Marx Collective in Bayangol told me that the annual cycle used to be to receive credits during the winter, which were more or less repaid in autumn with the harvest. But long-term debts were annulled several times. The last time debts were annulled was 1991.

52 Baragkhan is near the place named Sarankhur on Map 2.

53 The Baragkhan farm has a "business plan," according to which 20% of the total product is paid in wages (cream, meat, and grain), and regular supplies of grain and forage are given to all workers during the year to support their domestic livestock. The grain workers receive 15% of the total product of their sector, which is more profitable than the farm as a whole.

54 See Humphrey (in press).

55 This point is emphasized throughout Buryatiya, e.g., in Bichura, where local bakeries, sausage making, vegetable preserving, cedar nut processing, and sewing workshops are being set up (*Buryatiya,* 25 July 1997, p. 3).

56 Cream, from which butter is made, is sterilised at high temperatures in vats heated by a coal-fired boiler.

57 For example, a team of plumbers mending the collective's central heating boiler was paid in butter, though the team leader tried hard to bargain for money.

58 Such barter is conducted by reckoning money prices for the goods involved, though it is not clear in what sense these could be said to be "market" prices, since in many cases a market hardly exists.

59 The ex-communist Potapov was voted in as President of Buryatiya in 1994, and with this there was a change of personnel. Many reform-minded administrators were shifted to distant and less-influential posts. Nevertheless, the reform tendency is a prominent voice in local politics.

60 The old *kolkhoz* shepherding settlements consisted of two families per team, but the great reduction in sheep in the last few years has made half of the houses redundant.

61   It is possible, judging from what other shepherds told me, that Dulma gets a proportion of the lambs as her wages. If she cuts any wool over the contracted amount, she can sell it.

62   Information about this farm is derived from tape-recordings made by Raleigh International in 1993.

63   Such a large sum is almost impossible to borrow by an ordinary person. Katya must have had official links and advice. To obtain the loan she had to write a professional business plan, get this registered, and detail the function of each of the members of the farm.

64   The rent Katya pays to the collective might in theory be distributed to its shareholders as dividend, but as the collective is in debt and has not divided up its lands to shareholders (so no one knows whose lands Katya is using) this will not happen.

65   The "shares" of 15 to 20 people are required to obtain one tractor, and each share comes with a debt of one million rubles. It is not clear why land shares and shares in livestock do not seem to involve these debts.

66   In Buryatiya, as in Mongolia, wrestling has become the most popular of the traditional "three manly sports," the others being archery and horse racing. Wrestling is widely practised, and top sportsmen are considered true heroes, like football players in Europe. For the close connection between the manly sports and the epic hero, see Hamayon 1997.

67   In areas with extensive industrial unemployment, however, such as Dzhida, there are programmes to set households up as smallholders rather than support them through unemployment benefits. The *Moye Podvor'ye* programme took land from local collectives and allocated one cow per household to support 2,869 families this way (*Buryatiya,* 24 July 1997, p. 5).

68   Many villagers resisted privatisation, even though the costs were not high.

69   The idea of "outsider" even applies to near neighbours, such as the forestry organisation at Yubileinyi (pp. 152–3). It is acceptable for the Bayangol collective to lease hay land to Yubileinyi, but a request by a private farmer from Yubileinyi for some land was refused.

70   *Ogni Kurumkana,* 24 Feb. 1997, pp. 1–2.

71   Information from recordings made by Raleigh International.

72   *Barguzinskaya Pravda,* 4 Nov. 1996, p. 2.

10 Rural culture and visions of the future

1   It is most unlikely, said one girl from Bayangol, who is now a student in Ulan-Ude, that any young Buryat people would make a "wrong" marriage, since everyone is brought up to know about exogamous clans and parents, and a wide circle of kin take an active interest in vetting marriage partners from this point of view. Indeed, I learned that the *milaagod* festivity (pp. 398–9) also takes place before marriage, on which occasion kin trace all the relatives of various clans who must be invited to the wedding.

2   Clan vote blocs are important in Tunka, the district of origin of the Buryat politician Saganov, who was recently defeated by the Russian Potapov in presidential elections (Galina Manzanova, Sergei Panarin, pers. comm.). I did not hear of similar voting patterns, however, in Barguzin or Selenga.

3   For an explanation of why female spirits are so often the crucial ancestor spirits for patrilineal clans, see Humphrey 1996, 188, 284.

4 The cupboard contains no image of the spirit but, rather, grains and other offerings.

5 The Emege-Eezhi is worshipped communally twice a year, once at the Lunar New Year and once in summer.

6 This is the clan of Lyuba, the energetic Trade Union organiser of the collective.

7 The population of Tashir is about 35% Russian. Besides this, there are 4 Tatar, 4 Chinese, and 2 Chuvash families, while the rest of the 500 or so households are Buryat. Purbo said he did not attend the Emege-Eezhi festivities but worshipped instead at his own clan *oboo* further up the valley, "where my ancestors came from." Russians do go to other *oboo*s, and Russian drivers universally make offerings at Buryat wayside shrines.

8 Abayeva (1992, 88) notes that there used to be a funerary construction in the form of a log cabin at this place. In it was a trunk with clothing inside. People used to bring the clothing of ill people and those suffering from psychological disorders and place them in the trunk. The lid was left open. All this suggests shamanic exorcism and is similar to shamanic practises among the Daurs (Humphrey 1996, 272–85).

9 Physical evidence of the shamanic burial site has been removed and replaced with the cupboard shrine and Tibetan prayer in the Buddhist idiom. The Buddhisisation of the cult is seen also in the fact that it is not a *tailagan* sacrifice; in other words, animals are not slaughtered at the site. Cooked meat is taken up from the village. The more shamanic aspect of the Emege-Eezhi cult, however, is perhaps retained in individual visits to the shrine. People come with problems and questions for the Mother; they make libations and pray silently, and somehow in this process their queries are answered. There is no shaman in the Iroi Valley.

10 Burin Khan is said to have a warlike appearance. The Burin Khan mountain has 13 *oboo*s on its summit. Clans from all surrounding districts worship there, and only men may participate.

11 If this is not done, people told me, the marriage would be unhappy and dogged by misfortune.

12 The motif of prosperity linked to retention and boundedness appears in the story of Bull-Stone (*bukha-shuluun*) told to me in Bayangol in 1990. This bull-shaped rock lies just outside Bayangol, near the Russian Bodonskii State Farm. According to legend: "A Russian stole some Buryat cattle of the local type and drove them off in the direction of Barguzin town. He stopped for the night at Bodon, and in the morning when he woke up he was amazed to find that the whole herd had turned to stone. From this time no one has dared to drive off cattle. The local population became rich and prosperous and the place began to be called Bayangol [Rich Valley]. Bull Stone is a place of worship [*mesto pokoleniya*] for the Buryats." Another similar legend concerns Sturgeon Snout, a cliff located at the opening of the valley. This cliff spirit is said to "strictly follow who leaves and who enters the Barguzin Valley, and any Buryats going beyond the boundaries of Barguzin should make a libation to the being who inhabits the cliff."

13 This word is pronounced *tsagaalgan,* as in Mongolian, in Selenga, but the generally recognised Buryat spelling is *Sagaalgan.*

14 In Tunka, to the west of Selenga, in 1995 a family experienced a series of bad omens: sparrows hitting the windows, the son injuring his leg, a cuckoo flying into the yard, the grandmother having nightmares. These portents were explained by a shaman: the household had grazed its livestock on a hillside "owned" by "Grandfather" Sambuyev. The Grandfather is the spirit of a local shaman who

died in the 1960s, and the family had neglected to honour him. Further misfortune was averted by the sacrifice of a ram and four bottles of vodka to the spirit. In the same district rites are performed twice yearly to request the spirits to grant fertility of cattle (Zhukovskaya 1997, 100–101).

15 In addition to the local Bayangol sites (p. 402) there are five main sacred sites (*tavan sabdag*) in Barguzin Valley: (1) Boolon Tümer (lit. Sacred Iron), the lake from which the River Barguzin flows; (2) Barkhan Uula, the highest mountain in the Barguzinsk Range; (3) Shabogor Khada (lit. Sharp Cliff), the steepest peak in the Barguzinsk Range; (4) Bukha Shuluun (lit. Bull Stone, see n. 12), and (5) Khel'men Khoshuun (lit. Sturgeon Snout, see n. 12).

16 The sacred grove is located at the foot of the hill with a Buddhist *muukhan* mentioned on p. 402.

17 True, apathy hangs over many farms. In collectives which appear to be doomed or in which the best parts have already been hived off, such as Bayangol, communal meetings are sometimes so poorly attended that they do not reach a quorum.

18 The Prayer House was opened in 1995 on the request of the villagers in the building of the former chemists' station of the hospital. The spacious building has many rooms for worship and prayer. The lama in charge is a young, highly qualified young man from the Tamchinsk Monastery, near Gusino-ozersk. He was trained in St. Petersburg and knows English as well as Tibetan. He says prayers at people's request, gives Buddhist teaching to children, does astrological consultations, and conducts all the rituals at sacred springs (*arshan*), *oboo*s, and locality spirit cults.

19 I stayed in the hotel in 1996, along with a team of plumbers repairing the collective's furnace, but the hotel keeper said she thought the hotel might close soon.

20 A modest affair, which heats only the farm's offices and the houses of "the elite," as one or two people complained to me.

21 Not occupied in 1996 but in working order.

22 The kindergarten has 67 children, all from Tashir. The children of farm members pay much reduced fees (2,000 rubles a month, as opposed to the highest fees of 50,000 per month). There are 16 staff, including nurses, cooks, washerwoman, watchman. The collective supplies all the food for the kindergarten at low rates. Another kindergarten has closed.

23 The school has 11 classes and 460 children, with 70 boarders. The administration was unable to cover the costs of the boarding school in 1996, so richer parents were asked to contribute food. The first four classes are taught in Buryat and the higher classes in Russian. Many pupils go on to further training or education, around 15–20% go straight to work and around 5% into the army. The collective has stopped its training scheme which provided grants for further training for its brightest students. In recent years many school leavers have been unable to get work, especially girls, and they stay at home with nothing to do.

24 Founded in 1985, the school has a hall for performances and several practise rooms. There is (1996) one young teacher and 13 students who pay a small fee for their lessons. Singing and a range of European and Buryat instruments are taught: piano, accordion, *domra, bayan, chanza,* and the *morin khuur.* The collective farm built the school and provides central heating.

25 The library has a collection of around 25,000 books and a children's section of 6,000–7,000 books. The three staff have created a comfortable atmosphere, with armchairs and tables for study. They devotedly collect newspaper cuttings on subjects likely to interest the farmers (on local history, on the neighbouring mon-

astery, on legal aspects of contracts, taxes, and pension rights, etc.). The only service recently discontinued is the travelling library service to herders on distant pastures.

26 The hospital used to have 25 beds but now has only 10. Medical insurance is planned but not yet in place, so the hospital treats patients free (medicines have to be purchased, however). The head doctor of the hospital is the wife of the Chairman of the collective.

27 See the illuminating discussion of unequal access to *kul'tura,* based on the passport system, in Anderson 1996.

28 I was with an elderly man at an *oboo,* where he made a libation, and then descending from the summit he said: "What is wrong today? Traders (*torgovtsy*). They should be got rid of. Why? They make money only for themselves, and that makes other people poor."

29 *Barguzinskaya Pravda,* 20 Sept. 1996.

30 The school has a workshop where the children learned to make furniture, tables, chairs, and so forth. Later, people began to order coffins, because the school workshop was cheaper than ordering from distant towns. So the children began to make coffins, this impurity affected their minds, and they began to treat one another with brutality (Zhukovskaya 1997, 99).

31 The Russian families in the village also contributed, though they did not attend the rites.

32 One might posit that distance from markets would affect attitudes: a place like Tashir, close to Gusino-ozersk within a few hours drive of Ulan-Ude, might be more market oriented than Bayangol, which, even if one is lucky with the roads and river crossings, is a good two days away from the capital. But this does not seem to be the case.

33 Herders and milkers from Udunga I encountered at their summer pastures were living in deepest squalor, surrounded by rusting milking equipment, but with a TV to while away the day. "Of course I keep a gun," said one herder, "What if bandits were to turn up?"

34 "It is no accident that 78% of ordinary villagers questioned said, given the choice of working in a collective farm, a cooperative, a production group with contracts, a privatised farm, or a traditional (i.e., pre-collectivisation) household economy, that they prefer the collective farm (kolkhoz)" (Manzanova 1997).

35 The Russian term *pai,* not the indigenous *khubi,* is used for present-day land shares, though *khubi* was used for land shares in the nineteenth century. This indicates that the parallel drawn here between *pai* and *khubi* is my interpretation, not one current in the villages. Buryat farmers I talked to see *pai* as a modern idea, while *khubi* applies to traditional situations (sacrificial portions, shares of hunted game).

36 Ostrowski (1990, 537), discussing the influence of the Mongol Kipchak Khanate on Muscovy, wrote: "In contrast to Kievan Rus', where the landowner took his land with him, in Muscovy when a *votchinnik* left the service of the grand prince for another prince his property reverted to the grand prince. The grand prince could also grant property as a reward for past service. In contrast to the situation in European feudalism, future service was not a condition of the grant, nor was any reciprocal obligation required of the ruler. In Mongol, as in Muscovite society, each individual, as a matter of course, owed service to the ruler. One did not need to specify it in a contractual agreement."

37 In Mongolia itself a different system of rule, in which ruling princes were not

genealogically related to their subjects, took over with the Manchu Dynasty in the seventeenth century.

38 The kinship basis of clan membership could be extended to include nonkin, who thereby became "kin" (clan members) while remaining a separate subgroup. This was a common practise, called "territorial kinship" by Petri (1924), which permitted the clan as a political and fiscal unit to continue while allowing some mobility to households. I quote from a late-nineteenth-century Buryat document: "The natives and elders of the Sartul clan at a general meeting in the Torei settlement gave their agreement to the native of the Atagan clan, Tsynbylov and his colleagues, that they would be accepted according to their wish into our Sartul clan and that we will answer for them if they are unable to pay taxes and dues. Land, both hay-meadows and arable fields, will be given to them from our areas, and if in future their numbers multiply we guarantee to increase the amount of land without hindrance" (Sydenova 1992, 22).

39 Gerasimova has written about Inner Asia: "The specificity of clan ownership rights to land was that it was disconnected from economic use. Karl Marx wrote that the appropriation of land as a collective property, naturally belonging to a social collective, 'emerges not by means of labour, but precedes labour as its condition.' Such appropriation of land rests on representations of land as naturally or sacredly given to the group. In the traditional world-view, the appropriation of land by a kin group is defined as its sacred right, as its spiritual property" (1989, 257).

40 Commenting on this passage, Even and Pop (1994, 263) observe: "Consommer une part de cette nourriture sacrificielle – qui devait demeurer a l'intérieure du clan afin que la prospérité ne s'en échappe pas – permettait aux lignées de réaffirmer l'appartenance au clan et de tirer bénéfice des solidarités qui en découlaient."

41 "The expense of carrying out a *tailagan* are divided in advance into shares (Russ. *pai*), and for the sake of their honour the rich people take several shares, while poor people take only one. Complete paupers take part in the festivities along with everyone else, without contributing anything. In one of the clans of the Kudinsk district (*vedomstvo*) they celebrated 14 *tailagans* in 1887. Over that period the meat eaten, the bread and alcohol consumed, came to a sum of 2,620 rubles. The clan consisted of 108 households, so each one should have contributed about 24 rubles. But, in fact, the allocation was as follows: the poor households took a single share, equivalent to 8 rubles, while the rich ones took 4–5 shares, i.e., to a value of 32–40 rubles" (Astyrev 1891, 246).

42 I am grateful to David Sneath, who raised this point in discussion with me.

43 This is why it is common in Inner Asia for parents to closely scrutinize a newborn child for physical signs that he or she is a reborn ancestor.

44 The skeleton is a metaphor for the patrilineal line; *yahan* (B. clan) is also the word for "bone."

45 This idea is found among both philosophers and villagers. In the latter case it is used as an explanation for general disasters like floods or epidemics (Galdanova 1992, 156).

46 For example, there are regular visits by politicians, lamas, and intellectuals between the two peoples.

47 The deportation of 1943 resulted in the loss of one-third of the people and had other disastrous consequences; thirteen years of dispersal in alien lands broke the Kalmyks' economic abilities and cultural traditions and led to loss of Kalmyk as their main language.

48 A number of chess clubs called "Kirsan-Shatar" (Kirsan Chess) have been set up to encourage knowledge of the Mongolian native chess game as well as the international variant (*Pravda Buryatii,* 19 Sept. 1997, p. 6).

49 The election of Yosif Davydovich Kobzon brought the tiny polity of Aga to 'all-Russia attention in September 1997. Kobzon is famous not only for his singing but also because his close Mafia links and shady business deals have made him a dubious figure internationally (refused a U.S. visa, thrown out of Israel). In Buryatiya his huge vote (80%) was attributed to his "buying" of the local leaders and to patriarchal relations in Aga which incline people to vote as their leaders instruct them. His advent was greeted with criticism (he is "not ours") but also with some envy of the funding from Moscow he will bring to the region. Grants constitute 85% of the Aga budget (*Vechernii Ulan-Ude,* 17 Sept. 1997, pp. 1–2; *Inform Polis,* 18 Sept. 1997, p. 2).

50 Ries (1997, 26–30) gives a wonderfully nuanced description of *narod* as a keyword. Buryats have absorbed this Russian array of understandings as their own.

51 This type of representativeness of communities operates at various levels; the more famous the figure, the wider the community calling on their name.

52 *Ogni Kurumkana,* 25 Oct. 1996, p. 1.

53 The visiting young sportsmen at the tournament were addressed: "From our whole soul we welcome you to the wonderful Barguzin land, at the foot of the sacred Barkhan Mountain, to the homeland of manly people" (*Ogni Kurumkana,* 25 Oct. 1996, p. 1).

54 *Ogni Kurumkana,* 4 Oct. 1996, p. 3.

55 Soodei Lama lived at the turn of the century. He was a yogi who was the incarnation of Nagarjuna, the founder of the Mahadyamika school of philosophy. Highly educated and well travelled, Soodei Lama also had extraordinary powers, in particular prophesy.

56 Soodei Lama is presently incarnated in an elderly lama in India. It is devoutly hoped that the next incarnation will be again in Barguzin (*Ogni Kurumkana,* 18 Nov. 1996, p. 1).

57 *Ogni Kurumkana,* 25 Sept. 1996, p. 4.

Glossary

The spelling of Buryat words is taken from Cheremisov 1973.

aimak   Bur. *aimag*, administrative unit within Buryat ASSR, equivalent to the district (Russ. *raion*)

artel'   workers' cooperative, organised on the same basic principles as the collective farm; this term was used most commonly in the 1920s and 1930s but is still sometimes employed to refer to collective farms or units within collective farms

buluk   Bur. *büleg*, section, used in the first two decades of the twentieth century for the lowest level of administration on territorial principles; a land-holding unit consisting of several settlements (*khoton*)

datsan   Bur. *dasan(g)*, from Tib. *grva-tshang*, Lamaist monastery with teaching faculty

desyatina   Russian unit of square measurement used until approximately the mid-1920s, equals about 2¾ acres or 1.1 hectare

enzhe   Bur. *enzhe*, property given by bride's family to bride after marriage, usually livestock

esige   Bur. *esege*, lit. 'father', also used for sub-division of patrilineal descent group or lineage (*yahan*)

ferma   Russian term for livestock production unit within a collective or state farm

ispolkom   abbreviation of Russ. *ispolnitel'nyi komitet*, executive committee; commonly refers to committees in the structure of Soviets

khoton   Bur. *khoto(n)*, lit. pen or enclosure for livestock, used for settlement or camp

Komsomol   Youth Branch of the Communist Party

krai   region, equivalent to *oblast'*; used for some far-flung regions of the USSR (from Russ. *krai*, edge)

milaagod   Bur. *milaanguud*, festival to celebrate the birth of a child

obkom   Russ. abbreviation for *oblastnoi komitet*, regional committee, usually used for committees of the Communist Party

oblast'   region or province, administrative unit comprising several districts (*raion*); the Buryat ASSR is hierarchically equivalent to an *oblast'*

oboo   Bur. *oboo*, lit. a heap or cairn; used for ritual cairns situated

	on the top of hills where Lamaist ceremonies are carried out, often requests for timely rain, good luck and fertility
okrug	Russ. district, equivalent to *raion*
otara	Russ. sheep flock, used for sheep production unit within a collective or state farm
partorg	Russ. abbreviation for 'Party organiser', secretary of primary Party unit such as the Party section attached to a collective farm
raiispolkom	Russ. abbreviation for 'district executive committee', usually used for committees of the district level of the Soviets
raikom	Russ. abbreviation for *raionnyi komitet*, district committee; commonly refers to the Party committee or Party offices at the district level
raion	Russ. district (in Buryat ASSR briefly termed *khoshun* after the Revolution), comprising several lowest level administrative units such as the Russ. *selo*, village, or Buryat *somon* (see below)
rod	Russ. lit. race, genus, kind, used in ethnographic literature for 'clan' or 'lineage'; in the nineteenth century used by the Tsarist government as an administrative unit for ruling Buryats and other oriental peoples amongst whom kinship appeared to dominate over territoriality in the organisation of society
sel'sovet	Russ. term for the organisation of elected deputies (Soviet) at the level of the *selo* (village); in fact this unit, which is the lowest administrative level of the Soviet government, may comprise several villages or settlements
somon	Bur. *somon*, from Mong. *sum* 'arrow', originally a military unit, subsequently an administrative unit in the Mongolian Empire; adapted by the Buryats as equivalent to the *selo*, e.g. in *somonoi sovet*
subbotnik	Russ. term for day of voluntary labour on Saturday (*subbota*)
surkharbaan	Bur. *suur-kharbaan*, Buryat summer festival of archery with other sports such as wrestling and horse racing
tailgan	Bur. *tailga(n)*, large-scale communal sacrifices, usually of horses and/or sheep, carried out by Buryat shamanists
tsagaalgan	Bur. *sagaan sar* (or *hara*), lit. 'white month', New Year festival, held at the beginning of the first month by the Oriental lunar calendar, usually in February
ulus	Bur. *ulas*, Mong. *uls*, 'people' or 'state', used in ethnographic literature on the Buryats to refer to the village or group of settlements
ütüg	Bur. *üteg*, manured hay-field, often also irrigated; used sometimes to refer to the winter settlement of a household in general
üüse	Bur. *üüse*, meat from livestock killed in the autumn, frozen and kept to last through the winter
volost'	Russ. district in pre-revolutionary administrative system initiated on territorial basis at the beginning of the twentieth century
voskresnik	Russ. term for day of voluntary labour on Sunday (*voskresen'ye*)

567

Glossary

VUZ	Russ. abbreviation for *vysshee uchebnoye zavedeniye*, 'higher educational institution'
yahan	Bur. *yaha(n)*, lit. 'bone', 'skeleton', used by some groups of Buryats to refer to patrilineal descent group
zahal	Bur. *zahal*, dowry, consisting of jewellery, clothing, domestic utensils, etc. given to bride at wedding

References

Abayeva, L.L. 1992. *Kul't gor i Buddizm v Buryatii,* Nauka, Moscow.

Abramov, Fedor. 1962. *Vokrug da okolo,* Posev, Frankfurt am Main; trs. F. Abramov, *The Dodgers,* Flegon Press, London, 1963.

Abramov, Fedor. 1978. *Pryasliny* (Verandas), Lenizdat, Leningrad.

Amalrik, Andrei. 1970. *Involuntary Journey to Siberia,* Collins and Harvill Press, London.

Anderson, David. 1995. 'Hunters, herders, and heavy metals in arctic Siberia', *Cambridge Anthropology* 18 (2), 35–45.

Anderson, David. 1996. 'Bringing civil society to an uncivilised place: citizenship regimes in Russia's Arctic frontier', in C. Hann and E. Dunn (eds.), *Civil Society: Challenging Western Models,* Routledge, London and New York.

Anderson, David. 1997. 'Living in a subterranean landscape: identity politics in post-Soviet Khakassia', in Susan Bridger and Frances Pine (eds.), *Surviving Post-Socialism: Local Strategies and Regional Responses in Eastern Europe and the Former Soviet Union,* Routledge, London, 52–65.

Appadurai, Arjun. 1995. 'The production of locality', in R. Fardon (ed.), *Counterworks: Managing the Diversity of Knowledge,* Routledge, London and New York, 204–25.

Argunov, I.A., and N.V. Isakova. 1977. 'O professional'noi orientatsii vypuskov sel'skikh srednykh shkol' (On the professional orientation of graduates of rural secondary schools), in Boiko 1977.

Arutyunyan, Yu.V. 1973. 'Social mobility in the countryside', in Yanowitch and Fisher 1973.

Arutyunyan, Yu.V. 1974. 'Experience of a socio-ethnic survey relating to the Tatar ASSR', in Yu. Bromley (ed.), *Soviet Ethnology and Anthropology Today,* Mouton, The Hague, 1974.

Asalkhanov, I.A. 1959. 'Vlianiye vkhozhdeniya buryatii v sostav rossii na khozyaistvennoye i obshchestvennoye razvitye buryat' (The influence of the inclusion of Buryatiya in Russia on the economic and social development of the Buryats), *Trudy BKNII SO AN ASSR* (Ulan-Ude), 1.

Asalkhanov, I.A. 1960a. 'O buryatskikh rodakh v XIX veke' (On Buryat clans in the nineteenth century), *Etnograficheskii Sbornik* (Ulan-Ude), 1.

Asalkhanov, I.A. 1960b. 'Zemelnyye otnosheniya buryat barguzinskogo vedomstva vo 2-i polovine XIX veka' (Land relations of the Buryat of Barguzin district in the second half of the nineteenth century), *Kratkiye Soobshcheniye BKNII SO AN ASSR,* 2.

Asalkhanov, I.A. 1963. *Sotsial'no-ekonomicheskoye razvitiye yugovostochnoi Sibiri vo vtoroi polovina XIX veka* (The socio-economic development of south-east Siberia in the second half of the nineteenth century), BKI, Ulan-Ude.

Asalkhanov, I.A. (ed.) 1968. Issledovaniya i materialy po istorii buryatii (Investigations and materials on the history of Buryatiya), Trudy BION 5, Ulan-Ude.

References

Asalkhanov, I.A. 1974. 'Dorevolyutsionnyye sistemy zemledeliya u buryat' (Pre-revolutionary systems of agriculture among the Buryat) in V.I. Boiko *et al.* (eds.), *Rabochii klass i krest'yanstvo natsional'nykh raionov sibiri* (The working class and peasantry of national regions of Siberia), Nauka, Novosibirsk.

Astyrev, N. 1891. *Na Tayezhnykh Progalinakh,* Moscow.

Ayushiyev, B.A., (ed.). 1973. *Ekonomicheskiye problemy prigorodnogo sel'skogo khozyaistva buryatskoi ASSR* (Economic problems of agriculture in the suburban areas of the Buryat ASSR), BKI, Ulan-Ude.

Ayushiyev, B.A., and G.M. Radnayev. 1961. 'Razmeshcheniya proizvodstva i potrebleniya pishchevykh produktov v buryatskoi ASSR' (The coordination of the production and consumption of food products in the Buryat ASSR), *Krayevedcheskii Sbornik* (Ulan-Ude), 6.

Bahro, Rudolf. 1977. 'The alternative in Eastern Europe', *New Left Review* 106, Nov.–Dec.

Baldayev, S.P. 1959. *Buryatskiye svadebnyye obryady* (Buryat wedding rituals), BKI, Ulan-Ude.

Baldayev, S.P. 1961a. *Izbrannoye* (Selected works), BKI, Ulan-Ude.

Baldayev, S.P. 1961b. 'Materialy o buryatskikh plemenakh i rodakh' (Materials on Buryat tribes and kin-groups), *Etnograficheskii Sbornik* (Ulan-Ude), 2.

Baldayev, S.P. 1961–70. *Buryaad aradai duunuud* (Buryat folk songs), vol. 1 (1961), vol. 2 (1965), vol. 3 (1970), BNKh, Ulan-Ude.

Baldayev, S.P. 1970. *Rodoslovnyye predaniya i legendy buryat* (Genealogical stories and legends of the Buryat), vol. 2, *Bulagaty i Ekhirity* (Bulagats and Ekhirits), AN SSSR BION, Ulan-Ude.

Banzarov, Dorzhi. 1955. *Sobraniye sochinenii* (Collected works), including 'Chernaya vera ili shamanstvo u mongolov' (The black faith or shamanism among the Mongols), originally published Kazan, 1846, AN SSSR, Moscow.

Bartanov, P.I. 1972. 'Ukrepleniye kolkhosov i sovkhosov Buryatskoi ASSR rukovodyashchimi kadrami i spetsialistami v gody semiletki (1959–1965 gg)' (The strengthening of the collective and state farms of the Buryat ASSR with managerial cadres and specialists in the seven-year period 1959–65), in Z.N. Tsydypova (ed.), *Nekotoriye voprosy podgotovki kadrov i kommunisticheskogo vospitaniya trudyashchikhsya v buryatskoi partorganizatsii* (Some questions concerning the training of cadres and the communist education of the workers in the Buryat Party organisation), Min. Pros. RSFSR, Ulan-Ude.

Basayeva, K.D. 1962. 'Semeino-brachnyye otnosheniya u buryat' (Family and marriage relations among the Buryat), *Etnograficheskii Sbornik* (Ulan-Ude), 3.

Basayeva, K.D. 1965. 'Vospitaniye detei u buryat' (The upbringing of children among the Buryat), *Etnograficheskii Sbornik* (Ulan-Ude), 4.

Basayeva, K.D. 1974a. *Preobrazovaniya v semeino-brachnykh otnosheniyakh buryat* (Transformations in the family and marriage relations of the Buryat), BKI, Ulan-Ude.

Basayeva, K.D. 1974b. 'Traditsionnyye obychai i obryady zapadnykh buryat, svyazannye s rozhdeniem i pervymi godami zhizni rebenka' (Traditions, customs and rituals of the western Buryat associated with the birth and first years of life of the child), *Etnograficheskii Sbornik* (Ulan-Ude), 6.

Basayeva, K.D. 1980. *Sem'ya i brak u buryat (vtoraya polovina XIX-nachalo XX veka)* (Family and marriage among the Buryat—second half of the nineteenth and beginning of the twentieth centuries), Nauka, Novosibirsk.

570

References

Batorov, P.P. 1923. 'Narodnyi kalendar' alarskikh buryat' (The folk calendar of the Alar Buryat), *Etnograficheskii Byulleten* (Irkutsk), 3.

Bazheyev, D.G. 1968. 'Osvoyeniye tselinnykh zemel' v Buryatskoi ASSR (1954–1958 gg)' (The appropriation of virgin lands in the Buryat ASSR 1954–1958), in Asalkhanov 1968.

Belikov, V.V. 1974a. 'Izmeneniye sotsial'no-klassovoi struktury naselniya buryatii (1923–1970)' (Changes in the social class structure of the population of Buryatiya, 1923–1970), in Lubsanov 1974.

Belikov, V.V. 1974b. 'Sotsial'no-professional'nyi sostav rabotnikov sovkhoza "Kizhinginskii,"' (The socio-professional composition of the workforce of the 'Kizhinga' sovkhoz), *Etnograficheskii Sbornik* (Ulan-Ude), 6.

Belousov, A.A. (ed.). 1971. *Vosprosy preodoleniya perezhitkov lamaizma, shamanizma, i staroobryadchestva* (Questions of the overcoming of the survivals of Lamaism, shamanism, and 'Old Believer' orthodoxy), BKI, Ulan-Ude.

Bettelheim, Charles. 1970. 'State property and socialism', *Economy and Society* 2 (4).

Bettelheim, Charles. 1974. *La Lutte des classes en URSS,* Maspero-Seuil, Paris.

Bettelheim, Charles. 1975. *The Transition to Socialist Economy,* trs. Brian Pearce, The Harvester Press, London.

Binns, Christopher A.P. 1979–80. 'The changing face of power: revolution and accommodation in the development of the Soviet ceremonial system.' *Man* 14 (4), 1979 and 15 (1), 1980.

Bloch, Maurice. 1974. 'Symbol, song and dance, or is religion an extreme form of traditional authority?', *European Journal of Sociology* (Paris).

Bloch, Maurice (ed.). 1975. *Political Language and Oratory in Traditional Society,* Academic Press, London.

Bogdanov, M.N. 1926. *Ocherki istorii buryat-mongol'skogo naroda* (Studies in the history of the Buryat-Mongol people), Verkhneudinsk.

Boiko, V.I. (ed.). 1977. *Sel'skaya molodezh' yakutii, sotsial'naya mobil'nost', otnosheniye k trudu, professional'naya orientatsiya* (The rural youth of Yakutiya, its social mobility, attitude to work, and professional orientation), AN ASSR SO YF, YKI, Yakutsk.

Boldonova, T.M. 1959. 'Traditsionnyye pesni khorinskikh buryat, po materialam fol'klornoy ekspeditsii 1957 g' (The traditional songs of the Khori Buryat, from the materials of the 1957 folklore expedition), *Kratkiye Soobshcheniya BKNII SO AN SSSR* (Ulan-Ude), 1.

Bolonov, F.F. 1969. 'Ob izmeneniyakh v bytu i kul'ture russkogo (semeiskogo) naseleniya buryatii' (On the changes in way of life and culture of the Russian (Semeiskii) population of Buryatiya), *Etnograficheskii Sbornik* (Ulan-Ude), 5.

Bourdieu, Pierre. 1977. *Outline of a Theory of Practice,* Cambridge University Press, Cambridge.

Bridger, Susan. 1996. 'The return of the family farm: a future for women?' in Rosalind Marsh (ed.), *Women in Russia and Ukraine,* Cambridge University Press, Cambridge, pp. 241–54.

Bridger, Susan, and Frances Pine. 1997. 'Introduction: transitions to post-socialism and cultures of survival', in Susan Bridger and Frances Pine (eds.), *Surviving Post-Socialism: Local Strategies and Regional Responses in Eastern Europe and the Former Soviet Union,* Routledge, London.

Buruyev, M.T. 1974. *Spetsializatsiya khozyaistv skotovodcheskikh zony buryatskoi*

References

ASSR (Specialisation of enterprises in the cattle-farming zones of the Buryat ASSR), BKI, Ulan-Ude.

Buryatskaya ASSR za 50 let—statisticheskii sbornik (The Buryat ASSR after 50 years—a statistical collection), BKI, Ulan-Ude, 1967.

Buyakhayev, S.S. 1993. *Etnopoliticheskaya i etnokul'turnaya situatsiya v respublike Buryatiya* (The ethnopolitical and ethnocultural situation in the Republic of Buryatiya), Issledovaniya po prikladnoi i neotlozhnoi etnologii, no. 42, RAN IEA, Moscow.

Buyantuyev, V.P. 1959. *Barguzinskaya dolina* (The Barguzin valley), BKI, Ulan-Ude.

Carrère d'Encausse, Helene. 1978. *L'Empire eclatée: la revolte des nations en URSS,* Flammarion, Paris.

Castoriadis, Cornelius. 1997. *The Imaginary Institution of Society* (trs. K. Blamey 1987), Polity Press, Cambridge.

Chagdarsurung, Ts. 1975. 'La Connaissance Geographique et la carte des Mongols', *Studia Mongolica,* 3 (2), 1975, fasc. 20, Permanent Committee International Congress of Mongolists, Ulan-Bator, Mongolia, 1976.

Chalidze, Valery. 1977. *Criminal Russia: Essays on Crime in Soviet Union,* Random House, New York.

Charichina, A.G. 1958. *Rol' zheleznykh dorog v razvitii sel'skogokhozyaistva* (The role of the railways in the development of agriculture), Moscow.

Cheremisov, K.M. 1973. *Buryaad-orod slovar'* (Buryat-Russian dictionary), Sovetskaya Entsiklopediya, Moscow.

Chernoyarova, A.A. 1967. 'Trudovyye resursy Severa Buryatii, ikh formirovaniye i zanyatost' (Labour resources of North Buryatia, their formation and employment), in P.R. Buyantuyev (ed.), *Voprosy ispol'zovaniya trudovykh resursov buryatskoi ASSR* (Questions of the use of labour resources of the Buryat ASSR), BKI, Ulan-Ude.

Chubarov, A.P. (ed.). 1972. *Spravochnik predsedatelya kolkhoza* (Directory for the Chairman of a collective farm), Kolos, Moscow.

Clarke, Simon, Sarah Ashwin, and Vadim Borisov. 1997. MS. 'The non-payment of wages in Russia'.

Dalton, George (ed.). 1967. *Tribal and Peasant Economies,* University of Texas Press, Austin and London.

Dambayev, G.E. 1969. 'Sovremennoye zhilishche barguzinskikh buryat' (Contemporary dwellings of the Barguzin Buryats), *Etnograficheskii Sbornik* (Ulan-Ude), 5.

Dambayev, G.E. 1970. *Iz proshlogo i nastoyashchego barguzinskikh buryat* (From the past and the present of the Barguzin Buryat), BKI, Ulan-Ude.

Davies, R.W. 1980. *The Soviet Collective Farm, 1929–1930,* Macmillan, London.

Deryugina, V.N. 1968. *Proizvodstvennyye tipy kolkhozov i sovkhozov buryatskoi ASSR* (Productive types of collective and state farms of the Buryat ASSR), BKI, Ulan-Ude.

Dolotov, A.P., and S.N. Seleznev. 1978. *Tovarno-denezhnyye otnosheniya v kolkhoznom proizvodstve* (Commodity-monetary relations in collective farm production), Ekonomika, Moscow.

Dondukov, U.-Zh.Sh., and B.-N. Tsyrenov. 1960. 'Bai', *Etnograficheskii Sbornik* (Ulan-Ude), 1.

Dorzhiev, D.L. 1993. *Krest'yanskiye myatezhi i vosstaniya v Buryatii v 20–30 gody* (Peasant risings in Buryatiya in the 1920s–30s), Obshchestvenno-nauchnyi tsentr 'Sibir', Ulan-Ude.

References

Dorzhiyev, Zh.D. 1969. 'K voprosu ob obychayakh i obrayadakh aginskikh buryat' (On the question of the customs and ceremonies of the Aga Buryat), in Okladnikov and Lubsanov 1969.

Dorzhiyev, Zh., and B. Shagdarov. 1967. *V stepi aginskoi* (In the Aga Steppe), Sovetskaya Rossiya, Moscow.

Drykheyev, V. 1958. 'Nekotoriya voprosy vosproizvodstva obshchestvennogo stade ovets v kolkhozakh B-MASSR' (Some questions concerning the reproduction of the communal sheep flocks in the collective farms of the Buryat-Mongol ASSR), *Ucheniye Zapiski* (Ulan-Ude), 14.

Dugarov, D.G. 1968. *Khadyn azhalsha khünüüd* (Working people of the mountains), BNKh, Ulan-Ude.

Dunmore, Timothy. 1980. 'Local party organs in industrial administration: the case of the *ob'edinenie* reform', *Soviet Studies* 32 (2), April.

Dunn, Stephen P. 1971. 'Structure and functions of the Soviet rural family', in James R. Millar (ed.), *The Soviet Rural Community,* University of Illinois, Urbana.

Dyer, S. Rimsky-Korsakoff. 1979. *Soviet Dungan Kolkhozes in the Kirghiz SSR and the Kazakh SSR,* Oriental Monograph Series no. 25, Australian National University, Canberra.

Dylykov, Yu.G. 1962. 'Komsomol buryatii v borbe za sploshnuyu kollektivizatsiyu sel'skogo khozyaistva (1930–1932)' (The Buryat Komsomol in the struggle for total collectivisation of agriculture, 1930–1932), *Kratkiye soobshcheniya BKNII SO AN SSSR,* 4.

Dymbrenov, V.G. 1961. *Kolkhoz imeni Karla Marksa* (Karl Marx collective farm), BKI, Ulan-Ude.

Dyukov, V.V. 1979. *Oznovnyye napravleniya sovershenstvovaniya respredeleniya po trudu v kolkhozakh* (Basic directions in the improvement of wage distribution in collective farms), Izd. Kazansk. Universiteta, Kazan.

Eliasov, L.E. 1965. *Kritika ideologii lamaizma i shamanizma* (Criticism of the ideologies of Lamaism and shamanism), BKI, Ulan-Ude.

Ellman, M. 1973. *Planning Problems in the USSR: The Contribution of Mathematical Economics to Their Solution, 1960–1971,* Cambridge University Press, Cambridge.

Elyakov, A.D. MS. 'Printsip iyerarkhichnosti v upravlenii sotsialisticheskom obshchestvom' (The principle of hierarchy in the government of socialist society).

Emel'yanov, A.M. (ed.). 1977. *Osnovy ekonomiki i upravleniya sel'skokhozyaistvennym proizvodstvom* (The foundations of economics and management in agricultural production), Ekonomika, Moscow.

Etgarov, I.M. 1900. 'Svadebnyye obrady u alarskikh buryat' (Wedding rituals among the Alar Buryat), *Izvestiya VSORGO* (Irkutsk), 30 (1–2).

Even, Marie-Dominique, and Rodica Pop (trs. and eds.). 1994. *Histoire Secrete des Mongoles: chronique Mongole du XIIIe siècle,* Gallimard, Paris.

Fondahl, Gail A. 1998. *Gaining Ground? Evenkis, Land and Reform in Southeastern Siberia,* Allyn and Bacon, Boston.

Forsyth, J. 1992. *A History of the Peoples of Siberia: Russia's North Asian Colony 1581–1900,* Cambridge University Press, Cambridge and New York.

Fortes, Meyer. 1949. *The Web of Kinship among the Tallensi,* Oxford University Press, London.

Freedman, R. (ed.). 1976. *Marx on Economics,* Penguin Books, Harmondsworth.

Galdanov, Ts.B. 1969. *Ekonomicheskiye problemy intensifikatsii sel'skogo*

573

References

khozyaistva buryatskoi ASSR (Economic problems of the intensification of agriculture in the Buryat ASSR), BKI, Ulan-Ude.

Galdanov, Ts.B. 1970. 'Dostignutyi uroven' i osnovnyye napravleniya razvitiya sel'skogo khozyaistva bur. ASSR' (The achieved level and main directions of the development of agriculture in the Buryat ASSR), *Trudy otdel. ekon. issled. BF SO AN SSSR* (Ulan-Ude), 3 (7).

Galdanova, G.P. 1992. *Zakamenskiye Buryaty: istoriko-etnograficheskiye ocherki,* Nauka, Novosibirsk.

Gas'kov, M.M. 1970. *Sotsialisticheskoye sorevnovaniye v kolkhozakh i sovkhozakh buryatii* (Socialist competition in collective farms and state farms of Buryatiya) BKI, Ulan-Ude.

Gellner, Ernest (ed.). 1979. *Soviet and Western Anthropology,* Duckworth, London.

Gerasimova, K.M. 1957. *Lamaizm i natsional'no-kolonial'naya politika tsarizma v zabaikaliye v XIX i nachale XX vekov* (Lamaism and the national-colonial politics of Tsarism in Trans-Baikal in the nineteenth and beginning of the twentieth centuries), B-MNIIK, Ulan-Ude.

Gerasimova, K.M. 1964. *Obnovlencheskoye dvizheniye buryatskogo lamaistskogo dukhovenstva* (The reform/renewal movement of the Buryat Lamaist clergy), BKI, Ulan-Ude.

Gerasimova, K.M. 1965. 'Suchnost' izmeneniya buddizma' (The essence of the changes in Buddhism), in Eliasov 1965.

Gerasimova, K.M. 1969a. 'Kul't obo kak dopolnitel'nyi material dlya izucheniya etnicheskikh protsessov v Buryatii' (The oboo cult as additional material for the study of ethnic processes among the Buryat), *Etnograficheskii Sbornik* (Ulan-Ude), 5.

Gerasimova, K.M. 1969b. 'Lamaistskii pokhoronyi obryad v buryatii' (The Lamaist funeral ritual in Buryatiya), in Okladnikov and Lubsanov 1969.

Gerasimova, K.M. 1970. 'Lamaistskaya transformatsiya animisticheskikh predstavlenii' (The Lamaist transformation of animist conceptions), in B.V. Semichev (ed.), *Materialy po istorii filologii tsentral'noi azii,* vol. 4, BION, Ulan-Ude.

Gerasimova, K.M. 1971. 'Sotsial'naya funktsiya lamaistskoi obryadnosti' (The social function of Lamaist ritual), in Belousov 1971.

Gerasimova, K.M. 1980. 'Izmeneniya v bytovoi obryadnosti lamaizma v sovremennykh usloviyakh' (Changes in the practical ritual of Lamaism in contemporary conditions), in Mikhailov 1980a.

Gerasimova, K.M. 1989. *Traditsionnyye verovaniya tibetsev v kul'tovoi sisteme lamaizma,* Nauka, Novosibirsk.

Gluckman, Max. 1972. *The Ideas in Barotse Jurisprudence,* Manchester University Press, Manchester.

Gomboyev, B., *et al.* 1996. 'The present condition and use of pasture in the Barguzin valley', in Caroline Humphrey and David Sneath (eds.), 1996, *Culture and Environment in Inner Asia,* vol. 1, *The Pastoral Economy and the Environment,* White Horse Press, Cambridge.

Goody, Jack. 1962. *Death, Property and the Ancestors,* Stanford University Press, Stanford.

Goody, Jack. 1970. 'Sideways or downwards', *Man,* n.s. 5.

Goody, Jack., and J. Buckley. 1972. 'Inheritance and women's labour in Africa', *Africa,* 43.

Gorokhov, G.I. (ed.). 1977. *Zemleustroistvo kolkhozov i sovkhozov* (The system of land-tenure in collective and state farms), Urozhai, Kiev.

574

References

Gracheva, G.N. 1977. 'Izmeneniya v khozyaistve i bytu naseleniya pos. Ust'-Avam za poslednyye gody' (Changes in the economy and way of life of the population of the village of Ust'-Avam in recent years) in *Kratkoye soderzhaniye dokladov godichnoi nauchnoi sessii instituta etnografii AN SSSR 1974–76*, Nauka, Leningrad.

Grant, Bruce. 1995. *In the Soviet House of Culture*, Princeton University Press, Princeton.

Grant, Nigel. 1979. *Soviet Education*, 4th edition, Penguin Books, Harmondsworth.

Gregory, C.A. 1980. 'Gifts to men and gifts to god: gift exchange and capital accumulation in contemporary Papua', *Man* 15 (4).

Gregory, Chris. 1997. 'Hunting for water in Port Moresby', *Anthropology Today* 13 (4), 15–17.

Grossman, Gregory. 1977. 'The second economy of the USSR', *Problems of Communism*, 26, Sept.–Oct.

Guchinova, Elsa-Bair. 1996. 'Power relationships in an ethnocultural context: the perception of the president among the Kalmyks', *Études Mongoles et Sibériennes*, cahier 27, Paris, 299–304.

Gumperz, J., and D. Hymes. 1972. *The Ethnography of Communication*, Holt, Reinhardt and Winston, New York.

Gurevich, B.S. 1963. *Obshchiye sobraniya (skhody) grazhdan v buryatii* (General meetings *[skhody]* of citizens in Buryatiya), BKI, Ulan-Ude.

Hamayon, Roberte. 1990a. *La chasse à l'ame*, Société d'éthnologie, Nanterre.

Hamayon, Roberte. 1990b. 'Tribus, clans et ulus bouriates à la fin du XIXe siècle', *Études Mongoles et Sibériennes*, cahier 21, Paris, 85–122.

Hamayon, Roberte. 1996. 'Chamanisme, bouddhisme, héroisme épique: quel support d'identité pour les Bouriates post-soviétiques?' *Études Mongoles et Sibériennes*, cahier 27, Paris, 327–58.

Hann, C.M. 1980. *Tázlár: a Village in Hungary*, Cambridge University Press, Cambridge.

Hann, Chris. 1996. 'Land tenure and citizenship in Tázlár', in Ray Abrahams (ed.), *After Socialism: Land Reform and Social Change in Eastern Europe*, Berghahn Books, Providence and Oxford, pp. 23–50.

Hastrup, Kirsten, and Karen Fog Olwig. 1997. 'Introduction' in Olwig and Hastrup (eds.), *Siting Culture: The Shifting Anthropological Subject*, Routledge, London and New York, pp. 1–16.

Hegedüs, Andras. 1976. *Socialism and Bureaucracy*, Allison and Busby, London.

Hegedüs, Andras. 1977. *The Structure of Socialist Society*, trs. R. Fisher and revised by P. Szente, Constable, London.

Hivon, Myriam. 1995. 'Local resistance to privatization in rural Russia', *Cambridge Anthropology* 18 (2), 13–22.

Hivon, Myriam. 1997. 'Social pressure as a survival strategy', in Susan Bridger and Frances Pine (eds.), *Surviving Post-Socialism: Local Strategies and Regional Responses in Eastern Europe and the Former Soviet Union*, Routledge, London, 33–51.

Hough, Jerry. 1969. *The Soviet Prefects: The Local Party Organs in Industrial Decision-Making*, Harvard University Press, Cambridge, Mass.

Hough, Jerry F. 1971. 'The changing nature of the Kolkhoz Chairman', in James R. Millar (ed.), *The Soviet Rural Community*, University of Illinois, Urbana.

Hough, Jerry F. 1977. *The Soviet Union and Social Science Theory*, Harvard University Press, Cambridge, Mass., and London.

Humphrey, Caroline. 1974a. 'Inside a Mongolian tent', *New Society*, 31 October.

References

Humphrey, Caroline. 1974b. 'On some ritual techniques in the Bull-Cult of the Buriat Mongols', *Proceedings of the Royal Anthropological Institute 1973* (London).

Humphrey, Caroline. (1975). Magical Drawings in the Religion of the Buryats, Ph.D. Dissertation, University of Cambridge.

Humphrey, Caroline. 1978. 'Women, taboo and the suppression of attention', in Shirley Ardener (ed.), *Defining Females, the Nature of Women in Society*, Croom Helm, London.

Humphrey, Caroline. 1979a. 'Do women labour in a worker's state?', *Cambridge Anthropology*, 5 (2).

Humphrey, Caroline. 1979b. 'The uses of genealogy: a historical study of the nomadic and sedentarised Buryat', in *Pastoral Production and Society*, ed. L'Équipe écologie et anthropologie des sociétés pastorales, CUP—Editions de la Maison des Sciences de l'Homme, Cambridge—Paris.

Humphrey, Caroline. 1979c. 'Theories of North Asian shamanism', in Gellner 1979.

Humphrey, Caroline. 1989. 'Perestroika and the pastoralists: the example of Mongun Taiga in Tuva ASSR', *Anthropology Today*, 5 June, 6–10.

Humphrey, Caroline. 1995. 'Chiefly and shamanist landscapes in Mongolia', in E. Hirsch and M. O'Hanlon (eds.), *The Anthropology of Landscape: Perspectives on Place and Space*, Oxford University Press, Oxford.

Humphrey, Caroline. 1996. *Shamans and Elders: Experience, Knowledge and Power among the Daur Mongols*, Oxford University Press, Oxford.

Humphrey, Caroline. (Forthcoming). 'Traders, disorder and citizenship regimes in provincial Russia', in M. Burawoy and K. Verdery (eds.), *Uncertainties of Transition: Ethnographies of Transformation in the Former Socialist World*, Rowman and Littlefield, 1998.

Humphrey, Caroline, and Stephen Hugh-Jones (eds.). 1992. *Barter, Exchange and Value*, Cambridge University Press, Cambridge.

Humphrey, Caroline, and David Sneath (eds.). 1996. *Culture and Environment in Inner Asia*, vol. 1: *The Pastoral Economy and the Environment*, vol. 2: *Society and Culture*, White Horse Press, Cambridge.

Humphrey, Caroline, and David Sneath. (Forthcoming). *The End of Nomadism? Society, State, and the Environment in Inner Asia*, Duke University Press.

Isayev, V.I. 1977. *Vyravnivaniye i ratsional'noye ispol'zovaniya dokhodov kolkhozov* (The equalising and rational use of the incomes of collective farms), Kolos, Moscow.

Istoriya Buryatskoi Sovetskoi Literatury, BKI, Ulan-Ude, 1967.

Jagchid, Sechin, and Paul Hyer. 1979. *Mongolia's Culture and Society*, Westview Press, Dawson, Folkestone.

Kal'm, P.A., N.A. Pilichev, and F.V. Zinov'yev. 1977. *Osnovy nauchnoi organizatsii upravleniya v kolkhozakh i sovkhozakh* (The foundations of the scientific organisation of management in collective and state farms), Kolos, Moscow.

Kaneff, Deema. 1996. 'Responses to "democratic" land reforms in a Bulgarian village', in Ray Abrahams (ed.), *After Socialism: Land Reform and Social Change in Eastern Europe*, Berghahn Books, Providence and Oxford.

Katsnenlinboigen, A. 1977. 'Coloured markets in the Soviet Union', *Soviet Studies* 29 (1), January.

Kazakov, S.K. 1973. *Praktikum po bukhgalterskomu uchetu v sovkhozakh i*

576

References

kolkhozakh (Textbook for accounting methods in state and collective farms), Statistika, Moscow.

Kerblay, Basile H. 1968. *Les Marchés Paysans en URSS,* Mouton, Paris.

Khadalov, P.I., and A.I. Ulanov (eds.). 1953. *O kharaktere buryatskogo eposa 'Geser'* (On the characteristics of the Buryat epic 'Geser'), B-MNIIK, Ulan-Ude.

Khan, Azizur Rahman, and Dharam Ghai. 1979. *Collective Agriculture and Rural Development in Soviet Central Asia,* Macmillan, London.

Khangalov, M.N. 1958–60. *Sobraniye sochinenii v 3-kh tomakh* (Collected works in 3 volumes), BKI, Ulan-Ude.

Khaptayev, P.T. (ed.). 1954. *Istoriya buryat-mongol'skoi ASSR* (History of the Buryat-Mongol ASSR), vol. 1, B-MKI, Ulan-Ude.

Khaptayev, P.T. 1962. 'Aimachnoye i antiaimachnoye dvizheniya' (The *aimak* and anti-*aimak* movements), *Trudy BKNII SO AN SSSR* (Ulan-Ude), 10.

Khaptayev, P.T. 1974. 'Formirovaniye i razvitiye rabochego klassa v natsional'nykh raionakh sibiri' (The formation and development of the working class in national districts of Siberia), in A.P. Okladnikov (ed.), *Rabochii klass i krest'yanstvo natsional'nykh raionov sibiri* (The working class and the peasantry of national districts of Siberia), Nauka, Novosibirsk.

Khazanov, Anatoly M. 1997. 'Ethnic nationalism in the Russian Federation', *Daedalus* (Summer), 121–42.

Kim, N.V. 1967. 'Iz istoriya zemledeliya u buryat v kontse XVIII i pervoi polovine XIX veka' (From the history of agriculture among the Buryat at the end of the eighteenth and first half of the nineteenth centuries), *Trudy BION* (Ulan-Ude), 5.

Kisilev, I.P. 1975. 'Obshchestvenno-politicheskaya aktivnost' kak pedagogicheskoye sredstvo vospitaniya patriotizma' (Socio-political activism as a pedagogical means for the development of patriotism), in Yanovskii 1975.

Klaus, G. 1967. *Kibernetika i obshchestvo* (Cybernetics and society), Moscow.

Klements, D.A. 1891. 'O svadebnykh obryadakh zabaikal'skikh buryat' (On the wedding rituals of the Trans-Baikal Buryat) *Izvestiya VSORGO* (Irkutsk), 22 (1).

Kochetov, A.K. 1973. *Lamaizm,* Nauka, Moscow.

Kolakowski, Leszek. 1971. *Marxism and Beyond,* Paladin, London.

Konstantinov, Yulian. 1997. 'Memory of Lenin, Ltd.: reindeer-herding brigades on the Kola Peninsula', *Anthropology Today* 13 (3), 14–19.

Kosinskii, V.N., and G.F. Mikhailik. 1977. *Formirovaniye kolkhoznykh fondov i ikh ispol'zovaniye* (The formation of funds in collective farms and their use), Kolos, Moscow.

Kotlykova, V.P., and E.M. Erenprais. 1963. *Khonin bürihöö—khur'ga* (A lamb from every sheep), BNKh, Ulan-Ude.

Kotz, David, with Fred Weir. 1997. *Revolution from Above: the Demise of the Soviet System,* Routledge, London.

Kovalev, E.M. (ed.). 1996. *Golosa Krest'yan: Sel'skaya Rossiya XX veka v kresyanskikh memuarakh* (Voices of peasants: Rural 20th century Russia in peasant memories), Aspekt Press, Moscow.

Kowalewski, J.E. 1844. *Dictionnaire Mongol—Russe—Français,* 3 vols., Universitetskaya Tipografiya, Kazan.

Koz'min, N.N. 1924. *Ocherki skotovodcheskogo khozyaistva v Burrespublike* (Studies of the livestock economy in the Buryat republic), vol. 1, Gos. Planovaya Kommissaya, B-MASSR, Verkhneudinsk.

References

Krol', M.A. 1894. 'Brachnyye obryady i obychai u zabaikal'skikh buryat' (Wedding rituals and customs among the Trans-Baikal Buryat), *Izvestiya VSORGO* (Irkutsk), 25 (1).

Krol', M.A. 1895. *Brachnoye pravo inorodtsev Selenginskogo okruga* (Marriage law of the natives of Selenga okrug), Irkutsk.

Kryuchkov, N.I. 1971. 'Partiinoye rukovodstvo naucho-ateicheskim vospitaniyem trudyashchikhsya v Tunkinskom aimake' (Party leadership by the scientific-atheistic education of the workers in Tunka *aimak*), in Belousov 1971.

Kuibyshev, V.V. 1925. *Lenin i kooperatziya* (Lenin and cooperation), Moscow.

Kulakov, P.E. 1896. 'Buryaty Irkutskoi Guvernii' (Buryats of the Irkutsk Guberniya), *Izvestiya VSORGO* (Irkutsk), 26 (4–5).

Kuz'menko, P. 1927. 'Bor'ba za ozdorovleniye buryatskikh mass' (Struggle for the health of the Buryat masses), *Zhizn' Buryatii,* 10.

Kuz'mina, R.A. 1977. 'Nekotoriye aspekty otnosheniya k trudu molodykh rabochikh sovkhozov' (Some aspects of the attitude to work of young workers in state farms), in Boiko 1977.

Lampland, Martha. 1995. *The Object of Labour: Commodification in Socialist Hungary,* University of Chicago Press, Chicago and London.

Lane, Christel. 1981. *The Rites of Rulers: Ritual in Industrial Society—the Soviet Case,* Cambridge University Press, Cambridge.

Lane, David. 1971a. *The End of Inequality? Stratification under State Socialism,* Penguin, Harmondsworth.

Lane, David. 1971b. *Politics and Society in the USSR,* Weidenfeld and Nicolson, London.

Lattimore, Owen. 1934. *The Mongols of Manchuria,* John Day Company, New York.

Lattimore, Owen. 1962. 'Inner Asian frontiers: Chinese and Russian margins of expansion' in *Studies in Frontier History, Collected Papers 1928–58,* Oxford University Press, London.

Lavigne, Marie. 1978. 'Advanced socialist society', *Economy and Society* 7(4).

Leach, E.R. 1951. 'The structural implications of matrilateral cross-cousin marriage', *Journal of the Royal Anthropological Institute,* 81.

Leach, E.R. 1954. *Political Systems of Highland Burma,* Bell, London.

Lel'chuk, L.T. 1976. 'Yakutskiye i buryatskiye konovyazi' (Yakut and Buryat tethering posts), in I.S. Vdovin (ed.), *Material'naya kul'tura naradov sibiri i severa,* Nauka, Leningrad.

Lenin, V.I. *Pol'niye sobraniye sochinenii* (Full collected works), Moscow, quoted in Kal'm *et al.* 1977.

Lessing, Ferdinand D., M. Haltod, J.G. Hangin, and S. Kassatkin. 1960. *Mongolian-English Dictionary,* University of California Press, Berkeley and Los Angeles.

Levin, M.G., and L.P. Potapov (eds.). 1956. *Narody sibirii* (Peoples of Siberia), AN SSSR, Moscow, Leningrad.

Lewin, M. 1968. *Russian Peasants and Soviet Power: A Study of Collectivisation,* Allen and Unwin, London.

Lifshitz, Solomon. 1975. *History of the Jewish Kolkhoz in Siberia (1926–1934)* (in Russian), Soviet Institutions Series no. 4, Soviet and East European Research Centre, Hebrew University of Jerusalem.

Linkhovoin, L. 1972. *Zametki o dorevolyutsionnom byte aginskikh buryat* (Notes on the pre-revolutionary way of life of the Aga Buryat), BKI, Ulan-Ude.

Loseva, E.G. 1973. 'Ob etnicheskikh protsessakh u buryat' (On ethnic processes among the Buryat), *Trudy BION* (Ulan-Ude), 20.

References

Loseva, E.G. 1974. 'K voprosu o dvuyazychii u buryat' (On the question of bilingualism among the Buryat), *Etnograficheskii Sbornik* (Ulan-Ude), 6.

Lozy, Vaskhnil G.M. 1977. *Osnovy nauchnogo upravleniya* (The foundations of scientific management), a textbook for managers of collective farms, state farms and farm groups, 3d edition, Ekonomika, Moscow.

Lubsanov, D.D. (ed.). 1968. *Iz opyta konkretno-sotsiologicheskikh issledovanii* (From the experience of concrete sociological investigations), vol. 1, Trudy BION 11, BKI, Ulan-Ude.

Lubsanov, D.D. 1971. *Gazeta 'Pravda Buryatii' i eyë chitateli* (The newspaper 'Pravda Buryatii' and its readers), BKI, Ulan-Ude.

Lubsanov, D.D. (ed.). 1974. *Iz opyta konkretno-sotsiologicheskikh issledovanii* (From the experience of concrete sociological investigations), vol. 2, BION, BKI, Ulan-Ude.

McAuley, Alastair. 1979. *Economic Welfare in the Soviet Union,* Allen and Unwin/ University of Madison Press, Madison.

McAuley, Mary. 1977. *Politics and the Soviet Union,* Penguin Books, Harmondsworth.

Madason, I.N. (ed.). 1960. *Buryat aradai on'hon, khoshoo ügenüüd* (Buryat folk proverbs and sayings), BNKh, Ulan-Ude.

Makeyev, O.V., and A.D. Ivanov. 1961. 'Vodnaya i vetrovaya eroziya pochv v buryatskoi ASSR i zonal'nyye osobennosti protiveroziomykh meropriyatii' (Water and wind erosion of soils in the Buryat ASSR and zonal particularities of anti-erosion measures), *Krayevedcheskii Sbornik* (Ulan-Ude), 6.

Makhatov, V.P. 1964. *Stranitsy iz zhizni buryat kudarinskoi stepi* (Episodes from the life of Buryats of the Kudarin Steppe), BKI, Ulan-Ude.

Makovetskii, I.V. (ed.). 1975. *Byt i isskustvo russkogo naseleniya vostochnoi Sibiri* (The way of life and art of the Russian population of eastern Siberia), vol. 2: *Trans-Baikaliys,* Nauka, Novosibirsk.

Malinowski, Bronislaw. 1922. *Argonauts of the Western Pacific,* E.P. Dutton and Co., London.

Malinowski, Bronislaw. 1926. *Crime and Custom in Savage Society,* Kegan Paul, Trench and Trubner, London.

Mangutov, N.R. 1960. *Agrarnyye preobrazovaniya v sovetskoi buryatii (1917–1933 gg)* (Agrarian transformations in Soviet Buryatiya, 1917–1933), Academy of Sciences, BKNII, Ulan-Ude.

Manzanova, G.B. 1997. 'Trudovyye motivatsii zhiteli natsional'nykh grupp v period krizisa sel'skoi obshchnosti' (Labour motivations among inhabitants of national groups in a period of crisis for rural communities), MS.

Manzhigeyev, I.A. 1960. *Yangutskii buryatskii rod* (The Yangut Buryat lineage), BKI, Ulan-Ude.

Manzhigeyev, I.A. 1961. 'K voprosu o protsesse otmiraniya perezhitkov shamanstva u buryat' (On the question of the process of dying away of the survivals of shamanism among the Buryat), *Etnograficheskii Sbornik* (Ulan-Ude), 2.

Manzhigeyev, I.A. 1962. 'Prichiny sushchestvovaniya shamanisticheskikh perezhitkov i sposoby ikh preodoleniya' (Reasons for the existence of survivals of shamanism and means of overcoming them), *Etnograficheskii Sbornik* (Ulan-Ude), 3.

Manzhigeyev, I.A. 1978. *Buryatskiye shamanisticheskiye i doshamanisticheskiye terminy* (Buryat shamanist and pre-shamanist terms), Nauka, Moscow.

Matthews, Mervyn. 1972. *Class and Society in Soviet Russia,* Allen Lane, London.

References

Matthews, Mervyn. 1975. 'Top incomes in the USSR: Towards a definition of the Soviet elite', in *Economic Aspects of Life in the USSR,* Colloquium 1975, Brussels.

Matthews, Mervyn. 1978. *Privilege in the Soviet Union, a Study of Elite Life-Styles under Communism,* Allen and Unwin, London.

Medveyev, R.A., and Zh.A. Medveyev. 1977. *Khrushchev, The Years in Power,* Oxford University Press, London.

Meshcheryakov, Aleksandr. 1996a. '"Vidish' korovu? Eto televizor . . ."', (Do you see that cow? It's a television . . .), *Otkrytaya Politika* 15 (9–10), 52–7.

Meshcheryakov, Aleksandr. 1996b. 'Kollektivnyi avtoportret sel'skogo uchitelya v otdel'no vzyatoi postsovietskogo prostranstva selo Tory, Tunkinskii raion, Buryatiya, iyul' 1995 goda' (Collective autoportrait of a rural teacher in the particular post-soviet space of the village of Tory, Tunka district, Buryatiya, July 1995), *Vestnik Evrazii* 1(2), Moscow, 166–9.

Mikhailov, T.M. 1962. 'O perezhitkakh shamanizma u buryat' (On the survivals of shamanism among the Buryat), *Etnograficheskii Sbornik* (Ulan-Ude), 3.

Mikhailov, T.M. 1965a. 'Ob obychayakh i traditsiyakh buryat v sovremennyi period' (On the customs and traditions of the Buryat in the contemporary period), *Etnograficheskii Sbornik* (Ulan-Ude), 4.

Mikhailov, T.M. 1965b. 'O sovremennom sostoyanii shamanstva v Sibiri' (On the contemporary situation of shamanism in Siberia), in Eliasov 1965.

Mikhailov, T.M. 1968. 'O metodike izucheniya sovremennogo sostoyaniya shamanizma' (On the methodology of studying the contemporary state of shamanism), in Lubsanov 1968.

Mikhailov, T.M. 1969. 'Novoye v kul'ture i byte kolkhoznikov Aginskogo natsional'nogo okruga' (The new in the culture and way of life of the collective farmers of the Aga national region), *Etnograficheskii Sbornik* (Ulan-Ude), 5.

Mikhailov, T.M. 1970. 'O shamanskom fol'klor buryat' (On the shamanist folklore of the Buryat), in Ulanov 1970.

Mikhailov, T.M. 1971. 'Shamanskiye perezhitki i nekotoryye voprosy byte i kul'tura narodov sibirii' (Shamanist survivals and some questions of the way of life and culture of the peoples of Siberia), in Belousov 1971.

Mikhailov, T.M. 1979. 'Vliyaniye lamaizma i khristiyanstva na shamanizm buryat' (The influence of Lamaism and Christianity on the shamanism of the Buryat), in Vdovin 1979.

Mikhailov, T.M. (ed.). 1980a. *Sovremenniye problemy buddizma, shamanizma i pravoslaviya* (Contemporary problems of Buddhism, shamanism and Orthodox Christianity), BION, Ulan-Ude.

Mikhailov, T.M. 1980b. *Iz istorii buryatskogo shamanizm* (From the history of Buryat shamanism), Nauka, Novosibirsk.

Mikhailov, T.M., and P.P. Khoroshikh. 1973. *Buryatskii shamanizm, ukazatel' literatury (1774–1971 gg)* (Buryat shamanism, bibliography 1774–1971), BKI, Ulan-Ude.

Mikul'skii, K.I., *et al.* (eds.). 1995. *Elita Rossii: ó Nastoyashchem i Budushchem Strany* (Russian Elites: On the Present and Future of the Country), Vekhi, Moscow.

Miller, Robert F. 1976. 'The future of the Soviet kolkhoz', *Problems of Communism* 25 (2), March–April.

Miller, Robert F. 1980. 'The politics of policy implementation in the USSR: Soviet policies on agricultural integration', *Soviet Studies* 32 (2), April.

References

Mironov, N.A. 1960. 'Soderzhaniye i nekotoryye formy i metody antireligioznoi propagandy' (The content and some forms and methods of antireligious propaganda), in *Protif religioznykh perezhitkov,* BKI, Ulan-Ude.

Mironov, N.A. 1965. 'O sostoyanii nauchno-ateisticheskoi propagandy, provodimoi Buryaskoi organizatsiyei obshchestva "Znaniye"' (On the situation of scientific-atheist propaganda carried out by the Buryat organisation of the 'Knowledge' society), in Eliasov 1965.

Molonov, G.Ts. 1974. 'Sravnitel'nyi analiz uchebnykh interesov shkol'nikov goroda i sela' (Comparative analysis of the school interests of urban and rural pupils), in Lubsanov 1974.

Moore, Sally Falk, and Barbara G. Myerhoff (eds.). 1975. *Symbol and Politics in Communal Ideology,* Cornell University Press, Ithaca and London.

Mukayeva, O.D. 1997. 'Kalmytskaya natsional'naya ideya: etnopedagogicheckii aspekt' (The Kalmyk national idea: ethno-pedagogical aspects), in Urbanayeva (ed.), *Dokalady i Tezisy Mezhnunarodnogo simpoziuma "Buryat-Mongoly nakanune III tysyucheletiyu",* RAN, Ulan-Ude.

Nadneyeva, K.A. 1969. *Kritika nekotorykh nravstvennykh doktrin lamaizma* (Criticism of some moral doctrines of Lamaism), Summary of thesis, Moscow.

Naidakov, V.Ts., A.B. Soktoyev, and G.O. Tudenov. 1968. *Rol' literatury i iskusstva v bor'be s perezhitkami proshlogo* (The role of literature and art in the struggle with survivals of the past), BKI, Ulan-Ude.

Naidakov, V.Ts. (ed.). 1993. *Istoriya Buryatii XX vek, chast' 1,* (History of twentieth century Buryatiya, pt. 1), Obshchestvenno-nauchnyi tsentr 'Sibir', Ulan-Ude.

Naidanova, S.B., and T.G. Dumnova. 'Sotsialno-ekonomicheskiye posledstviya stagnatsii: snizheniye urovnya i kachestva zhizni', in I. S. Urbanayeva (ed.), *Dokalady i Tezisy Mezhnunarodnogo simpoziuma "Buryat-Mongoly nakanune III tysyacheletiya",* RAN, Ulan-Ude, 132–5.

Narodnoye khozyaistvo buryatskoi ASSR—statisticheskii sbornik (The economy of the Buryat ASSR—a statistical collection), BKI, Ulan-Ude, 1953.

Narodnoye khozyaistvo buryatskoi ASSR—statisticheskii sbornik (The economy of the Buryat ASSR—a statistical collection), BKI, Ulan-Ude, 1963.

Narodnoye khozyaistvo buryatskoi ASSR v devyatoi pyatiletke—statisticheskii sbornik (The economy of the Buryat ASSR in the 9th five-year plan—a statistical collection), BKI, Ulan-Ude, 1976.

Narodnoye obrazovaniye i kul'tura v SSSR, statisticheskii sbornik (Education and culture in the USSR—a statistical collection), Statistika, Moscow, 1977.

Nemtsov, V.F. (ed.). 1978. *Organizatsiya i planirovaniye proizvodstva v kolkhozakh i sovkhozakh* (The operation and planning of production in state and collective farms), Vysshaya Shkola, Moscow.

Nimayev, D.D. 1979. 'Istoriko-etnograficheskiye issledovaniya v buryatii v 1977 g' (Historical-ethnographic studies in Buryatiya in 1977), in *Polevyye Issledovaniya Instituta Etnografii,* Nauka, Moscow.

Nimayev, R.D., et al. (eds.). 1994. *Elbek-Dorzhi Rinchino: dokumenty, stat'i, pis'ma* (Elbek-Dorzhi Rinchino: documents, articles and letters), Komitet po delam arkhivov pri sovete ministrov respublika Buryatiya, Ulan-Ude.

Nora, P. 1989. 'Between memory and history: les Lieux de Mémoire', *Representations* (Spring), 7–25.

Nove, Alec. 1961. *The Soviet Economy,* Allen and Unwin, London.

Nove, Alec. 1977. *The Soviet Economic System,* Allen and Unwin, London.

Nove, Alec, and D.M. Nuti. 1972. *Socialist Economics,* Penguin, Harmondsworth.

581

References

Novozhilov, V.V. 1972. 'Problems of planned pricing and the reform of industrial management' in Nove and Nuti 1972.

Obreski, J. 1976. *The Changing Peasantry of Eastern Europe,* Schenkman Publishing Co., Cambridge, Mass.

Obyaznitel'naya zapiska k etnograficheskoi karte sibiri (Explanatory note to the ethnographic map of Siberia), AN SSSR, Moscow, 1929.

O'Hearn, Dennis. 1980. 'The consumer second economy: size and effects', *Soviet Studies,* 32 (2), April.

Okladnikov, A.P. 1937. *Ocherki iz istorii zapadnykh buryat-mongolov* (Sketches from the history of the western Buryat-Mongols), Leningrad.

Okladnikov, A.P. 1970. *Yakutia, Before Its Incorporation in the Russian State,* ed. H.M. Michael, Arctic Institute of America no. 8, McGill—Queen's University Press, Montreal.

Okladnikov, A.P., and D.D. Lubsanov (eds.). 1969. *Voprosy preodoleniya perezhitkov proshlogo v bytu i soznanii lyudei i stanovleniya novykh obychayev, obryadov i traditsii u narodov Sibiri* (Questions of the overcoming of survivals of the past in the way of life and understanding of people and the establishing of new customs, rituals and traditions among the peoples of Siberia), BION, Ulan-Ude.

Osokin, G.M. 1906. *Na granitse Mongolii. Ocherki i materialy k etnografii Yugo-Zapadnogo Zabaikal'ya* (On the Mongolian frontier. Studies and materials on the ethnography of south-west Trans-Baikaliya), St. Petersburg.

Ostowski, D. 1990. 'The Mongol origins of Muscovite political institutions', *Slavic Review* 49 (4) 525–42.

Pamyatka uchastnika sorevnovaniya za kommunisticheskii trud (Record book for a competitor for communist labour), Michneveskaya tipografiya, 1960s.

Panarin, Sergei. 1997. 'Buryatskaya selo Tory v 90-e gody: sotsial'naya i kul'turmaya readaptatsiya maloi poselencheskoi ohshchnosti' (The Buryat village of Tory in the 1990s: The social and cultural readaptation of a small rural community), in Proceedings of the IV International *Conference Rossiya i Vostok: problemy vzaimodeistviya,* Omsk, 1997.

Panchenko, N.F., and V.A. Lomakhin. 1976. *Nakopleniye v kolkhozakh* (Accumulation in collective farms), Kolos, Moscow.

Parkin, David. 1975. 'The rhetoric of responsibility: bureaucratic communications in a Kenya farming area', in Bloch 1975.

Patnakov, S. 1912. *Statisticheskaya dannyya, pokazyvayushchiya plemennoy sostav naseleniya Sibiri* (Statistical data showing the tribal composition of the population of Siberia), vol. 3, *Irkutsk Gub., Zabaykal'sk, Amur, Yakutsk., Primorsk., i.o. Sakhalin,* Zapiski Imperatorskogo Russkogo Geograficheskogo Obshchestva po otdeleniyu statistiki, vol. 11, no. 3, St. Petersburg.

Peshekhonov, V.A. 1980. *Rol' gosudarstva v ekonomicheskom razvitii kolkhozov* (The role of the state in the economic development of collective farms), Izd. Leningradskogo Universiteta, Leningrad.

Pesterev, A.M. 1930. 'Polovoi byt buryat' (The sexual life of the Buryat), *Zhizn' Buryatii,* 4.

Petri, B.E. 1924a. *Brachnyye normy u severnykh buryat* (Marriage norms of the northern Buryat), Izd. VSORGO, Irkutsk.

Petri, B.E. 1924b. 'Elementy rodovoi svyazi u severnykh buryat' (Elements of clan relations among the northern Buryat), *Sibirskaya Zhivaya Starina* (Irkutsk), 2.

Petri, B.E. 1925. *Vnutrirodovyye otnosheniya u severnykh buryat* (Intra-clan relations among the northern Buryat), Irkutsk.

582

References

Pine, Frances. 1995. 'Kinship, work and the state in post-socialist rural Poland', *Cambridge Anthropology* 18 (2), 47–58.

Platz, Stephanie. 1996. "Pasts and Futures: Space, History and Armenian Identity, 1988–94," Ph.D. diss., University of Chicago.

Plenkin, F.I. 1930. 'Sel'skoye khozyaistvo buryato-mongolii' (The agriculture of Buryat-Mongols), *Severnaya Aziya* (Moscow), 1 (2).

Pleshakov, P.B. (ed.). 1974. *Ocherki istorii potrebitel'skoy kooperatsii v buryatii, 1923–73* (Sketches of the history of the consumers' cooperative in Buryatiya, 1923–73), BKI, Ulan-Ude.

Plishkina, A.A. 1971. 'Otnosheniye k religii nekotorykh sotsial'no-professional'nykh grupp trudosposobnogo sel'skogo naseleniya buryatii' (The attitude to religion of several socio-professional groups in the rural working population of Buryatiya), in Belousov 1971.

Plishkina, A.A. 1975. *Povysheniye kul'turnogo urovnya i ulushcheniye uslovii byta sel'skogo naseleniya buryatii (1959–70)* (The raising of the cultural level and the improvement of the conditions of life of the rural inhabitants of Buryatiya 1959–70), BKI, Ulan-Ude.

Poppe, N.N. 1933. *Buryat-Mongol'skoye yazykoznaniye* (Buryat-Mongol linguistics), Trudy Instituta Vostokovedeniya AN SSSR, Leningrad.

Poppe, N.N. 1934. *Yazyk i kolkhoznaya poeziya Buryat-Mongolov Selenginskogo Aimaka* (The language and kolkhoz poetry of the Buryat-Mongols of Selenga District), AN SSSR and Gosudarstvennogo Instituta Kul'tury B-MASSR, Leningrad.

Poppe, N.N. 1936. *Buryat-Mongol'skii fol'klornyi i dialektologicheskii sbornik* (Buryat-Mongol folklore and dialect collection), AN SSSR, Moscow, Leningrad.

Poppe, N.N. 1978. *Tsongol Folklore* (Translation of the collection 'The language and collective farm poetry of the Buryat Mongols of the Selenga Region'), Otto Harrassowitz, Wiesbaden.

Posepelov, I.M. 1962. 'Komsomol buryatii v podgotovitel'nyi period kollektivizatsii sel'skogo khozyaistvo (1928–1929 gg)' (The Komsomol of Buryatiya in the appropriation period of the collectivisation of agriculture, 1928–1929), *Kratkiye Soobshcheniye BKNII SO AN ASSR,* 4.

Pospelov, P.M. (ed.). 1978. *Kollektivizatsiya sel'skogo khozyaistva Yakutskoi ASSR (1928–1940 gg)* (The collectivisation of agriculture of the Yakut ASSR, 1929–40), YKI, Yakutsk.

Pospielovsky, Dimitry. 1970. 'The "link system" in Soviet agriculture', *Soviet Studies* 21 (4), April.

Potapov, L.P. 1960. 'Ocherki narodnogo byta tuvintsev' (Studies in the way of life of the Tuvinians), *Trudy Tuvinskoi Kompleksnoi Ekspeditsii Instituta Etnografii AN ASSR,* vol. 1, ed. L.P. Potapov, Moscow, Leningrad.

Prozorov, N.Z. 1967. 'Oplata truda v kolkhozakh buryatii' (Payment for labour in the collective farms of Buryatiya), in P.R. Buyantuyev (ed.), *Voprosy ispol'zovaniya trudovykh resursov bur ASSR* (Questions of the use of labour resources in the Buryat ASSR), BKI, Ulan-Ude.

Ptitsyn, V.V. 1896. *Selenginskaya Dauriya, ocherki zabaikal'skago kraya* (Selenginsk Dauriya, studies of Trans-Baikaliya), St. Petersburg.

Pubayev, R.E. 1965. 'Zadachi nauchno-ateisticheskoi propagandy po preodoleniyu perezhitkov lamaizma i shamanizma' (Tasks of scientific-atheist propaganda in overcoming the survivals of Lamaism and shamanism), in Eliasov 1965.

Pubayev, R.E. 1969. 'Perezhitki lamaizma v bytu i soznanii buryatskogo sel'skogo

583

naseleniya' (Survivals of Lamaism in the way of life and understanding of the Buryat rural population), in Okladnikov and Lubsanov 1969.

Radnayev, E.R. 1965. 'Barguzinskii govor' (The Barguzin dialect) in Ts.B. Tsyden-dambayev and I.D. Burayev (eds.), *Issledovaniye buryatskikh govorov* (The study of Buryat dialects), vol. 1, BKI, Ulan-Ude.

Randalov, Yu.B. 1967. *Sotsialisticheskiye preobrazovaniya khozyaistva, byta, i kul'tury buryatskogo ulusa za gody Sovetskoi vlasti* (The socialist transformation of the economy, way of life, and culture of the Buryat *ulus* in the years of Soviet power), BKI, Ulan-Ude.

Randalov, Yu.B. 1969. 'K voprosu o formirovanii novykh obshchestvennykh prazdnikov v buryatskikh kolkhoznykh ulusakh' (On the question of the formation of new social festivals in Buryat collective farm villages), *Etnograficheskii Sbornik* (Ulan-Ude), 5.

Rigi, Jacob. 1997. 'Economic change and identity construction in Kazakhstan', MS.

Roerich, N. 1929. *The Heart of Asia,* New Era Library, New York.

Romash, M.V. 1977. *Khozraschetnyye otnosheniya kolkhozov s gosudarstvom* (Self-accounting relations of collective farms with the state), Nauka i Tekhnika, Minsk.

Romashev, I.A. 1928. 'Byt i sotsial'nyye bolezni ol'khonskikh buryat' (The way of life and the social diseases of the Ol'khon Buryats), *Severnaya Aziya* (Moscow), 4 (22).

Ruble, Blair A. 1995. *Money Sings: The Changing Politics of Urban Space in Post-Soviet Yaroslavl,* Woodrow Wilson Center Press and Cambridge University Press, Washington and Cambridge.

Rukavishnikov, I.A. 1923. 'Ocherki khozyaistvennogo byta buryat selenginskoi daurii' (Studies of the economic life of the Buryats of Selenga Dauriya), in *Selenginskii Aimak,* Irkutsk.

Rumyantsev, G.N. 1956. *Barguzinskiye letopisi* (Barguzin chronicles), B-MKI, Ulan-Ude.

Rupen, Robert A. 1964. *Mongols of the Twentieth Century,* vol. 1, Indiana University Publications Uralic and Altaic Series no. 37 part 1, Mouton, The Hague.

Sahlins, Marshall. 1972. *Stone Age Economics,* Tavistock Publications, London.

Sandanov, B.D. 1969. 'Surkharban—massovyi sportivnyi prazdnik buryatskogo naroda' (Surkharban—a mass sports festival of the Buryat people), in Okladnikov and Lubsanov 1969.

Sanzhiyev, G.L., and Yu.B. Randalov. 1968. 'Ob izmenenii sotsial'noi struktury sel'skogo naseleniya buryatii' (On changes in the social structure of the rural population of Buryatiya), in Lubsanov 1968.

Semenov, Bato. 1967. *Narodnyy kontrol' v deistvii* (People's Control in action), Soviet of Ministers of Buryat ASSR, Ulan-Ude.

Semichev, B.V. (ed.). 1960. *Protif religioznykh perezhitkov* (Against religious survivals), BKI, Ulan-Ude.

Semin, S.I., P.I. Gusev, and N.P. Pisarenko. 1977. *Razvitiye sotsialisticheskikh proizvodstvennykh otnoshenii v sel'skom khozyaistve* (The development of socialist productive relations in agriculture), Moscow.

Serebrennikov, I.M. 1925. *Buryaty, ikh khozyaistvennyi byt i zemlepol'zovaniye* (Buryats, their economic life and use of land), Verkhneudinsk.

Serruys, Henry. 1974. *Kumiss Ceremonies and Horse Races,* Asiatische Forschungen vol. 37, Otto Harrassowitz, Wiesbaden.

Shagdarov, B.Sh., and Zh.D. Dorzhiyev. 1971. *Aga stepnaya* (Steppeland Aga), BKI, Ulan-Ude.

References

Simmel, Georg. 1978. *The Philosophy of Money,* trs. Bottomore and Frisby, Routledge and Kegan Paul, London.

Sitnikov, V. 1975. 'Skol'ko derevne lyudei nuzhno' (How many people does the village need), *Liternaturnaya Gazeta* 31 (30 July).

Skinner, Quentin. 1980. 'Language and social change', in Leonard Michaels and Christopher Ricks (eds.), *The State of the Language,* University of California Press, London.

Slepenkov, I.M., and B.V. Knyazev. 1976. *Rural Youth Today,* trs. James Riordan, Oriental Research Partners, Newtonville, Mass.

Smolev, Ya.S. 1898. 'Tri tabangutskikh roda selenginskikh buryat' (Three Tabangut clans of the Selenga Buryat), *Trudy Troitskosavsko-Kyakhtinskogo otdela Priamurskogo otdeleniya RGO* (Moscow), 1 (3).

Sneath, David. (Forthcoming.) *Changing Inner Mongolia: Pastoral Mongolian Society and the Chinese State,* Oxford University Press, Oxford.

Snelling, John. 1993. *Buddhism in Russia: The Story of Agvan Dorzhiev, Lhasa's Emissary to the Tsar,* Element, Shaftesbury, Dorset, Rockport, Mass., and Brisbane.

'Sokrashchennaya istoriya Barguzinskikh buryat s prisovokupleniyem dokumentov' (Abbreviated history of the Barguzin Buryats with additional documents), in Rumyantsev 1956.

Soloukhin, Vladimir. 1974. *Izbrannyye proizvedeniya (Kaplya rosy)* (Selected works ('Drops of dew')), vol. 1, Khudozhestvennaya Literatura, Moscow.

Stewart, Michael. 1997. *The Time of the Gypsies,* Westview Press, Boulder.

Stuart, Robert C. 1971a. 'Managerial incentives in Soviet collective agriculture', *Soviet Studies* 22 (4), April.

Stuart, Robert C. 1971b. 'Structural change and the quality of Soviet collective farm management, 1952–1966', in James R. Millar (ed.), *The Soviet Rural Community,* University of Illinois, Urbana.

Suleimanov, Sh. 1975. *Vosproizvodstvo i ispol'zovaniye proizvodstvennykh fondov v kolkhozakh* (The reproduction and use of the productive funds in collective farms), Uzbekistan, Tashkent.

Sydenova, R.P. 1992. 'Iyerarkhiya obshchinnykh obrazovanii v Buryatii (vtoraya polovina XIX–nachalo XX v.),' in K.M. Gerasimova (ed.), *Traditsionnaya obryadnost' Mongolskikh narodov,* Nauka, Novosibirsk.

Takhanov, A.D. 1969. 'O preodolenii perezhitkov proshlogo v bytu i soznanii sredi nasleniya Tunkinskogo aimaka' (On the overcoming of survivals of the past in the way of life and understanding of the population of Tunka district), in Okladnikov and Lubsanov 1969.

Ten Dyke, Elizabeth A. (Forthcoming.) 'Memory, history and remembrance work in Dresden', in D. Berdahl, M. Bunzl, and M. Lampland (eds.), *Altering States: Ethnographies of Transition in Eastern Europe and the Former Soviet Union,* University of Michigan Press, Ann Arbor.

Tiktina, Dora. 1978. *A Rural Secondary School in the Ukraine, 1948–1962* (in Russian), Soviet Institution Series no. 2, Soviet and East European Research Centre, Hebrew University of Jerusalem.

Tivanenko, A.B., and V.G. Mitypov. 1974. *V taige za Baikalom* (In the taiga forest beyond Lake Baikal), BKI, Ulan-Ude.

Tonayevskaya, N.S. 1978. *Rabochiye sovkhozov zapadnoi sibiri (1959–1965 gg)* (Workers of the state farms of western Siberia, 1959–65), Nauka, Novosibirsk.

Trebukhovskii, A.F. 1929. *Svad'ba balaganskikh buryat v proshlom i na-*

585

References

stoyashchem (The wedding of the Balagansk Buryat in the past and the present), Verkhneudinsk.

Tsibikov, B.D. 1961. 'Tsagalgan, provedennyi po-novomu' (The *tsagalgan* festival conducted in a new way), *Etnograficheskii Sbornik* (Ulan-Ude), 2.

Tsibikov, B.D. 1969. 'Tsagalgan', in Okladnikov and Lubsanov 1969.

Tsibikov, B.D. (ed.). 1970. *Obychnoye pravo Selenginskikh buryat* (The customary law of the Selenga Buryat), BKI, Ulan-Ude.

Tsibikov, B.D. (ed.). 1992. *Obychnoye pravo Khorinskikh Buryat* (The customary law of the Khori Buryat), Nauka, Novosibirsk.

Tsybikov, G. 1927. 'Tsagalgan' (Buryat New Year festival), *Buryatiyevedeniye* (Verkhneudinsk), 3–4.

Tsybikzhapov, V.B. 1971. 'Sovremennaya tserkovnaya organizatsiya lamaizma v Buryatii' (Contemporary church organisation of Lamaism in Buryatiya), in Belousov 1971.

Tsydendambayev, Chimit. 1970. *Buryatskiye uzory* (Buryat decorations), Sovetskaya Rossiya, Moscow.

Tsydendambayev, Ts.B. 1972. *Buryatskiye istoricheskiye khroniki i rodoslovnyye* (Buryat historical chronicles and genealogies), BKI, Ulan-Ude.

Tugolukov, V.A., and A.S. Shubin. 1969. 'Kolkhoznoye stroitel'stvo u evenkov severnoi Buryatii i ego vliyaniye na ikh byt i kul'turu' (Collectivisation among the Evenki of northern Buryatiya and its influence on their way of life and culture), *Etnograficheskii Sbornik* (Ulan-Ude), 5.

Tugutov, I.E. 1958. *Material'naya kul'tura buryat* (The material culture of the Buryats), BKI, Ulan-Ude.

Tugutov, I.E. 1960. 'V Baragkhanskom sel'skom muzee' (In the Baragkhan Rural Museum), *Sovetskaya Etnografiya*, 2.

Tugutov, I.E. 1961. 'Obshchestvennyye igry buryat' (Communal games of the Buryat), *Etnograficheskii Sbornik* (Ulan-Ude), 2.

Tugutov, I.E. 1965. 'Stanovleniye novykh semeinykh obryadov' (The establishing of new family rituals), *Etnograficheskii Sbornik* (Ulan-Ude), 4.

Tugutov, I.E. 1969. 'Obshchestvennyi i semeinyi byt sovremennykh buryat' (The social and family life of the contemporary Buryat), in Okladnikov and Lubsanov 1969.

Tugutov, I.E. 1978. 'The tailagan as a principal shamanistic ritual of the Buryats', in V. Dioszegi and M. Hoppal (eds.), *Shamanism in Siberia*, Akademiai Kiado, Budapest, 1978.

Tyushev, V.P. 1947. 'Iz istorii kolkhoza Zagustaiskogo somona' (From the history of the kolkhoz in Zagustai *somon*), *Ucheniye Zapiski B-M Pedinstituta* (Ulan-Ude), 1.

Tyushev, V. 1958. 'Leningradskaya mnogotirazhnaya gazeta "Skorokhodovskiy Rabochiy" kak istochnik po istorii kolkhoznogo dvizheniya v buryatii' (The Leningrad wide-circulation newspaper 'The Skorokhod Worker' as a source for the history of the collective farm movement in Buryatiya), *Buryat-Mongol'skiy Gosudarstvennyi Pedagogicheskii Institut im. Dorzhi Banzarova Uchenyye Zapiski* (Ulan-Ude), 14.

Ulanov, A.I. (ed.). 1970. *Buryatskii fol'klor* (Buryat folklore), BION, Ulan-Ude.

Urbanayeva, I.S. 1997. 'Tsentral'no-aziatskaya tsivilizatsiya i sud'ba buryat-mongolov, tysyatileitiya stepnoi kul'tury i put' natsional'nogo dukha v orbite Rossii' (Central Asian civilization and the fate of the Buryat-Mongols: a thousand years of steppe culture and the path of the national spirit in Russia's orbit), in Urbanayeva (ed.), *Dokalady i Tezisy Mezhnuna-*

References

rodnogo simpoziuma "Buryat-Mongoly nakanune III tysyacheletiya", RAN, Ulan-Ude.

Urtyubayev, D.Ts. 1961. 'Molochnaya pishcha barguzinskikh buryat' (The milk foods of the Barguzin Buryat), *Etnograficheskii Sbornik* (Ulan-Ude), 2.

Urzhanov, A.D. 1969. 'Ob odnom sanaginskom spiske "serzhema" Bukha-Noionu na tibetskom yazyke' (On a Sanagin text, the 'sershem' of Bukha-Noion in Tibetan), *Trudy BION* (Ulan-Ude), 12.

Ushnayev, F.M. 1961a. 'Denezhnaya oplata truda v kolkhoz imeni Karla Marksa Selenginskogo aimaka Buryatskoi ASSR' (Money wages in the Karl Marx collective farm of Selenga district of the Buryat ASSR), in O.V. Makeyev (ed.), *Voprosy razvitiya narodnogo khozyaistva buryatskoi ASSR* (Questions of the development of the economy of the Buryat ASSR), BKI, Ulan-Ude.

Ushnayev, F.M. 1961b. 'Sotsial'nyye izemeneniya truda krest'yan pri sotsializme' (Social changes in the work of peasants in socialism), *Trudy otd. ekon. issled. BF SO AN SSSR*, 1 (5).

Ushnayev, F.M. 1968. 'Rabochee vremya i uroven' zhizni kolkhoznikov' (Working time and the standard of living of collective farmers), *Trudy BION* (Ulan-Ude), 11.

Ushnayev, F.M. 1969. *Trudovyye resursy kolkhozov buryatskoi ASSR i ikh ispol'zovaniye* (Labour resources of the collective farms of the Buryat ASSR and their use), BKI, Ulan-Ude.

Ustav kolkhoza buryatskoy ASSR (Collective farm statutes of Buryat ASSR), Soviet of Ministers of Buryat ASSR, Ulan-Ude, 1970.

Vainshtein, Sevyan. 1980. *Nomads of South Siberia: The Pastoral Economies of Tuva*, Cambridge University Press, Cambridge.

Vasil'yev, N.V. 1977. 'Kharakter i tendentsii sotsial'no-professional'nykh peremeshchenii evenskoi i evenkiiskoi molodezhi' (The character and tendencies of social-professional movements among the Even and Evenki youth), in Boiko 1977.

Vasyukin, M.K., and A.S. Davydov. 1978. *Gosudarstvennyye zakupki kolkhoznoi produktsii: ekonomicheskii analiz* (State purchases of collective farm production: an economic analysis), Ekonomika, Moscow.

Vdovin, I.S. (ed.). 1979. *Khristianstvo i lamaizm u korennogo naseleniya sibiri* (Christianity and Lamaism in the native population of Siberia), Nauka, Leningrad.

Verdery, Katherine. 1995. *What Was Socialism and What Comes Next?* Princeton University Press, Princeton.

Vinogradov, Georgii. 1926. 'Zamechaniya o govorakh tunkinskogo kraya' (Remarks on the ways of speech of Tunka district), *Buryatovedcheskii Sbornik*, 2.

Vlasova, I.V. 1975. 'Poseleniya Zabaikal'ya' (The settlements of Trans-Baikaliya), in Makovetskii 1975.

Voinovich, V.N. 1975. *Zhizn' i neobychainyye priklyucheniya soldata Ivana Chonkina* (The life and amazing exploits of the soldier Ivan Chonkin), YMCA Press, Paris.

Voinovich, Vladimir. 1979. *Putem vzaimnoi perepiski (kem ya mog by stat')* (By mutual correspondence (who I might become)), YMCA Press, Paris.

Voronin, G.I (ed.). 1977. *Buryatskaya ASSR, administrativno-territorial'noye deleniye na 1 aprelya 1977 goda* (The Buryat ASSR, administrative-territorial divisions on 1 April 1977), 3d edition, BKI, Ulan-Ude.

Voskoboinikov, M.G. 1960. 'Evenki severnoi buryatii' (Evenki of northern Buryatiya), *Etnograficheskii Sbornik* (Ulan-Ude), 1.

References

Voskoboinikov, M.G. 1961. 'Nekotoriye danniye po etnografii evenkov buryatii' (Some data on the Evenki of Buryatiya), *Etnograficheskii Sbornik* (Ulan-Ude), 2.

Vostrikov, A.I., and N.N. Poppe. 1935. *Letopis' barguzinskikh buryat, teksty i issledovaniya* (Chronicle of the Barguzin Buryats, texts and investigations), AN SSSR, Moscow, Leningrad.

Vreeland, H.H. 1957. *Mongol Community and Kinship Structure,* HRAF, New Haven.

Vyatkina, K.V. 1960. *Mongoly Mongol'skoi Narodnoi Respubliki* (Mongols of the Mongolian People's Republic), Trudy Instituta Etnografii AN SSSR, vol. 9, Moscow.

Vyatkina, K.V. 1969. *Ocherki kul'tury i byta buryat* (Studies in the culture and way of life of the Buryat), Nauka, Leningrad.

Waddington, Caroline (C. Humphrey). 1967. 'Simvolicheskii aspekt v razvitii buryatskogo zhilishcha' (The symbolic aspect in the evolution of Buryat dwellings), in *Etnicheskaya istoriya i sovremennoye natsional'noye razvitiye narodov mira,* Institut Etnografii AN SSSR, Moscow.

Wädekin, K.-E. 1971. 'Soviet rural society: a descriptive stratification analysis', *Soviet Studies,* 22 (4), April.

Wädekin, K.-E. 1975. 'Income distribution in Soviet agriculture', *Soviet Studies,* 27 (1), January.

Yandanov, A.G. 1975. *Povysheniye kul'turno-teknicheskogo urovnya kolkhoznogo krest'yanstva buryatii* (The raising of the cultural-technological level of the collective farm peasantry of Buryatiya), BKI, Ulan-Ude.

Yanov, Alexander. 1977. *Detente after Brezhnev: The Domestic Roots of Soviet Foreign Policy,* Institute of International Studies, University of California, Berkeley.

Yanovskii, R.G., *et al.* (eds.). 1975. *Voyenno-patrioticheskoye vospitaniye molodezhi v sovremennykh usloviyakh* (The military-patriotic education of youth in contemporary conditions), SO Institut Ist, Filologii i Filosofi, AN SSSR, Novosibirsk.

Yanowitch, Murray. 1977. *Social and Economic Inequality in the Soviet Union,* Martin Robertson, London.

Yanowitch, Murray. 1979. *Soviet Work Attitudes: The Issue of Participation in Management,* M.E. Sharpe and Martin Robertson, New York and Oxford.

Yanowitch, Murray, and Wesley A. Fisher (eds.). 1973. *Social Stratification and Mobility in the USSR,* International Arts and Science Press, White Plains, New York.

Yefimov, Igor'. 1979. *Bez burzhuyev* (Without the bourgeoisie), Posev, Frankfurt am Main.

Yegunov, N.P. 1952. 'K istorii organizatsii odnogo iz pervykh zhivotnovodcheskikh kolkhozov B-MASSR' (Toward a history of the first livestock collective farms of the Buryat-Mongol ASSR), *Zapiski B-MNIIK* (Ulan-Ude), 16.

Yegunov, N.P. 1963. *Kolonial'naya politika tsarizma i pervyi etap natsional'nogo dvizheniya v buryatii v epokhu imperializma* (The colonial policies of Tsarism and the first stage of the national movement in Buryatiya in the imperialist period), BKI, Ulan-Ude.

Zaitsev, Yu.V. 1974. 'Iz istorii razvitiya vnutrikolkhoznoi demokratii v pervyye poslevoyennyye gody (1946–1950 gg)' (From the history of intra-kolkhoz democracy in the first post-war years, 1946–1950), in N.Ya. Gushchin (ed.), *Obshchestvenno-politicheskaya zhizn' sovetskoi sibirskoi derevni* (Socio-political life of the Soviet Siberian village), Nauka, Novosibirsk.

588

References

Zemtsov, Il'ya. 1976. *Partiya ili Mafiya?* (Party or Mafia?), Les Editeurs Réunis, Paris.

Zhalsarayev, A.D. 1974. 'Nekotoriye predvaritel'nyye itogi issledovaniya natsional'nogo samosoznaniya podrostkov v natsional'no-smeshannykh sem'yakh' (Some preliminary results of the study of the national consciousness of adolescents in nationally mixed families), *Etnograficheskii Sbornik* (Ulan-Ude), 6.

Zhamtsarano, Ts. 1906. 'O pravosoznaniye buryat' (On the law-consciousness of the Buryat), *Sibirskiye Voprosy* (St. Petersburg), 2.

Zhukovskaya, N.L. 1969a. 'Modernizatsiya shamanstva v usloviyakh rasprostraneniya buddizma u mongolov i ikh sosedei' (The modernisation of shamanism in the conditions of the spread of Buddhism among the Mongols and their neighbours), *Etnograficheskii Sbornik* (Ulan-Ude), 5.

Zhukovskaya, N.L. 1969b. 'Sovremennyi lamaizm (na materialakh buryatskoi ASSR)' (Contemporary Lamaism, on the basis of materials from Buryat ASSR), *Mysl'* (Moscow).

Zhukovskaya, N.L. 1977. *Lamaizm i ranniye formy religii* (Lamaism and early forms of religion), Nauka, Moscow.

Zhukovskaya, N.L. 1981. 'Iz istorii dukhovnoi kul'tury mongolov ("podarok-ot-darok" i ego mesto v sisteme tsennostei)' (From the history of Mongolian spiritual culture—the 'gift and counter-gift' and its place in the system of values), in V.I. Vasil'yev and G.P. Vasil'yeva (eds.), *Vsesoyuznaya konferentsiya 'Etnokul'turnyye protsessy v sovremennom mire'* (All-union conference 'Ethnocultural processes in the contemporary world'), AN SSSR, Elista.

Zhukovskaya, N.L. 1992. 'Buddhism and problems of national and cultural resurrection of the Buryat nation', *Central Asian Survey* 11 (2), London, 27–41.

Zhukovskaya, N.L. 1995. 'Religion and ethnicity in Eastern Russia, Republic of Buryatiya: a panorama of the 1990s', *Central Asian Survey* 14 (1), London, 25–42.

Zhukovskaya, N.L. 1997a. 'The shaman in the context of rural history and mythology (Tory village, Tunka District, Buryat Republic)', *Inner Asia* 2 (1), Cambridge, 90–107.

Zhukovskaya, N.L. 1997b. *Vozrozhdeniye buddizma v Buryatii: problemy i perspektivy,* (The rebirth of Buddhism in Buryatiya: problems and perspectives), Russian Academy of Sciences IEA, *Issledovaniya po prikladnoi i neotlozhnoi etnologii,* no. 104, Moscow.

Zinov'yev, Aleksandr. 1978. *Svetloye budushchee* (A bright future), L'Age d'Homme, Paris.

Index

590

Index

buluk (pre-revolutionary territorial unit), 5, 51, 272
Buryat ASSR, 4, 24, 114, 171, 193, 380
Buryat ethnographers, 3, 12, 17, 21, 375, 403
Buryat Filial of Academy of Sciences, 17, 20
Buryatiya, comparison with E. Europe, 489–90
Buryats
  age-structure, 48–9, 512
  birth-rate, 542
  'class' structure, 32–3
  clothing, 19–20, 30, 240, 276, 388
  culture, 35, 289, 434–7, 441–2
  ethnicity, xv, 20, 28, 32, 257, 318–19, 110 12, 115, 117, 123 4; *see also* identity
  food, 18, 235, 276, 291
  history, 23–5, 30–2, 434, 437, 507
  housing, 239, 272, 276, 283–5, 289
  intelligentsia, viii, 30–1, 418, 440, 501, 505
  language, xxii, 3, 18, 20, 23, 34, 346, 437, 544
  nationalism, xxii, 31, 51, 60, 419, 424, 442
  population, xx, 23–4, 171, 509, 513
  pre-revolutionary stratification, 28, 53, 61, 437
  representation in Soviets, 477
  'repressed nation' status, xv, xxi
  settlement in collective farms, 34; *see also* migration
  tribes and clans, xviii–xix, 24, 51–5, 55–60, 483–6, 495–6, 548, 564; and difference, 488

Central Asia, 14, 15, 347, 445
Chair (*predsedatel'*) of collective farm, 20, 348, 449, 520–1, 525
  appointment of, 122, 150, 161, 318, 326, 331
  authority of, 16, 103, 108, 111, 119–24, 135, 160–1, 331, 352, 503
  income, 15, 84, 261–2, 533–4
  kin network of, 344–6
  relations with district authorities, 317–29
  relations with workers, 185, 219, 304, 318; post-Soviet 466–7, 479–91
  responsibilities of, 262, 266, 331, 450, 503
  view of farm structure, 103, 105
Chair of Rural Soviet (*sel'sovet*), 16, 120, 126, 346, 348, 354
childbirth, 70, 516, 541

children, 38–45, 285, 287, 291, 297, 300–1, 343, 369; *see also* school
  attitude to farmwork, 230–1, 311–16
  burial of, 425
  Buryat attitudes towards, 68–72, 550
  choice of nationalisty, 36–7
  juvenile offenders, 362
  kindergartens, 451, 516
  labour, 292, 301, 302–3, 328
  'lending' of, 412
  mortality, 68–72, 541
  reincarnation and, 427
Chinese, 23, 28, 64, 493, 509
  traders, 469
Chinggis Khan, xxi, 495, 497, 500
clans, *see* Buryat, tribes and clans
Clarke, S., 452, 465
class, 5, 28–9, 32–3, 148–9, 277, 505, 543
climate, 66–7, 195, 207
collective farming (post-Soviet), ix
  attitudes to, 460–2, 465, 475
  based on contracts, 445, 478–9
  in Bulgaria, 489
  among Evenki, 491–2
  'insiders' collectives, 446, 482, 491
  new forms in 1990s, viii, 447–8, 556
  shareholders' collectives, 445–6, 490, 493–5, 503–5
collective farm (*kolkhoz*), 3–4, 13, 120, 130, 140–2, 153–4, 159, 447, 453–4
  accounts, 16, 159–62, 196–200, 224, 468
  amalgamations of, 142, 147, 149–51, 351
  Auditing Commission, 104, 200, 449
  Buryat compared with others, 14–17, 181, 347, 443–4
  charter (statutes) of, 73–5, 77, 111, 132, 164, 329–30, 448, 516–7, 556
  club, 19, 317, 328, 361, 367–8, 370
  'commandments' (*zapovedi*), 111–12
  committee (*pravleniye*), 103, 123–4, 137, 317, 332–3, 356
  early forms of, 143
  ethnic composition in, 34, 39
  general meeting, 103–4, 109–10, 160–1, 327, 330–2, 449, 521
  hospital, in, 18, 328; *see also* medical care
  'indivisible funds' of, 94
  office (*kontora*), 20
  radio, 360
  school in, 222–3, 328, 361, 367–8, 370; *see also* school
  shops in, 19, 21, 204, 222, 328, 332
  Soviet theory of, 73–92, 95–117

591

Index

Malinowski, B., 118, 520, 524
'man-day', 14–15
Manchuria, 24, 25
  Barga district, 60
'manipulable resources', 9, 170, 195, 204,
    210, 217–24, 225–7, 326, 382, 435,
    468–9
markets, 28–9, 76, 221, 279, 452, 462, 560,
    563
  black, 145, 221
  'kolkhoz', 145, 186, 217–18, 305–6
marriage, 39–46, 58, 270, 401
  age of, 39–45, 453
  brideprice, 54–5, 274–5, 383–4, 387,
    395, 437, 536
  bride-service, 55
  dowry, 55, 168, 252–5, 274–5, 315, 369,
    383–5, 387, 392, 536
  endowment of bride (enzhe), 275, 383,
    387, 546
  exchange marriage, 55, 436
  exogamy, 47, 53, 56–8, 288–9, 385,
    395, 414, 483, 560
  'generalised exchange,' 53
  local endogamy, 45
  occupations of spouses, 40–5, 394
  polygyny, 71
  'restricted exchange', 56, 58
Marx, Karl, ix, 73, 76, 80, 81, 86–7, 97,
    105, 428, 517, 564
Marxism, ix, 7, 74, 76–81, 86–8, 97–8
  neo-Marxist theory of 'ownership',
    151–2
match-makers, 385–6, 388, 390, 392,
    398
meadow-workers, 255–7, 266
meat, 166–7, 170, 178, 189, 210–12
  ritual and, 375, 386–7, 390, 405, 408,
    412, 423
  üüse (B. meat for winter), 493, 495
mechanisation, 178–9, 228, 238
medals, 328, 351, 354–8
medical care, 18, 71, 269; see also collective
    farm, hospital in
  by lamas, 422
  by shamans, 410
Meshcheryakov, A., 459, 460, 465–6, 558
migration, 24–5, 46–7, 63, 181, 309, 456,
    513
Mikhailov, T. M., 376, 381, 408, 410, 414,
    416
milaagod (family ritual), 273, 377, 394,
    398–9, 516, 548, 560–1
military service, 35, 45, 133, 314, 350,
    363–4, 549
  shamanist ritual for, 407

milk, 178, 184, 189
  cost of production, 528
  milk foods, 378
  problems of production, 208–9
  problems of sale
milkers, 229, 242–7, 266, 313–16, 356–7,
    376
  in political life, 359
Ministry of Agriculture, 14, 46, 84, 94–5,
    137, 152, 330, 454, 467, 517
money, 366–7, 370–1, 387, 415, 451, 461–
    2, 466
  attitudes towards, 188–9, 190–2, 394–5,
    459, 468
  inflation, 459
Mongolia, xii, xv, 23–4, 27, 30, 37, 60, 63–
    4, 130, 346, 378, 454, 508, 553–4,
    564
Mongols, 23, 48, 52, 373, 430, 563–4; see
    also Chinggis Khan
monopolies, 468, 470
morality, 76, 189–92, 195, 360, 362, 417,
    449, 479
  kinship and, 410–13
  and 'hard work', 354–8, 479–80

names, 240, 273, 398
  use of Russian, 346
  use of Tibetan, 424
nationalism, see Buryats, nationalism
New Economic Policy (NEP), 145
newspapers, 32, 76, 144, 356, 529
  local, 111, 165–6, 192–5, 231
  national, 193–5
nomenklatura (elite holders of official posts),
    147–8, 323, 331, 358–9, 370, 540

oboo (ritual cairn), 374, 378, 402, 422–3,
    429, 432, 485, 498, 504, 548, 563
officials, 11, 304, 306, 309, 398, 400
  as match-makers, 385, 399
  in-marriage of, 394
omens, 69, 422, 562
orders, 109–11, 448, 449–50

Panarin, Sergei, 465, 490–1
Party Secretary in collective farm (partorg),
    120, 124–6, 147, 316, 326–9, 330, 348
  relation with Chair of kolkhoz, 326–9,
    348–9
  role in rituals, 400, 415
passports, 13, 123, 132–3
pastoralism, 'traditional', 11–12, 28, 146,
    174, 189
  compared with collectvised, 230–2, 233,
    240, 296

Index

wages, x, 192, 444, 533–5
  bonuses, 88–9, 108, 169, 180, 215, 220, 238, 244, 254, 261, 429
  Buryat compared with USSR averages, 471
  differentials in farm, 239, 259–60, 377
  for 'man-day', 15
  for 'workday', 86, 149
  guaranteed minimum, 13, 15–16, 182, 184, 187, 215, 217, 244, 248–9, 254, 429
  in kind, 220, 466–7, 532, 560
  of officials, 84, 466, 534
  post-Soviet decline, 466
  shepherds', 238
  Soviet theory of, 86–8, 100, 108, 110, 260
war
  First World War, xiv, xxi
  Second World War, xiv, xxi, 462
wealth, 181, 242, 285, 394; see also consumerism, money
  in Buryat culture, 284–5
  display of, 384, 388–9
  education as, 370–1
  in post-Soviet times, 459
weddings, 171, 270–1, 272, 298, 331, 382–402; see also marriage
  'komsomol', 383, 391–2, 399–400
  'traditional' ritual at, 383, 385–91, 398
women,
  Buddhist monastery for, xvi, xxii
  cultural attitudes towards, 35, 69, 272, 287–8, 346–7, 393, 430, 530, 552
  in division of labour, 189–92, 229, 233–4, 247, 248, 287–8, 527
  education, 537
  inter-marriage, 34–8
  numbers of employed, 15, 39, 133, 301–2

'over-qualification', 539
patriliny and women's status, 287–9, 298
in political life, 114, 148, 347–8, 354
property rights, 268, 287
in household, 151, 272, 284, 287–8, 294–5, 302, 458, 521, 535–7
single, 291, 297
women's attitudes, 190, 298–9
women's organisation, 360
women's rituals, 377
working life as milkmaid, 242–3, 246
working life as shepherd, 237
work, xvii, 252–3, 354, 439
  attitudes to (post-Soviet), 489–91
  hours, 188–9, 235, 242–4, 249–50
  illegitimate benefits of, 254–5, 463–4
  increase in Soviet period, 180–1, 189
  norms, 149, 258–9, 261, 542
  numbers working in collective farm, 301–2; by month, 537–9; by region, 539
  in post-Soviet period, xvii, 448–9, 460, 489
  Soviet ethic of, 112–13, 133, 191, 236–7, 245, 252–3, 254, 256–7, 354, 357–8, 479–80
  'traditional' Buryat attitude to, 189–92, 258–9, 282–3, 307–8
'workday' (trudoden'), 86, 149, 220
  post-Soviet reintroduction of, 450, 466
'workers' dynasties', 357

Yakutiya (Sakha), 381
Yanov, A. 156, 461
Yeltsin, B., xx, 450, 468, 471, 503
yields, grain, 15, 279; see arable farming

Zhukovskaya, N. L., xxi, xxii, 408, 423, 426–7, 435, 488, 544, 554, 555